JEFFERSON COLLEGE

3 6021 00026 421

66-352

P9-BXW-365

PN4121
B7139    Brigance
1961     Speech

66-352

# SPEECH

## Its Techniques and Disciplines

## in a Free Society

*Chicago Historical Soc*

The painting, "Stump Speaking" by George Caleb Bingham (1854), depicting a typic
scene in early American political life, illustrates Macaulay's statement: "Parliamenta
government is government by Speaking."

# SPEECH

## Its Techniques and Disciplines
## in a Free Society

**By** **WILLIAM NORWOOD BRIGANCE**

*Late of Wabash College*

SECOND EDITION

*New* **AC** *York*

**APPLETON-CENTURY-CROFTS, Inc.**

JUNIOR COLLEGE DISTRICT OF
JEFFERSON COUNTY, MISSOURI
LIBRARY

NO LONGER
PROPERTY OF
JEFFERSON
COLLEGE
LIBRARY

Copyright © 1952, 1961, by

APPLETON-CENTURY-CROFTS, INC.

*All rights reserved. This book, or parts thereof, must not be reproduced in any form without permission of the publisher.*

635-19

LIBRARY OF CONGRESS CARD NUMBER: 61-5128

PRINTED IN THE UNITED STATES OF AMERICA

E–12612

# EDITOR'S FOREWORD

DURING THE 1959 convention of the Speech Association of America, I sat at luncheon with the author of the second edition of this college textbook on speechmaking. When I told him that I had just finished reading it and had found it to be a substantial improvement over its predecessor which already had established itself firmly in the esteem of discriminating teachers of public speaking, he seemed gratified. How little did I then think that I should never see him again!

Professor Brigance was a skilled practitioner of the principles and techniques which he set forth in his writing and taught to his classes. His profound grasp of subject matter; his vivid and cogent rhetoric; his powerful, resonant voice; his expressive visible action; and his strong ethical appeal made him one of the great platform speakers of our time.

Long ago publishers learned that William Norwood Brigance could not be hurried in preparing a manuscript but that, when it reached the editor's desk, every i would be dotted and every t crossed. He had an eye and a taste for excellence and, wherever he employed a word or a phrase in an unusual way, there was likely to be a marginal warning: "Printer: Don't change this! I want it just this way!"

Brigance did not revise his books with a pair of scissors and a tube of paste. In this volume there is scarcely a page that does not reflect the author's careful reconsideration of subject matter, terminology, and phrasing. Even before the ink on the pages of the first edition had dried, he was already planning how he could improve it; the twenty-four folders in his desk, representing the chapters, had begun to fill with items which he thought might be useful in a revision.

For a third of a century Brigance was a dominant force in the field of speech education. His popular textbooks cover the whole range from high school to graduate school. He was one of the select few chosen to serve the American Speech Association in both of its top positions—the Presidency and the Editorship of the *Quarterly Journal*. Further, the indelible imprint of his scholarship is on the monumental two-volume *History and Criticism of American Public Address* which he assembled and edited.

Within the covers of this volume, we have the distilled wisdom of a balanced mind deeply grounded in educational philosophy and illumined with brilliant insight into human history. The very title of the book betokens a long and broad view of speech as a dynamic essential in the life of the individual and of a democratic society. In a very real

sense this book is the last will and testament of a great teacher. Those
who study it thoughtfully will become his beneficiaries. I rejoice to feel
that I may play even a minor role in transmitting to college students the
rich heritage that he left to them.

ANDREW THOMAS WEAVER

# PREFACE

SOMEONE WILL SURELY ASK of this revision as is asked of every one by anyone, "Why another revision?" I hope those who feel this way will be patient enough to read not only why this revision was made, but also why, as a textbook writer, I think reasonably frequent revisions are vital.

First, no textbook that communicates living meaning to students can ever be written without deliberately including what Emerson called "the conventional, the local, the perishable." A book of pure thought, even were it possible, would be understood only by the scholars and the experts. To students it could be only embalmed darkness. Therefore, in writing the first edition I deliberately included all the "conventional, the local, the perishable" that would help make it rich in meaning for students of the 1950's. For others I cannot testify, but for me over one-half the time given to writing or revising any book goes into collecting, rejecting, selecting, and putting into apt words the illustrations, specific instances, and other references that give this meaning to principles. The test of each one is: "Will a student know what this reference means five years hence, or eight, or will he have to look up the meaning in a reference book?" I find that for a high-school textbook I need to re-examine these references every five years, for a beginning college textbook every seven to ten years, and for an advanced college textbook every twelve to twenty years. If I don't, there arises a new student generation "which knows not Joseph," and knows not the meaning of references that were meaningful to students of a short generation before. My first responsibility in this revision, therefore, has been to replace references that gave the book added meaning to students of the 1950's but that would have less meaning to students of the 1960's.

Second, I have made available within this revision an explanation of all significant new discoveries recently made on the nature of persuasion. These range from reports now available on experiments in planned persuasion made by the United States government during World War II to tentative conclusions recently derived from motivational research. Like the discovery of the Dead Sea scrolls to scholars in religion, these discoveries on the nature of persuasion change almost nothing basic, but they do throw great light on things already known. Especially they modify and amend things already known—as the sleeper effect in persuasion, the effect of order of arrangement, and how the ways of communicating ideas to people of lower economic levels differ from the ways of communicating them to people of upper economic levels.

Finally, behind every revision there is a deeply personal reason. It was described once by Louise Closser Hale as it applied to actors, but it also applies to writers. On Broadway, she said, if she spoke lines or acted in scenes that failed to measure up to expectations, she could say, "I can do that better tomorrow," and tomorrow she would. But in Hollywood she met with a painful new experience. There she would sit in a darkened room and see herself on the screen, speaking lines and doing scenes that she knew were not her best. She would start to say, "I'll do that better tomorrow," only to remember the dreadful reality that her acting was recorded irrevocably on film. For her now there was no tomorrow.

So with a writer. I write a book. I rewrite all of it five, six, and seven times—and parts of it ten or twenty times. Then when I see it in irrevocable print I say of many paragraphs and pages, "I can do it better." But there is no doing it better until that distant day arrives for a new revision. It may mean little to teachers who use this book, and mean less to students who read it for the first time, but for me there is deep satisfaction in knowing that some of its pages carried over from the first edition now read easier and carry more meaning because they have been torn up and recast without regard for time or labor.

As always I am troubled about acknowledgments. Packed into three filing cabinets in my library are voluminous digests of books and articles. Filed there are also notes on papers I have heard at speech conferences, and especially also notes on conversations held in hotel lobbies. One group of these is arranged into 25 folders, one each for the Foreword and 24 chapters of this book. How many hundreds these would number I would not want to guess. How much they have influenced my thinking is easier to assess, for they are like water and cultivation to crops: they have improved the harvest. To these authors and colleagues—from Bower Aly to J. Jeffery Auer through Wilbur Samuel Howell (I am jumping from A to Z, not calling the roll) to Otis M. Walter and E. William Ziebarth—I remain in continuous debt.

Other acknowledgments will be indicated by the footnotes. I have not wearied the reader by expressing thanks in each footnote, so I herewith do express thanks to all so cited.

Finally, to the following persons I must repeat the indebtedness expressed in the first edition:

Victor M. Powell, a colleague whose sound judgment and advice on knotty problems of advice on planning was especially valuable.

Andrew T. Weaver, University of Wisconsin, who read the manuscript in its final form and gave it the benefit of his usual unusual judgment.

Four additional acknowledgments that appeared in the first edition must be repeated:

James A. Winans and Charles H. Woolbert whose contributions to the field of speech during its early days of renaissance became a permanent part of my professional heritage.

George Campbell, onetime of Marischal College, Aberdeen, Scotland, whose *Philosophy of Rhetoric* published in 1776 contains a body of enduring substance. Especially his treatment of the four purposes of speaking seems to me superior to the traditional ends of speech used by later writers; hence they are the basis of the purposes of speech as set forth in Chapter 9 of this book.

Aristotle—court adviser to Hermias, tutor to Alexander the Great, analyst of constitutional government, and founder of the Lyceum—for his brushing aside the confusion of Plato's vision "half seen and half communicated," establishing rhetoric as a science, and demonstrating its necessity to citizens in a free society. With the general semanticists I share the protest against the extremes of Aristotelianism propagated by little men who followed after. With leading semanticists I agree that Aristotle returned among us would be a dissenter against such Aristotelianism.

W. N. B.

# CONTENTS

## Part V: OCCASIONS AND FORMS

## Part VI: THE INFLUENCE OF SPEECHMAKING

# SPEECH

Its Techniques and Disciplines

in a Free Society

# INTRODUCTION

# Why Speak? Who Listens?

WHEN ANY HUMAN BEING stands up to speak and others sit down to listen, more than 3,000 years of human struggle, sacrifice, learning, and culture are involved in that simple act. The ground rules started with the beginning of civilization, as aptly stated by Curtis Bok: "In the whole history of law and order the longest step was taken by primitive man when, as if by common consent, the tribe sat down in a circle and allowed only one man to speak at a time."

That was the beginning. During the centuries since, mankind has been developing, slowly and painfully, the ground rules under which speakers speak and listeners listen. Unfortunately they are not the same in all parts of the world. They differ in the Communist world, and even in that insular world of the Middle East, from the ground rules of Western democracies; and this difference is a constant, inevitable source of friction. But whatever else the ground rules of Western democracies include, they presume that *the purpose of speechmaking is to energize thought and humanize truth.* Some of the greatest men who ever lived gave the best years of their lives learning how, and recording their findings for the benefit of mankind.

Some will say, of course, that all this has no place in a modern textbook on speechmaking, which ought to deal unashamedly with "speaking for results." The answer is that such knowledge is vital to those who would "speak for results," and if it is not made available to them in a speech textbook, they are likely never to learn it at all. This book, first of all, is a guidebook on how to "speak for results," a book for future leaders who must learn how to promote thought, plan, organize, build, and sell. But it is more than a guidebook. It is also a book about the role of speechmaking in the democracy we are dedicated to defend. It is concerned with how the ground rules got started, why speechmaking grew out of the struggle of free people to govern themselves, and why in a democracy it must inherently be different from that in totalitarian countries. It includes this because the survival of democracy in this dangerous twentieth century will depend on how effectively its leaders use this accumulated knowledge.

This introduction focuses on speechmaking in a democracy. Chapter I will start the ground-clearing on how to become an effective speaker. In succeeding chapters both streams of thought will merge in proper proportion.

## I

Why do we have speechmaking at all? In every generation a jubilant minority has hailed it as a formula for personal success: "The way to dominate a hundred people, or a thousand," or "The secret of how to overcome resistance by a magnetic personality," or a method by which you can "engineer consent" from others. Also in every generation a frustrated minority has disputed the worth of speechmaking altogether: "It is medieval, outworn." Or "Scientists do not settle things by speaking; they investigate." Or "Even the best-intentioned of public speakers probably do more harm than good" because they use "irrelevant tricks" to "persuade people to the rightness of a good cause." The last indictment happens to be in the frenetic words of Aldous Huxley, but the tune is twenty centuries old.

Both groups rely on vehemence instead of reason. We shall not engage them in controversy. Let us instead turn to the pertinent questions of how speechmaking got started in the human race, and why it survived?

About 470 B.C. people in the city-states along the Mediterranean Sea began to change their governments. They had endured both autocracy and tyranny. Now they began to cast off both oligarchies and tyrants, and to try to rule themselves. This was man's first democracy, his first free society. *At once these Greeks discovered that they could not have a democracy without developing a system of public address.* A wronged citizen appealed to the new people's government: "Ten years ago the dictator took my land. I want it back." The dictators had banished and confiscated. They had effaced towns and transferred people, just as was done in north central Europe during the 1930's and 1940's. They had carefully destroyed old land titles. Now people were asking for justice. There were true claims and false claims. So these people had to invent a jury system to find out who really owned the land. Their juries were not small like ours. They were made up of 101, or 501, or even 1,001 freemen. There were no lawyers. Each citizen was a freeman, and each freeman was required to speak for himself. A wronged citizen had to stand up before the huge jury and explain why the land was his. To his dismay, he found that truth and justice were not enough, either to make the jury believe him or even understand him. He also needed speaking skill, for the man with speaking skill too often got the land! Eight hundred years later St. Augustine was to state the situation in immortal words: "Who dare say that the defenders of truth shall be unarmed against falsehood? . . . While advocates of falsehood know how to state facts

*Fratelli Alinari, Florence*

St. Augustine (354-430 A.D.) was the last of the major classical writers on rhetoric, whose work *On Christian Doctrine* was begun *ca.* 396 and finished 427. From a photograph found in Italy taken about a hundred years ago by Alinari of a painting by Era Fillipo Lippi in the Gallery of the Uffizi at Florence.

concisely, clearly, and plausibly, shall defenders of truth speak so they tire their listeners, make themselves hard to understand, and hard to believe? . . . Who is so foolish as to think this to be wisdom?" (*On Christian Doctrine*, 4. 2. 3). So these pioneers of democracy learned in the fifth century B.C.

Not only did they need public speaking in their courts, but also in their new legislatures. In these city-states nobody was elected to the legislature. Every freeman automatically was a member; and they met—1,000 or 5,000 of them—at stated times. Some freemen might say, "We need such-and-such new law." But the city-state would not get that new law merely because it needed it. Somebody had to explain why it was needed, and explain it so the whole 1,000 or 5,000 freemen could hear him, explain it in terms of their wants, hopes, and immediate needs—explain it even with the winds blowing and miscellaneous noises drifting through the out-door forum.

At once these people were forced to establish a *system* of speechmaking. Within ten years after the first democracy emerged, there appeared the first book on speechmaking. As every teacher of speech knows, the place where this system of speaking started was Syracuse—Italy, not New York—and the beginning year was about 460 B.C. But neither place nor year are primarily significant. *The significant fact is that democracy and the system of speechmaking were born together, and grew up together. Since that early day we have never had a successful democracy unless a large part, a very large part, of its citizens were effective, intelligent, and responsible speakers. Today, as twenty-three centuries ago, a system of speechmaking is imperative for preserving democracy.*

There are today two kinds of nations, and two kinds of people, in the world: Those who in disagreements and crises want to *shoot* it out, and those who have learned to *talk* it out. To shoot it out is the way of the machine gun, the bomb, the concentration camp. To talk it out is the way of mediation, parliamentary discussion, and political campaigns settled by the ballot. That is what Macaulay meant by his famous and sometimes misunderstood statement that "Parliamentary government is government by speaking." That is what is meant by democracy being described as "government by talk." In a democracy problems are not settled by force, but are "talked out of existence, or talked into solution." But democracy is not government by mere talk alone, or by any kind of talk. Talk in a democracy requires three conditions:

*First, its leaders must know how to talk effectively, intelligently, and responsibly.* People must give up the notion that "anybody can talk," merely because he can utter sounds. They must learn that effective public talk is a discipline that requires skill and training. One critical need in America today is people who can talk effectively. We have scientists who can crack the atom. We have engineers who can build bridges and skyscrapers. We have authors who can write great books; well, anyhow, write books. But we don't have enough competent speakers to carry on the everyday business of living together in a democracy.

*Second, we must maintain a society in which everyone has an equal right to speak his mind, and where both sides of every public question are fairly heard and fairly decided.* Of course, there are always people in a democracy—good people who mean well—yet who want to suppress the discussion of "dangerous views." They "believe in free speech— but. . . ." They succeed at times in restricting the discussion of both sides of public questions. In the long run, however, in every democracy that survives, the majority permits people to speak their minds freely on both sides. In other words, they believe it is just as important to have the right to be wrong as to have the right to be right; for where you don't have the right to utter a wrong opinion you won't long have the right to utter the right opinion. Even if a man is a fool or a quack, the best safeguard, they have found, is to let him notify the world by speaking freely.

*Third, there must be "popular intelligence," a public that can listen and judge.* Down the centuries, of course, skeptics have not believed in "popular intelligence." They have insisted that the multitude lacked both intelligence and judgment, and could not acquire them even through education. Plato's distrust of the multitude is well-remembered. He would forbid them even freedom of speech and freedom to travel. He would regulate the games of children, lest they grow up with dangerous ideas. Plato had no faith in the democracies of his day. Nor was this view confined to early aristocrats. In 1770 Lord North, the new British Prime Minister, said tartly: "The drunken ragamuffins of a vociferous mob are not exalted into equal importance with men of judgment, morals and property. I can never acquiesce in the absurd opinion that all men are equal." In 1857 Thomas B. Macaulay, who believed in a top-drawer democracy by the better class, wrote that if "the supreme authority in any state" should be "intrusted to the majority of citizens" it "must sooner or later destroy liberty, or civilisation, or both." Even today some thinking people are disturbed at the rising power of the multitude. So eminent a thinker as Walter Lippmann, as late as 1954, said: "The public opinion of masses cannot be counted upon to apprehend regularly and promptly the reality of things. There is an inherent tendency in opinion to feed upon rumors excited by our own wishes and fears." This distrust of the multitude has been the prevailing view through most of human history.

Aristotle, to be sure, suggested over twenty-three centuries ago that the final power should rest with the multitude, even though he much preferred the middle class. Nicolò Machiavelli before his death in 1527 had made the bold assertion that the multitude, in spite of their inconstancy, were in general more prudent and stable, and therefore more likely than a dictator to display a sound judgment. In the seventeenth century Descartes had declared that "good sense" was the most widespread thing in the world. But these were lonely voices. The majority of the "better classes" agreed with Plato and Macaulay. Not until a bit more than a hundred years ago did the multitude rise to ultimate control in the enlightened nations of the Western world. Not until 1859 could John Stuart Mill write: "It is almost a triviality to say that public opinion now rules the world."

But does the multitude, which now controls the democracies of the world, really have "popular intelligence"? Frankly, the answer is yes, yet only recently have we really been sure. First, these democracies survived the onslaught of governments ruled by dictators. When only the fit could survive they proved they were fit. Next, there is now scientific evidence that comes from the public-opinion studies of the past three decades. I know, of course, that the scientific study of man's behavior makes some scholars dreadfully uneasy, just as the rapid growth of mathematics and physics three hundred years ago made those scholars dreadfully uneasy. Back in that day the scholars wrote books attacking the rise of science, just as some today attack social science. In that wonderful day three hundred years ago those who controlled the curriculum at the Universities of Oxford and Cambridge refused to permit even mathematics to be taught. At Cambridge, Sir William Hamilton declared "the study of Mathematics to be no part of the business of this University." At Oxford, it was ruled out as one of "the black arts." The same type of intellectual today attacks the scientific study of man, and for the same reason: It upsets that beautiful dream-world picture of a changeless world in which everybody can learn about life by reading Plato.

Meanwhile, the scientific study of man's behavior goes right on. Through trial, error, and correcting mistakes we are learning what we never knew before about man's behavior. The scientific measurement of public opinion during the past three decades shows that the mass of people have a remarkably high degree of common sense. Repeatedly their answers were logically sound, even when the persons answering did not evidence the logic. Repeatedly their answers confirmed the verdict of Samuel Butler over half a century ago, whose parish work among the poor in London had quickened his insight: "The public may not know enough to *be* experts, but they know enough to judge between them." Research on the behavior of man has given statistical proof of the wisdom of the people; and, in the words of Stuart Chase, has "vindicated political democracy from a scientific standpoint" in a way that no logic and no sentiment down the centuries had ever been able to do.

In other words, for over twenty centuries we had been wrong on this point. We thought that the multitude was not to be trusted, that it had no "popular intelligence." Now we have discovered the awful truth. The failure was not with the multitude, but with the leaders. The multitude *is* capable of sound judgment *when the leaders are capable of supplying the ideas and capable of communicating them intelligently, effectively, and responsibly.* As William Lydgate stated in his summary after measuring public opinion for fifteen years, the average voter's mistake stems from lack of information, not from lack of intelligence or judgment; and when people have the information, they move on to form the right opinion, and do so two years ahead of Congress! George Gallup, with the mass of evidence piled high in front of him, wrote that, "The public is almost always ahead of its governmental leaders," and that social scientists now know this from "an overwhelming volume of evidence amassed during . . . two decades on nearly every conceivable issue—political, social and economic."[1]

This, therefore is the point of departure for this book: *The system of speechmaking was born of man's early struggle for democracy. It is still inherent in a free society, and unless an adequate portion of leaders in all areas of human life can speak intelligently, effectively, and responsibly—among themselves and to the people at large—we must live in constant danger of internal breakdown. A course on speechmaking ought to be founded on this premise.*

## II

Next, students of speechmaking should know that *for twenty-three centuries effective speeches have been prepared in accordance with a theory of public address.* Uninformed people, to be sure, mouth loose statements to the contrary, such as, "Most great speakers ignore rules and regulations." (This statement is copied from a book by an "authority" on the "new scientific techniques" of "modern" speaking.) Whose rules? Whose regulations? On what evidence? Isocrates, that doughty speech teacher who left his permanent stamp on both theory and practice, knew better as early as 392 B.C. After 2,350 years even the slow-minded have had time to catch on. The evidence need not be repeated here. It is available in authoritive histories of public address, and in such standard references as R. C. Jebb's *Attic Orators,* Donald L. Clark's *Rhetoric in Greco-Roman Education,* Wilbur Samuel Howell's *Logic and Rhetoric in England, 1500-1700,* and Thonssen and Baird's *Speech Criticism,* not to mention volumes dealing with specific instances such as Sister Miriam Joseph's *Shakespeare's Use of the Arts of Language.*

Every examination of the evidence shows there never was any really effective speaking until speeches began to be prepared in accordance with a theory of public address. As Jebb stated, "It was of the essence of Greek oratory . . . that its practice should be connected with a theory.

---

[1] William Lydgate, *What Our People Think* (New York, Thomas Y. Crowell Co. 1944), Chapter 1, "The People, Yes." George Gallup, "The Changing Climate for Public Opinion Research," *The Public Opinion Quarterly,* XXI (Spring, 1957), No. 1, 27.

Art is the application of rules . . . and the Greek conception of speaking as an art implied a Rhetoric." (*Attic Orators,* II, 370.) Furthermore, the later decline in quality of Greek public address did not come from "loss of freedom" as scholars once assumed. It began before freedom was lost, and its contributing cause was a depravation of theory taught in the schools. "The Old Oratory was an art, and was therefore based upon a theory. The New Oratory was a knack, and was founded upon practice [only]." (*Attic Oratory,* II, 441.) Here is a lesson of history before which teachers of speech should pause in sober reflection. Are we today teaching a *theory* of public address? Or merely a *knack?* Let's face it frankly. Some among us teach only a knack.

Knowing the theory, of course, is not enough. "All the rhetorician's rules teach nothing but to name his tools," wrote Samuel Butler.[2] Naming the tools is only the first step. Using the tools is what makes the theory count, and effective speakers have used them for twenty-three centuries. Whether any individual speaker was personally trained in classroom speaking is beside the point. Most of them were, to be sure, from Daniel Webster to Franklin D. Roosevelt. *But the essential thing is the existence of a theory of public address in each generation and the example in public life of a nucleus of speakers who apply that theory.*

I hardly need say that this book has no claim of "public speaking made easy," nor any formula for "the modern speaker of the new school." Instead it sets forth the theory of public address as developed by human experience and experiment through twenty-four centuries, fusing both the fundamental contributions of the old rhetoricians and the enormous and invaluable research of modern times. Above all, it postulates that effective speaking requires the application of a theory, exactly as effective surgery and effective airplane building require it.

### III

We come now to *Who Listens?*

A loose notion, here to be challenged, is that the influence of the public speaker has declined in modern times. That lament is hoary with age. It was invented centuries ago. It was voiced conspicuously by Edward T. Channing in 1819: "We hear constantly how it [public address] has fallen from its old supremacy." In that year, particularly unhappy for such a lament, Clay was 42 years of age, Webster and Calhoun were 37, Lincoln was ten, Douglas and Beecher were six!

Only recently has the history of modern public address been carefully investigated on a wide scale, and it shows the opposite to be true. Two centuries ago even representative governments were, in the words of Disraeli, "for the few, and the very few." Even when Thomas Jefferson in 1776 wrote that "all men are created equal," in America less than one

---

[2] Samuel Butler (1612-1680) here quoted is not to be confused with Samuel Butler (1835-1902) quoted above on page 6.

adult in five was eligible to vote or hold any form of political power, and Roger Sherman of Connecticut voiced the opinion of the majority of the Founding Fathers when in the Constitutional Convention of 1787 he said: "The people should have as little to do as may be about the Government. They . . . are constantly liable to be misled." But the people who had read Thomas Paine's *Rights of Man* and the Declaration of Independence intended to have those rights of men, including the right to vote; and by 1832 they had established universal manhood suffrage in practice, even though not all states had it by actual law. "You are summoned to give history a fresh start," Barère de Vieuzac had said to the French Assembly in 1789. In a sense that is what universal suffrage did in America. It changed the nature of our political society. It altered the pattern of *Who Listens?* It gave history a fresh start.

Down to 1840, for example, no Presidential nominee had ever made an active speaking campaign. Jefferson had not. The Adamses had not. Jackson had not. But in 1840 William Henry Harrison, in the words of Robert G. Gunderson, "took his cause to the people in what many considered a blatant disregard for tradition." Already universal suffrage was changing the pattern of *Who Listens?* Thereafter for more than half a century speaking during Presidential campaigns was tame and restricted. But if the politicians were slow in catching on, in the end they were sure. Today every Presidential nominee travels by plane and train to city and hamlet, and 100,000 miles is a campaign minimum. He speaks in person at the crossroads. He speaks on television to the nation. Over 100,000,000 people will see his face and hear his voice.

This, of course, has fundamentally affected the nature of public address. Aristotle commented on the select Athenian audience of his day—when hardly one adult in forty voted or sat in the popular assemblies—that "There are people whom one cannot instruct," and that speakers must remember that they are talking to "persons who cannot take in at a glance a complicated argument, or follow a long chain of reasoning." It is even more true today when every adult has the right to vote and the right to listen. Pale theorists and anemic academic intellectuals may complain of speakers who are "popular." They are misfits, born centuries too late. In a free society the speaker's compulsion is to be "popular," if by that derogatory term it is meant to be understood by the masses. But to be "popular" does not mean to be careless in reasoning, weak in judgment, or irresponsible in talk. It means to be *understood by the people.* This is a distinction that students must be taught to recognize, and to which they should be held accountable from the beginning.

As *Who Listens?* has expanded from the select few to the whole people, there also has come an incredible increase in the amount of speaking. Two hundred years ago few speakers traveled far, and few listeners went far to listen, because of physical reasons. Land transportation had not changed since 500 B.C. It was still by the horse and the highway. Then in swift succession came the steamboat and the railway, and later the automobile and the airplane, all of which multiplied the amount of speaking beyond the dreams of man. Consider a few particulars. In 1828 there were perhaps 100 branches of the lyceum; in 1834 there were 3,000. In 1835 Emerson confined his speaking largely to his own state; in 1855 he was making annual western tours to places like Chicago and Milwaukee, and in that year at far-away Davenport, Iowa, he crossed the river on ice to keep a speaking engagement. A hundred years ago there was no National Association of Manufacturers, no United States Chamber of Commerce, no AFL-CIO, no Speech Association of America—and therefore there were no conventions held by them and no speaking before their members. A hundred years ago there were no service clubs and no women's clubs, and no speaking before groups of that sort. The truth is that even a hundred and fifty years ago there was very little speaking compared with the per capita amount that exists today.

*Who Listens?* More people listen, and they listen to more speeches.

Not all people, of course, listen equally in either amount or effectiveness. Elmo Roper, unconsciously perhaps adapting an idea once propounded by John Fiske, has tentatively but discerningly classified the "United States public" into six levels in terms of their members' influence (*Saturday Review*, July 31, 1954). First, are the most influential, the *Great Thinkers*, of whom probably there are not more than half a dozen now living in the world. They come forth with important ideas that influence the world, like Aristotle and Einstein. Second, are the *Great Disciples*, of whom there might be a dozen now living in this country. They are the protagonists and explainers of ideas of the great thinkers, like Abraham Lincoln and Thomas Huxley. Third, are the *Great Disseminators*, of whom there are probably less than a thousand in the United States. They are the influential communicators who disseminate basic ideas to ordinary intellectuals and to people of action. Typical of this group would be Thomas Edison and Walter Lippmann. Fourth, are the *Lesser Disseminators*, the influential teachers, editors, labor leaders, and others who "locally and popularly" communicate ideas and influence public opinion. These number perhaps 25,000. Fifth are the *Politically Active*, which is a group of some 10,000,000 people—plus an additional 15,000,000 who are "somewhat active." These politically active have a persistent interest in public affairs. They vote, attend meetings, give money to worthy causes, and work for a better community and better nation. Sixth, are the *Politically Inert*, numbering over 100,-000,000. By "politically inert" is meant that they are inert most of the time, but not all of the time, for large sections of this group become intermittently active. They compose the so-called "masses" whose intermittent activity is a vital democratic check on the "excesses of the experts."

*Who Listens?* The whole people. Not all listen in equal amounts or with equal effectiveness, but at vital moments even the inert listen actively and act positively.

## IV

But after all, *Why Speak?* Cynics repeatedly have said that "all the speeches ever given never changed a vote or altered an opinion." If true, this would not decrease the necessity for speechmaking, as we shall see in a moment, but it would alter the theory of speechmaking. Indeed it would alter the whole structure of free societies, and of Western civilization. Is it true?

Not too many years ago even the scientific polltakers believed for a brief moment that it was true. In 1948 Dr. George Gallup writing as a Scientific Expert, an authority on New Knowledge, asked himself the question: "Do speeches change many votes?" and answered that his polltakers had "tested political opinion just before a candidate arrives in a state for speaking and again after he has left. The difference is almost always negligible." Of course he had forgotten those frequent 5 per cent shifts of opinion shown by his own polltakers in previous years, and had ignored the gigantic 20 per cent shift following one speech in the 1936 campaign. He learned better in the hard bitter way that year when the shift-of-opinion votes totaling almost 10 per cent for President Truman upset his predictions of a Dewey victory and made him a false prophet. After the election all of the leading polltakers met in conference. The best summary of that conference was stated by Archibald M. Crossley, one of the leading experts: "We *assumed* that campaigns did not change many votes and we stopped polling too early." Nearly twenty years later George Gallup admitted wryly: "The 1948 election, bitter experience though it was, proved a blessing in disguise. We learned that political sentiment can shift. . . ."

Now Aristotle, Quintilian, St. Augustine, and George Campbell— masters of the theory of public address—could have told the polltakers that in the first place. As early as 450 B.C. it had been discovered that speechmaking did change the votes of jurors and lawmakers, and a great deal had been discovered about how it changed votes.

This knowledge that people's opinions are altered and modified by speechmaking has been known for twenty-four centuries. More important, it is the foundation of all free societies, and the *one* factor whereby the Hellenic and Western civilizations rose above the other 19 civilizations that flourished for a time on this planet. Walter Bagehot posed the question and gave the answer in his monumental *Physics and Politics*, published in 1873—a book that certainly every speech teacher ought to read: "A large part, a very large part, of the world seems to be ready to advance to something good . . . , and then to have stopped, and not advanced. India, Japan, China, almost every sort of Oriental civilisation, though differing in nearly all other things, are alike in this. They look as if they had paused when there was no reason for pausing." Why? These arrested civilizations were not governed by talk. Nor were they free societies. They allowed no varieties of thought, but only fixed custom "imposed on all minds." In contrast, the civilization to which we belong "was made in states where the government was to a great and growing extent a government by discussion. . . . In this manner all the great movements of thought in ancient and modern times have been nearly connected in time with government by discussion." (*Physics and Politics, passim* pp. 53-166.)

Likewise, Arnold J. Toynbee's *Study of History* rests on the premise that civilizations are never created by the masses of people, but only by the "dominant minorities," and that members of the dominant minority must lead the masses, never by force, but always by "charm" (i.e., persuasion). When they resort to rule by force instead of persuasion, he finds, they are destroyed by their numerical superiors. In other words, in a democracy the multitude holds final power, and every group within it is a minority: management, labor, lawyers, physicians, farmers, educators. Every group, therefore, if it is to enjoy social or economic health, must constantly present its case to the public. It must do this constantly because every day thousands of old people pass on, and thousands of lusty boys and girls are born who do not know that Revlon makes "living lipstick," or that their dog will be happier on Gaines Food. They do not know the special problems of other groups that live among them: management, labor, lawyers, physicians, farmers, and educators. They will soon forget unless each group presents its case constantly. For them it may not be literally, as Wallace Carroll once said, "Persuade or perish," but it is "persuade or be neglected, misunderstood, or even persecuted."

This is the law of a free society. An educational system that ignores it is betraying the people it would serve.

Nevertheless, even were it not possible to persuade by speechmaking, and even were persuasion not the keystone of a free society, the making of speeches would still be inherent in human life. It has other functions than modifying opinions. People need continually to have their faith renewed and their courage strengthened. Again and again they need to be told that the righteous shall be saved, that truth can be made to triumph, and that democracy is the hope of the world. Continually and without ceasing, they need to be told that life has a purpose, and that they have a duty. This cannot be done wholly while people are separated as individuals. It must come to them also while they sit together elbow to elbow and are stimulated by the presence of others. They must see and hear the man who talks, take measure of him, and find his deeper meanings. "My voice goes after what my eyes cannot reach," exclaimed Walt Whitman.

Hence you cannot have a church without a minister and a meeting place, nor a political party without political rallies and speakers, nor any movement, intellectual or industrial, without conventions and conferences. And correspondence-school universities have never seriously competed with those who put their students in the classroom face-to-face with the teacher.

*Why Speak?* To keep a free society free. To settle differences by talk instead of force. To alter and promote thought. To water and cultivate ideas, hopes, sentiments and enthusiasms in a way and to a degree that cannot be done while we are separated one from another.

## V

Finally, in what language shall we teach students to speak? I do not refer to whether it shall be English or French or German. The question is more penetrating.

For over three centuries, roughly until the end of World War II, our Western civilization constituted "the modern world." It was a world created by the Renaissance, a world pioneered by men like Galileo, Erasmus, Hobbes, Locke, and Newton. But the concepts we used to describe it, and the language, came mainly from one man: René Descartes. It was Descartes who redefined and reapportioned old terms and gave them modern meanings.

During the century in which Descartes and these other intellectual pioneers lived most of the leading ideas and beliefs that influence our lives today took their modern form. In government, the struggle for freedom of speech, trial by jury, the privilege of *habeas corpus,* freedom of press, freedom of religion and of man's conscience—all of these began to take their modern form some three hundred years ago. In science, the foundations were laid by Kepler, Newton and others on which the twentieth century built. Even in business, current economic theories and practice had many of its foundations laid down some three hundred years ago in vexing problems that still vex us today: creeping inflation, currency control, government deficits, tariff and foreign trade.

As a result, until around the end of World War II an educated man three hundred years ago could still understand an educated man of today, and still be able to make himself understood; for both of them spoke the language of Descartes.

But since the end of World War II, or about that date, we have been moving with high speed toward a new view of the world to replace the old one we have been using for three hundred years. It is as if the atom bomb not only had thrust us into a new age of energy, but also into a new age of concepts; and this new age of concepts is forcing us to speak in a new language.

I pass by the new language of physics and mathematics. If you are acquainted with these fields the recent change of language is well known. If you are not, it is too complicated for quick explanation.

But let us look at the new language in psychology. In psychology Descartes set up that famous dual world of mind and body. Mind dealt with "intellect" and "reason." Mind operated on a different set of principles from body. Psychologists used this language almost entirely until about 1910, and most of them for many years after. In terms of Descartes' language education was a *mental* process. Now psychologists have given up the mind-body dualism. They say that you cannot separate the human mind from human behavior. They say further that learning is not "mental" but is a process that involves the whole organism. This has led to a lively conflict in education, part of which comes from two groups of educators talking to each other in two languages. The traditional educators since World War II have been attacking the public schools with almost psychopathic fury. They are persons who by most standards would be called "men of good will," yet they have been driven to using violent words like *quacks* and *charlatans* in discussing public school educators. Now *these critics of education write and think entirely in the language of Descartes!* Education, they say, has lost its "mental discipline," and its "intellectual values." The trouble here is that modern psychologists and educators do not even think in those terms. According to their concepts there is no such thing as "mind" or "mental discipline," or "intellectual values." According to their concepts education is a whole process. In short, according to their concepts Robert Hutchins, Whitney Griswold, and Arthur Bestor are talking in a dead language. I don't mean in an ancient language, but a dead one.

Where does that leave us? Physicists long ago said that there was no "matter." Now psychologists say there is no "mind." One wit has summarized it well: "No matter, never mind."

In economics we have also developed new concepts and have begun to talk in a new language. A student of economics forty years ago would never have heard of such current concepts as *management, administered prices, concentrated industries, commodity credit, gross national product,* and of *disposable* personal income. These are new concepts and new terms. As I read those who discuss economic problems today they are in serious language trouble. We've had those "16 revolutions" of the twentieth century which have changed the nature of government and business, and changed their relationship to each other. Electronics and automation have made corporations bigger today than old governments were in the past. The role of government has been revolutionized. It must supply information on which business bases its plans. It must shape the policies of money and credit. It must stabilize the economy. Yet writers, and even a few economists, still talk about new concepts in old terms: *big business, monopolies, government interference,* and *the welfare state.* As a result, their using an old language to discuss new concepts creates what Mark

Twain termed "confusion of the mind and congestion of the ducts of thought."

In speech and language, of course, we could not escape language trouble for we deal with it *per se*. Against the anguished protests of parents and traditional educators, we talk less of *grammar* and more of *communication*. Grammar is a concept of the *parts* of speech, dear to the world of Descartes. Communication looks at the *whole process* of speech: what is said, to whom, through what media, under what conditions, and in what frame of reference. It may even concern itself with what was not said, and why.

Here is the essential difference between the world of Descartes and the world of today, whether in speech, economics, science, or anything else. In Descartes' world the whole was the sum of its parts. It had to be, for the world of Descartes was mechanical. It was static. *But in the new view of the world emerging since World War II, perhaps the greatest single departure from the old concepts lies in our understanding that the whole is more than the sum of its parts. For the whole adds "process," what the physicists call "energy" and what the psychologists call "function."* This new concept recognizes growth, development, dynamism. It postulates that the basic principle of all phenomena is not mass but *energy*, and that what we used to call "matter" and "mind" are merely special forms of energy. This explains why in speech *grammar* is no longer a basic concept. It explains why *communication*—in spite of the disdain of older members in the field of speech—has become the new concept. Communication does not deal with static subject matter, or with parts of speech, but with the whole process.

Now this has a direct impact on every student of speech. Half a century ago college teachers of the old classical subjects found their classes getting smaller, and saw with dismay that classes in "new" subjects like speech and psychology were getting larger. They accused these new departments of teaching courses that had no "content" or "subject matter." The controversy, of course, arose out of the empty classrooms of frustrated educators; yet these educators had power on certain campuses and their arguments had to be dignified by a reply. What kind of answer did we teachers of speech give? Proudly we pointed to our "subject matter," which was older than Aristotle. We presented evidence to show that in Greek and Roman education speech was the core around which other subjects were grouped, so much so that its institutions of higher learning were known as "schools of rhetoric." This was an adequate answer, but you will note that it was based on the assumption that "subject matter" and "content" *were* the only tests of respectability in education. Indeed everybody who lived in the world of Descartes believed that the important thing in education was "content" and "subject matter."

We know better now. We know now that "content" and "subject matter" are not enough. Looking back we can see that our proud insistence that these "new" courses of half a century ago had "subject matter" missed the essential fact. Actually, the new outlook in the field of speech during the 1920's and 1930's was doing to education what Einstein's formula was doing to the scientific world. It was rising above static subject matter. It was insisting that *function* was part of education. It was demonstrating that the *whole was more than the sum of its parts*. It was discarding the inept adage that "knowledge is power," and replacing it with the new concept that "only the *use* of knowledge is power."

What has all this to do with you? Simply this. You are living in a world which has produced not merely new inventions, but also new concepts of thinking. Yours is not merely a generation which has nylon and ball-point pencils, jet planes and man-made satellites. It has also developed new concepts and new levels of thinking. In the half-century ahead this brave new world, like the world of Locke and Newton, will be changing under the impact of more new discoveries and more new concepts. You must learn to discuss these new concepts intelligently, effectively, and responsibly.

You will have trouble on two fronts. First, in the various fields of human thought we have now reached a maddening confusion of tongues. Each field has its own new language, and to everybody on the outside it is jargon. As a result, scientists have trouble explaining even to Congress what they are doing with money appropriated for national defense, until one United States Senator groaned, "It sounds like unscrewing the inscrutable." That same blackout is likely to arise when specialists in any field try to talk with specialists in any other field.

You face also a second problem. During the next half-century this world in transition will be groping for more new concepts and more new terms in which to communicate them. We shall be living in a time of confusion, language confusion. You can't do much about all this. It is the price you pay for living in such an interesting and strenuous world. But one thing you can do. You can decline to confuse people by using old terms when you talk about new concepts. You can refuse to talk about "mental training" in education, and use instead the concepts and language of today. You can refuse to engage in economic double-talk, to use seventeenth-century words in discussing twentieth-century concepts. Already in fields like mathematics people in midstream have had to unlearn an old vocabulary and learn a new one. They have had to give up the concept that a line was the "shortest distance between two points" and learn that a line is a "set of points," discard old terms for new concepts like "Cartesian products," "null sets," and "strict inequalities." During the next half century we shall need to do this in all fields of human affairs.

This is the frame of reference. In the pages that follow we shall proceed to the treatment of ways and means.

PART

* I *

# GETTING STARTED

# The Rights of Listeners

AMERICA IS FACED with a shortage of scientists, we are warned, and of engineers, technical experts, and even skilled workers. True. But we are also faced with another shortage just as critical. It is a shortage of enough competent speakers to carry on the business of 180,000,000 people living together in a free society.

Among the most precious possessions of mankind is an inherited civilization that must be preserved under all circumstances. But civilization is never static. It is changing continuously so that now, as in that day when the proverb was first written, "all things are in perpetual flux and fleeting." It calls for constant examination and continuous intelligent discussion by people who can humanize truth and energize knowledge. It calls for people who can do this, not merely through the indirect written channels, but also through the immediate, direct, face-to-face spoken word, formally and informally, around a table and from a platform, before small groups and large.

These speakers cannot be set apart into a separate profession like the law, medicine, education, industrial management, or the clergy. We cannot say, "These experts will teach the schools, and those experts will give the speeches." Or "These specialists will manage industry and those specialists will do the speechmaking." No group of experts can long hire others to speak for it. It must do its own speaking, or in the end be misunderstood, needlessly criticized, or even persecuted. We are here concerned with how to produce speakers to carry on the necessary business of living together in this American democracy.

Unhappily we now have three kinds of speakers: effective, ineffective, and defective. People don't become effective speakers merely because they have ideas, or even because they have learned to write important ideas in clear English. Ideas are vital and skill in writing is vital, yet some of the most brilliant writers of important ideas have remained among the world's defective speakers. The reason is obvious. One writes in solitude, and sets down ideas to be read in solitude. But public address requires a living speaker to talk with living people. They sit before him.

They are visible to him (except in radio and television where they are not physically visible, but are sharply in his mind's eye and are listening at the moment of utterance.) The speaker talks *to* them. He talks *with* them. He looks *at* them. He sees their nods of understanding or telltale expressions of misunderstanding, their attentive look which says "I am interested," or bored restlessness which says "I am tired of listening." Public address, then, is not set down on paper for somebody to read next week or next month. It is spoken to people listening at the moment of utterance. It not only requires previous composition of material. It requires also that *the speech be created on the instant and in the presence of the listeners.*

The speaker, of course, has the more difficult role, but the listeners' role is more important, for public address exists, not to serve the speaker, but to serve the listener. From the listeners' standpoint entirely too much public talk is trite, dull, boring, or simply worthless. Too much is perpetrated by self-made speakers who have never learned to manage ideas, or to manage themselves in public, or to create a speech while standing before listeners. Public speaking requires professional skill, just as playing the violin or building jet planes, and the painful truth is that most would-be speakers attempt to substitute pious intentions for professional skill. They believe that "anybody can talk," and vengefully demonstrate their false belief. So each day and each night thousands of men and women stand up to speak to a variety of listeners, and most of these speakers are inept. Yet they speak for hours on end, until listeners feel numb on one end and dumb at the other. If all such speakers were laid end to end their audiences would applaud heartily!

In short, we have not yet become an enlightened democracy capable of communicating effectively by speech. We shall not become so until the usage becomes law that *no speaking is worth listening to unless it delivers useful goods to the listener.* These two things, then, in an enlightened democracy—every listener has a right to demand of every speaker:

1. *Useful* goods
2. Ability to *deliver* these goods

Let us consider each in detail and in more formal language.

### From a speaker, listeners have the right to expect interesting and useful ideas

The average educated person hears approximately one hundred speeches a year. Why listen to so many? Why listen to *any*? Not because we are forced outwardly, for outwardly we are free to listen or not.

We are rather driven by forces within us. We are human beings, living in an entangled world. In that world we face problems which must be understood by responsible people; we are beset by choices and temptations; we are haunted by the shadows of fear. We listen to speakers because we hope they will illuminate life and make irrelevant facts seem significant. We listen because we hope they will give us new information, new ideas, or will simply water and cultivate old ideas. We listen because we want to be given encouragement, to renew our faith, to strengthen our determination. We listen because we want to be shown the beauty, the goodness, and the glories of life. We listen perhaps because we want to escape from reality for a time, to laugh and forget our troubles.

These are the services expected of speakers, and listeners have the inalienable right to demand that every speaker who consumes public time shall deliver the services expected. The following are three types of parasites who do not so deliver, and who ought to be put out of business:

1. *The Bafflegab*—who uses words that cover everything but fit nothing, like this:

> The extent to which we control the future depends upon our adherence to the ideals that have made us great.

If you ask what these noble words mean you won't find out, not from the Bafflegab. He deals in generalities. The Bafflegab also winces at straightaway English. His sentences are shapeless bundles of words. Here is a specimen bundle:

> In most cases where retirement dissatisfaction existed advance activity programming by individuals had been insignificant. [In straightaway English this means "Most people who did not want to retire had not planned how to use their leisure time."]

Not only does the Bafflegab use imprecise words and rumple them into shapeless bundles. He ties his bundles together with what Sir Winston Churchill called "woolly phrases" that could "be left out altogether, or replaced with a single word":

> It is also of importance to bear in mind the following consideration. . . . [Meaning "also."]

How do speakers get that way? Face it frankly. Clear thinking is hard work. Clear thinking takes time. The Bafflegab's foggy language comes from foggy thinking. He does not take the time to think himself clear. He does not take the time to find the right words, or to line them up in the right order. He does not make the effort to illuminate thought by an illustration, or to relieve a tired audience with humor. Of him it could never be said what Charles I said of Edward Coke, that listeners were "never weary with hearing him, he mingled mirth with business to so good purpose." The Bafflegab, in other words, does not meet the test. He fails to water and cultivate ideas with clear ideas, plain facts, and precise words.

2. *The Witless Wit*—who believes in the salvation of man by funny stories. He is determined to set the audience in a roar, and comes armed with twenty anecdotes—but no thought. He recites with gusto his hodge-podge of jests, which illustrate no theme, and measures his success by the amount of laughter. To listeners who have previously heard part or all of the jokes, they are no longer funny.

3. *The Phonograph*—who reproduces a magazine article and thinks it makes a good speech. The Phonograph is a common species among students. He puts off preparing a speech until the night before, then evades the issue by seizing a magazine article, swallowing it and attempting to reproduce it undigested, as a speech. He does not plagiarize outright; that is, he does not recite verbatim the words of the article. But he does reproduce the outline and the contents, and he adds nothing of his own. He is a Phonograph, and his speech is a failure, because even a good article when recited is not a speech. "The voice is Jacob's voice, but the hands are the hands of Esau." The magazine article was written six months or a year ago. It was intended for a reading audience of perhaps a million people, a people of varied educational levels, scattered over the entire United States and in foreign lands. In contrast, the speech is to be given *today* to *one* particular group of thirty people who have already heard two speeches on the same topic during the past month, and it is given by a student whose voice and manner proclaim loudly that he knows nothing about the subject except what he is reciting from the magazine. In other words, the student has failed to focus the speech on the particular audience meeting at a particular place on a particular day. Being a Phonograph, he simply reproduces another person's thoughts.

### Listeners also have the right to see and hear a human being who talks with the audience, and not a dull or nervous creature who talks to himself

Some people, of course, believe that "delivery" is not important. A speaker, they think, needs only to "say what he thinks" and these thoughts will find their way into the minds of the listeners. A fair summary of this belief is, "It does not matter how you deliver a speech; the only important thing is what you say." Now this is a comfortable belief. It relieves a speaker from any responsibility beyond writing a paper. But the belief does not square with the facts of life. It assumes that you literally do "deliver" a speech in the same way you deliver a loaf of bread. It assumes that when delivered, the speech, like the loaf of bread, arrives intact and cellophane-wrapped no matter how long the delivery man took, whether he arrived drunk or sober, or how many detours or breakdowns he had along the way. These are grand assumptions indeed, but only assumptions. Actually there is no such thing as delivering a speech. The very word "delivery" is a turn of expression and not a statement of fact.

## WHY NO SPEAKER CAN REALLY "DELIVER" A SPEECH

You can deliver a book, a pencil, or a loaf of bread. You carry them to their destination and give them up to another's keeping. You cannot so deliver a speech. *To "deliver" a speech you have to telegraph it by using sound waves and light waves; and the methods you use in telegraphing determine how much the listeners get, how well they get it, and how long they remember it.* This telegraphing goes through seven stages from your mind to the listener's mind:

1. You start with a *thought* in your mind.

2. This thought is coded into a series of impulses and sent through your nervous system. These impulses are roughly like the dot-dash telegraph code, and are known as a *neurogram*.

3. This neurogram is coded further into phonetic symbols by *muscular movements* of the tongue, lips, face, diaphragm, etc.

4. These phonetic symbols, thus produced by muscular activity, are coded still further into *sound waves* that travel invisibly through the air. When these sound waves reach the listener, the decoding process begins.

5. The sound waves *strike the listener's ear drums* and produce a mechanical action in the bones of the middle ear and in the fluid of the inner ear. In this process the sound waves are decoded again into phonetic symbols.

6. These decoded phonetic symbols are sent in the form of impulses along the nerve fibers to the brain. These impulses, as in stage 2, are roughly like the dot-dash telegraph code and compose a *neurogram*.

7. In the listener's brain this neurogram is decoded further into a *thought*. This last step is the semantic stage, wherein the various brain assemblages translate the incoming symbols into meaning. The amount of meaning in each instance will depend: ( *a* ) on the distinctness and

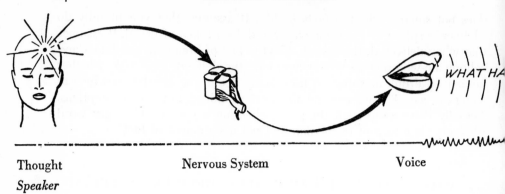

Thought             Nervous System           Voice

*Speaker*

PRO(

clarity of incoming symbols, and (*b*) on the variety of brain connections, built-in and temporary, that are available for use.

Thus you do not "deliver" a speech at all in the way you deliver a book, a pencil, or a loaf of bread. There is no "delivery" to it. Instead, you *use sound waves and light waves to create thought in the listener's mind.*

So far, of course, we have discussed only sound waves. This was not because light waves are not important or not inherent, but solely and simply because the complex process glibly miscalled "delivery" is more easily understood if taken one part at a time. We can now consider light waves. They follow a process parallel with that of sound waves: (1) The *thought* in the speaker's mind is coded into (2) a *neurogram* in the nervous system, then (3) further coded into *muscular movements* of posture, body, hands, face, and head. These in turn are (4) transmitted by *light waves* that are (5) received by the listener's *eyes* where it is (6) decoded into a *neurogram* via nerve impuses sent along the optic nerve to the brain. Finally, in the brain this is (7) decoded into a *thought*. Now this thought is not so refined and exact as the thought conveyed by words, but it is older in the human race, is written deeper in the human organism, and carries more basic meanings. Sound waves carry the refined, precise thought. Light waves carry the broad basic background of meaning. To the listener they say, "That speaker does not mean what he says; his actions deny his words." Or, "He is not thinking, but is only reciting." Or, "I see exactly what he means, for he both *shows* and *tells* me." The inherent part of light waves in communication will be covered more fully in Chapter 16.

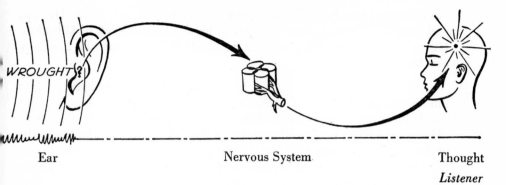

| Ear | Nervous System | Thought |
|---|---|---|
| | | *Listener* |

WROUGHT?

PEECH

## WHY SPEAKERS FAIL IN "DELIVERY"

The following are common types of speakers who create barriers that prevent their creating full thought in listeners' minds:

1. *The Fidgeter*—whose actions distract the listeners' attention. The eye is quicker than the ear. What the listener sees take priority over what he hears. Hence the Fidgeter's actions interfere with his words. Behold his behavior: If his hands are in his pockets, he takes them out; if they are out, he puts them in. If his coat is unbuttoned, he buttons it; if it is buttoned, he unbuttons it. If he is at one side of the platform, he paces to the other side; when he gets there, he paces back again. He rocks from heel-to-toe. He stands on one foot, and hoists the other as though to cool off the sole of the shoe. His hands and feet are always in the way, and he has the air of having too many of them.

2. *The "And-Er" Vocalist*—those pauses mutilate instead of punctuate. Instead of a clean pause at the end of a thought unit, he creates static like this:

I—*Er*—want to compare the—*Er*—stage plays of—*Er*—today—*Er*—with those of a—*Er*—century ago.

To *Er* is human. But the most unforgivable human *Er's* are those inflicted on suffering audiences by speakers who neglect their home work. They deserve cruel punishment. They should be forced to listen to a recording of their own voices.

3. *The Mumbler*—who can hear himself and does not care about anyone else. He looks at their ceiling, at the floor, or out the window, but not at the audience. He keeps his mouth closed "like the front room in an

old-fashioned farmhouse," and opens it only to eat and yawn. His lips and tongue are on vacation. His jaw is fixed, like the Rock of Gibraltar. His voice is flat, and his tones are weak. He believes that talk is cheap, and his talk *is* cheap.

4. *The Sleeping-Pill Voice*—whose listless tones lull listeners into intellectual slumber. He talks loud enough to be heard, of course, but his words have no color, warmth, life, friendliness, or informing inflection. "Though the earth be moved and the mountains be carried into the midst of the sea," he gives nothing any meaning. He is a *tranquilizer* who leaves the listeners unmoved, untouched, and undisturbed. Over two centuries ago a famous author and clergyman, Jonathan Swift, warned a young man entering the ministry against such speaking; and his words are as apt today as then: "If your arguments be strong, in God's name offer them in as moving a manner as the nature of the subject will probably admit." Or as Emerson put it: "Eloquence wants anthracite coal. Coldness is the most fatal quality."

Of course, it is self-satisfying for a listless speaker to imagine that it does not matter *how* he talks, that *what* he says is the only thing that counts. But whosoever says that varnishes nonsense with the charms of sound. Down the centuries wise men have known better, and experimental evidence has given statistical validity to their wisdom. This evidence suggests that listeners will remember only about 40 per cent as much of what speakers say in a listless voice as compared with what they say in a lively voice having emphasis, inflection, and tone color. Imagine two speakers. Both talk loud enough for every word to be heard, but one speaks with color, warmth, and informing inflection; the other speaks in a dead-flat tone. The audience will remember only about 40 per cent as much of what the listless speaker says as compared with what the lively speaker says.

To summarize: *In speaking, the know-how as well as the know-what is important; and listeners have the right to demand that speakers have both.*

## TALKING WITH THE AUDIENCE

Every speaker should ask himself three questions. First, "Can I be heard?" Second, "Can I be understood?" If he can answer yes to those two, he then comes to the formidable third question: *"Can I be enjoyed?"* Unless a speaker is enjoyed, he will not long be listened to.

We cannot here look into all the elements that make listeners enjoy a speaker, but the first and basic one is that a speaker should talk *with* the entire audience.

Public speaking is *enlarged conversation.* It should be enlarged enough to fill the room, and to reach that slightly hard-of-hearing listener in the eighth row who leans a little forward as you begin to talk. This takes not only physical energy, but also mental and moral qualities well stated by James A. Winans:

1. *Full realization of the content of your words as you utter them,* and
2. *A lively sense of communication.*[1]

If you don't *fully* realize the content of words at the *instant* of utterance, your delivery is absent-minded. If you don't have a *lively* sense of communication, you seem to be talking to yourself. Enlarged conversation, in others words, requires you to think foremost of your listeners, and not of yourself. You must present your ideas to *them,* interest *them,* look for *their* response. It is not enough even to talk *to* them. You must talk *with* them. When you talk with them you are concerned that they listen, understand, and enjoy.

Now this takes courage as well as self-control. "It is four-fifths will power," admitted a speaker who had finally learned how. If you won't exert will power, but weaken and back up inside yourself, you lose control of yourself, and obviously lose control of your audience. Speakers who do that mumble, or gaze at the floor, or stare out the window. They lack courage, or lack self-control; or having only a little of either they talk in a *half*-direct way. They don't entirely lack a sense of communication, but still we must say, they are only half-way creatures. Arthur Schopenhauer's statement, "Style is the physiognomy of the mind, and a safer index to character than the face," is more true of delivery than of composition. So in a roundabout way we are saying that listeners have the right to demand that speakers be men and women of character, people who have something to say and not just an emotion or prejudice, people who know that truth is not enough if you neglect the homework required to create a speech—people, in short, who make it worth while for listeners to listen.

## Assignments

ON SPEAKERS HAVING INTERESTING AND USEFUL IDEAS

1. Report on two speakers you have recently heard, one good and one poor. A suggested analysis for each speaker:
   a. In what way was the subject worth (or not worth) listening to: a new idea? cultivated an old idea? gave stimulation or encouragement?
   b. How was it made interesting: facts and figures? illustrations? comparisons? suspense? humor, etc.?

2. Make a brief report on the most interesting speaker you have heard during the past year or two. Analyze *why* he was interesting in terms of the principles set forth in this chapter.

[1] James A. Winans, *Public Speaking* (New York, Appleton-Century-Crofts, Inc., 1915), p. 31.

ON SPEAKERS WHO REALLY TALK TO LISTENERS VERSUS DULL OR NERVOUS
PERSONS WHO TALK MAINLY TO THEMSELVES

3. In terms of principles found in this chapter, report on the "delivery" of each of the speakers selected in the above assignments. Why was it good? Or why was it poor? Or why merely a sad average?

4. As an ice-breaker start with a speech introducing another member of the class. The instructor will divide the class into pairs, and each student will obtain pertinent information from his partner: full name, home city, high school, activities, honors, travel, hobbies, etc. Outline your speech (better not write it or it might sound like memorized recitation instead of talk), rehearse it, and deliver it. Apply the principles of this chapter on respecting your listeners' rights.

5. Give a two-minute demonstration speech on something of interest to class members: a blackboard sketch of football plays, a demonstration of camera equipment, showing how to apply first-aid bandages, etc. Apply the principles of this chapter on respecting your listeners' rights.

6. Give a two-minute reading of any prose selection that you happen to like especially well. Remember that before the printed words of this selection can reach the audience, they must go through *seven stages*. Review them, then rehearse reading the selection until you can carry the thought through all seven stages.

ON PLANNING AHEAD

7. There are two kinds of speakers: those who "have something to say," and those who "have to say something." Obviously, not much can be expected of the latter group, and you will want to plan now to keep out of it. Therefore, copy and fill out the following Speech-Subject Analysis Form. Its purpose is twofold: (*a*) to examine your background and locate speech subjects that others may want to hear you talk about; (*b*) to collect a list of subjects that you would like to hear other speakers talk about.

After the forms are turned in, the instructor, or a committee of class members, can assemble a list of subjects that one or more students would like to hear. Preferably this list should be mimeographed and given to each student. If this is not possible, then it can be posted in an available place.

## SPEECH-SUBJECT ANALYSIS FORM

Name_____ Course No._____ Section No._____
    (last name)   (given name)

College address_____ Phone_____ Date_____

1. Where you were born, where you have lived or travelled, and what schools you have attended

_____

2. Your special interests and hobbies

_____

3. Your extracurricular activities in college

4. Jobs you have held in the past, or now hold

5. Your probable major study in college, and why you chose it

6. Your probable minor study, and why you chose it

7. Other courses you have especially enjoyed

8. Your reading preferences, including both areas (history, drama, or science, etc.) and particular individual books

9. Your political affiliations or sympathies

10. Your economic (labor-management, etc.) affiliations or sympathies

11. Your religious affiliations or sympathies

12. Your social affiliations or sympathies

13. Your possible or probable vocation

14. On the basis of the above analysis, list ten subjects you might use for speeches. Place a check before those you think the class would especially like to hear:

15. List ten subjects you would like to hear other class members discuss:

# Four Fundamentals
# for Speakers

BEFORE LOOKING at the details let us examine the four fundamentals on which good speaking is based. These are the principles which good speakers use, consciously or unconsciously.

## FIRST FUNDAMENTAL

*Effective public speaking is a technique as definitely as are the techniques of designing airplanes and removing appendixes, except that it is older and more complex than either*

Centuries upon centuries have gone into developing this technique, and some of the greatest men who ever lived gave their lives to it.[1] Now a technique requires a method of procedure. This method is not set down in fixed rules, for as Charles Henry Woolbert repeatedly said, "There is only one rule in public speaking and that is that there are no rules." Or as some wit later put it, "Rules are for when brains run out." Instead of rules, effective speaking is founded on a procedure derived from judgment, understanding, trial and error, and research.[2] Don't be misled by

[1] Among earlier eminent persons who made noteworthy contributions to this technique are Corax (about 470 B.C.), Aristotle (384-322 B.C.), Cicero (106-43 B.C.), Quintilian (35-100 A.D.), St. Augustine (354-430), Erasmus (1466-1536), and Francis Bacon (1561-1626). Significantly, Shakespeare, not a public speaker but a playwright, has mastered the technique of public speaking, and his mastery is seen in the scores of speeches made by the characters in his plays. The most famous example, of course, is Antony's speech at Caesar's funeral. "I come to bury Caesar, not to praise him. . . . ," which is a model of classical speech composition. George Campbell (1719-1796) should also be added. First of the famous Scotch rhetoricians, he was also the most penetrating and original. His analysis of persuasion was sustained by later research, and his classification of speech purposes surpasses that of most later writers.

[2] This explains the fallacy of the popular notion that "most great speakers ignore rules and regulations." In truth, research has shown that great speakers—Daniel

Six eminent men who contributed to the theory of speechmaking. *Reading down:*
Aristotle, Cicero, St. Augustine, Francis Bacon, Erasmus, George Campbell.

the cheap notion that you can substitute bypaths, or bag-of-tricks magic for a technique that has taken centuries to develop. This has been tried before.

Nor can you be an effective speaker, as some people want to believe, by having a rich voice or a fluent tongue. These may be assets, but they have handicapped many aspirants who tried to use them as substitutes.

Nor yet can you become an effective speaker simply because you have untrained natural ability. As Sir Arthur Quiller-Couch said of writing, which also requires a technique, "You will not get there by hammering away on your own untutored impulse." And as Horace put it centuries ago, "Neither training without rich gifts nor genius rude and untrained is sufficient." In other words, natural ability helps just as it helps in music or surgery; but people do not become musicians or surgeons from natural ability alone. They also must have training, and it takes training likewise to become a competent speaker. The slogan, "You Can Master It in Ten Easy Lessons," appeals to a certain type of people. Therefore, it might be interesting to know that men were looking for short cuts to effective speaking and for bag-of-trick substitutes long before Columbus sought his short route to India by going west; and, like Columbus, they never found the way. The whole idea was satirized by old Lucian of Samosata about the year A.D. 179 in the following words:

> Never let it disturb you that you have not been through the laborious preliminaries with which the ordinary system besets the path of fools; they are quite unnecessary. . . .
>
> Bring then above all ignorance, to which add confidence, audacity, and effrontery; as for diffidence, equity, moderation, and shame, you will please leave them at home; they are not merely needless, they are encumbrances. . . .
>
> The tongue is an unruly member; do not attempt to rule it; never care whether your firstly is logic's firstly, or your secondly and thirdly in the right order; just say what comes. . . .
>
> People of sense, remember, are rare, and they will probably hold their tongues out of charity; of if they do comment, it will be put down to jealousy. The rest are awed by your costume, your voice, gait, motions, falsetto, shoes, and sundry; when they see how you perspire and pant, they cannot admit a moment's doubt of your being a very fine . . . performer.[3]

This answer nearly 1,800 years ago to the short-cut seekers came from a competent and celebrated speaker who knew that short cuts were a delusion. It is an answer affirmed by the centuries. Public speaking is

---

Webster, Abraham Lincoln, Woodrow Wilson, Franklin D. Roosevelt, Winston Churchill, to mention a few modern ones—were careful students of speaking techniques. The supposed "rules" they ignored were false rules set up by inept writers.

[3] *The Works of Lucian of Samosata,* trans. by H.W.Fowler and F.G.Fowler (Oxford, 1905), III, 224-227.

a technique. Like every technique, it requires an expert method. Don't look for short cuts.[4]

## SECOND FUNDAMENTAL

### *Effective speaking is also an intellectual discipline*

Effective speaking is not merely a technique and nothing more. It is very much more. It is also an intellectual discipline. Now what is an "intellectual discipline"? *It is the ability to produce and manage ideas.*

Consider first the ability to produce ideas. William Hawley Davis quotes the amusing plight of a master of technique who complained, "I can express anything, but I have nothing to express." Let us have no nonsense about the importance of ideas. To speak well, you must be able to produce ideas, to test them for soundness, to know when you are doing straight thinking or crooked. But the ability to produce is not come by easily. Whence arises the maxim, "Thinking is hard work but prejudice is a pleasure." Even when we have ideas on a subject, they are not full-blown in our minds at the moment. They are dormant, they are forgotten, they are scattered about, unrelated, half-thought-out. Even worse, we may not have any ideas, or hardly any, and must go forth to find them.

This hunt for ideas is part of what we call "intellectual discipline." Really there is no discipline about it, and no orderliness. Says Barzun:

> Thinking is inwardly a haphazard, fitful, incoherent activity. If you could peer in and see thinking going on, it would not look like that trimmed and barbered result: A Thought. Thinking is messy, repetitious, silly, obtuse, subject to explosions that shatter the crucible and leave darkness behind. Then comes another flash, a new path is seen, trod, lost, broken off, and blazed anew. It leaves the thinker dizzy as well as doubtful: he does not know what he thinks until he has thought it. . . . Young scholars should believe all this if only in order to overcome their too frequent discouragement at the sight of their first thoughts. . . . Too much has been talked about "cold reason" and "orderly processes of mind." The impression has got about that Euclid began with a fresh sheet of paper, wrote down "Proposition I," and pushed on through to the end of the book without an erasure.

[4] Here are three interesting sidelights. Daniel Webster, at the age of forty-six, read Richard Whately's *Elements of Rhetoric* then just off the press, and commented that he had "found in it twenty things which I have thought of often, and been convinced of long, but never before saw in print." Henry Ward Beecher in later life said he did not preach his first sermon until after he had been speaking some ten years in college (during which he had about three years of formal speech training) and in the pulpit; he had preached *at* sermons for ten years until he learned how to preach "the first real one." Franklin D. Roosevelt reached maturity as a speaker in 1932 at the age of fifty; his apprenticeship included two years of classroom training in preparatory school and college plus more than twenty years of apprentice speaking in public life.

Even if his manuscript was neat, which I doubt, his previous fits and starts were doubtless many. The momentary glimpse that shows a relation, a truth, or a method of proof does not come at will. It is watched for like big game, and only when captured and tamed with others like it can it be shown off in orderly sequence.[5]

This is old knowledge to experienced speakers, and as early as 336 B.C. Aristotle listed twenty-eight sources of ideas that could be found within the speaker's mind. Yet each new generation must learn it anew—that ideas must be stalked with persistence and patience.

All of this is only the first step. Assume that with patience and persistence you have finally assembled the ideas. Do you now have a speech? No. You have, in fact, only finished preparing to begin. *The real steps of intellectual discipline are: (1) meditation, (2) judgment, and (3) finally the management of ideas.* In this three-fold process the ideas must be sifted, sorted, and tested. Those found fit for human use must be formed in line—in marching order. In other words, the speech must be given structure and its parts be proportioned. Here are some of the problems involved:

Where does your speech begin? Where does it end? What have beginning and end got to do with the listener?

What shall be the main topics? Where and how shall each topic begin, and what are their internal relationships and how can these be made instantly clear to the listener?

How shall the orientation of main topics toward one another and toward the final speech purpose be maintained?

Where is the best place for this or that theme to enter, how far shall it be developed there, and where shall it re-enter?

How shall vitally important shades of emphasis and subordination be effected?

What is the most effective way of developing any given main topic?

Can suggestion or humor sharpen or illustrate this part of the speech?

How shall emotion be handled?

How shall the time limit be handled?[6]

These are problems in the managing of ideas, and they constantly confront everyone who gives a speech. If at first they seem acute, remember that as H. L. Mencken said, "Thinking is something new to man and he does it very badly. We have lost the baboon's sureness of instinct and have not yet perfected sureness of reasoning."

Added to them is another problem particularly sharp and constant. Throughout, you must be reminding yourself: *My listeners will hear this*

[5] Jacques Barzun, *Teacher in America* (Boston, Little, Brown and Co., 1945), pp., 306-307.

[6] Many of these questions were stated in sharpened form by Bernard De Voto, as they related to historical writing, in "The Easy Chair," pp. 50-55, *Harper's Magazine,* April, 1949. To him I owe a debt for the sequence here used.

*speech but once.* They can't go back and read it again. They must get it instantly as I speak, and I must at all times make it possible for them to do so. Therefore, I must present ideas with proper labels: *firstly, secondly,* and *thirdly.* Each part I must define, or explain, or illustrate, or perhaps do all three. I must point ahead to the place where I am going, and point back to the place where I have been. For the listeners hear it but once, and that once they miss it, they miss it forever. Can I, then, enable listeners to say of my speech what was said of Hobart D. McKeehan's: "One thing I like about your speeches is that you have *handles* on them. A man can pick them up and carry them home with him." Or as W. T. Snead, a newspaper editor, wrote after thirty-five years of reporting speeches for the press, "Two things should never be lost, your temper and the thread of your discourse."

This, then, is the intellectual discipline of effective speaking, the problem of producing and managing ideas.

### THIRD FUNDAMENTAL

## *You must earn the right to give every speech*

"How long did it take you to prepare that sermon?" a listener once asked that powerful preacher, Henry Ward Beecher. "Forty years," was the significant answer. A youth once approached Daniel Webster with a question on how he might learn to speak impromptu. Retorted Webster, "Young man, there is no such thing!"

Many persons, of course, possessed by the lust to speak, are not impressed with the necessity of earning the right. Emerson remarks with unusual sharpness for him on "those who prematurely boil, and who impatiently break silence before their time," and of "a small-pot-soon-hot style of eloquence," in which the speaker thinks of his own enjoyment without regard for the suffering audience.

In contrast, the characteristic note of effective speakers is thorough preparation. You may go back as far as you will, back even to that day when Quintilian thought (he was writing 95 A.D.) that "men of the earliest ages did not speak with our exactness and care," and still the characteristic note of good speakers was thorough preparation. Of *Demosthenes* (384–322 B.C.) a scoffing critic complained that his speeches "smelled of the lamp," for he was known to spend copious hours in preparation. *Cicero* (106–43 B.C.), after listing the details of speech preparation, a preparation that he was known to give to his own speeches, concluded, "Let us then cease to wonder at what is the cause of the scarcity of good speakers." To *Father Massillon,* eloquent French cleric of the early eighteenth century, Louis XIV said, "Father, I have heard many great

*Wide World Photos*

Even the most experienced speaker has to earn the right to give every speech. Here we see Adlai Stevenson deep in thought as he prepares his speech accepting the nomination for the Presidency in 1956.

orators in this chapel, and have been highly pleased with them; but for you, whenever I hear you, I go away displeased with myself, for I see more of my own character." These sermons that so touched Louis were written and rewritten many times. *Edmund Burke,* English speaker of the late eighteenth century, "more than Cicero in the senate, almost Plato in the academy," spent more labor on his speeches than any of his great contemporaries. *Patrick Henry* was once thought to have flashed his "Give me liberty or give me death" on the inspiration of the moment. He is known to have rehearsed it for months before backwoods audiences. *Daniel Webster* was notoriously slow and thorough in his preparation. He once explained to Edward G. Parker that after he had finished lining up what he wanted to say, he did not write it out, but would "walk up and down the room thinking it over" until he had "put it in shape, eye to eye and face to face" with his audience.

Among twentieth-century speakers, *Franklin D. Roosevelt* spoke with consummate skill. Competent authorities agree that he drew freely upon a selected group of advisers for general ideas, that the final draft was in his own words, and that it represented from the fifth to the twelfth revision. *Sir Winston Churchill,* probably the most effective British speaker of the past two centuries, memorized his important speeches, then rehearsed them before a mirror in order to study his gestures. In later years, when recording machines had been perfected, he recorded and edited them for "clarity, voice inflection, tone quality, and general structure." Churchill was not at all a natural speaker. It took as much unremitting work at the age of 70 for him to prepare a speech as it had at 26. As Lord Birkenhead once said, he "devoted the best years of his life to the preparation of his impromptu speeches."

Sir Austen Chamberlain, after a careful study of British speakers, put it in a nutshell: "Those who say to public men, 'Oh, speaking is no trouble to *you*,' have not seen them in the hours of preparation. Their wives and their private secretaries tell a different tale."

*A good part of every college speech course is wasted by students who try to speak without earning the right. Their technique is feeble, their ideas are fuzzy—the stuff is simply not there—not because they are beginners and not because they cannot learn or have no talent, but because they do not put forth the effort. Months go by, and a large part of the course is gone, and yet they have not learned one simple fundamental —that a speaker must earn the right to give every speech.*

**FOURTH FUNDAMENTAL**

*A speech is not an essay on its hind legs. It does not become a speech until you put it out to the audience by sound waves and light waves*

You may have a splendid plan on paper—organized in detail and every part of it thought out—but it is not yet a speech. It is still only an idea on paper, an outline, an essay, or a set of notes—but not a speech. It will not become a speech until you lift the thoughts off the paper and create them into a speech. As James A. Winans put it, a speech is not an "essay standing on its hind legs." In saying this Winans possibly was remembering his many students who had had difficulty turning an outline into a speech, and of the many distinguished scholars he had known—wise and learned, but innocent and inept at lifting a speech off paper.

How to turn an outline or a manuscript into a speech, this is one of the real problems of speechmaking. It is a problem that confronts students and older persons alike. A lecture bureau manager stated it in these words: "We try to book among others, a few eminent thinkers. But it often gets us in trouble. For example, we might capture a real prize, a Nobel prizewinner, a Pulitzer prizewinner, a college president famous for his ideas, or someone who has written a book or produced ideas that everybody knows about and wants to know more about. We book him for a series of lectures. Then letters and telegrams start arriving, saying he was 'disappointing,' or 'failed to satisfy,' or 'could not speak,' or was just plain 'terrible.' This sort of thing keeps us awake at night, for we never know whether anybody famous for having ideas can make a speech."

Mere ideas, then, do not make a speech. The best of plans put on paper do not make a speech. *There is no speech until you carry the thought to the listener. Nor can you "deliver" the speech as you would deliver a book or pencil. Actually there is no "delivery" to it. You must use sound waves and light waves to tell the audience what you are thinking. You have no other media.*

Other elements of so-called "delivery" will be discussed later (pages 321-422), but the basic principle is this: *Get enthusiastic about what you have to say. If you are enthusiastic, your "delivery" will probably be earnest and moving. If you are enthusiastic, you will not bother about how you stand, gesture, breathe, or use your voice—and later through practice you can clear away faults and barriers. If you are enthusiastic, you can forget yourself into reasonably good speaking. Enthusiasm is contagious. Unless you have a good time talking, your audience will not have a good time listening. This is the basic foundation of "delivery."*

These are the four fundamentals: (1) that effective speaking is a technique, (2) that it is also an intellectual discipline, (3) that you must earn the right to give a speech, (4) that a speech is not an essay on its hind legs. Throughout the centuries in which speechmaking has played its important part in human life they have been the fundamentals of effective speakers. Some have followed them partly by intuition. Others have learned them through the painful process of trial, error, and discouragement. But in one way or other, they have used them. A circuit rider of the last century stated his method of use in homespun words. Asked the secret of his power as a preacher, he replied: "It's simple. I read myself full. I think myself clear. I pray myself hot. And then I let go."

## Assignments

ON EFFECTIVE SPEAKING REQUIRING A TECHNIQUE

1. Make a list of speeches you have heard during the past month or so. Include the incidental speeches, such as announcements, introductions, explanations, etc. Go over the list and check speeches that were positively superior—i.e., those you could easily hear and easily understand, those that held your attention closely, and those whose content you still remember. (Obviously you won't check many! But there ought to be a few.) Now go over the *unchecked* speeches on your list, and itemize the reasons that prevented each from being as good as it ought. Finally, draw up a general list of five or six barriers that most often prevented these speeches from being their best. Make a permanent entry of the list in your notebook, and in the future note how many of them injure your speaking.

2. Prepare a short speech relating to the technique of speaking on one of the following subjects:

   *a.* An effective teacher I know; how he uses effective techniques
   *b.* A poor teacher I know: techniques he needs but fails to use
   *c.* Our preacher: techniques he uses well and those he fails to use
   *d.* Techniques used by salesmen
   *e.* Techniques used by short-story writers
   *f.* Any other subject that fits this assignment

3. Prepare a speech on one of the following subjects, using the procedure described below:

   *a.* What a man or woman should get out of college
   *b.* What employers expect of college men
   *c.* My favorite author: and my reasons for thinking so
   *d.* Poetry I like best, and why
   *e.* Shows I like best, and why
   *f.* The college course from which I profited most, and why
   *g.* What I like (or dislike) about the college fraternity system
   *h.* Campus politics: an analysis of how it is run
   *i.* The ablest man in Congress: an analysis of his ability
   *j.* Things about the race problem on this campus that disturb me
   *k.* What religion means to me
   *l.* Any other subject that fits this assignment.

   Pick this subject ten days or two weeks before your next speech and develop by the following procedure:

   *a.* Without doing *any* reading or conversing on the subject, make an outline of what you already know (if you don't know how to make an outline, turn to the next chapter, pages 56-62).
   *b.* The next day make a *second* outline and note whether time, and perhaps unconscious meditation, has added to your stock of ideas.
   *c.* Now do some reading on the subject, or talk it over with other persons. Then after three or four days make a third outline. Obviously this should

be a more mature outline than either of those preceding. In it your best judgment will be used in testing, sifting, and arranging ideas.

d. After a few days more, expand this third outline into the final one to be used for the speech, and on the day you speak hand it to the instructor.

ON EARNING THE RIGHT TO SPEAK

4. Prepare a report on how one particular speaker, or a group of speakers, prepared speeches. The following useful bibliography can be expanded by library research:

Braden, Waldo W., and Gehring, Mary Louise, *Speech Practices* (New York, 1958). (Chapters 2 and 3 contain information on twenty speakers.)

Brandenburg, Earnest, "Preparation of Franklin D. Roosevelt's Speeches," *Quarterly Journal of Speech*, XXXV (April, 1949), 214-221.

Brigance, W. Norwood, ed., *A History and Criticism of American Public Address*, Vols. I and II (New York, 1943). (Twenty-eight speakers.)

Chamberlain, Austen, "How Great Speakers Prepare Their Speeches" (Pitt, Gladstone, Disraeli, Macaulay, John Bright, etc.), *Living Age*, January 3, 1925.

Feris, Frances, "Speech Preparation of John Bright," *Quarterly Journal of Speech*, XVII (December, 1931), 492-504.

Goodrich, Chauncey A., *Select British Eloquence* (New York, 1852, etc., also on microcard). (Twenty speakers, mostly in the eighteenth century.)

Hatch, Alden, "Men Around Dewey," *Harper's Magazine*, October, 1948, pp. 38-46, esp. pp. 44-45 on Dewey's methods of speech preparation. This article is significant, not because it tells about Dewey's method, but because his method is typical of most men in public life in this age of radio and television.

Hochmuth, Marie K., ed., *A History and Criticism of American Public Address*, Vol. III (New York, 1955). (Twelve speakers.)

McGlon, Charles A., "How I Prepare My Sermons: A Symposium," *Quarterly Journal of Speech*, XL (February, 1954), 49-62. (Six living ministers: Jewish, Catholic, Protestant.)

Taylor, Robert Lewis, *Winston Churchill: An Informal Study of Greatness* (Garden City, N.Y., 1952); especially Chapter 28, pp. 425-426.

*Time*, November 4, 1940, p. 4, on Wendell Willkie. Like Hatch's article on Dewey cited above, this article is significant, not because it describes one man's method in particular, but because it describes one method used by superior speakers in public life.

5. Prepare a four-minute speech on one of the subjects you listed in the Speech-Subject Analysis Form in Chapter 1 (see pages 28 and 29). Use the following general method:

a. Read yourself full

b. Think yourself clear

c. Sift, sort, and test your materials

d. Arrange the materials into a simple, easy-to-follow outline

e. Remember that your listeners will hear the speech only once, and therefore help them get each separate part. Present the parts with proper

labels: *first, second,* etc. Forecast where you are going. Summarize what
you have said.

*f.* Rehearse the speech five or six times over a period of several days.

6. Make a Time Table of your speech preparation. In it record both the total
time spent and the distribution of time, to wit:

> September 25—35 minutes
> September 26—0 minutes
> September 27—2 hours, 15 minutes

*a.* Hand a copy of this Time Table to the instructor along with the outline
when you deliver the speech.

*b.* Make a permanent record of this Time Table in your notebook, and do
the same with the following speeches. In this way, throughout the course
you can compare each speech grade, and your over-all general progress,
with the *total* time and with the *distribution* of time spent in earning the
right to speak.

ON A SPEECH NOT BEING AN ESSAY

7. Prepare one of the following selections to read before the class, using the
following general procedure:

*a.* Make sure you know what the selection as a *whole* is trying to say.

*b.* Get the author's structural parts.

*c.* Look up unknown words. Absorb the full meaning of sentences, Note
how each one is related to the sentence before and the sentence after.

*d.* Now practice reading it aloud until you can—by means of mind, imagination, voice, and action—lift the black marks off paper and turn them
into a living thought.


## THE VALLEY OF THE THAMES AND THE FARMS OF KANSAS

I am not a native of this land. I come from the very heart of America. In the
superficial aspects by which we ordinarily recognize family relationships,
the town where I was born and the one where I was reared are far separated
from this great city. Abilene, Kansas, and Denison, Texas, would together
equal in size possibly one five-hundredth of a part of great London.

By your standards those towns are young, without your aged traditions that
carry the roots of London back into the uncertainties of unrecorded history.
. . . Hardly would it seem possible for the London Council to have gone farther
afield to find a man to honor with its priceless gift of token citizenship.

Yet kinship among nations is not determined in such measurements as
proximity of size and age. Rather we should turn to those inner things—call
them what you will—I mean those intangibles that are the real treasures
free men possess.

To preserve his freedom of worship, his equality before law, his liberty
to speak and act as he sees fit, subject only to provisions that he trespass

*Dwight D. Eisenhower,* 1945, on being made an honorary citizen of London.

not upon similar rights of others, a Londoner will fight. So will a citizen of Abilene. When we consider these things, then the valley of the Thames draws closer to the farms of Kansas and the plains of Texas.

## HAMLET'S ADVICE TO THE PLAYERS

Speak the speech, I pray you, as I pronounced it to you, trippingly on the tongue: but if you mouth it, as many of your players do, I had as lief the town crier spoke my lines. Nor do not saw the air too much with your hand, thus, but use all gently; for in the very torrent, tempest, and, as I may say, whirlwind of your passion, you must acquire and beget a temperance that may give it smoothness. O, it offends me to the soul to hear a robustious periwig-pated fellow tear a passion to tatters, to very rags, to split the ears of the groundlings, who for the most part are capable of nothing but inexplicable dumb-shows and noise: I would have such a fellow whipped for o'er-doing Termagant; it out-Herods Herod: pray you, avoid it.

Be not too tame, neither, but let your own discretion be your tutor: suit the action to the word, the word to the action; with this special observance, that you o'erstep not the modesty of nature: for anything so overdone is from the purpose of playing, whose end, both at the first and now, was and is, to hold, as 'twere, the mirror up to nature; to show virtue her own feature, scorn her own image, and the very age and body of the time his form and pressure. Now this overdone or come tardy off, though it make the unskillful laugh, cannot but make the judicious grieve; the censure of the which one must in your allowance o'erweigh a whole theatre of others. O, there be players that I have seen play, and others praise, and that highly, not to speak it profanely, that, neither having the accent of Christians nor the gait of Christian, pagan, nor man, have so strutted and bellowed that I have though some of nature's journeymen had made men and not made them well, they imitated humanity so abominably.

SHAKESPEARE

## THE GREEN PASTURES

NOAH. Yes, suh, dis seems to be complete. Now 'bout the animals, Lawd, you say you want everythin'?

GOD. Two of everythin'.

NOAH. That would include jayraffes an' hippopotamusses?

GOD. Everythin' dat is.

NOAH. Dey was a circus in town las' week. I guess I kin fin' dem. Co'se I kin git all de rabbits an' possums an' wil' turkeys easy. I'll sen' de boys out. Hum, I'm jest wonderin'—

GOD. 'Bout what?

NOAH. 'Bout snakes. Think you'd like snakes, too?

GOD. Certainly. I want snakes.

NOAH. Oh, I kin git snakes, lots of 'em. Co'se some of 'em's a little dangerous. Maybe I better take a kag of likker, too?

GOD. You kin take a kag of likker.

NOAH. (Musingly.) Yes, suh, dey's a awful lot of differ'nt kin's of snakes, come to think about it. Dey's water moccasins, cottonmoufs, rattlers— mus' be a hund'ed kin's of other snakes down in de swamps. Maybe I better take two kags of likker.

GOD. (Mildly.) I think de one kag's enough.

NOAH. No. I better take two kags. Besides I kin put one on each side of de boat, and balance de ship wid dem as well as havin' dem fo' medicinal use.

GOD. You kin put one keg in de middle of de ship.

NOAH. (Buoyantly.) Jest as easy to take two kags, Lawd.

GOD. I think one kag's enough.

NOAH. Yes, Lawd, but you see forty days—an' forty nights—(*There's a distant roll of thunder.*)

GOD. (Firmly.) One kag, Noah.

NOAH. Yes Lawd, one kag.

MARC CONNELLY[7]

## A LETTER TO THE CORINTHIANS

If I speak with the tongues of men and of angels, but have not love, I am a noisy gong or a clanging cymbal. And if I have prophetic powers, and understand all mysteries and all knowledge, and if I have all faith, so as to remove mountains, but have not love, I am nothing. If I give away all I have, and if I deliver my body to be burned, but have not love, I gain nothing.

Love is patient, and kind; love is not jealous or boastful; it is not arrogant or rude. Love does not insist on its own way; it is not irritable or resentful; it does not rejoice at wrong, but rejoices in the right. Love bears all things, believes all things, hopes all things, endures all things.

Love never ends; as for prophecy, it will pass away; as for tongues, they will cease; as for knowledge, it will pass away. For our knowledge is imperfect and our prophecy is imperfect; but when the perfect comes, the imperfect will pass away. When I was a child, I spoke like a child, I thought like a child, I reasoned like a child; when I became a man, I gave up childish ways. For now we see in a mirror dimly, but then face to face. Now I know in part; then I shall understand fully, even as I have been fully understood. So faith, hope, love abide, these three; but the greatest of these is love.

PAUL (1 Corinthians, 13; Revised Standard Version)

---

[7] Copyright, 1930; renewed, 1958, by Marc Connelly, and reprinted by permission of Holt, Rinehart and Winston, Inc.

# ✿ 3 ✿

# First Steps in
# Managing Ideas

WE HAVE SEEN why people don't become effective speakers just because they have pious intentions. We have seen why they can't get there by hammering away on their own untutored impulse. We have seen that the adage "anybody can talk" is only a half truth, and is more misleading than if wholly false. We have seen, in other words, that effective public speech takes professional skill, and that to learn that skill takes training. Here you face the first problem. You can't first study all the principles involved, then go forth with a head full of principles to begin the first steps in practice.

To get you started, therefore, we shall set down, in this chapter and the next, a few of the first steps. These first steps are only a postage-stamp miniature of the full size principles. They won't carry you beyond the first few simple speeches. But they will get you started. Later these principles will be developed more fully.

For your first speeches, then, here are the seven steps for you to follow. Each is explained in this chapter:

1. Choose a subject of interest to you, and one that can be made interesting to the audience.

2. Do not try to cover the whole subject, but select one specific part for your central idea.

3. Phrase the central idea into a Purpose-Sentence so you will know where you are going.

4. Make a list of two or three main points of your central idea, or not more than four at the most.

5. Obtain specific and interesting supporting material for each of these main points.

6. Organize the speech into an outline.

7. Practice delivering the speech until you have it well in mind.

## *Choose a subject of interest to you, and one that can be made interesting to the audience*

You ask, "Where can I find an interesting subject?" Not so fast, please. Look at your audience first. They are college students, mostly about your age. They are not engineers or industrialists or factory workers, and you cannot talk to them as such. Nor are they high-school students; and so you cannot work off on them that speech you prepared back in high school. Better forget it entirely and get a new subject. Your audience is a class made up of college students with a wide range of interests. Some might be called scholars; they are interested in books and ideas. Some are athletes; they spend several hours a day in athletic practice, and for several hours more the subject is on their minds. Some are interested in the sciences, and much of their time is spent in laboratories. Some are interested in the humanities; for them literature and languages are life's deepest currents. Some are interested in economics and business. Some are going to become teachers, physicians, lawyers, engineers, what-have-you.

How can anyone find a subject to fit people with such widely separated interests, you ask. Finding a subject is never easy, of course, yet it is easier to find them for college audiences than for most others. Their range of interest is wider. Here is your guide:

1. Choose a subject you know something about, and about which you can find out more.
2. Choose a subject the audience may know a little about, but wants to know more.

Are you majoring in literature? Tell the class who the newest writers are, and what they are trying to do. Or what the *Canterbury Tales* were really about. Or what is blank verse or free verse. Or let them enjoy meeting Homer, Lewis Carroll, or Sarah Bernhardt.

Are you majoring in science? Then explain to the class how antibiotics work. Or which new ones have been recently developed. Or how the latest earth satellite was developed. Or what Newton did. Or Pasteur. Or Einstein.

Are you majoring in economics or business? A wealth of subjects is yours: cost of living, wages and prices, taxes, social security, labor, industrial management, the profit system, small business. . . .

Are you an athlete? Increase your listeners' pleasure in seeing an athletic contest by explaining it to them from the *inside*, things that players try to do or try to avoid, things to be seen from the outside that tell the experts how the game is going.

Actually a wide range of subjects can be made interesting to college audiences. Already most students are specializing in what is to become their "earning field" in future years. Yet the eager-minded want to know something of other fields, and perhaps most of them have an uneasy feeling that beyond their own "earning field" is an array of useful knowledge they really need, but have no chance to get. Terence, the Roman playwright, brought thunderous applause with the line, "I am a man, and interested in all *manly* things." So are intelligent and educated people always. So are your listeners. In choosing a subject this is your opportunity.

## Do not try to cover the whole subject, but select one specific part for your central idea

Young speakers at first want to cover the moon, the sand, and the stars in a five-minute speech. But five minutes can't be stretched that far. You must learn to narrow the subject until you can cover it interestingly and specifically.

Is your subject art? Here is a speech that tries to cover all:

> Why we have art
> Greek and Roman art
> Italian painters
> Dutch, Flemish, and French painters
> English and American painters
> Oriental types of art
> The Moderns: Realism, Impressionism, etc.

Now you might cover all that in a book, if it were a *big* book, but you could not cover it in a two-hour speech. So for a classroom speech you take a fraction of the first topic: "Why we have art," and use the following central idea:

> How lines and colors can improve your looks

Is your subject labor unions? Here is a speech that covers too much:

> History of labor unions
> How unions are operated today

From this vast area you might take the following single point for your central idea:

> How grievances are handled in Union Local 604

A good speech is like a good photograph. It is in focus. It centers on one specific thing. And a good close-up is worth a dozen distant shots.

*Phrase the central idea into a Purpose-Sentence so you will know where you are going*

As this is stated you may not at first see what it means, or why you should do it. Yet it is important, and if you don't do it you can later run into trouble. It is important because a speech, unlike a private conversation, needs a definite purpose. A private conversation may be aimless, but a good public speech moves straight toward a goal. The speaker is going somewhere. He is aiming at a target. He wants the audience to *know* something, to *understand* something, to *believe* something, to *do* something. Therefore, to keep in mind where your speech is going, put it down in writing.

You are going to talk about television drama, let us assume, and have chosen the following central idea:

Television plays compared with stage plays

With such a central idea you may have at least a dozen specific purposes. Three of these are indicated by the following three Purpose-Sentences:

The television play differs from the stage play because it must be done in a more limited time, using limited sets, with a limited number of actors, and projected on a screen of limited size [i.e. *information*], or

Television plays are necessarily poor because they are produced for the vast public instead of for the intelligent few [i.e. *argument*], or

Television plays really represent a higher art than stage plays because they communicate to the whole people instead of merely to the ivory-tower intellectuals [i.e. *argument*].

Now any one of these three could be a good speech purpose, but don't wander across all of them in a single speech. Choose *one*. Write it out in a clear-cut Purpose-Sentence, and stay with it as you plan the speech.

## AVOID ARGUMENT AND CONTROVERSY IN FIRST SPEECHES

A final suggestion: For these first speeches, better avoid subjects involving argument and controversy. At its best, argument is an explosive and you have to know how to handle it. *"Win an argument and you lose a soul,"* said Bishop Fulton J. Sheen. And in the same vein Burton Hillis added: "The more hot arguments you win, the fewer warm friends you'll have." There will be plenty of time later for controversial speeches, but right now avoid them. Start with the fundamentals; and *the most funda-*

*mental thing in speaking is to be able to explain an idea clearly and interestingly.* It is the foundation for all other kinds of speaking.

## Make a list of two or three main points of your central idea, or not more than four at the most

These main points should cover the whole central idea. Later (see pages 56-62) we shall take up the various formal methods of arranging main topics, but for the present rely on common sense plus your general knowledge of composition. Make these main points simple and obvious. Don't have too many, for listeners simply can't remember too many. Five main points are probably always too many. Other things being equal, three are better than four, and two are better than three.

Then when you have reduced them to as few as possible, set them down in straightaway English. Your first draft, for example, might have five points, and your language might still be involved:

PURPOSE-SENTENCE: Your looks can be improved by using art skillfully.
   *Main Points:*   I. Looking your best can help you socially and professionally.
             II. Stout people can be helped by artistic lines.
             III. Thin people can also be helped.
             IV. Blue eyes and light hair can be enhanced by one set of colors.
             V. Dark hair and eyes can be enhanced by another technique.

Too many main points! And that's not all. Read those sentences again, and you'll find that not one has power to make the thought *move*. Instead, each sentence lets the thought lie still, and makes the *listener* lift it up. Why? Each is a roundabout sentence. Note the language: *"Can be helped by," "can be enhanced by."* So we have two problems, yet they come from a single source. The speaker has not thought himself clear, hence both words and ideas are still foggy. When he thinks himself clear, he can make the two changes seen below. First, reduce the main points from five to two, and so make each really a *main* point. Second, recast them in straightaway English:

PURPOSE-SENTENCE: You can improve your looks by skillful use of lines and colors.
   *Main Points:*  I. If you are either fat or thin, skillful use of *lines* can improve your looks.
             II. If you are either blond or brunette, skillful use of *colors* can improve your looks.

## *Obtain specific and interesting supporting material for each of these main points*

Each main point, you will note, is the statement of an idea or principle. Such a statement, in the technical language of speechmaking, is called an *Assertion*. Now an Assertion does not, in itself, explain, prove, or elaborate. It only asserts. Taken alone, it is not worth much, for it leaves the idea simply hanging in the air unsupported. Merely to assert that "modern music is degrading," or that "Bernard Shaw was a great playwright," does not increase a listener's knowledge or change his beliefs. Standing alone, it is "as broad and general as the casing air."

Assertions, then, state the speaker's main ideas. But Assertions in speechmaking are usually worthless *until they are supported or elaborated*. In fact, listeners seldom even remember them unless they are supported, for they hear a speaker's words only once, and, unlike a reader, they cannot pause to think back, to weigh and judge, or to consult a dictionary. They must go right on listening to the speaker's words as they come through the air. In the hundred or so speeches a year which the average educated person hears, therefore, they remember very few of the unsupported Assertions. Unsupported Assertions are like drifting clouds. They catch our attention for a moment, but we do not later remember one from another. What we *do* remember are the things kept vividly before our attention. What we remember are ideas supported by a succession of details, examples, comparisons, or illustrations. What we remember are ideas hammered in by vivid supporting material.

## HOW TO USE SUPPORTING MATERIAL

How can a speaker develop his Assertions with effective supporting material? The following five kinds are especially useful:

1. Facts and Figures    4. Comparisons
2. Specific Instances    5. Testimony
3. Illustrations

The manner of using these supporting materials can be seen in the following cross section of an outline:

I. ASSERTION
  A. Supporting material
  B. Supporting material
  C. Supporting material

Or the speech might be more elaborate and have two or more levels of Assertions. But no matter how many levels it has, a good speech in the end gets down to the bedrock of solid supporting materials. The following is a cross section of outline for *two* levels of Assertion:

I. ASSERTION (FIRST LEVEL)
    A. *Assertion* (*second level*)
       1. Supporting material
       2. Supporting material
       3. Supporting material

    B. *Assertion* (*second level*)
       1. Supporting material
       2. Supporting material
       3. Supporting material

### FACTS AND FIGURES

This is the most elementary type of supporting material, plain Facts and Figures. Yet student speeches are notably weak in Facts and Figures. In general, students don't get the pertinent facts, and don't use what few facts they have. They rely on Assertion, as if anyone cared about their assertions unsupported! Therefore, make this your basic rule: Where Facts and Figures are to be had, get them, verify them, and use them. Beware of alleged facts. Remember that much printed material is deliberately planted for propaganda. The "facts" may be accurate (though not always), but their selection—and careful omissions—make them misleading. Check your sources! A first test of educated people is to read suspiciously, and know how to detect propaganda.

The following example demonstrates the use of verified Facts and Figures as supporting material:

MAIN POINT (ASSERTION):
I. The accusation that education has recently declined in quality does not square with the facts.

*Facts and Figures*
A. An identical test was given to 8th-grade students in Boston in 1845 and over the whole U. S. in 1919; the 1919 students scored 21 per cent higher in grammar, history, arithmetic, and geography—and made only one-third as many errors of spelling.

*Facts and Figures*
B. An identical test was given high-school seniors in Indiana in 1919 and 1941, and the 1941 seniors outscored the 1919 seniors, 152 to 137.

*Facts and Figures*
C. An identical test was given to grades 3, 4, and 5, in Dearborn, Michigan, in 1926 and 1951; and the 1951 students led all the way, from one semster in arithmetic to two years in English

*Facts and Figures*          D. The Armed Forces Institute developed tests in English, social studies, science, and mathematics, which were first given to armed forces students in 1943. In 1955 these tests were given to a representative 5-per-cent sample of all public high schools in the U.S., and the 1955 students made higher average scores on *each* of these tests than had those in 1943.

*Facts and Figures*          E. In Cleveland, Ohio, in 1947 was found a copy of the first interschool examination ever given in that city, which had been in 1848 covering arithmetic, history, grammar, geography, and definitions. The *Cleveland Press* asked the schools to give the same test again to students of the same age and educational level. The result was that the 1947 students beat the 1848 students, 955 to 924.

### SPECIFIC INSTANCES

Specific Instances are condensed examples. They are brief, but specific. For them to be effective, the audience must know enough about them so they carry an instant meaning. Suppose, for example, a speaker says: "The early English parliaments did not always succeed in resisting encroachments by the early English kings [*Assertion*]. Encroachments were made by such kings as Edward III, Henry VII, Henry VIII, and James I [*Specific Instances*]." These Specific Instances would not carry an instant meaning to listeners, excepting to the scant few who knew English history intimately. Don't use that kind of Specific Instances. Use those that listeners will understand.

The following example shows how Assertion might be supported by effective Specific Instances:

MAIN POINT (ASSERTION):    I. Great achievements have been made by men and women under 30 years of age.

*Specific Instance*          A. At that age Elizabeth Barrett Browning had published two volumes of poems.

*Specific Instance*          B. Margaret Mitchell had finished half of *Gone With the Wind*.

*Specific Instance*          C. Lord Byron had written *Childe Harold* and published 14 volumes of poems.

*Specific Instance*          D. Mozart had published over 200 of his musical compositions.

*Specific Instance*          E. William Pitt, the Younger, had been Prime Minister of England for 6 years.

*Specific Instance*          F. Alexander Graham Bell had invented the telephone.

| | |
|---|---|
| *Specific Instance* | G. Henry Ford had produced his first automobile. |
| *Specific Instance* | H. Herman Wouk had been writing professionally for 10 years, and even though service in the Armed Forces had taken four years of his life, was within two years of completing his first Book-of-the-Month selection, *Aurora Dawn*. |

## ILLUSTRATIONS

An Illustration is a narrative of events, usually told in the order of happening. It tells the full story, but skillfully eliminates the nonessentials. As with Poe's properly constructed short story, a good Illustration will have the events so closely interwoven that not one can be removed without breaking the entire chain. A single Illustration at times is enough to support an Assertion, as in the Parable of the Good Samaritan ("And who is my neighbor?") and that of the Prodigal Son (There is joy over "one sinner that repenteth"). At other times two or more are used, like this:

| | |
|---|---|
| MAIN POINT (ASSERTION): | I. People now and then used to think that the world had really attained security, or was about to attain it. |
| *Illustration* | A. I remember way back in that wonderful normal year, 1913. Our dean of the Law School had been elected to the U.S. Senate the year before, and had just come home from his first session in Washington. A few of us students went over to visit him one afternoon, and he gave us copies of a new law passed that month, December 1913, by Congress. It was a famous law, and one that all of you know about even now, the Federal Reserve Bank Act. Well, I was only a sophomore, but I wanted to join the conversation, so I asked an omnibus question: "Senator Sterling, what is this law for?" He answered, "Young man, this is a bill to prevent depressions." I knew about depressions. I'd been born during the depression of the 1890's and I remembered the depression of 1907 that left my family with only $5.00 in cash. I asked, "Will it really prevent depressions?" He replied, "I think it will," and explained why. We'd made progress. After centuries, we were finally safe from depressions! |

*Illustration*                       B. Five months rolled by. It was now May
                                        1914. In my economics class some student
                                        asked the professor just how a modern
                                        democratic government—without a power-
                                        ful king or oligarchy—could raise the money
                                        to carry on a modern war. The professor
                                        answered: "You don't need to worry about
                                        a long modern war. Today wars are so ex-
                                        pensive that their fantastic cost would bank-
                                        rupt little nations in six weeks and the
                                        strongest government in the world in three
                                        months. We cannot have world wars today
                                        as we used to have in the days of Napoleon."
                                        We'd made progress. After centuries, we
                                        were finally safe from war, as well as safe
                                        from depressions. That was May 1914!

## COMPARISONS

Comparisons show likeness and difference. Especially are they valuable supporting materials for the following purposes:

*To connect something meaningless with something meaningful.* If you say, "Scotland has 30,405 square miles" the statement has less meaning than if you say, "Scotland is slightly smaller in size that the state of Maine." (But check your comparisons to be *sure* they are accurate. A check on fifteen sets of comparisons sent through the mails by organizations attempting to influence public opinion, showed that *nine* were not accurate!)

*To explain something new, about which people are suspicious, with something old which they accept.* People are often suspicious of new things, even as they were once suspicious of democracy, of the printing press, of Christianity. Therefore when you advocate or explain something new, you can often best do it by showing that it is like-this or like-that, which people already know about and believe in. Thus St. Paul compared a newly-converted Christian to a man who had grown up and "put away childish things" of his former religion. And young Benjamin Franklin, looking for work in a London printing office, met a foreman who was disdainful of anyone trained in America, until 19-year-old Franklin set in type before his eyes a persuasive comparison: "Can any good thing come out of Nazareth? . . . Come and see."

In the following outline Comparisons are used as supporting materials:

MAIN POINT (ASSERTION):   I. New York is a fabulous city where foreign-born,
                              children of foreign-born, and Americans live
                              together as Americans.
*Comparison*                  A. It has as many Irish (500,000) as Dublin.
*Comparison*                  B. It has more Jews (2,250,000) than the
                                 whole nation of Israel.

| | |
|---|---|
| *Comparison* | C. It has almost as many Italians (1,095,000) as Rome. |
| *Comparison* | D. It has half as many Poles (412,000) as Warsaw. |
| *Comparison* | E. It has more Negroes (1,150,000) than Tennessee and Florida combined. |

**TESTIMONY**

Testimony is the authority of others. In effect, the speaker says: "I am not the only one who believes this. There are two of us, or three of us, and these others are famous, or experts, or in a special position to know." The use of Testimony has been abused by modern advertisers, for intelligent people are not impressed by the testimony of Home-Run Hopwood on which cigarettes are the smoothest, always spoken in words written out for him by the advertiser. Yet intelligent people do live by authority, the right kind of authority. We accept the authority of our church, our social groups. We respect the authority of courts and judges. On questions of judgment and on complex ideas, we accept the authority of qualified experts. On reading a book we must accept, or reject, the authority of the author.

To present the Testimony of competent authorities, therefore, is one of the important forms of supporting materials. The following example illustrates its use:

| | |
|---|---|
| MAIN POINT (ASSERTION): | I. For 24 centuries intelligent and educated people have been saying that education has been getting steadily worse. |
| *Testimony* | A. In this generation President A. Whitney Griswold of Yale is typical. He writes of the "serious setback to education," of its "lost character," and its being "diluted," and says that unless we return to older kind of education we shall neglect it "at our peril." |
| *Testimony* | B. In 1894, at a time when President Griswold now thinks of as our having an excellent curriculum, a Faculty Committee reported to the Harvard Board of Overseers on the sad state of education. Young men entering Harvard, the Report said, were 19 years old, yet they still had "immature thoughts . . . miserably expressed," they wrote still in "a crabbed slovenly hand," and they still spelled "wretchedly." Education had declined from the Good Old Days of half a century before. |
| *Testimony* | C. In 1845 the Boston Grammar School Committee made an official report on the decline |

of education: "boys and girls of 14 and 15 years of age, when called on to write simple sentences . . . cannot write, without such errors in grammar and spelling, and in punctuation, as we should blush to see in a letter from a son or daughter of their age." To them the Good Old Days of education of half a century and more ago had declined.

*Testimony*  D. In 1773 Dr. Samuel Johnson testified at length that "learning had declined" since those Good Old Days when he had been a student in Oxford University in 1728-1729.

*Testimony*  E. About 81 A.D. Tacitus wrote of "our striplings" who are "drawn off" into "schools of impudence" for an education that "is likely to do their talents more harm." The educational system he disliked produced Dionysius of Harlicanassus and, almost unchanged, it produced St. Augustine considerably later.

*Testimony*  F. In 423 B.C. Aristophanes wrote scathing satires against the "new learning" in Greece. He said the schools had lost their "old discipline and virtue" and they were now practicing "quackery." One teacher in particular he indicted of practicing quackery was a young man named Socrates. The educational system Aristophanes disliked produced both Plato and Aristotle.

## USING COMBINED METHODS OF SUPPORT

Not often does a speaker limit himself to one kind of supporting material. He uses two, three, or four, in order to give each Assertion its best kind of support. The following illustrates the use of *four kinds* of supporting material for a single Assertion:

MAIN POINT (ASSERTION):  I. Europe has been afflicted by barriers against money and trade.

*Facts and Figures*  A. I don't mean the mere inconvenience of different kinds of money, for travelers get used to handling 26-cent guilders, 24-cent marks, 23-cent Swiss francs, 2-cent Belgian francs, and until recently ¼-cent French francs.

*Illustration*  B. One day I spent 250 Italian lire for breakfast, 9.10 Austrian shillings for lunch, and 5.05 Swiss francs for dinner; and it took only a minute to figure that in U.S. money breakfast cost 40 cents, lunch 36 cents, and dinner $1.15; that's a nuisance, but not a barrier.

*Specific Instances*

C. The money barriers come from countries who try to fix by law the rate of exchange on their currency, and to regulate the amount of money that comes in and goes out of that country. You could take 10 pounds into England, and 5 out; 100 guilders into Holland, and 50 out. France for 12 years fixed its rate at 350 francs to the dollar, when on the black market in France and in the open exchanges of other countries the franc sold over 400 to the dollar.

*Specific Instances*

D. The trade barriers came only slightly from high tariffs; more especially they came from private artificial barriers known as cartels. These cartels assigned quotas to their members, and had power to force into bankruptcy any member who violated his quota.

*Testimony*

E. The Common Market Treaty of 1957 undertook to erase these barriers and permit goods and workers to move as freely in Western Europe as between New York and California in the U.S. As Konrad Adenauer said: "We must part with concepts of the past."

## Organize the speech into an outline

A distinguished novelist, Martin Flavin, after serving as a judge in a writing contest said that as he read the new novels two things stood out. First, there was lack of plan. Second, there were too many scenes that did not advance the story but merely interrupted it. These are characteristics also of beginners' speeches, and both are inherent in that first weakness, the lack of an outline.

Anyone can learn to make an outline. Following are the basic steps:

1. Set down the Purpose-Sentence so you can keep in mind where you are going. (We have already discussed this, see pages 47 and 48.)

2. Make a list of the two or three main points of the central idea. (We have already discussed this; see page 48.)

3. Arrange these main points in the most effective order for your audience. In doing this rely for the time being on common sense.

4. Develop each of these main points with specific and interesting supporting material. (For discussion of this see above, pages 49-56.)

5. Plan an introduction that will explain the subject if necessary and will capture the attention of the listeners. Most introductions total about 10 per cent of the whole speech, but this proportion obviously varies.

6. Plan a conclusion that in some way will round out the speech. This may be a summary to enable listeners to remember the main points, or it may be other material that will leave the listeners with a lasting impression. Usually, a conclusion is even shorter than the introduction. The average is perhaps 5 per cent of the whole speech, although this also obviously varies.

The following shows a complete outline for an eight-minute speech that has been developed through the above six steps:

## WHY READ BOOKS?

*Purpose-Sentence:* Read books if you would develop intelligence and remain free.

### INTRODUCTION

I. A few years ago Rudolf Flesch wrote a book called *Why Johnny Can't Read.* Johnny can't read, said Flesch, because he was not taught properly.
II. I don't know about that, but I think I do know one reason why Johnny *doesn't* read.
  A. Look at his home; a typical middle-class home, one of the new modern homes with everything, including a two-car garage.
    1. But when you enter that home one thing is missing; there are no bookshelves.
    2. Now in his father's home there were bookshelves; before 1940 over twenty per cent of the new homes even had built-in bookshelves.
    3. But a recent survey shows that only 9 per cent of the homes have built-in bookshelves, and 51 per cent don't have shelves of any kind.
  B. In the TV den we meet Johnny's mother, absorbed in a serial, *Edge of the Night.*
    1. She has lots of time to kill until supper, thanks to her electric washer and other appliances.
    2. That night Johnny falls asleep to the tune of the *Late, Late Movie* which his mother and father are watching.

### DISCUSSION

I. Book reading in this country seems to be going the way of the old one-room country school.
  A. But you say, "I read. I have to read to stay in college. I will keep on reading after I leave college."
    1. Some of you will, no doubt, but some of you won't, as shown by these figures compiled by Dr. George Gallup on reading habits of college graduates:

a. Only one in ten could name the author of *Tom Jones* (first novel).

b. Only one in four could name the author of the *Wealth of Nations* (economic bible).

c. Only four in ten could name the author of *Vanity Fair* (the first step toward "realistic" writing).

d. One college graduate admitted he hadn't read a book since he left college ten years ago. He "guessed that" Shakespeare wrote *Canterbury Tales.*

2. Of course, this might be true of graduates of lesser colleges and universities, you say, but it simply could never be true of *our* institution! Let's see.

a. Last week I took a poll of 156 typical students on this campus. In selecting both the number and the persons, I had advice from the Department of Psychology. I asked each student to identify the authors of a list of twenty books.

(1). Six out of ten could not name the author of the *Life of Samuel Johnson,* the first great biography of the English language. Several said Mrs. Johnson wrote it. One said Johnson's mistress wrote it!

(2). Seven out of ten could not name the author of *Democracy in America,* a book that after 150 years is still a classic discussion of American government and society.

(3). Six out of ten could not name the author of *Coming of Age in Samoa,* one of the most significant studies ever made of primitive society; and is besides a report on a way of life where there are no taboos on the behavior of young people!

(4). (In case you are wondering, the authors of these three are Boswell, de Tocqueville, and Margaret Mead!)

(5). On the encouraging side, I am happy to report that nine out of ten *could* name the authors of the following: *Wealth of Nations, War and Peace, Canterbury Tales, Candide,* and *The Divine Comedy.*

b. For the whole list of twenty books, the average person answered five out of ten correctly. This is not bad, but hardly outstanding.

B. The American Institute of Public Opinion reports other significant facts on reading.

1. In England, at the time of interview, 55 per cent of the English were reading a book. In America the figure is 17 per cent.

2. In America, 57 per cent of high-school graduates and 20 per cent of college graduates had not read a single book in the past year.

3. In America, the percentage of adults reading a book at the time of interview was 29 per cent in 1937, and is only 17 per cent today.

C. People do read, of course, even adults.

1. Some reading is unavoidable: sign posts, interoffice memoranda, recipes, and TV commercials. We might call this "necessity reading."

2. A second type is "escapism reading." The magazine *Life* falls into this class.

     *a.* Because of the large number of pictures, you don't exactly read it; you just *look* at it.

     *b.* That explains why *Life* and *Look* are among the magazines with largest circulation—even above the unmentionable *Confidential*—and why special magazines like *Better Homes and Gardens* rely more on pictures than on articles.

   3. The third type of reading is the one that really counts. It's done neither for necessity nor escape. It is done by people who want to learn, to know, to expand the horizons of living.

   (*Transition:* By now most of you are probably saying, "All right, I don't read much, but I don't have the time, and that's that." I admit we haven't much time outside our studies, but I believe that if we think it's worth while, we will *make* time.)

II. Reading books will enable you to live 2,000 years or more within the span of your one lifetime.

  A. Observe how you can escape from living only at one place and at one time.

    1. Émile Zola's *The Gin Palace* is a fascinating expose of the evils of alcohol. After reading it, I seriously considered never touching liquor again.

    2. Niccolò Michiavelli's *The Prince* is a book that had a part in causing World War II and the way it was fought. Both Hitler and Mussolini read it, and both relied on it as a dictator's handbook.

    3. Shakespeare's *Othello* could be called "The Big Lie Repetition in the 16th Century." The main character, Othello, is an honorable man who allows Iago to deceive him. Othello is like the Germans who were led astray by Hitler's Big Lie tactics; and like Americans led astray for a time by the Aaron Burrs, Bilbos, and McCarthys.

     *a.* Iago is a model of such behavior, who uses half-truths, insinuations, and evasion to convince Othello that his wife is unfaithful.

     *b.* Iago, of course, is serving personal ends; he is jealous of Othello's wife.

  B. By reading books you can avoid mistakes of thought and action made even by the most intelligent people who live only in the present.

    1. If you have read Arnold J. Toynbee's *A Study of History* you will know why we cannot arrest communism just by arresting Communists.

    2. If you have read English institutional history you will appreciate liberties that today we take for granted, but which were won for us by great men of the past who died in the right way and at the right time. And you won't be tempted to barter away freedom of speech and trial by jury just to suppress some group which is a danger of the moment.

    3. If you read good current books, like Stuart Chase's *Proper Study of Mankind*, you will learn how much knowledge we really have that we don't use in handling everyday problems—from how to study to how to get along with your employer.

CONCLUSION

I. Now what does this all add up to? We see that there are three types of reading: for necessity, for escapism, and for what we may truly call *living*.
   A. We could call these the easy, the standard, and the fairly difficult.
   B. Or we might label them the comic books, *Saturday Evening Post,* and *Boswell's Life of Johnson.*
II. If you want to live 2,000 years during your next fifty you can do so by learning to read up: up from standard books to the fairly difficult, up from the fairly difficult to the difficult, and up from the difficult to the very difficult.

This is a detailed outline for an eight-minute speech, and it contains about 60 per cent the number of words as the full speech. Each idea, even the smallest, is set down. It thus affords a guide for a speaker who might want to pick up the outline next week or next month, refresh his mind from the outline, and give the speech again.

For your first speeches you will probably find it advisable to make outlines as complete as this one, although this is not a rule. Each speaker will develop his own particular system, yet by and large *responsible* speakers—as contrasted with loose talkers and demagogues—are characterized by having longer and more detailed preparations on paper. If a student starts early to develop glibness at the expense of thoroughness and accuracy, he puts a ceiling on his own progress.

## Practice delivering the speech until you have it well in mind

Each of the previous six steps has been concerned with developing ideas in your mind and getting them down on paper. You do not yet have a speech. It is not yet even an "essay on its hind legs." You have only thought lying flat on paper. Now comes the task of creating the speech out of these thoughts-on-paper. How can you be sure, when you stand up, of not forgetting, of not rambling and getting ideas misplaced? How can you avoid those long pauses filled with *ah* and *er*? How can you keep within the allotted time? These are no idle questions. When you try to speak in public and the words come, the failure becomes real and personal.

Many people deserve to fail. This is a hard unsympathetic way of putting it, but it is true. To create a speech out of an outline requires skill, and those who fail have refused to face the facts. Often they even tried to use short-cuts.

First, remember that extemporaneous speaking is not impromptu speaking. To be sure many people still think so, even as they once thought the world was flat. They think that extemporaneous speaking is speaking without preparation. Of course, this is wrong, completely wrong. Unprepared speeches are *impromptu,* and we are not here interested in them simply because real impromptu speeches usually are not good. Other people think that extemporaneous speeches are those "given with hasty or meager preparation." This, of course, is also wrong, completely wrong. These are simply poorly prepared speeches, nothing more. "It was with awe as well as eagerness that I braced myself for the supreme effort," wrote Winston Churchill of his first speech in Parliament, an extemporaneous speech. "I need not recount the pains I had taken to prepare, nor the efforts I had made to hide the work of preparation."

*A true extemporaneous speech, then, is a speech in which the ideas are firmly fixed in mind, but the exact words are not memorized.* A speech haphazardly planned is not extemporaneous, but just a haphazard speech. "What I call my best passages," said that eloquent Irishman John P. Curren, "my white horses, I have all ready beforehand."

Next, assuming that you have a good outline, how do you turn it into a good extemporaneous speech? You have taken part in a play, or at least seen a play, so let's start from there. The actors start with a script, complete with every word set down. But the script is not the play, for the play is a *living* thing. In the same way, an outline is not a speech.

How do the actors turn a script into a play? (1) They study the lines to find their meaning and their mood. (2) They learn the lines. (3) They perfect their memory and develop the play by rehearsals.

In creating a speech out of an outline you don't follow the same steps, but you do use the same *process*. You don't need to study the outline to find the meaning, since you made it and you know the meaning and mood. Nor do you "learn the lines," as in a play, which is to say you don't memorize it word-for-word. Individual methods vary, but in general they use the following procedure:

### PICTURIZE IN MIND THE SEQUENCE OF IDEAS

First, fix in mind the two or three main points. Next, "picturize" in your mind the arrangement of supporting material. Please note that you don't memorize these, as you would memorize a play or poem. Instead, you "picturize" the arrangement in your mind, so you *see* each illustration, specific instance, comparison, testimony, etc., and see *why* you put it at that place. For doing this, these are the steps that psychologists have found to be the most effective:

1. First, read the outline *silently* from beginning to end. Read it slowly, feeling your way along, but do not back-track even once, for back-tracking breaks the memorizing of sequence.

2. Next, read the outline *aloud*, thoughtfully, but again without backtracking.

3. Now put aside the outline and rehearse the speech aloud, still without back-tracking. If you forget parts of the speech, go right on. Don't look at the outline, and don't back-track. You are trying to get the whole thought pattern in mind, therefore, don't get entangled in details.

4. Study your outline again and note the places where you skipped parts of the speech or got the sequence out of order. After patching up these parts mentally, read the outline again *aloud,* slowly and thoughtfully, but still without back-tracking.

5. Put aside the outline and rehearse the speech aloud from start to finish without back-tracking.

### REHEARSE THE SPEECH FORMALLY FROM FIVE TO TEN TIMES, REHEARSE ON YOUR FEET AND PREFERABLY IN A LARGE ROOM

The above rehearsals were intended merely to fix the outline in your mind. Now come the rehearsals for creating the speech. From centuries of experience man has accumulated the knowledge of how to create a speech from thoughts-in-the-mind. This is the way:

*Rehearse on your feet.* You don't remember merely with you brain. You remember with your nerves and muscles also. This is often called "muscle memory," and it is essential to any speaker. You are going to give the speech while standing up. Therefore, rehearse the speech standing up. Then you can get the muscular set you will use in the final speech. Also by standing up you can pay attention to posture and action. These, too, are part of the rehearsal.

*Rehearse in a room roughly the size of the classroom.* This is not necessary for all rehearsals, although it is preferable, but certainly for a few rehearsals you need to stand up in a full-size room and get the feel of your voice as it comes back to you from the four walls. For this use one of the college classrooms in late afternoon or evening. Sometimes groups of students organize practice sessions, meet together, and practice on one another. Sometimes two students pair off, hold a practice session together, and criticize each other.

*Rehearse where you are free from interruptions.* This is so obvious that it needs no elaboration.

*Rehearse the speech formally from five to ten times.* The number of needed rehearsals is not fixed, and these numbers are suggestive. Few students will need less than five. Some will need more than ten. But one thing is positive: Most students need more rehearsals than they think. During the first few rehearsals you are still fixing the speech in mind. The next few allow you to work on posture, action, and especially *poise*— that imperative plus of all good speaking. The last rehearsals allow you to make sure that the fine shades of thought—the humor and suspense and all the other elements that make up what is known as *feeling, mood,* and *attitude*—are projected to every listener in the room.

## CLASSIFIED SPEECH SUBJECTS

### THE STORY OF (NARRATIVE)

College life in colonial days
McGuffey's readers
Noah Webster's dictionary
The 1949 Gold Rush
Appomattox
The Hoover Dam
The St. Lawrence Seaway

Modern music
The microscope
Antibiotics
Modern hog raising
How Washington, D.C. got located
Printing
Trial by jury

### THE CAUSE OF (ANALYSIS)

Tornadoes
California climate
Detroit being the automotive center
Iowa being the corn center
Hollywood being the cinema center
Poe's erratic genius
Mexico City's summer climate

U.S. foreign aid
High prices following World War II
The low living standard in Spain
Dictatorships in Latin America
The Asians' attraction to communism
Low value of the French franc
Universal liking for music

### A CRITICAL EXPOSITION OF (DESCRIPTION)

The curriculum of this institution
A course I am taking
A book I recently read
A play I recently saw
A speech I recently heard
The Flemish painters
Early American artists

The situation in Israel
Russian scientists
U.S. public school education
Jet plane development
The stock market
Modern short stories
Newspapers

### HOW IT WORKS

A woman's mind
A man's pride
Univac
Running a student paper
A county political organization
Focal plane shutters
Color photography
Offset printing

Coaxial cable
Radar
Photoelectric cell
Acoustically treated rooms
Grading beef
The corn picker
Fingerprinting
A city credit bureau

### WHAT IT IS

Medians, means, and averages
Dow-Jones Industrial Average
Bull markets and bear markets
Realism in literature
Impressionistic art
Rock 'n roll
Royal Doulton china

Gobelin tapestry
Chippendale furniture
Industry-wide collective bargaining
Closed shop
Union shop
Check off
Shop steward

### WHAT IT IS

Farm parity prices

Hope Chest

Octane rating

Honor system

Grade-point system

Democracy

Socialism

Communism

Social security

Blue Cross and Blue Shield

### HOW TO DO IT

Choose a husband or wife

Win friends and influence people

Get along with professors

Get elected to office

Read a book

Study

Get a date

Give first aid

Take pictures

Navigate

Draw a cartoon

Handle a fly rod

Hit a golf ball

Buy a secondhand car

Make a speech

Apply for a job

Sell life insurance

Raise money for a cause

Write a good business letter

Budget study hours

Use a slide rule

Develop color prints

Take action pictures

Put on makeup for stage or television

Read with meaning

Manage a political campaign

Make Easter flowers bloom for Easter

Understand the fine points of football

### BOOKS, ART, AND MUSIC

Sacred music

Classical music

Popular music

Richard Strauss

Beethoven and Bach

Victor Herbert

Rodgers and Hammerstein

Literary magazines

Pulp magazines

Detective-story magazines

Western stories

Carl Sandburg, poet and biographer

William Faulkner and Tennessee
Williams, modern Southern writers

Margaret Fuller: "I accept the universe"

Cooper's *Leatherstocking Tales*

The origin of the comic strips

Who were the early American artists?

The art collectors

How to tell a genuine old master

### HISTORY AND BIOGRAPHY

The first legislature in America

Samuel Adams and the Boston Tea
Party

How the Declaration of Independence was written

Steamboats on the Ohio and Mississippi

The early railroads

The San Francisco Vigilantes

How Lincoln was nominated

Florence Nightingale

Dolly Madison

Man 25,000 years ago

Genghis Khan

Hannibal's Carthage

Samuel Johnson's England

Winston Churchill's England

William F. Cody's American West

The Chinese 3,000 years ago

How the American Indians got here

Travel 200 years ago

Early forms of money

PERSONAL AND OTHERWISE

"See this show"
"Listen to this symphony"
"Read this book"
"See this art exhibit"
"See this television program"
"Take this course"
"A teacher who made me study"
"What I believe about religion"
"What I believe on marriage and family"
"Why am I here? Where am I going? How shall I get there?"
"Why I came to college"

"What I ought to learn in college"
"What I must unlearn when I leave college"
"What different courses I would take if I could do it over again"
"Why I believe in extracurricular activities"
"Don't make up your mind about this yet"
"Learn to doubt intelligently"
"Hold fast to your faith"
"Learn to live with other people"

# Assignments

ON OBSERVING HOW OTHERS DO IT

1. Go to hear a speaker and evaluate his extemporaneous ability:

   a. Is his speaking disrupted by mental gaps like these:
      "I should—*er*—first like to say that—*er*— . . ."
      "The reason for this is that—*the reason is that*—we cannot. . . ."
      "First, I want to say—*to say*—that our policy is. . . ."
   b. As you make a key-word outline of the speech, do you find that the speaker has wandered from the line of thought?
   c. Does he waste time and words simply because he has not thought the subject out until it was clear in his own mind?

2. Analyze one of your instructors in the manner explained in Assignment 1.

ON FINDING AND PHRASING PURPOSE-SENTENCES

3. Select a subject. (For possible subjects see Classified Speech Subjects just above. See also subjects listed in your Speech-Subject Analysis Form, Chapter 1, pages 28 and 29.):

   a. Select three specific phases of this subject, each of which would be suitable for a speech.
   b. Phrase each of these three specific phases into a suitable Purpose-Sentence using the principles found in this chapter.

ON USING SUPPORTING MATERIAL

4. To study the use of Supporting Material, prepare a one-cell section of an outline after the manner seen on pages 57-60. Set down your Assertion as a main topic, then beneath it in subhead form organize the Supporting Material—Facts and Figures, Specific Instances, Illustrations, Comparisons, and Testimony.

5. Read one of the speeches listed in the Appendix. From various parts of the speech, outline three one-cell sections showing how the speaker used Forms

of Support. Follow the general method of outlining one-cell units as shown in this chapter, pages 57-61.

## ON OUTLINING

6. Make a three- to five-page outline of one of the speeches listed in Assignment 5 above. Include everything: Purpose-Sentence, main heads, Supporting Material in the subheads. For the general form and arrangement, see the specimen outline on pages 57-61.

7. From the subject you used in Assignment 3 above, or any other suitable subject, prepare an outline for a speech. Include everything a good outline should have: Purpose-Sentence, main heads, Supporting Material in the subheads. For the general form and arrangement, see the specimen outline on pages 57-61.

## ON PUTTING THE SEVEN STEPS TOGETHER

8. Prepare a four-minute speech, following the Seven Steps set forth in this chapter. In order not to overlook or treat casually any step, use the following procedure:

   *a.* Make a Time Table of your speech preparation, and hand it in with the outline. On it list the Seven Steps, and show when you *started* each and when you *completed* it. This is a mechanical procedure, and is for beginners only. For them it is excellent, for it shows the source of trouble or failure in the first speeches.

   *b.* Make a permanent record of this Time Table in your notebook, and do the same with later speeches. You can then compare each speech grade, and the over-all general progress, with the amount and method of speech preparation.

# ❉ 4 ❉

# First Steps in Managing Yourself

BERNARD SHAW once wrote to H. G. Wells: "When you first spoke . . . I told you to hold up your head and speak to the . . . back wall. To shew me that you were not going to be taught by me, you made the commonest blunder of the tyro; you insisted on having a table; leaning over it on your knuckles; and addressing the contents of your contracted chest to the tablecloth." Shaw thereupon tartly admonished Wells to "stand on your heels instead of your knuckles." Wells at the time was around forty years old, author of nineteen books, and recognized as one of the foremost writers in the world. His behavior was typical of what audiences endure from mine-run speakers, even though they be famous or gifted, who have never learned to manage themselves in public.

Many such persons simply don't know that public speaking involves a technique; and—like H. G. Wells—they won't believe it, even when told by a Bernard Shaw. They believe that "anybody can talk," and are blithely unaware how painfully their performance disproves it. Others have what Emerson tartly described as a selfish enjoyment of their sensations, "and loss of perception of the sufferings of the audience." Many speak in a half-direct manner, really talking to themselves and not to the listeners. They don't open their mouths wide enough to allow clear-cut speech. They don't use energy enough to lift their voices above the hum line of noise. Their hands and feet are out of control.

Face it frankly. Most self-made speakers are the product of unskilled labor. They may be as famous as H. G. Wells, but as speakers they are defective, as Wells was defective. You are to avoid their example, not imitate it. Man has spent more than 2,400 years learning how to humanize knowledge and energize truth, and you have the opportunity of learning this accumulated knowledge of 2,400 years. One part of it deals with how to manage yourself in public, and with that part we are concerned in this chapter.

## Stage fright

The first besetting problem is stage fright. "How can I overcome stage fright?" is perhaps the most frequently asked question about public speaking. Surprising numbers of men and women, even in middle life, approach speech instructors wanting to learn the formula for overcoming stage fright. As with all the problems of human life, there is no formula. It must be done through understanding and intelligent effort.

### EXTENT OF STAGE FRIGHT

First, you should know that stage fright is almost universal among singers and actors as well as speakers, among old-timers as well as beginners. That grand old prima donna Madame Schumann-Heink, after nearly fifty years before the public frankly said, "I grow nervous, . . . I become sick, almost; I want to go home." The actress Eva Le Gallienne was interviewed after she had just finished her one-thousandth performance. The reporter wanted to know if she still had stage fright. "Yes," she said, "and its gets worse every year." A British cartoonist, David Low, once told an audience that every time he made a speech he felt a block of ice, nine by nine inches, in the pit of his stomach. Sir Winston Churchill was in the audience and afterwards came forward to ask: "How large did you say that block of ice is?" Replied Low: "Nine by nine inches." And Churchill commented, "What an amazing coincidence. Exactly the same size as mine." Abraham Lincoln would have understood; he had stage fright all his life. When he first rose to speak, he "froze in his tracks," and "had a far away prophetic look in his eyes." Even Cicero, more than two thousand years ago, struggled with stage fright: "I turn pale at the outset of a speech, and quake in every limb and in all my soul."

### THE CAUSE AND NATURE OF STAGE FRIGHT

Why do people have stage fright? One of the paradoxes of human nature is that most of us *want* an audience, yet *fear* it. We possess a deep craving to be noticed by others, and are beset by a fear—sometimes a terrible fear—of being neglected or ignored. But when we get attention (as in giving a speech), or know we are going to get it, we become afraid. If we are inexperienced, we are afraid to stand alone against the audience, afraid of forgetting, afraid of being made a spectacle, afraid of failure. Even if we are speakers of experience we are afraid of not doing our best, of having it said of us, "He is slipping; he used to do better." In both cases the fear arises from our feeling "inadequate to meet a situation."

Stage fright is not merely mental, but is also physical. This comes from the incredibly potent doses of the endocrine glands that travel to every organ and reach every bit of living bone and muscle tissue of the body. In stage fright these come especially from the adrenal glands, and possibly also the thyroid. When the impulse is telegraphed to these glands, at once adrenalin (and possibly also thyroxin) is shot into the blood stream. At the same instant a trigger is pulled that dumps glycogen (a special form of sugar) from the liver into the blood stream. When these secretions hit your heart, it starts to thump. When they hit the respiratory center in the brain, you start to gasp. When they hit the blood vessels going to the brain, they contract and you feel woozy. These are the obvious effects. Less obvious effects are even more profound. Blood is drawn away from internal organs and transferred to outer muscles—arms, legs, etc.—and this transfer slows down or stops the digestive process altogether. (Ergo, don't eat too much just before you give a speech!) The blood now clots more easily. Muscles become tense all over; hence your tense throat muscles tend to produce harsh shrill tones. Salivary glands stop secreting, the mouth becomes dry, and you feel thick-tongued. In contrast, sweat glands increase secretion, so the skin becomes moist and beads of perspiration may stand on your forehead. You are short of breath, for the breath stream is shallow and jerky. All of this takes place in the body when you have extreme stage fright. In mild stage fright, the body undergoes the same changes in lesser degree, and we feel faintly seasick, have faint disagreeable sensations, or are simply keyed up and tense.

## THE PROBLEM RESTATED

When you have stage fright, therefore, remember that others have it too. Many of the best are like Henry W. Grady who found that "every nerve in my body was strung tight as a fiddle-string." But seasoned speakers have learned to control and use stage fright.

Your problem is not to overcome it, but to control and use it. For stage fright if properly controlled helps a speaker instead of hinders. What Amelita Galli-Curci said of singers is just as true of speakers: "The person who does not get the least bit nervous at the prospect of stepping on a stage will never move an audience to wild ecstasy." Indeed, Cicero had discovered this twenty centuries ago: "For the better the speaker, the more profoundly is he frightened of the difficulty of speaking, and of the doubtful fate of a speech, and of the anticipations of an audience." Cicero did not know *why* this was true, but now psychologists have learned the reason. We have already given the explanation in the section just above on the cause and nature of stage fright, namely that stage fright is accompanied by chemical changes in the blood—the most important being the excessive secretion of adrenalin (and possibly of thyroxin). *But psychologists have further discovered that adrenalin is also secreted by vigorous bodily action, even in the absence of stage fright or other emotion. Finally, they have discovered that the physiological changes produced in the body by such means, if they are controlled and directed, "increase our adequacy" of performance.* In others words, a reasonable amount of stage fright, if controlled and directed, makes you a better speaker.

Restated, then, the problem is not how to overcome stage fright, but how to reduce it, control it, and give better speeches because of it.

## CONTROLLING STAGE FRIGHT

There is no formula for controlling stage fright, but there are tested procedures, especially the following four:

1. *Get an interesting subject.* Ask yourself whether you are really afraid of your audience or whether down at the bottom you are afraid of your *subject.* Many students are afraid of their subject, and for a good reason. They don't *know* much about it. They don't *care* much about it. But a speech is coming up, and they've *got* to have a subject, so they picked this one—a little desperately perhaps—and are going through the motions with it. They don't have stage fright. They have *subject* fright.

Therefore, the first step in controlling stage fright is to get an interesting subject. You have read about this already (page 45). Possibly you have finished making that Speech-Subject Inventory (pages 28 and 29), and you have a list of subjects that other class members say they would like to hear. If so, you ought to have on hand half a dozen really good subjects. Meanwhile, stay off dry and dusty subjects, and avoid talking about something because "it might be a good subject." Instead, get a subject that really interests you, one that fires you up when you think of it. Ask yourself: What do I mostly think about when I am not working? (There you have a *good* subject.) Or ask: Which course in college do I like most of all, and why? Which do I like least, and why? (Here are two more good subjects.)

2. *Be well prepared.* Often severe cases of stage fright are the result of inadequate preparation *without the student himself being aware of it.* Sometimes he has simply tried to memorize something that he has not digested, memorize a whole solid paragraph or page without absorbing it into his own thinking. The slightest distraction can destroy his cues, and he does not know enough about the content to carry on. Or he may have

started the speech too late and tired himself by working long hours the night before, or even crammed his preparation into the period immediately preceding the class. He meant to do better, but never got around to it. Often he really gave ample time to it, but started too late. The same amount of time spread over several days or several weeks would have produced a better speech and given him more assurance. Not always, then, does lack of preparation mean "too little too late." Often it means "enough work started too late."

The second step in controlling stage fright is to be well prepared. If you want to review the ways and means of preparation, turn again to pages 47-62.

3. *Use physical action.* The person who has stage fright is physically tense all over. This tension is not merely the effect of fear; it is also in part the cause of fear. One is not simply tense because he is afraid; but in part he is afraid because he is tense. He is caught in a vicious circle: Because he is afraid he becomes tense, and because he becomes tense he becomes still more afraid. At some point he must break this vicious circle.

To prescribe a cure is easy. *Relax.* Use only those muscles needed to keep the body poised and erect, and relax all others. Free the tension in the arms, the hands, and, above all, in the face. In short, get the body tonus back to normal, and stage fright will be reduced.

You cannot do this, of course, merely by commanding the body to relax. You can do it by *doing* something with the head, hands, and feet. Take a step, no matter how heroic the effort. Nod the head, or shake it. Smile, or at least raise the eyebrows. Use the hands in some way or other. Then the instant any part of the body is free, use it to help carry your thought to the audience. Remember that mere vigorous action is not enough; it may fly off at loose ends, and you may merely pace the floor, fumble at your clothes, and scratch your face. You need to *use vigorous action for communicating your thought to the audience.* When this is done, you will be freed from the grip of fear. Ultimately will come to you that great sense of self-mastery, the triumph of *using* stage fright to give a *better* speech.

Here are detailed suggestions for using physical action:

BEFORE YOU SPEAK

1. During those minutes of tension before you speak, sit upright and start breathing *deeply* and *regularly.* One of the bodily changes that accompanies stage fright is irregular breathing. Watch particularly, therefore, that your breathing is not only deep, but is regular.

2. Relax your hands. (Aren't they clinched, or your fingers fidgeting?) Press the fingertips of one hand against those of the other until the fingers when opened feel easy and relaxed.

3. Relax the muscles of your face and jaw and throat. Let your jaw "flop like an idiot's" said Woolbert. Lean the head forward as if you were almost asleep and let every muscle in the face sag. Finally, *yawn* (even in public you can hide a yawn behind a hand or a handkerchief!) A yawn is the best of all exercises for relaxing the whole region of the face and throat.

4. With the yawn still lingering and the face relaxed, think again about your breathing. Is it regular? And deep?

WHILE YOU SPEAK

5. When you stand up before the audience, *get set to speak* first of all. This "getting set" needs to be rehearsed beforehand, using the following procedure:
   a. Set both feet firmly on the floor, so they will not be tempted to shift or wander.
   b. Stand up to your *full* height, with no sagging in your chest, and no drooping of the hip or knee.
   c. Draw in a deep breath. (You need power to fill that room!)
   d. Open your mouth *wide* to give your voice a decent chance of getting out. The very sound of your voice coming out full and strong will go a long way toward getting you over the hump.

6. During the speech use communicative action. Use gestures that show listeners what you are talking about. Use gestures that explain your idea. Nod your head to emphasize a point. Lift the eyebrows when you ask a question. Throw the weight of your whole body behind emphatic words. Action like this will divert the stresses and tensions of your body to their proper use. (But action will not at first come spontaneously. You must rehearse it.)

4. *Don't think of yourself, but of your subject and audience.* Perhaps the majority of frustated people in the world are victims of the inability to forget themselves. Among these is the speaker who keeps asking himself, "How am I doing?" for putting your mind on "How am I doing?" tends to make you self-conscious and to manufacture stage fright.

> A centipede was happy quite
> Until a frog in fun
> Said, "Pray, which leg comes after which?"
> This raised her mind to such a pitch,
> She lay distracted in a ditch,
> Considering how to run.

During much of our lives we think of ourselves, but if we would speak effectively we must acquire what Ralph Dennis called "a vital sense of the brotherhood of man." We must lose ourselves in the welfare of those to whom we talk. Can they hear us? Can they understand us? Do they enjoy listening? Are we throwing light on problems that have puzzled them? Are we showing them something of the beauty, the goodness, or the glories of life? As Cardinal Manning advised a young man making his first important public speech: "Be full of your subject and forget yourself."

## IF YOU FORGET WHILE SPEAKING

Suppose you do forget in spite of everything, then what? It's a fearful point.

First, rest assured that if you have prepared thoroughly, and have followed the other steps set forth in this chapter, you just won't forget more than momentarily, if at all. Even if your mind goes blank and the room blacks out, you will keep on talking—*if* you have prepared thoroughly and have rehearsed the speech while standing on your feet.[1] More than one beginner has had the room grow dim and his conscious mind go blank, only to regain full mental possession and find his voice going right on with the speech! But this does not happen to people who have not thoroughly prepared.

Suppose that in spite of careful preparation you forget anyhow. What then? Be assured that all is not lost, even then. There are the ways and means, such as the following:

*Don't go into a panic, but take a deep breath and try to remember the next point.* A deep breath will tend to keep you from tightening up. Perhaps a step forward will help put your mind on the track. (But don't back away from the audience. They won't harm you, and you really are not afraid of them!) After three or four seconds if a deep breath, or a step forward, does not help, then move on to the next method, as follows:

*Summarize aloud what you have already said.* By summarizing you will get started down the track again, and this tends to lead you into the next idea. Or if it does not lead you into the next idea, it may lead you to some idea that follows. If so, go right ahead. You are on the track again, and if it is not exactly where you got off the track, don't worry about it. If summarizing out loud does not work, then turn to the third method, as follows:

*Tell your listeners frankly that you cannot remember the next point.* When you forget, everybody in the audience knows it anyway. Your freezing up is as visible as a fire wagon. Be sensible, then, and talk about it frankly. How much better it is to hear a student say, "Well, friends, for the life of me I can't remember what I was going to say next, but you

---

[1] Soldiers in combat have been known to black out completely, yet never falter. They even give orders, and the right ones, during the blackout. This is the result of rigid military drill, which fixes behavior patterns so firmly that a momentary blackout will not change them. In the same way speakers will carry on through a momentary blackout *if* the rehearsals have fixed the behavior patterns.

know how rough public speaking is on beginners. I had been saying
[here he goes back for another summary]." In other words, if you have
forgot you might as well be gracious about it and bring the sympathy of
the audience over to your side. By the time they chuckle and you smile
back, you will feel far more comfortable than you were a few moments
ago. You will be able to move about. You will have felt the warm sympathy of those people out front, who won't be monsters any longer but
kind, friendly people who want to be nice to you. By that time, you can
*say something*, just as though you would speak if you met a friend on the
street. After that, you can *say something about your subject*. It may not be
what you had planned to say, but no matter what it is, you can follow
it through like a conversation. Maybe you will get back onto your planned
speech. Maybe not. But you will have the thrill of discovering that the
people out front are not enemies, but are really friendly; and that if
you treat them as friends they will listen earnestly, laugh with you, and
applaud you. Under that uplift, you will not need to worry about forgetting.

## The mental attitude for good speaking

Stage fright was discussed first because it is often a barrier in the
student's mind. Actually, stage fright is part of a larger and more important problem of developing the mental attitude for good speaking. Behind much of the beginner's excessive stage fright, behind much of the
mumbling and fumbling and fidgeting that one hears from self-made
speakers, lies a poor mental attitude. " 'Tis hard for an empty bag to
stand upright," observed Benjamin Franklin.

### A SENSE OF COMMUNION

"I knew a very distinguished man once who memorized every word of
each address," said Clarence B. Randall, "and did it with amazing skill,
but I always felt that his slight preoccupation with the effort of memory
drew an unfortunate veil between him and his audience." Randall's judgment deserves respect. He was one of the half-dozen most important
businessmen in America when he retired. He gave nearly twenty years
of his life to public service. He was a recipient of a U. S. Speaker-of-the-
Year Award. He was one of the most discerning analysts on why speaking
in American public life was effective and why it was ineffective. What
he says about memorizing, therefore, commands respect. Now there is
nothing inherently wrong with memorizing, of course. Actors memorize,
and many earlier speakers did it. They spent years learning the art,

and spent weeks rehearsing and perfecting memory for each performance. In earlier centuries people admired the art of memorizing, and applauded one who perfected the art. They applauded often for the art itself. Not so today. The tempo of this twentieth-century industrial civilization simply does not fit that kind of speaking. Audiences don't admire speeches primarily as an art. They need information. They need help in problem-solving. They need to have ideas watered and cultivated. They want to hear the strongly-held convictions of the speaker as he stands before them. He won't reach them by reciting polished memorized phrases. He won't lead them, or influence their thinking, until he projects *himself* into their minds. You can sum it up in one word. In real public speaking you participate in *communion* with your audience. Memorizers don't participate in communion. They recite.

Speakers face the same handicap in using notes and manuscripts. A speaker who is looking on paper for his next idea is not in communion with the listener. The mind-to-mind contact is broken. Each time it is broken it has to be re-established. "There is no gesture in the world," said Clarence B. Randall, "more persuasive with an audience than for the speaker after he has addressed the chair to turn out the reading light. No one can doubt that such a man is voicing his own opinions, and no matter how bad his phrasing or how broken his sentences, there is a rugged integrity about what he says that can be deeply moving. When he looks them in the eye and lets them have it they listen, and they respect him even when they differ."[2]

Let us grant that most speakers today use notes or manuscripts. Let us grant that some do it well, and a few superbly. The bald fact is that most do it badly, and it is not possible for them ever to learn to do it well. As John W. Davis explained in the midst of an address to the U. S. Supreme Court, "There is something about a sheet of paper interposed between a speaker and listener that walls off the mind of the latter as if it were boiler-plate. It obstructs the passage of thought as the lead plate bars the X-rays."

We talk a great deal of the differences between public speaking and private conversation. Actually, the differences are largely superficial and the likenesses are fundamental. How do they differ? Where is the dividing line? James A. Winans in his *Public Speaking* raises the issue in a vivid way. He imagines a man who has seen a great battle, or is fired with a great enthusiasm, meeting a friend on the street and pausing to talk. Others gather; he lifts his voice so all may hear. Still others gather; and they want to see him as well as hear him, so he mounts a cart and goes on with his talk. Obviously, the man started with a conversation and ended

[2] Clarence B. Randall, *Freedom's Faith* (Boston, Little, Brown and Company, 1953), p. 143. The preceding quotation is from pp. 145-146.

with a public speech. Where did the conversation become a public speech?

We might pick any given place as the passover point. We could say that conversation becomes public speaking when the number of listeners reaches 15, or when it reaches 50, or when the speaker stands on a cart or platform. But these are arbitrary points. Not one is the real passover point between a conversation and a public speech.

Actually, conversation *gradually* becomes public speaking, and public speaking is simply *enlarged* conversation. Therefore, get rid of the idea that you are "making a speech" when you stand on a platform. You are not talking *at* people merely to enjoy the sound of your own voice. You are not declaiming to the walls, the ceiling, or simply into the air. You are not, as distinguished writers so often do when they try to speak, merely testing the acoustics in the empty echo-chamber of your own ego. You are talking *with* people, and right soon you should learn the ways and means by which they talk; for plainly will they say to you: "I agree, go ahead," or "I don't quite understand that; say it again," or "I am bored; will you please stop."[3]

Enlarged conversation, of course, has problems of its own. Not all people are good conversationalists. Some bore you in private, and on the platform they bore everybody. In class, these present a delicate problem, for when the instructor comments on their tiresome tones they are likely to reply in perfect innocence, "But that's the way I talk naturally." Shall the instructor tactfully avoid the issue? Or shall he say with brutal honesty: "Exactly. In private conversation you bore two or three. In public speech you bore thirty." Other people speak passably well in private, but when their speech is enlarged into public address cracks and flaws show up. All in all, then, we should look at some of the attributes of good enlarged conversation:

### LOOKING THE AUDIENCE IN THE MIND

Did you ever observe people in earnest conversation? Try it. They don't gaze out the window, or at the floor, or at the ceiling. They look one another directly in the eye. But their looking-into-the-eye is only an outward sign of an inward state of mind. Actually, they are trying to *look each other in the mind.*

---

[3] You can read agreement and query in listeners' faces. All you have to do is *look* at them. When you see a question mark in the expression of half a dozen at one time, you know it is time to *stop,* put aside your prepared speech, and *explain again* whatever has puzzled them. Boredom is even easier to read. If a speech is interesting, listeners don't shift much, perhaps *once* every 60 seconds. But if they are bored, up goes the rate of shifting all over the room, until it reaches as much as *five to ten* shifts per minute for each person. Now all of this is as visible to a speaker as a neon sign. You may ask, "Why don't speakers *do something* when listeners look puzzled or start shifting?" The answer is that these speakers are not paying any attention to the listeners. They are talking *at* them or declaiming to the walls or mumbling to the speaker's stand.

This is the mental attitude of a good public speaker, no matter how large the audience or how small. His manner will vary to fit the occasion. His posture, action, and voice may change to fit the size of the audience or the formality of the occasion. But one thing does not change: his direct looking-the-audience-in-the-mind mode of communication. Adam Smith, that great university lecturer of the eighteenth century, will serve as an example. He was great because he spoke not only to the patient ear of the earnest student, but also because he spoke to the shallow ear of the poorest student and to the callous ear of the great outside world, "which must be tickled in order to be made attentive." He attributed his success, said his biographer, "very largely to the vigilant care with which he watched his audience; for he depended very much upon their sympathy. 'During one whole session,' he is reported to have said, 'a certain student with a plain but expressive countenance was of great use to me in judging my success. . . . If he leant forward to listen, all was right; but if he leant back in an attitude of listlessness I felt that all was wrong, and that I must change either the subject or the style of my address."[4]

### BEING EARNEST

Some speakers talk as though spraying water out of a garden hose. They spray words into the air, and let them fall on listeners like drops of water. But the word-sprayer is not *earnest*, and unless a speaker is earnest something is forever lacking. As William Jennings Bryan said of Lincoln, "He possessed the two things that are absolutely essential to effective speaking—namely, information and earnestness." Of earnestness James A. Winans, one of the greatest speech teachers of this century, said: "An audience will forgive a speaker almost any lack, if he is manifestly earnest. . . . Earnestness moves our emotions, thaws our indifference, and gives us faith which a leader must create." If you don't have earnestness, nothing else matters too much. Edward Everett, who labored a hundred hours and more over a single speech, did not always have it, and after one of his memorized recitations a critic said, "When you hear him, you button your coat to keep from taking cold."

Of course, it is not easy to be earnest the first time you stand before an audience. You have not had enough experience with this sort of thing. You stand up alone, like a man before a firing squad, and the eyes of the audience gleam at you like shining gun barrels. You wish you were at home, or in a foxhole on a battlefield, or anywhere—to escape those gleaming eyes. Faced by this crisis, you tend to do one of two things, both wrong. Either you shrink within yourself, like a turtle drawing in his head, to escape those eyes. Or you bellow defiantly in a loud voice to prove that you are not afraid.

Both are bad. Both come from the wrong mental attitude. Uppermost

[4] Francis W. Hirst, *Adam Smith* (London, Macmillan Company, 1904), pp. 34-35.

in your mind, even in your first speech, should be this thought: "I am here to tell this audience about this subject, just as I would tell someone in an important private conversation. I must magnify and intensify my manner and my voice. I must reach them all, especially on the back row. I must make them see this subject and feel about it as I do. To do this I must talk *to* them and *with* them. Above all, I must be earnest."

### PHYSICAL VITALITY

Said an English newspaper reporter of that brilliant Italian speaker, Alessandro Gavazzi: "As I listened to him I first understood why Demosthenes insisted so strenuously on . . . delivery as the first, second, and third secret of successful" public speaking. "For Gavazzi did not merely speak with his lips. He was eloquent to his finger tips, and to the soles of his sandaled feet." Such action requires physical vitality. The truth is that enlarged conversation demands what seems to beginners like an unbelievable amount of physical vitality. Talking to one or two persons close by takes relatively little energy. Listless conversation takes almost no energy. But when you speak to twenty people in a classroom, or a hundred in an auditorium—incredible though it may seem—it takes five, ten, fifty, or a *hundred* times the energy of good private conversation; all this energy for the speaker's voice to sound as loud, earnest, and direct as in good private conversation.[5]

The earnest public speaker, therefore, is a fountain of vital force. He opens his mouth wider than he would ever dream of doing in private conversation. He makes sure that even those farthest away can hear easily. He communicates uninhibitedly with head, body, and arms. This is the compulsion of good "enlarged" conversation.

### PERSONALIZED SPEAKING AND THE RHYTHM OF TALK

In private conversation we use those personal pronouns, *we* and *you* and *I*. We also use "talking words," those short words of the English language known to everybody. Thus when talking we commonly say *but*

[5] The following pertinent data is taken from Lyman S. Judson and Andrew T. Weaver, *Voice Science* (New York, Appleton-Century-Crofts, Inc., 1942), pp. 285-288:

1. Speech power:

|  |  |  |
|---|---|---|
| of soft whisper | 0.001 | microwatts |
| of soft speech | 0.1 | microwatts |
| of average speech | 15.0 | microwatts |
| of loud speech | 1000.0 | microwatts |

Thus loud speech requires 66 times the power of average speech, 10,000 times the power of soft speech, and 1,000,000 times the power of soft whisper.

2. Sound intensity and distance: The intensity of sound varies inversely as the square of the distance from the source. A speaker, let us assume, produces a sound of given intensity at a certain distance. At twice the distance this sound has one-fourth the original intensity, and at three times the distance it has only one-ninth the original intensity. (See pages 389-392, for further discussion of this.)

*Brown Brothers*

"Teddy" Roosevelt, the apostle of the strenuous life, was a dynamo of physical vitality in delivering his campaign speeches.

instead of "however," *go* instead of "travel," *think* instead of "reflect," and *want* instead of "desire."

Good speakers also use these personal pronouns and talking words. But this comes hard for college students. Why? You *write* your outlines and often even write your speeches! In these written outlines and speeches you don't use short "talking words," like *but, go, think,* and want. Instead you use the abstract written form, like "however," "travel," "reflect," and "desire." You also tend to avoid personal pronouns. You are afraid to say "I think," and often back in, crab-like, with "It is my thought that." Add it all up, and it means that when you stand before the class you are not "woman talking" or "man talking." Your talk doesn't sound as it did last night at the dinner table. It's not the same. *On the platform you're not talking, but only rerunning what you wrote on paper. Before you can learn to use talking words and personal pronouns on the platform you must learn to write them in the outline.*

Finally, is the rhythm of talk. In private conversation we talk in contractions. We say *don't, won't,* and *it's*—not "do not," "will not," and "it is." Only when we want to emphasize a negative do we say "He is *not* here." As Harold Whitehall said pointedly in *Webster's New World Dictionary,* "English spoken without the natural rhythm of English is scarcely English at all." And as Dorothy McCleary, prize-winning master of dialogue writing, added, "It is only persons who are unsure of the language who use the full forms of speech, because they lack the intimate feel for the contraction." Here is the nub. Stage-frightened students *are* unsure of their language. That's why they tend to avoid contractions, and hence to sound artificial. Read aloud the sentences below, and compare the stilted rhythm with the genuine speech rhythm:

| STILTED RHYTHM | SPEECH RHYTHM |
| --- | --- |
| *It is* over there | *It's* over there |
| I *do not* think so | I *don't* think so |
| He *is not* here | *He's* not here, (or) He *isn't* here |
| I *have not* found it | *I've* not found it, (or) I *haven't* found it |

This use of contractions is the basis of speech rhythm. One reason (though not the only one) why most people sound artificial when they read aloud is that they don't use contractions. They read the full written forms which forces them to use stilted rhythm. To compare stilted rhythm with real speech rhythm, read aloud the following passage without using contractions:

> The world is divided into peoples that own the governments and governments that own the peoples; and it is the first kind we are determined to defend in America.

Now read it again, using the contractions that permit speech rhythm:

> The world's divided into peoples that own the governments and governments that own the peoples; and it's the first kind we're determined to defend in America.

Finally read it still again, this time using not only contractions, but also giving heavy emphasis to important words and unstressing less important ones:

> Th'-world's-*divided* / into-peoples-that-own-th'-governments / an-*governments*-that-own-th'-peoples / and-it's-th'-*firstkind*-we're-determined-to-defend / in-*America*

Read in this way, it does not sound like recitation but like real talk.

## A SENSE OF HUMOR

"Show me how a man reacts to humor and I'll tell you how he reacts to life," runs an adage of the social scientists. It fits speakers like a glove.

What do we mean by *humor* and by having a *sense of humor*? At times we speak loosely of humor as being the same as *fun*, and at other times as being the same as *wit*. Actually, it is not the same as either. *Fun* is a capacity for laughing, for making others laugh, or for finding things to laugh about in other people. *Wit* is "intellectual brilliancy and quickness of perception"; it is not mere calisthenics with words, but is truth expressed in a sparkling manner. Above these is *humor*. Humor springs from deep insight, an insight that carries understanding and wisdom. It implies human sympathy, human tolerance, human kindliness. It includes not only the readily-perceived absurdness of characters, situations, and consequences, but also the not-readily-perceived pathos.

Thus *fun* suggests boisterous laughter, and *wit* denotes intellectual subtlety, often sharp and biting; but *humor* is understanding and gentle and sympathetic. Hence we speak of the *fun* of playing children; and writers distinguish the *wit* of Washington Irving from the *humor* of Mark Twain.

Humor is not the opposite of seriousness, but is rather the opposite of solemnity. Serious men—from Julius Caesar to Benjamin Franklin and Winston Churchill—have been men of humor. Fanatics, by contrast, are lacking humor because they lack perspective. They are zealots, often unable to laugh or smile, and unable to see their subject in a human light. That is why great movements are better led by men of humor than by zealots whose fanaticism burns away their common sense.

Students in their first attempts at speaking are serious to the point of dullness and as spontaneous as a doorknob. They lack humor. Sometimes this comes from lack of preparation, for when the time they give to homework is "too little too late" the result is immature, even childish; and the speaker is not capable of humor that comes from insight, wisdom, human tolerance, and humankindliness. But even well-prepared students usually lack humor. They speak at first in a doleful, jaundiced manner. They are not yet at home on the platform. They look solemn and are solemn, for they are thinking only of themselves. They are in no mood for humor, for they have not yet learned to think foremost of their listeners.

So when we say a speaker should have a sense of humor, we are saying far more than first meets the eye. We are saying that a speaker should think foremost of his listeners, not of himself. We are saying that he should have sympathy, tolerance, and kindliness; insight, understanding, and wisdom; perspective and maturity. We are saying that, *as he speaks, these qualities should be seen and heard.*

Some speakers are like owls. They claim to be wise by hooting at everything. The hoot-owl method soon wears out, and the hooting becomes a noisy nuisance. But a sense of humor is enduring. It wins the sympathy of those who listen. It earns respect from those who disagree. It leaves a friendly, lingering memory and an unspoken welcome to return again.

## A SENSE OF LEADERSHIP AND SELF-RESPECT

In a true sense the speaker is a *leader*. He cannot escape the implications of leadership. What do they imply?

To gain the respect of others, a leader must respect himself. You wish to be believed? Then believe in yourself. But you may say: I *don't* believe in myself; I have doubts and fears about the whole business! Of course; and so does every speaker and every leader in those long years of growth; only they learned with Emerson that "Do the thing you fear and the death of fear is certain." Within reasonable limits self-respect can be cultivated, if you cultivate the foundations on which to base it. How?

First, *prepare thoroughly.* If you have not really prepared the speech, you do not deserve self-respect, and down in your own heart you know it. If you have not earned the right to speak, you have not earned the right to self-respect. If you have waited until the night before, and are then wondering frantically what to do, it is time to take an honest inventory of yourself.

Second, *get enthusiastic about your subject.* Enthusiasm is not a rare quality, but it is a precious one, without which speaking—and life itself —would lose much of its interest and meaning. We can almost say that without it speaking is futile. Certainly it cannot rise above the level of routine; and routine speaking is seldom heard with pleasure, or looked forward to with expectancy. A Midwestern Town Hall director complained to Harold Peat of the scarcity of dynamic and convincing speakers. "I can't understand," he protested, "why men who know their subjects thoroughly, and their trade equally well, leave an audience cold and unconcerned. They believe what they are saying, but they can't make anyone else believe it." The answer is, that though they believe in their subjects in a sort of way, they don't burn to make the audience believe. They lack a sense of leadership and its essential element, enthusiasm. Said Emerson, "Nothing great was ever achieved without enthusiasm." Without it, no speech is effective.

Third, *act as if you had self-respect and confidence.* Emotions and mental attitudes can be induced by deliberately assuming the physical positions and by going through the actions that characterize such emotions and attitudes. Double up your fists, grit your teeth, stomp the floor, and frown—all the while thinking of something that provokes your wrath—and you can work up a right good state of anger. Or smile, relax your muscles, and think things cheerful, and you can get a good start toward ridding yourself of a grouch. In the same way, stand straight, chest up and eyes front, thinking how vital it is that people believe you —and you will tend to acquire self-respect and confidence.

Fourth, *don't overdo self-respect!* In plain words, beware of egotism or conceit. "For by the grace given to me I bid every one among you not to think of himself more highly than he ought to think, but to think with sober judgment." You need self-respect, but need it tempered with modesty. Don't stand, on the one hand, with the manner of one who has a "please kick me" sign pinned to your coattail. Don't assume, on the other, the manner of one who thinks that with some assistance from God he has created the universe.

## LEARNING TO RECOGNIZE THE AUDIENCE FEEDBACK

One of the achievements of the twentieth century is the electronic computer, able to solve in a few minutes an equation that might take a team of mathematicians the rest of their lives. All of these machines have built into them one conspicuous quality of the human brain. They have a *feedback* to check their performance, correct deviations, and keep them on the planned course. Man's body is full of feedbacks. An upright human being, for example, is a preposterous physical arrangement because the center of gravity is too high for physical stability. Two legs alone could not keep him in balance without feedbacks in the ear canals, in the horizon sense of the eyes, and in the nerve ends of the feet. But with these feeding-back messages to the muscles, man, instead of capsizing, stays upright and mobile.

A speaker also must constantly rely on feedbacks to find out whether the circuit is still open between him and the audience. Do listeners nod their head in agreement? Their feedback tells the speaker he is being understood. Do they look at him with a puzzled frown? The speaker knows something has gone wrong. He failed to speak loud enough. Or he fluffed his words. Or he used foggy language. Or the audience refuses to accept his opinion. He'd better find out exactly where the circuit broke down, or he might as well quit talking. Do listeners look away as though uninterested? The speaker has lost their attention. He must win it back, or be counted out.

In other words, speaking is not a one-way circuit, but two-way. You talk to the audience, and they feed back their response to you. You won't get far as a speaker until you learn to read their feedback. Here is where those speakers fail who read manuscripts. A master reader like

Charles Laughton or Franklin D. Roosevelt, of course, instantly adjusted
to audience feedback. But they spent *years* learning to read in public.
The self-made reader, of course, knows nothing of the complex art of
reading (and how incredibly complex it is!). He mumbles at his manuscript. Unhappily nobody has yet invented a Univac manuscript with
a built-in feedback!

The only way you can judge the effect of your speech is to read
the feedback. It tells you whether to change pace, to indulge in humor,
to rephrase or repeat an important item that the audience has failed
to understand.

## Physical appearance and activity

The moment you step on the platform you are like a fish in a glass bowl.
Things you once did unconsciously are now enormously magnified.
Those staring eyes are upon you, and you cannot escape them. Even
your smallest movement is under their scrutiny, and they never let you
go. You cannot "act natural," for there is no such thing as "acting natural,"
and furthermore you are not in a "natural" situation. To "act natural"
would be to act nervous, awkward, and ill at ease. How, then, do you
go about the business of behaving under the spotlight of eyes?

An opening wedge was described by Margaret Lee Runbeck in telling
about her growing terror as the time grew near to speak at her high-
school graduation. In desperation she confessed her stage fright to the
visiting commencement speaker seated at her side. "I'm scared too,"
he said. "I've got a speech written down, but I don't think it's much good,
and besides. . . ." "But *you* don't have to be afraid," she protested, for
though a young man he was already famous. "Neither do you," he replied.
"I'll tell you a secret; then you'll never need be frightened again. Everyone on earth is shy, self-conscious, and unsure of himself. Everybody is
timid about meeting strangers. So if you will just spend the first minute
you are in the presence of a stranger trying to help *him* feel comfortable,
you will never suffer from self-consciousness." This famous young man,
then in his early thirties, was later to become even more famous for his
ability to put strangers at ease and to overcome stage fright. She had not
known his name, but the program told her who he was: "Commencement
Address by the Honorable Franklin D. Roosevelt, Assistant Secretary of
the Navy."

This, then, is the opening wedge: Think of helping the audience, and
not of your own afflictions. Remember how often they have suffered at
the hands of self-made speakers who thought foremost of their own
enjoyment and lacked perception of their listeners' suffering. Put them
at ease. Reassure them that you know at least one law of speechmaking,

namely that the listeners' minds can absorb only so much as their seats can endure. Make sure to speak so they can hear. *When you have thus helped your audience, you won't be frightened or unsure of yourself any more.*

## DRESS AND MANNERS

A classroom speech begins the moment you rise from your seat. But in the big outside world it begins long before that. When you first walk into the room you are under observation. Do you stand with hands scrouged into your pockets? Do your arms barricade your chest? If so, you've told them who you are. If it is a dinner speech, how you handle a knife and fork can lift you up or knock you down in the minds of people out front. Even how you talk with others, smile or scowl, are weighed and measured—for you or against you.

Especially your clothes are put under the X-ray. The clothing man will see your suit. The shirt man will see your shirt. The tie man will see your tie. The shoe man will see your shoes. If you are a woman— well, women know what women see in other women. This poor author is a mere man and will not attempt to offer words without wisdom. But women know what women see, even if men do not know.

All of this some students learn the hard way. They come to class for a speech in unkempt clothes, or rolled-up sleeves, or slacks. These are handicaps you cannot overcome in a short speech.

## GETTING TO THE PLATFORM

It's a long walk from your seat to the platform. The eyes of everyone are on you. *With every step of that long walk you are talking.* Not with words but with action. Do you slink, shuffle, tiptoe, or drag like Shakespeare's schoolboy ". . . creeping like snail, unwillingly to school"? Do you stride belligerently as if to show who's running the show? Or do you walk as though you were going forward to meet a friend, a friend you were glad to see? The audience sees all, and knows all. You've told them, not with words but with action.

Now you are on the platform. But there are two obstacles you must dispose of before you start the speech. First, do you know where to stand? Don't stop over at one side. Go to the center! If there's a speaker's stand, get squarely behind it, or get positively on one side of it. But don't hover at the corner as though you cannot make up your mind. (That's why speakers *do* hover. They *can't* make up their minds.)

After you've decided where to stand comes the next critical moment.

The temptation is to start speaking before you are set, mentally or physically. Don't! Before you speak, pause and get ready. Make sure of your posture. Take a deep breath, or take two, until deep breathing seems normal. Then look at your audience as you would look at friends. Smile if you can. (You would smile, remember, if you met them off the platform.) Wait a few moments until they are all looking at you, and ready to hear your first words. Then begin your speech, and *be sure that your first words reach listeners even on the back row.*

## POSTURE

Remember that you talk first, not with words, but with the way you walk to the platform and the way you stand after arriving there. *During every minute of the speech your posture keeps talking to the audience,* indeed sometimes drowning out your spoken words. It tells every listener whether you are thinking of yourself or communing with them, whether you have self-control or are an unguided missile sputtering at loose ends.

No single posture is best for everyone, but some are bad for everyone. From the listener's standpoint, a good posture should not call attention to itself. From the speaker's standpoint, a good posture should allow ease of movement, ease of breathing, and ease of voice projection.

To develop a good speaking posture, first start with a military posture, then modify it to a speaking posture. A military posture, of course, is not a good speaking posture. It is too stiff and formal. But it is a good point of reference, so we shall start with it:

1. Heels together.
2. Feet turned out, forming an angle of about 45 degrees.
3. Hips level; body erect, resting equally on hips; chest lifted; shoulders squared, but not lifted.
4. Hands and arms hanging at sides.
5. Head erect; chin drawn in; eyes front, and not on ceiling or floor.
6. Weight of body resting partly on the balls of the feet; heels on the floor.

Hold this military posture until you get the feeling. Then soften it down into a good speaking posture that lets you move easily, breathe deeply, and project your voice to fill the room.

Next, *"stand tall"* as you speak. To stand tall, reach *up* with the top of your head. Reach *up* with your spinal column. Reach *up* with your chest and abdomen. And reach *down* to the floor with your legs.

You won't learn posture from reading a book. Professional actors spend about a year of drill on how to walk, how to stand, and how to sit on stage or before a camera. Football players each year drill day after day on that one single "set" which players hold before the ball is snapped. Each reaffirms John Dewey's axiom: "If you are going to learn any habits, you are going to have to *practice* those habits." So with posture. To have a good posture, one that looks casually and deceptively "natural," you must pay the price. Rehearse it five minutes a day for a week before each speech. Practice in private situations how to *sit tall, walk tall,* and *stand tall.*

Three universally bad postures especially should be avoided:

*The Fence-Straddle Posture.* In the fence-straddle posture the feet are spread wide apart, and the speaker resembles an inverted Y. The weight is distributed equally and constantly on both feet. In fact, the speaker cannot change posture or shift weight without a tremendous visible effort. He is battened down for the duration of the speech. This posture is bad because it looks grotesque. It is bad because it prevents easy bodily movement.

*The One-Legged Sag.* In this posture the speaker stands on one foot and lets the other foot go for a free ride. At its extreme, one whole side of the body sags. One shoulder sags, one hip sags, one knee sags. Usually the neglected foot is restless, and it wanders, seeking a comfortable place of rest and never finding it. This posture is bad because it is inert. Primarily, only one side of the body is used. Breathing is perforce shallow, the voice tends to be weak and dull. The eyes of listeners tend to look at the conspicuous knee and follow the wandering foot instead of following the speech.

*The Rigor-Mortis Posture.* In the rigor-mortis posture, the body is tense and rigid. The speaker fixes himself into what might have been a good posture, but freezes it and is incapable of moving. It is bad because it permits no bodily action. It is bad because it tends to tire the audience by making them also tense. A good posture must allow freedom of movement.

## USING THE BODY TO COMMUNICATE THOUGHT

In conversation, normal people are animated. They use sight waves as well as sound waves to tell others what they think and how they feel. They talk with their bodies as well as their hands, and of the two hundred muscles in the human body they use them all. As Charles Henry Woolbert once said, "Why use two hundred muscles when you talk? Because there aren't any more."

Of course, some will say, "But gestures are not natural to me." What do they mean by "natural"? It is "natural" for people to think of themselves first and last. It is "natural" to be selfish and ill-mannered. In a "natural" state, people are without education, government, hospitals, or churches. Education, indeed civilization itself, consists of purging "natural" habits and desires in favor of higher forms of behavior.

On the platform, of course we don't feel "natural," for we are the center of all eyes and we cannot escape. "Naturally," we think of ourselves instead of our listeners or our speech, so "naturally" we freeze up until it seems "unnatural" to use action. But that is the wrong way out. Gestures talk. Lack of gestures talk. Gestures tell listeners what you mean and how you feel. Gestures reinforce words, give added meaning. Lack of gestures tell listeners that you are tense, inhibited, ill at ease, don't know your way about. *You can't escape talking with your body. You can only talk badly or talk well.*

Bodily action, of course, is not confined to the hands. We talk also with the eyes, the face, the mouth, the eyebrows. We carry meanings with a shrug of the shoulders, with step forward or backward. In a later chapter (see pages 321-340) we shall discuss action in detail. For the first speeches, rely on your experience in conversation, observe others, and give attention to the ways and means that normal people use in communicating thought by bodily action.

## USING A TABLE OR SPEAKER'S STAND

The purpose of a speaker's table or stand is to make the platform look less bare, and serve also as a resting place for a water pitcher, a vase of flowers, or the speaker's notes. It looks harmless. But beware! It's a booby trap, and the unwary speaker is caught as inexorably as the night-flying moth who wings to his death in the flame. As inevitably as the moth, and with the same lack of self-control, the unwary speaker is caught in the coils of the speaker's stand. He uses it as a crutch. He uses it as a stanchion on which to rest his weary frame. He uses it as a shelf for paper clips, watch, or other trifles which he fingers and fondles to the distraction of the audience.

For a beginner, it would be better probably if he had no such dangerous contraption around. He has enough to think about anyhow. Yet sooner or later he must learn to master speaker's tables and stands, or be mastered by them.

How does a speaker handle such a booby trap? Exactly the same way a combat soldier learns to handle a hand grenade. You learn the nature of the danger, learn how to handle it without getting hurt, and finally learn how to use it to protect yourself. Here is a working formula, but just reading it won't save you; you've got to practice it until you can do it right under fire:

First, stand behind it, squarely in the middle. (Remember that standing off-center will make some people in the audience uncomfortable by

pulling their muscles off center. This phenomenon is known as *empathy*.)
Next, rest one or both hands on it, but *don't put your weight on it!*
Furthermore, don't (1) push it, (2) pull it, (3) kick it, (4) scratch it
with your foot, (5) stiff-arm it, (6) elbow it, (7) slump over it, or (8)
think up any new way of getting caught with it. These mannerisms
distract the audience. They are likely not to remember what you said
until tomorrow, but only that you wrestled with the table and lost. Later
you can explore other possibilities of behavior, but not at first. Your first
duty is exactly the same as a combat soldier's with a hand grenade, not
to get hurt.

## GETTING OFF THE PLATFORM

The following are common errors of getting off the platform:

*The I-Thank-You Exit.* To say "I thank you," at the close of a speech
is a habit that is meaningless and hackneyed. What is the speaker thank-
ing the audience for? If the speech is a good one they will want to
thank him. If it is not good, they may also want to thank him—for sitting
down. In truth, the phrase "I thank you," is a cover-up for the speaker
who wants to get off the platform and does not quite know how. It leaves
a bad flavor. Don't use it.

*The Talk-While-I-Walk Exit.* In this exit the speaker beats a retreat
as he nears the end of his speech. Of course the surprised audience pays
no attention to what he is saying. Their amused interest is centered on
his hasty quitting the scene of action. Better stay put until you finish
the speech.

*The Change-of-Character Exit.* This is an exit peculiar to certain types
of students, and is not found among mature students or older speakers.
It is an exit where the student changes character as he leaves the platform, and by his manner plainly says, "I really didn't mean what I said;
I was only giving a speech." Do we need comment further?

How, then, does a speaker best get off the platform when he has
finished? Simply pause a moment, as you would in leaving a friend's
house; and then, without confusion or any I-thank-you cover up, walk off
—without haste or without lagging.

## Assignments

ON UNDERSTANDING STAGE FRIGHT

1. Give a four-minute talk, and after finishing it fill out the following chart:
    a. I felt the following aspects of stage fright (write 0 if you felt none, 1
       if you felt it mildly, 2 if reasonably strong, and 3 if extremely so):
       (1). Rapid heartbeat _____
       (2). Dry mouth _____

(3). Perspiring body or forehead _____
(4). Felt cold or chilly _____
(5). Trembling body _____
(6). Weak knees _____
(7). Muscles tense or partially paralyzed _____
(8). Felt dizzy _____
(9). Felt clumsy _____
(10). Felt I was not doing my best _____
(11). Weak voice _____
(12). Voice sounded distant or unnatural _____
(13). Felt like running away _____
(14). Felt like apologizing _____
(15). Could not think clearly _____

b. I chose the subject for the following reasons:
(1). Suggested by a magazine article _____
(2). My own experience _____
(3). A college bull session or other discussion _____
(4). Reading _____
(5). One of my courses _____
(6). A student or friend _____
(7). A faculty member _____

c. My quality of preparation was as follows:
(1). Started the speech last night, spent little time on it _____
(2). Started the speech yesterday, and worked hard on it _____
(3). Started it 2 to 4 days ago, but did little work on it _____
(4). Worked hard on it for 2 to 4 days _____
(5). Worked hard on it for over 4 days _____
(6). (Other) _____

d. My speech material came from the following sources:
(1). Personal experience _____
(2). Discussion, conversation, listening _____
(3). Observation _____
(4). Reading _____
(5). Combination of above _____

2. Check the above chart against the suggestions given in this chapter on controlling stage fright, then write out a diagnosis on where you were weak in preparing your last speech and a prescription on what you ought to do in preparing the next one. If necessary, talk with your instructor, but not until *after* you have written your prescription and the diagnosis for the next speech.

3. Prepare a report on stage fright. For further information consult other speech textbooks, biographies of speakers or other public performers, or works on psychology. The psychologies probably will not offer a discussion of stage fright *per se,* but will include it under social stimulation, fears, inhibitions, frustrations, etc. Therefore, consult these topics in the indexes.

4. Give a two-minute talk on muscle tensions during stage fright, and in the speech *use movement* to demonstrate its use in relieving stage fright.

TO DEVELOP A SENSE OF PERSONALIZED SPEAKING AND RHYTHM OF TALK

5. Listen to a good television speaker or announcer, and evaluate his sense of communication. (Avoid announcers who have acquired the *patternized,* television-announcer tone. This is recognized by a forced enthusiasm which tries not to say, "I know this advertising script is ridiculous, but I've got to read it for a living and make the sponsor believe I think it is wonderful.") Before starting the assignment, make a brief outline of the suggestions contained in this chapter on how to develop an effective mental attitude, and note especially the matter of stilted rhythm compared with genuine speech rhythm.

6. Hear a speaker and write a brief report on his earnestness, vitality, directness, and rhythm of talk. Before hearing this speaker, better make a brief outline of the suggestions contained in that part of this chapter. Then you can check the speaker against these items.

7. Read aloud the following passage. In preparing to read it, change the stilted-rhythm form into genuine speech rhythm, and mark the changes on your copy. Then rehearse and read it so that it sounds exactly like superior earnest talk:

What is democracy? It is not a form of government. It is not easy to define. Indeed we might say of it as Lincoln said of Liberty, "The world has never had a good definition, and the American people, just now, are much in want of one." But the inner spirit of democracy is respect for human dignity. It is a rule of the majority with protection of the rights of the minority.

8. Prepare a short story and tell it to the class in your own words. Remember that not all short stories are adaptable to telling. Some move too slowly. Others are too complex in detail, or are too subtle in atmosphere for any but a skilled and experienced story teller. The best type for your purpose is a story with a simple plot, a minimum of character analysis, and a maximum of action and of vivid description—like the stories of O. Henry and Kipling.

   Since your time is limited and you cannot tell *all* the story, cut unnecessary scenes and even characters. In general this is done easiest by cutting from the earlier part of the story (summarizing it like the magazine summary of a serial), then treating the climax in detail.

   The following procedure will help you prepare the story:

   a. Read the story through silently to get the atmosphere, setting, characters, plot, etc., using your imagination and entering into the spirit of the story.

   b. Familiarize yourself with the plot by writing down the incidents in order, noting how one leads to the next and how all lead to the climax.

    *c.* After looking over this chain of incidents, decide which parts can be omitted without losing the dramatic effect.

    *d.* If you desire, plan to read certain parts of the story directly from the book. But know the danger of this, for most people read poorly, flattening their tones, speeding up the rate of utterance, and losing the meaning and feeling of the words. Blend your reading and speaking so smoothly that a person with his eyes shut could not tell one from the other.

    *e.* Rehearse the story 5 to 8 times. If that is not enough (and for some it is not enough), then rehearse it still more. Give the class a finished product, not a midpoint rehearsal.

TO DEVELOP AWARENESS OF PHYSICAL APPEARANCE AND ACTION

  9. Attend a moving picture or television play, and report on the amount and type of action used by the actors. To simplify this, do not attempt to study all of the actors, but concentrate on two or three:

    *a.* How were special attitudes carried by posture, and by changes of posture?

    *b.* Study facial expressions. How did they reinforce the actor's words? List some of the special meanings carried by facial expression.

    *c.* What conventional head gestures were especially used? How were they timed with the actor's words?

    *d.* How was action used to hold attention?

  10. Study the physical appearance, muscular tone, and bodily action of a speaker who is notably ineffective. Select a fellow student, a teacher, a minister—any speaker who is invariably dull.

    *a.* Observe his posture. Is it inert, sagging, or stiff?

    *b.* Observe the over-all muscular tone. Is it listless, inert, or merely awkward?

    *c.* Observe the changes of posture. Are they related to changes of thought, do they distract from what he is saying, or do they seem unrelated to anything he is saying?

    *d.* Observe the specific actions of his head, arms, and hands. Are they listless? Are they awkward? Does he merely fidget? Does it make you uncomfortable to look at them?

    *e.* Assess the speaker's mental attitude behind all of this. Does he seem to be also mentally inert? Is he seemingly ill at ease? Does he show a desire to communicate his ideas to others?

# ☼ 5 ☼

# Efficient Listening

WE LAID THE GROUNDWORK in the last four chapters for getting started as a speaker. But if we may paraphrase Emerson, it's a good listener that makes a good speech. We want now to consider listening. Hearing and listening, of course, are not the same. When you merely hear, the input may be only "as sounding brass or a tinkling cymbal." When you listen, you make sense out of what you hear.

How well do you listen? In private conversation you get along right well, for each bit of conversation is short. Such listening is a simple hook-and-eye process, and when in doubt you can ask questions on the spot. But listening to a speech or classroom lecture is something else. You must take hundreds of single units and weave them into a large complex whole.

Thirty years ago nobody knew much about listening efficiency. Since then we have investigated it painstakingly. Two conclusions stand out, both of them almost startling discoveries. First, most of us are outright poor listeners. When college students are asked to write in their own words a summary of what a speaker said, only rarely can more than 25 per cent do it. What they summarize is not what the speaker actually said. They have missed the essential point. Even when students try hard, knowing they are going to be tested, and are given plain multiple-choice questions that call for identifying right from wrong, they can hang on temporarily only to about 50 per sent of what they hear. Within a few weeks they can retain less than 25 per cent even of the essential points emphasized in classroom lectures.

The second discovery is almost equally startling. Listening efficiency varies more widely than intelligence. Some college students have a 70-per-cent efficiency, and some only 10-per-cent.[1]

[1] Irving J. Lee, *How To Talk With People* (New York, Harper & Brothers, 1952), p. x. Stuart Chase, *Power of Words* (New York, Harcourt, Brace and Company, 1954), pp. 165-167. Ralph Nichols and Thomas R. Lewis, *Listening and Speaking* (Dubuque, Iowa, Wm. C. Brown Company, 1954), pp. 3-4. Ralph G. Nichols, and Leonard A. Stevens, *Are You Listening?* (New York, McGraw-Hill Book Company, Inc., 1954), p. ix.

## Listening and literacy

Does it matter? It does; and matters now more than ever before. For nearly five hundred years after 1450 A.D. the printing press was our only medium of mass communication. We had no other way to "get words out of town" to large numbers of people. As a result, education was built primarily on the reading-writing process. Now, after nearly five centuries, have come in swift succession the radio, talking pictures, and television. In the short space of three decades they displaced print as the most influential mass medium. Educators may cry out in protest that books are vital, and must remain so. True. But the brutal facts are that even educated adults no longer get most of their ideas directly from books. The elite few do, but not the majority even of college-educated people. The Book Manufacturers Institute sadly admits that 60 per cent of people's current ideas come from television, radio, and movies; and of the 40 per cent that comes from print, only 8 per cent comes from books, and 32 per cent from newspapers and magazines. To be literate in this disturbing twentieth century you must be able to listen efficiently as well as read efficiently.

Why should television and radio so swiftly have outstripped print in influence? Education had largely ignored these new media. Some educators had condemned them, and some educational organizations had even published official reports that they tended to prevent people from "becoming reasoning, critical beings." Education emphasized books, yet most people after learning how to learn from books went out in life, relegated books to second place, and turned to television and radio. Why? *Most people are ear-minded, not print-minded.* After learning in school how to decode meaning from print, they are still more ear-minded than print-minded. During all those five centuries when the printing press was the only mass medium, these unhappy ear-minded people belonged to the lost generations. Now they have come into their own.

At once you ask why, if these people are ear-minded, can't they listen more efficiently? The answer is that they have spent years learning how to read (and most even then don't read too well), but they have spent no time whatever in learning how to listen. They are more interested in listening, and they are more gifted, but they do it with their own untutored impulse. To borrow a phrase from frontier days, they go at it "with main strength and awkwardness." As a result, they don't try to listen to complex ideas. The millions treat television as a vending machine, and listen only for entertainment and escape. When Sophocles' Greek play *Oedipus Rex* was televised more people heard it in one hour than had heard it in all the combined stage audiences during the past

2,500 years. This excites human imagination. Yet remember that during that hour over 15,000,000 television sets were tuned to run-of-the-mill programs. Their owners were not interested in this play that had lived for 2,500 years!

Can people really learn to listen efficiently? Or is listening a gift from on high? Until a few years ago we assumed that listening depended on hearing acuity and intelligence, and schools could do little about either. This assumption, we know now, is wrong. Listening is a skill. It has something to do with intelligence, but they are not identical. Many highly intelligent people are poor listeners. Others who are less intelligent listen far more efficiently. (For reasons we don't know, college students from farm families are the best listeners, yet they don't take the top honors in intelligence tests!)

We now know that with training the poorest listeners in college can increase their listening efficiency from 25 to 40 per cent. The average listener can almost double his listening efficiency within one semester. In other words, even ear-minded people don't listen at highest efficiency without learning how; and their poor listening habits handicap them not only in college but all through life. Literate listening is now what Ralph G. Nichols calls, "The Missing 'L' in Learning." You belong to a generation that presumably was taught how to read. You were born too soon for the educational system to have set up a curriculum that would teach you to listen. You now have a chance to make up that deficiency.

You are in a favored position in a speech class. You will hear a hundred or more speeches, and each of them offers opportunity to apply the principles of systematic listening. You ought to do two kinds of listening. First, listen to get meanings. That is the kind of listening we have been talking about so far in this chapter.

*Second, you ought to listen to evaluate speech techniques.* Most of you will take only this one speech course before entering a world where one of the "ten plagues," as Mark H. Ingraham put it, is the "inability of intelligent people to communicate with one another." Vital to your success, as Peter F. Drucker stated in his famous *Fortune* article to college graduates, will be your ability to organize and communicate ideas in writing and speaking, and "if you do not lay these foundations during your school years, you may never have an opportunity again."[2]

What you get out of this one speech course, then, will do more to determine how effectively you live, and how successfully in a material sense, than what you will get out of almost any other course in college; for it will greatly determine how effectively you *use* what you learn in other courses. You can read this textbook, take a series of examinations,

[2] Peter F. Drucker, "Some Truths that Every Young College Graduate Should know," in "How to Be an Employee," *Fortune*, XLV (May, 1952), No. 5, p. 127.

and find out how much you have learned about the system of speech-making. You can give five or ten speeches, look over the instructor's grades and comments, and see where you have succeeded and where you have failed in communicating effectively. You can thus make progress. But if you want to make maximum progress, you will listen critically to every speech given by every student in class, and will evaluate critically how he uses speech principles. Instead of five or ten chances to learn, you will have a hundred or more. In short, here's your chance to learn without the chips being down.

Don't fade into a coma, then, while others speak. Don't listen half-consciously, and rouse yourself only at a pause, change of pace, an occasional emphatic word, or an interesting tidbit. Learn from other speakers' mistakes; you haven't time to make them all yourself! Learn to do *two* kinds of listening at the same time:

First, listen to find out, "*What* did the speaker say?" That is, listen to get the idea and evaluate its worth: What is the essential point? What are the supporting ideas? Are his facts accurate? Can you trust his judgment? Can you trust the speaker? Or is he just another propagandist?

Second, listen to find out, "*How* did the speaker say it?" That is, you listen, note and weigh his speaking techniques: What kind of introduction was that? Was he too slow getting to the point? Did he make his proposition clear? Did he state it too soon, or too late? Ought he to have used a summary of that topic? If he had talked louder would listeners have got more? If he had used action to explain this point or that would listeners have got more? He made that point clear in two minutes; I wonder if I can use that method in my next speech? He certainly knows how to use examples; ought I to look into how to use them better? Note how he drove that topic home with a climax; that's where I fell down in my last speech.

## Levels of listening

There are at least five levels of listening. Literate listeners at different times use each of them. Semiliterate listeners use only the three lowest. In ascending order of difficulty these five levels are:

1. *Listening for entertainment.* This is listening merely for enjoyment to funny stories and interesting talk. It is the kind of listening we do to variety shows on radio and television. It is the kind of listening we do at popular moving-picture shows.

2. *Listening for escape or sublimation.* Men like to listen to sportcasts. Women like soap operas. Such programs let us escape from the humdrum and responsibilities of daily life. They epitomize our wishes and

ambitions in the stories of other people. For a moment in the imagination we can become Superman or Cinderella, and can live in an unreal world. Listening for escape allows a release for our wishful thinking.

3. *Listening for inspiration.* We listen also for a renewing of faith, an uplift of spirit, an inspiration to be better and do more. Sermons and religious music, inspiring drama, patriotic themes, all are founded on the human quest for inspiration.

4. *Listening for information and ideas.* Sometimes we listen for information only. This generally is the type of listening done, or at least attempted, in classroom lectures, explanations of technical subjects and new discoveries, and newscasts. We want to know what is to be known, to keep up with the world. At other times we want to have the meaning of facts explained to us. At still others we want ideas on problems that face us. In short, this type of listening is a search for facts and a quest for ideas.

5. *Listening to evaluate and form opinions.* Most listening on controversial subjects is done with a closed mind. We listen, not for facts or ideas or to form opinions, but simply to ratify old beliefs. Nevertheless, some people can listen critically, to weigh and judge and modify old opinions. Not all want to do it, or can do it. They prefer to listen only for entertainment, or for escape into a dream world, or to gain pleasure from hearing what they already believe. Some try to listen critically, but get tired after a few minutes and give up. They have never been trained to listen literately, and they go through life listening only at lower levels. Critical listening is not learned in a day. It is cultivated by slow degrees.

The kinds of listening with which we are henceforth concerned are the last two levels: listening for information and ideas, and listening to evaluate and form opinions. The third level, listening for inspiration, is useful indeed; but you can learn it easily once you have acquired efficiency in the final two.

## The listening process

Before considering specific listening techniques we should examine the nature and limitations of listening.

*Listening is instantaneous.* In reading you can stop and ponder. You can reread. In listening there is no backtracking. A skillful speaker will help you by repetitions and summaries, but no full rehearing is possible. Therefore, you get it straight the first time, or you don't get it straight at all. Hence an active intelligent mind that gets meanings instantly will have about the same efficiency in listening as in reading. But if the mental activity is lowered, a reader can compensate by rereading, whereas the listener is left behind. In some degree, then, a listener is like Long-fellow's daughter:

> When she's good, she's very, very good;
> When she's bad, she's horrid.

*In listening you can get meanings from voice and action that cannot be given you by print.* Assuming a competent speaker, a listener can get meanings that no reader can get out of print. These come from the speaker's color of voice, informing inflection, pause, emphasis, and by action that points, describes, divides, discriminates. Talk is older than print. Man has evolved a code of meaning by action, a sign language, that is understood over all the world. He has also evolved an exact and subtle code of meaning by voice inflection and pattern which is far older than any words of the English language. Print is a newcomer. It offers mere black on white. It cannot carry as full meanings as effective talk.

On the other hand, the run-of-the-mill speaker lacks know-how. His voice goes drip-drip in a dull dead tone. He interrupts the flow of thought by *ah* and *er*. His action distracts you, or misleads you. You are tempted to dismiss him in disgust. Yet if you really *want* to, you can compensate for poor delivery in reasonable measure, and make a poorly-delivered speech more effective than you might think. But you must really want to, and it takes an enormous amount of energy.[3]

*Efficient listening depends on (1) attitude, (2) attention, (3) retention, and (4) evaluation.* Here we are summarizing the complicated process that goes on in a listener's mind. First, consider *attitude*. Research shows that strongly opinionated listeners learn less than others. Those who tend strongly to disagree or agree also fail more than others to get the speaker's central ideas and to form valid inferences. Apparently such people spend their listening time in rationalizing their own opinions rather than in listening to the speaker's ideas. In a sense they are not listeners. Those who disagree tend to become disputers, and those who agree tend to become applauders.

*Attention* means that you take an active part. Note the word "active." Many people think listening involves merely receiving communication from the person giving it. This is partly right, but you don't receive it like a gift or a judgment from the court. Listening is an activity, like catching a baseball. You don't wait for the ball to hit you and stick there. You reach out and take hold of it. If you don't, the ball bounces off or goes on past. Listening is like catching a ball in still another way. It takes skill. Listening is unlike catching a ball in one respect, however. You either catch the whole ball or miss it, whereas in listening you can catch merely a piece of the thought. But the analogy is a good one. Listening is

---

[3] For a summary of research on this, see James I. Brown, "The Objective Measurement of Listening Ability," *Journal of Communication*, I (May, 1951), No. 1, p. 45.

like catching a ball. You get set for it, watch the windup, follow the throw. This demands attention. You watch the speaker, catch each point as he delivers it, relate it to the other points, and try to guess what is coming next.

Next, is *retention*. Listening is not efficient unless you remember the main lines of thought. To continue the baseball analogy, you keep track of the innings, the number of strikes, balls, outs, and the total score.

Finally, is *evaluation*. Here the baseball analogy no longer holds, for in baseball an out is an out, a score is a score, and the umpire's decision is final. Not so with listening. Here you make up your own score, and it may be a different score from those made up by other listeners. It depends on your intelligence, understanding of the subject, previous attitude toward it, and listening ability. Before evaluating, you first must be able to say with reasonable certainty, "I *understand*." Until you do understand, evaluation is folly. But once you do understand, you then talk back—silently, of course. You say, "I understand, and agree." Or "I understand, and agree with reservations or modifications." Or "I understand, and suspend judgment until I can think further." Or "I understand, and disagree, for your analysis was superficial . . . or your reasoning was illogical . . . or your evidence was rigged." In this way you sift, measure, and judge. You place one fact against another, one judgment against another, and emerge with a concept fused out of material already in your mind plus new ideas presented by the speaker.

Evaluation is the highest listening skill. Some listeners fail on the bottom step; they don't *understand* what the speaker says, hence their evaluation is worth little. Others fail on the second step. They get the details—what we call the speaker's Supporting Material—but they can't put them together or judge their relevancy. As Louis Agassiz, famous fact-finding naturalist, always reminded his students, "Facts are stupid things until brought into connection with some general law." These listeners can't find the relation of the speaker's facts to his general laws. Finally, we have those undisciplined minds found in every class who are in love with their prejudices. They are often rude, and almost always insensitive to the feelings of others. Their prejudices to them are the Voice of God, and intelligent judgment is the Whisper of the Serpent. Such persons cannot evaluate. They can only dispute.

## How to listen effectively

From this background we can set down seven steps of efficient listening:

1. *Get ready to listen.* Have you observed how many like to sit at the back of the room, or near an exit where outside noises mask the speaker's voice? Have you seen students enter a classroom, and slouch down in a

seat, feet out and head back? These people seldom listen efficiently. Many don't want to listen efficiently. In getting ready to listen, seat yourself where you can see and hear, take a comfortable but alert posture, focus your eyes on the speaker and your attention on what he is about to say.

2. *Switch off emotional attitudes.* Most people listen through a filter of wishes and prejudices. But research shows that people with strong emotional attitudes don't listen well. They fail to make relevant judgments. They fail even to get the speaker's central idea. You can't listen efficiently when strong emotions are chasing themselves through your mind, when you are saying to yourself, "Of course he's right; any fool can see that," or "There's nothing to be said on that side of question," or "I wish I weren't stuck with this assignment." You can't yield to emotions and listen efficiently, both at the same time. Emotions win, and listening comes in second. Therefore, switch off emotional attitudes.

3. *Start listening on the first sentence.* Most students begin their listening too late, after too many words are spoken and gone forever. Printed words you can reread, but a speaker's words you hear only once. If you don't get them when uttered, you don't get them at all. A speaker may state his central idea within the first minute or so, sometimes even in the first few seconds. Or he may delay it until after warming up the audience for five minutes. You can't know which method any speaker will use. So start listening on the first sentence. If it is mere windup, let it pass, but keep set for the statement of the central idea, or for definitions, or ground clearing of any sort. In listening, the first part of the speech is critical. After that it becomes a little easier.

4. *Get the central idea.* Every speech worth listening to has one central idea supported by several organized parts. When you listen be on the lookout for that central idea. Remember that facts, examples, and all the other parts are put there to hold up the central idea, so concentrate on it. If the speaker does not put it into exact words, do it yourself. If, when the speech is over, you can't state the central idea, you really have not listened. You may have picked up interesting tidbits, but the speech will be what William James said the world is to a baby: "a big, buzzing, blooming confusion."

5. *Relate the chief supporting ideas to the central idea.* If you get the central idea you will find that, almost miraculously, the chief supporting ideas are easier to remember. Why? A good speech is like a good house. It is all under one roof, but has different rooms, and each room is used for a different purpose. To some extent each room is independent; it has its own walls, ceilings, and doors. Yet no room is independent from the rest of the house. They are connected by hallways, stairways, arches, and

doors. (In speeches these connections are called *transitions,* and a good speaker attends to them as carefully as an architect plans a doorway.) Also each room has its own special use: bedroom, kitchen, living room; and each major part of a speech has its own special use: to show the cause, or the effect, the problem, or the solution.

You may say these look as if they were rules of speaking instead of rules of listening. So they are. Speaking and listening are reciprocal. If speakers don't organize their ideas, if they don't have a central idea and a room-like arrangement of parts, there is not much point in speaking, or in listening. Neither would get you very far. That's what we meant in the Foreword by saying that down through human history "there never was any really effective speaking until speeches began to be prepared in accordance with a theory of public address."

A skillful speaker helps you get the major parts. So watch for the cue phrases as "First," or "At the beginning." They tell you that here comes the first major part. Then watch for cue phrases like "Another consideration," or "Second," which tell you that the speaker now is coming to the second major part. If you have trouble at first in carrying these parts in your mind, write them down. A little practice in writing down the major parts will help soon to carry them in your head.

Watch also the cues the speaker gives you at the end of a major part. He may wrap it up, round it out, or even summarize it: "What I have been saying, then, amounts to this," or "To put it another way," or "In summary."

Especially watch the summary that often comes at the end of the speech. Here you have a chance to get a bird's-eye view of all the speaker has said, and to pick up points and relationships you missed the first time.

6. *As you listen, think back on what the speaker has said and think ahead on what he is likely to say.* You may say this is impossible, that it takes all your attention to grasp what the speaker is saying at the moment, and there is no time to think back or think ahead. Not so. Here is a discovery made not long before you were born, and most of you never heard of it. *You can think almost five times as fast as speakers talk.* In other words, most speakers talk 100 to 150 words a minute, but you can think 400 to 750 words a minute, and even 1,200 words a minute is not uncommon. This is known as the "rate differential" between speech and thought. It means that to get the speaker's words takes only one-fourth to one-fifth of your time. But this vast amount of idle time can get you in trouble. You can cruise at 400 to 750 words a minute. So while the speaker drags along at 125, off goes your mind chasing rainbows, and when you get back you've missed the speaker's essential point. Learning to listen, then, is in a large measure learning how to use this spare time. Especially there are two ways.

First, think back on what the speaker has said. In listening clinics it was discovered that people learned to listen better when afterward they had to tell a third person what the speaker said. Remember the adage that repetition helps you to remember? This helps prove it. So while the speaker is talking, you give a supplementary speech to yourself on what he is saying. That is, you summarize each point and fasten it in your memory. Then you fit each point into knowledge already in your head.

Second, try to look ahead and guess what is coming next. Ask yourself: What does this speaker want me to believe or understand? Right now he's giving me the problem; is he next going to propose this solution, or that one? Now he's talking about the effect; what's he going to claim is the cause? Whether you guess right or wrong, this guessing game pays off. If you guess right, you will remember the point because you got there before the speaker did. If you guess wrong, you will test it, weigh it, and remember it by comparing the speaker's point with the one you prophesied. Either way you win.

7. *Weigh and consider.* So far we have been talking about getting clearly what the speaker says, for before you weigh or judge you must be able to say, "I understand." "Yea, with all thy getting get understanding," said the men of wisdom who wrote the Proverbs. After you have got understanding, you are ready for the final purpose of listening: evaluating what you understand. You can pronounce any sort of judgment—biased, bickering, undisciplined; or mature, reflective, relevant. You can refuse to evaluate, but simply forget it. You can damn with faint praise, then put it aside. But if you have the ability to judge critically, or want to develop it, you can undertake this final step of criticism, judgment, and evaluation. Criticism, of course, is not disagreement. It is not listening to doubt or to scorn. It is evaluating as Francis Bacon said readers should: "Read not to contradict or confute; not to believe and take for granted; nor to find talk and discourse; but to weigh and consider."

## Assignments

1. If you want to take a standardized listening test and compare your listening efficiency with other college students, use the following: *Brown-Carlsen Listening Comprehension Test* (World Book Co., 313 Park Hill Avenue, Yonkers 5, N.Y.).

2. Another standardized test is the *Clyde W. Dow Listening Comprehension Test.* It requires that your instructor record the test items and that two pages of mimeographed material be prepared for each student. For the test and full instructions, see *The Speech Teacher,* IV (November, 1955), No. 4, pp. 239-246.

3. Test your ability to listen for information. Your instructor will read a 5-minute article from *Time, U.S. News & World Report*, etc. Take no notes during the reading, but immediately afterward write a brief summary of the central idea and its most important Supporting Material.

4. Test your ability for listening to evaluate. Listen to the recording of a speech of some outstanding person in public life, and write a report as follows: (*a*) the speaker's central idea, (*b*) the main supporting ideas, (*c*) any supporting material that you remember, (*d*) your evaluation of the speaker's facts, assumptions, and inferences.

5. Test your listening ability on the next round of classroom speeches, and grade yourself as follows: (*a*) After the speech is over each speaker will read his central idea (i.e. purpose-sentence in his outline); if you have written it down correctly, score it 10; if partly correct, score it 5; if omitted or wrong, score it 0. (*b*) Each speaker will then read his first main head, and you will score it the same way. (*c*) Each speaker will read his second main head, and you will score it the same way. (*d*) Continue until all main heads are read. Then add up your total score and compare it with other members of the class. Often everybody will miss a speaker's central idea or a main head. That's the speaker's fault for not making it clear. But when some listeners get an idea and others miss it, that means that some are listening more efficiently than others.

6. Draw up a list of the factors that make it difficult for you to listen efficiently. Prepare your next speech with these factors in mind, taking special care to organize, word, and deliver the speech so these missing cues are given your listeners. Attach your list of factors to the outline. On the left margin of the outline explain the methods you plan to use for giving special aids to listeners.

7. In listening to a later round of class speeches, evaluate the speaking techniques of each speaker. Which were well used? Which were poorly used? Which were ignored?

PART

·II·

# THE AUDIENCE

*You have now covered that miniature introduction of speechmaking principles promised in Chapter 3. We begin here to examine these principles in detail. Again we shall start with the audience, the people to whom you talk.*

# The People to
# Whom You Talk

"DOES AMERICA NEED A HEARING AID?" asked Robert Redfield, and added: "I do not think we listen enough to the sound of what we say in the ears of him to whom we say it."[1] This question and warning faces all speakers everywhere. The people to whom you talk live physically in the same world as you, but they don't all think and feel in the same world. Each listener is a human satellite flying in his own space orbit. Unlike earth- and moon-satellites, however, each person can change his orbit within reasonable limits. His navigating instruments are intelligence, education, and pressing self-interests. Yet he dares not change too much, for no man travels alone on a solitary orbit. He travels in a cluster, along with others in his group. Since birth he has been influenced by the culture of this group until he is surprisingly like the others, sometimes embarrassingly like them. His group, in turn, travels in a cluster near other groups and is influenced by them. Individually or collectively, each person is a member of many groups and is influenced by each: his nation, state, city; his church; his political party; his business, professional, or working group; his social stratum.

Now there are only two means by which individuals or groups can be changed—by force or by persuasion. "Civilization," said Plato, "is the victory of persuasion over force." Force is the method of dictators and autocracies. Persuasion is the basis of democracy. It rests on belief in man's right to life, liberty, and the pursuit of happiness. It rests on governments deriving their just powers from the consent of the governed. Democracy, therefore, demands that the multitude make decisions— whether wise or not—and benefit or suffer the consequences thereof.

In democracy, then, competition for the minds of men is keen. In

[1] "Does America Need a Hearing Aid?", *The Saturday Review*, XXVI (September 26, 1953), No. 4., p. 11.

recent years it has become scientifically organized. By the turn of the mid-century, advertisers had established "advanced laboratories in psychology" to discover people's goals, needs, and motives—both conscious and subconscious. They had developed a "depth approach" for "motivational research," through which they probed deeper into our thought processes than ever before. They had created techniques for persuading people to buy goods they never bought before, and which previously they did not know they wanted.

But the advertisers were not alone. There were also the public-relations experts who used this depth approach to "engineer consent" of people to their propositions. Today these experts are hired by political parties, labor groups, business corporations, and minority racial groups to manage their efforts at winning friends and votes.[2]

Public-welfare organizations also must "persuade or perish." Hence the Red Cross, March of Dimes, National Safety Council, organizations for better schools, and organizations for financial aid to higher education must employ the services of experts. These experts have been called that "little-known band of men and women" who are "Persuaders in the Public Interest."

In this day of high-speed mass communication, then, if you want to sell aspirin or create a climate of good will for the Red Cross you will call on the services of experts. The advertisers, of course, are the single-cell amoebas who work on the elementary level of human behavior. From them we can learn of simpler forms of human behavior. They offer release from fear ("Not a Whisper of Bad Breath"). They offer to upgrade your social standing ("Men of Distinction"). They offer adventure ("Excitement Rides with You Every Mile"). They offer release from inhibitions ("I Dreamed I Went Walking in My Maidenform Bra!").

Persuading people to accept *ideas* is more complex, of course, than persuading them to buy aspirin. New ideas compel us to reshape our thinking or behavior. They are often in conflict with deep-seated attitudes. So don't for one moment think that mere talk will persuade, or that merely "giving the facts" will persuade, or that people will follow you merely because you have truth and justice on your side. Ponder that

[2] A few examples: (a.) The American Medical Association hired Clem Whitaker and Leone Baxter (whose corporate name is *Campaigns, Inc.*) to manage its campaign against compulsory health insurance and in favor of voluntary insurance like Blue Cross and Blue Shield. (b.) The California Teachers Association also hired Whitaker and Baxter to manage its campaign for a badly-needed salary increase; and this firm "succeeded in raising the payroll from $77 million to $400 million a year." (c.) The Republican Party, starting in 1952, engaged the firm of Batten, Barton, Durstine & Osborn to "represent us at campaign time and all the time in between on a retainer. We're a regular account." (d.) The Democratic Party has repeatedly engaged the services of Norman, Craig, and Kummel. See *Time*, December 26, 1955, pp. 11-12; Stanley Kelley, Jr., *Professional Public Relations and Political Power* (Baltimore, The Johns Hopkins Press, 1956), pp. 67-106 and 144-201; Vance Packard, *The Hidden Persuaders* (New York, David McKay, Inc., 1957), pp. 181-200.

classic statement of Aristotle, made about 336 B.C. and now validated by the test of twenty-four centuries: that truth and justice are stronger than falsehood and injustice, hence when falsehood and injustice win it is not the fault of depraved voters, but is the fault of inept speakers who neglected to learn the science of persuasion. Remember Adolf Hitler, who in the "enlightened twentieth century" trained sinister men to speak well, and overran an almost helpless German educational system that had neglected to train good men to speak at all.

In this complex twentieth century the welfare of man is being determined by "organized persuasion." You will learn the science of persuasion, or be counted out.

## The influence of reason, logic, and evidence

Observed Justice Oliver Wendell Holmes, "As I grow older I realize how limited a part reason has in the conduct of men. They believe what they want to." Was Holmes just a cynical old man, or had he seen through human pretenses? Actually he was just about right, but human behavior cannot be understood from so brief a statement. Let us examine it in detail.

We use reason right along in simple two-times-two problems. A garage mechanic connects a tester to your car to find out how much life is left in the battery. A scientist tests human fossils by atomic radiation to determine how old they are. Each uses reason. But note the two special conditions: First, each faces a specific problem capable of a specific answer. Second, neither problem involves any cross-current of human prejudices, wants, hopes, ideals, or group pressure. On such two-times-two problems we use reason, limited only by our information and skill in handling logical methods.

But when we face problems of human relationships, the hurricanes of prejudice, self-interests, and preconditioned responses usually make a shambles of logic. "Should the Bible be read in the public schools?" "Should 'indecent' literature be permitted in the bookstores of a free country?" "Should we have Federal aid to education?" On such questions we take sides according to preconceived bias, prejudice, or self-interest, *then use reason to defend our position!* Hence Bernard Shaw's statement that we use reason only to support our prejudices. Shaw's statement, of course, is not universally true, but it draws blood because exceptions are hard to find. An adage spells it out: "Five per cent of the people think; 10 per cent think they think; and 85 per cent want a slogan so they won't have to think."

Now that you are in college, it would be delightful to say that education will change all that, that the multitude to be sure is ruled by prejudices, but that really intelligent people, when educated, henceforth are ruled by reason. This would be delightful indeed, but total nonsense. Of this myth Woodrow Wilson said, "We talk a great deal about being governed by mind, by intellect, by intelligence, in this boastful day of ours; but . . . men, no matter what their training, are governed by their passions, and the most we can hope to accomplish is to keep the handsome passions in the majority."

Experimental psychology confirms this judgment. Maria Zillig, a German psychologist, for example, experimented with both pupils and teachers. First, she had elementary-school children select by ballot the best-liked class members and the least-liked. Keeping the results secret, and supposedly choosing persons at random, she had the five most-liked and the five least-liked stand before the class, and she then arranged them in alternate order. Privately ahead of time she had instructed the five best-liked students to do the *opposite* of whatever she commanded. Now she told all ten to raise their right hand. The five least-liked did so, but, of course, the best-liked raised their left hand. Zillig now asked the remainder of the class to list the names of pupils who did the exercise wrong. After this first trial run, she instructed the class to use utmost care in observing and listing accurately the names of all who might do it wrong. Following this, she repeated the experiment four times more— with the best-liked pupils always raising the wrong hand and the least-liked raising the correct hand. For the total experiment, then, the best-liked pupils were 100 per cent wrong and the least-liked were 100 per cent right. *But when the class scores were totalled, it was found that the best-liked pupils had been graded higher than the least-liked!* (If you are my friend, you're right. If I don't like you, you're wrong!)

Zillig next turned her attention to the teachers. From eighteen teachers she got the names of the two students they liked best and the two they liked least. Then she procured copies of a spelling test that had been graded by these teachers. On checking the test, she found that *the teachers had overlooked over 38 per cent of the errors of the best-liked students, but only 12 per cent of the errors of the least-liked.* (Moral: Don't get on your teacher's least-liked list.)

But lest you think teachers are especially irrational, consider the impressive research of Edward L. Thorndike. For each of 117 cities he computed a *factual*-index. Then he asked people distinctly above average in ability to give him their opinion on the quality of government, schools, morals, culture, etc. To these people he stressed that he did not want guesses, but only judgments based on facts. His list included 99 business-men, 97 educators, 72 clergymen and social workers, and 31 reformers —all *leaders* in their respective fields. When their judgments were checked against the factual-index, where did they stand? Here are the correlations. They speak for themselves:

| 97 educators | ·59 |
| 31 reformers | ·51 |
| 72 clergymen and social workers | .36 |
| 99 business men | .27 |

All of the groups gave "far too little weight to the facts." Instead, they tended to believe what they *wanted* to believe, and the (hard-headed?) businessmen were the least objective of the groups. Thorndike significantly adds that these results are typical and are statistically valid, and would be altered only slightly if the number of persons interviewed had been "increased tenfold or more."[3]

A. T. Poffenberger, psychologist, summarized his experiments on the conditions of belief: "Belief is rarely the result of reasoning. . . . We tend to believe what arouses our desires, our fears, and our emotions generally." F. H. Lund undertook to answer by research such questions as: (1) Is belief conditioned by emotional factors? (2) Is the *rational* an ideal among people? (3) What is the relation of belief to knowledge, etc.? In presenting the results, he noted that "there is a marked tendency to idealize the rational principle, and to conceive of it as the most important" factor in determining belief, whereas in truth the "non-rational factors appear to outweigh it so largely." Furthermore, he found the college students used in this experiment tended to rate *themselves* as being more rational than other people. ("Lord, I thank Thee that I am not as other men.") Reduced to statistics he found the following correlations:

| Between belief and evidence | +.42 |
| Between belief and knowledge | +.64 |
| Between belief and desire | +.88[4] |

Belief and *desire*, as you see, have the highest correlations; belief and evidence have the lowest.

Wherever the social scientist probes he finds the same pattern of response. At the midcentury UNESCO, for example, investigated the attitudes of people living in eight countries, as part of the information

[3] Zillig's experiments are reported in William H. Burnham, *The Wholesome Personality* (New York, Appleton-Century-Crofts, Inc., 1932), pp. 92-104. Thorndike's is reported in "Facts *vs.* Opinion: An Empirical Study of 117 Cities," *Public Opinion Quarterly*, II (January, 1938), 85-90. All three are reported in Robert T. Oliver, *The Psychology of Persuasive Speech* (New York, Longmans, Green and Co., 1957), pp. 48-51.
[4] A. T. Poffenberger, "The Conditions of Belief in Advertising," *Journal of Applied Psychology*, VIII (March, 1923), 4-9. F. H. Lund, The Psychology of Belief," *Journal of Abnormal and Social Psychology*, XX (April, 1925), 174-196. These were pioneer studies followed since by hundreds of others. See also "The Behavior of Public Opinion," in Wilbur Schramm, *The Process and Effects of Mass Communication* (Urbana, University of Illinois Press, 1954), pp. 321-340. For the similar findings of public relations experts, see Vance Packard, *The Hidden Persuaders* (New York, David McKay Company, Inc., 1957), in every chapter, almost any page.

it was assembling on how nations might live together in harmony. The following significant sample shows what the people of two countries who speak the same language think about each other:

|  | PERCENTAGE OF PEOPLE SAYING "YES" | |
|---|---|---|
|  | *In U.S.* | *In Great Britain* |
| Are people in the U.S. hardworking? | 68 | 32 |
| Are people in Great Britain hardworking? | 43 | 57 |
| Are people in the U.S. domineering? | 9 | 37 |
| Are people in Great Britain domineering? | 33 | 6 [5] |

Such is the nature of man's behavior. We tend to see what we want to see and believe what we want to believe. Most of our so-called reasoning consists in finding arguments to go on believing what we believe already.

But pause for a moment before you condemn such behavior too much. Remember that man has lived on this planet for tens of thousands of years. To survive he was forced to adjust himself first to his physical world, then later to his social environment. To survive he developed basic wants and patterns of culture. These are *old*, and they are man's means of survival. Reason and logic are new. When they interfere with man's older drives, they must go the way of the weak who wage combat. Ralph Linton, studying man from the standpoint of anthropology and sociology, remarked that "We are anthropoid apes trying to live [in social groups] like termites while lacking most of the termite equipment. One wonders whether we could not do it better with instincts."[6]

Nevertheless, as we shall see in the next chapter, logic and reason are extremely important to man's living, in spite of the low estate to which they seem to be assigned at the moment.


## The influence of wants and impelling motives

### WHY THEY INFLUENCE PEOPLE

To persuade others you must talk in terms of their wants. You must know their needs, their hopes, their ambitions, their fears. Know to "what gods they pray and what kind of fights they love," know what songs they sing, and what sentiments they applaud.

Wrote John Ruskin: "The first and last, and closest trial question to any living creature is 'What do you like?' Tell me what you like, and I'll tell you what you are. Go out into the street, and ask the first man or

[5] William Buchanan and a Hadley Cantril, *How Nations See Each Other* (Urbana, University of Illinois Press, 1953), pp. 46-47.
[6] Ralph Linton, *The Cultural Background of Personality* (New York, Appleton-Century-Crofts, Inc., 1945) p. 15.

woman you meet, what their 'taste' is and if they answer candidly, you know them, body and soul."[7]

Frederick J. E. Woodbridge, psychologist, put the premise in scientific form:

> We ought to stop talking about what is consciousness and what is behavior and what is sentiment and what is emotion and what is sensation and what is idea and all this, that, and the other thing, and tackle these more obvious things: what do people want? How do they go about getting it? How effective is their way of getting it? I confess it all seems to me to be as simple as that.[8]

What are the basic human wants found in all people? Natural man has only two wants, said Sir William Osler: *"to get and to beget."* This oversimplification can be expanded into five basic wants that are behind every human belief and act. They fall into five levels, starting with basic biological wants, and rising to the levels that represent higher human development. These five wants influence or determine everything people believe or do:

*1st level:*   Basic physiological needs, including hunger and sex.
*2nd level:*  Safety, including self-preservation and security.
*3rd level:*  Love, including affection, friendship, and tender emotion.
*4th level:*  Esteem, including self-respect, pride, reputation.
*5th level:*  Self-realization, including personal achievement and artistic tastes.

But human nature is not so elementary as this might suggest, for these motives do not operate singly or in simple form. Indeed civilization is a process of multiplying and institutionalizing human wants, of intellectualizing and socializing them. Hence civilized man has split and combined and refined his wants into many channels. He has developed institutions like governments and churches and social clubs to protect and promote them. Especially there are three forces that determine how these wants will operate within any given person.

First, is the conflict of opposing motives. Do I want comfort more than I want freedom? Do I want security above reputation? Do I put the

[7] *The Works of Ruskin: The Crown of Wild Olive* (New York, Oxford University Press, 1921), Lecture II, "Traffic," p. 267.

[8] *Minutes of the Dartmouth Psychological Conference, August, 1925,* privately printed. There are many schools of psychologists, of course, including gestaltists, behaviorists, organismists, functionalists, reflexologists, hormists, and other -ists. They use different terminologies and often dissent vigorously from one another. Almost all have made significant contributions to human behavior, public opinion, and the nature of persuasion. But none holds a monopoly, and the weakness of most is their tendency to become a self-sealing system. The viewpoint here is, therefore, deliberately *selective.* It presents the major contributions of Greek thinkers, and the pertinent concepts of early psychologists. Especially also it uses the invaluable research of modern psychologists, anthropologists, and sociologists. Of the latter groups, none quite brings into focus the problem of persuasion, but they have uncovered valuable tangent material which speakers ought to have at their disposal.

immediate wishes of my family above their remote welfare, say, ten years hence? Current events and personal circumstances will vary the strength of these motives in human lives, just as the winds vary that blow across the surface of this planet.

Second, motives vary in strength according to one's social or economic level. Old established families and the prominent new rich, for example —those who compose the sociologist's Upper Class—strive less than others for recognition. They already have it. They oppose most twentieth-century changes in politics and economics. They conform least of all to current fashions. In contrast, the Lower Middle Class, the "white-collar" class, conforms most of all both in fashions and to the moral code. It is the most church-going, and the most serious section in all society.[9]

Third, motives have different strength at different age levels. As Aristotle bluntly observed centuries ago: "Young men have strong passions and tend to gratify them indiscriminately. . . . They are hot-tempered and quick-tempered, and apt to give way to their anger. . . . While they love honor, they love victory more; for youth is anxious for superiority over others." As for Elderly Men, "They are not generous, because money is one of the things they must have." "They are continually talking of the past." They "are often supposed to have a self-controlled character; the fact is that their passions have slackened."[10] This provocative analysis, by the man who has influenced the thinking of the Western World more than any other, shows how he thinks a speaker should compose his speech to fit the motives of his audience.

## SPECIFIC WANTS

The following list of 20 specific wants will serve as a useful guide. Necessarily, they are incomplete and overlapping, for specific motives are indefinite in number. But they offer a useful analysis of the main-springs that cause people to reject or accept a speaker's idea. They are the *universals* shared by all human beings everywhere:[11]

| | | | |
|---|---|---|---|
| 1. | Security | 6. | Self-respect and Pride |
| 2. | Property | 7. | Honor and Duty |
| 3. | Freedom | 8. | Fair Play |
| 4. | Recognition | 9. | Love and Friendship |
| 5. | Reputation | 10. | Loyalty |

[9] Pierre Martineau, *Motivation in Advertising* (New York, McGraw-Hill Book Co., Inc., 1957) pp. 164-169.

[10] *Rhetoric*, II, 1389a-1390a.

[11] Psychologists generally agree that these wants or motives include urges, drives, sets, tendencies, instincts, propensities, unlearned behavoir, and habits. Thus a motive may be biological, physiological, or social. Often it is all three.

11. Sex Attraction
12. Sympathy
13. Physical Enjoyment
14. Competition and Rivalry
15. Adventure
16. Conformity
17. Curiosity
18. Artistic Tastes
19. Fear
20. Reverence and worship

#### SECURITY

"Give us this day our daily bread," is a universal prayer, and not the prayer of Christians only. It is more than a prayer for food, it is a prayer for Security. To be secure from loss of job, or property, or income. To be secure from the uncertainties of tomorrow. To be secure even from the *change* of daily habits. In crises people have sold even freedom and the right to rule themselves, because they wanted Security more. Thomas Paine in *The Crisis,* written in 1776, noted how Security overrode desire for freedom in the minds of many: *"Well! give me peace in my day."* Forest L. Whan, after long research, summarized the attitude of a typical section of the American public in 1858, on the eve of another crisis: "They seemed to place security above comfort."[12] In this strenuous twentieth century, people are as unchanged in their desire for Security as was the Cro-Magnon Man 25,000 years ago. When a motion picture producer not long ago sent out several thousand letters to librarians asking which books had been most in demand during the past decade, he was astounded that sex was not the most popular subject. The most popular was survival, and the next was the "search for security." (In this chapter both are classed as Security).[13] One is tempted to say, not seriously of course, that only a person from Hollywood would ever have thought that sex was a stronger want than Security.

Of this desire, Mr. Justice Oliver Wendell Holmes said, "The timid and faint-hearted long for security and repose, not knowing that security is an illusion, and repose is not the destiny of man." The timid and faint-hearted include most of the human race.

You may challenge people to adventure, or rouse them to conflict, or impel them to take risks. These, too, are human wants. A few, a very few, are willing to live by the standard that "There is no security; there is only opportunity." The multitude may also be challenged momentarily by that standard. But broad and deep in human behavior is the want for Security. At times you can base persuasion on this basic want. More often human problems will demand that you overcome the listeners' want for immediate Security. But recognize it for what it is, a want that's old and deep in human behavior.

[12] *History and Criticism of American Public Address,* W. Norwood Brigance, ed. (New York, McGraw-Hill Book Co., Inc., 1943), II, 782.
[13] *Quote,* XXXII (September 23, 1956), No. 13, p. 5. The producer was Jerry Wald.

### PROPERTY

The desire for Property overlaps the desire for Security, but is not identical. It means the desire for lands, goods, money in all their forms: machinery and tools, a city home and a country retreat, stocks and bonds, coins and currency, wages, interest, dividends, profits. Here is a desire that drives management to create jobs for workers, that sends workers into the shops and factories, that keeps the stores open, the trains running, and the airplanes flying. It is the foundation of our industrial momentum. Remove it, and the machinery would slacken pace. The Russians quickly found that out and had to recognize it in their Communist state.

### FREEDOM

Freedom is a proud want. We boast that our forefathers "fought for freedom," and that we now have it. For centuries our literature has upheld the theme, " 'Tis Liberty we seek, . . . 'Tis that or Death," and we sing the refrain, "Sweet land of liberty."

Actually Freedom is a nurtured want. Like an exquisite flower, it has to be fertilized and kept free of growths that choke it out. In every generation people who say they want Freedom have surrendered it for security, and have consoled themselves after the manner Antonio Giolitti consoled a Communist colleague who was troubled by Soviet tyranny: "Don't lose your spirit. Remember, liberty is not everything." Increasing mass fears in the twentieth century have seriously endangered Freedom over much of the so-called free world.

Many who want Freedom for themselves would deny it to others, by law or social pressure. No free society allows complete freedom of discussion. Each group restrains its members. People will speak freely of the weather and the soil, but they do not speak freely of powerful groups in their community, or speak out against common views held by such groups. "Whose bread I eat, his song I sing," was a warning proverb in England long ago when men were fighting for their freedom. It is still a warning proverb. Freedom continually tends to be restricted by laws, by judicial procedure, by executive authority, and by popular pressure. Hence the adage, "Freedom degenerates unless it has to struggle in its own defense."

### RECOGNITION

Nobody wants to be the Common Man. We want to be noticed, to be the object of attention, to be complimented, to be acclaimed as the Uncommon Man or Woman. This want moves in different directions with different people, and differently at times in the same people, but its force is as ceaseless as the infinite flow of a river. It impels young men to seek athletic prowess, and be applauded on the playing field or floor.

It impels others to seek recognition of intellectual powers, to graduate with honors or a Phi Beta Kappa key. It impels some to seek political power, industrial power, or society leadership. It operates in forms and with power that cannot be described in a few sentences. One example will have to serve. William H. Whyte, Jr., after an extensive investigation of American business methods, noted that Recognition was one of the surprising, almost startling, forces in modern business. A large corporation, for example, almost lost one of its valuable vice-presidents. Why? In shift of offices, inadvertently he was given a metal desk instead of a mahogany desk as other vice-presidents had. He mistook this for a deliberate lowering of status, and thereafter began to read hurts and hidden meanings in every casual conversation. Finally he was on the brink of a nervous breakdown. Said Whyte: "Silly? Ask the man who's had one."[14] Recognition is one of the most powerful forces in all human behavior. It puts grim truth in that husband's quip to his wife: "What a system! We spend money we don't have for things we don't need in order to impress people we don't like!"

### REPUTATION

Reputation comes from the same basic desire to be superior as found in Recognition. It might be defined as the status of one who knows he is already recognized. Such people want to be thought of as honest, kind, generous, noble. They want never to be thought of as knavish, spiteful, stingy, contemptible. They want to feel that "eyes are turned kindly toward them and that tongues speak their praise." Rather than lose reputation, people have been known to sacrifice life itself. "Of course you have a reputation for fair-mindedness (or good judgment); therefore, I know you will listen fair-mindedly to what I say." What listener wants to deny such a reputation?

### SELF-RESPECT AND PRIDE

People are linked together in groups, and each person has a strong desire to be accepted by others of his group. The standards of their job associates and their social group thus become a magnetic North Pole by which each guides his behavior. In American middle-class society, for example, no man would wear a monocle or go to work in a top hat. "Let me ask the man," said Lincoln, "what compensation he will accept to go to church some Sunday and sit during the sermon with his wife's bonnet upon his head?" Nothing could compensate such an act. Why? Pride and Self-respect.

Never say to listeners, therefore, "Since you don't know much about this subject I want to discuss it," or "How many of you ever stopped to realize that . . ." Blunt words like these hurt the listeners' Self-respect

[14] *Is Anybody Listening?* (New York, Simon and Schuster, 1952), p. 119.

and Pride. They hurt the speaker's chance of success. The tactful speaker uses Self-respect and Pride. Says he: "You remember so-and-so," or "I'm sure you want to hear the unpleasant facts rather than pleasant fiction."

### HONOR AND DUTY

"A plain duty, like a plain woman, attracts few wooers," hence the speaker who says bluntly, "It's *up to you*," or "It's your *duty*," won't get far. Listeners have heard this banality so often from self-made speakers, that they tend to rebel at duty when pushed at them bluntly and often.

Yet the sense of Duty is strong. "England expects every man to do his duty," Lord Nelson signalled his ships as the Battle of Trafalgar began; and men died doing their duty. "This generation has a rendezvous with destiny," said Franklin D. Roosevelt to Americans who were flinching from the prospect of war. "Let us therefore brace ourselves to our duties," said Winston Churchill to Britons who stood alone after the fall of France, "and so bear ourselves that, if the British Empire and its Commonwealth last for a thousand years, men will still say, 'This was their finest hour.'" Leaders have always lifted men by the challenge to Honor and Duty. But they use it with tact and they use it sparingly.

### FAIR PLAY

"Play the game," is an impelling slogan. "Fair play" is a motive to which men are ashamed not to respond. We hate to feel that we have ever been unfair or unjust. Worse, we hate to have it said about us, "He won't play according to the rules," or "He plays with loaded dice." Many a speaker has softened hostility by saying skillfully, "*I know you disagree with me, and that is your right. But I know, too, that you believe in Fair Play, and that you'll listen to those who sincerely disagree.*" Many a skillful trial lawyer, while selecting a jury panel, has quickened their sense of Fair Play: "*You know the background of this case. . . . Now you wouldn't want not to be fair, would you? So will you just tell the court whether you have any opinions that would be unfair to my client.*"

### LOVE AND FRIENDSHIP

We crave Friendship and want to be an accepted member of groups of friends: a fraternity, club, church, social caste, or informal circle. In these groups, members largely think as we do, feel as we do, and hold the same values and ideals. They share our pleasures, and perhaps our fears. What we think is good, they think is good; and what they hold to be bad, we hold to be bad. Therefore, these people are our friends, and we feel kindly toward them. Others are our friends too. Our neighbors. Our business associates. Those who when we need help don't

ask, "Is there anything I can do?" but who come and say, "Here I am."
Man *needs* Friendship, and without it he withdraws too much into
himself, becomes embittered, or even frustrated.

*Love* is a more intensive human want, biologically older than Friendship. "Children feed on love as they do on fresh air." The casebooks
of child clinics and juvenile courts reveal that children who are denied
Love develop sulkiness, suspicion, lying, thievery. The emotional starvation develops poison within the organism. In adults the lack of a normal
amount of Love often leads to bitterness or suspicion or despair. Love
or Friendship, then, is not a mere sentimentality. It is a basic want, a
need in human life.

### LOYALTY

Loyalty arises from the desire to identify ourselves with the welfare
of our group. It takes many forms: family pride ("My Mother bakes the
best pies in all the world"), school spirit ("It is *my* school, and it is the
best in the land") state pride ("You must admit that this is the most
wonderful state in the union, though I have been in but four states
myself"), patriotism ("My country, right or wrong").

For a speaker to use this motive is easy and obvious. "Will . . .
[you] withhold, save in strained courtesy, the hand which straight from
his soldier's heart Grant offered to Lee at Appomattox?" Henry W. Grady
asked his New England audience. Their answer was "tumultuous cheering and shouts of 'No! No!'" Socrates long ago observed that "it is not
difficult to praise the Athenians to an Athenian audience."

### SEX ATTRACTION

This is one of the confused forces in human persuasion. Men (the
male sex) want the attention and admiration of women, and women of
men. To keep this want within social bounds, they have developed a
conventional code of behavior toward each other. This code varies with
different cultural groups, but in Western civilization men are the
"stronger" sex, the more "aggressive," and the more "intellectually
capable." Women are the "weaker" sex, the "gentler," and the "purer."
Of course biologically most of this is not true at all; women can endure
more than men, they live longer than men, and they are equal in intelligence. But these old concepts were the basis of the patriarchal family
in which the man was head of the house and woman was protected from
worries of the outside world which she did not understand! The patriarchal family has now disappeared. In the modern home, the man is
just another member of the family who baby-sits, helps with the shopping
and with the heavy housecleaning. The woman mows the lawn, takes care
of the family car, pays the bills, and watches the bank balance. She wears
slacks and man-tailored shirts, and does things only men used to do.

She goes into business, skiis, plays golf, races sail boats, and manages race-horse stables. The centuries-old masculine-feminine relationship has broken down. In the home they are co-managers. In the world they are becoming co-equal.

Yet all of this matters little as this want operates in public address. There both sexes keep up the old pretenses. Publicly toward women, men represent Gallantry, the Armed Knight, and Protection from Danger. Publicly toward men, women represent Virtue, Beauty, and Helplessness. Now all this is make-believe, but we act it out on the human stage. "A man needs a woman to take care of him," runs the adage, "so she can make him strong enough for her to lean on."

Therefore, recognize the code in public address. Whatever men do in private, gentlemen in public rise in the presence of women. They place taboos on their speech. Some things they do not talk about in public before women, and certain kinds of stories they do not tell. As for women, they are now equal to men, but the emancipated woman does not talk like a man. She talks like the Mother of Men, who rules the world because she rocks the cradle, or can rock it. She talks with a woman's sense of values, a woman's concern, a woman's deep sympathy. When she speaks as Woman, she speaks impellingly; but let her speak as a man-among-men, and she becomes merely a female.

### SYMPATHY

One of the permanent themes of great literature is compassion, for it reflects the deep-felt sense of Sympathy in human beings. We pause to comfort a crying child, to visit a sick neighbor, or send flowers to friends in hospitals. These things we do not merely because others are in distress, but because if we fail others in distress we are left with an inner feeling that we have not been true to ourselves. Down the centuries comes the question, always impelling: "Which now of these, . . . thinkest thou, was neighbor unto him?" Nor is individual Sympathy enough. We have organized the Red Cross, the March of Dimes, the Heart Foundation, the Community Chest to care for human needs too great for us to sustain as individuals.

If you would arouse Sympathy, describe vividly the people who need it. (Mere facts and figures will not arouse Sympathy; don't use them for that purpose.) Make listeners *see* and *feel* and *hear* the human need— sense that "when the Devil takes the hindmost, the wrench is felt by the topmost—and felt to the very marrow of his bones."

Sympathy is used in another manner also. If you would describe the greatness of a man or woman, in a eulogy or speech of tribute, remember that his capacity for Sympathy is a quality by which you can measure greatness. Did he have Sympathy of a particular quality, or a particular magnitude? Can you demonstrate it by a story or example or comparison?

### PHYSICAL ENJOYMENT

Consider the life of modern man. He eats food that comes from distant places, rides in an airplane or train or taxicab or elevator. He plays golf or tennis, goes fishing or hunting. He attends a moving picture, or listens to the radio, or watches television. In America, at least, the average man has comforts that Alexander the Great would find incredible and George Washington would envy. Behind this attainment is the motive of Physical Enjoyment. It is not merely physical *comfort* or *ease*. It is rather *enjoyment*, which may include effort and action.

Modern advertising relies strongly on Physical Enjoyment. ("Air conditioned comfort." "Come stand in history's wagon tracks." "Good living twelve months a year.")

### COMPETITION AND RIVALRY

We want to equal or surpass others. If they can do something (run, shoot, drive, have social ease or beauty), we want to be able to do it as well or better. If they possess something (a better house, car, clothes, reputation, or social standing), we want as much or more. Hence we have athletic contests, business competition, social rivalry, and keeping-up-with-the-Joneses. Competition and Rivalry are fierce motives. Research on fourth- and fifth-grade children, for example, found that those who were competing increased both speed and accuracy in arithmetic far beyond those who were not competing (.63 in speed for those not competing; but 3.93, or over six times as much, for those who were competing).

Speakers premise arguments on Competition and Rivalry who say, "Let us not be outdone," or "Remember the victory of last year when the odds were against us," or "Which one of you will win this award?"

### ADVENTURE

"Why do you want to climb this mountain?" a reporter asked the famed Alpinist George Mallory. His answer was the answer of all men who seek adventure: *"Because it's there!"* This is not a mere child's want, nor is it basically a desire for thrills. It drives human beings to give up ease and security in order to do something they want more than ease and security. It drives them to do "the useless, brave, noble, divinely foolish and the very wisest things that are done by man," wrote Walter Lippmann. Perhaps it might be said that out of the dust from which man is made there is also fire, that this is true of no other animal on this earth, and that the fire within man can be lighted by the great winds of *Adventure*.

Speakers use this motive in many forms. One says, "Here is a story of adventure." Another says, "All of this I saw, and a part of this I was." Still another, "I have nothing to offer but blood, toil, tears, and sweat."

## CONFORMITY

Every group exerts pressure on its members to conform to the beliefs and behavior of the majority. The aberrant person who fails to conform is brought into line by degrees of force that range from subtle pressure to blunt ostracism. Odd-sticks are not tolerated. Members who resist too much learn quickly the price of nonconformity. Those who conform learn that it brings safety and security. We conform in the kind of clothes we wear. Men wear bow ties with dinner jackets, but four-in-hands with cutaways. They don't wear skirts. They go without shirts on the beach, but not in stores. Women may not go uncovered above the waist even on the beach. By contrast in other parts of the world are places where women of high rank receive their guests formally, with breasts completely bare, and who think that any wife who dressed herself above her waist could be aiming only at adultery. Not so in Western civilization! But we applaud the speech whether we like it or not. We accept ideas, not because we have thought them out for ourselves, but because our group accepts them; monogamy, private ownership of property, private initiative. In effect we say, "People have believed this for a long time. I believe it too."

Here is a motive with obvious virtues and equally obvious defects. Man is a social animal. He must conform to survive. But he is also an individual, and democratic society survives only by having enough people question outworn ideas and develop new ones.

## CURIOSITY

Pascal once said, "Curiosity is mere vanity. Most people want to know only in order to talk." That would be reason enough, but man has learned far more about human nature than Pascal knew. We now know that the adage "Curiosity killed the cat," is closer to the truth. From Curiosity a boy tears down a clock to see why it ticks. From Curiosity adults go to see celebrities-in-person, in a sense to see why they tick. From Curiosity psychologists experiment on the behavior of man, to see why man ticks. From Curiosity physicists experiment on dynamics, to see why the universe ticks. Civilized man is insatiably curious, and we are debtors to generations of curious men who lived before us.

A speaker says, "As I crossed the street I saw two boys. . . ." (Curiosity: who were they? what were they doing? why is the speaker telling about them?) Or, "What caused people to think they saw flying saucers? There are three reasons. . . ." (Curiosity: "I know only one. What were the other two?")

## ARTISTIC TASTES

These are the esthetic wants. They are old and deeply embedded. The Cro-Magnon man mixed his pigments and drew colored pictures of reindeer on the walls of his caves some 25,000 years ago. Thousands of years later man developed a word-skill, and at once he used this new-found skill to produce poetry and drama. So it has been with every skill that man developed. He makes it not only useful, but *beautiful*. Our Artistic Tastes include appreciation of nature, architecture, sculpture, painting, music, poetry, and drama. They include also appreciation of harmonious color and form in clothes, furniture, pictures, silverware and dishes, kitchen utilities—and such unsuspected things as washtubs, fishing rods and reels, football uniforms, and the format and type of this book you are now reading.

In using Artistic Tastes, a speaker must know the artistic *level* of his audience. Educated and cultured people probably do not have stronger Artistic Tastes than the less educated and less cultured, but certainly theirs are *different*. Educated people may appreciate classical music, others may prefer hillbilly music or bebop. The educated may prefer the literary novel, others may prefer the pulp magazines. Make clear to the person of culture that your course of action will enable him to hear drama of highest type, or own pottery of exquisite design. Demonstrate to woman that these particular lines and colors fit best her individual personality. Persuade any group that here is something to please their particular level of Artistic Tastes. To all, you have given a motive for action.

### FEAR

Not only are we impelled by things we like. We are held back from doing things, not alone by inertia or dislike, but also from fear of unpleasant consequences. The truth is that man lives much under the dominion of Fear. First, there are social fears. We are afraid of what people will think if we don't belong to the right clubs and societies, use the right fork, or wear the right clothes. We are afraid of public dis-approval if we stray from the accustomed path. Also, there are more primitive fears. The mother is afraid for her children. The worker is afraid for his job. The owner is afraid for his business. The man who has gained property and power under the status quo is mortally afraid of *change*—of new taxes, new laws, New Deals. Finally, there is acute anxiety over what will happen to the world in the struggle for power between communism and democracy? Will it end in atomic war? If so, what will be our place in the world—if there is any world—after the atomic war has ended? This is a new form of an old fear. Around 2,800 B.C. a wise man in Assyria chiselled on stone: "The earth is degenerating. . . . It is evident that the end of the world is speedily approaching." In every generation people have feared world disaster.

The world was not a safe place in which to live, not even before the appearance of communism, but people need to be told that over and over again in words they will remember. The world always has been a bad world for the timid and weak, and always a good world for the brave; but people need to be told that too over and over again.

### REVERENCE AND WORSHIP

Man wants to reach out and up to something beyond himself. A common level of this desire is found in *hero worship*. It may be the star on the varsity team, the Sultan of Swat in baseball, a national hero—a Washington or Lincoln, Edison, or Einstein. We reverence also *tradition*. Among reverenced traditions are Home, Mother, Flag, Democracy, Freedom, Free Enterprise, Science, and the Scientific Method. Such traditions, we tend to think, are infallible and above criticism. Finally, there is *reverence for Deity*. "If there were no God," said the agnostic Voltaire, "it would be necessary to invent one." True, indeed. You may travel across all the face of the earth—from the high plateaus of Tibet, through the valleys of civilizations, into the jungles that are the last retreat of primitive man—and everywhere you will find worshipping men. What they worship may differ. Whether they worship is never a question.

Speak, then, with respect of things that men reverence and worship. And if you must disagree with tradition, or must question the greatness of accepted heroes—do so with extreme tact, and with reverence for other traditions or heroes not in question. Walk softly and speak gently, "for thou goest among snares and walkest upon the battlements of the city."

## The influence of culture patterns

You were born in a society that had certain customs and ways of thinking, and from the moment of birth you have been conditioned to accept them. Japanese babies reared in America by Americans will be Americans. American babies reared in Japan by Japanese will be Japanese. Any baby can be brought up to be German, Turk, Eskimo, or Arab. By the time you could talk, you were already a creature of your culture. Before you were grown, its beliefs were your beliefs, its habits were your habits. Every child born into your group will share these things with you, and no child born into one on the opposite side of the world, as Ruth Benedict points out, "can ever achieve a thousandth part." A speaker must know the role of culture, its laws and varieties, its influence and limitations. Whence came these Cultur Patterns?

*First, some came from 6,000 years of civilization.* These are common to all civilized peoples in the world. Among these are writing, architecture, and a system of taxation.

*Second, some were developed in our Western civilization.* These make us different from the peoples of the Orient and the Middle East. Among the culture patterns of Western civilization are the Christian religion, nationalism, and the scientific method.

*Third, a narrower and sharper set of culture patterns came from Anglo-Saxon culture.* These include the English language, the right to vote, *habeas corpus,* freedom of speech and religion, political democracy, and a strong sense of superiority over foreigners.

*Fourth, came the culture patterns from English-speaking North America.* These include a sublime faith in education, the acceptance of mass production, the new suburbia, habits of television and radio listening, love of baseball and jazz music, and installment buying.

*Finally, come the culture patterns of our immediate locale:* New England, Lower South, Middle West, Far West, etc. They shall not be considered here (but see Locale, below, pages 135-136).

We are not slaves to these culture patterns. Instead they are useful garments that come to us, as Ralph Linton points out, like suits of ready-made clothes. We do not wear them just as they are, but alter them to fit us—take them in at one place, let them out at another. Naturally there are limits on how much they can be altered, but the limits are wide enough to accommodate most people. Yet in spite of these minor variations in different people, and in the same people at different times, most people in a given culture will respond to a situation in much the same way.

We shall consider, therefore, a selected list—very selected indeed—of culture patterns that influence the American people:

| | | | |
|---|---|---|---|
| 1. | Political Democracy | 4. | Race |
| 2. | Private Property and Enterprise | 5. | Religion |
| 3. | Marriage and Divorce | 6. | War and Force |

## POLITICAL DEMOCRACY

The American people believe in Democracy as a way of life. This includes belief in the Declaration of Independence, the constitution, the Bill of rights, *habeas corpus,* trial by jury. We believe in the principles, and often in the sacredness, of these documents, even though we may not quite know what is in them. (In a poll, 79 per cent of adult Americans did not know what the Bill of Rights was.) Yet our belief in democracy stems not from mere belief in its charters and documents. Instead, it comes from the universal feeling that this is a way of life we want. Political democracy gives us freedom of speech, the first and foremost freedom that lifts us above animal existence. It lets us work off frustration without too much restraint. To be sure, no one is wholly free, in a democracy or elsewhere. All must conform to certain patterns. Yet in a democracy we feel that we are free to *be* free, if we *want* to be free, and we do not have to avoid trouble by being inconspicuous, as people who survive under totalitarianism have learned to do so well.

Belief in political democracy includes belief in universal suffrage and in the right of majority rule. But it includes also belief in protecting the rights of minorities. Thus in English-speaking North America (and in parts of Europe) no defeated candidate is compelled to flee, nor even to refrain from speaking out in public against those in office. Bear in mind that this is not true of defeated candidates in all so-called democracies. In some cultures people simply do not understand our viewpoint. They believe it proves that opposing political parties are secretly conspiring together against the people. Speaking in the British Parliament, shortly after his defeat as Prime Minister in 1945, Sir Winston Churchill dryly observed the bewilderment of people in the Balkans: "A friend of mine, an officer, was in Zagreb, when the results of the late General Election came in. An old lady said to him, 'Poor Mr. Churchill! I suppose he will be shot.' My friend was able to reassure her. He said the sentence might be mitigated to one of the various forms of hard labor which are always open to His Majesty's subjects." To us this is humor. To people of certain other cultures, it would simply be confusing.

### PRIVATE PROPERTY AND ENTERPRISE

The culture patterns on Private Property and Enterprise are intricate and conflicting. A survey would lead us into a labyrinth of economic history and practice. Hence here we can offer only a snapshot hastily exposed and hastily developed, in the effort to call attention to the subject.

Americans believe in private ownership of property, and not in communal ownership. Even mineral rights, and hunting and fishing rights, belong to the owner—and not to the government, as in Latin-American and other cultures.

We say we believe also in private enterprise, and often call it "free private enterprise." Actually we believe in it with enormous modifications. Immediately after our forefathers adopted the Constitution they passed a tariff act, which amended the free enterprise concept. Later they needed railroads, and gave grants of public lands to persuade private companies to build them. Then big business became too powerful, so they passed an antitrust law. These were the preliminaries. Now came the speedup. The proverbial wicked English had invented the Industrial Revolution, and the proverbial practical Americans now jet-propelled it by inventing mass production. Thereupon our culture patterns on "free private enterprise" were changed most radically. In World War I the draft act brought the federal government into the American family; and wartime economic controls brought it into almost every business. Then came the Great Depression of 1929, and people began to say that if the federal government could draft young men out of the family and send them off to die, it ought to use that same power to save the family home from foreclosure, or the family itself from starvation. World War II with its rationing, price controls, and total economic regulations, very nearly made permanent a new culture pattern. Americans no longer have the old sharp fear of the encroaching state. For better or worse, they have come to accept government aid and regulation as a general principle, and to believe in it. Whether this is good or bad is here beside the point. We are simply defining the culture pattern for use of public speakers.

Now it is not easy to apply this change of pattern to public address without becoming a tempting and vulnerable target, tempting because it is likely to arouse political animosity, and vulnerable because the animosity will be based on emotional grounds and thus not be subject to a rational answer. But with so vital a change in this culture pattern the risk must be assumed. Applied to political speaking, this change means simply that *whereas a generation ago it was effective to demonstrate that a proposed reform meant increasing federal control, this is no longer true.* Intelligent minorities, to be sure, are more fearful of the dangers of federal control than ever before, especially chambers of commerce, manufacturing associations, medical and legal professions; *but not the mass of people!* They have a Federal Social Security number. In times of crisis they look toward the federal government for succor. To them you can't argue the danger of federal control. You need to find other bases or argument: too much loss of money in getting it from the taxpayer to Washington and back again, higher taxes, increasing debt burden, etc.

Political and economic leaders must learn to know the *possible* from the impossible. In this day when the study of man has become a science, leaders can learn the possible by engaging experts on public opinion to discover the "trend curve" of public opinion. (The polltakers can do that; it's their business.) These experts can learn where the public might be persuaded to alter their views, and where they have gone beyond the point of no return. None of this will prevent change of public opinion, for change is as inevitable as death and taxes; but it will give intelligent leaders a chance to direct the change.

### MARRIAGE AND DIVORCE

In many parts of the world Marriage is arranged by the families involved, and not by the persons. The reasons are not pertinent here, but involve social class and transfer of wealth. Not so in our culture. With us the only proper basis for marriage is romantic love. This is the recurring theme of literature, from Romeo and Juliet to Edward Streeter's father-of-the-bride who yields to his daughter's announcement of love by saying, "Okay, puss, if that's the way you feel about it, I love him already."

As for Divorces, we recognize them, but we do *not* approve them as ideal. A growing divorce rate is cause for concern. Hollywood actors may get divorces in private life, but not on the screen. Everywhere the ideal marriage is for keeps.

Though marriage is a legal act, regulated by law, it also has a religious side. In both Protestant ethic and Catholic theology marriage is a religious sacrament. The home and family is not only a patriotic theme but also a religious theme.

Not everybody follows the code. (If you think so, read the *Kinsey Reports.*) But there is a strong and constant pressure on those who don't. Young intellectuals are sometimes slow in finding this out. In class speeches they advocate free love, or regulated prostitution, or what-have-you, as the way to solve certain pressing problems of youth; then they are shocked at the backfire of their audience, and blame it on stupid listeners, forgetting that the lowest form of stupidity, as John Morley said, is to criticise the stupidity of others. These inexperienced young speakers simply don't know that they drive their arguments point-blank against the culture patterns of our society, and thus defeat themselves. You cannot attack a culture pattern head-on, but must go about it obliquely.

### RACE PREJUDICE

Race Prejudice is not an instinct. It's a culture pattern. You are not born with it; you learn it. In over half the world it does not exist; these people never learned it. In Western culture it's fairly recent, but very strong. It is not confined to America, but exists over all Anglo-Saxon civilizations. It varies in form from one part of the Anglo-Saxon world to another, but it varies less in intensity that we would like to believe. As Isidore Ziferstein, formerly a psychiatrist in New York, summarized it: "Studies show that 80 per cent of the American people show some degree of prejudice, and that children in an all-white school in New York City show the same basic prejudice as children in Georgia."

Emery S. Bogardus over thirty years ago measured the feeling of "social distance" felt by 1,725 native-born Americans. They lived in every part of the United States: East, South, Middle West, Far West. They represented both sexes, different occupations and different religions. But all had a high-school or college education, and all spoke for the more thoughtful and forward-looking segment rather than the narrow-minded and backward. Of this top-level group only 9 per cent were willing to admit a Negro to their club as a personal chum, only 12 per cent to admit one to their street as a neighbor, and only 39 per cent to admit one to employment in their occupation. Toward Jews there was also a "social distance." Of the best-liked Jews, the German Jews, 22 per cent of these Americans would admit to their club, 25 per cent would admit them to their street as neighbor, and 40 per cent would admit them to employment in their occupation.[15]

These attitudes have been modified since then by time and human events, but they have not disappeared. The National Opinion Research Center found the following changes for white people of the United States over the 14-year period, 1942-1956:

|  | PERCENTAGE | |
|---|---|---|
|  | *1942* | *1956* |
| Favoring integration with Negroes on public transportation facilities | 44 | 60 |
| No objection to living near Negroes | 35 | 51 |
| Favored school desegregation | 30 | 48 |
| Believed Negroes are as intelligent as whites | 40 | 75[16] |

Race prejudice varies also according to the intensity of exposure to other races. For example, in London it existed in mild form until black citizens from Jamaica emigrated there, whereupon it became intense and bitter, until finally it exploded into violence. In America, no survey has been made of how it varies in rural areas of the North, which has no contact with the problem, compared with industrial Northern cities where two races live side by side. But the American Institute of Public Opinion on July 16, 1954, published its survey among white people of the United States on how many would object to having their children attend a school where the majority of pupils were Negroes. In the North, 45 per cent objected. In the South 82 per cent objected.

Now to discuss this culture pattern in terms of speechmaking is even more dangerous than discussing the explosive culture pattern of private enterprise. Yet we must assume the risk, for in the opinion of both races—in the North and in the South—this is the most important question facing the United States today, more important than taxes, inflation, or even the atom bomb or cold war.[17] Yet of the 123 national organizations working on race relations today, most of them are working blind, ignoring the laws of human relations, not understanding either culture patterns or the tenets of persuasion. Much of their effort boomerangs, and makes bad conditions worse. This is a job for people who know how.

First, let us define "race prejudice." Actually it is not a single simple prejudice. Instead it is a *group of social conflicts*, some of which are stronger than others. For example, Negroes resent all discrimination, but the one they resent *most* is economic discrimination. American whites

---

[15] Theodore M. Newcomb and Eugene L. Hartley, *Readings in Social Psychology* (New York, Holt, Rinehart and Winston, 1947), p. 504.

[16] For the entire survey see *Scientific American*, Vol. 195 (December, 1956), No. 6, pp. 35-39.

[17] Poll by the Ben Gaffin Associates, Inc., for the *Catholic Digest*, 1956.

show exactly the reverse attitude. Most of them flinch at full racial equality, but object *least* to economic equality.[18] Now people's attitudes, you will remember, are changed most easily on the *circumference*, and not at the hard-core center. If, therefore, you have free choice you will find it easier to improve economic race relations than any other. In other words, recognize frankly that you can't attack *any* culture pattern head on. A head-on attack will fail. It will backfire, and do more harm than good. Start, therefore, at the circumference and take it piecemeal. Don't attack race prejudice outright, but work on race *discrimination,* for race discrimination is on the circumference, exposed to conflict with two other culture patterns: democratic tradition and Christian religion.

Next, you should know that the majority of whites *and* Negroes in both the North *and* South agree on the following assumptions. These are the assumptions on which you can safely base arguments:

1. The race problem is one of the biggest problems in the country today.
2. It is a tough problem to solve.
3. Whites worry more about it than Negroes do.
4. Southern whites worry more about it than other whites do.
5. The problem needs to be kept in front of people.
6. All men are created equal.
7. Education does more good than laws in solving the problem.
8. Churches have not done all they should to help solution.
9. Slum clearance and low-rent housing help toward solution.
10. Younger whites are more friendly toward Negroes than older whites are.

You should know also that the majority of Southern whites disagree with the predominating opinions of Negroes and Northern whites by believing the following propositions:

1. We are now getting farther from solving the problem, not closer.
2. Both whites and Negroes are more friendly in the South than in the North.
3. The two races should be kept apart.
4. Negroes in their own neighborhoods are more friendly toward whites than are Negroes in mixed neighborhoods.
5. Laws against segregation hurt solution of the problem.
6. Most Negroes want segregated schools.

Finally, you should know that the majority of Negroes disagree with the predominating opinions of whites in both sections of the country by believing the following:

1. Whites living in mixed neighborhoods are more friendly to Negroes than are other whites.

[18] William Samuel Maron Banks, "Rank Order of Sensitivity to Discrimination," *American Sociological Review*, XV (August, 1950), 529-534.

2. We don't need more laws so much as enforcement of present laws.

3. It doesn't matter to most Negroes whether they live in white or Negro neighborhoods.[19]

Not all of these opinions are fixed, of course, for never will life sit still. Some will change with the years; perhaps many will change. But these are the assumptions with which you must now deal. When you discuss race problems, whatever your purpose, you must treat with respect the assumptions of any group to which you speak. Your task is to compose these differences into a more or less successful image of justice, bearing in mind that each group wants justice according to its own assumptions.

### RELIGION

In Western civilization the culture pattern of Religion has undergone one important change during the past three hundred years. For centuries before that, Christian nations waged religious wars, and communities engaged in witchhunts. No government granted religious tolerance, and the hangings, beheadings, and burnings make unpleasant reading today. We have got over the more violent aspects of this. We don't fight religious wars any more; and most Western nations grant freedom of worship. This does not mean that we have developed full religious tolerance. We really have not. We are sensitive about religious differences, and as a rule refrain from open and friendly public discussion of religious differences. Indeed, religious difference is one of the least-discussed subjects in modern life, less so than social, economic, and political differences. But people of different religious faiths do live peaceably together, and the religious rights of minorities are protected by law. In this sense, our culture pattern of religion includes religious tolerance.

Are people as intensely religious as they were in earlier centuries? Some people say not. But you must remember that some people always say that the Good Old Days were best, and now the world is getting worse. Wise men chiselled that on stone tablets 2,800 B.C. Homer remarked on it constantly in the ninth century B.C. Learned men from Samuel Johnson in 1760 to Whitney Griswold in 1960 have lamented the decline of education, religion, etc. We brush aside this lament of old men with old nervous systems, and try to get at the truth. Three centuries ago Christian religious attitudes began to alter. Change began with the advancement of learning and the beginning of scientific progress. Soon a group of intellectuals proclaimed the arrival of the "Age of Reason," in which religion was out of date, churches were no longer necessary, and "my own mind is my own church." As the tempo of modern education and scientific discoveries increased, this has been a recurrent theme with

[19] This is based on the findings of the Ben Gaffin Associates, Inc. Research Agency, made for the *Catholic Digest* as "the first comprehensive survey of public attitudes toward suggested solutions to the racial problems in the U.S." It was published in five parts in the *Catholic Digest*, June through October, 1956.

many intellectual leaders. Indeed, churchmen themselves have constantly feared that modern scientific thought would weaken the spirit of worship.

Actually, while all this intellectual ferment was going on church membership was steadily *increasing*. In the United States, for example, it increased from 20 per cent of the total population in 1860 to 62 per cent in 1957. Of these members, seemingly about the same percentage attend church today as a century ago.

Religion is universal. No people ever lived without it, whether prehistoric primitive man or modern civilized man. It is not confined to church attendants or to church members. It has been altered, but not weakened, by modern scientific thought. And today, as centuries ago, *it is less strong in young people than among middle-aged and older people*. There are many individual exceptions, but the basic pattern is that increasing religious faith comes with increasing experience and age.

Young people who are impatient with religious ceremony should remember that they are not the first to feel that way, nor will they be the last. In discussing religion, remember that most people hold it in respect; hence topics based on respect for religion are likely to be listened to with respect. Remember also that most people are sensitive even to mild criticism of religious practice; you cannot attack religion head-on, and even the mildest criticism must be handled with tact. Witness the tact of the man who filed a court petition to compel radio stations to grant him the right to criticise certain religious practices: "I do not throw stones at church windows. I do not mock at people kneeling in prayer. . . . But I abhor and denounce those who seek to prevent others from expressing contrary views."

### WAR AND FORCE

If war were an instinct there would be no hope of man living long without war. Fortunately, it is a culture pattern, not an instinct. Peoples like the Eskimos and Mission Indians of California never learned this culture pattern. To them the idea of a whole village going to war against another village is unthinkable. To them killing is murder, and they have no separate concepts whereby if one man kills another it is murder, but if the people of one village kill the people of another, it is war. To them all killing is murder.

In Western civilization, however, people have been conditioned to accept cycles of War and Peace, "much as mankind accepts the coming and going of the season." A military writer, Homer Lea, points out that from the fifteenth century B.C. until the present time, a cycle of over 3,400 years, we have had less than 234 years of peace.

In conflict with this culture pattern of War and Force, we have more recently developed another of peace and justice. We take pride that we do not wage wars of aggression, that we fight instead to resist aggression and to attain "enduring peace, world democracy, and the rights of oppressed peoples." We are, therefore, living with these two conflicting culture patterns. One is for settling world differences by peaceful methods. The other is to wage war rather than surrender national sovereignty or submit to foreign aggression.

## Other influences

Reason, wants, and culture patterns, which we have just studied, are the basic forces of public opinion common to all. But when people assemble in individual audiences still other influences operate. These we shall consider under five headings:

1. Age
2. Sex
3. Locale
4. Education and Economic Status
5. Activity Level

### AGE

Young people more than older are prone to romance and adventure. In romance they find an outlet in hero worship: in stars of screen, television, and the sports world. At the peak, for example, there were 2,000 "Frank Sinatra Clubs," averaging 200 members each. The fans of a radio disc jockey, Howard Miller, organized 300 fan clubs and wrote him 1,200 fan letters a week. The fans of second-baseman Nelson Fox, called themselves "Fox's Mighty Mites," and organized 150 fan clubs in 29 states including Hawaii. In his name they bought Christmas gifts for the poor, visited hospital children's wards and homes for the aged. These groups are teen-agers. They crave excitement, and find it harder than older people to listen to ideas. Instead, they prefer thriller pictures, action stories, and helping others in the name of their current hero.

We used to think that youth was vitally interested in public affairs, and was an impatient reformist eager for change. But when the social scientists began their relentless probing, they found that in the United States youth were *less* concerned with public affairs than were older people. At first this discovery was so disconcerting that people questioned its validity. But as the research continued, the evidence mounted, until now we know it is true. Not only that, but it's true at *each* educational level that younger people are less interested in public affairs than are older people.[20] Young people have not yet paid taxes, and don't comprehend the staggering cost of government. Older people have, and do.

But young intellectuals tend to be radical. They don't like "that mess

[20] This research is summarized by Charles A. Siepmann, *Radio, Television, and Society* (New York, Oxford Press, 1950), pp. 98-100.

in Washington." They don't like the state of the world. They want a quick change. As they grow older, their impatience lessens, and their ardor cools. They are more content with the world. As they grow still older, they tend to resist change, especially changes advocated by young, impatient reformists, and to wonder why youth nowadays has such dangerous ideas. To put it humorously, at 18 young intellectuals want to reform the world. At 25 they are content to reform America. At 40 they would settle for reforming their own children. At 60 they give up trying to reform themselves.

Finally, young people have not lived so long as older ones, they have had a narrower range of experiences, and have accumulated less knowledge. Therefore, they tend to accept what they are told, less critically than do older persons.

In speaking to young people, therefore, topics based on Adventure, Competition, Pride, Loyalty, and Hero Worship are stronger than such topics would be with older persons. In speaking to older people, topics based on Security, Property, Reputation, Conformity, and Worship of Tradition or Worship of Deity are stronger than they would be with young persons. In speaking to older people, remember that they will weigh and judge more suspiciously, and that they will tend to resist accepting new ideas more than do young people.

### SEX

Women are more passive, receptive, long-suffering, and enduring of pain than men. As a compensation, they have developed an especially strong inner bulwark of self-respect and pride, which finds expression in the desire for beauty and charm, and in simply "being a woman." Hence women need to be admired and loved, and will pay great attention to clothes, cosmetics, and beautifiers.

Men are more aggressive than women. They rely more on *doing*, and women rely more on *being*. Hence it is still unusual to have a woman legislator, a policewoman, or a woman who manages a business involving risk of investment. Most women prefer to be homemakers, to preserve and protect rather than to create.

For this reason perhaps women are less concerned than men with politics and political affairs. To them the problems of running a home put out of mind the problems of running a democracy. In studying a presidential election, for example, the investigators found that only 26 per cent of women wanted to hear evening radio political talks or discussion about public issues—far below the men. They ran into such remarks as "I don't care to vote. Voting is for the men." "I think men should do the voting and the women should stay home and take care of their work." The workers concluded that not only did women feel no compulsion to vote, but some "actually consider aloofness a virtue."

Men are prone to say that women are more emotional than men. This is not quite true, since men are about as emotional as human beings can be. Yet the adage points vaguely toward a difference between men and women, a difference that can be stated in more precisely these terms: *Women care more about what other people think than about following a set of abstract laws or regulations.* Thus boys adapt themselves more readily to rules, whereas girls are more sensitive to the wishes of others. In the main, laws are still made by men, and observance of law is upheld by men. It is a man who would send his daughter from the home if she had broken the code, not a woman. It is a woman who would plead for a son to be excused from the penalty of reckless driving; only a man would let the boy take his medicine and learn his lesson.

Women probably have stronger artistic tastes than men, or at least they are more refined. They have a greater appreciation of good music and art, even though this taste is strong also in men. They are more sensitive than men to beautiful housefurnishings, tableware, and clothes. (The sterling silver industry could never survive on men's desire.) "The thing that sells a house more than anything else," explained a man who had loaned tens of millions on homes, "is a beautiful kitchen, and it is usually the women who decide which house they want."

Women, finally, have a stronger sense of worship and reverence of God. With men the sense of worship comes in some degree from their allegiance to the moral law, or to the sense of order in the universe. With women it tends to be reverence for a personal God who has a personal concern for their personal welfare.

These are the major lines of difference between men and women as they concern the speaker. With women, topics will be especially strong that rest on worship and reverence, artistic tastes, inner privation, or welfare of home and family and friends. Don't expect too many women to be interested in the welfare of government (though some will be), or the preservation of abstract principles like liberty or freedom of speech.

### LOCALE

People of different regions tend toward specific differences in outlook. In the Middle West isolationism lingers in many disguises. Vermont votes Republican. Mississippi votes Democratic. Wisconsin is "progressive." Pennsylvania is "conservative." The South is "solid." These are gross differences. There are many finer ones. Upstate New York does not vote the same as New York City; for that matter even their speech is different. Downstate Illinois votes differently from Chicago. In the Old South, the piedmont is different in outlook from the older tidewater. In the Far West, Southern California already has developed different characteristics from those in the region of San Francisco Bay.

There are also differences between those who live in city and country.

They follow different occupations, and live in different tempos and rhythms. They enjoy different pastimes.

Many books and magazines are published primarily for people of different locale. Still more so must a speaker recognize the influence of locale on his immediate audience.

### EDUCATION AND ECONOMIC STATUS

America is a political democracy in which all men are equal before the law. We like to say we have no class-consciousness like Europe's. Actually we do, but it is based on a different standard from Europe's. America's social classes rest chiefly on Education and Economic Status; but make no mistake, they are social classes nevertheless. A rich man is not just a poor man with money. He is a different man who moves in a different group on a different level. He is disciplined by associations with that group and by wanting to be accepted without reservation. As a result he develops different ideals, different standards of right and wrong, different concepts of politics and economics, and often a different church membership.

Now we don't like to talk much about this, because in our ideology all men are created equal, socially as well as politically. We verbalize this ideal in casual thinking. Political office-holders emphasize it in public speeches. But without bringing it right out in the open, we sense that some people are above us, and some are below us, on some kind of a scale. We know we live in a dual world. One is the ideal world of our dreams in which all men are equal in all ways. The other is the concrete world in which we live where people reside in different residential districts, belong to different clubs, and move in different circles. All our talk about all men being equal does not fool anybody, not even ourselves. We sneer at the "social climber." Why? Our sneer accuses him of trying to adopt the standards of a class higher up to which he does not belong. We speak scornfully of "snob appeal." Why? Our scorn is for people who belong to a class that behaves in a way different from ours.

In short, every American knows that we have social classes, even though he might not admit it, even to himself. The primary index of social class is not peerage or nobility, but money and education. Not money or education alone, but what these lead to.

They lead seemingly to five social classes in large industrial cities. At least a three-year study of the social structure of metropolitan Chicago directed by W. Lloyd Warner found the following five classes, which probably are typical:

1. *The Upper Class* (0.9 per cent) composed of manufacturers, financiers, and top advertising executives. These are the traditional leaders in any large American city. It is limited to people who have learned how

to behave "properly," to fill their lives with "good deeds," give money to "approved philanthropy," yet keep their arrogance within manageable proportions. This class constitutes less than 1 per cent of Middle Western or Far Western cities, but may rise to 3 per cent in older Eastern cities.

2. *The Upper Middle Class* (7.2 per cent) composed of professional and businessmen such as store owners and top-level salesmen. These are people who get things done. In civic affairs they provide the active front for the Upper Class. A few are born into this class, but most get there on their own through two factors: First, they *want* to rise to this class; second, they have the ability to do so.

These two classes constitute the levels above the Common Man.

3. *The Lower Middle Class* (28.4 per cent). This class includes the top-level of the Common Man. It is the white-collar class, made up of small tradesmen, clerks, office workers, technicians, and ordinary salesmen. Members of this class are not leaders but most of them are good followers. This is the most conforming of all classes, the most church-going, and morally the most serious. You don't see much divorce at this level; divorces come from the top and bottom class levels, but not here. This is the group, above all others, that establishes the American moral code.

4. *The Upper Lower Class* (44 per cent). Most of the Common Men are in this class. Formerly it was composed of people said to be "the real poor people, but honest and fine." Today they are no less honest and fine, but far less poor. They compose the factory production worker, union-labor groups, and skilled workers. Interestingly, it also includes labor union leaders and some politicians who stay in it because if they moved out they would lose their power.

5. *The Lower Lower Class* (19.5 per cent) composed of unskilled laborers, racial immigrants from other parts of this country, and people in nonrespectable occupations like garbage hauling. This group tends to get more fun out of life. Its members don't get in the rat race that besets all of the classes above them. They are less willing to save for a rainy day, and comprise most of the people who depend at times on public or private relief.

*Studies in communication abilities reveal that the two classes at the top show striking differences in their modes of thinking from the three at the bottom, and presumably show the same differences in their modes of listening. Members of the top two classes, for example, can tell a story like a movie director who switches from one camera to another. But members of the three lower classes can use one camera only. Members of the top two classes can think in abstract categories, but members of the*

*three lower classes can think in concrete terms only. Members of the
top two classes can organize an idea, and hold it in mind even when
departing from it to bring in side lights. Farther down the social level
people are less able to organize an idea, until at the bottom some cannot
"tell a straight story or describe a simple incident coherently."*[21]

This research into the nature of the American public reveals at least
three critical problems in persuasion. First, the three lower groups cannot communicate effectively. Yet they do have feelings, responses, and
attitudes toward common problems. Second, between the lowest groups
and the highest are wide differences in moral viewpoint, in sophistication,
in standards of right and wrong, and even in what constitutes humor.
Can a woman with an Upper-Middle-Class background, belonging to the
top 8 per cent of American society, speak for the factory worker's wife?
On some things they have like viewpoints. On others they live in different
worlds. Can a man from the Upper Class, belonging to the top 1 per
cent of society, speak for the small tradesmen, union laborers, and unskilled workers? In our history a few men have. In government, Thomas
Jefferson did, Franklin D. Roosevelt did, and Nelson Rockefeller did. In
religion, Henry Ward Beecher did and Harry Emerson Fosdick did. If
America remains healthy, more men at the top must speak for those at
the bottom; but before they can speak they must learn the latter's values,
responses, attitudes, and listening limitations.

A third danger is the fear of change found in most members of the
two higher groups. Gaston Berger, director-general of higher education
in France, diagnosed it tersely: "In general, there are now two groups
of people in the world: those full of hope but living in poverty, and those
enjoying prosperity but haunted by fear of the future." The latter fear
most of the political changes of the twentieth century. They fear "creeping socialism." They fear that the Common Man's desire for security has
led to his corruption by politicians who have given him something for
nothing. These are understandable fears, for the upper groups under
the old order could amass vast wealth scarcely touched by taxation. They
want to go back to those Good Old Days, yet know they cannot. Since
they cannot, most of them attack vehemently anybody who rocks the boat
any more.

For students of public address this fear of change by men of property
and education is one of the most significant forces in political history.

[21] Pierre Martineau, *Motivation in Advertising* (New York, McGraw-Hill Book Co.,
Inc., 1957), p. 164; W. Lloyd Warner, *Social Class in America* (Gloucester, Mass.,
Peter Smith, 1957), pp. 11-15, 66-67; Leonard Schatzman and A. L. Strauss, "Social
Class and Modes of Communication," *American Journal of Sociology*, LX (January,
955), 329-338; Vance Packard, *The Status Seekers* (New York, David McKay Company, Inc., 1959), *passim*. Warner's classification for New England cities shows six
classes instead of five, and a slightly different percentage for each group, but the
difference is not significant from the standpoint of this book.

Plato, wealthy philosopher, opposed the coming of democracy in Athens. French nobility before 1789 resisted change, until they were marched to the guillotine in the Revolution. White Russians before 1917 resisted change, until they were destroyed by the Red Russians. In America, most (though conspicuously not all) of the men of property opposed the American Revolution of 1776, the Jeffersonian revolution of 1800, the Jacksonian democracy of the 1830's, and the Roosevelt New Deal of the 1930's. In resisting change, the educated and men of property ignored too much the bitter need of the less educated and those without property. By refusing to allow a little change, or enough change, they created pressure that led to the violence, and to their own disastrous defeat. In future crises, can the educated and privileged be persuaded to change enough, or must they always be overpowered by force?

Partly the answer depends on their education, which obviously needs to be changed from the education of the past. Partly also it depends on the skill of those who undertake to persuade them. Here enters a dangerous new factor. Down until the twentieth century men of property and education controlled governments except during special moments of history. They could be overthrown only by revolution. None publicly subscribed to the cynical dictum of the Marquis de Sade, that "it is a danger to love men, a crime to enlighten them," but they feared the raw power of the masses and gave them no political power. Now for the first time in human history the masses have come to power. Also for the first time there are now the mass media to reach them—radio and television.

After the centuries the chips are down. Leaders henceforth must have greater skill than ever before in persuading the less educated and less intelligent to a wise course of action. As Wallace Carroll put it, it is "persuade or perish." If men of good will disdain to learn this, rest assured that demagogues will not disdain it, and henceforth we shall be ruled increasingly by men who make slight distinction between "what sounds good" and "what is good and sound."

### AUDIENCE ACTIVITY LEVEL

Last is the Activity Level of each particular audience. For convenience we divide these into three levels: excited, normal, and depressed.

At the *excited activity level* the listeners are under tension. It may be extreme tension, as when they are deeply involved, aroused, or excited— like a cocked gun waiting for a finger to pull the trigger. It may be milder tension, as with partisans or enthusiasts who are deeply interested in a subject or a speaker or an occasion. Examples of excited-level listeners are students at a football rally, partisans at a political convention, persons at a religious revival, or any group prearoused by the nature of the meeting such as a labor union local discussing whether to strike, or a Congress in the final discussion of a critical bill.

You will not meet the excited activity level in the classroom. But when you do meet it, you had better be prepared for its demands: (1) Waste no time on tedious details, but get to the heart of the subject at once. (2) If listeners are in an unreasoning mood, don't try to reason, for they won't listen. You can state impellingly, and in terms of their wants, the *results* of reasoning; but do so with the process left out. (3) If it is an audience concerned with finding the answer to an acute need (Shall we strike? Can we win the election with this man, or that one?), reduce the problem to its simplest terms, and keep repeating it in simplified form. (4) Speak like a man who *can* and *will* lead. Whosoever speaks in dull accents and limpid manner will not satisfy the needs of listeners at the excited activity level. They need to hear the voice of Authority, and to see behind it a man.

The *normal activity level* is one where the audience has little tension, excitement, or special interests involved. Its members are entirely willing perhaps to listen—but only if the speaker delivers the stuff. Most audiences are at the normal activity level, and the procedures of this book center on speaking to them at this level.

The *depressed activity level* you will meet often in classroom speaking. It's a Monday morning, and your class has not yet recovered from the weekend. It's any morning at eight o'clock, and they are not yet fully awake. It's the day after a heavy date, a great night, or a big social event; they are awake, but responses are slow. Or it's just another day, and they've heard seventy speeches in the course already. Ho hum, now comes the seventy-first! All of this is good training for you, because outside of class you will also meet audiences at the depressed activity level. Perhaps the program has been too long, and the hour is late. Or the preceding speaker was an *And-Er-r-*Vocalist, or was perhaps a dealer in hollow banalities. He depressed the audience, and now they are yours. Again, it may be a program that follows a meal, the audience is relaxing on a full stomach, and the demands of digestion have left them drowsy. No matter what the cause. You will meet audiences at the depressed activity level. You must learn now to deal with them. The methods are thoroughly covered throughout the remainder of this book, starting with the next chapter, but basic suggestions are inserted here: (1) Wake yourself up and use vigorous mental and physical action. Said a disgruntled drowsy listener, "I wanted to go to sleep, but that confounded speaker talked so loud he kept me awake, and I had to listen." Be that kind of speaker if you have an audience at the depressed activity level. (2) Use human interest stories and humor. Make them laugh. Get their interest, and you have a chance to keep it.

## Assignments

1. From a popular magazine take a sampling of advertisements (i.e. not an assortment that you happen to like, but a stratified sampling, such as all the full-page advertisements in an entire issue, or all the advertisements in a given number of pages, etc.)

   a. Classify them into four groups: Those based primarily on (1) reason and logic, (2) wants and impelling motives, (3) culture patterns, and (4) reason plus wants, or reason plus culture patterns.

   b. Classify the strongest motives or culture patterns on which the advertisements were based in the last three groups above.

2. Write an analysis of your attitudes and beliefs on one of the following topics. Include the influence of reason and evidence, of wants and impelling motives, and of culture patterns. Remember that your instructor will be aware of the tendency discovered by Poffenberger of people (see above, page 111) to idealize and magnify the influence of reason in their own conduct:

   a. Why I belong to my church

   b. Why I joined (or did not join) a fraternity or sorority

   c. Why I came to this college

   d. Why I like dates

   e. Why I like athletics

   f. How I developed my political and economic beliefs

3. Read some influential speech given at a critical moment in history, such as Abraham Lincoln, "Gettysburg Address," Franklin D. Roosevelt, "We Have Nothing to Fear but Fear Itself," (First Inaugural), or Winston Churchill, "Blood, Toil, Tears, and Sweat":

   a. Select the strongest motive on which it is based, and classify it in terms of this chapter.

   b. Explain how the speaker based the speech on this motive, whether through reason and evidence, vivid description only, irrational play on emotions, etc.

4. Read a speech found in this volume, in *Vital Speeches,* or in A. C. Baird's annual volumes on *Representative American Speeches:*

   a. On what wants, impelling motives, or culture patterns does the speaker base the speech?

   b. Do you think the speaker chose the most effective ones? If you were speaking to this audience on such a subject, what other wants, impelling motives, or culture patterns would you use?

5. On what wants, impelling motives, and culture patterns would you base speeches on the following topics:

   a. Why the U.S. college curriculum should (or should not) be like that in Russia

b. Why students should engage in extracurricular activities

c. Why they should study foreign languages

d. Why they should study the fine arts

e. Why they should study science

f. Why they should study

g. Why they should prefer democracy to communism

ON USING REASON, WANTS, AND CULTURE PATTERNS IN SPEAKING

6. Prepare a 2-minute speech based on *one* want or culture pattern. Use as many different techniques as possible for making this speech effective, especially reason, evidence, and vivid description, but under no circumstances resort to illogical emotional appeal.

7. Choose a subject for a longer speech, one in which you intend to cultivate a change of attitude:

   *a.* Determine as accurately as you can the wants or culture patterns of the class members that would cause them to resist changing attitude.

   *b.* After studying your subject, select the strongest available *other* wants or culture patterns for which you have supporting material. For example, if the chief obstacle to change of attitude is desire for Security, you may be able to use against this the desire for Freedom or Property. Concentrate on the strongest motives, and reject weak or doubtful ones even though you have supporting material for them. Having thus chosen the strongest wants or culture patterns, you will now proceed to reinforce them with all the best available reason and supporting materials that can be used within the time limit.

8. Prepare a speech to win specific action from an apathetic audience, such as "study harder," "don't take snap courses," "attend the college lecture series," or "vote on election day." Choose the strongest possible want (or wants) on which to base the speech, and use as many techniques as possible to make the want effective.

9. Give a speech on how you think the principles studied in this chapter could be used in some particular field, such as (*a*) dormitory management, (*b*) student-and-teacher relations, (*c*) personnel work, (*d*) labor relations, (*e*) law enforcement, (*f*) salesmanship, (*g*) politics, (*h*) religion.

# * 7 *

# The Architecture of Persuasion

A SPEAKER IS in the position described by Catherine the Great when Denis Diderot, a great scholar and personal friend, urged her to change her form of government by simply renouncing the old form. Replied Catherine: "These fine-sounding principles of yours may be all very well in the world of books, but they do not suit the world of affairs. You do your work on patient paper. I, who am only an empress, have to work on human skins, and they are ticklish." A speaker, like Catherine, works on human skins, and they are ticklish. In this chapter we shall summarize the accumulated knowledge of 2,400 years on how to do this.

There are two types of persuasion. First is *short-range* persuasion where the aim is immediate action, as in speeches to courts, or juries, or in committee discussions. These groups are *already committed to action*, and the question is *which* action. Chief Justice John Marshall testified to the importance of this kind of speaking by reversing a former decision of the United States Supreme Court and apologizing for the error, explaining that the error had been made because the previous case "had not been argued by counsel."[1] Another short-range persuasion occurs during "times of decision" when people know that by a given time they must make up their minds. An example is a political election. In a typical Presidential election over half the voters will listen to the candidates by radio or television, and roughly 15 per cent will change their minds, either from hearing the speakers or from talking with others.[2] Under such

---

[1] See *Congressional Record*, 44th Congress, 1st Session, Part 7, pp. 320-321.

[2] See George Gallup, "The Changing Climate for Public Opinion Research," *The Public Opinion Quarterly* XXI (Spring, 1957), No. 1, pp. 26-27. See also Paul F. Lazarsfeld, Bernard Berelson, and Hazel Gaudet, *The People's Choice* (New York, Duell, Sloan and Pearce, 1944) for an analysis of the percentage of change and reasons for change of voters in Erie County, Ohio, during the 1940 Presidential campaign. See W. Norwood Brigance, "The Effectiveness of the Public Platform," *Annals of the American Academy of Political and Social Science*, Vol. 250 (March, 1947), pp. 71-72 for the influence of certain speeches in the 1936 Presidential campaign, which was the first to be measured scientifically.

special conditions any given speech, or group of speeches, may influence immediate action.

But even short-range persuasion does not produce erratic public opinion. Nobody hears a speech today, then changes a deep-seated attitude before the sun goes down. Nobody can be persuaded by one speech today to the virtues of Buddhist monasticism, by another tomorrow to the blessings of Moslem polygamy, and by still another next week to the beneficence of Western monogamy. The public cannot be persuaded today that college education promotes success and happiness, then persuaded tomorrow that college education is a waste of time and money. Human society survives only from having reasonable stability of public opinion, yet adequate change to meet changing conditions. Persuasion is inherent in both.

The pre-eminent purpose of persuasion, then, is *long-range*, the slow shifting of attitudes and slow changes in the climates of opinion. Human attitudes must change whether people want them to or not, for time moves on at a relentless pace, and no human hand can hold it back. We may protest its relentless pace, as man always has done:

> Backward, turn backward, O Time in thy flight;
> Make me a child again, just for tonight.

But the flow of time is never backward. It pushes man and events onward at a rate that never slackens and never falters. "Time and tide wait for no man." As they thrust us into the future, they thrust us also into new problems, new needs, new duties, new challenges. Constantly they compel us to reshape our opinions and alter our behavior. Constantly they compel us to redefine issues about which we have thought little, or have not been concerned. We dare not think today as we did yesterday about education, taxes, wages, art, leisure, literature, or youth. We must meet their new problems and new challenges. Our ability to do this depends in a large measure on how effectively our ideas are watered and cultivated by others. "No man is an Iland, intire of itselfe," said John Donne, "every man is a peece of the Continent, a part of the maine."

The architecture of persuasion was not invented in the twentieth century. The basic principles are described by Aristotle, Cicero, Quintilian, and the medieval and Renaissance rhetoricians. But during the past fifty years scientific research has demonstrated that these early thinkers were right, and has increased enormously our understanding of details and methods. This research has come from separate fields: from anthropologists, psychologists, sociologists, political scientists, and advertisers, as well as experts in speech. This research can be summarized as follows:[3]

[3] The evidence is so extensive that its bibliography would require a dozen pages. The following references will be a start for those who want to inquire further: Joseph T. Klapper, "What We Know About the Effects of Mass Communication . . . ," *Public Opinion Quarterly* XXI (Winter 1957-1958), No. 4, pp. 453-474. Erik Barnouw,

United Nations

e U.N. Security Council in Session (1960). The hope of humanity is that the long-
ge result of such international discussion will be a world "conceived in liberty and
dedicated to the proposition that all men are created equal."

1. The cumulative effects of mass communication are powerful. They influence all phases of American life: family relationships, politics, business and social activities. They contribute to attitudes and opinions which remain after the sources are forgotten.

2. Radio was more effective than newspapers, television is now more effective than radio ever was, and face-to-face speaking is still more effec-

*Mass Communication* (New York, Rinehart & Co., Inc., 1956), pp. 203-270. Leo Bogart, *The Age of Television* (New York, Frederick Ungar Publishing Co., 1956), pp. 37-40, 208-230. William Albig, *Modern Public Opinion* (New York, McGraw-Hill Book Co., Inc., 1956), pp. 436-485. Still pertinent is Wilbur Schramm, "The Effects of Mass Communications," *Journalism Quarterly* XXVI (December, 1949), No. 4, p. 397. The most popular treatment of modern advertising methods is Vance Packard, *The Hidden Persuaders* (New York, David McKay, Inc., 1957).

tive than television. Both radio and television create "the illusion of real-ism" and the "illusion of intimacy" within the family home. Repeated experiments demonstrate that "the human voice is more persuasive, more friendly, more compelling than the written word," and that "the physical presence of a speaker" is more effective than "the mere sound of his voice."

3. The amount of learning from mass communications, other things being equal, depends on the listener's attention, and hence on the motivation which compels attention.

4. To say a thing once is not enough. You must keep presenting it, keep talking about it "systematically and persistently." Especially repetitions with variations increases both factual learning and attitude change. Repetition via different channels—magazine, television, face-to-face—also increases both factual learning and attitude change.

5. Persuasion is more effective, other things being equal, when related to people's wants. "Men think critically and precisely only under specific conditions of motivation, and then only in response to the particular problem."

With this background we proceed to methods available to the speaker for influencing public opinion. Primarily there are seven:

1. Get the listeners' attention
2. Get them to accept *you*
3. Rest reason and evidence on deep-seated wants and culture patterns
4. Know your listeners' prevailing attitudes at the time you speak
5. Use indirect methods as well as direct
6. For long-run persuasion, remember that organized information is usually more effective than attempts to force immediate change of opinion
7. To reaffirm old attitudes, vitalize human hopes, ideals, desires and values

## *Get the listener's attention*

Remember that most audiences are restless in their seats. So every time you give a speech have a curb conference with yourself when it's over, and ask: "Did I get their attention in my first ten words?" If you didn't, reform yourself. There's no communication if listeners can't *hear* your first words. And there's no communication if listeners don't *listen*. Do you say airily, "Oh, these problems don't worry *me*"? Exactly. They *don't* worry most speakers. Most speakers ignore them, and let them worry the audience.

## TWO IRON CURTAINS BETWEEN SPEAKER AND LISTENER

Two iron curtains commonly hang between speaker and audience during those first two minutes. First, the speaker fidgets and mumbles. He's tense, as all good speakers are when they start. Unless he has planned deliberately *not* to fidget and mumble, and rehearsed if necessary, his opening words will torture the listeners. As an experiment, before writing this paragraph I kept an inventory of the last ten speakers heard outside of the classroom. They were typical. Six were self-made. Four had been trained. Yet all the self-made and two of the trained speakers—eight of the ten—fidgeted or mumbled or did both during the first two minutes. The average number of fidgets for the whole ten—i.e. putting hands in pockets, jerking them out, twirling a paper clip, etc.— was 18 for the two minutes. That's nine fidgets per minute! The average number of *ers* and unintelligible words for the ten speakers was 14 for the two minutes. That's seven per minute! Listening to that kind of speaking is like having a tooth pulled.

The second iron curtain is the speaker's common tendency to start with foggy abstractions instead of with plain simple narrative, incident, or information that throws interesting light on the subject. In other words, they start at the back end instead of the front end. They start with the conclusions instead of the facts. Instead, they ought to start at the beginning, with the facts, the evidence, the narration, then lead the audience step by step toward the conclusions. The result is that during the first few minutes this iron curtain hangs between the speaker's idea and the listeners' minds. "You cannot make a man want you," runs the feminine adage, "but you can attract his attention." You cannot make men always accept your ideas, but you can get their attention. In the section below we shall see how.

### NATURE OF ATTENTION

What is the nature of attention? How long does a single span of attention last? How long, for example, can a listener "attend" to what a speaker is saying? *Attention comes in spurts and lasts for only a few moments at a time.* Even when you give attention to such simple things as a dot on a paper, or the noise of a buzzer, it is not possible to fix attention for longer than from one to three seconds. Complex stimuli will allow longer periods of attention, but not much longer. When you face an audience, therefore, remember that you are never more than a few seconds away from losing the attention of any person who sits before you! You cannot "get attention" at the beginning of a speech and expect it to remain fixed to the end. You must recapture that attention every few seconds, or else it is soon lost and gone.

The common-sense ways of holding attention have been confirmed by experimental psychology. Some of them we have discussed already under Forms of Support (pages 49-56). They include the use of *facts and figures, specific instances, illustrations, comparisons, and testimony.* Another method of holding attention, already discussed, is of unsuspected importance: namely *arranging ideas into a simple, obvious, and meaningful pattern.* Listeners can then see the whole thought arrangement, know where the speaker has been, know where he is, and forecast where he is likely to go. In this sense, *careful outlining,* then, is a means of holding attention.

Consider the following two examples. In the first, the speaker has not one single specific instance, illustration, comparison, or testimony. Nor has he humor, suspense, or juice of any kind. He starts with one of those foggy abstractions that lowers the iron curtain between him and the audience.

> Internal weakness is invariably the prime cause of breakdown. All history warns against short-cuts to progress. Where the uncreative majority follows the leadership of a creative minority by a species of drill, a mechanical and superficial imitation of the inspired original, the invariable danger is that the leaders become infected by the mechanicalness of their followers. The result is an arrested civilization in which the leaders substitute the whip of compulsion for persuasion.

This kind of speaking confirms the tart maxim that most speakers are like those old-time store keepers, "they are dealers in dry goods and notions." Contrast the above failure with the means of attention used by Hungarian-born Nicholas Nyaradi:

> A few months ago, . . . my car developed engine trouble on the winding highways of southern Indiana. It was late at night, the rain was pouring, and I was helpless and hopeless. Not that I did not know what was wrong with my car, but there wasn't a single thing I could have done about it. Car manufacturers here in America must be so confident about the quality of their make that they fail to include even so much as a screw driver in their equipment.
>   So there I stood on the edge of the road in despair, and suddenly one of those huge interstate trucks drove up, stopped, and the driver . . . climbed out of his seat to give me a helping hand in my trouble. While the trucker was working on my engine we started a conversation, and . . . it did not take him more than about twenty-five seconds to discover that I was not talking with a Midwestern accent.
>   He suddenly looked at me and asked . . . "By the way, Buddy, what are you doing here in the United States?" And I said to him, "Well, Buddy, that

is difficult to answer; because I am traveling all across this great and beautiful land to tell you happy, smug, comfortable Americans how terrible life is behind the Iron Curtain. Then, I am also writing articles for such publications as the *Saturday Evening Post, Fortune Magazine,* and the Scripps-Howard newspapers, . . . and I am also a college professor." . . . "Buddy" looked at me and said, in obvious disgust, "Ah, isn't that too bad; I thought you were at least a traveling salesman."

. . . I suppose you might call me a traveling salesman, although the merchandise I am trying to sell you people is difficult to sell, because it hurts.[4]

You will listen to a speech like that. First, it goes into the subject with a narrative instead of a foggy abstraction. Further, the narrative is studded with specific instances: "southern Indiana," "screw driver," "*Saturday Evening Post.*" Finally, it uses direct quotation: "Say, Buddy," "Ah, isn't that too bad."

If you don't get attention and keep it, nothing else really matters. William Trufant Foster, after nearly fifty years of speaking in public, testified on how hard it is for a speaker to learn this vital prelude to persuasion:

Unhappily I was slow to learn [that] knowledge and righteousness on a man's side are not enough [and that] in addition, he must know how to speak. Over and over again I found that out. . . . Uncle Joe Cannon, Speaker of the House of Representatives . . . giving a campaign speech declared that the United States is a great nation; great largely because of the Republican Party. Then he said it all over again with violent waving of his arms. It was the first time I had heard "the eagle scream." I [also campaigning for the Republicans] was disgusted; and when the audience applauded lustily, I felt still worse. My own speech was based on research and analysis. I marshalled evidence—accurate, documented, logically devastating. To my dismay the audience did not care a campaign button for what I said. . . . I began to realize that in place of half the heavy substance of my speeches, I should have substituted lightness of touch: concrete examples, humor, anecdotes, color, and adaptation to each audience. No audience can attend to serious discourse for more than a few moments at a time. I was stupidly slow in learning that. Last month I spoke to a club in Winter Park, Florida, the University Club, which takes pride in the large proportion of its members who are listed in *Who's Who in America,* who are members of Phi Beta Kappa and who have doctor's degrees. Even a highbrow audience can not stand much. If a speaker does not provide relief from abstract seriousness, his hearers will provide it for themselves, at the speaker's expense.[5]

[4] Address to the Minnesota Editorial Association, *Vital Speeches,* XXII (April 1, 1956), No. 12, pp. 367-368.

[5] "Random Notes on Public Speaking," *Quarterly Journal of Speech,* XXXIII (April, 1947), No. 2, pp. 141-142.

## *Get the listeners to accept you*

To persuade a man you must first get him to listen to you; we've just discussed that. When he starts listening, then you must get him to believe what you say. But he won't do that until he believes *you*. Said Kenneth Burke: "You persuade a man only insofar as you can talk his language by speech, gesture, tonality, order, image, attitude, ideas, *identifying* your way with his."[6] This, then, is the key: You must *identify* yourself with the listener, identify your way with his, or in some way become "substantially one" with him. We call this persuasion by "identification." No one has defined it better than St. Augustine, about 427 A.D.: A man is persuaded if "he likes what you promise, fears what you say is imminent, hates what you censure, embraces what you commend."

*First,* you may identify yourself with the listener by personal association: "I once lived in this community," or "Once I, too, was a college student," or "I am a member of your church, your profession." Said former President Herbert Hoover, speaking at his birthplace on his 80th birthday: *"I am glad to come to West Branch. My grandparents and my parents came here in a covered wagon. In this community they toiled and worshipped God. They lie buried on your hillside. . . . My roots are in this soil."* Even an ex-President speaking only to friends makes sure of identifying himself with his listeners.

*Next,* you may identify yourself with the listener's beliefs, desires, or welfare: "These things we believe," or "These goals we seek together." Said Patrick Henry to the quarreling delegates of the Continental Congress: *"I am not a Virginian, but an American!"* As he reinforced this concept the 43 delegates sat spellbound. What he was saying was crazy; they knew it was crazy. There was no such thing as an American; there were only Virginians, New Yorkers, etc. To call one's self an American was sheer madness. Yet in this madness and this man "there was contagion." Patrick Henry in this critical moment of history persuaded bickering Colonial delegates to take one step forward together by *identifying* himself with the welfare of delegates from other colonies.

*Third,* you may identify yourself with that which is respectable: religion, home, family, science, freedom, the American way of life, community spirit. There is danger in this. Most speakers do it ineptly and do it too much. They become dreadful bores and earn a low-rating in listenership. Franklin D. Roosevelt did it with a master's hand. On the night before each election he spoke briefly to the American people, but

[6] *A Rhetoric of Motives* (Englewood Cliffs, N. J., Prentice-Hall, Inc., 1950), p. 55.

spoke not one word about politics itself. Instead, he reminded Americans that this was one of the free countries of the world, and that he knew they would keep it free by being vigilant citizens. He closed with a prayer for God's blessing on America. He did not solicit votes. He simply *identified* himself with those who believed in a free America and those who believed in God.

*Fourth,* be vigilant in avoiding unfavorable identifications. In other words, when speaking on education don't identify yourself with prohibition, segregation, civil rights, foreign aid, labor, small business, big business, Democratic Party, Republican Party, the Catholic Church, or a Protestant church. Discuss frankly the differences of opinion on education, but confine yourself to the differences inherent in the subject. Avoid unfavorable identifications not pertinent to the subject.

Student speakers here have a special problem. Thoughtlessly, they often identify the audience as ignorant folk who need enlightenment and uplift, and identify themselves as wise men about to give enlightenment and uplift. More than once from tactless students you will hear these words: "Since you don't know anything about this, I'm going to explain it." And "Did you ever stop to realize . . . ?" (Meaning, "You never did, so now I'm doing it for you.") And "How many of you ever thought about it this way before?" (Meaning, "You've been thinking wrong, and now I'm telling you what's right.")

*Finally,* be vigilant to display the appropriate signs of character that will persuade an audience to trust you. You cannot do this directly. You cannot say bluntly, "I am honest," or "I am a man of good judgment." Yet you must *identify* yourself with honesty and judgment if you are to persuade fully. If members of the audience know you personally, your life has told them about you already and your words while speaking will alter only slightly their willingness to accept you. If you are known only slightly, they will judge you in part by your pronunciation, language, courtesy, general manner, and even by the clothes you wear. They will also judge you by how you handle speech material. "The lady doth protest too much, methinks," said the queen in *Hamlet* when the show was overplayed, and listeners will so judge any speaker who does the same. After the first two full-length speeches you give in class, most other members of the class "will have your number." You will have given it to them. They will know whether you have judgment and the ethics of accurate statement, or whether you fall short, and if so, how short. There is not much that any of you will do about all this, for you cannot long display signs of character if you don't have that character; and character for most of you was established before you entered college. But for those who want to check themselves, and really want to improve, here are the commandments, distilled from the wisdom of centuries:

1. Thou shall not parade thy prejudices.

2. Thou shall not name-call, nor shall thou praise or damn any person or group indiscriminately, but shall rest thy cause on the power of facts.

3. Thou shall not be gullible, nor shall thou pass on to others information that has not been tested for trustworthiness. Let it be said of you, "His evidence can be trusted, for this man readeth suspiciously and falleth not into the trap by the propagandist."

4. Thou shall not pretend to be an expert on all things, but shall know how to cause experts to speak for thy cause.

5. Thou shall not pretend to prove too much, but shall exercise judgment and moderation on how much can be proved and how far the boundary can be moved in any one speech.

## Rest reason and evidence on deep-seated wants and culture patterns

At last we come to the place of reason and argument in persuasion. Do we really use them? Do they play an important part in human behavior? To both questions the answer is yes. Men are not primarily rational beings. They don't think analytically all the time, or even most of the time. But they do try to think analytically under specific conditions of need and on particular pressing problems. In other words, when we get in a jam and must find a way out, we resort to Reason.

*We use Reason, then, to solve our problems, to satisfy our desires, to lift ourselves upward toward higher values of life. We use Reason only as a means of satisfying human needs and wants. In persuasion, therefore, we use Reason to show others how to get what they want, how to reach a goal, how to lift themselves toward an ideal. Hence the maxim that those who persuade must rest Reason and Evidence on deep-seated wants and culture patterns.*

At this point we must pause to pay respect to the concept held by many good people that a speaker must either "appeal to emotion" or "appeal to reason." This concept usually implies that "appeal to emotion" is unethical, that it panders to human weakness, and hence the ideal speaker should "appeal to reason" only. It is a concept that lingers among would-be educated people, even though it came from arm-chair psychology and was disproved by experimental psychologists almost a century ago. Yet this concept persists, and we can expect to hear often in the future that complaint made recently by a well-meaning educator: "You should teach students to appeal to reason instead of appealing to emotions."

People who live in the twentieth century should know that this concept misses the bases of human behavior. It ignores the nature of man.

It ignores the motives that down the centuries have led people to struggle for survival and uplift and enlightenment. Leaders who work on "ticklish human skins" have known all along that they cannot separate persuasion into "appeal to emotion" and "appeal to reason." Long afterwards, experimental psychologists confirmed what leaders through the centuries had known intuitively.

*First,* there is no "either-or." People don't have compartments, with the "intellect" in one compartment and the "emotions" in another. We know how silly it would be to say that a woman must either have "good clothes" or "good sense," for she may have either, neither, or both. We now know it is just as silly to say a speaker must "appeal to reason" or "appeal to emotion."

*Second,* that word "appeal" can be misleading, and often is. If one describes a man walking down the street as "appealing his feet to the sidewalk," you have the right to say he is not using apt language. So with using the word "appeal" in speaking. True, a speaker can use "appeals," but in effective speaking he does not need to, usually does not do so, and often dares not do so. Good speakers, instead, use Logic and Reason to show listeners how to solve a problem, attain a goal, or lift themselves toward an ideal. That's what we mean by saying that speakers should "rest Reason and Evidence on deep-seated Wants and Culture Patterns."

*Finally,* use of the word "emotion" can be misleading. People have emotions, to be sure. But effective speakers usually don't deal with them as such. Rather they deal with wants, motives, hopes, ideals, ambitions, and those habits of society known as culture patterns. Therefore, it is more effective for speakers to think in terms of these human drives with which they must deal: wants, motives, hopes, ideals, ambitions, and culture patterns.

So put aside the myth that you "appeal to reason" or "appeal to emotion" or "appeal" to anything. Give up that notion that man is made up of compartments like the mail boxes in a post office, that Box No. 1 is "Intellect," Box No. 2 is "Emotion," Box No. 199 is "Religious Instinct," and that each box is unlocked with a different key. Recognize that you can't remove a belief with logic alone, that as Elmer Davis once observed, "it hurts more to pull a belief than to pull a tooth," and that when you try to pull a belief there is no intellectual novocaine to be had. Recognize that you cannot even uproot a prejudice with logic, for

> A man convinced against his will
> Is of the same opinion still.

It is, in fact, "easier to smash an atom than a prejudice," and you must usually go around them. Recognize, finally, that it does no good to protest that God should never have created man that way. Be humble, confess that God knew his business, and admit that He expects you to study man's nature, not decry it. From the scientific study of man we find that communication operates through, not one, but *two* transistors in a manner crudely depicted in the diagram below:

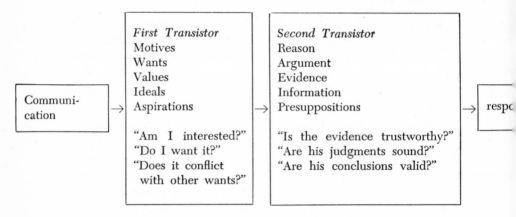

Bertrand Russell stated it precisely:

> If, in the name of Reason, you summon a man to alter his fundamental purpose . . . you will fail, and you will deserve to fail. . . . And you will fail equally if you attack deep-seated prejudices while your argument is still open to question. . . . But if you can prove, by evidence which is convincing to every sane man who takes the trouble to examine it, that you possess a means of facilitating the satisfaction of existing desires, you may hope, with a certain degree of confidence, that men will ultimately believe what you say.[7]

To summarize: We use Reason to solve problems, to satisfy wants. We don't use it to make others change beliefs *per se* or give up their prejudices. Most people use Reason badly. Some can hardly use it at all. Yet it is man's highest intellectual achievement, his instrument for solving problems, his fulcrum for lifting mankind from savagery to civilization. Democracy can survive only when its creative minority uses Reason effectively, and then persuades the multitude to accept that reasoning.

### Know your listeners' prevailing attitudes at the time you speak

In the preceding chapter we discussed the universal wants of all peoples, and the culture patterns of the American people in particular.

[7] *Power: A New Social Analysis* (New York, W. W. Norton & Co., 1938), p. 139.

These are the foundations of behavior, public opinion, and persuasion. But persuasion is not a matter of matching a list of motives to a group of listeners in simple one-to-one relationship. Persuasion is not a matter of saying, "Here is the want," and pressing its button to release the listeners' springs of action. At best a standardized list of motives describes behavior under only a few and simple conditions, whereas in life the conditions of behavior are neither few nor simple. At best a standardized list of motives is not enough. To persuade, one must know *how* these motives operate and *why* in the behavior of the specific people to whom he talks at the moment.

Social scientists now think there is no such thing as a pure single motive for anything. Behind people's acts is a battery of dominant motives, and behind that is another battery of subordinate motives. These motives exist side by side but they don't stay fixed in strength or fixed in arrangement. They change from time to time, group to group, and person to person. If people get excited, angry, or frightened, or hungry one motive can temporarily block another motive entirely. More significant, motives are amplified or diminished by human events. Does the cost of living go up again? Does unemployment increase, or corporation profits fall? Does education inside Russia threaten to surpass ours in quality or quantity? Are you about to get married, to buy a home, or to have a baby? Each of these human events changes the dominant motives in the people affected.

Finally, remember that people's prevailing attitude is largely decided by the group to which they belong. They don't like to be at odds with others in their church, political party, social group, or business group. They want to "belong," to be accepted, to be offered the glad hand of fellowship. Hence they are influenced more by the prevailing group attitude than by their individual motives. The way this operates was illustrated by Willam H. Whyte, Jr., through an informal experiment that anyone can try out on his friends. A prolabor cartoon was clipped from a labor-union magazine, but the label was changed and it was credited to a manufacturing journal. Then it was shown to twenty members of that labor union. The result? Fourteen damned it as antilabor, which, as one said, "makes me want to spit."[8] Do you say that is only labor-union prejudice? Then talk to a professor of languages and literature about public-school education! Or talk to members of a chamber of commerce about income taxes and big government! Most of the members of each group will take an *identical* stand, and give you almost *identical* answers. They stand with their group, and the prevailing group attitude usually becomes the prevailing attitude of each member.

Persuasion hinges on knowing the prevailing attitudes *at the moment you speak*, of the individual or of the group as the case may be. It hinges

[8] *Is Anybody Listening?* (New York, Simon and Schuster, 1952), p. 22.

on knowing when a subordinate motive becomes dominant, and when a dominant motive fades into subordination.

A few examples will serve. In 1858 Abraham Lincoln argued the startling proposition that, " 'A house divided against itself cannot stand.' I believe this government cannot endure permanently half slave and half free." Some friends had advised him against using this argument; they said it would cost him the election as senator that year. He overruled their advice and did it anyway. He lost the election as senator in 1858, and seemingly that was one of the reasons. But he was elected President in 1860 and certainly his startling proposition in 1858 was one of the reasons. Lincoln had sensed the coming prevailing attitude of the majority of the North, and based his argument on it.

In 1936 dictators around the world were rattling their swords: Mussolini in Italy, Hitler in Germany, Stalin in Russia, and the war lords in Japan. In the face of this, the prevailing attitude in America was "Let's be isolated." No speaker could ignore this prevailing attitude, and no national spokesman could attack it head-on. Franklin D. Roosevelt, therefore, could not argue that America must no longer be isolated. Instead he talked about people in other lands who had "grown too weary to carry on the fight," had "sold their freedom for the illusion of a living," and challenged Americans to make democracy work at home so it might "revive it in those parts of the world where it had died." All of this he wrapped up in one phrase that people could remember: *"This generation of Americans has a rendezvous with destiny."* Now most Americans in the 1930's did not want a rendezvous with destiny. They just wanted jobs, and job security. But in that "rendezvous" idea was something of old Thomas Paine's "These are the times that try men's souls." It stirred a dormant sense of greatness, and when the chips went down with the bombing of Pearl Harbor in 1941, that "rendezvous with destiny" became the prevailing American attitude. Roosevelt had avoided attacking the prevailing attitude of isolation, and had instead cultivated a subordinate attitude until time and events made it dominant.

In contrast, at the height of his popularity, Roosevelt attacked the Supreme Court for obstructing what he called social justice. He was defeated in both houses of Congress, and his action was disapproved in every public opinion poll. Why? The prevailing attitude of Americans was that the courts should be beyond attack from other branches of government.

As a final example, consider the prevailing attitude of people who attend church on the Sabbath. Through the week they have been concerned with material problems: work, food, paying bills, and cleaning house. On the Sabbath they want to escape these material things. They want a sermon that will light up moral problems that disturb them, will quicken their heart and conscience, ease their tensions, renew their faith, restore their hopes. They want to be lifted to that plane where man does not live by bread alone. Their prevailing attitude on the Sabbath is not their prevailing attitude on work days.

## Use indirect methods as well as direct

There are two methods of persuasion, the Direct and the Indirect. The Direct Method attacks the issue head-on. The Indirect Method takes the roundabout approach. Thus the Direct Method would show the need for old-age pensions; and the Indirect—without arguing need—tells the story of an aged couple on relief. The Direct Method would present the proposition: "The Irish are a noble people." The Indirect Method would say: "Let us see the Irish at work and play, hear the songs they sing and the deeds they do."

The Indirect Method is generally more effective than the Direct. The reason is fairly obvious. If a listener does not like the speaker's viewpoint, with the Direct Method he assumes a mental set against it. ("I don't like the Irish; in my city they win the elections and hold the city jobs.") Now when a person has said "No," all his pride and self-respect demands that he stand by it. Even when he later feels he was wrong, he yields slowly and reluctantly, for pride is a precious motive. Thus pride and the mental set may prevent persuasion. But the Indirect approach avoids this. The listener's preconceptions are not on guard, and the speaker's viewpoint gets a fair hearing.

James A. Winans' story of the farmer's hog shows the use of the Indirect Method at its best:

> Dr. Wiley tells a story of a member of a certain Middle West legislature who sought an appropriation of $100,000 for the protection of public health; but could secure only $5,000. One morning he put upon the desk of each legislator before the opening of the session, a fable which ran something like this: A sick mother with a baby is told by a physician that she has tuberculosis and that she should seek a higher altitude. Lack of means prevents her going. She applies to the government and is told that not a dollar is available to save the mother and her child from death. At the same time a farmer observes that one of his hogs has cholera symptoms. He sends a telegram, collect, to the government. An inspector comes next day, treats the hog with serum and cures it. Moral: Be a hog!
>
> The $100,000 appropriation was promptly granted.[9]

The Indirect Method, however, has limitations. In the first place, the speaker who overuses it can get the reputation of deliberately looking in one direction while walking toward another. ("That man won't look you in the eye with an argument; he sneaks up on you.") Next, the In-

[9] James A. Winans, *Public Speaking* (New York, Appleton-Century-Crofts, Inc., 1915), p. 209.

direct Method cannot treat a subject *comprehensively*—explore all phases
and answer questions that thinking people will need answered. At best,
it is either a hit-and-run method (as in the "Be-a-hog" argument), or is a
longer treatment that hovers near the proposition yet never comes to
grips with it. (Telling the story of an aged couple on relief would be an
example. Such a story would present vividly the need, but would not
explain where the money is to come from, or how to prevent malingering,
etc.)

Students should be warned not to confuse the Indirect Method with
that common inept one known to the trade as the Barbed-Wire-Entanglement method. The Barbed-Wire-Entanglement method consists of crawl-
ing painfully through several subjects that the speaker is *not* going to
discuss before coming to the true one. Here is an example:

| | |
|---|---|
| *Barbed wire; first row* | In 1787 our forefathers framed the Constitution which set up the government under which we live. Under this Constitution a federal government was created and the American people were guaranteed freedom of speech, press, and religious worship. |
| *Barbed wire; second row* | Under this Constitution the American people have survived many crises. The first was external. Would nations of the old world—Spain, France, England—hem us down on the Atlantic seaboard, or would we be free to expand westward to the Pacific? That crisis was settled during the first half of the nineteenth century. The second crisis was internal. Would the U.S. become one nation or two? That crisis was was settled in 1865, during the second half of the nineteenth century. |
| *The break-through! Here's the subject!* | But none of these are problems that I want to discuss today. I want instead to talk with you about another American problem, the problem of American art. What tastes in art have the American people developed since the founding of this government? What have been the crises in art faced by people of artistic tastes? |

Of the two methods, Direct and Indirect, the Direct is the normal
to-be-expected method. The Indirect has limitations, yet within these
limitations it can be more effective than the other. A skillful speaker will
learn to use both.

## For long-run cultivation of attitudes, remember that organized information usually is more effective than attempts at immediate persuasion

A speech seldom changes people suddenly. Its influence is slow, like
watering and cultivating a garden. *In this slow changing of opinion, presenting organized information is generally more effective than attempts at*

*quick persuasion. Give the listeners truthworthy facts, and in time the facts will change their attitudes.*

This is known as the "sleeper" effect in persuasion. It is a new discovery, made by the investigators of mass communication after the invention of radio. It has compelled even the advertisers to adopt a new axiom: "The more you tell, the more you sell." The investigators are not yet able fully to account for it. But there are plausible reasons. First, we are suspicious of many speakers—members of an opposing political party, a competing business or labor group, a rival social group—and we assume a mental set against such speaker's ideas. Our attitude is, "I don't quite trust you; therefore, I don't trust your ideas." Now what happens when such a speaker does not present "ideas" *per se?* What happens when instead he presents *carefully organized information,* tested information with facts-as-they-really-are instead of half-facts or selected-facts-with-omissions that mislead? The listener, of course, is still hostile, but the facts hit him in the mind anyhow. Weeks later, the facts have sunk in, are buried and forgotten. But in the sinking they have done their work.

Next, when a listener is given truthworthy and pertinent information, it has much the same effect as water on a plant. It sinks in and is lost from sight. It mingles with the water that fell last week. It will mingle with the water that is to fall next week. In the case of a speech, the information makes up part of the total experience of the listener. The new facts blend with the old, and the sum of the whole influences beliefs and attitudes.

Finally, after the facts sink in and disappear, often long after, comes the harvest. *New attitudes and opinions, based on these and other forgotten facts, tend to emerge. These are known as "generalizations beyond the evidence," and they are profoundly important in determining what people think.*[10]

A large amount of persuasion, then, does not come from persuasion *per se,* but from speeches of information that influence the listener's attitudes and beliefs during the weeks and months after the information has sunk in and been forgotten.

This "sleeper" effect may have been suspected by early writers on rhetoric, but they dared not boldly say so, and none suspected its potency. Yet here and there were scattered references, as John Morley's assessing the effect of Richard Cobden's speaking: "He produced that singular and profound effect which is perceived . . . when a speaker leaves party recriminations, abstract argument, and commonplaces of sentiment, in

---

[10] Wilbur Schramm, "Information Theory and Mass Communication," *Journalism Quarterly,* XXXII (Spring, 1955), No. 2, 131-146; Joseph T. Klapper's summary in Wilbur Schramm, *The Process and Effect of Mass Communication* (Urbana, University of Illinois Press, 1954), pp. 296-299; C. I. Hovland, A. A. Lumsdaine, and F. D. Sheffield, *Experiments on Mass Communication* (Princeton, Princeton University Press, 1949), especially pp. 192-200. The latter volume presents the effects on soldiers of facts and attitudes after five-day and nine-week intervals.

order to inform his hearers of telling facts."[11] The earliest scientific studies of public opinion confirmed this "singular and profound effect . . . of telling facts" to a degree that even Morley did not suspect. William Lydgate, after carefully examining the first fifteen years of polltaking, found that the average voter's mistake as judged by time stemmed generally from lack of information, not lack of intelligence or judgment, and that when the public has the information it moves on to form the right decisions *two years ahead of Congress*. Later research repeatedly confirmed this.[12] This reaffirms the axiom of Raymond Clapper: "Never overestimate the people's knowledge, nor underestimate their intelligence." The sum of the whole is that a lot of people now trying to influence other people need to change their methods radically, give up their attempts to inject ready-made doctrines, turn off the propaganda pressure, and resort to cultivating opinions with telling facts.

## *To reaffirm old attitudes, vitalize human hopes, ideals, desires, and values*

So far we have been discussing, too largely perhaps, speechmaking that changes belief and action. Yet a large amount of speechmaking is not for this purpose at all, but is to *reaffirm old attitudes*. There are times when human beings, being human, need be told to "Do your duty." At other times they need to hear the call to "Renew your faith," or "Strengthen your determination." And still again they need to be inspired to "Rededicate yourselves," or simply to hear the voice of a leader who can say, "Come unto me, ye who are weary and heavy laden, and I will give you rest."

In times of crisis, when people are driven to defend themselves by force, they must be told (though they believe it already) that their cause is just, and that right increases their might, "for who will defend our cause if we have no faith in it ourselves?" In placid times, they need to be aroused from lethargy, lest their virtues decay and the spirit that made them great be lost.

Never underestimate the power of sentiments and ideals. At Gettysburg in 1863 a tall gaunt man spoke 266 words beginning with, "Four score and seven years ago. . . ." Lincoln's words are now part of the nation's heritage. So long as the English language lives, its peoples will remember the words of Sir Winston Churchill: "I have nothing to offer but blood, toil,

---

[11] *Life of Richard Cobden* (Boston, Roberts Brothers, 1881), p. 119.

[12] William A. Lydgate, *What Our People Think* (New York, Thomas Y. Crowell Co., 1944), Chapter 1 on "The People, Yes." George Gallup, "The Changing Climate for Public Opinion Research," *The Public Opinion Quarterly* XXI (Spring, 1957), No. 1, pp. 26-27.

tears, and sweat.—Never in the field of human conflict was so much owed by so many to so few.—We shall fight on the beaches, we shall fight in the fields and in the streets, we shall fight in the hills; we shall never surrender." At a critical moment these words became one of the resources of the British Empire, along with her ships and tanks, guns and planes.

Of Emerson, whose words often roused contented intellectuals, James Russell Lowell testified that:

> There was a kind of undertow in that rich baritone of his that sweeps our minds from their foothold into deeper waters with a drift that we cannot and would not resist. . . . Behind each word we divine the force of a noble character, the weight of a large capital of thinking and being. We do not go to hear what Emerson says so much as to hear Emerson. . . . If asked what was left? what we carried home? . . . we might have asked in return what one brought away from a symphony of Beethoven?

Arnold J. Toynbee, after examining all of the civilizations both past and present, concludes that perhaps the greatest single force in sustaining any civilization is the spirit of its people. He points out that old civilizations have declined at the exact moment its people were improving techniques, and that civilizations have risen during times when techniques remained static. The vitality of any civilization, he concludes, is more closely related to the spirit and morale of its people than to its command over its physical environment.[13] Not always is Toynbee valid in his philosophy of history, but this conclusion is valid. One of the constant purposes of public address, therefore, is and must be to revitalize convictions, hopes, sentiments, and enthusiasms—to give them fresh meaning and renewed force.

In such speaking, of course, you cannot use certain forms of support. First, you cannot use mere facts, figures, and formal proof; for a people's faith is not renewed, nor are their hopes uplifted, by syllogisms, logarithms, and binomial equations.

Further, you cannot use argument; for how would you *prove* that patriotism is noble, and if you did, whose pulse would be quickened? Said Oliver Wendell Holmes, Jr., in one of his most brilliant addresses:

> I cannot argue a man into a desire. If he says to me, Why should I wish to know the secrets of philosophy? Why seek to decipher the hidden laws of creation that are graven upon the tablets of the rocks, or to unravel the history of civilization. . . ? I cannot answer him; or at least my answer is as little worth making for any effect it will have. . . . You must begin by wanting to. But although desire cannot be imparted by argument, it can be by contagion. Feeling begets feeling, and great feeling begets great feeling.[14]

[13] *A Study of History* (New York, Oxford University Press, 1947), pp. 254, 255-267, 290, 555-557.
[14] Address to the GAR, Keene, N. H., 1884; W. N. Brigance, *Classified Speech Models* (New York, Appleton-Century-Crofts, Inc., 1928), p. 337.

The methods of vitalizing hopes and ideals are these:

1. *Revive common ideals, common history, and common memory of the past.* This is done by making the speech fragrant with the memories of yesterday. It may paint the picture of battlefields: Lexington, Yorktown, Gettysburg, Iwo Jima. It may call the roll of great names and great deeds. Or it may picture great ideals, as done by Frank Pace, Jr., in speaking on "Religion and American Life":

> America has always been the land of promise. When the second and third and fourth waves of immigration swept over this country, they came to the Golden Land, and they sought the pot of gold at the end of the rainbow. To some, the pot of gold was a material pot of gold, to be earned by sweat, by perseverance, by ambition, by keenness of mind, by the capacity to better the other fellow. To others it was a spiritual pot of gold because here was the place where the free mind and the free heart were allowed full scope of operation. But to all it was a land of promise. . . .
>
> We've grown since those early days when this nation was young and just starting, but today America is still the land of promise. I've traveled in the last six months to the Far East and I've traveled to South America. You have only to see the face of the boy—or the girl—who says to you, in his own language, "One day I hope to come to America." . . .
>
> I remember during the period of the Korean War . . . when I was given the difficult and challenging assignment of awarding the Medal of Honor—in most cases posthumously—I thought what a strange alchemy it was that took a Tennessee farm boy, a New York boy from the streets, a rancher from Montana, and brought out in him such acts of heroic valor. It was then that I knew that we, as a nation, inherently had greatness that could come only from dependence on God.[15]

2. *Reaffirm your faith, hope, and determination in a way that listeners will want to share them.* This uses the Indirect Method of persuasion. Instead of urging listeners to "Renew your faith," it says, "This I have seen, this I believe, and in this faith will I live." Herbert Hoover, well past 80 years of age, used this method in speaking to American manufacturers:

> The minds of Americans are today greatly troubled. We have . . . domestic shortcomings. . . . Troubles beset us from abroad. . . .
>
> I have lived a long life, and I have seen our country exert its strengths to overcome as great dangers as those which beset us today. . . .
>
> I have witnessed our people deny themselves to save the world, including our enemies, from the inevitable and gigantic famines which followed two of these wars. And among them we saved the lives of 15,000,000 Russians, then under the Communistic Government, from their terrible famine in 1922-1923. And there is no less humanity in the American heart today.
>
> Within my years I have seen our institutions of higher learning expand until today they turn out more trained men and women each year than all of the rest of the world combined.

[15] *Vital Speeches*, XXIV (July 1, 1958), No. 18, pp. 555-556.

In my adult lifetime I have passed through several economic recessions and two great economic depressions which swept over our country. Each time we came out economically stronger than ever before. . . .

I have watched our countrymen rise and fight two world wars to victory in defense of our country. The skill of our military leaders, the courage of our men, and the willingness of our people to make sacrifices are no less today than then. . . .

And from whence comes this strength? It lies in freedom of men's initiative and the rewards of their efforts. It comes from our devotion to liberty and religious faith.[16]

3. *Make your lines of thought vivid by illustration, specific instance, comparison, and suspense.* As we have seen, you cannot use formal "evidence" or "argument" or "proof," in this type of speaking, for they deal largely in material values and not with hopes and sentiments. Nor can you rely on *assertion* only, for assertion cannot long hold attention. Therefore, you must find vivid forms of support outside these areas. This leads us straight to those forms always required for vividness and inspiration: illustration, specific instance, comparison, suspense, and their related forms. Harry Emerson Fosdick, for example, used four illustrations in support of his topic that "Great people live greatly in times of crisis," and increased the vividness of these illustrations by quoting one poem, using five direct questions, and citing 15 specific names of persons and places:

In a commencement address delivered by Douglas Freeman, author of the great life of Robert E. Lee, he described what some people had done amid the horror of their days to keep the light of beauty and of goodness burning for the souls of men to return to. When did Wordsworth write some of his greatest poetry? When Napoleon was collecting at Boulogne the armada for his planned assault on the English coast at Dover. When did Beethoven write the *Fifth Symphony?* The first year of the Peninsular War, with Napoleon's shadow dark over Europe. When did Beethoven finish that glorious *Seventh Symphony?* When Napoleon was assembling his army on the line of the Niemen River for his assault on Russia. Everybody knows John Keats' immortal sonnet, "On First Looking Into Chapman's Homer";

> Then felt I like some watcher of the skies
> When a new planet swims into his ken.

When did Keats write that? The summer that Waterloo was fought.

What am I pleading for—an ivory tower to escape from the appalling facts? No! Such souls as these never found in this life an ivory tower of escape, but tension—terrific tension—between the brutal and the beautiful, the evil and the good, the actual and the possible, the temporal and the eternal; and they refused to escape that tension by surrendering the higher realm.[17]

---

[16] *Vital Speeches*, XXIV (December 15, 1957), No. 5, pp. 154-155.
[17] *Living Under Tension* (New York, Harper & Brothers, 1941), pp. 4-5.

## Assignments

ON THE USE AND INFLUENCE OF MASS COMMUNICATION

1. Make a report on the amount, nature, and seeming effect of attempts to influence public opinion by some particular group or organization:

   a. Start with the 5-step summary of research given in this chapter (pages 145-146). Consult also, if you wish, any other studies on mass communication and public opinion including those listed in footnotes 2 and 3.

   b. Using this knowledge as a basis, analyze the attempts to influence public opinion used by your newspaper, or by news magazines like *Time, Newsweek,* and *U.S. News & World Report.* Each of these magazines, for example, has its own presuppositions, and in some cases outright prejudices, on politics, segregation, public-school education, etc. If you want to read these magazines, yet remain intellectually free, you must learn the bias of each.

   c. Make a list of the various channels you have observed being used by the Democratic Party, Republican Party, AFL-CIO, United States Chamber of Commerce, Farm Bureau, or National Education Association. Rate the effectiveness of its efforts, and consider how they might be improved. Consider also the ethical level of these methods.

ON GETTING AND HOLDING ATTENTION

2. From *Vital Speeches* or other sources study the introduction to six speeches. Imagine yourself sitting in each audience, and decide whether the introduction would really get your attention if effectively spoken. Don't be discouraged if all of these introductions seem to fail. Remember that most speeches today (though conspicuously not all) are given by people who may be experts on their subject, but who have never learned how to speak in public.

3. Explain the methods used to get and hold attention found in one of the speeches printed in the back of this book.

4. Rework your last speech, using new supporting material that better holds attention, and by making the speech more vivid throughout.

ON RESTING REASON AND EVIDENCE ON WANTS AND CULTURE PATTERNS

5. Read one of the following historically important speeches, and determine the extent to which it rests reason and evidence on basic wants and culture patterns. That is, (a) outline its main lines of thought and decide whether basically they are supported by reason and evidence, (b) determine what problem the speaker was trying to solve, and which basic wants or culture patterns would be satisfied by accepting the speaker's solution. Each of these speeches, of course, may be found in many library sources, but below one source is listed for each:

   a. Franklin D. Roosevelt, "We Have Nothing to Fear But Fear," (First Inaugural) *Public Papers & Addresses of F. D. Roosevelt,* II, 11-16.

*b.* Woodrow Wilson, "For Declaration of War Against Germany," *Selected Literary and Political Papers of Woodrow Wilson,* II, 234-247.

*c.* Booker T. Washington, "At the Atlanta Exposition," Booker T. Washington, *Up From Slavery,* Chapter 14.

*d.* Henry W. Grady, "The New South," W. N. Brigance, *Classified Speech Models,* pp. 287-297.

*e.* Henry Ward Beecher, "Liverpool Address," W. N. Brigance, *Classified Speech Models,* pp. 40-65.

*f.* Abraham Lincoln, "Cooper Institute Address," J. M. O'Neill, *Models of Speech Composition,* pp. 341-357.

6. Prepare and deliver a persuasive speech in which you make the most effective possible use of the principles of persuasion. First, choose the subject and gather the speech material, then proceed as follows:

*a.* Draft the purpose-sentence carefully so that it is impelling, i.e., rests on the strongest available wants or culture patterns.

*b.* Choose main heads that not only will develop the purpose-sentence logically, but will also reinforce the impelling want or culture pattern on which the purpose-sentence rests. Phrase these heads so they are quickly understood, and use as few as possible. Other things being equal, three are better than four, and two are better than three.

*c.* Develop these heads with compelling reason, evidence, and supporting materials.

ON USING THE INDIRECT METHOD OF PERSUASION

7. Prepare and deliver a 1-minute speech using the *indirect* ("Be-a-Hog") method of persuasion.

ON THE EFFECT OF INFORMATION FOR LONG-RUN CULTIVATION OF ATTITUDES

8. Write down the basic changes of *attitude,* as well as you can now recall them, that you have experienced during the past one or two years toward one of the following subjects *as a result of learning new information about it in a college course*: Poetry, modern art, labor problems, industrial management, England, Russia, China, physics, biology, psychology, religion, or any other. Discuss the implications of this for persuasion.

9. Prepare and deliver a speech of information, which, *because* of the information, will influence the listeners' attitude toward the subject. You must, of course, know enough about the subject to speak with adequate authority.

ON REAFFIRMING OLD ATTITUDES

10. Report on the most inspiring speech you ever heard. Explain both *what* the speaker said that made it inspiring, and *how* he said it.

11. Prepare and deliver a speech to reaffirm old attitudes, in which you use the principles set forth in this chapter. Possible subjects for such a speech would be:

This is a great university

Remember the home, and keep it a home

"Faith of our fathers, living still, we will be true to thee till death."

CHAPTER

# ⁕ 8 ⁕

# The Seven Lamps of Planning a Speech

EVEN AFTER you have studied the foundations set forth in the two preceding chapters you are a little like the man who took that correspondence course in aviation. "He knew all about flying, but he couldn't fly."

This chapter is on how-to-do-it. As John Ruskin lighted the seven lamps of architecture and Goldwin Smith lighted the seven lamps of fiction, so we here light the seven lamps of speechmaking. Each lamp lights one step of the stairway. The seven light up everything in this book on persuasion, not only in chapters that have gone before but in those to follow after (for you are now far enough along to understand something about things to come). *They are set forth here in a system of preparing the speech.* Therefore, *every* time you prepare a speech open the book to this chapter and keep these Seven Lamps visible for reference, until using them becomes habitual.

### Lamp One: *Focus on a definite response that you can win from your audience*

This step has two parts. The first is "focus on a definite response," which already has been discussed briefly (pages 47-48) and will be further discussed in detail (pages 188-191). This means focussing *exactly* on what you want, instead of a hazy focus on the whole universe.

The second part belongs to a higher order: focus on a response "*that you can win from your audience.*" Don't try the impossible. Ask yourself, first: Why haven't they already done what I urge? Habit? Inertia? Lack of information? Lack of interest? Lack of need? Conflicting wants or culture patterns? Then ask: *How far can I lead them in my direction?*

You can lead only so far in one speech, and no farther. If you try to push listeners too far, they will not merely balk but back up.

The following checklist will serve as a guide:

1. *Am I attempting a response that runs headlong into their wants or culture patterns?* (You can't get it. You can only discredit yourself for having bad judgment. A culture pattern or prevailing want must be approached obliquely with finesse, not head-on.)

2. *Am I asking for too much?* (College students can't be persuaded to "Landscape your homes artistically," but can be persuaded to take a favorable attitude toward the idea. Elderly people won't become missionaries, but can be persuaded to give money to carry on the work of missions. Labor groups can't be converted into pro-management groups, but can be persuaded that co-operating is more profitable than fighting.)

3. *Am I trying to use the audience as a cat's paw?* (You can't win a response unless it meets the audience's need, not yours.)

4. *Am I asking for something the audience "ought to do if they would only be reasonable about it"?* (There is no such thing. First, remember that the concept of Logical Man is a myth, and if you insist on believing the myth all you will get is a bloody nose. Second, don't confuse man's *nonlogical* behavior with *illogic,* for they aren't the same thing. Third, if people seem irrational it's simply because you have not discovered the prevailing wants and culture patterns on which their attitudes are based. Especially perhaps, you have mistaken the surface reasons for the real cause.)

## Lamp Two: *Phrase this response into an impelling proposition*

What makes a proposition impelling? From Chapter 5 we know that a proposition becomes impelling if it *satisfies a prevailing want or reinforces a culture pattern.* (Wants, of course, include needs, hopes, aspirations, ideals.) Remember that you cannot argue a man into a want; many people never learn this and always wonder why they are being clipped from behind. You must start with prevailing wants and culture patterns, then (1) quicken them and make them stronger, (2) show how to attain them, i.e. solve a problem, get out of a difficulty, or make progress toward it. Or (3) replace one want by another. Thus people who want Security might be challenged to Adventure (difficult but possible within limits). People who want Property can be persuaded to give it away because of other wants: Reputation, Sympathy, Competition and Rivalry, Conformity, Fear, Reverence, and Worship.

Therefore, set down the following as a convenient working definition of persuasion:

1. *If the purpose is to stimulate, to inspire, to create morale, or to intensify ideals—persuasion is attained by vitalizing old desires, ideals, or culture patterns.*

2. *If the purpose is to secure acceptance of new beliefs, development of new attitudes, or adoption of new courses of action—persuasion is attained by substituting new desires, ideals, or culture patterns in place of old ones.*

Whether men shall pursue an immediate want or a remote one, whether they accept satisfaction of a high idealistic desire or a low material one, depends, and always will depend, in a large measure on how impellingly these alternatives are presented to them by leaders, thinkers, writers, and speakers.

A speech proposition, therefore, ought to be stated in terms that impel the audience to accept it. Here we must pause to insert a warning. Before any proposition can be impelling it must be clear, and before it can be clear it must be *understood*. Said Sir Winston Churchill of his having to stay in one grade for three years while in a British public school: "But I was taught English. Thus I got into my bones the essential structure of the ordinary English sentence—which is a noble thing." A proposition needs be put in an ordinary English sentence, whose essential structure "is a noble thing." But if it crawls in backwards like a crab, or circles around in periphrases instead of going straight to the point, or conceals the idea under woolly abstract words—it can's be impelling because it can't be understood. Here is an example of a proposition that can't be impelling because it's foggy:

> It is important that students understand that in college they cannot get the fullest education possible until they have acquired the ability to listen in a manner which is efficient.

It needs straightaway English like this:

> You can't get a full college education unless you learn to listen efficiently.

Being understood, of course, is not enough; that merely clears the way. The real test is whether the proposition is stated in terms that will impel the audience to accept it. Those listed below illustrate both the poor and the good:

UNIMPELLING

1. It's up to you to learn to read better. ["Up to you" is trite; don't use it. Also, it rests the proposition on Duty, an overworked want.]

IMPELLING

1. The big switch today in the business world is from brawn jobs to brain jobs, which are open only to people who can *read*. [The proposition now rests on, not on Duty, but on Security and Recognition.]

UNIMPELLING

2. I want to tell you about art. [*You want to, eh? That means you want listeners for a cat's paw. Go talk to yourself!*]

3. It's up to us to do our duty and save ourselves from socialism. [(a) "Up to us" is still trite. (b) "Save ourselves from socialism," is like crying "wolf! wolf!"; it has been overworked in the past by speakers who argued that woman suffrage, parcel post, income tax and Federal Reserve Banks would destroy us because they were socialistic; most people now are amused but not alarmed when a speaker cries "socialism." (c) Duty is an overworked want; use it skillfully or don't use it at all. (d) Beware of that conjunction "and" in a proposition; usually it's a sign of a two-headed monstrosity; you want *one* response, not two.]

IMPELLING

2. From art you can learn which clothes will make you look fatter or thinner, taller or shorter, more poised or less poised. [The proposition now rests on Curiosity and Artistic Tastes, with Recognition and Sex Attraction not far behind.]

3. Unfair railroad regulation today may force the railroads so deeply into debt that the U. S. government 25 years hence will be compelled to take over the railroads outright as a means of national defense. [Most people want government regulation, but not government ownership. This proposition now rests on Fair Play to the railroads plus the culture pattern of Political Democracy.]

## Lamp Three: *Support this proposition with main heads that touch the "springs of response" in the audience*

Main heads are the pillars that support the proposition. Every speech has them. Here we are concerned with their *choice* and *wording*. First, beware of Mother Hubbard main heads that cover all, but reveal nothing. Here is an example:

I. The causes of the problem are complex.
II. There are a number of things we can do.

What's the speaker talking about: The Russians? High cost of education? Or feeding hogs? Who knows? Nobody. Not even the speaker, for if he did he would say so.

Second, beware of foggy main heads. Young speakers are like Bishop Gerald Kennedy's preacher who was "divinely dull." Someone asked what he meant by "divinely dull," and Kennedy replied, "No man could be that dull naturally. He *had* to have divine aid." Some students seem to feel that if by divine aid they can get a sentence involved enough, they somehow have produced a main head. All they have really done is to make it foggy. Here is a cherished example from the files, written by a student as the main heads of Thomas Paine's *The Crisis*:

> I. Because of repeated disasters the American patriots are now abandoning hope and are beginning to think that maybe we should not have undertaken such an advanced step as to declare that we are an independent nation.

> II. But it is important that these patriots continue to believe that the Divine Providence will not forsake us and will not give help to the King of Britain against us.

Thomas Paine himself used short straight speech:

> I. These are the times that try men's souls.

> II. But God has not given us up, nor can the King of Britain look to heaven for help against us.

Third, select main heads that, when stated clearly, will touch off the listeners' "springs of response." Consider the two sets of main heads below, one that fails to meet the test and the other that does the job:

| POOR | GOOD |
|---|---|
| I | I |
| I. Speech courses are practical. | I. After college you can't escape having to give speeches in public. |
| II. They are also sound in principle. | II. So learn all you can in college about speechmaking, then keep on learning more after you get out. |
| ["Practical" and "sound in principle" touch off no springs of response.] | [These heads touch off springs of response because they rest on Recognition, Reputation, Self-respect and Pride, with a measure of Security also.] |
| II | II |
| I. Bernard Shaw's early failure. | I. For nearly 20 years every play Bernard Shaw wrote was too poor to be produced or published. |
| II. His later successes. | II. Yet he later became the greatest English-speaking playwright since Shakespeare. |
| [These are incomplete phrases, not main heads. A speaker who | |

| POOR | GOOD |
|------|------|
| *knew* what his main heads were might use such phrases, but they would simply continue the confusion of one who had not thought himself clear.] | [These heads would enable the speaker to show the causes of Shaw's early failure and later success. They rest on Artistic Tastes plus Curiosity.] |

## Lamp Four: *Arrange these main heads in the order most effective for your audience*

A speech must fit each audience, and each audience is a special group alive and warm with interests, wants, prejudices, habits, and culture patterns. Ergo, where do you start, and in which order do you unroll a speech?

This question of order has taunted the experts since the day of Corax in 460 B.C. Some of them, to be sure, wrote positively about it, but their very vehemence testified to lack of evidence. School-boy debaters and U. S. Presidents alike still ponder whether to save the "best" argument for the end of the speech or to lead off with it. Finally, in the 1920's social science had advanced to the point where it was possible to investigate order scientifically. As a result, the confusion at first was worse than ever, for one experiment would show that speakers should lead with their strongest topic, and another that they should hold back the strongest until last!

At last, however, tentative conclusions have begun to emerge. The following seems to be the best order of arrangement. But there is yet no substitute for a speaker studying the audience *feedback* (see pages 83-84) while presenting disagreeable topics:

1. When you present *contradictory* information in a speech, the items presented *first will have more effect* than those presented later.

2. When you present information on how to satisfy a need, the following is the best order:

I. Motivate it; show that the need is real.

II. Give the information on how to satisfy the need.

If you reverse this order, you will reduce the response, and even three months later the response will still be reduced in the listener's mind.

3. If the audience is only mildly interested in the topic, *start with the topic that interests them most*. Otherwise, many will switch off attention and only halfway listen; others won't listen at all. Likewise, if you have a topic *highly desirable* to listeners (i.e. based on their prevailing motives), put it *first*. If you reverse the order and save the desirable topic

until last, listeners not only change opinion less, but also remember less about the less desirable topic.

4. If you discuss pro and con arguments on any topic, *put the pro arguments first*. When the pro arguments are put first and the con arguments come later, the listener seldom switches from pro to con. But when the con arguments are put first listeners commonly will resist accepting the pro arguments.[1]

For detailed discussion on arranging main heads, see pages 217-227.

## Lamp Five: *Develop each main head according to the audience's attitude toward it*

For convenience, we shall recognize four levels of attitudes:

1. *Is the audience actively favorable?* Then develop the topic by the IMPRESSIVE OR DYNAMIC METHOD. This consists of telling people what they already know—old stories, old examples, old ideas. People like to relive the past, to think romantically of glorious days that are "past and gone." College graduates return to the campus after many years. Societies meet to renew old memories. Nations commemorate their great moments of the past:

> No meetings can compare with those
>    Reunions that we hold
> To live again in memories
>    Those moments made of gold
>
> They are the bonds of kindred souls
>    That tie around the heart
> And seal the lasting promise that
>    Old friends will never part.

In doing this you don't try to *prove* what listeners believe already. You revive cherished memories. You vitalize them, give them richer meanings. The following forms of support will be especially effective:

| | |
|---|---|
| Illustrations | Narration |
| Specific Instances | Suspense and Climax |
| Comparisons | Direct Quotation |

2. *Is the audience indifferent?* Then use the MOTIVATIVE METHOD to show why the topic is important. Is it a problem dimly seen that soon will become acute? Is it a neglected problem about to catch listeners unawares? Is it a once-settled problem that now returns to life? Is it an unpleasant problem that we want to forget and Let George Do It?

[1] Research on order is found in almost a hundred books and magazine reports on research. The best summary is found in Carl I. Hovland (ed.), *The Order of Presentation in Persuasion* (New Haven, Yale University Press, 1957).

Suggested modes of development are these:

*Motivate it* by showing the involved wants, needs, hopes, and ideals. Possible forms of support for this are:

| | |
|---|---|
| Facts and Figures | Explanation |
| Testimony | Restatement |

*Vitalize it* by making the ideas vivid. For this the following are especially effective:

| | |
|---|---|
| Illustrations | Narration |
| Specific Instances | Suspense and Climax |
| Comparisons | Direct Quotation |

3. *Is the audience doubtful or uninformed?* Then develop the topic by the INSTRUCTIVE METHOD. You present interesting information, specific information, trustworthy information, organized information.

Here is a vital purpose of speechmaking. Modern man has a mind littered with promiscuous information. Much of it is simplified and predigested, and was served to him in catchwords to further the interests of some organized group. Much of it is shallow and unconnected with any thought system. Much of it is inaccurate. He has been bombarded by speakers who claim to present "the facts," but their "facts" turn out to be, not facts, but *conclusions* that support the speaker's propaganda purpose. People need to have speakers make sense out of what is already in their minds by *organizing* it, showing what is *trustworthy*, and what has *meaning*. As Matthew Arnold said, we don't change our minds as a result of logic and refutation, but as *"we learn more, the ground gently shifts beneath us, and we no longer look at things as we formerly did."*

In presenting such information, a speaker will not state his conclusions at the start, as if to say: "I'm going to prove that these are the conclusions, and that those who doubt it are stool pigeons." A good speaker does not talk that way because he does not think that way. He asks the listeners to go over the ground with him: "What are the facts on this question?" Then when they've searched for the facts, sifted the false from the true, the pertinent from the irrelevant, he asks listeners to go with him on the next leg: "What caused it to happen?" Again, he inquires and searches out, but does not set it forth in a manner that says: "Here's your answer; I've wrapped it in a package for you."

Especially useful are the following modes of support:

| | |
|---|---|
| Defining the terms | Illustrations |
| Explanation | Specific Instances |
| Testimony | Comparisons |
| Repetition and Restatement | Narration |
| Facts and Figures | Concrete Language |

4. *Is the audience opposed?* "Why try such a thing?" someone will say. "Who ever heard of anyone changing his mind because of a speech?" Well, people *do* change their minds in this changing world, and they are constantly making shifts of attitude. But they don't change them from hearing bull-headed argument. Thomas Jefferson was right when he said, "No one will ever change his mind on account of a mere argument" and he was justified in his intense dislike of personal arguments. With prophetic wisdom (for scientific investigation later proved he was right) he added that a man might "change his mind as a result of his own reflections" and of what he has "slowly digested."

People who understand man have always sold goods and won votes, lifted men's faces toward new ideals, and sent them forth for the Holy Grail. But they have done it by harnessing the drives that impel men to action. The steps in this process are simple to set down in print, but are beset with thorns when you try to apply them in practice. Basically there are four:

a. *Don't provoke argument.* An opposed listener is like a cocked gun. It takes only a slight pull on the trigger to shoot it. Therefore keep your hand off the trigger. Don't name-call. Don't use hate-provoking words like "*selfish* business interests," and "*radical* labor leaders." Students find it hard to resist name-calling. They hold it while the pressure mounts, then relieve themselves by one hefty name-calling term which they hope won't do any harm. But one is enough. Just one. Like Mercutio's wound, it may not be wide as a church door, nor as deep as a well, but it will do the business in the end. Face it frankly. Name-calling is an index of character. People who lack the character to restrain themselves will name-call. Face it frankly again. Name-calling is effective before partisan audiences. But a speaker injures himself when using it before opposed or nonpartisan audiences.

b. *Seek first to get a Yes-Response.* Says one speaker, "Campus politics are rotten, and everybody in office got there by secret bargain." Listeners who voted for those in office, instantly retort (mentally, of course), "That's false, and you know it." This is their way of saying "No," and their "No" is far more than uttering a single word. It triggers their whole personality. It shoots their wants and culture patterns at the speaker. No matter if later that listener feels that his "No" was wrong. He stands by it to save his face. So note how a competent speaker goes about it: "I am proud of this institution. I am glad I came here. I would not want to go any other place." *Everybody agrees with this* (i.e. he gets a Yes-Response") so he continues: "I want to talk about campus politics. We must have politics, of course, for we can't have officers without candidates, nor candidates without supporting groups. So I'm for politics." Listeners again give him a Yes-Response, and he then continues: "But I'm not so happy about that last campus election. A faculty-student committee has investigated it, and this committee's report disturbs me. It says. . . ." So far, not a listener has had the chance to say "No." The first speaker committed suicide in the first sentence. The second will go far.

c. *But beware of being ingratiating.* Listeners will not be fooled, and they will not be mocked. They will see through insincerity as through cellophane. They will see both faces of a two-faced speaker. Call two-facedness what you will: apple-polishing, soft-soaping, laying-it-on, or other names less printable that students all know—it comes to the same end. To seek Yes-Response on a common ground is a way of honestly settling differences by talk, a way of people learning to live together. To talk out of the other side of your mouth is something else. It does not take intelligence to know the difference, but it does take character to separate them in practice.

d. *Follow up by developing the subject so that hearers either (1) forget their objections, or (2) have them removed by logical processes.* It is a curious commentary on human nature that some people can be persuaded simply by causing them to forget their objections, or to *suspend judgment.* Thus a moving illustration, or sustained narrative that focuses people's attention somewhere while they are forgetting, may serve to persuade. But frankly, this is not the best method. What Archbishop Fénelon wrote around 1679 has since been established as scientifically valid: Such words "delight you at the moment but are not easily recovered afterwards. Even though you should remember them and should repeat them in other terms, they are not any longer the same thing—they lose their grace and strength." The best of all known methods is to follow that Yes-Response with impelling argument (not to be confused with "provoking an argument"). This impelling argument is not "argument" as such at all. It is *information, organized, trustworthy* and *pertinent* that is related to listeners' wants, hopes, aspirations, or ideals—actually very much like Step 3 described above.

## Lamp Six: *Remember that listeners think in images; be therefore specific, pictorial, and vivid*

"With words we govern men," said Disraeli. "Give me the right word and the right accent, and I will move the world," said Joseph Conrad. These simplifications point in the right direction. Catchwords and seductive slogans do not influence public opinion as much as formerly supposed. "But truth and force are Siamese twins." A speaker's task is to overcome mental laziness and find the exact words with which to speak the truth about what he thinks.

"Logicians may reason about abstractions; but the great mass of men must have images," said Macaulay. Therefore, beware of dullness! Never lose sight of the purpose of speech—to give people images, the right image, a bright image. Use words with verve and dash, and even audacity. Says the dull-minded bore: "It is necessary that all citizens should participate in election of public officials in order to have a government that fulfllls the essential functions of a democratic society." Nonsense! Say, "If you want good government, vote on election day."

Be specific. Rather than say vaguely, "There were several things they could do," come to the point, and say, "They could do three things: Pay the fine, appeal the case, or go to jail."

Know what effect you want to get—polished, elegant, learned, vigorous, gentle, shocking—then use the words that will get it.

Finally, sustain and develop the picture with vivid illustrations, comparisons, and direct quotation.

## Lamp Seven: *Keep the speech marching toward a goal*

"Absolute stillness is death," said Pascal. He was not thinking at the moment of speeches, but it applies to them. It takes movement to hold attention, and without movement a speech is only a dead carcass.

But movement alone is not enough. It must move *toward a goal,* and the speaker must show listeners glimpses of this goal along the way. A good speech keeps it fixed in view through a "recurrence of emphasis on the central idea."

Best of all is movement toward a goal that is half-revealed and half-concealed—revealed enough to follow the thought, and concealed enough to create suspense in the final end.

These are your Seven Lamps. Use them for light and guidance in preparing each speech.

## Assignments

ON APPLYING THESE PRINCIPLES TO SPEECHMAKING

1. Use these Seven Lamps to prepare a persuasive speech that will really *influence* the opinion of the class:

   a. Choose a subject you are concerned about, and have thought about for a long time. Especially consider subjects listed in your Speech-Subject Analysis Form in Assignment 7, Chapter 1.

   b. Reinforce your own ideas and experiences with material gathered from the library. Talk with others. Be alert to materials that always come to the speaker who is on the lookout.

   c. Follow the Seven Lamps of this chapter.

   d. Do not try to be an authority on government, politics, or world affairs. If you need authority, get it, and tell when and where your authority testified.

   e. Do not use this speech as an excuse for airing thinly-veiled prejudices. Do not damn or praise indiscriminately the military, the President, Russia, Egypt, capital, labor, democracy, communism, art, literature, nor anything else.

*f.* Instead, if you discuss a controversial issue, get your facts (and be sure they *are facts,* and are not rigged), assemble your ideas, rest them on impelling wants, and present your views. Hit as hard as you want with the facts, but don't call names and don't sing a hymn of hate. No question is too controversial to *discuss,* but name-calling and mud-throwing produce heat without light.

*g.* Don't pretend to have proved more than you have proved. In short, don't give hearers a chance to call you Baron Munchausen or claim that you put the truth on stilts. So present your case that those who disagree will say willingly, "He was fair and honest."

PART

### • III •

# THE SPEECH

# ❄ 9 ❄

# Selecting the Subject
# and Purpose

Two KINDS OF SPEAKERS, like the poor, always we have with us: those who "have something to say," and those who "have to say something." The difference between them is like that between lightning and lightning bugs. This is a chapter about that difference.

## Selecting the subject

Never is it easy to find a subject. In class the date for your next speech is announced. You will be one of five, or ten, who will speak that day; and one of fifteen, or thirty, who will speak during that round. Your first question is like everyone else's: What can I talk about?

Students are not the only ones harrassed by that question. It haunts experienced speakers also. You might think that out in the world people give speeches only when they have an idea they want to talk about. Not so. A large amount of speaking is done because a speaker's position requires him to say something appropriate, and he is faced by the question: What *is* appropriate? This includes speeches given by presidents of the parent-teacher association, the local insurance salesmen's association, the city medical society, business corporations, and Presidents of the United States. At other times an audience faces a problem and needs to find a speaker who can discuss it profitably. At still other times the group meets at regular intervals, weekly or annually, and want to have their thinking stimulated on any suitable topic. Lord Balfour, British statesman, voiced the troubles that most speakers have in selecting a subject:

> I will confess to you at the outset that I have been much embarrassed in the selection of a subject. [My address], so I was informed, might be about

anything. But this "anything" is too apt, upon further invesigation, to resolve itself into nothing. Some topics are too dull. Some are too controversial. Some interest only the few. Some are too great a strain upon the speaker who has to prepare them. Some too severely tax the patience of the audience which has to listen to them. And I confess to have been much perplexed in my search for a topic on which I could say something to which you would have patience to listen, or on which I might find it profitable to speak.

Fortunately, out of the experience of others a helpful procedure has been developed for finding and testing subjects. It can be classified into four steps:

1. The audience    3. The occasion
2. The subject     4. Special problems

## THE AUDIENCE

Good subjects are often found in the audience. What are their particular problems, needs, tastes, or interests? *Choose a subject about which the audience may know something, but wants to know more.* For example:

*Does the age or sex of the audience suggest a subject?* Young people are especially interested in subjects like these:

Making a success of marriage

Living on a modest income

Religion in the home

What makes one a business executive,
or simply a white collar worker

Women, by comparison with men, are more actively interested in subjects like the following:

The home

Their children's school

Women in business

Music

Literature

How to escape from worry or fear

*Do the social, economic, political, or religious beliefs of the audience suggest a subject?* Club women are interested in the status of women in the Middle East. Business men want to hear more of private initiative and stabilizing the dollar. Taxpayers are concerned with where the money goes. Democrats always will listen to speeches on Jefferson or Jackson or Franklin D. Roosevelt. Republicans want to remember Hamilton or Lincoln or Theodore Roosevelt. Religious groups want to hear their tenets restated and reaffirmed.

*Does the local background of the audience suggest a subject?* The local background of college students is rich in appropriate subjects:

> Drab weekends
>
> Recreation
>
> Social life
>
> Snap courses and tough ones
>
> Required courses and electives
>
> Good teachers and poor ones
>
> Fraternities and sororities
>
> Athletics
>
> Scholarships—local, state, and federal
>
> The rising cost of education
>
> Vocational education or liberal education

## THE SUBJECT

Good topics are also found by looking directly at the subject matter itself. A safe rule is this: *Choose a subject about which you know something, and can find out more.* For example:

*Do you have any first-hand or special knowledge from which a subject can be taken?* Everyone has had first-hand experiences in some field or other, and is to some degree an expert in that field. About such things you can speak in the manner of one who says, "All of this I saw, and a part of it I was." Perhaps you have worked on a factory assembly line; you know the worker's sense of not belonging and his deep desire for recognition. You may have lived among the Navajoes; and you know how their culture patterns differ from ours. You may have lived on a farm that employed migratory workers for harvesting; you have observed how they work and play, and perhaps why they prefer to be migrants rather than stay-at-home workers. You may have been a cowpuncher on a Western ranch, an employee at a tourist resort, an office girl, or a baby-sitter; you have seen things from a different viewpoint than those who look at the occupations from the outside.

In addition to first-hand experiences there is also special knowledge of another sort. You are an engineering student; you know something —and can find out more—about roadbuilding, jet airplanes, or what we are now doing with missiles. You have studied banking; you know something—and can learn more—about how the stock market serves the public, or how banks came into existence, or what their current problems are. You are majoring in literature; you can discuss why people read literature, or what kinds of literature there are.

Students often try to avoid subjects they know about. They are afraid it will be "too personal," or protest that "I really don't know enough about it to give a speech." Well, speaking *is* personal. Every speech is from the speaker's *experience*. He has had the experience in the flesh mayhap, or mayhap in the spirit or the imagination through books. But he must have *been* there.

*Have you recently read a book, heard a speech, or had a conversation that suggests a subject?* It may be an old book—Homer's *Iliad*, Plato's *Republic*, or Jane Austen's *Pride and Prejudice*—or the latest *selection* of the Book-of-the-Month Club. It may be as well known as *Huckleberry Finn*, or as forgotten as Hervey Allen's *Anthony Adverse*. It is not the book, but what the book has done to you. Has it made you think? Aroused impulses? Created resentment? Has it caused you to feel that here is something that ought to be more widely known—or steadfastly refuted? A speech or a conversation might affect you the same way. Again, it is not the ideas it gave you so much as the prodding, the spurring-on, it did. You disagree with what was said; and your mind won't forget it. You thought it missed the real point; and you keep going over it again to see where it got off the track. These represent the birth of a thought —and a thought, by careful nurture, can become a speech.

*Is a subject to be found in some topic before the public eye?* It may be a new discovery, invention, or process. It may be an industrial crisis, like a strike or antitrust suit. It may be an economic crisis, like another rise in the cost of living. It may be a crisis in foreign affairs. It may be an urgent political topic, an election, a new tax, a new program of federal aid. Listeners are concerned about these topics. Your job is to do what newspapers cannot do—analyze the question, show which way it is moving and why; in short, tell what the day-to-day headlines really mean.

*Do you want to defend or criticize some cause or subject of persistent controversy?* Always there are plenty, of which the following are typical:

> Behavior of young people today
> Modern education
> Modern art
> Modern novels
> Modern poetry
> Jazz and bebop
> Automobiles and highways
> Racketeering
> Big labor unions
> Big business
> Big government

Campus topics like these are persistent topics of controversy:

> Subsidized athletics
> Grading system
> Class attendance
> Examinations
> Professors
> Graduation requirements
> The fraternity system
> Student marriages

*Do you want to change some present custom, tradition, or established law?* Some people contend that when time outmodes a custom or law it ought to be abolished. Others hold that customs and laws ought to be left alone unless they become actively dangerous, because stability is a form of self-preservation. The first group believes that this cultural lag stagnates a people. The other group believes that most people are incapable of accepting quick changes, no matter how much he may want to, because people live mainly by habit, "acting as they have been taught to act without stopping first to think." Ergo, we have scores of political legacies, social legacies, educational legacies that are hang-overs from the past. The perennial question is: Ought these legacies to be scrapped or kept? They make good speech topics. The following list suggests their nature:

The 21-year-old voting requirement

Latin and Greek in modern education

Requiring four years of science and mathematics

Requiring anthropology and sociology for the proper understanding of man

Requiring speech for the "profession of citizenship"

The Presidential electoral college

The two-term limitation for U.S. Presidents

## THE OCCASION

Good subjects may also be found by considering the occasion. For example:

*Does the occasion itself suggest a subject?* Henry W. Grady, a Southerner, spoke to the New England Society of New York on the rewards to be gained from co-operation instead of antagonism between North and South. John W. Davis, American, spoke at the festival of Shakespeare's birth, at Stratford in England, on the proposition that "all men of English speech share in the legacy of Shakespeare." John A. Brett, a lawyer, addressed a state bar association on the subject, "Who Is a Good Lawyer?" Humble occasions may also suggest subjects: An alumni banquet, a fraternity annual meeting, a founders' day meeting.

*Does the occasion suggest a related idea?* You have a speech on the eve of final examinations; an idea related to the occasion would be "How to Study for Final Exams." (There is a lot of published research on how to study to be found in your library.) You have a speech on the eve of preregistration for next semester; a related idea would be, "Here Is a Course You Will Want to Take Next Semester." It is National Music Week; and you speak on a great composer, on modern music, or on the influence of radio on musical taste. It is Constitutional Week; and you speak on "The Constitutional Convention of 1787," or "*The Federalist, a Little Known but Important Political Document,*" or "How the First Law Was Declared Unconstitutional." Every occasion is rich in related ideas.

## SPECIAL PROBLEMS

A few special problems should be considered, mostly by way of warning on testing a subject for suitability:

1. *Don't choose a subject above or below the intellectual level of the audience.* You cannot discuss the psychology of music with people who don't know the diatonic scale. You cannot discuss the implications of the quantum theory with people who know nothing at all of physics. Conversely, college students will not listen patiently to a discussion on the values of being a boy scout, or on high-school ways of life. What's one man's meat is another man's poison, and a speaker must know whose meat, and whose poison.

2. *Don't use a subject too difficult for oral presentation.* Some subjects are simply not adaptable to a speech, and it is a waste of time to talk on them. The following are illustrations:

   a. *Complicated processes* requiring mental visualizing and accurate memorizing of a series of steps, by the listener—such as how a rotary press operates, how to tie a knot, how to fly an airplane.

   b. *Technical subjects* requiring the audience to possess a specialized vocabulary and thought-concepts, and to follow the speaker's close reasoning without the opportunity to review it and keep it fastened in the mind—such as "An Experimental Analysis of Dynamic and Static Equilibrium," or "The J-Curve Hypothesis of Conforming Behavior." These are better fitted to the printed page, not the ear.

   c. *Complex subjects* requiring the listener to carry in mind a long chain of reason, master large quantities of statistics, etc.—such as "The Postulates of Symbolic Logic," or "Deviations in Actuarial Statistics."

*d. Intimate subjects* about which people might read alone without embarrassment, but which would embarrass them to listen to in a group.

## Whittling your speech down to size

It takes students a long time to learn this vital requirement, that you must whittle every speech down to size. They want to start from the Garden of Eden and work down. They take a subject big enough for a *book,* and sail over it in five minutes—high up where the air is thin. They will talk on "music"—all of it—in one speech. But you can't cover "music" even in a book; it would take an encyclopedia. In a classroom speech you can't cover the whole subject of modern jazz, or grand operas, chamber music, Bach, Beethoven, Victor Herbert, or George Gershwin. You can take only a selected portion of any of these topics.

A good speech must cover "more and more about less and less." Take an example. A student spoke on "photography," and tried to cover all of it in one speech—cameras, films, lighting, composition, prints, and transparencies. Of course, the speech was a failure. In fact, it wasn't a speech, but merely a bundle of woolly assertions that bored the listeners. Next, he drafted an outline on "cameras" only. Like every beginner, he tried to cover all of it, from the "history of cameras" to the "kinds and purposes of cameras used today." But this, he soon found, would take more than *ten hours!* In the end, he gave two good speeches: one on "How Daguerre Invented the First Camera," and the other on "Why a Good Lens Costs So Much Money." Of course the latter subject was far too big for one speech, so he whittled it down by talking only about why it took 28 pages of mathematical formulas to make a simple 4-element lens. (That really *interested* everybody in the class!) Later he started to plan another speech on "films" but found it would take at least five speeches to cover all of it. So he left out color films, and focused on only two black-and-white films, then discussed the different effects a photographer could get with each. His title forecast the speech purpose: "Why a Photographer Gets Better Results by Using Two Films Instead of One."

After you have read this it would be delightful to say: "Go forth and select your subject with confidence, for now you know how to whittle it down to size." But you don't! By the record (made from speech courses over a period of *six years*) 80 per cent of students, after reading every warning a textbook can put in print, still march right out and select a subject so big they need from one hour to twenty hours to cover it! Some will even take a subject like that described in a newspaper not long ago: "The speaker, who talked on 'Nature,' narrowed her topic down to astronomy, biology, geology, heavenly bodies, living things, and earth formations." For you, the exciting question is, "Am I one of the 20 per cent, or do I belong to the multitude?"

## Selecting the purpose

You have a subject. Where are you going with it? What do you plan to do when you get there? Like any traveler, you want to find out what detours and blocked roads there are along the way. Then when you finish, no one will wonder, "What was he driving at?" They will know.

Does this seem like unnecessary advice? Not so. How many times do people listen to a speaker for half an hour, or even longer, then come out of the room trying to figure what he was talking about. He used fine phrases. His ideas were lofty. But you just couldn't get sense out of what he was trying to say. He used words you hear day in and day out, but you couldn't pin him down to any concept that had meaning. He reminds you of a bad dream in which you are suspended in the sky, with your head in a cloud, trying to communicate to someone down on the ground. Therefore, when you give a speech, find out where you want to go, then get on the road.

What possible speech purposes may a speaker have? Fundamentally, he has just *one*. He wants the audience to *respond* to his speech, to *do something about what he says*.

Not all responses are equally easy to get. Some are easier, some are more difficult. We here divide them into four groups, known as General Purposes, and arrange them according to increasing difficulty:

### TO INTEREST THE AUDIENCE

Why speak at all, no matter how good the speech is, if the audience does not *listen?* Every speech must *interest* the audience enough to make them listen. Interest, then, is the common denominator of *all* successful speaking.

But there are times when you will speak just to interest the audience, and for no other reason. You don't speak to inform, to stimulate, or to convince. You speak only to interest them. You deal in wit, repartee, and dramatic movement. You tell stories. You relax the audience and take their thoughts from the tensions of modern living.

To interest is the purpose of most private conversation, of the toastmaster's introductions, of those "filling-in" speeches at meetings, of much after-dinner speaking, and of story-hour talks for children.

### TO INFORM THE AUDIENCE

Next is the speech to inform. Typical of these are class lectures, speeches on "what's behind the newspaper headlines," on what modern artists (or poets) are trying to do, on how college life has changed during the past fifty years, and all the many types of speeches that "relate yesterday's facts to today's events to produce tomorrow's meaning."

The purpose of these speeches is to tell people something they don't know, or to give meaning to facts they already know, or to separate trustworthy information from myth, rumor, and propaganda. This is more difficult than giving a speech just to interest; for the information must be tested and processed, then presented so listeners can understand and use it. *A speaker can never merely pass out information. He must see that listeners get it in usable shape.* Especially he must bear in mind the following essentials:

1. *Arrange the information under two or three topics, or not more than four at most.* You can't string out information like the links in a long chain, for listeners can't remember ten or twenty links of information. Instead, group your information into the fewest possible units. Two headings are best. Three are harder to remember, but all right. But if you have more than three, be careful! Unless you write them on a blackboard, or put them on large placards, the listeners won't remember them.

2. *In giving the speech, fasten these topics in the listeners' minds.* When you come to the first topic, tell them it is the first: *"The first step is. . . ."* When you get through with that topic, say so, and summarize it so they will remember. Then as you begin the second topic, tell them it's the second topic: *"We now come to the second topic. . . ."*

3. *Make your information specific.* There is no such thing as abstract information. If it is abstract, it's not information. You say, "It's *hot.*" That is a value judgment, but not really information. The temperature of a hot day makes cold soup; the temperature of hot soup makes a cold airplane motor; the temperature of a hot airplane motor won't produce nuclear fission. How hot *is* hot? Be specific. Now this does not mean to confuse listeners with decimal points, but means for you to be specific, to give details, to illustrate and compare. For example, you would not say, "This distance was 449.8 miles," for the listener would tend to remember the ".8 miles"—which is not important—and forget 449 miles. Better say, "It was just under 450 miles," which is your essential figure. In other words, make it easy for listeners to remember the essential.

4. *Use charts, graphs, and diagrams if the material is technical or complex.* The eyes sees proportions easier than the ear can follow explanations about them. So present complex or technical data so listeners can *see* as they hear.

5. *Make your information interesting.* Remember that listeners are just plain human beings. They can absorb only so much, and no more.

After mental fatigue sets in all facts begin to seem much the same to them. So use anecdotes and illustrations. Make interesting comparisons. Flavor your facts with humor.

## TO STIMULATE ATTITUDE OR ACTION

We come now to the more difficult levels of response that are found in persuasive speaking.

*What is persuasion? We know already that it consist of vitalizing a proposition so as to make it a dynamic force in the thinking and action of other people.* But people have many levels of beliefs. Some beliefs are shallow, temporary, or subject to easy change. Some are deep-rooted and hard to change. The listeners' level of belief determines the speaker's mode of approach. For convenience we here divide them in two levels. First are beliefs we hold in a mild form. Second are those we hold vigorously and sometimes obstinately.

*Speeches to stimulate attitude or action are concerned only with the first kind, where belief is held only in a mild form, or where lip service is given to the proposition but where the listener fails to practice it in the actual conduct of life.*[1]

We may, for example, believe that we ought to study our lessons, get eight hours of sleep, attend that lecture series, go to all the college plays, and really start preparing every speech on time—but we believe some of these propositions so mildly that we don't do what we believe we ought. Actually, we have many mild beliefs that hardly influence our behavior at all.

Most speechmaking aims at vitalizing these mild beliefs. They include commencement speeches, inaugural addresses, eulogies, dedications, college pep talks, inspirational talks to businessmen, speeches at reunions, celebrations, anniversaries, most sermons, and most political speeches. These are speeches to *stimulate the listener's attitude* into an active acceptance of mild beliefs, or to *stimulation action* on propositions to which they agree, give lip-service, but do nothing.

A speech to stimulate attitude or action is more difficult than a speech to interest or to inform. Interest it must have, and information also, but more yet. It must be fitted to the prevailing wants of the listeners. It must set up an "adequate system of rewards" for those who accept the

---

[1] We use the word *stimulate* in the exact sense defined by *Webster's New International Dictionary*, second edition: "to excite, rouse, or animate, to action *or more vigorous exertion* by some pungent motive or by persuasion." Other writers have used the word *impress* to designate this speech purpose. But literally *impress* means to stamp or imprint. It implies that the speaker merely stamps or imprints an idea on the listener's inert mind. In contrast, the view here taken is that the listener's mind is not inert, and that a speaker can't stamp it the way the post office stamps a letter. The listener's mind is *active*, and takes an active part in listening, like a player catching a ball. The appropriate word for this is *stimulate*.

speaker's proposition. It must *motivate* the proposition in terms of the listeners' wants, hopes, inspirations, until it vitalizes their conduct.

### TO CHANGE ATTITUDE OR ACTION

*The speaker here is dealing with propositions that are not accepted by the listeners. He is asking the listeners to change direction in some form or other, to alter an opinion, to vote, to join, to go, to give, to do!* He may be asking listeners to "believe this thing earnestly," or to "do this thing actively." The first is change of attitude. The second is change of action. Both are change.

To change attitude or action is the aim of the lawyer who defends a client, of the legislator who argues for a change of farm policy or of conducting foreign affairs, or of the speaker who says that literature is as essential to society as material things.

This is the hardest of all speech purposes, because it calls for everything required by the other three purposes, plus more besides. The speaker must interest, inform, and stimulate; but those three are not enough. He must make listeners *want* to change their attitudes, to vote, to join, to give. He must present evidence to show the logic of his cause. This evidence in itself may not persuade, in fact it usually will not, yet he must present it as a token of good faith, and without it he cannot expect to succeed.

Let us summarize the speech purposes. (1) All speeches have one fundamental purpose—to gain a response. (2) But some responses are harder to gain than others; there are, in fact, four levels known as General Purposes, with each successive level becoming more difficult than the one preceding:

1. To Interest $+$
2. To inform $+ +$
3. To Stimulate $+ + +$
4. To change $+ + + +$

## Assignments

ON FINDING SPEECH SUBJECTS

1. Consult again the Speech-Subject Analysis Form you prepared in Assignment 7, Chapter 1 (pages 28-29). You may now want to revise and add to it.

2. Consult the Classified Speech Subjects at the end of Chapter 3 (pages 63-65), and from it select five to ten subjects that would be suitable for your speeches.

3. Evaluate the subjects used by students in this class. Classify them into groups you would regard as: (*a*) excellent, (*b*) fairly satisfactory, (*c*) poor. State briefly your reasons.

4. Read the table of contents in recent issues of such magazines as *Atlantic, Harper's, Fortune, New Yorker, Commonweal,* and *Christian Century.* These will give you a look at the subjects these editors think are important at the moment.

5. Look at two or three issues of *U.S. News & World Report, Time,* or *Newsweek,* and note what news the editors think is currently important. Do you find additional speech subjects?

ON SELECTING THE SPEECH PURPOSE

6. Go to hear some speaker. Determine the subject, general purpose (i.e. to Interest, Inform, Stimulate, or Change). Note how the speaker narrowed the subject to the limits imposed by time and audience.

7. Read three speeches in *Vital Speeches, Representative American Speeches,* or any other collection. Determine the general purpose, the specific purpose-sentence, and note how the speaker narrowed the subject to the limits imposed by time and audience.

8. List four speeches that you have heard during the past year, each having a different general purpose.

9. From one of the subjects that you listed in Assignments 1, 2, 4, or 5, select a subject for your next class speech. Determine the specific response that you want, then carefully phrase that response into a purpose-sentence. Decide whether you want: (*a*) merely to interest the audience, (*b*) to present significant information, (*c*) to stimulate attitude or action, or (*d*) to change attitude or action. Select the supporting materials best adapted to your purpose, and if you don't have enough, go forth and get more. Outline the speech, rehearse it, and give it to the class.

# Earning the Right to Speak

AS A YOUNG MAN Sir Winston Churchill wrote a novel about a man of action who made many speeches:

> This man [said Churchill] knew that nothing good can be obtained without effort. These impromptu feats of oratory existed only in the minds of the listeners; the flowers of rhetoric were hothouse plants. . . . His ideas began to take the form of words, to group themselves into sentences; he murmured to himself; the rhythm of his own language swayed him. . . . He scribbled down a rough sentence, scratched it out, polished it, and wrote it in again. The sound would please their ears, the sense improve and stimulate their minds.

Churchill knew. He was young, but on his way to become one of the most effective speakers in the history of man. His was not a new discovery. Epictetus, about 100 A.D. had summarized knowledge already old: "No great thing is created suddenly, any more than a bunch of grapes or a fig. If you tell me that you want a fig, I answer you that there must be time. Let it first blossom, then bear fruit, then ripen."

Some people find it incredible that a speech must blossom, bear fruit, then ripen. "Good speakers," they argue, "talk off the cuff." That notion, of course, is pure fantasy. Shakespeare's *Hamlet* was not written off the cuff, nor was Churchill's "Their Finest Hour," nor is the President's latest address to the American people. (For one of President Eisenhower's addresses to Congress the reporters got a record of the amount of work —over one hundred hours for a 51-minute speech.) William DeWitt Hyde, onetime college president, struck a good average: "I make it a rule to spend one hour in preparation for every minute I speak." Food for thought is like any other food—it takes time to prepare and serve it.

In this chapter we shall summon what science and experience has learned on how a speaker best develops ideas and turns them into a speech: The process involves four steps:

1. Starting in time
2. Thinking on the subject
3. Gathering material
4. Processing the material

## Starting in time

You can't prepare a speech the way you prepare a history lesson. You must *cultivate* a speech as you cultivate a crop. This takes time. You need time to think. You need time to read, and talk with others. You need time for ideas to incubate, grow, and bear fruit. You need *time*! As Oliver Wendell Holmes, Sr., said:

> Knowledge and timber shouldn't be much used till they are seasoned. . . . Put an idea into your intelligence and leave it there an hour, a day, a year, without ever having occasion to refer to it. When, at last, you return to it, you do not find it as it was when acquired. It has domiciliated itself, so to speak,—become at home,—entered into relations with your other thoughts, and integrated itself with the whole fabric of the mind.[1]

By starting on time you gather material without work. You are reading a magazine, and an idea or fact, that fits the speech meets your eye. You are studying a lesson in biology, economics, literature, nutrition, or diesel engines—and an illustration lies there, ready and waiting. You enter the library, and a book stares at you. You walk down the street, and ideas flash through your mind.

By starting the speech on time you can get rid of immature ideas and get around roadblocks. An idea that today seems splendid, may next week turn out to be immature. An outline that today seems perfect, may a few days later prove to be superficial. Or you reach a roadblock and simply come to a halt. (People who *think* run into roadblocks right along). So you put the speech aside and go on your way—then suddenly tomorrow finds you have got around the roadblock, without quite knowing how. Everyone who does any sort of creative thinking, knows that it takes *time* to get around a mental roadblock. Said John Dryden of one of his best plays, *The Rival Ladies* (1664), ". . . long before it was a play . . . it was a confused mass of thoughts, tumbling over one another in the dark."

## Thinking on the subject

A British scholar, Isaiah Berlin, said of American college students:

> Many of these excellent young people could not . . . either read or write, as these activities are understood in our best universities. That is to say, their thoughts came higgledy-piggledy out of the big, buzzing, booming confu-

[1] *The Autocrat of the Breakfast Table* (Boston, Houghton Mifflin and Co., 1858), p. 134.

sion of their minds, too many pouring out chaotically in the same instant. . . .
Somewhere in their early education there was a failure to order, to connect,
and to discriminate. . . . They tended [therefore] to look to their professors
to tell them not merely what books to read but sometimes what chapters
and what pages; on being told, the more serious among them would throw
themselves upon the recommended pabulum and would try to absorb it in
a very frenzied fashion. They read rapidly, desperately, and far too much.
And because they tended to believe that all facts (and only facts) were
important, and, what is more, equally important, the result was often a
fearful intellectual congestion from which many of them will probably suffer
the rest of their lives.

Berlin overstated the case. But there is painful truth in part of what he
says, and you might want to assess your own habits, especially your habits
when writing a paper or preparing a speech. Are you one of those who
read, without thinking, in a frenzied fashion? Here is disturbing evidence? More than five hundred students were asked, "How do you prepare your speeches?" Over half said the *first thing they did was to look
for speech material in the library!*
That method brings to mind the cowboy's dream of heaven:

> The road to that bright, happy region
> Is a dim, narrow trail, so they say;
> But the broad one that leads to perdition
> Is posted and blazed all the way.

These students have taken the trail that's posted and blazed, but leads
to perdition. At the end they become editors of somebody else's thoughts,
not speakers in their own right. At the end they must stand up and say
to all the world: "This is my voice, but the thoughts belong to *The
Reader's Digest* (or this book, or that article). The first step is to "look
for material" all right, *but to look first in your own head!*
Speakers face two hazards when they start preparing a speech. On the
one hand, a speaker may have only an emotion, a prejudice, or a slogan.
He may be one who scorns homework, and depends on righteous indignation. He gives off heat, but no light. He may be another variety of the
same species, one who looks around for half-facts to prove he is right,
or uses rigged evidence in the solemn pretense that it is the whole truth.
Such a speaker delights his partisans. He does not win friends or influence
human behavior outside his group.
On the other hand, he may be that really honest student who never
tells the truth. He doesn't willfully deceive or deliberately falsify. He
just does not trust himself, but only echoes what others say. He goes to
the library without first thinking, comes forth with "the people I read
in the library think this," and calls it his own. Wrote Emerson, out of the
fullness of experience, "Speak what you know and believe; and are

personally in it; and are answerable for every word." This is a pointed way of saying: Do your own thinking, stand on your own judgments. You cannot do this by rushing first to the library to look up the ready-made thoughts of others.

At this point you may say, "But I'm not sure I know how to think, or where to begin." All right, now is the time to learn. There are no hard-and-fast rules about thinking—just hard rules. The first step we have already discussed: *Get started on time.* When you cultivate ideas you must give them time to grow. The second step is: *Take stock of what you know already.* Again you may say, "But I don't know anything about the subject." Actually, this is not so. Rather you mean that you lack specific information or matured ideas. True, but let's look at what little you do know, and "think" about it. You start by looking at the subject with X-ray eyes to find its skeleton. You ask yourself questions like these:

### PRELIMINARY

1. Why did I choose this subject?
2. What do I know about it first-hand?
3. What does the audience know about it?
4. What do they want to know?

### DIAGNOSIS

1. What is the problem, or point in question?
2. What are its symptoms?
3. What have been its effects?
   Visible effects?
   Less visible effects?
4. What is its present status?
5. What caused it to arise?

### HYPOTHESES ON WHAT TO DO

1. What are the motives of persons who have been talking or writing on this subject?
2. How far can I trust their facts and ideas?
3. Must I discard them as untrustworthy, or can I correct for a standard deviation—and then use the corrected materials?
4. What do they think ought to be done?
5. After discarding or correcting for their bias, where do their recommendations seem to be inadequate, and where adequate?
6. What do I think (tentatively) might be done (i.e. several things)?
7. What are the advantages and disadvantages of each?
8. Which seems (tentatively) to be the final best way?

### FURTHER VERIFICATION

1. What further knowledge do I need to help verify my tentative diagnosis?
2. What knowledge do I need to help verify my tentative hypothesis on what to do?

When you X-ray a subject by this process you are *thinking*. You are also *calling up ideas from the subconscious mind*. You may not know it, but you rarely, perhaps never fully, forget any experiences or ideas you ever had. They lie below the surface, hidden but not entirely forgotten. Many can be brought to light by self-questioning. "It was then that I made the great discovery," said Mark Twain, "that when the tank runs dry you've only to leave it alone and it will fill up again in time, while you are asleep—also while you are at work at other things and are quite unaware that this unconscious and profitable cerebration is going on."

The road won't be smooth. Often there will be times when you seem to get nowhere. Be of good cheer; Aristotle and Einstein had those periods too. They are the "plateau periods" in thinking. You *seem* to be getting nowhere, but these are the periods when ideas *incubate*. They incubate even when you are not working on them, for they are working on you. Then comes that next period of thinking, the *sudden flash*, that makes things clear. You've been puzzling over a knotty problem for days, or weeks. Then suddenly, out of nowhere, the solution appears. "Why didn't I think of that before?" you wonder. The answer is: It was incubating, and it just now hatched. That's how we conceive original ideas, or see an old problem in a new light. Archimedes discovered specific gravity while taking a bath. Charles Darwin's idea of natural selection came to him while riding in a carriage. He wrote: "I can remember the very spot in the road . . . when to my joy the solution occurred to me." Newton discovered the law of gravity while sitting under an apple tree; and legend has it, after a falling apple had hit him on the head. College students have testified to getting sudden flashes of insight while listening to music and listening to uninteresting speakers! (Interesting speakers keep their listeners' attention. Uninteresting ones leave them free to think!)

But these sudden flashes of insight don't happen except after a lot of hard work, spread over many days, that seemed absolutely fruitless. In other words, nobody gets a big idea when he is not relaxed—and nobody gets a big idea when he is relaxed all the time.[2]

About now you are ready to *assemble your ideas into a skeleton outline*.

---

[2] Two short valuable discussions on the process of thinking are: Otis M. Walter, "Creativity: A Neglected Factor in Public Speaking," *The Speech Teacher*, III (September, 1954), No. 3, pp. 159-168; and A. Grove Day, "Writer's Magic," *AAUP Bulletin*, XXXIII (Summer, 1947), No. 2, pp. 269-278.

Part of the outline will contain the facts and ideas you dug out of your mind. Part of it will be simply unanswered questions. It will be shadowy —but it's *yours*. Later you will discard it and make another outline, or several more. But this first skeleton outline is time-saving, for it will enable you to compare new material with old, new ideas with old, to weigh both and take the better.

Now you are ready to gather material and expand the subject.

## Gathering speech material

Americans have turned the old Greek maxim "Know thyself" into the gospel "Know thy stuff." From the Nile to the Ganges a speaker may hold throngs by the utterance of postulates, conclusions, and suppositions; and his unattested thought may be received as beatitudes. Not in America. Americans want factual content, not facts alone but facts with meaning, information that adds up, knowledge that makes sense. As an intelligent American businessman put it: "These speakers who play tiddledywinks with ideas burn me up. I want to *know* about things, and *know* the *meaning* of what I know." To meet this demand you must turn especially to three sources of ideas and information:

1. Conversing and listening
2. Investigating
3. Reading

### CONVERSING AND LISTENING

If you are speaking on a campus question, talk to other people. They supply you with ideas. There is a lot of waste in this sort of talk, to be sure, but it takes no extra time—for man is a talking animal and all you need do is to talk to a point when you meet others. Talk with them on the campus, in dormitories, at meal times—and listen to what they think, and learn whether they think. You may find significant trends, for example, in what the freshmen think, or the seniors, or the science majors. You may find that they are not interested in the question, or not informed, or have strong prejudices. All of this is useful information. "I never met a man," exclaimed Henry Ward Beecher, "from whom I did not get an idea for a sermon."

You may also interview people who are authorities. What does the athletic department think about the new penalty rule, or eligibility requirement? What background can a chemist give you on that newest antibiotic? What do the political scientists think of that new book on political theory?

Conversing not only brings in new information and ideas; it especially enables you to *test* your ideas. You are planning a speech on examination methods, the honor system, fraternity pledging, or the vacation schedule. You have certain ideas about the subject. These you can test in advance by talking with others. You may find unexpected objections to your plan, or find that you did not explain it clearly the first time, or discover that your line of approach antagonized listeners. All this is useful preparation. It may interest you to know that Dwight Eisenhower in preparing an address to Congress consulted with the following persons: First, with all the members of his Cabinet. Next, with his speech writer, Kevin McCann. Third, with constitutional lawyers. Fourth, with McCann again while revising the third and fourth drafts. Fifth, with the Vice-President and entire Cabinet again. Still later, he consulted again with three Cabinet members, three Presidential advisers, and leading members of his party in the House and Senate.

## INVESTIGATING

Wherever possible, go and see for yourself or write and find out first-hand. A student gave a speech on diseases of trees; he dug it out of books (a commendable thing), but never thought to supplement his knowledge by looking at campus trees or to note that the tree outside the class windows was afflicted with one of the diseases he discussed. A student spoke on the city-manager plan of government, citing his information from distant cities; but a visit to the city hall would have refuted the biased and out-of-date figures he got from a propaganda article. Students give speeches on chain stores without ever going downtown to compare, on their own, chain-store with independent-store prices. They will criticize postal service without talking with anyone in the post office to get their side of the problem. They will advocate new methods of purifying milk (swallowed from a *Reader's Digest* article!) without knowing first-hand what method and what equipment is used at local dairies. Make it a cardinal rule, therefore, to investigate whenever possible and to see for yourself.

If you need specific information that others have first-hand, often you can get it by writing a letter. (But you can do this only if you start a speech on *time!*) For best results: (1) Make the letter brief. (2) State why you want the information. (3) State exactly what information you want. (4) Verify the initials and spelling of the name of the person you address. (5) Enclose a stamped and self-addressed envelope for reply.

*H. Armstrong Roberts*

While the library is an excellent resource in gathering speech material, the speaker should not fail to supplement his reading with first-hand investigation, whenever possible.

## READING

Reading, of course, is the most abundant source of speech material. But random reading can waste time, and leave you still with spotted knowledge. Better make the reading systematic, and start with a bibliography.

### HOW TO COMPILE A BIBLIOGRAPHY

You don't want a "complete" bibliography. Indeed a complete bibliography might fill fifty pages and take a month to compile. You want a *selected* bibliography containing perhaps four or five times as many references as you will be able to read. A selected bibliography, of course, is not a hit-and-miss affair made up from the first list of references that meets the eye. It is compiled by a systematic process of selection and rejection according to date, source, author, and availability. The obvious sources of bibliography are the library Card Catalogue and *Readers' Guide,* but all the following useful sources ought to be considered:

## COMMON SOURCES OF BIBLIOGRAPHIES

*How and Where to Look It Up: A Guide to Standard Sources of Information,* Robert W. Murphey. The title explains the contents, a reference work on where to find everything.

Library Card Catalogue.

*Readers' Guide to Periodical Literature.* Index of articles appearing in approximately 115 general magazines. Published since 1890. Cumulated approximately semimonthly, monthly, quarterly, and annually. Permanent cumulated volumes since 1935 at two years to a volume.

*Poole's Index.* The pioneer index, covering 105 years: 1802-1906.

*International Index to Periodicals.* Index of articles in approximately 170 magazines in the humanities and social sciences. Since 1907.

*The Education Index.* Index of articles in about 120 British and American magazines; also books and pamphlets. Since 1929.

*New York Times Index.* A newspaper index from which can be located the dates on which similar stories appeared in other newspapers. Since 1913. Semimonthly. Annual cumulation.

*Public Affairs Information Service.* Index to books, documents, pamphlets, articles, in public affairs. Weekly. Cumulated five times a year. Permanent annual volumes.

*Vertical File Catalogue.* Lists current pamphlets and booklets. Since 1932. Monthly. Annual cumulations. Use with caution, for some listed pamphlets are propaganda or advertising.

*United States Government Publications Monthly Catalog.* Lists publications of the largest single publisher in the world, the U.S. Federal Government.

*Biography Index.* Accumulative index to biographical materials in books and magazines. Monthly since 1946. Cumulated into annual volumes. Permanent cumulation in three-year periods.

*Essay and General Literature Index.* Lists over 40,000 essays and articles that appear in over 2,000 volumes of collections. Since 1900.

Winchell, Constance M., *Guide to Reference Books.* Presumably will be revised infrequently and will issue supplements.

In addition to the above, there are also special indexes such as the following:

*Agricultural Index* (since 1916), *Art Index* (since 1929), *Engineering Index* (since 1884), and *Industrial Arts Index* (since 1913). Consult your library for additional ones.

There are three tests of a good bibliography:

*Is it accurate?* There are about five items on each listing where an error can occur: (1) Spelling of names, (2) wording of titles, (3) name of magazine (or publisher), (4) date of issue, (5) pages. With only a 10-item bibliography, there are fifty chances for error. Better proofread carefully, and save time.

*Is it complete?* Consider the dewy-eyed person who lists "Smith, Standards of Practice." Which Smith? Adam Smith was an economist, Joseph Smith was a religious leader, Al Smith was a governor, MacDonald Smith was a golfer. *Who's Who in America* lists 474 Smiths, and one typical city directory lists 14 pages. Beware even of "J. E. Smith; for *Who's Who in America* lists five. Get the full name as listed: "J. Eugene Smith." Next, where is the item found? Is it a book—and if so, when published and where published? Is it an article—and if so, in what magazine and in what issue and on what pages? Is it a pamphlet or document —and if so, when issued and by whom? A complete bibliographical reference would be as follows:

Elvidge, Ford Q., "The Two-Party System," *Vital Speeches,* XXIV (July 15, 1958), No. 19, pp. 586-588.
Gunderson, Robert Gray, *The Log-Cabin Campaign* (Lexington, University of Kentucky Press, 1957), p. 163.

*Is it consistent?* There are variant forms of listings, but a standard form is to list items in the following order:

### BOOKS

1. Author's name, last name first
2. Title of book, underlined (also underline pamphlet titles, etc.)
3. Place of publication
4. Name of publisher
5. Date of publication
6. Pages (not merely the beginning page)

### MAGAZINES

1. Author's name, last name first
2. Title of article, set in quotation marks
3. Title of magazine, underlined
4. Volume number, usually in Roman numerals[3]
5. Month and year of issue
6. Pages (not merely the beginning page)

1. *Is the author uninformed?* (Don't take it for granted that everyone who gets in print is informed.)
2. *Is he misinformed?* (A United States Senator wrote an article for a magazine with the largest circulation in the world; he was in error on certain figures by 200,000 per cent.)
3. *Is his analysis complete?* (Your X-ray reading will show this.)
4. *Is he illogical?*
5. *Does his evidence sustain his assertions?*

---

[3] The magazine volume number is often omitted in informal bibliographies; but it is included in complete ones.

### HOW TO CHECK UP AND FILL IN

When you have done critical reading there will be facts and ideas that you want to check, and open spots you want to fill in. The following are obvious sources:

#### GENERAL ENCYCLOPEDIAS

*Encyclopedia Americana*
*Encyclopædia Britannica*
*Collier's Encyclopedia*
*New International Encyclopedia*

#### SPECIAL ENCYCLOPEDIAS

Carter Alexander and Arvid J. Burke, *How to Locate Educational Information and Data.*

Carter V. Good, *Dictionary of Education.*

Walter S. Monroe, *Encyclopedia of Educational Research.*

Philip Lawrence Harriman, *New Dictionary of Psychology.*

E. R. A. Seligman, *Encyclopædia of the Social Sciences,* 15 vols.

James Truslow Adams, *Dictionary of American History,* 5 vols.

Robert E. Spiller, *Literary History of the United States,* 3 vols.

*The Catholic Encyclopedia,* 15 vols., plus index, and extensive supplements.

*The Interpreter's Bible,* 12 vols.

*The New Larned History for Ready Reference,* 12 vols.

I. F. Henderson and W. D. Henderson, *Dictionary of Scientific Terms.*

*Van Nostrand's Scientific Encyclopedia.*

### HOW TO READ

Any speaker worth his salt must go beneath the surface of the subject he talks about. He must bring to light things people don't know or don't understand. If his background comes from reading, then it must not be just ordinary reading, but critical reading to weigh and consider. Critical reading is active reading. You must really dig in. It demands especially three kinds of action on your part:

*First, read behind the book or article.* Find out what *kind* of book or article it is. Loosely, there are two kinds, theoretical and practical. Theoretical ones tell you *"that* something *is."* Practical ones teach you *"how* to do something you think you *ought* to do," or the author thinks you ought to do. Find out which kind you are reading. Then you know by which standard you must judge it. . . . Next, find out something about the author. What are his basic beliefs and assumptions? Why is he presenting his explanation or argument? What philosophy or interest-group does he represent? Often he will tell you by his line of approach, by his choice of facts, examples, and testimony—or too often by his name-calling adjectives. Most authors, like most speakers, are reasonably transparent to people who look for the signs. But don't hesitate to check the author in one of the several biographical sources (see just below), or check on other things he has written.

*Second, read to get the content.* This is not so simple as it sounds. First, you X-ray it as you read, and locate the proposition. You X-ray further, and find the main supporting parts (i.e. main heads). In other words, you get the structural whole and the related parts—the entire framework of thought beneath the words. You don't have to read a whole book, or even the whole of a long article, to do this. In a book the preface and table of contents will often serve. In an article the opening paragraphs plus a quick skimming of its contents will do it. Now you can examine the forms of support—the facts, figures, illustrations, specific instances, comparisons, and testimony—which sustain the various parts. You know about these things, because you have studied them in this book. Now you turn them around and apply them to the authors you read.

*Third, read for critical evaluation.* Of all the possible things in the world, the three easiest for your mind are to (1) believe everything, (2) believe nothing, (3) believe what you want to believe. None requires judgment. But in critical reading you must *judge.* You must decide whether you agree or disagree, and this decision cannot be either a snap-judgment or a want-judgment. Therefore, you don't judge until after you have finished reading for the content. In other words, you don't say "I agree," or "I disagree," or "I suspend judgment," until you first can say, "I understand." This means that you must know and respect the difference between knowledge and *opinion.* There are specific standards for agreement or disagreement:

### BIOGRAPHIES

Eminent Persons of the Past

*Appleton's Cyclopedia of American Biography.* Long sketches of selected names.

*New Century Cyclopedia of Names.* Many names, short sketches.

*Dictionary of American Biography.* Selected names, long sketches.

*Dictionary of National Biography.* British, similar to American Dictionary.

*Lippincott's Universal Pronouncing Dictionary of Biography and Mythology.* Includes men and women of all nationalities including the ancient. Some long and some short sketches.

*Webster's Biographical Dictionary.* Many names, very short sketches.

*Who Was Who in America.* Sketches of deceased persons who while living were listed in *Who's Who in America.* Since 1897.

*Who Was Who.* British, similar to the American. Also since 1897.

Living Persons

*Who's Who in America.* Includes living persons subject to inquiry or discussion.

Various regional volumes issued by the same publisher of the above volume, including *Who's Who in the East, Who's Who in the Midwest,* etc.

*Who's Who in Commerce and Industry.*

*Who Knows—and What.* A cross-indexed dictionary of living authorities, experts, and especially informed persons.

*Biographical Directory of American Scholars.* Learned writers and scholars, largely confined to colleges and universities.

*Biographical Directory of Leaders in Education.* Includes both administrators and scholars.

*American Men of Science.*

*Who's Who.* British, similar to American.

*Monthly Supplement of Who's Who in America.*

*Current Biography.* Monthly publication of biographies of persons recently prominent. Since 1940. Annual cumulation and cumulative index.

(The above volumes contain reliable biographies of living persons. They list only persons who meet certain standards and accept no money from any person listed. But there are others which are less reliable. Some have been suspended by the Federal Trade Commission, like *Who's Who in the Western Hemisphere.* Others, which libel laws prohibit naming here, will include almost anyone who pays to have his name included. Still others, like *Who's Who in American Education,* have standards for admission, but do not include biographies unless the person listed buys a copy of the volume, or pays for the cost of having it printed, etc. Such volumes are irregular, since they do not include biographies of persons who decline to buy a copy or pay for the cost of having their names included.)

### STATISTICAL INFORMATION

*Statistical Abstract of the United States.* The most comprehensive summary published of statistics on the industrial, social, political, and economic affairs of the U.S. Annually since 1878.

*United Nations Statistical Yearbook.* Contains international statistics from over 150 countries or territories including East Germany and the USSR. Annually since 1949 by the United Nations. In French and English.

*World Almanac.* A yearbook of facts. Vast array of information in inexpensive volume.

*Information Please Almanac.* Similar to *World Almanac,* but not identical coverage.

CURRENT HISTORY

*Americana Annual.* An encyclopedia of the events of the year.

*Britannica Book of the Year.* Contains events of the year, like the Americana.

*New International Year Book.* Contains a history of the year, like the above two volumes.

*Facts on File.* A digest of world news. Issued biweekly. Accumulated into monthly, quarterly, and annual indexes, with each in a different color to make identification easy.

*U.S. Government Organization Manual.* The official organization handbook of the Federal Government. Descriptions of agencies in legislative, judicial, and executive branches. Supplemental information on quasi-official agencies, and list of names with reference to pages where found in the manual. Published annually.

## HOW TO TAKE NOTES

You can't carry in mind all you read. It fades out, gets disordered, or you remember parts of it wrong. Therefore take notes. But the popular hit-and-miss note taking leads to hit-and-miss results. Therefore, take systematic notes. The following is a tested method:

1. Use reasonably *large* cards (4 × 6 or 5 × 7 inches), or a *looseleaf* notebook.

2. Write one *one* side only.

3. Record each idea on a separate page.

4. Remember that direct quotations are usually, though not always, more useful than abstract summaries. Record direct quotations exactly and enclose in quotation marks.

5. Use an ellipsis (three spaced dotes, thus: . . .) to indicate omissions in a quotation; and use brackets [   ], and *not* parentheses, to indicate insertions of your own words, as in this example:

We, the People of the United States [note that it is not "We the States"], in order to form a more perfect Union, . . . do ordain and establish this Constitution for the United States of America.

6. Check facts, figures, and quotations and do this immediately to be sure of accuracy.

7. Record the source immediately, including the exact pages, and do this for each card or sheet. You may need to consult the source again without wasting time.

8. Use a heading on each card or sheet that accurately labels the material recorded. (This heading is commonly put at the upper left.)

9. Note the classification of the material according to where it fits into your first tentative outline. (This is commonly put at the upper right, and written in light pencil so you can erase and change as you revise the outline.)

### NOTE-TAKING SPECIMEN

| (HEADING) | (CLASSIFICATION) |
|---|---|
| Early U.S. education | The first professor of speech |

In 1804 the " 'rules, directions, and statutes of the *Boylston professorship of rhetoric and oratory* in Harvard college,' . . . were approved by the board of overseers.

"In June 1805 the honorable *John Quincy Adams* was chosen, by the corporation, the first professor on this foundation. . . . Mr. Adams accepted the appointment with a reservation, which should leave him at liberty to attend his public duties in Congress; he being at that time a senator of the United States from Massachusetts. . . .

"He was installed June 12, 1806; . . ."

John Quincy Adams, *Lectures on Rhetoric and Oratory* (Cambridge, 1810), I, pp. iv-v, in the Publisher's Advertisement, dated February 26, 1810.

### HOW TO CLASSIFY SPEECH MATERIAL

When the notes really begin to pile up you may get confused, because your mind cannot carry so large an array of *unsorted* material—not even with it on cards. So before the notes become too numerous, you will want to classify them. There are many methods, of which the following are typical:

*Time order.* Here the notes are arranged according to the years, months, days, or hours.

*Place order.* Notes in place order are arranged according to nation, state, city, up-and-down, north-and-south, in-and-out, etc.

*Topic classification.* Such classifications might be (1) educational, (2) military, (3) religious, (4) political, (5) physical, (6) economic, (7) social, (8) sex, (9) age, etc.

*Cause-effect.* First will be grouped notes on causes or alleged causes. Next will come the notes on effects or alleged effects. Or you may reverse the order, and put the effects first and the causes second.

*Problem-solution.* Grouped in one set are notes on the problem— definition of, cause of, visible effects of, etc. Grouped in another set are notes relating to proposed solutions.

## *Processing the material*

### METHODS OF PROCESSING

Of course you don't wait for all the speech material to be gathered before processing it. From the first, this is continuous. The following steps are helpful:

1. Begin on time. (We've talked about that.)

2. Make a tentative outline before you start gathering speech material. (We've talked about that also.)

3. Classify your notes as you go along. (That, too, we have talked about.)

4. As soon as you start preparing the speech, *start also copying down ideas, information, examples, and exact phrases that come to mind. Do this at once, or you will be disturbed at finding that a perfectly clear thought has vanished an hour hence. This means to keep at hand pen or pencil, and paper or cards, both ready to use on the spot.*

5. At reasonable intervals reclassify your notes. This is merely another way of revising your tentative outline—which, in turn, is another way of *rethinking* the subject.

6. When you are ready to start on the final outline, lay out your notes in rows on a table. (Remember that you have only *one* idea on a sheet or card, and that you have written on *one* side of the paper only. Here is where the method pays off.) Now you can arrange and rearrange the main heads. You can lay out the subheads and subsubheads under your eye. You can insert illustrations, comparisons, testimony—even humor and spice—exactly where you anticipate they will be needed. And if you don't like the first outline, you don't have to do any erasing or rewriting. You simply pick up your notes and start rearranging them. This is the time-saving—the pay off—for what you may have thought was "extra work" involved in systematic note-taking.

### GETTING TO THE ESSENTIAL IDEA

Repeatedly we have said that a speaker should know his facts, should find them, test them, and process them for listeners to understand them. Later we shall stress this again, for no intelligence can go beyond the threshold of information. There is too much talk by people whose assertions are supported only by assertions, who don't have ideas but only prejudices, and who weigh the facts with their thumb on the scales.

People have too many doctrines dreamed up out of wishful thinking, too many beautiful ideas that are brutally destroyed by ugly facts. So we say that in this dangerous twentieth century we need facts to think with, and a speaker's job is to get them.

But you've got to learn that a set of indisputable facts does not always add up to the whole truth. Sometimes every statement in a speech may be true, yet the speech as a whole gives a false impression. As Pulitzer Prize Winner Harry S. Ashmore said of reporters who wrote about race friction, they "got their facts, and in great abundance," yet produced an "odd, distorted, and grossly incomplete image" of what happened. This was not because of personal prejudice, but because they failed to put their facts "in meaningful perspective." They were so busy telling *what* happened that they never were able to tell *why* it happened.[4]

Therefore, hunt for the *essential* fact, the keystone fact that gives others meaning. Put your illustration in the exact spot in the framework that gives it significance. Select specific instances that focus on the ultimate truth. Be sure that your facts add up, and make sense. Few have ever been able to do this with the power shown by that master of the essential fact, Sir Winston Churchill, but let his epilogue to the Battle of Gettysburg serve as an example:

> When that morning came, [Robert E.] Lee, after a cruel night march, was safe on the other side of the river. He carried with him his wounded and his prisoners. He had lost only two guns, and the war.[5]

## INTEGRITY OF IDEAS

Also involved in the handling of ideas is integrity, and especially so in a free society where there are no "approved" thoughts. In a democracy, therefore, are crackpots, emptyheads, and propagandists—all free to speak. There are even disloyal persons in the pay of foreign governments who use freedom of speech to destroy freedom of speech. Even in the classroom some students will talk banalities, and others will parade only their prejudices, developing a skill in discussing a *part* under the solemn pretense that it is the *whole*. In a free society we always have this kind of speaking. There is no way of purging it without purging freedom itself.

But in a free society people have the right to decide *which kind of speakers they trust*. In colleges and universities—that presumably exist for the preservation and uplift of free society—the instructor has a right to decide whether there shall be a standard of integrity. Toward this end two assumptions are offered:

[4] "The Easy Chair," *Harper's Magazine*, Vol. 216 (June, 1958), No. 1297, pp. 10, 12.

[5] *A History of the English Speaking Peoples* (New York, Dodd, Mead & Co., 1958), IV, p. 241.

### KNOW A FACT FROM AN OPINION

"Every man has a right to his opinion, but no man has a right to be wrong in his facts," said Bernard Baruch. There are various ways of being wrong with facts. First, there are speakers with "a 155 mm. mouth and a .22 caliber brain," who can never learn to know fact from opinion. In a speech class probably nothing can be done to change either the mouth or brain caliber. Let them stand as pots marred in the making. Next, there are others who have yet to *learn* the difference between facts and opinions. Typical of them are students who, early in the course, listed the following opinions as *facts:*

Modern poets are really insane.

God forbids capital punishment.

The Republicans have always wrecked the country when they came to power and the Democrats have had to save it.

When the Democrats get in power, they always get us in war.

Now these *opinions* are certainly held by particular groups of people, but in their nature they are not *facts*. What, therefore, are facts, and what are opinions? They belong to different categories, like color and size, and ought to be kept separate in the mind.

*Facts are "what has really happened"—the physical or mental event.* They are often hard to locate, but somewhere down beneath are the facts.

*Sound opinions are thought-out conclusions derived from a sound analysis of facts.* Loose opinions, of course, are those colored by feeling, sentiment, and bias. On them facts have little influence.

### KNOW SOUND OPINION FROM LOOSE OPINION

Make no mistake about it, this is rough going, for man is not a thinking animal except under certain limited conditions. Nevertheless the procedure is known. In simplified form it involves four steps:

1. Do you have an adequate and reliably established body of facts?

2. Do you proceed from warranted assumptions instead of prejudices?

3. Do you substitute part for the whole—by overlooking facts that disprove what you want to believe—and use only the facts that prove what you want proved?

4. Do you use righteous indignation in place of facts and ideas?

## ACKNOWLEDGING THE SOURCE OF IDEAS

When Adlai Stevenson gave one of his famous 20-minute commencement addresses he quoted the words or cited the opinions of other people seven times. When Alfred E. Perlman, president of the New York Central Railway System, spoke to business men in Detroit, he also, in 30 minutes, cited the opinions or quoted the words of other people seven times. When Wendell Phillips—that old "firebrand set to music"— gave his eulogy on Daniel O'Connell he quoted or cited the opinions of others twenty-nine times. Man needs to be refueled intellectually, so inevitably he turns to the ideas of other people. "He who never quotes, is never quoted," said Charles Haddon Spurgeon.

Now one of the foundations of persuasion, one of the means by which you persuade listeners to accept *you*, is to let them know where your ideas and information came from. When you use the words or the idea of another person, give credit to that person. When you present information, tell who gathered the information—and if necessary, *when* and *how*. In a sense one is known by the company he keeps; and when listeners find that you have been keeping company with eminent people of ideas and with expert collectors of information, they are impelled to accept you and your ideas.

Unfortunately, students often feel that they must *hide* their sources of speech material. They will talk on American foreign policy—about which they know nothing first-hand—and present information without revealing their source, or will propose courses of action without explaining who originally thought them out. They will talk on missile defense, Russian education, a crisis in the Middle East—on which they are not themselves authorities—and leave the listeners wondering whether they really know anything, or are peddling irresponsible notions in place of knowledge.

This has two unhappy results. First, it damages the speaker's reputation for honesty and judgment. Listeners know the speaker is not talking from personal experience, and suspect he's hiding his sources because they won't bear inspection. Second, it raises a question on the ethics of concealing one's sources of ideas. Both of these harmful side-effects are unnecessary, and usually not intended. The student simply does not know how to reveal his source of ideas. He has not the experience or the skill.

Therefore, *tell* the audience who collected your facts. Quote freely the words of others, and use freely their ideas. But tell who they are, and take pride in being in their company. And remember that righteous intention is not enough. You need to learn how to do it smoothly. You don't want to do it awkwardly the way typical beginners do:

Edward W. Barrett in his book *Truth Is Our Weapon*, published in 1953, says on page 6—quote—"Unless we Americans are bent on suicide, we have no wise choice but to master the techniques of international persuasion"— end of quote.

That is worse than awkward. The title, date, page, "quote," and "end of quote" distract from what the authority said. Listeners have been known to remember only that "Barrett said something in 1953, but I don't know what." Better smooth it out like this:

> Edward W. Barrett in his book *Truth Is Our Weapon* says that "Unless we Americans are bent on suicide, we have no wise choice but to master the techniques of international persuasion."

Or if you want to build up the author as an authority, tell how he knows and give weight to his opinion, you might state it this way:

> Edward W. Barrett was paid an unintended compliment by Radio Moscow. It called him the "possessor of the foulest voice in the world—the Voice of America." He earned that compliment. He was a top executive in General Eisenhower's Psychological Warfare Branch. He was director of the international operations of the Office of War Information. In 1950 he was called back from an editor of *Newsweek* to develop a new government "campaign of truth." After these years of service, Barrett says that "Unless we Americans are bent on suicide, we have no wise choice but to master the techniques of international persuasion."

Observe how experienced speakers go about the business. Said Douglas MacArthur:

> The world has turned over many times since I took the oath on the plain at West Point, and the hopes and dreams have long since vanished, but I still remember the refrain of one of the most popular barracks ballads of that day which proclaimed most proudly that old soldiers never die; they just fade away.

And Dorothy Thompson:

> It is a truism to say that we live in a time of crisis, or what the great British historian, Arnold Toynbee, calls a "time of trouble."

And C. Keith Funston:

> A great industrialist, Benjamin Fairless, summed this up not long ago. He commented wryly that with our new automation, detail work may well disappear into the innards of a computer. But he added: "If the apple which fell on Sir Isaac Newton's head had happened to fall on a Univac, the machine might have blown a tube . . . but it never would have come up with the law of gravity."

And Henry Watterson:

> Turning to the *Cyclopaedia of American Biography*, I find that Webster had all the vices that are supposed to have signalized the Cavalier, and Calhoun all the virtues that are claimed for the Puritan.

# Assignments

ON FINDING SPEECH MATERIAL

1. List the library sources for material on the following: (*a*) Higher education in colonial America, (*b*) Commercial use of atomic energy, (*c*) American folk music, (*d*) The early railroads, (*e*) Flemish painters, (*f*) the Greek jury system.

2. Locate and write down where each of the following references is found in your library. Note whether any are not there, and list other seemingly useful references not included below:

   *a.* The ten common sources of bibliography listed in this chapter
   *b.* The thirteen general and special encyclopedias
   *c.* The seventeen biographical references
   *d.* The nine references on statistical information and current history

3. List the reference containing the best biographical material for each of the following: (*a*) Edward R. Murrow, (*b*) Marie Curie, (*c*) Mark Twain, (*d*) Isaac Newton, (*e*) St. Augustine.

4. Hand in notes properly documented giving the following information:
   *a.* Total number of students in U.S. colleges last year
   *b.* Circulation of the four leading U.S. magazines
   *c.* Area and population of your home state
   *d.* Winners of the high jump and 100-meter race in the last Olympic Games
5. Find the date of newspaper articles on each of the following: The first sputnik (1957), the first atom bomb (1945), Lindbergh's flight across the Atlantic (1927), death of Woodrow Wilson (1924).

ON THINKING, FINDING SPEECH MATERIAL, AND
ASSIMILATING IDEAS INTO A SPEECH

6. Select a subject from the speech lists you have prepared previously (see Assignments 2-5, Chapter 9, pages 191-192): (1) Think on it, using the X-ray, how-to-think process described in this chapter. (2) Make a preliminary outline.

7. *Without studying or reading on the subject,* see what information and ideas you can gather during the next week. Do this by listening, conversing, and being generally on the alert.

8. Prepare a selective bibliography of perhaps 10-30 titles on your subject: (1) Do not rely only on the library card catalogue and *Readers' Guide,* but consult also the other common sources given in this chapter. (2) Do not take merely the first items you find, but sort carefully from the whole available bibliography those that seem best to fit your speech purpose. (3) Make sure that your items are accurate, complete, and consistent.

9. Use this bibliography for gathering speech material. Remember to read cautiously, not gullibly, and always with an eye for critical evaluation. Take notes, not by a hit-and-miss method, but by using a tested method such as

described in this chapter. Be prepared, if the instructor calls for them, to hand in your notes with the final outline.

10. Classify your notes, process your material, and revise your first tentative outline. *For at least this one time use the loose-leaf method of outlining as described in this chapter, and rearrange your notes several times until you get them in best order.* Perhaps you will want to revise this outline still again before you copy it in final form. Now you are ready to rehearse the speech for delivery.

# Organizing the Speech

JEAN CLAUDE, an almost forgotten writer of three centuries ago, warned the clergy of his day, "it ought to be remembered that the greatest part of the hearers are simple people," hence "it is impossible to edify them unless you are very clear." Then sagely he added, "and the learned have fatigue enough without increasing it at church." A sense of order regulates the minds of men, both simple and learned. They want to see ideas presented "as organized platoons—in marching order."

Now this "marching order" does not have to be a *logical* order, even though we pay lip service to the superiority of logical structure. Henry Ward Beecher insisted that "facts placed in juxtaposition" rather than in logical sequence was "best suited to the wants of uncultivated minds," and modern research shows he was right. Franklin D. Roosevelt once spoke in the Pittsburgh baseball stadium, and arranged his speech like the box score of a baseball game. Edmund Burke at times sought for a "dramatic conception" instead of a logical structure. Other speakers organize their speeches to fit the prevailing attitude of the listeners—i.e. they put first the points on which speaker and listener are most likely to agree, and save for last those topics on which speaker and listener will disagree. Speakers use many methods of organizing ideas, but all methods must pass one compelling test. The organization, first, must be *simple*, and, second, must be *instantly clear*.

How does one organize a speech into orderly form? The five steps in Lyman Abbott's famous Open Letter on Speechmaking offer an excellent start:

1. What is the object of this speech? What end is it to serve? What verdict is it to win? What result is it to accomplish?

2. Central thought. What thought lodged in the mind of an auditor will best accomplish the desired result?

3. Analysis of this central thought into three or four propositions [main heads], the enforcement and illustration of which will serve to fasten in the minds of the hearers the central thought, and so to secure the desired result.

4. Some illustrations or concrete statements of each one of these separate propositions [main heads].

5. These four points firmly fixed in the mind; then an endeavour on these lines of thought to win this result with this audience, exactly as one would endeavour to win assent from an individual.[1]

## Examining the so-called one-point speech

In the study of vertebrate zoology a useful method is to start with the one-cell amoeba. So with speeches. Imagine a one-cell speech, an amoeba. This single cell would consist of two kinds of subcells:

1. A single assertion
2. Supporting material (facts, figures, specific instances, illustrations, comparisons, testimony, etc.)

In outline form it would appear something like this:

ASSERTION      I. Having a baby is a real crisis.

*Specific instance*      A. You hold the new baby in your arms and say, "So this is my baby"; and now you know what the phrase means, "It's your baby."

*Specific instance*      B. You ask, "What will I do with it?" for you can't start it, stop it, and steer it like an automobile; it has no steering wheel.

*Specific instance*      C. It wakes up when it wants to, cries when it wants to, and if it decides to have you walk the floor at 2:00 A.M., you walk the floor—in undress parade.

*Specific instance*      D. You say, "I'm stuck; I have this baby on my hands 24 hours out of every day, with no double pay for overtime. How long does this last?" It lasts until the baby grows up and goes to college.

There are occasions on which speakers actually use a one-cell speech like these, but these occasions usually are limited to where *a speaker is himself giving only part of a whole speech,* and where the other parts are given by other persons on the program. Among such occasions are the one-point speeches given in discussion groups, in a series of short reports or explanations, in committee meetings, in business conferences.

The one-point speech, then, like the amoeba, is a one-cell animal. Also like the amoeba, it is not often seen in everyday life; but it is a useful specimen to illustrate the structure of real speeches.

[1] In Brander Matthews, *Notes on Speech-making* (New York, Longmans, Green, and Co., 1901), p. 90.

## *Dividing the speech into well-chosen main heads*

In well-organized speeches the central theme is supported by *two or three main heads or topics, occasionally four, and almost never more than five*. What about long speeches? Don't they have more main heads than short classroom speeches? No. If you read a hundred well-organized long speeches, and a hundred short ones, you will find that the short ones have as many main heads as the long ones. Daniel Webster once spoke for two days—four hours each day!—with two main heads, one each day. The difference between long speeches and short ones is not in the number of heads but in amount of support. In the longer speech each head has more information, illustrations, specific instances, and other forms of support. We point this out so you will understand that in giving classroom speeches you will use the same speech structure as twenty years hence when you may be called on to give a thirty-minute speech.

Students often ask: Why not have just *one* main head? The answer is you *do* have one central idea, but we call that the proposition, or purpose-sentence. We are here talking about how to divide this proposition into two or more simple parts so listeners can understand it. These two or more simple parts we call "main heads."

What is wrong with six or seven main heads? And why are two better than four? There are two stern answers. One lies in the subject. The other lies in the minds of the listeners. If you analyze any subject into its *basic* parts, you usually have only two or three main heads. The speaker who has six or seven has not analyzed the subject. He has merely swept together miscellaneous incidental units. As Harry Emerson Fosdick said of one of his sermons delivered as a young man: "I preached a sermon . . . with six points. It came out like a broom, in a multitude of small straws."

Furthermore, an audience cannot remember too many topics. Two they can remember with ease, three with more difficulty, but beyond that is like climbing Mt. Everest. It's hard work, and only a few make it. As Joseph Glanvill said back in 1678, the main heads "should be *obvious*, and plainly laid down." Nor should they be too intricate, for "the main things to be said may be reduced to a small number of heads, which being thorowly spoken to, will signifie more than a multitude slightly touch'd."[2]

## THOUGHT PATTERNS

"When you divide, it is necessary to divide simply, naturally," said François de Fénelon around 1679. "One must have a division that is

[2] Joseph Glanvill, *An Essay Concerning Preaching* (London, Printed by A. C. for H. Brome, 1678), pp. 39, 40.

found ready-made in the subject itself; a division that clarifies, that puts the materials into classes, that is easily remembered, and helps one to retain everything else."[3] We quote these men of the past because they perceived from experience and judgment what has now been verified by scientific study of audience understanding. In organizing a speech you must look for a plan that is "simple," "natural," "ready-made in the subject," or, we may add, that fits the prevailing attitude of the listeners. Among the common thought patterns are these:

1. *Time Order.* You begin at a given date or period of history, then move forward—or backward—with time. The divisions are marked by the clock or calendar. For example:

#### TEACHING READING IN AMERICAN SCHOOLS

I. In the 1840's when McGuffey's Readers were being written teachers used the phonetics method, stressing the alphabet at first and later the syllable.

II. After 1900 they developed the thought method, first using the word as a thought unit and later using the whole sentence.

III. Now they blend all these methods together, and motivate them with games and slides.

2. *Space Order.* You arrange material according to any pattern of space—east-to-west, far-to-near, top-to-bottom, inside-to-outside. Especially is this pattern useful for simple exposition or description, like this:

PROPOSITION: To form a clear idea of Australia, imagine that the United States is an island without Florida.
   I. From Maine to North Carolina is the Great Barrier Reef.
      A. Behind the Reef are no large natural harbors.
      B. The climate is semiarid, and the population is sparse.
  II. From North Carolina around to Louisiana lies the region best suited for for habitation.
      A. The soil is rich, and the rainfall abundant.
      B. Within this area lies the great cities of Brisbane, Sydney, Melbourne, and Adelaide, each with a population between 500,000 and 2,000,-000.
 III. The remainder of the country is largely an arid desert plateau which rises on the west coast to barren rolling hills.
      A. On the Australian west coast, in place of our Los Angeles, is Perth, somewhat smaller than San Diego; and it is the only real city in the vast reaches of Western Australia.
      B. Where we have San Franciso and Seattle, Australia has an empty coastline with villages of less than 1,000 people.

[3] *Fenelon's Dialogues on Eloquence,* translation by Wilbur Samuel Howell (Princeton, Princeton University Press, 1951), p. 61.

C. Along the northern border there is only Darwin, a city of less than 5,000, located roughly where we have Minneapolis and St. Paul.

3. *Classification Order.* You classify by identifying related forms and activities. The following are typical forms of classification:

1. *Classification according to fields of inquiry:*
> Educational
> Religious
> Physical
> Economic
> Political
> Social

2. *Classification according to the groups involved:*
> Young and old
> Men and women
> College and noncollege
> Northern and Southern
> Producer and consumer
> Labor and management

3. *Classification according to cause, as:*
> *a.* The primary cause was. . . .
> *b.* The contributing cause was. . . .
> *c.* The precipitating cause was. . . .

Other miscellaneous forms of classification include the following:

4. Prose and poetry

5. Plants and animals

6. Public and private

7. Function and structure

8. Inherited and learned

9. Experimentation and investigation

4. *Cause-and-Effect Order.* You arrange material according to causes and results. You seek to determine causes by asking, "What events, factors, or circumstances caused—or partly caused—this result?" You search for the kinds of causes by asking, "Which were the primary causes? Which were contributing causes? Which were immediate causes?" You seek to forecast results by asking, "What events, factors, or circumstances result (or have resulted) from this situation?"

*Beware of False Causes.* Don't mistake that which merely *precedes* for that which actually *causes.* This is an old error for which the Romans had a famous name: "*Post hoc, ergo propter hoc.*" "After this, therefore on account of this." It is probably as old as Methuselah, but people still get caught. Note some air-tight "after-this" situations: (1) As women stopped wearing corsets and took to girdles, women deaths from pneumonia fell to one-fifth its former rate. Does that prove that wearing corsets caused pneumonia, or did antibiotics happen to be discovered about that time? (2) For the past hundred years when ministers' salaries in Massachusetts have gone up, the price of rum in Havana has also gone up; and when the ministers' salaries have gone down, the price of rum has also gone down. Does this prove that the preachers hiked the price in good times by drinking more rum than Havana could produce, or did U.S. prosperity have something to do with both the rise in salaries and rise in prices? (3) In England as the imports of bananas increased, so did the victims of tuberculosis. After a time the alarmists were crying, "Forbid banana imports, and save our children's lives." Did bananas cause tuberculosis, and if so why did the Polynesians, who ate more bananas than any other people in the world, have no tuberculosis? (4) During the first ten years after radio broadcasting reached its peak (i.e. 1926-1936) the United States suffered the worst droughts within the memory of living people. Many farmers muttered, "Radio is to blame." Were they right, or was this a coincidence? (5) Statistics show that as the sale of comic books increase, juvenile crime also increases? Does one cause the other? Maybe so; maybe not. But no cause has been established as this book goes to press; and persons old enough to remember the dime novels that passed from hand to hand in the good old days (always out of sight of parents), ask themselves: "What have the modern comic books got that the old dime novels did not have, except more pictures and less dirt?"

*Beware of Single Causes.* We almost never have a situation in which one-cause equals one-effect. An effect—"whether a stomach-ache or a revolution"—usually is the result of several causes; and this effect in turn often produces still more effects. Most effects actually are the result of a *spiraling process in which one cause reinforces other causes.* They are much like ballistic missiles. A good one can't get under way with just a one-stage rocket. It takes a two-stage or a three-stage rocket. Look, therefore, for the whole process of causes, and don't be fooled into thinking that one thing caused all of it.

In using Cause-and-Effect arrangement skillful speakers usually—though not always—turn it around and present it to listeners in Effect-to-Cause sequence. This sequence allows them to present first a vivid picture of "what happened?" then rouse suspense over "What caused it?" Here is an example:

### WAR CAUSES INFLATION

EFFECT:      I. Inflation has accompanied every major war in U.S. history.
             A. The U.S. Department of Labor compiles a monthly Consumer Price Index, and has projected it back into early American history. In doing this it found that prices

during the American Revolution increased at least 200 per cent.

   B. During the War of 1812 prices, as measured by our Consumer Price Index of today, rose from 39 to 54.

   C. During the Civil War prices rose from 30 to 54.

   D. During World War I prices rose from 42 to 85.

   E. During World War II and the Korean War prices rose from 60 to 115.

CAUSE:    II. The cause goes back to Adam Smith's law of supply and demand.

   A. War creates a demand for military supplies.

      1. In the American Revolution our government spent $75 million.

      2. In the Civil War the Federal and Confederate governments all together spent $6.5 billion.

      3. In World War I our government spent $26 billion.

      4. During World War II and the Korean War it spent roughly $500 billion on military operations alone.

   B. These expenditures created a sudden intense demand which prewar industry machinery could not supply; and the sudden demand inflated prices.

   C. In addition, during recent wars we have had to open new factories in new locations, give bonuses to workers to move there, pay more bonuses for overtime work, and boost farm prices so farmers would grow more crops even though their sons and workers were away in the armed forces.

SUMMARY    I don't mean that other causes don't also cause inflation. There are probably at least four other operating causes. But war remains a leading cause that man has never yet learned to control.

5. *Problem-Solution Order.* Here you diagnose the problem and attempt to find a way to relieve it. But mark well that when you attempt probelm-solving the route is trapped with pitfalls. Some speakers lament an ill and cry, "There ought to be a law," but the law they want is to change human nature, and make it retroactive to the Garden of Eden. They have not solved the problem. They have only shed tears over it.

Before you can solve a problem you must first diagnose its ultimate causes, and in doing that keep in mind the warning of Dr. Charles H. Mayo of the famous medical clinic. When asked what type of illness most of his patients had, he replied, "Mistaken diagnosis." Social, political, economic ills suffer from the same malady: mistaken diagnosis. To avoid it analyze your problem in this manner:

   1. What are the effects, nature, external manifestations of this problem? *Sort and classify them!*

   2. On the basis of this classification—what *seem* to be the causes?

*The ability to ask the right questions is more than half the battle of finding the right answer!*

On complex questions the solutions are more complicated than the above two questions would indicate, but the key still lies in asking the right questions and getting to a clear statement of the problem. When you have done this, you can then consider the four master questions involved in problem-solving:

1. Is there a "felt difficulty" that makes a change desirable or necessary? (This you've already covered, so go to the next three questions.)
2. Would the change I advocate remedy the situation?
3. Might it not bring on new evils worse than the present ones?
4. Is not some other solution more satisfactory?

Or for the sake of vividness you might ask:

1. Is the man sick?
2. Will my medicine cure him?
3. Will it make him worse?
4. Is there another medicine that's better?

Of course you won't automatically convert each of these four steps into a main head. Never would your final heads turn out to be: I. The problem; II. My solution; III. Refuting the dangers of new and worse evils; IV. Refuting other solutions. These are simply your *steps of inquiry* by which you get to the bottom of the problem and test the various ways to get rid of it. Here is an example of a Problem-Solution thought-pattern that presents a three-step solution:

PROBLEM:   I. Higher education will continue to face its financial crisis for the rest of the twentieth century.
A. College enrollments will continue to rise.
1. In 1870 the U.S had 60,000 college students.
2. In 1941 we had 1,500,000.
3. Today it is approaching 4,000,000.
4. By 1970 we shall have between 6,000,000 and 8,000,000.
B. The cost of instruction *per student* continues to rise.
1. In 1830 Henry Word Beecher's tuition, board, room, and laundry cost $93 a year; and this was typical for 1830.
2. In 1930 the Associated Press estimated that the median cost of going to college was $500 in state institutions and $1,000 the more expensive private Eastern institutions.
3. By 1960 records kept by selected students showed the median cost to be over $1,500 plus clothes and tuition,

and a United Press survey showed that many families set the total cost at close to $3,000 a year.

4. Dr. Ernest V. Hollis of the U.S. Office of Education estimates that by 1969 the cost of college education will be double what it was in 1960.

5. Yet in spite of this increasing cost paid by students, they are actually paying a smaller percentage of what their education costs than their parents paid in 1940; for even the $1,400 tuition charged by private universities in 1960 covered less of the student's cost of education than $400 tuition paid by their parents in 1940.

SOLUTION II. This crisis needs the joint action of three groups: public officials, private corporations, and parents.

A. The people should urge their state legislators not to dodge the issue, or wait until the rising tide of students flood the campuses.

1. They should appropriate now the money for buildings they are going to need, and for professors they cannot do without.

2. If it helps to reduce the pain, let them remember that money spent on education is not cost but *investment* in the future.

B. Business corporations should face the fact squarely that if private colleges decline, students of the future will move into state institutions; and when that happens taxes on corporations will be increased to pay for educating these transferred students.

1. Giving now to private institutions won't "cost" anything; it will only prevent more money being taxed out of corporations in the future.

2. Therefore let them save taxes tomorrow by giving to private institutions today.

C. Parents must face reality by recognizing that colleges in the future must charge tuition that covers a higher percentage of education cost; the old day of charging a student $600 for an education that cost $1,200 is gone.

1. That means they must look upon the education of sons and daughters as a *capital* expenditure, and not as a current cost; in other words, they must borrow to finance such just as they borrow to buy a home.

2. This, in turn, means long-range planning, like buying educational insurance, or arranging with a bank to finance the education.

a. Bank-financed education started about 1958, when the banks set up special accounts known variously as "Learn Now, Pay Later," and "College Education Assured."

b. They vary in detail but follow the same principle; the bank each month pays to the college and student the money needed to cover the cost of education; the students' parents make monthly payments for 6 to 10 years to repay the loan: or the student himself takes over the monthly after he gets a job.

*Beware of patent-medicine solutions.* Remember that we really "solve" few problems in life. Through the centuries, we have never "solved" the problems of marriage, divorce, crime, taxes, war, tolerance, and equal justice under the law. Instead, we *keep at* solving them. In real life, sometimes the only solutions open to us are to "Watch this problem carefully," or "Act with courage," or "Be tolerant," or "Make these few adjustments." There are times when even the President and the Congress and the Courts can advise us only of the general direction we should go in solving pressing political questions. It comes with ill grace, at such times, for a college student to point the way out in a five-minute speech with a patent-medicine remedy. It brings to mind Winston Churchill's apt retort to free-lance advisers: "It is easy to give advice if you have not got to carry it out."

## PRINCIPLES OF SELECTING AND ARRANGING HEADS

For easy reference let us draw together the basic principles, most of which already have been stated or implied:

1. *Arrange the speech according to one consistent pattern.* Observe the confusion caused by two overlapping patterns in the following outline:

A NICARAGUAN CANAL

CASUAL PATTERN:    I. The Panama Canal cannot long handle future traffic.
                  II. It is also too vulnerable to air attack or sabotage.
TIME ORDER:       III. Negotiations for a Nicaraguan Canal were begun in 1826.
                  IV. Early investigations were held on feasibility in 1876.
                  V. Later investigations were again held in 1929-1931.

The trouble arises in part from the speaker having *two* speeches. He needs to make up his mind which he will use, cut off the unused one, and arrange the final speech according to one consistent pattern.

2. *Divide the speech so different heads don't overlap.* The following overlapping heads would confuse the listener simply because the speaker himself is still confused:

I. In flying from Los Angeles to New York you travel faster than in flying from New York to Los Angeles.

    II. This is something that anyone notices who makes the trip both ways.

    III. You naturally wonder why, and it is easy to find out.

    IV. The reasons are. . . .

We start over, and look for heads that don't overlap. We ask two questions: *What?* and *Why?* (Useful questions always.) We get the following clearcut heads that don't overlap:

EFFECT:        I. You fly faster from Los Angeles to New York than from New York to Los Angeles.

CAUSE:        II. This is because prevailing winds, including the jet stream, blow from west to east.

3. *Compose the parts so nothing essential is left out.* Please note the word "essential." Nothing is so dull as the speech that tries to cover the earth, the moon, and the stars—for it can only be dehydrated and tasteless, without the juice that makes a real speech. If you have tried to cover too much, narrow it down. But once the proposition is settled on, cover the essential parts. Look carefully at the following main heads:

PROBLEM:      I. Too many farmers don't get fair prices on the open market.

SOLUTION:    II. The Federal Government should guarantee fair prices to the farmers.

Note the essential parts left out: (1) How much would it cost the American people to guarantee fair prices? (2) What would keep farmers from using more fertilizer to get more crops to get more guaranteed government money? (3) If the government guaranteed fair prices to farmers why not guarantee fair profits to businessmen? (4) If the farmers deliver price control to the government, must it not also ask the government to control the price of farm machinery and farm methods—in fact, control the farmer's life? (5) Would not some other method—like a soil bank— be more effective and less dangerous? Obviously the speaker has not considered whether "new and worse evils" are involved or whether there are "other solutions more satisfactory?"

4. *Beware of fewer than two main heads, or more than four or five.* This has already been discussed (page 48), but will bear repeating. Wherever possible use two heads instead of three, and remember that when you have more than three heads it's like climbing Mt. Everest. It can be done, but it is rough going.

## Phrasing the main heads effectively

The bulk of your speech is made up of facts, illustrations, explanations, and argument, but these are *tied together by the framework of main heads.* Therefore, phrase them carefully, and, if possible, impellingly. Consider the following poorly-phrased heads:

I. The purpose of literature is the foundation of its writing.

II. Great literature is great.

III. The failure to produce great literature today is caused by several things.

(These main heads are not thought-up atrocities. They really are copied from the outline of a class speech!) Such heads make no sense because there is no analysis behind them. Better toss them out and start over.

At a higher level, but still not acceptable, is the speaker who substitutes *transitions* for main heads, like this:

I. What were the causes?

II. What were the effects?

Now these are excellent transitions. They lead right into the idea. But transitions are *not* main heads—not any more than a sign saying, "To the zoo" *is* the zoo. Transitions say "To the main head." They are *not* themselves main heads. Oftentimes—more often than not—the speaker will indeed start developing a main head with a transition ("What were the causes?"), will unfold it gradually, and not come to the full statement of the head until near the end. This is the inductive method, and it is very effective. But all along the speaker has each main head phrased in his own mind. He knows what its boundaries are. And when he gets through unfolding it he *tells the listeners* exactly what the main head is. These, for example, could be the real main heads of the above transitions:

CAUSE: I. The coming of radio and television has changed the nature of the American government.

EFFECT: II. The people once thought of government in terms of their Senator or Congressman, whom they often knew personally; now they think of it more in terms of the President whose face they see in their homes almost every week.

The following is a useful checklist for testing the effectiveness of phrasing main heads:

1. *Have you used straightaway English?* If you want to be understood, don't circle around an idea, don't go in backward, and don't bundle it up like a ball of worms. Try unraveling the meaning of this bundle:

First in importance are the early enviornment factors which developed in Bernard Shaw the ability to produce the type of plays he did.

Put in straightaway English it means:

Bernard Shaw's plays show the influence of his early life in Ireland.

Especially beware of overworking that lifeless verb *is*. Note how it makes the following idea lie down like a corpse:

I. There *is* a lack *of* social life in college this year.

II. As a result there *is* a disorganization *of* school spirit.

With a live verb you can put it into straightaway English like this:

I. We don't have the social life we enjoyed last year.

II. You see it reflected in our listless school spirit.

2. *Have you phrased your main head impellingly?* Impelling main heads are based on listeners prevailing needs, impelling motives, or culture patterns. Review these principles of motivation discussed in Chapters 6 and 7, and put them to use. For example, take the following distinctly unimpelling main head:

The basic principles of psychology are of great importance in modern life.

This need not be unimpelling. Rephrase it in terms of listeners' wants and you get the following impelling main head:

You can get along better with other people if you use psychology.

3. *Have you whenever possible helped listeners by parallel phrasing?* Main heads are the co-ordinate parts of your speech. They are roughly equal, and often parallel. At least they are parallel if well-chosen according to one consistent thought pattern. Very well, whenever possible phrase them so they *sound* parallel. The following heads fail to do this:

I. Understanding of the past in one quality of an educated man.

II. Also an educated man ought to know about the present.

III. And using knowledge is also inherent in an educated man.

Recast them in parallel form and you will get main heads that are easy to be instantly understood:

I. An educated man should understand the past.

II. An educated man should understand the present.

III. An educated man should know how to use his knowledge to influence the future.

## Arranging the supporting material so it really supports

1. *As an operating principle don't make an assertion without backing it up with supporting material that develops, proves, or clarifies.* You know what supporting material is. You have already studied it (pages 49-56), and will now study it further in more detail. Observe its use in a speech of simple explanation:

## LITERARY CRITICS AND THE GREAT AMERICAN PUBLIC

I. ASSERTION

I. For over a hundred years Nathaniel Hawthorne has been acclaimed, in the words of John Erskine, as a writer of "distinction in American literature."

   A. *Supporting material*

   A. His most famous novel, *The Scarlet Letter,* never sold over 10,000 copies during his lifetime.

   B. *Supporting material*

   B. Yet *Uncle Tom's Cabin,* published in the same decade and assigned by Carl Van Doren to a low status in art of fiction, sold 3,000,000 copies.

   C. *Supporting material*

   C. A few years later appeared Lew Wallace's *Ben Hur,* which Van Doren thought to be "a long, dull romance"; but it sold 4,000,000 copies.

   D. *Supporting material*

   D. Mark Twain was the only American author of the late nineteenth century accepted both by the critics and by the public; his *Huckleberry Finn* sold 1,000,000 copies and *Tom Sawyer* sold 1,500,000.

II. ASSERTION

II. At the turn of the century the critics acclaimed William Dean Howells' domestic realism and Henry James's psychological realism to be the best of their time.

   A. *Supporting material*

   A. Their novels sold in the 10,000 and 20,000 bracket.

   B. *Supporting material*

   B. About that time came Harold Bell Wright and Gene Stratton Porter, whose names will not be found in any anthology, be it Van Wyck Brooks's or the *Cambridge History of American Literature.*

      1. *Supporting material*

      1. Yet six of Wright's novels on the Ozarks sold 5,600,000 copies.

      2. *Supporting material*

      2. And six of Porter's novels on the Limberlost Country sold 9,500,000 copies.

III. ASSERTION

III. During the last generation since the paper backs have been put into drugstores, the critics would certainly rate three novelists among the best.

A. Assertion

   1. *Supporting material*

   2. *Supporting material*

   3. *Supporting material*

B. Assertion

   1. *Supporting material*

   2. *Supporting material*

   3. *Supporting material*

   4. *Supporting material*

A. All three won the Nobel Prize.

   1. Pearl Buck's most popular novel was a social chronicle, *The Good Earth*, of which critic Nancy Evans said, "To read this story . . . is to be slowly and deeply purified." It sold 1,800,000 copies.

   2. William Faulkner's most popular book was the one most widely criticized by the critics, *The Wild Palms*; it sold 1,700,000 copies.

   3. Ernest Hemingway's most popular novel was that impressionistic realism, *A Farewell to Arms*, which Clifton Fadiman thought was, "The very apotheosis of a kind of modernism." It sold 1,400,000 copies.

B. But the three most popular authors were not the Noble Prize winners.

   1. Margaret Mitchell's *Gone With the Wind*, was thought by critic I. M. Paterson to be "redundant and devoid of distinction," but it sold 5,000,000 copies.

   2. Grace Metalious' *Peyton Place* was called by *Time*, "a dreary splash in a small-town sex sump," but it sold 7,300,000 copies.

   3. Erskine Caldwell's *God's Little Acre* was thought by critic Robert Cantwell to have characters "all distorted and enlarged," but it sold over 8,000,000 copies.

   4. And of course this does not include the unmentionable Mickey Spillaine's sale of over 30,000,000 copies.

The following pattern shows how supporting material would be used to develop a Cause-Effect arrangement.

I. Assertion:

   A. *First subassertion*
      1. *Supporting material*
      2. *Supporting material*
      3. *Supporting material*
      4. *Supporting material*
      5. *Supporting material*

I. Causes of the situation are. . . .

   A. Primary Cause is. . . .
      1. Facts
      2. Figures
      3. Comparison
      4. Illustration
      5. Testimony

|                              |                              |
| ---------------------------- | ---------------------------- |
| B. *Second subassertion*     | B. Immediate cause is. . . . |
|   1. *Supporting material*   |   1. Illustration            |
|   2. *Supporting material*   |   2. Illustration            |
|   3. *Supporting material*   |   3. Facts                   |
|   4. *Supporting material*   |   4. Specific instances      |
| II. ASSERTION. . . .         | II. Effects are. . . .       |

*2. Arrange supporting material in a consistent thought pattern.* You have already studied thought patterns as applied to main heads—Time Order, Space Order, Classification Order, Cause-Effect Order, and Problem-Solution Order. These thought patterns are also used for arranging supporting material. For each head choose whichever pattern seems most effective. For example, the supporting material of Head I could be arranged in Time Order, that of Head II in Space Order, and that of Head III in Classification Order. Shift from one pattern to another as much as you please when you move from one head to another, but generally don't shift patterns within any particular head or co-ordinate series. The following is an example of three main heads arranged in Classification Order, but with the supporting material under Heads I and II arranged in Time Order:

CLASSIFICATION         **PATENTS THEN AND NOW**
ORDER

TIME ORDER          I. Patents have encouraged American inventors since
WITHIN                 the beginning of our national history.
HEAD I-A               A. The original patent act was passed in 1790.
                          1. The first patent went to Samuel Hopkins
                             that year, signed by George Washington;
                             it was for the making of pot and pearl ash
                             ($K_2CO_3$).
                          2. There were three patents granted that year.
                          3. Abraham Lincoln received a patent for a
                             device to lift river boats off sand bars.
                          4. Thomas Edison received more patents than
                             anyone else; altogether he received 1,100.
                          5. The 1,000,000th patent was granted in
                             1911, after 121 years; but the 2,000,000th
                             patent took only 24 years more; it was
                             granted in 1935. Now we've passed the
                             3,000,000th.
                       B. Getting a patent today is more complicated
                          than in the early days.
                          1. There are now some 78,000 applications a
                             year; that's over 250 applications for each
                             working day in the year.
                          2. Each of these must be investigated to de-

termine whether it infringes on any previous patent; almost half of them do, so of the 78,000 applications only some 40,000 are granted.

    3. Most patents take about three years to go through, but some may take 10 years. For example, the patents on the processes that produced the first atom bomb were applied for in 1945, but were not granted until 1955.

**TIME ORDER**
**WITHIN**
**HEAD II**

II. You can still get patents today if you have patience and know-how.

    A. Suppose you invent a wonderful dandelion picker with pincer-jaws at the end of a 4-foot handle.

        1. Chances are that someone else already has invented it.

        2. But your invention may be sufficiently different to get a patent.

    B. You write the U.S. Patent Office for a list of patent attorneys and agents; cost $1.75.

        1. You hire one of these experts.

        2. He cannot divulge secrets; he would be disbarred.

        3. But he'll search the Patent Office records for similar inventions.

        4. If everything is all right, he'll advise filing for a patent; cost $30.

        5. If the patent is granted, it will cost you $30 more.

        6. All of this, remember, takes about three years.

    C. When you get the patent, suppose you haven't found anybody who wants to manufacture it, then what?

        1. You can have your invention listed among patents which are for sale.

        2. This is known as the "Register for Patents."

III. Behind this principle of granting patents is the belief that it encourages men of genius to create new products and processes.

## Assignments

ON PRELIMINARY PRACTICE IN ORGANIZING IDEAS

1. As the first step in using the principles of this chapter, make a one-cell, amoeba outline of any subject of your choice. Let it consist of a single assertion supported by three or four subheads of solid speech material.

2. For the next phase of applying principles, read three speeches, each having a different thought pattern (cause-and-effect, problem-solution, etc.). You may find them in *Vital Speeches*, in this book, or anywhere else. For each write the purpose-sentence and main heads, and identify its thought pattern.

3. We are now ready to apply principles on a more complex level. For each of the five thought patterns discussed in this chapter: (*a*) Select a subject for which such an arrangement would be fitting. (*b*) Phrase an impelling purpose sentence for it. (*c*) Select and arrange main heads so they form one consistent thought pattern. (*d*) Phrase the main heads concisely and impellingly; and if possible use parallel phrasing.

4. After the above preliminary practice you are ready to examine the full-scale organization of a speech. Make an outline of one of the speeches found at the back of this book, and especially criticize the following: (*a*) Adequacy of thought pattern found in the main heads. (*b*) Consistency of thought pattern found in the supporting material (subheads, etc.). (*c*) Amount and quality of this supporting material.

5. Listen to a good speaker and make a rough-draft outline of his lines of thought. Study it critically: (*a*) Did he have a thought pattern, and was it consistent? (*b*) Did these lines of thought overlap, or leave out essential parts? (*c*) Did he state these main lines of thought so they "had handles on them," and you could remember and carry them away? (*d*) Were they impelling, and were they stated impellingly? (*e*) Was the supporting material arranged in a clear and consistent thought pattern, or did it seem to be a waste-basket arrangement? (*f*) If you were giving this speech how would you change the main heads, change their arrangement, change the supporting material, and rearrange the thought pattern of supporting material?

ON ARRANGING YOUR SPEECHES INTO ORDERLY FORM

6. Pair with a classmate and criticize each other's outlines for the remaining major speeches of this source. Especially be watchful whether:

   *a.* The main heads are arranged in a consistent thought pattern, and that it is the best thought pattern for this subject.
   *b.* The main heads do not overlap and do not leave out essential parts.
   *c.* Each main head is a simple, single, complete statement, and is phrased impellingly.
   *d.* The group of main heads, where possible, are stated in parallel form.
   *e.* Assertions are supported by ample and adequate supporting material.
   *f.* Supporting material, like the main heads, are arranged in a consistent thought pattern.

7. In all future class speeches use the principles of this chapter to make more effective what you have learned from previous chapters on thinking, finding materials, making ideas impelling, etc.; and cross-check them with at least one classmate as designed in Assignment 6.

# Beginning and Ending
# the Speech

WHEN YOU STAND before a live audience, you realize at once that you face
two acute side-problems. The first rolls toward you like a giant ocean
wave: "How can I get all those people to turn loose other thoughts, shake
off their indifference, and give me attention *right now?*" The second is
over the horizon, but you know it is coming at you, and you later will
meet it head-on: "How can I make them *remember* what I say as I close
the speech, so they won't just walk out and forget it?"

We shall consider these problems one at a time.

## Getting attention and orienting the audience

When you begin a speech you face not one problem, but two. First, to
get attention and good will. Second, to orient the audience, tell what
the subject is about, and supply the necessary background. *But you can't
deal with the second problem until you first get attention!*

### GETTING ATTENTION AND GOOD WILL

Remember that in Chapter 7 (pages 147-151) we pointed out that two
iron curtains commonly hang between the speaker and audience during
the first two minutes of a speech. One was the common tendency of speakers to start with foggy abstractions—often to state their conclusions in
dense terminology—instead of starting with interesting material that
throws light on the subject. This shatters the communication line, of course.
It's the equivalent to a ten-yard loss in football. We repeat what was said
on Chapter 7, that if you don't get the listeners' attention in the first ten

words you should have a curb-conference with yourself when the speech is over. In that chapter we discussed the psychology of getting attention and good will. Here we shall set down specific techniques for doing so:

1. *Get attention and good will by establishing common ground with the audience.* Establishing common grounds with the audience has nothing whatever to do with the subject. It does not tell what the subject is about, nor does it supply any necessary background. From a logical standpoint it may seem ridiculous for a speaker to waste time on what appears to be nonsense. If you think so, you are not the first. A great intellectual, whom some say was the greatest intellectual of all time, had to warn his students that they did not talk "to ideal hearers, but to hearers as we find them," and hence speakers often had to say things that had "nothing to do with the speech itself," but only with "the weak-minded tendency of the hearer to listen to what is beside the point." So said Aristotle around 336 B.C., and so you will find next week when you address that next audience. Actually we now know that this is not a "weak-minded tendency," but simply that listeners are not IBM calculating machines. They are human beings, alive with human judgments and human values. Before they will accept your ideas they must first accept *you.* Therefore, one of the surest ways of getting attention and good will is to establish common ground so the listeners will accept *you.* Even persons of high prestige, like Presidents and Prime Ministers, must recognize this compulsion. Said Dwight D. Eisenhower, speaking in Oklahoma on the fiftieth anniversary of its statehood:

> First, I should like to extend my thanks to the people of Oklahoma for this chance to share in celebrating the fiftieth anniversary of Oklahoma's statehood.
>
> Born in the Lone Star State just to your south, and reared in the Sunflower State just to the north, I have tonight a fine feeling of coming home again.[1]

Likewise Harold Macmillan, British Prime Minister, established common grounds with his American audience when speaking at DePauw University:

> For a Prime Minister of Great Britain to be invited to your great university is an unusual occasion. But I feel sure that my present office was not the only, nor indeed, perhaps the main reason for your invitation. My real claim to be here is on account of my birth, or at least on one side of it. For I am half Scot and half American. . . .
>
> Like my great predecessor in office, the greatest of living and perhaps of all Englishmen, Sir Winston Churchill, I took the precaution on entering life to make sure that I was born of an American mother. . . . For my mother's father, Josua Belles, as you know, was one of the first graduates

[1] *Vital Speeches,* XXIV (December 1, 1957), No. 4, 98.

of DePauw's Medical School. My mother was born in the state of Indiana—I think in Indianapolis. I was able, two years ago, to visit Spencer where she lived all her life until she left America, and to attend service in the Methodist Church in whose choir she used to sing.[2]

2. *Get attention and good will by paying the audience an honest compliment.* A visiting lecturer begins: "It gives me great pleasure to address college men and women today, for they are the most intelligent of our youth, and our youth today will become the leaders of tomorrow. . . ." No, it won't do. Those college students have heard that before.

A political candidate says: "I am glad to come to this splendid community with its wonderful schools, its magnificent churches, its noble people. They represent the best in America—the honest, God-fearing people who pay their debts and do good to their neighbors." No, it won't do either. People aren't that dumb. To be sure, the candidate's partisans forgive with easy tolerance ("The old boy was spreading it around, eh?"), but such methods win neither votes nor respect.

If you have a compliment to pay, do it skillfully, for audiences are speech-wise and skeptical of them. But it can be done—if you have the compliment and the know-how. General Willard G. Wyman went from Virginia to Massachusetts to address former members of the armed forces, and did it with the perfect touch:

> I appreciate this opportunity to come back again to the place where so much that is America began, and to talk to people who have done so much to defend America. Actually, New England is my country. I began up here, too, so just being here today gives me a lift for which I am warmly grateful.[3]

3. *Get attention and good will by reference to the occasion or surrounding.* Sometimes a speaker seizes on some small reference of interest value, and turns it to account, as the speaker who said:

> On the platform behind me you will notice, among others, a Catholic priest and a Protestant minister. They don't know it, but they are a symbol of what I am going to talk about—for my subject deals with the need for tolerance and cooperation between Catholics and Protestants in America.

At other times—like anniversaries and ceremonies—the occasion is the heart and core of the program, and the speaker is expected to recognize it. Woodrow Wilson's introduction to his address at Independence Hall in Philadelphia, July 4, 1914, remains a classic:

> We are assembled to celebrate the one hundred and thirty-eighth anniversary of the birth of the United States. I suppose that we can more vividly realize the circumstances of that birth standing on this historic spot than it would be possible to realize them anywhere else. The Declaration

[2] *Vital Speeches,* XXIV (July 1, 1958), No. 18, 552.
[3] *Vital Speeches,* XXIII (September 15, 1957), No. 23, 717.

of Independence was written in Philadelphia; it was adopted in this historic building by which we stand. I have just had the privilege of sitting in the chair of the great man who presided over the deliberations of those who gave the declaration to the world. My hand rests at this moment upon the table upon which the declaration was signed. We can feel that we are almost in the visible and tangible presence of a great historic transaction.

4. *Get attention and good will by reference to matters of special interest to listeners.* Every special group has common knowledge, interests, and desires—college students, physicians, lawyers, retailers, executives— that can be used to capture attention and good will. In addition to the special interests of special groups are the universals of special interest to all groups. Thus Rabbi Charles E. Shulman, speaking before the Illinois Bankers Association, got attention and good will by reference to common history and universal values held by all Americans:

In the *Cleveland Plain Dealer* there recently appeared an article written by the Financial Editor and headlined "Invest in America." It went on to say:

"A solid answer to the usual May Day show of muscle by the Communists is being forged in Cleveland by business leaders from many industries. It will culminate in a civic luncheon. This is the 'Invest-in-America' week celebration which is part of the national celebration to be held in more than seventy cities in the country. . . . The purpose of 'Invest-in-America' week, it was pointed out, is to emphasize what has made America a great country with the highest standard of any nation in history is the willingness of men to invest their savings in present and new business with all the people being the real winners. . . . It is the best defense against the isms that today threaten our national life. . . ."

Reading the article, I could not help wondering: Is this all we should invest in America? Only the dollars we have saved? . . . Is this what drew the Pilgrim Fathers to these shores and caused us to rebel against England? Is this what inspired the Gettysburg Address? Is this what the teeming immigrants from all corners of the world were thinking about when they gratefully entered our gates? Is this an adequate answer to the challenge of communism? . . .

Our gadget-loving, gadget-dominated age has had ample warning from history not to put its trust in material strength and power alone. Long ago Kipling wrote this warning in the stately lines of his "Recessional":

> For heathen heart that puts her trust
> In reeking tube and iron shard,
> All valiant dust that builds on dust,
> And guarding calls not Thee to guard,
> For frantic boast, and foolish word,
> Thy mercy on Thy people, Lord!

America is built on investments more solid than dollars which keep our machines running and our employment pails full. To invest in the real

America is to bolster the qualities that have made this nation unique among the peoples of the world. . . .

What are these solid American investments that can yield us rich and satisfying dividends?

One is freedom. A second is faith in our system of government. A third is brotherhood. And a fourth is religion. They are all related to the essential character of American life.[4]

5. *Get attention and good will by pleasantry or humor.* Usually the prepared joke is a poor beginning, because it is just plain trite—and listeners are bored with radio and television gags. A short apt funny story, of course, is good. But be sure that it is short, apt, and funny. Experienced speakers tend to rely more on other types of humor or pleasantry. Thus G. Keith Funston, President of the New York Stock Exchange, in speaking to Women's National Press Club in Washington, began:

> Never before, when in the presence of more than two ladies, have I had such an excellent chance to do all the talking—and perhaps even to get in the last word. Certainly, this has not been my experience with the three ladies of my own household.[5]

Likewise Senator Edmund S. Muskie of Maine, addressing the American Forensic Association, began with a short sharp thrust of humor:

> I feel very much like the mosquito who found himself unexpectedly in a nudist colony. I don't know where to begin.[6]

6. *Get attention and good will by direct reference to the significance of the subject.* When the audience has an intense interest in the subject, you may not need to get attention. You can then gain their good will by coming at once to a significant statement of your proposition or first main point. Bernard S. Van Rensselaer, a research specialist in government affairs, did this in addressing the Economic Club of Detroit:

> To travel here I boarded an airplane in Washington, D. C., at 2:40 P.M. yesterday, I arrived in Detroit three and a half hours later. In that very brief space of time our Federal Government spent $1,500,000 for military and economic aid to foreign countries.
>
> I mention this because I think it illustrates two of our national characteristics. We move fast, and we do things in a big way.[7]

But note, please, that most speeches cannot be started by direct reference to the subject. If the audience is apathetic, a direct reference to the subject will leave them apathetic. If they are doubtful about you,

[4] *Vital Speeches,* XXIV (July 1, 1958), No. 18, 560-561.
[5] *Vital Speeches,* XXIV (November 15, 1957), No. 3, 89.
[6] Vital Speeches, XXIV (October 15, 1957), No. 1, 30.
[7] *Vital Speeches,* XXIII (July 1, 1957), No. 18, 555.

or doubtful about the subject, a direct reference to the subject—without any human warm-up—won't reach them. This is an introduction you use when the listeners' interest is really intense.

7. *Get attention and good will by a narrative or illustration that leads into the subject.* Other things being equal a narrative or illustration is probably the easiest way to get immediate attention, and the surest. A good one is specific and easy to follow. A good one has suspense that makes people want to listen in order to find out what happened. And a good one will lead them right into the heart of the subject, much as the modern automobile expressways take one over the network of obstacles right into the heart of the city. Walter Lippmann's narrative in speaking at Freedom House, New York City, on wars and revolutions of the twentieth century, is an ideal example:

> Many years ago while I was still a student at college, I read a book about which I have forgotten almost everything, including the name of the author, except one specific incident. The book contained the recollections of an Englishman who visited France a few years after the fall of Napoleon. One day, as I recall it, he found himself talking to an old peasant, who had been working on his farm, which was a day's journey from Paris, for more than fifty years. He had lived there under the Bourbon Kings, during the Revolution, during the Terror, and during the Napoleonic Empire and its downfall.
>
>   . . . So the Englishman tried to draw out the peasant, feeling I suppose, that when he returned he would then be able to tell the people of England what the people of France were thinking. But what was his surprise when he found that his excellent friend had somehow contrived to live near Paris for the past fifty years and yet never to have heard anything about Napoleon Bonaparte.
>
>   I remember asking one of my old teachers about the story and whether such a strange thing could really have happened, and I remember his saying, "Yes, it could have happened . . . it happens in every age, and what is more it happens to most of the people in any age, and it will happen to you, too, in one degree of another, to live in an age when history is made and not to know what that history is."[8]

A word of advice to college students on looking for illustrations and narratives: You can find them as abundantly as you find plants on the earth, in history, literature, psychology, science, religion—and especially from personal experience. Don't waste time searching for rare ones, like four-leaf clovers. Take the everyday apt ones all around you. Here are a few samples drawn at random from superior classroom speeches:

Last month I had a blind date. . . .

The first day I was in college I met a senior. He said. . . .

[8] A. Craig Baird, *Representative American Speeches, 1943-1944* (New York, H. W. Wilson Co., 1944), pp. 248-249.

When I was a senior in high school the English teacher one day. . . .

I remember the first time I tried a scientific experiment. The boy next door had one of those do-it-yourself-kits. . . .

## ORIENTING THE AUDIENCE

You may have noticed that each one of the Introductions given in the few pages previous not only gained attention and good will, but also did one additional significant thing. *Each oriented the listeners to the speaker's point of view.* That is, at the same time the speakers were getting attention and good will, they also told the audience what the subject was about, adjusted them to the speaker's viewpoint concerning it, and (when necessary) supplied them with background facts for understanding the discussion. These are two separate purposes of the Introduction: (1) to get attention and good will, (2) to orient the audience. They are not necessarily, or even usually, done in two separate parts, however. A skillful speaker can blend them into one smooth whole.

There is no formula for orienting the audience but the following are helpful procedures:

1. *Orient the audience by explaining the subject background.* Consider the follow-the-rule debater who opens his speech in this manner:

> We are to discuss whether the federal government should continue price support to farm crops. By the "Federal government," we mean that government established in 1787 under the Constitution and which is now centered in Washington, D. C. By "continue" we mean to vote taxes to carry on without essential change the policy of the past five years. . . .

No, this won't do at all. He is telling listeners what they already know. He is taking simple words and explaining them in complex words. This is not "explaining the subject background." It is muddying the issue. In explaining the subject background, you waste no words telling listeners what they already well know, for elaboration of the obvious tends to lose good will, and certainly loses attention.

But when the background facts are not known, or when they are not fresh in mind, a vivid background sketch permits the audience to see the subject in its perspective. Samuel B. Pettengill, in a radio speech on communism, began by explaining the subject background:

> It was 101 years ago that Marx and Engels wrote the *Communist Manifesto* which began with the words, "A specter is haunting Europe, the specter of communism." This sounds like today's newspaper. That was the year gold was discovered in California, before the covered wagon began to roll across the plains. Please keep this date in mind. It is significant.
>
> A little later, Marx, in London, wrote *Das Kapital,* the bible of the Communists and Socialists. As a reporter of facts, Marx was accurate. The con-

ditions of the workers in England a century ago, as he points out, were very grim. Women pulled canal boats along the tow-path with ropes over their shoulders. Women were harnessed, like beasts of burden, to cars pulling coal out of British mines. In the textile mills, children began to work when they were 9 or 10 years old, and worked 12 to 15 hours a day. In many cases, the beds in which they slept never got cold, as one shift took the place of the other. It was said that they were machines by day and beasts by night. Tuberculosis and other occupational diseases killed them off like flies.

Conditions were terrible. Not only Marx, but other warm-hearted men, such as Charles Dickens, Ruskin, and Carlyle, poured out a literature of protest which was read around the world.

On his facts, Marx can scarcely be challenged. But his diagnosis was wrong and, therefore, the remedy he prescribed was wrong also.[9]

2. *Orient the audience by stating and explaining the proposition.* Before a hostile audience the one thing you don't do is to state your proposition openly at the beginning, lest the listener's minds snap shut like a steel trap. Instead you start on common ground, take up the facts of the situation before you offer opinions, approach the proposition inductively, and state the proposition after the evidence is in. Before a hostile audience you orient the audience in the Introduction by supplying the background facts, but you don't state the proposition openly.

Nonhostile audiences, however, can be oriented by making the proposition clear early in the speech, usually as soon as you get the listeners' attention. Eric Johnston, for example, speaking at a Motion Picture Day luncheon in New York, came almost at once to his proposition and main heads:

This afternoon I'd like to talk to you about Hollywood—the Hollywood I've known for the past dozen years—the Hollywod that is America's traveling salesman to all the world, a salesman of goods and services, of language and culture, of ideals and hopes. . . .

I want to discuss these two points:

First, the Hollywood motion pictures as the great stimulator of mass production—the assembly line—at home and overseas.

And, second, the Hollywood film as the pioneering and still tireless agent for American democracy and the fruits of democracy throughout the world.[10]

Hugh G. Grant, former U.S. Minister to Albania and Thailand, skillfully used an orthodox method in addressing a Woman's Club in Athens, Georgia. He first got attention by an illustration that led into the heart of his subject, then came to an open statement of his proposition:

Near the end of World War II, in 1945, while the United Nations was in the making in San Francisco, I sat in on some of the sessions as an observer.

[9] *Vital Speeches*, XV (May 1, 1949), 442-443.
[10] *Vital Speeches*, XXIII (July 1, 1957), No. 18, 572.

I met and talked with a number of the leading foreign statesmen who were delegates at the United Nations Organization meeting. One of these statesmen was Jan Masaryk, Foreign Minister of Czechoslovakia.

In an hour's conversation with Masaryk, I asked him the pointed question as to whether, in his opinion, a United Nations Organization could establish and maintain world peace. . . . Masaryk replied: "Unless the great nations work together, there will be no peace in the world." He named the United States, Great Britain, France, Russia, and China as the great powers.

That conversation took place 11½ years ago. Masaryk is no longer around. A short time later he was either a suicide or was murdered in his foreign office in Prague. What about Masaryk's prediction?

. . . With the exception of China, the great powers mentioned by Masaryk are all there, but they are not working together. In fact, the United States and Russia are not only not working together, but they are at daggers' points with the threat of global war ever present.[11]

3. *Orient the audience by explaining how you propose to develop the subject.* Sometimes this is done simply to make instantly clear where the speaker is going. J. T. Fields thus began his popular lecture by stating the subject in the opening words and explaining at once how he proposed to develop it:

Ladies and Gentlemen: I am to speak to you this evening, without pretense, but in all earnestness, if I may do so, a few thoughts on a subject which I shall call "The Masters of the Situation," and as example is always better than precept, and as it is much better to go and do a thing than to say how it ought to be done, I shall hope to interest you with now and then a short story illustrative of my theme, rather than by a long sermon, had I the ability to preach one.

This method is especially useful in treating a *complex* subject, for listeners are able to follow complex ideas more easily when the plan of arrangement is deliberately explained at the beginning. Thus a lecture on "Economic Theory" might begin by explaining that

There are three prominent schools of economic theory today, the Ricardian, the Marxian, and the Keynesian. I shall discuss first the disciples of Ricardo, who believe that the government should keep out of practically everything. Next, I shall discuss the disciples of Marx, who hold that the government ought to get into practically everything. Finally I shall discuss the disciples of John Maynard Keynes, who stand midway between the first two theories. Let us look, first, at the disciples of Ricardo. . . .

Finally, this method of orienting the audience is used when the speaker faces an audience that has *doubts or reservations about him or about his subject.* Roger M. Blough, Chairman of the Board of the United States Steel Corporation, used it when addressing a Committee of the United States Senate that was investigating monopolies:

[11] *Vital Speeches,* XXIII (March 1, 1957), No. 10, 299.

I have read with deep interest, and with understandable perplexity, the conflicting testimony of the distinguished economists who have appeared before you at these hearings. I have studied their differing definitions of the term "administered prices"; I have sought to comprehend that . . . economic concept called the "zone of relative price difference"; I have struggled with that . . . paradox known as "monopolistic competition"; and pursuing my research even farther into the semantic stratosphere of economic literature, I have encounted "atomistic heteropoly" and "differentiated polypoly."

Clearly this is no place for simple iron puddlers; so with your permission, I'll just try to keep it simple by avoiding the pitfalls of economic theory and by sticking to the practical economic facts of life which every businessman must face if he is to survive the rising tide of costs, meet his competition, and keep his plant intact in the absence of adequate depreciation allowances.

Now as I understand it, the main purpose of this investigation is to inquire into the warmed-over theory that "administered prices" in the so-called "concentrated industries" are responsible for inflation. Freely translated, I suppose that means: "Is Big Business to blame for it all?"[12]

## Producing a final effect with the conclusion

A conclusion has one purpose, *to give your proposition a lasting effect so listeners won't just walk out and forget it.*

Do this quickly. Do it skillfully if you can, but regardless of skill do it quickly, for it is fatal to let listeners ask, "Is he never going to stop?" An old rhyme voices this universal feeling of people who listen to speeches:

> There are speakers who please me,
> To whom I'll allude:
> They say, "Now, in conclusion"
> And promptly conclude.

"Learn the delightful art," said H. A. Overstreet, "of closing with a snap." This does not mean that a full-length speech is broken off with a sentence—although Robert G. Ingersoll did close his encomium on Voltaire with the terse summary, "This was the work of Voltaire." Rather it means that a good conclusion moves swiftly, without passing a stop sign.

The following are seven different types of conclusions:

1. *A Challenge.* This is the most frequently used method. In some ingenious way the speaker presents a short compelling challenge for the audience to take a positive attitude, position, or action—in short, to *do* something. Sir Winston Churchill's address to the British Parliament and people after the fall of France in 1940 stated a challenge in words that are likely to be remembered as long as the English language is spoken:

[12] *Vital Speeches,* XXIII (October 1, 1957), No. 24, 754.

What General Weygand called the Battle of France is over. I expect that the Battle of Britain is about to begin. Upon this battle depends the survival of Christian civilization. Upon it depends our own British life, and the long continuity of our institutions and our Empire. The whole fury and might of the enemy must very soon be turned upon us. Hitler knows that he will have to break us in this Island or lose the war. If we can stand up to him, all Europe may be free and the life of the world may move forward into broad, sunlit uplands. But if we fail, then the whole world, including the United States, including all that we have known and cared for, will sink into the abyss of a new Dark Ages made more sinister, and perhaps more protracted, by the lights of perverted science. Let us, therefore, brace ourselves to our duties, and so bear ourselves that if the British Empire and its Commonwealth last for a thousand years, men will still say, "This was their finest hour."

2. *A Quotation.* A speaker reinforces his theme with an apt quotation. This is perhaps the second most widely used method today. On most occasions the best quotations are short and pointed, as the one used by General Willard G. Wyman at the Commissioning Exercises for an ROTC:

> As Douglas Southall Freeman recorded the incident, the wife of one of Robert E. Lee's officers brought her son for him to bless during the General's farewell visit to northern Virginia. General Lee looked at the boy for a moment in the gathering dusk, then gave the child back to his mother and said: "Teach him that he must deny himself."[13]

But a quotation may be longer if the occasion permits, and if it suits your particular talents. Dr. Walter H. Judd, member of Congress and onetime medical missionary in Asia, thus closed an address to college graduates:

> Surely God did not bring our beloved country to its position of unprecedented influence and power in the world for no great purpose. Surely He expects and has a right to call you at the beginning of this new chapter of your lives, and all of us in this hour of crisis, to rise to the occasion, to be worthy instruments of His will that all men should be free.
>
> > He hath sounded forth the trumpet
> > Which shall never call retreat.
> > He is sifting out the hearts of men
> > Before His judgment seat.
> >
> > O be swift, my soul, to answer Him;
> > Be jubilant, my feet;
> > Our God is marching on.
>
> God bless you as you go with Him.[14]

[13] *Vital Speeches,* XXIII (July 15, 1957), No. 19, 603.
[14] *Vital Speeches,* XXIV (August 1, 1958), No. 20, 627.

3. *A Summary.* If the speech is complex, or if the speaker's purpose is to present information, then you had best draw together the important points in condensed and unified form. "If you can sum up your arguments," said J. H. Gardiner, so that listeners "will go off and unconsciously retail your points to their neighbors, you probably have them." Likewise, if you can sum up your information so that listeners can carry it away in condensed and unified form, they likely will remember it. Bruce Barton, in that widely-quoted speech, "Which Knew Not Joseph," closed with a skillful summary of each main point:

> So I say to you that there is a certain technique about this matter of dealing with the public, and if you have anything seriously the matter with you —whether it be a big advertising problem or merely a bad letterhead (and some of you have wretched letterheads)—there probably is some advertising doctor in your town who has made a business of the thing, and it may be worth your while to call him in. But in the meantime . . . I say to you, "Be genuine, be simple, be brief; talk to people in language that they understand; and finally, most of all, be persistent." You can't expect to advertise in flush times and live on the memory of it when you are hard up. You can't expect to advertise when you are in trouble, or about to be in trouble, and expect to get anything in that direction. It is a day-by-day and hour-by-hour business. If the money that has been thrown away by people who advertised spasmodically was all gathered together it would found and endow the most wonderful home in the world for aged advertising men and their widows. Don't throw any more of that money away. If advertising is worth doing at all, it is worth doing all the time. For every day, gentlemen, the "king" dies, and there arises a new "king" who knows not Joseph.

4. *An Appeal.* This is a classic form of conclusion, heavily used by the ancients. When well done it is effective, but when it lacks substance it is trite or mawkish. Abraham Lincoln's Second Inaugural address closes with an appeal that is an enduring part of the American Heritage:

> With malice toward none; with charity for all; with firmness in the right, as God gives us to see the right, let us strive on to finish the work we are in; to bind up the nation's wounds; to care for him who shall have borne the battle, and for his widow, and his orphan—to do all which may achieve and cherish a just and lasting peace among ourselves and with all nations.

5. *An Illustration.* An illustration is one of the easiest for beginners in that it is simple in structure and requires no skill beyond that of story-telling. But you need a story that carries the core of the proposition or the action you want listeners to take. President Charles F. Phillips of Bates College used a homespun illustration to close a speech on free competition:

May I conclude with one of my favorite stories, one which illustrates the kind of spirit needed to make a competitive economy function successfully? It concerns a former president—Mr. Stuyvesant Fish by name—of one of our well-known railroads, the Illinois Central.

There walked into Mr. Fish's office one morning an Irishman, hat on and pipe in mouth, who said: "I want a pass to St. Louis."

"Who are you?" asked President Fish, somewhat startled.

"I'm Pat Casey, one of your switchmen."

Mr. Fish, thinking it was a good chance to impart a lesson in etiquette, said, "Now, Pat, I'm not going to say that I will refuse your request, but there are certain forms a man should observe in asking a favor. You should knock at the door; and when I say, 'Come in' you should enter and, taking off your hat and removing your pipe from your mouth, you should say, 'Are you President Fish?' I would say, 'I am. Who are you?' Then you would tell me, and the matter would be settled. Now you go out and come in again and see if you can't do better."

So the switchman went out. About two hours later there was a knock on the door and President Fish said, "Come in." In came Pat Casey with his hat off and pipe out of his mouth.

"Good morning," he said, "are you President Fish of the Illinois Central Railroad?"

"I am. Who are you?"

"I am Pat Casey, one of your switchmen."

"Well, Mr. Casey, what can I do for you?"

"You can go to hell! I got a job and a pass on the Wabash."[15]

6. *Visualizing the Future.* The speaker ends on the high note of looking forward into the future. He may, if his prestige is high, say "I shall in the future do this thing, and I ask men of courage and wisdom to join with me." Or he may merely express personal faith and hope. Thus Rear Admiral Hugh H. Goodwin closed a commencement address by visualizing a personal faith in the future:

> We can not maintain our present position of world leadership, not to mention advancing it, unless our form of government is supported by good citizens of the present and future. . . .
>
> You are the citizens of the future and I am confident that this destiny of our country will be safe in your hands.
>
> As we say in the Navy, "May fair breezes and smooth seas be yours on the voyage upon which you are now embarking."[16]

7. *Rounding Out the Thought.* With simple speeches, sometimes even with more complex ones, a speaker may simply round it out with a few swift strokes. Adlai Stevenson closed an address to a convention of lawyers with a quotation followed by one brief sentence:

[15] *Vital Speeches,* XXII (August 15, 1956), No. 21, 670.
[16] *Vital Speeches,* XXIII (June 15, 1957), No. 17, 523.

When Sparta was frightening the Athenians, Pericles said, "I am more worried about our own faults than about the plans of our enemies." And so am I.[17]

Whatever kind of conclusion you use, remember that its purpose is to give a final motivated impetus. Make it short. Make it motivated.

### LENGTHS OF INTRODUCTIONS AND CONCLUSIONS

How long is an Introduction? How long is a Conclusion? It may serve a useful purpose, and certainly will satisfy the curiosity of some, to supply the answer. Across the board, Introductions average about 10 per cent of the total speech, and Conclusions average about 5 per cent. These, mind you, are *averages* of wide extremes. Introductions of reasonably good speeches have been known to range from 1 per cent to 38 per cent, and Conclusions from less than 1 per cent to 15 per cent. Nor do these figures tell you what proportions a speech *ought* to have. They are merely a measurement of what other speakers in other days have done. Faced by the same conditions, you may possibly use approximately the same proportions.

## Assignments

ON ANALYZING THE CAUSES FOR GOOD AND POOR INTRODUCTIONS AND CONCLUSIONS

1. Examine the introductions and conclusions of five printed speeches, preferably using speeches you have previously read in this course:
   a. Rank them as good, poor, or sad averages.
   b. Classify the method used in the introduction to get attention and good will (establishing common ground, humor, etc.).
   c. Classify the method used in the introduction to orient the audience (explaining the subject background, explaining the proposition, etc.).
   d. Weigh these introductions critically and decide what methods *you* would use if it were your speech.
   e. Classify the method used in the conclusion to give the final impetus (challenge, quotation, etc.).
   f. Consider these conclusions critically and decide what methods you would use if it were your speech.

2. Analyze the introductions in one round of class speeches: (*a*) List the two best and two poorest, and give your reasons. (*b*) Explain how you would improve the two poorest.

3. Do the same for conclusions in one round of class speeches.

ON LEARNING TO BEGIN AND END SPEECHES EFFECTIVELY

4. Analyze the introductions and conclusions of two or three of your own class speeches given previously. Use the principles of this chapter to recast and improve them.

[17] *Vital Speeches*, XXIV (December 15, 1957), No. 5, 134.

5. Using one of your speeches previously given in class, draft three introductions suitable for three different audiences (women's club, high-school students, business men, etc.). Consider also whether you would use the same or different conclusions.

6. Assume that you are speaking on a controversial subject: Farm policy, segregation, racial minorities, U.S. education, a political election, labor union policies, etc. Draft two introductions to get attention and good will, one for a favorable audience, and one for an opposed audience.

7. Draft two conclusions for the above speech: (a) One intended to persuade listeners to respect your viewpoint even though they disagree, (b) One intended to arouse partisans to enthusiasm and determination.

# •13•

# Supporting the Ideas

Mr. Justice Oliver Wendell Holmes once wrote sarcastically, "The chief end of man is to frame general ideas—and . . . no general idea is worth a straw." Mine-run speakers do exactly that. They fill speeches with general ideas, *without supporting material.* Sometimes these general ideas are "big thumping generalizations, salted with popular prejudices." Sometimes they are merely foggy ideas put into murky words. Sometimes they are valid ideas, but cloudy because the speaker uses opaque words instead of supporting material. This sort of speaking is excellent for listeners who need sleep, but not for those who need light.

*Each basic unit in a good speech has two parts: First, a general idea. Second, supporting material.*

(Remember, of course, that on the platform many excellent speakers, possibly most, reverse this order. They give their supporting material *first,* and the general idea last.)

Why? because an audience is made up of human beings with a limited span of attention. Many can't—and most others won't—listen to general ideas. Intellectuals often lament this. They now blame it on the modern "decline in education," and on the "unfortunate" influence of newspapers, magazines, and television which nowadays prevent most people from "becoming reasoning, critical beings." This lament, of course, is fortified nonsense. The span of human attention has not decreased during the history of man; and twenty-four centuries ago Aristotle had to warn his students—all of them intellectuals who spoke almost entirely to intellectuals—about the listening comprehension of audiences: "Anything vague puzzles them, so give them a grasp" of something tangible at the beginning, so "they can hold fast to it and follow the argument."

What Henry J. Taylor said of Dwight D. Eisenhower applies to most intelligent listeners and all of the less intelligent. If the informant is vague, said Taylor, and the words beat about the bush, they "do not seem to touch Eisenhower's brain at all. . . . He simply loses interest in the obscure. Facts are his tools, and he can't work without them. But let the facts begin to flow and a sign lights up in his eyes: 'Brain at work.'"

Most listeners' minds are that way. Better minds want the tangible evidence so they can sort and sift, then judge the framework of thought. Average minds want word pictures, simply because they cannot follow abstractions. Therefore, to make an idea count, support it with concrete materials, picture it so listeners can see it as well as hear it, or create a situation of which listeners feel themselves to be a part.

The purpose of Supporting Materials, then, is to reinforce the original statement and make it live in the mind's eye of the listener. By a succession of details they direct the listener's mind again and again to the original point. They reinforce the point, heap it up, until the listener can understand and is motivated to action. Technically, Supporting Materials can be defined as materials that (1) clarify, (2) intensify, (3) amplify, or (4) prove the original statement. Twice previously they have been discussed briefly (pages 49-56 and 115-124). Here the Forms of Support previously mentioned are amplified and additional ones are included, as follows:

1. Definition and Explanation
2. Factual Information
   a. facts
   b. figures
   c. statistics
3. Illustrations
4. Specific Instances (Undeveloped Illustrations)
5. Comparison and Contrast
6. Testimony
7. Repetition and Restatement
8. Description
9. Narration
10. Visual Aid Material

Often, of course, several Forms of Support are combined into one—as in an Illustration that contains Figures, Comparisons, and Repetition—but for purposes of explanation we shall consider them separately.

## Supporting ideas by definition and explanation

Napoleon gave three instructions to the secretaries who relayed his messages: "(1) Be clear. (2) Be clear! (3) *Be Clear!*" A speaker is under the same compulsion. One of the first essentials of clarity is to *define the essential terms of your speech*. Especially are there two types of terms that will need defining:

1. The first is technical words, complex words, or strange words. They are words that listeners don't know. In this age of specialization, thousands of such words are in common use by specialized groups but are not known by the general public. Typical of a few appearing in recent student

speeches are: *inertial navigation* (naval warfare), *consciousness of abstracting* (semantics), *Oedipus complex* (psychology), *odd-lot sales* (stock market), *color temperature* (photography). When you must use such words, define them, restate them in simple terms, amplify them, illustrate what you mean.

2. Next, there are familiar words that we use frequently and loosely, but which have many meanings to different people. What do you mean, for example, by *liberty, freedom of speech, democracy,* or *Americanism?* What do you mean by such two-dimensional words as *justice, fairness, right,* or *wrong.* To many people, these words have no meaning, but only emotional assocations. When spoken glibly, they don't communicate thought; they merely pull a trigger that releases pious feelings. Yet speakers must use them, and ought to use them. To speak with clarity and precision, however, they must define what meaning they propose to use.

Listeners may know the dictionary meaning of these words, but that does not mean that they know the meaning you give to them, for a dictionary at best furnishes only a general scheme into which many meanings may be inserted. Real meanings, like all things human, depend upon the human beings involved; and your task is to make clear your personal and particular meaning. Note how Judge Clyde S. Shumaker made clear the meaning of American citizenship to newly-made citizens:

> Here you may worship God as you know Him according to the dictates of your own conscience and in the faith of your fathers, as did our founding fathers—without fear of imprisonment. . . .
>
> "At last a citizen" and as such you may now have a dog, own a gun, obtain a fishing and hunting license, and vote. . . .
>
> But being a citizen carries with it certain responsibilities, some of whch I now call to your attention.
>
> You have pledged allegiance to this country, and by doing so you are required to protect and defend it and may be called upon, in case of national emergency, to bear arms and to serve in one of our fine branches of military service. Like those born here you may, but God forbid, be required to lay down your life that our democracy and way of life may continue, and that our land may not be invaded or destroyed by aggressive nations, classified as our enemies.
>
> Your citizenship entitled you to become a registered voter and I call upon you to make inquiry concerning . . . our political parties, choose one, register to vote, and at election learn what you can about the candidates for public office and issues being submitted to voters, and make your choice . . . by entering your voting booth and casting your ballot.[1]

Suppose, for example, you were discussing "democracy." How would you define it? Is it the same as a "republic"? Can a "monarchy" like Great Britain also be a "democracy"? Is communism really a "democracy," as

---

[1] *Vital Speeches,* XXIII (July 1, 1957), No. 18, 546-547.

the Communists claim? Note how Henry M. Wriston carefully defined the word in a speech on "Who Besides the Russians?" If you read his definition carefully you will find that he uses the following four methods of definition:

1. Definition by authority (Shaw, Lincoln, Carlyle, Declaration of Independence).
2. Definition by classification ("More than . . . an economic order").
3. Definition by negation ("Not a form of government").
4. Definition by comparison or illustration ("What Lincoln said of liberty").

Wriston's definition is a follows:

> Who besides the Russians imperils the American system? The answer can be categorical: All who directly or indirectly tarnish the ideal or retard the attainment of democracy. Maybe that seems categorical without being clear, for many have doubts that there is such a thing as democracy; at least they would agree with the cynical comment of George Bernard Shaw, "Democracy may be defined as a word that all public persons use and none of them understands."
>
> Admittedly it is difficult to define. We could say of democracy what Lincoln said of liberty: "The world has never had a good definition . . . and the American people, just now, are much in want of one." The word has been utterly prostituted by the Communists at one extreme—and many ultra-conservatives, at the other end of the spectrum, tend to feel that despair expressed by Thomas Carlyle who said, "Democracy is, by the nature of it, a self-cancelling business; and gives in the long run a net result of zero."
>
> The difficulty arises from the fact that democracy is more than a political idea, an economic order, or a social system—it is vastly more fundamental than any of those things. Democracy is not a form of government. It exists within many forms—wherever, in fact, the consensus of mature public opinion governs public action. . . . Democracy must not be confused with ballots or any other procedural device. Instead, it is a spirit which animates political, social, and economic institutions. And the essence of that spirit is a profound respect for human dignity. . . .
>
> Respect for individual human dignity is the inner meaning of the most striking phrase of the Declaration of Independence: "We hold these truths to be self-evident,—that all men are created equal."[2]

## Supporting ideas with factual information

"Facts," Owen D. Young once observed, "are our scarcest raw material." Especially is this true in student speeches. Young people can seldom speak with authority. They need to have behind them the power of facts.

[2] *Vital Speeches,* XVI (June 1, 1950), No. 16, 503.

But what *is* a fact? It is not an opinion, prejudice, or value judgment. It is a thing that has actually happened. It is an event seen by competent observers. It remains the same when seen from different places or viewpoints. There are no affirmative facts, negative facts, Catholic facts, Protestant facts, American facts, or Chinese facts. There are *facts* that remain the same when seen from every direction. The dictum of the *Manchester Guardian* is a standard for every speaker: "Comment is free, facts are sacred."

Once you have the facts, the next step is how to use them. The adage, "let the facts speak for themselves," is a myth. They just won't. Sometimes every fact in a story may be true, yet the whole give a false conclusion. Sometimes, as Mark Twain noted, facts can be presented so they create "confusion of the mind and congestion of the ducts of thought." *Facts will speak clearly only when they are told in proper perspective and in proper order.*

The best order is narrative, when you can use it. If narrative cannot be used, then arrange facts in one of the other Thought Patterns discussed in Chapter 11 (see pages 217-221). Victor Hugo, for example, explained the battlefield at Waterloo by using Space Order:

> Those who wish to gain a clear idea of the battle of Waterloo have only to place, mentally, on the ground, a capital A. The left leg of the A is the road to Nivelles, the right one the road to Genappe, the tie of the A is the hollow road to Ohain from Braine-l'Alleud. The top of the A is Mont-Saint-Jean, where Wellington is; the lower tip is Hougomont, where Reille is stationed with Jerome Bonaparte; the right tip is the Belle Alliance, where Napoleon is. At the center of this point is the precise point where the final word of the battle was pronounced. . . .
>
> The triangle comprised in the top of the A, between the two limbs and the tie, is the plateau of Mont-Saint-Jean. The dispute over this plateau was the whole battle.

*Figures* are an effective kind of factual information if used wisely and sparingly. You don't want to load a speech with too many, for the audience won't remember a shower of figures, and most of them won't even listen to them. But used sparingly and wisely, figures can make clear many an otherwise vague idea. You say, "Traffic accidents are increasing," but how can you demonstrate this without presenting figures? You say, "Unemployment is increasing (or declining)," but how can you know— or the audience understand—without figures of comparison with previous years? Albert W. Hawkes wanted to show that "young men had made great achievements." For him it was not enough to assert without proof. He presented figures as follows:

> Alexander Hamilton was a lieutenant colonel at 20, a framer of the Constitution of the United States at 30, and Secretary of the Treasury at 32;

Alexander Graham Bell invented the telephone at 28; George Eastman produced dry plates for photography at 26; George Westinghouse . . . invented the air brake at 22; Henry Ford produced his first motorcar at 29; Thomas Edison . . . invented the incandescent lamp at 32; the Wright brothers were 32 and 36, respectively, at the time of their first air flight; Woolworth established his first store when 24; John D. Rockefeller organized the Standard Oil Co. when 31; John Wannamaker opened his first department store at 31; Lord Byron published his first book of poems at 19; Charles Dickens published his first book of Pickwick Papers at 24; John T. Delane was editor of the *London Times* at 23; Edward W. Bok was editor of the *Ladies Home Journal* at 26; Luther Burbank produced the Burbank potato at 22; Dr. Hyde became president of Bowdoin College at 27; Mark Hopkins became president of Williams College at 34; Dr. Eliot became president of Harvard at 35; Dr. Robert Hutchins became president of Chicago University at 30. . . .

This is the "march of youth" instead of the "march of time."[3]

*Statistics* are not the same as ordinary figures. They are groups of facts or figures that are assembled, classified, and tabulated so as to present a general truth about a complex physical matter. They are used to report mass data on economic and social trends, business conditions, and public-opinion polls.

But you must handle statistics with care. Remember that a well-wrapped statistic can distort the facts more than any Communist Big Lie. We can see in a moment how it can be "true," yet tell a barefaced falsehood. The following four tests may help you detect statistics intended to deceive:

First, *whose* statistics are they? The U.S. Bureau of the Census is competent and unbiased, and so are the other bureaus set up to supply information to the public. But most other high sources must be checked with care. A typical newspaper, the *Indianapolis Times*, carried the headline, "Average Water Cost Up 111.2 Per Cent Since 1951." The compiled statistics below the headline showed that the extreme was 111.2 per cent and the median increase was 103 per cent. But the principal joker was that from 1939 to 1951 there had been no increase in rates, even though the cost of living had almost doubled and the company operated at a loss during the last of those years. Taking the change of rates and the change in cost of living from the base year 1939, we get the following comparison: Increase in cost of living, 108 per cent. Increase in cost of water, 103 per cent.

The news magazine *Time* is as accurate as most, but don't believe that all its statistics tell the truth. The following is typical of its bias against the U.S. public schools: "Two out of three high school students [in the U.S.] do not take chemistry, three out of four avoid physics, seven out of

[3] *Vital Speeches*, XII (August 1, 1950), No. 20, 632-633.

eight get no trigonometry or solid geometry." The raw figures are true, but omits the keystone fact that in the U.S. some 87 per cent of youth go to high school compared with about 10 per cent in Western Europe and a lower percentage in other parts of the world. So these deceptive figures can be translated into meaningful statistics as follows: "In the U.S. 55 per cent of all youth take chemistry, in Western Europe not more than 10 per cent take it; in the U.S. 22 per cent of all youth take physics, in Western Europe not more than 10 per cent take it; and in the U.S. 10 per cent of all youth take trigonometry or solid geometry, and in Western Europe not more than 10 per cent take it." Remember that people who want to plead a cause will make their statistics do it for them. So know *whose* statistics you are using, then unwrap them to find what they are like inside.

Second, look for the "built-in-bias":

House-to-house survey shows that more Americans read *Harper's* than read *True Story*.

Now the survey did show this, yet the circulation of *Harper's* was less than 200,000 whereas *True Story* had about 2,500,000. Was it rigged investigation? Not at all. It was an accurate report of a survey made in all sorts of neighborhoods over the country. But when the interviewers asked people what magazines they read, most *True Story* readers would not admit it. They claimed they read more respectable magazines like *Harper's*. The same built-in-bias appeared in the report of another famous survey:

The average Yaleman, Class of '24, makes $25,111 a year.

The letter questionnaire produced this figure all right, but letter questionnaires have a built-in-bias In this case, members of the class of '24 who inherited wealth or earned high incomes proudly answered the questionnaire; but those who were ashamed of their income tossed the questionnaire in the wastebasket; and the lost sheep—so unimportant professionally or economically that they could not be located—had no chance to answer. In 1936 the *Literary Digest* polled 10,000,000 upper-income voters, got 2,376,523 replies, and prophesied the election of Alfred M. Landon as President by an electoral vote of 370 to 161. On election day Mr. Landon was defeated, 523 to 8. The poll had a built-in-bias. It included only upper-income voters.

Third, look for the "well-chosen average":

The average income of workers in that office is $22,077 a year.

But what do you mean by "average"? There are three kinds of "averages": the *mean, median,* and *mode.* You can make an "average" mean just about what you want it to mean, and still be telling the "truth." Let's see

how. The "office" in the above example is the head office of a manufacturing company. The "workers" are all the people who work there, as
follows:

1 president: $100,000 a year

2 vice-presidents: $75,000 each

3 secretaries: $5,000 each

1 file clerk: $4,000

6 stenographers: $3,000 each

If we want a high "average," we just add the total salaries and divide by
13 (total number workers), and we get the arithmetical *mean* of $22,077.
But if we want a lower "average," we take the *median*. That would be the
salary exactly in the middle, with half above it and half below. The file
clerk has six above and six below, so that salary is the *median*: $4,000.
But if we want the lowest "average," we take the *mode*. That is the salary
which occurs most frequently. The *mode*, then, is the salary of the six
stenographers: $3,000. With a simple set of figures, therefore, a statistician
can give you an "average" of $3,000, $4,000, or $22,077. The *median* is
generally the most accurate, though not always.

Fourth, look for the "unknown deviation":

Four places in the U.S. have the same mean temperature of 61 degrees:
San Nicolas Island off the south coast of California, Sacramento, Oklahoma
City, and Norfolk, Va.

True, but on San Nicolas the temperature ranges between a comfortable
47 and 87 degrees, whereas at Sacramento it ranges from 114 to 27, at
Oklahoma City from 113 to 17 below zero, and at Norfolk from 105 to 2.
Having the same mean temperature does not mean having the same
climate.

Finally, look for the "elusive error":

The Gallup Poll shows that 55 per cent of the American people favor this
policy.

Does it? The Gallup Poll operates usually on a sampling that allows a
4-per-cent standard error, so actually such a figure means 55 ± 4. In
other words, the percentage who favor this policy *probably* lies between
51 and 59, but there is a *slight* chance of it being above 59 or below 51.
Don't ignore that significant standard error.

Said Disraeli: "There are three kinds of lies: lies, damned lies, and
statistics." Said H. G. Wells: "Statistical thinking will one day be as
necessary for efficient citizenship as the ability to read and write." Both
men are right. When you use statistics, handle them with care. First,
don't cover loose talk by proclaiming that "Records prove. . . ." or
"Statistics show. . . ." Tell your audience whose statistics they are. Next,

before using statistics, unwrap them to find what they really mean. Finally, don't push a snarl of statistics at any audience. Untangle them, and give their down-to-earth meanings.

## Supporting ideas with illustrations

"They say I tell a great many stories," explained the master speaker, Abraham Lincoln, ". . . but I have found in the course of a long experience that common people—common people—take them as they run, are more easily influenced and informed by illustrations than in any other way, and as to what the hypercritical few may think, I don't care."[4] After years of groping, and frequent bitterness at what he thought was failure, Lincoln finally *learned to argue by analogy and to explain by stories*.

"Tell us a story," has been the demand of the ages, and the speaker who complies with this demand will not likely become "just another speaker" to whom the audience only half listens. "I have seen an audience," said Henry Ward Beecher, "time and again, follow an argument, doubtfully, laboriously, almost suspiciously, and look at one another, as much as to say, 'Is he going right?'—until the place is arrived at, where the speaker says, 'It is like—' and then they listen eagerly for what it is like; and when some apt illustration is thrown out before them, there is a sense of relief, as though they said, 'Yes, he is right.'" Beecher also said— and this you must remember if you ever become a good speaker— that, "Illustrations, while they make it easier for all, are absolutely the only means by which a large part of your audience will be able to understand at all the abstruse processes of reasoning."[5]

Harry Emerson Fosdick reaffirmed by example what Beecher and Lincoln had said in words. For fifty years Fosdick preached to one of the most intellectual audiences in America, and his published sermons sold millions of copies, mostly to intellectuals. His sermons "were essentially arguments," yet "he was not argumentative in the details. He did not so much prove his points as illustrate them. Rather than pile up fact on fact or biblical citation upon biblical citation . . . , he seized upon an illustration and used it like a lens to bring his proposition into sharp, clear focus."[6] *Illustrations are the most powerful form of support yet discovered by man.*

[4] D. K. Dodge, "Abraham Lincoln: The Evolution of His Literary Style," *University of Illinois Studies*, I, No. 1 (May, 1900), 35.

[5] Henry Ward Beecher (Yale), *Lectures on Preaching* (New York, J. B. Ford and Co., 1872), pp. 157-158.

[6] Robert D. Clark, "Harry Emerson Fosdick," in Marie Kathryn Hochmuth, ed., *A History and Criticism of American Public Address* (New York, Longmans, Green and Co., 1955), III, 444.

Students often ask, "But what *is* an illustration?" for in popular usage it means almost any form of support. A speaker may say, "Let me illustrate," and even cite statistics. This broad use of the term is all right out in the wide world. But when we speak of illustrations as a Form of Support we mean a *story about a connected series of events.* For a speech, the best illustrations are short and simple. They have no flashbacks and no subplots. They simply start at the beginning and roll onward, as straight as possible, to the climax at the end. Eric Johnston used two such short illustrations to demonstrate the influence of American motion pictures in foreign countries:

> I went to a screening in Warsaw given by the Communist minister of labor for Stakhanovite workers, the elite of the Communist labor force. An American film was shown, a rather inocuous romance, and it went over big. What most moved the audience was a scene in which the heroine met her fiance at a factory where he worked. Outside the factory were thousands of American workers' cars.
>
> The minister of labor was deeply disturbed. "Why do you try to fool us?" he asked me. "What do you mean, fool you?" I said. "Oh, now, you know your exploited workers don't have cars like that!" he said. "That's just propaganda!" But he didn't really believe it was propaganda, nor did the Stakhanovites. I still remember them as the party broke up, talking eagerly about American workers and their cars.
>
> I remember another evening on a mountain-top near Djakarta, Indonesia, where our motion-picture representative lives. Each Saturday night he puts up a bedsheet on his front lawn as a movie screen and invites the whole countryside to attend an American film. I watched the audience arrive at sundown, women walking up the mountainside with their babies on their shoulders, workers from the local tea estates, soldiers from the nearby garrison. I was told that even the guerrilla fighters turned up for these shows, parking their guns outside along with the police. . . .
>
> The movie that night was a rather antique but complicated Western without subtitles. I doubted that the audience could make head or tail of it. But they cheered and responded in the right places, and afterward a native priest came up to me. "Americans believe as we do," he told me through an interpreter. "How do you mean?" I asked. "Well," he said, "our religion tells us that good men prosper and evil men don't. From your fine movie, we see that you Americans believe this too!"[7]

A Great Speaker twenty centuries ago wanted to make clear who one's neighbor was. He did not argue. He did not explain. He did not deal in exposition. He told a story:

> A certain man went down from Jerusalem to Jericho, and fell among thieves, which stripped him of his raiment, and wounded him, and departed leaving him half dead.
>
> And by chance there came down a certain priest that way: and when

[7] *Vital Speeches,* XXIII (July 1, 1957), No. 18, 573-574.

he saw him, he passed by on the other side. And likewise a Levite, when he was at the place, came and looked on him, and passed by on the other side.

But a certain Samaritan, as he journeyed, came where he was: and when he saw him, he had compassion on him. And went to him, and bound up his wounds, pouring in oil and wine, and set him on his own beast, and brought him to an inn, and took care of him. And on the morrow when he departed, he took out two pence, and gave them to the host, and said unto him, Take care of him: and whatsoever thou spendest more, when I come again, I will repay thee.

For two thousand years that story has been told over and over again. On the face it is a story pure and simple. Beneath the surface it is an argument. Between the lines it is a sermon.

## *Supporting ideas with specific instances*

A Specific Instance is a condensed illustration. That is, it is not a story about a connected series of events, but is one single event or incident. It is specific, precise, exact. It names the person, place, date, or event— but does not develop it by giving details.

The Specific Instance is so brief that one or two, without any other form of support, is seldom enough to develop an idea. Usually a battery of five or ten will be used. Lyndon B. Johnson used twelve:

> I have complete trust and faith in our people. . . . They may speak with a different accent. They may plow corn land in Iowa or sew clothes in New York City. They may work on the docks in Seattle or run a department store in Kansas City.
>
> They may be Northern Yankees or Southern Rebels. They may be Catholics, Protestants, or Jews. It makes no difference because they are all Americans.
>
> I am not afraid to have them listen to Nikita Khrushchev or Karl Marx or Nikolai Lenin himself. They have the intelligence and the independence to make up their own minds.[8]

Or a speaker may lead with an Illustration or Comparison, then reinforce with a battery of Specific Instances. Or he may lead with a battery of Specific Instances and follow with other forms of support. Loren D. Reid in the quotation below opened with four Specific Instances followed by an Illustration:

> Over the last few years I have seen evidences that studying is a mislaid, or forgotten, and even, perhaps, a lost art. . . .
>
> As you know I have a special interest in British orators. I have spent much time overseas peering into the careers of men like Fox, Burke, Pitt,

[8] *Vital Speeches*, XXIII (July 15, 1957), No. 19, 584.

Gladstone, Churchill, and others. I read how Fox spent several weeks read-ing Restoration plays, and how, upon visiting Italy, he immediately began to learn the language. I looked through scores of notebooks Gladstone kept as a student at Eton and Oxford, and realized that as a teenager he knew more about Aristotle's *Rhetoric* than any undergraduate of my acquaintance. I read how Churchill, who was unable to meet college entrance requirements, nevertheless spent the long, hot, India afternoons reading history and aesthetics. I turned the pages on Disraeli's journals and read his observa-tions, as a young man, on history, literature, and oratory. This, I say to myself, is the art of study. Where today can I turn for similar examples?

During my overseas experience I got to know exceptionally well professors from English institutions. One day I had an enlightening conversation with a professor of French. He asked me whether it was true that American professors were insistent that students attend class punctually and regularly. . . . "Oh, yes," I replied, ". . . we regularly take the roll. . . . What is your practice?"

I knew the answer as well as he, but I wanted to hear him put it in his own words. "Why," he said, "we don't really care whether a student comes to class or not."

"I know, of course, that you do not hold regular classes in the sense that we do," I continued. "But at times you offer special lectures. Don't you require students to attend them?"

"Oh, no, not at all," said he, . . . "We would think he was smart to stay away. . . . We would conclude that he did not need that particular segment of information—that he had dug it up for himself."

I offer no brief for the British system of education as opposed to ours. In this country about one person in 60 is now going to college or university. In Great Britain the ratio is about one in 800. . . . So the British universities operate with a relatively limited and selected group. . . . They must be *students* in every sense of the word. In this country we seem to have lost the art of study.[9]

## Supporting ideas with comparison and contrast

*Comparison* measures similarities. It connects the known with the unknown, the more familiar with the less familiar. Sometimes compari-sons are brief and pithy, like the traffic expert's description of safety:

The driver is safer when the roads are dry; the roads are safer when the driver is dry.

At other times it is more detailed. Observe Prime Minister Harold Macmillan's blunt comparison between socialism and communism given at a political rally to members of his own party:

[9] "The Lost Art of Studying," delivered at the University of Michigan 1956 Sum-mer Speech Conference. Privately printed, 1956, by the University of Michigan De-partment of Speech.

> There is no difference between socialism and communism, except this: socialism is soft, communism is hard; socialism is pink, communism is red; socialism gets you down bit by bit by a kind of anesthetic process. It might be called mercy killing. Communism just knocks you in the head.[10]

At times a comparison makes an idea more clear, more vivid, or more interesting, as follows:

> Take one year, and let it represent the whole of time since the beginning of the world. How long—on the scale of one year—has the human race lived? The earliest prehistoric man arrived about 14 hours ago. The first pyramids were built 63 seconds ago. Christ was born 21 seconds ago. And the American Revolution was fought two seconds ago. Man is a newcomer to this planet which he now claims to dominate.

*Contrast* is a measurement of opposites. We often see a thing more clearly when we see its opposite, heightened by contrast. Witness the intensified effect given by Maxwell Droke's contrast of American civilians at home with Americans in the armed forces overseas:

> In 5 American cities—Omaha, Dayton, Chattanooga, Topeka and Terre Haute—there are well over 1,000 arrests a week for *serious* violations of civic statutes.
>
> The *combined* population of these cities—ranging from infants in arms to senior citizens in their dotage—total slightly less than the number of prime-of-life young men we have on foreign soils the world around.
>
> When you consider that the more than 800,000 of our armed forces are stationed outside the U.S. in a peacetime period, the amazing consideration is that we haven't had far more headline "incidents" involving our troops.[11]

## Supporting ideas with testimony

Often listeners will not take your unsupported word, but will respect the judgment of others. If you assert that the cost-of-living index has gone up or down by 5 points, the statement will carry more weight if you refer to the United States Department of Commerce as your source of information. If you assert that modern art lacks realism—or has high aesthetic values—your assertion will produce more effect if you reinforce it with testimony from the Cincinnati Art Museum Director, a University of Cambridge Professor of Art, or other accepted authority. Observe how Robert G. Gunderson skilfully condenses the testimony of five eminent people to support his opening assertion:

> Foreign travelers invariably testified that nineteenth-century citizens were bold, articulate champions of democracy—convinced of their own stake

[10] *The Times* (London), March 19, 1957.
[11] *Quote,* XXXIII (June 16, 1957), No. 24, 2.

in the American experiment—and of their own important role in it. Charles Dickens was dismayed because politics was the "national amusement." Count Adam Gurowski noted that "the thirst for knowledge" was a major "characteristic of the American mind." Though admittedly most citizens lacked a formal education, de Tocqueville found "hardly a pioneer's hut" which did not "contain a few odd volumes of Shakespeare." Philip Hone, onetime mayor of New York, observed that an American blacksmith "would think meanly of himself if he could not argue a point of law with the village lawyer." James Bryce reported a kindly sense of "human fellowship" in which citizens valued the integrity of others and felt that citizenship itself constituted "a certain ground" for respect.[12]

Obviously you cannot use any sort of testimony that pleases your fancy. There are rigorous tests for acceptable testimony:

1. Is he an expert in the field? Does he have special training and experience in this field?

2. Is he speaking from first-hand knowledge?

3. Is he influenced by self-interest? Does he represent an interest group that would profit from having people believe what he wants them to believe?

4. Is he known and acceptable to your listeners?

5. If he is not known to listeners, can he be made known by virtue of his position and achievements?

Testimony is used not only for proof; it is also used for vividness. Others have stated ideas so vividly that you can often reinforce argument, or make ideas clear, simply by quoting their lucid words. Among these are the testimony of great men, great books, and great anonymous sayings immortalized in folklore. How better, for example, can you phrase the following ideas than in the words of the persons quoted?

Wooden legs are not inherited, but wooden heads may be.

EDWIN GRANT CONKLIN

Whether there will be another war is known only to God and Drew Pearson.

BISHOP FULTON J. SHEEN

The high school tennis courts were laid out next to the rectory of St. Andrew's church. Exuberant youngsters occasionally whammed a ball over the fence onto the trim lawns of the rectory. The courts had been in use only a few weeks when a player chasing a stray ball came face to face with a large "No Trespassing" sign on the rectory's lawn.

The sign came down overnight, however, when the tennis club erected its own sign directly opposite. Their sign read, "Forgive Us Our Trespasses."

LESTER KROEPEL

[12] *Vital Speeches,* XXI (September 1, 1955), No. 22, 1464.

## Supporting ideas with restatement and repetition

Study the following example of restatement:

[1] We will walk on our own feet; [2] we will work with our own hands; [3] we will speak our own minds. [4] The study of letters shall be no longer a name for pity, for doubt, and for sensual indulgence. . . . [5] A nation of men will for the first time exist, because each believes himself inspired by the Divine Soul which also inspires all men.

RALPH WALDO EMERSON, "The American Scholar"

In the above specimen of restatement you will observe that the speaker presents no proof. He cites no Comparisons, Illustrations, or Specific Instances. He simply says the same thing five times in different words.

This is known as Restatement. Its value to the audience is plain. When an idea cannot be understood through one single statement, then Restatement gives the audience time to think it over, and digest it slowly as they come to understand its full meaning. In short, a speaker uses Restatement when it takes time for the original statement to soak in.

Now study the following example of *Repetition*:

We shall defend our island, whatever the cost may be. *We shall fight* on the beaches. *We shall fight* on the landing grounds. *We shall fight* in the fields and in the streets, and *we shall fight* in the hills. We shall never surrender.

WINSTON CHURCHILL, After Dunkerque

Here the speaker repeated the same idea four times in the same words. This is known as Repetition. Skillful repetition drives an idea home. It reinforces memory. As early as 44 B.C. Marc Antony was using Repetition to fix the guilt of Brutus in the minds of Roman citizens. In Shakespeare's version, Antony, in a short speech, repeats *nine* times with irony that Caesar's murderers are "honorable men"—until slowly the citizens grasp the intended contrary meaning and rush forth shouting, "We'll burn the house of Brutus!"

## Supporting ideas with description

Description tells how a thing looks, feels, tastes, smells, or how it acts. In words, it recreates places, things, and people for the listener's personal inspection. If you say, "In the Middle West summer winds blow constantly," that is explanatory fact. If you say, "Beginning with moist winds in May and continuing into dry winds in August, the summer winds are constant in the Middle West," you narrate events. But Ernie Pyle *described* those winds so you could feel them blow against your face:

To me the summer wind in the Midwest is one of the most melancholy things in all life. It comes from so far and blows so gently and yet so relentlessly; it rustles the leaves and the branches of the maple trees in a sort of symphony of sadness, and it doesn't pass on and leave them still. It just keeps coming, like the infinite flow of Old Man River. You could—and you do—wear out your lifetime on the dusty plains with that wind of futility blowing in your face. And when you are worn out and gone, the wind—still saying nothing, still so gentle and sad and timeless—is still blowing across the prairies, and will blow in the faces of the little men who follow you, forever.[13]

The following are suggestions for effective description:

1. Determine the purpose of the description. Suppose you are to describe a storm, for example. Do you want to tell how it arose and what it did? That is factual. Do you want to demonstrate its power and malevolence? That is imaginative. Do you want to describe a physical thing? Or a mental state? Determine one purpose, and stay by it.

2. Make description brief. Few speakers have the power to hold attention long by description.

3. Strip away the cluttering adjectives that mar most amateur efforts. Let the nouns and especially the verbs do the heavy work.

4. Follow a systematic order. Describe from right to left, front to back, top to bottom.

## Supporting ideas with narration

Narration makes clear who performed the action, what was done, when it was done, where it was done, how it was done, and why it was done. Effective speakers use it often, for they know its tremendous power. Students at first neglect it, for they have not discovered its power.

Narration takes many forms—among which are the illustration, story, fable, historical incident, and anecdote. All have one common element. They are a moving picture told in words, but they do not argue or provoke controversy. They are concrete, interesting, have action. They can create suspense, arouse laughter, or depict tragedy.

Good narrative seems so simple and natural, that anyone can do it. Unhappily, not so. It, too, has a technique, of which the essentials are these:

1. Tell the events in the order in which they occur.

2. Tell them in the form in which the listener might have seen them.

[13] *Home Country* (New York, William Sloan Associates, Inc., 1947), p. 3.

3. Organize the narration so it goes from somewhere to somewhere else—and sits down when it arrives.

All of these are illustrated in Mrs. Jennie H. Graves' speech on "The Impact of Taxation on Small Business":

> When I started manufacturing dolls and dolls' clothes to support my children after the death of my husband . . . , my business was operated in the rumpus room in my cellar. One of our bedrooms was a stock room—my garage a shipping room. My son's wagon was used to truck the orders back and forth between cellar and garage. When neighbors finally complained about the express trucks that called each day, I had to find manufacturing space outside of my home. We rented a small store with an apartment above. A hole was cut in one of the bedroom closets for a dumb waiter, which served as a freight elevator between the first and second floors.
>
> Our products, fortunately, met with public acceptance and the business expanded steadily. New ideas were developed. Sales increased. We added more employees to our staff. . . . We introduced an undressed doll with a complete line of clothes and accessories. Her name is "Ginny" and she is known as the "Fashion Leader in Doll Society." . . .
>
> Our new merchandising idea with "Ginny" was so successful that we were overwhelmed with orders. Within a very short time our sales increased from $500,000 to $1,500,000, and, although we earned $200,000, our federal taxes amounted to $140,000 or 72 per cent of those earnings. . . . There we were—a company caught in the web of excess profits taxes because our earnings base was small and fixed on minimum exemptions. . . .
>
> We paid the $140,000 tax bill and financed peak inventories of $500,000 and receivables of $340,000. . . . That year everyone told me how marvelous our business was. But, what I remembered most was my fear of the $300,000 loan I had to negotiate in order to remain in business.[14]

## Supporting ideas with visual aid material

The first nine types of Supporting Material were verbal. There remains a tenth—the use of visible materials such as charts, diagrams, maps, models, and pictures. A statistical curve or plan of battle are more easily demonstrated from a map or blackboard than from word-of-mouth description. An airplane design or the anatomy of a vertebrate are better understood from a drawing, a model, or a specimen. With films and slides you can bring distant scenes to the audience.

But the use of visual aid material is neither automatic nor foolproof. After listening to fumbling speakers for twenty-five years, J. R. Van Pelt summarized their abuse of visual aids "on a thousand platforms" as follows:

---

[14] *Vital Speeches,* XXIII (January 15, 1957), No. 7, 215.

We have seen overcrowded slides projected by machines that could not be focused. We have watched while speakers in a large room tried to use maps or charts that could not be read beyond arm's length. We have listened in vain as able scholars talked confidentially to a blackboard while writing illegible symbols with invisible chalk. We have fidgeted, mentally if not physically, as the remarks of a renowned scientist came to a dead stop while he readjusted some ill-arranged piece of apparatus or hunted for a scientific specimen to illustrate his point. The habit of badly using bad visual aids is rampant among those who "speak to inform." It is an occupational disease of university professors. Severe epidemics break out at every scientific, engineering, and medical convention."[15]

Let us, then, examine the techniques of using visual aids.

## USING CHARTS, MAPS, AND DIAGRAMS

The rules are simple enough, but the mistakes are many and costly:

1. *Make the charts large enough to be seen.* If the design on a chart is not large enough to be seen, it will be only an annoyance. Do not guess at the proper size, or try to decide about it while standing near by. Draw an experimental chart or diagram beforehand, and go to the back of the room to see whether its outlines can be easily seen in detail. If in doubt, make it larger.

Next, make the lines of the chart or diagram heavy and broad. A light, thin line which is perfectly visible to the speaker up close to it may be barely visible or wholly invisible from the back of the room. Even the writing on a blackboard ought to be carefully checked for size and heaviness of line. Otherwise it will almost surely be so small and light that persons at a distance cannot read it easily, if at all.

In training soldiers certain sizes of maps and charts have been standardized, because they were found to be the most effective size. In drawing maps to explain large military operations, for example, before audiences of one hundred or less, a scale of 3 inches to the mile is commonly used. This is large enough to show terrain features, cities, and other necessary items, yet small enough to show a large area of operations on one map or blackboard. Close-ups of military operations, however, are often mapped at 6 inches to the mile.

The use of different colors on maps and diagrams also may help to make distinctions clear. For example, a blackboard diagram of the human anatomy may show the bones in white, nerves in yellow, cartilages in green, and muscles in red.

[15] "Lantern Slides and Such," *Quarterly Journal of Speech*, XXXVI (February, 1950), 45.

2. *Don't crowd too many details into one chart.* Too many details lead to confusion. They distract attention, and provoke curiosity. Therefore, cut details and stick to bare essentials. In most charts cut the title, since that is covered in spoken context. Remember that an audience can read only 10 to 20 words without losing the speaker's thread of thought.

If there are several explanations to be made, or a series of steps in a process to be explained, don't try to put them all on one diagram. Instead, use a series of diagrams, each as simple as possible, and put only *one* central idea on each. When you put several points on one chart, the audience races ahead and speculates about the others while you are talking about the first one. Therefore, use a series, each as simple as possible.

Also, remember that *maps* or *graphs* are usually better than tables unless you are talking to specialists. They represent pictures that are easy to understand; and in graphs the figures will carry meaning to those who understand figures, but will not repel those—of which there are many— who dislike figures. You have a large variety of graphs from which to choose:

The *line* graph shows a rise-and-fall comparison of any item—like the cost of living—over any given number of years. This generally is best for specialists, but it can also be understood by a general audience if you know how to explain it.

The *bar* graph shows a series of bars or columns, either vertical or horizontal. It depicts a contrast in a series of facts and hence is easily understood by all types of audiences.

The *picture* graph, commonly called *pictograph*, is a simplified picture that compares two or more sets of numerical facts in stylized figures or objects. It appeals to audiences who know little about the subject or are not accustomed to handling technical data.

There are half a dozen others, ranging from the *piece-o'-pie* circle to the *cut-a-way* drawing. The simple ones will almost tell their own story. The complicated ones call for skillful explanation. All of them enable a speaker to communicate ideas that would be difficult with words alone.

3. *Talk to the audience instead of to the chart.* The young speaker finds a chart or a diagram to be a welcome refuge from the eyes of his listeners. He tends to turn away from them and to fix his gaze on the blackboard. Soon he is talking to the blackboard instead of to the audience. Of course, he feels silly talking to a blackboard in a strong and positive tone, and so he begins to mumble.

*Don't* look at the blackboard except when pointing to something specific on it. Even then, a glance is enough to give you the location, and you can turn again to the audience. *Learn the art of keeping a pointer properly placed on the blackboard while you are looking at the audience.*

4. *Don't stand between the audience and the chart.* The fault opposite to ignoring the audience while talking to the blackboard is that of ignor-

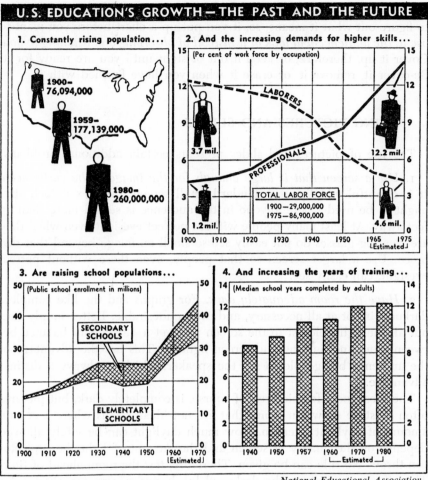

## U.S. EDUCATION'S GROWTH—THE PAST AND THE FUTURE

**1. Constantly rising population...**

1900—
76,094,000

1959—
177,139,000

1980—
260,000,000

**2. And the increasing demands for higher skills...**

(Per cent of work force by occupation)

LABORERS

PROFESSIONALS

3.7 mil.

12.2 mil.

1.2 mil.

4.6 mil.

TOTAL LABOR FORCE
1900—29,000,000
1975—86,900,000

1900 1910 1920 1930 1940 1950 1965 1975
LEstimated⌐

**3. Are raising school populations...**

(Public school enrollment in millions)

SECONDARY
SCHOOLS

ELEMENTARY
SCHOOLS

1900 1910 1920 1930 1940 1950 1960 1970
⌐Estimated⌐

**4. And increasing the years of training...**

(Median school years completed by adults)

1940 1950 1957 1960 1970 1980
⌐ Estimated ⌐

*National Educational Association*

Various types of graphs are shown in this chart: a pictograph (*upper left*), a combination of a simple line graph and pictograph (*upper right*), a shaded line graph (*lower left*), and a bar graph (*lower right*).

ing the blackboard while talking to the audience. Remember that your chart or diagram has been put on the board because the audience needs to see it. Stand out of the way so they can see it completely. If the audience is seated close to you, this usually means that you must stand at least *three or four feet* to one side. In such situations it is best to use a pointer; this enables you to stand far enough away to keep out of the audience's line of vision.

5. *Don't let an unused chart distract attention.* If possible, charts ought to be kept out of sight until needed, and removed from sight when they

are done with. The moment a chart appears, people will look at it and try to figure out what it means; so, if you put up a chart before you want to use it, *the audience will look at it instead of observing and listening to you.* Cover it up, therefore, or keep it out of sight until you are ready for it. Re-cover it, remove it, or erase it when you have finished with it.

## USING PICTURES AND SLIDES

The use of pictures and slides presents certain additional problems:

1. *Use a screen that is large enough for the image to be easily seen.* It is doubtful whether the standard small screen, the 39 x 48-inch size, ought to be used where anyone in the audience is seated more than 35 feet away. At least many people without perfect eyesight even when they are wearing glasses do not easily see so small an image beyond that distance. Use a larger screen so that people, even those without perfect eyesight, can easily see.

2. *Have the room adequately dark.* For graphs and the like complete darkness is not at all necessary, and even undesirable. Better simply turn out all the lights closest to the screen and get a satisfactory balance between room and lighting and screen lighting. This has the advantage of the audience being able to see the speaker, which is always a distinct advantage.

The ideal room for pictures, of course, is completely dark, but pictures often must be shown in rooms that are not ideal, rooms where a certain amount of daylight filters in. How much daylight can be safely allowed depends on the quality of screen and the amount of light the projector can throw. No rule can be given. Therefore, *test* the room ahead of time. Then if necessary it can be darkened by draperies, curtains, shades, tar paper—anything at hand, even blankets and or paper stuffed into cracks —until the screen image is obviously bright enough from all parts of the room.

Color pictures, be it noted, require a very much darker room and a brighter screen than black-and-white, because in color pictures the brilliancy of hue depends on the darkness of the room. Even if a small amount of outside light filters into the room, it will change the color hues. The effect is literally as though one had mixed paint to exactly the right tint for an especially attractive interior decoration, then, when the color was exactly what was wanted, one dumped into it a bucket of white paint. White light (sunlight) that filters into a room where color pictures are being shown has the same effect as white paint being poured into colored paint. The original color is faded out.

Other details, too, demand attention—shielding corridor lights, exit lights, and especially the lectern light to avoid shining into the eyes of the audience.

3. *Don't seat any members of the audience directly behind the projector.* No matter how well housed a projector may be, a certain amount of light escapes. This escaping light strikes the pupil of the eye of any person behind the projector, *causes the pupil to contract,* and so makes it difficult for the person to see the image on the screen. If your projector is set up in the room itself, and not housed in a booth, either place it behind the entire audience (this is by far the best method), or move your audience out of the V zone of light behind the projector. (*See diagram.*)

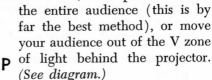

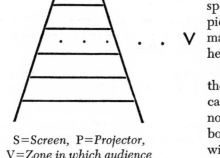

S = *Screen,* P = *Projector,*
V = *Zone in which audience*
*should not be seated.*

4. *Pay especial attention to making yourself heard and understood.* For three reasons speakers who are using moving pictures and slides tend not to make themselves adequately heard.

First, they are speaking in the dark where the audience cannot see them. The speaker's nod of the head, turn of the body, or indication of an idea with the hand are lost. The audience now must depend on the speaker's voice alone. That speaker who does not truly project his tones, who compels the audience to a partial lip-reading, is now wholly ineffective.

Second, if the speaker operates his own machine (and there are obvious advantages in the speaker's doing so), he must speak from the rear of the audience or perhaps from the rear of center. The picture is in front of the audience, but the speaker's voice comes from behind. This creates a mental interference, perhaps even a physical interference, *unless the speaker uses enough energy to build up room resonance so that the direction of voice is secondary to its easy audibility.*

Third, if moving pictures are being used, the projector makes a continuous noise. This noise, although not loud, is *at a pitch that masks the intelligibility of the speaker's words.* Therefore, unless the speaker realizes this and uses adequate energy of utterance to override the projector noise, he may quite literally be *heard* but not *understood.*

# Assignments

1. Go over the outlines of speeches you have previously given in class. On the left margin note the forms of support you have used. Draw up a list showing the number of times you have used each different form of support. Does this list reveal weaknesses in your use of supporting material, such as too little support and too much assertion? too few different kinds of support? overuse of weaker forms of support and underuse of stronger forms? Can you draft a plan for revising and improving your use of supporting material in future speeches?

2. Examine two speeches, preferably those you have previously read in this course. Classify their major supporting materials in terms of the ten forms of support explained in this chapter.

3. Give a two-minute speech of definition in which you classify, compare, illustrate, and if possible use testimony to make clear the meaning of a rarely-used, complex, or technical word.

4. Give a two-minute speech of definition on some common word or phrase used loosely by different people, such as *Americanism, communism, the common man, apple-polisher, regular fellow, etc.*

5. Give a two-minute speech in which you support an idea with factual information. Identify and list your thought pattern for arranging this material.

6. Give a two-minute speech supporting an idea with valid statistics. For suggested subjects leaf through the *World Almanac, Information Please,* etc.

7. Give a two-minute speech supporting an idea with half a dozen specific instances.

8. Give a two-minute speech supporting the idea with one good illustration.

9. Give a two-minute speech in which you compare and contrast such ideas as: (*a*) prose and poetry, (*b*) East and West, (*c*) education and training, (*d*) comedy and melodrama, (*e*) art and science, (*f*) learning and memorizing, (*g*) literature and popular novels.

10. Give a two-minute speech supporting an idea with acceptable testimony from two or more sources.

11. Give a two-minute speech supporting an idea only with restatement or repetition, or both.

12. Give a two-minute speech supporting an idea with description. Determine in advance whether you want the description to be factual, imaginative, etc.

13. Give a two-minute speech supporting an idea with a story, historical incident, or some other form of narration.

14. Give a two-minute speech supporting an idea with charts, maps, or diagrams. Each member of the class will write out and hand in a statement evaluating how well you satisfied the tests for effective visual aids as explained in this chapter.

# Making the Outline

WHY MAKE AN OUTLINE? Because you must create a speech on the instant before the audience, and you cannot create one out of nothing. Because an outline is like the runway on an airfield; it enables you to start down the runway with thoughts-on-paper, and take off with enough lift to stay up.

Why make an outline? Because an outline is a blueprint for the speech. It sets down the thought pattern in plain view. It enables you to test the analysis and order of arrangement. It shows at a glance the nature and amount of supporting materials, whether you have enough, and have the right kind. It allows a final check on that vital question: whether you plan to develop each topic according to the audience's attitude toward it, or whether you intend to plunge ahead blindly like the bull about to be killed by the matador.

Why make an outline? For the same reason an architect outlines a building, a playwright outlines a play, and a general outlines his plan of battle.

## The outline and the modes of delivery

The nature of the outline depends somewhat on your mode of delivery. There are four modes.

*Reading the speech.* First, you can read the speech from a manuscript. Because of radio and television, reading speeches is today more common than ever before in the history of man. Yet it is still as poor as ever. For now, as always, when a speaker stands before an audience, with his eyes looking at the manuscript instead of the people, he loses personal contact. Is that so bad, you ask? Frankly, it is. *Remember that a speaker talks three languages simultaneously: word language, tone language, and sign language. Remember also that sign language is half a million years older than man's word language and more deeply imbedded in his nervous system.* When a speaker glues his eyes to a manuscript, he is using only *one* of these three languages. He loses the tone language with its informing inflection. He loses the rich meanings that come from earnestness and changes of time and pitch. He loses all of the language that talks to the eye. As some wit put it: "Using a manuscript in making a speech is like courting a girl through a picket fence. Everything you say can be heard, but there's not much contact."

Let's face it. *It is harder to read with meaning than to speak extemporaneously with meaning.* I suspect you won't believe that. Well, I would not either at your age. But after teaching a class in reading for thirty-nine years, and teaching classes in speaking over the same period of time, I am prepared to testify that *never* in thirty-nine years has *any* class in reading learned to communicate as effectively as the classes in extemporaneous speaking, even though every student in the reading class had previously been in one of the speaking classes. In extemporaneous speaking you can *see* your thoughts, and speak them as you see them. In reading you see black type on paper, you see letters all the same size, all the same color, and all set evenly on the lines. No matter how hard you try, it will take a long time—certainly more than a year—for you to communicate black type on paper as effectively as you can communicate live thoughts in your mind.

This explains why most of the speeches read by public men are poor. It may explain why only one man in public life since the invention of radio has become a superior reader, namely Franklin D. Roosevelt. He became one by paying the price. In college he was influenced more by Charles T. Copeland, so he told his wife in later life, than by any other man. Copeland, be it remembered, was one of the greatest teachers of reading of all time. Later, in the early days of radio, before broadcasting a speech he recorded it twice, listened carefully to each playback, then changed and improved his reading. He *knew* how every speech was going to sound to others. He had already heard it twice.

Henry Ward Beecher dryly informed ministerial students that, "Peter, on the day of Pentecost, did not put on his specs and read." Norman Vincent Peale reported the result of reading his first sermon to his father. Said his father, "Well, Norman, there are several things I would do with that sermon if I were you. First, I would burn it up." Bishop Fulton J. Sheen throws away even his outlines. For every speech he will make five or six outlines, throw away each before he makes the next one, and throw away the last one before he gives the speech. What he forgets, he explains, was not worth remembering; and what he remembers is the good portion that listeners will remember when they hear the speech.

In summary, remember that most speech readers are inept. They are simply clumsy performers who think reading is the easy way out because "anybody can read," not knowing that good reading is more difficult than good speaking. If you are willing to invest *several years* in learning how to read—(1) learning to stretch your eye span so as to take in an entire paragraph at a glance while keeping contact with the audience, (2) learning how to make typed words on paper become living thoughts in your mind, (3) learning word-grouping and (4) tone-copying, (5) learning how to change pace and (6) change speech pattern—then go ahead and become a speech reader. If you are not willing to invest time to do all this, then burn your manuscript. For those who intend to become expert readers, the outline can be short, consisting only of a clear division of the main topics plus catch phrases that show how you propose to organize the supporting material.

*Memorizing the speech.* This is popular with students—too popular. They feel "safe" with a memorized speech. Safe from what? Safe from the fear of fear, but from little else. Are they safe from forgetting? Well, they have hundreds of words now to remember instead of a simple thought pattern. The very thing that makes them feel "safe" leads to danger, for a memorized speech *sounds* memorized. It sounds "canned" like the music of a hurdy-gurdy. The speaker, like the monkey, shuffles through his performance—then waits at the end for the applause. People applaud both in much the same spirit. It was pretty good for a monkey.

Many great men indeed have memorized their speeches, though probably only a fraction of those who were reputed to memorize them actually did so. As Fénelon said of that pair of great speakers of antiquity, Demosthenes and Cicero: "We have several reasons for believing that they did not memorize [their speeches] word for word." Of those who did, the best were consummate readers of lines. They came to the habit after years of training, and were willing to expend unlimited labor to attain artistic perfection. Let's have no nonsense comparisons. Students are not consummate readers of lines. They lack the experience. They lack the time. Memorizing may be useful for special exercises in voice training, or perfecting bodily action, but not for the main business of original speaking.

*Speaking impromptu.* This is speaking without preparation. More accurately it is speaking without *immediate* preparation, for an impromptu speaker, of course, uses his background of experience and information. We speak impromptu almost entirely in certain restricted ways, notably in club and committee meetings, where we ask a question, make a comment, or raise an objection in discussing matters of business. But formal impromptu speaking—where a speaker goes to the platform and gives a full-blown speech without preparation—is something else. Loosely, there are two kinds of such speaking. In one the speaker flounders, backtracks, scrambles and unscrambles his ideas—because he has had no chance to process or arrange them. Or if he belongs to the "Aw-Gosh" school of speaking, one who prides himself he can speak anytime on anything, he will proudly recite a stream of platitudes. Disraeli aptly labelled such speaking as "the hare-brained chatter of irresponsible frivolity." Impromptu speaking is useful as a training exercise, and most of us are caught in places where we have to make them. But don't trust to impromptu speaking when the speech is really important.

*Speaking extemporaneously.* You know what extemporaneous speaking is (see page 61). It is not impromptu. It is not speaking with slight preparation. It is speaking by one who thinks deeply on the principles of the subject, who knows intimately the details, who has put them in order in his mind. It is speaking by one who knows everything he must say, and the place where he must say it. In others words, it is speaking from thoughts carefully organized in outline instead of in manuscript. Obviously, such an outline would be more detailed than one used for writing a manuscript, for this outline is the takeoff for the speech itself. This is the type of outline to be considered in this chapter.

## Requirements for good outlines

Outlines for class speeches serve two purposes: (1) They are the construction blueprints for students learning to make speeches. (2) They are a diagnostic aid to the instructor; they tell him the kind of speech that was *planned.* From hearing the speech—and examining the outline—he can tell whether any particular problem arose from faulty planning, or from imperfect execution. Therefore, on two counts the classroom outline is not quite comparable to the outline used by experienced speakers. It will be more complete, and more attention will be paid to diagnostic details. Follow the procedure given below, except where modified or changed by your instructor:

1. *Prefix to the outline a clear and complete Purpose-Sentence.*

*Wrong*

This is the best solution to this problem. (What problem? What solution?)

*Right*

You had better borrow the money to go to college than not to go at all.

2. *Organize the outline into three parts: the beginning, the body, and the ending. Ordinarily these are known as Introduction, Discussion and Conclusion.*

*Right*

INTRODUCTION

I. _____

DISCUSSION

I. _____

II. _____

CONCLUSION

I. _____

3. *Use a consistent set of symbols to indicate main heads and each descending order of subheads.* From generations of usage the symbols given below have become almost common law. To avoid being misunderstood probably you had best follow general usage:

*Right*
I. Roman numerals used for main heads.
    A. Capital letters used for 1st level of subheads.
        1. Arabic numbers used for 2nd level of subheads.
           a. Small letters used for 3rd level of subheads.
              (1) Arabic numbers in parentheses used for 4th level of subheads.
                 (a) Small letters in parentheses used for 5th level of subheads.

4. *Number each part of the outline (Introduction, Discussion, Conclusion) as a separate unit.* The entrance and exit should not be confused with the thought pattern of the discussion. Thus if you have two parts in the Introduction, the first main head (Discussion) is numbered I, not III.

*Wrong*

INTRODUCTION
I. _____
II. _____

DISCUSSION
III. _____
IV. _____
V. _____

CONCLUSION
VI. _____

*Right*

INTRODUCTION
I. _____
II. _____

DISCUSSION
I. _____
II. _____
III. _____

CONCLUSION
I. _____

5. *Show the logical relationship of headings also by proper indentation.*

*Wrong*
I. This symbol is partly concealed by the word underneath, whereas every symbol ought to stand alone in the open, easily visible to the eye.
    A. Likewise this subhead symbol is partly concealed by being absorbed into the line beneath.
1. This subhead symbol is partly concealed, like the two above.

*Right*
    I. Note how this symbol stands alone and is instantly visible to the eye.
        A. Likewise this subhead symbol is instantly visible because it stands apart and to the right.
            1. Even sub-subheads like this are instantly visible when given proper indentation.

6. *Use complete sentences only.* This is done for two reasons: (*a*) Although catch phrases are perfectly all right for experienced speakers (though relatively few good speakers use them), you are *learning,* and in learning you need to be sure to think through each idea and phrase it into exact words. (*b*) Your outline is also to help the instructor diagnose your individual speech problems. A catch-phrase outline is a poor diagnostic aid.

7. *Write down each main head in a simple sentence, usually with an active verb; beware of compound sentences, complex sentences, winding sentences, and dangling clauses.*

*Wrong*
    I. Problems of higher education. (Not a sentence, but only a meaningless clause.)
*Poor*
    I. It is because of the fact that we have a large increase in population as well as the fact that a greater percentage of youth today go to college that the financial side of education has become critical. (Winding and dangling!)
*Good*
    I. The financial crisis in education comes from more babies being born now than ever before, with a larger percentage going to college when they grow up.

8. *Check your group of main heads to insure a consistent and simple thought pattern.*

*Poor; no thought pattern*
    I. Education ought to produce benefits to the individual.
    II. It fails when it does not.
*Good; simple thought pattern*
    I. An educated person ought to be able to entertain others.
    II. An educated person ought to be able to entertain himself.
    III. An educated person ought to be able to entertain a new idea.

9. *Check the main heads to be sure that they sustain the Purpose-Sentence.* This point is so elementary that the sight of it in print seems our of place. But in the hard school of experience it is a necessary reminder.

*Poor; main heads don't sustain Purpose-Sentence*
PURPOSE-SENTENCE:   You can't understand the heritage of Western Civilization without knowing the Bible.

    *Main Heads:*    I. Before the day of printing we did not have a true Western civilization.

                  II. Now we do and the Bible is a vital part of it.

*Good; main heads sustain Purpose-Sentence*

PURPOSE-SENTENCE:    You can't understand the heritage of Western Civilization without knowing the Bible.

    *Main Heads:*    I. Without knowing the Bible you can't understand the literature of Shakespeare and Milton, of Pope and Byron.

                  II. Without knowing the Bible you can't understand the Christian religion; or as St. Jerome stated it, "to be ignorant of Scripture is not to know Christ."

10. *Beware of trying to support any head by one subhead; use two or more.* You really can't "divide" an idea into one subhead, for "division" implies two or more parts.

*Wrong*

    I. One danger to the American democracy is the tendency to glorify the common mind.

        A. It exists in many forms.

            1. Schoolgirls imitate the television and movie stars.

*Right*

    I. One danger to the American democracy is the tendency to glorify the common mind.

        A. Every day we see it done in many ways.

            1. School boys collect autographs of baseball heroes and television celebrities, but not of great scientists, writers, or statesmen.

            2. School girls imitate the walk, hairdress, and bathing suits of sex stars who cannot act.

        B. Yet in this critical 20th century, it's the spiritual, political, economic, and scientific leaders whom we must follow if we are to survive.

    II. etc.

11. *See that the subheads at all levels develop the heads above them.*

*Wrong*

    I. Advertising today is based on impelling wants discovered through the advertisers' "motivational research."

        A. Until a short time ago it had been based on behaviorist psychology.

        B. This psychology assumed that a person would respond to a given stimulus if it were repeated often enough.

            1. This placed people in the status of Pavlov's dogs who salivated when the bell rang.

            2. But advertisers thought that this was the way to sell goods.

*Right*

    I. Advertising today is based on impelling wants discovered through the advertisers' "motivational research." (*for example*)

        A. Motivational research found that one impelling want of human beings is the assurance of vitality. (*consequently*)

1. Tea sales rose 13 per cent in two years when the slogan was changed from, "Tired? Nervous? Try tea," to "Make it hefty, hot and hearty. Try Tea!" (*and*)
2. In 1955 Phillip Morris decided to alter the sex of its Marlboro cigarettes.
    a. For years it had been sold in a white box as a woman's cigarette. (*but*)
    b. Motivational research showed that a red box would attract male customers, so the color was changed to red. (*and*)
    c. Then the advertisements were changed to show a virile young man, with a tatoo on his arm or hand, commanding a ship or doing some other job that made him a man's man. (*and*)
    d. Following this advertising change, Phillip Morris sales, which had declined over $31 million during the five years preceding, now increased $126 million; and its income increased over 38 per cent, from $11.4 million to $15.7 million. (*also*)
B. Motivational research found that another impelling human want was the desire for security. (*for example*)
    1. Wrigley's Gum found through a survey that some people chew gum to release tension and express hidden aggression; so they decided to exploit this want. (*and*)
    2. In a Pennsylvania coal-mining town where there was more than normal frustration from high illiteracy, low pay, and a mixture of racial groups, they ran a new series of advertisements; it was simply a cartoon showing a child overcoming all sorts of stupendous obstacles merely by popping in his mouth a stick of Wrigley's Spearmint. (*and*)
    3. Sales in this area nearly doubled the national average.

12. *Generally use personalized language, or echo the words of the actual speech.* Personalized language is wordy, but is the easiest takeoff from the outline into the speech. Less personalized language that echoes the words of the actual speech allows a shorter outline, but makes the takeoff a bit harder. Whichever you use, avoid the banal indirect phrasing, "I shall show the audience that. . . ."

*Wrong*
    I. Here I shall tell the audience about why baseball fans like the game
*Better*
    I. One reason for baseball fans is the colorful baseball players.
        A. Ted Williams is an example.
        B. Yogi Berra is another.
    II. Another reason is the umpires, for fans can always blame them when the game goes wrong.
*Wordy, but often the best*
    I. Colorful players make millions of baseball fans.
        A. For almost 20 years some fans booed Ted Williams and others

cheered him, but they came to see him play, and they liked to read stories about him.

1. In batting practice one day, peppery Billy Martin was kidding Ted. "Let's see you hit one down the right field line," said Martin, and Ted drove one right over first base. "How about left field?" yelled Martin, and Ted drove one over third base. "How about fouling one off?" chanted Martin, and Ted ticked it back to the screen.
2. Then Ted started talking, "You're supposed to be a good fielder, Billy. Show us how," and Ted blasted one between Martin's legs so fast that Martin fell down trying to get out of the way.
3. That was the last time Martin kidded Ted Williams about being a place hitter.
4. Of course, Ted was always cocky; when he met Ty Cobb he had the nerve to ask: "Have you ever played baseball, Mr. Cobb?"

B. Yogi Berra and Mickey Mantle were another pair of colorful players.
1. Yogi put a special solution in his eyes to improve his batting average.
2. One day when Yogi had 3 for 3 and Mickey had 0 for 3, Yogi said: "Here, Mick, why don't you try this stuff?" "Okay," said Mantle, and he drank the whole bottle in one gulp.
3. "You'll die. Call a doctor," shouted Yogi. Mantle laughed, went to bat, and hit a 400-foot home run.

C. But the umpires help make the game, for fans can always blame them when the wrong team wins.
1. "Where's your dog? asked an irate fan when his team was losing. "Don't have any," said the umpire crisply as he signalled for play to start. "Well, you're the first blind man I ever saw walking around without a dog," said the fan.
2. Even the umpires have fun at this. Lon Warneke was an old Cub pitcher who went on to become an umpire; and a Warneke fan asked him, "What happens when a player's eyes go bad? Isn't he through with the game?" Warneke replied solemnly, "Oh, no, they make an umpire out of him."

13. *Include the supporting materials in the outline.* An outline that contains only assertions—with no illustrations, factual information, comparison, testimony, etc.—is just about worthless. Better use the paper for doodling. For an example of an outline segment with supporting material included, see the last two illustrations under No. 12 just above.

14. *Include also, if you wish, the transitions and signposts.* These will not be numbered parts of the outline, of course, since they are signposts and not parts of framework of ideas. But signposts are useful, on highways and in outlines. Standard practice is to insert them, without numbers, in parentheses.

*Right*

I. The literary quality of American novels has fallen almost as low as their heroine's décolleté dresses.

   A. I know that people in every age criticize contemporary literature.

   B. But I submit that novels like *God's Little Acre* and *Peyton Place* have only small literary value compared to their amount of broken-field running in bedrooms.

     (You may say, "That's true, but these novels are best-sellers, and therefore what the American people want to read." That's right.)

II. Thanks to our reading taste, authors have found it more profitable to write sex novels than to write literature.

By examining the outline an experienced speaker, often at a glance, can spot inherent weaknesses in the speech; but these are not so obvious to the inexperienced. Fortunately, even for them, there is a method for bringing hidden weaknesses to light. It is known as the Technical Plot.

To test a speech by its Technical Plot, leave a margin of two or three inches on the left of the outline. In this space set down *what you are doing in the outline.* Where you have an illustration in the outline, write in the left margin, "illustration." Where you have used specific instances, write "specific instances." Where you have attempted to use suspense or to build a climax, write "suspense," or "climax."

If you do this accurately you can quickly test each part of the outline. Have you relied too much on assertion, or used real supporting material? Have you overworked explanation, or restatement and repetition (which are the weakest forms of supporting materials)? Have you based your speech on the strongest available human wants, or relied too much on the weaker ones? All of this you can discover by examining an accurate Technical Plot.

*I*

In the following outline, suitable for a five-minute speech, the speaker develops a speech of information on a reasonably simple subject. The main supporting materials were figures and specific instances. Each main head was developed by the *instructive method* (see page 173).

### THE U.S. POPULATION BOOM

*Technical Plot*                    *Outline*

PURPOSE-SENTENCE: The mid-century population boom in the United States caught us unprepared.

INTRODUCTION

I. The U.S. census of 1950 showed that we had an unexpected problem on our hands.

### THE U.S. POPULATION BOOM—Cont.

| *Technical Plot* | *Outline* |
|---|---|
| THOUGHT PATTERN: CAUSE-EFFECT | DISCUSSION |

I. Since 1940 the U.S. has had an unexpected, almost explosive growth in population.

*Figures*

   A. In the 10 years 1940-1950 it increased nearly 20 millions, or over 14 per cent.

*Figures*

   B. In the 10 years 1950-1960 it increased nearly 30 millions, or over 18 per cent.

   C. This increase of nearly 50 millions in 20 years caught every forecaster by surprise.

*Figures*

     1. The Thompson-Whelpton projections of 1937, based on assumptions of medium $mmO$, forecast a 1950 population of only 140.6 millions, or an increase of but 6.4 per cent; but the actual population was 150.7 millions.

*Comparison: figures*

     2. Out of a series of six such projections made in 1937-1938, each using a different $mmO$ assumption, the lowest forecast for 1950 was 137.1 millions and the highest was 144.2 millions.

*Comparison; figures*

     3. The Census Bureau projection had forecast a population gain 1940-1950 of 8 millions, to 139.6 million people; actually the gain was 19.5 millions, to 151.7 million people.

*Explanation*

     4. Statistically these forecasts were accurate, but the young American parents changed their ideas about having babies.

     5. Unless they change their minds again, we shall have over 210 millions of people by 1970.

| *Technical Plot* | *Outline* |
|---|---|

II. This explosive growth created unexpected problems which we have not yet solved.

| Technical Plot | Outline |
|---|---|
| | A. In education, a record number of children enter school each year for whom there are still not enough schools or teachers. |
| |   1. Experts had said that the school population would reach its peak in 1960, and after that would remain stationary or would decline. |
| *Testimony* |     a. As James B. Conant wrote in 1938: "The ever-enlarging school system, the ever-increasing college and university student body. . . . This is all past. . . . By 1960 or thereabouts we shall have a stationary population." |
| *Explanation* |     b. But 72 million babies born 1940-1960 confounded all the experts. |
| |   2. Note how this increasing population affected the schools. |
| *Comparison* |     a. In 1940, 2,259,000 babies were born; but since 1954 over 4,000,000 have been born each year. |
| *Explanation* |     b. This great wave hit the elementary schools in 1960; it will hit its second beachhead in 1968 when the first 4,000,000-a-year baby crop enters high school; and hits its third beachhead in 1972 when it enters college. |
| *Testimony* |     c. Even before this wave hit the elementary schools—back in 1958—*The Rockefeller Report on Education* found that U.S. public schools had a shortage of 142,000 classrooms, had 1,943,000 pupils in excess of classroom capacity, and that some schools had to drop mathematics, physics, and chemistry because they could not get the teachers. |

### THE U.S. POPULATION BOOM—Cont.

| *Technical Plot* | *Outline* |
|---|---|
| Testimony | d. Oscar Handlin of the U.S. Office of Education says we now need 150,000 additional public school teachers, plus at least 20,000 college teachers, and they are not in sight. |

B. Next, look at farming.

| | |
|---|---|
| Comparison | 1. By 1975 this population growth will call for additional cattle production equal to the 1950 production in Texas, Oklahoma, and Minnesota. |
| Testimony | 2. *Time* looked at the census projection and noted that it will by 1957 demand additional sheep production equal to that produced in 1950 in Montana, Wyoming, Utah, and Nevada combined. |

C. Finally, look at business.

| | |
|---|---|
| Figures | 1. In housing 1,400,000 new or rebuilt units must be built each year, just to keep even with population growth. |
| Comparison | 2. In electric power the utilities companies must increase capacity each decade as much as during the whole 75 years before 1950. |
| Comparison | 3. The pivotal auto industry, which accounts for 7.6 per cent of all U.S. manufacturing production now has 28 million more customers of buying age (19 and over) than experts had predicted in 1940. |

CONCLUSION

I. Dry figures published by the census bureau affect the happiness and well-being of the American people many years hence.

## II

In the following outline for a six-minute speech, the speaker develops a speech of information on a more complex subject than in the first outline. The main supporting materials are specific instances, testimony, illustration, and restatement. Because listeners *wanted* to know how to study, each main head was stated openly at the beginning, and each was developed by the *instructive method* (see page 173).

## HOW TO STUDY

| *Technical Plot* | *Outline* |
|---|---|
| | PURPOSE-SENTENCE: Studying, thinking and remembering go hand in hand, so that the absence of one leads to the loss of all three. |

### INTRODUCTION

| *Getting good will by pleasantry* | I. In selecting a subject for this Monday morning's speech, I remembered that it would be the Monday after our Big Weekend. |
| *Getting attention and orienting the audience by direct reference to a topic of vital interest* | II. I knew that most of you wouldn't be awake yet, so I chose one that would keep *me* awake, and one that would make you wish you were awake; for final exams are just three weeks ahead, and I'm going to talk this morning on *how to study*. |
| *Supporting the Purpose-Sentence by testimony* | III. William James once said that, "The art of remembering is the art of thinking," and I propose to show that studying, thinking, and remembering all go hand in hand, so that the absence of one leads to the loss of all three. |

THOUGHT PATTERN:
CLASSIFICATION ORDER

### DISCUSSION

| *Assertion* [1] | I. In order to study, you must think. |
| *Assertion* | A. The fact that we are conscious is not proof that we are thinking. |
| *Hypothetical illustration* | 1. We may take a train ride and at the end of the ride say to ourselves, "I've been thinking." |
| | 2. In truth, you probably have not thought for a single minute. |
| *Assertion* | B. Actually you think only when you are faced with a problem. |

[1] In the Technical Plot usually you do not list Assertions, because the purpose of a Technical Plot is to show the *amount and kind of Supporting Material being used to uphold the Assertions.* They are listed here only to illustrate what Assertions are as the term is used in speechmaking.

### HOW TO STUDY—Cont.

| *Technical Plot* | *Outline* |
|---|---|
| Hypothetical illustration | 1. If your train had suddenly lurched to a stop with screaming brakes, you would have started thinking, "Is there danger?" and "How can I escape it?" because you would have faced a problem that was immediate and urgent. |
| Restatement | 2. But if you were faced with no problem on your train ride, you probably would not think. |
| | a. You would look at people's faces. |
| Humor | b. You would admire or deprecate their figure, form, and clothes. |
| Assertion | C. The process is the same with formal study. |
| Specific instance | 1. You clear your desk of *Esquire, Look,* and the letter from home— then sit down to study "How to organize a speech into concise and orderly form." |
| Assertion | 2. In the next half hour a parade of ideas marches through your head. |
| Specific instance | a. You wonder about that assignment in Math. |
| Specific instance | b. Your girl in Ohio gets on your mind again; "What's she up to now?" you wonder for the fifteenth time. |
| Specific instance | c. "What about next weekend?" you wonder. |
| Specific instance | d. "Those confounded exams, only three weeks away," you think. |
| Specific instance | 3. Also, and naturally, you talked with a couple of other people who happened by. |
| Summary and climax that makes hearers wiggle uncomfortably | 4. In short, you have not been studying at all; you have been playing mental hop-skip-and-jump. |

| Technical Plot | Outline |
|---|---|
| *Assertion that relieves some of the discomfort* | 5. This is the *normal* way the mind and body behaves; both are restless. |
| *Explanation* | a. The human body is restless. |
| *Specific instance* | (1) I'm restless as I give this speech. |
| *Specific instance* | (2) You're restless as you listen to it. |
| *Specific instance* | (3) Even at night you turn over from 20 to 45 times while you are asleep. |
| *Explanation* | b. The human mind is quite as restless as the body. |
| *Explanation* | (1) Attention comes in "spurts" and we can think of nothing longer than a few seconds at a time. |
| *Explanation* | (2) What we call prolonged attention is simply repeated spurts of attention on the same subject. |
| *Testimony* | (3) William James once said that the only difference between his mind and any poor mind was that he could keep his spurts of attention from getting off the subject. |
| *Transition* | (So when we study our problem is to keep our repeated spurts of attention right on the subject, and to do this we must narrow our thoughts to the point where only the problem, or point in question, is in view.) |
| *Assertion* | II. First, we should attend to the physical aspect of study. |
| *Assertion of the first principle* | A. Clean up your study area of all probable sources of interruptions. |
| *Analysis of A, step one* | 1. Have a definite place to study, and at that place do nothing else but study. |
| *Specific instance* | a. Don't write letters there. |
| *Specific instance* | b. Don't play cards there. |
| *Specific instance* | c. Do nothing there but study. |

## HOW TO STUDY—Cont.

| *Technical Plot* | *Outline* |
|---|---|
| *Analysis of A, step two* | 2. Avoid disturbances. |
| *Specific instance* | a. Pictures on your desk or nearby wall can be a distraction. |
| *Specific instance* | b. A turned-on radio is certain to distract you; that popular notion that you can study while listening to a radio is wishful thinking. |
| *Analysis of A, step three* | 3. Above all, don't get too comfortable. |
| *Restatement* | a. Over comfort is good for sleeping, but not studying. |
| *Restatement* | b. A good idea is to lean forward and put your elbows on the desk. |
| *Assertion of the second principle* | B. Follow a definite study program. |
| *Analysis of B, step one* | 1. Review the previous lesson first. |
| *Restatement* | a. This will put you in the mood to study. |
| *Restatement* | b. It will also give you something to tack your new lesson to. |
| *Analysis of B, step two* | 2. Look at the *whole* lesson before you begin. |
| *Explanation* | a. You can then plan your method of learning. |
| *Explanation* | b. The important points will thus come easier. |
| *Analysis of B, step three* | 3. Underlining the book is a good idea, but a better one is to *write* in your own words on the margin. |
| *Analysis of B, step four* | 4. Finally, recitation is a great help to learning. |
| *Restatement* | a. Recite it to yourself a few times. |
| *Restatement* | b. The more times an idea enters your head, the better the retention. |
| *Assertion* | III. Next, we should observe the mental aspect of study. |

| Technical Plot | Outline |
|---|---|
| *Analysis of III, step one* | A. Study with the *intent* to remember, not just to pass an examination. |
| *Figures* | 1. Extensive experiments show that it is possible to remember from 20 per cent more to 400 per cent more simply because of the intent. |
| *Factual information* | 2. These experiments showed that those who studied to pass an exam, forgot when the exam was over; those who studied to remember kept on remembering when the exam was over. |
| *Analysis of III, step two* | B. Immediately apply to life what you study. |
| *Illustration* | 1. Harry Overstreet gives a significant example of this; he asked a philosophy student studying Spinoza to go to Coney Island and see what philosophy he could find there. |
| | a. The student stared in astonishment. |
| | b. Respectable young Ph. D. candidates did not do that sort of thing; they got philosophy out of books. |
| | 2. This man had not learned to apply his knowledge to life. |
| *Analysis of III, step three* | C. Try to develop and maintain your interest in the subject. |
| *Restatement* | 1. When you tire of one subject, switch to the study of another. |
| *Restatement* | 2. If you have no interest in a subject, you will be less likely to remember it. |
| *Analysis of III, step four* | D. Find a good reason for studying a subject. |
| *Restatement* | 1. A good reason supplies motivation for remembering it. |
| *Illustration* | 2. Everybody knows the story of the boy who was dull in physics until |

### HOW TO STUDY—Cont.

*Technical Plot*                                                        *Outline*

he learned one day that physics explained what made a baseball curve; and this boy, who wanted to be a pitcher, had no trouble thereafter remembering physics.

CONCLUSION

*Summary*

I. If you get nothing else from this speech, get these three points: 1) Clear your study area, 2) retain your interest in the subject, 3) apply your knowledge to life.

*Humor*

II. Follow these rules, my lords and ladies, and I'll guarantee that you'll know and understand your freshman English by the time you leave graduate school!

*III.*

The outline below is for an eight-minute speech. Listeners will *not want* to believe either of the two main heads, so the outline develops them by *conciliation plus impelling argument* (see pages 174-175). Notice that neither *main head was stated at the beginning, but each was opened by a transition, followed by a step-by-step presentation of the supporting materials. Only when the evidence was presented, did the speaker come to a full statement of each head.* The chief supporting materials are factual information, testimony, explanation, specific instance, and comparison.

### A COLLEGE EDUCATION IS NOT A FREE TICKET

*Technical Plot*                                                        *Outline*

PURPOSE-SENTENCES: Your college education won't have the money worth in real life that you want to believe it will.

INTRODUCTION

*Getting attention by reference to recent events of special interest*

I. Last week there were forty representatives of business corporations on campus interviewing seniors.

   A. They are talent scouts looking for college graduates to become junior executives who 20 years hence may earn

*Technical Plot*                                    *Outline*

$25,000, and 35 years hence may draw
one of those $100,000 salaries plus a
$200,000 bonus.

B. That's enough to excite your blood,
and it has excited some of the boys
at my house, until they are dreaming
of yachts and country clubs—and
falling behind in their studies.

II. I want to take a sober second look at what
we've been reading and hearing about the
money value of a college education.

A. I take you know I think a college
education is valuable; otherwise I
would not be working 55 hours a week
all summer—at two jobs—and four
nights a week all winter, to get that
magic college degree.

B. But I don't want to indulge in false
notions about its value.

(Let's look at some of the enthusiastic claims
about higher education.)

THOUGHT PATTERN:
  CAUSE-EFFECT                              DISCUSSION

Main head set in brackets        I. [Statisticians have misled you on the cash
because it was *not* stated          value of college education.]
at the beginning, but was
unfolded gradually.

*Testimony*                          A. In the last few years I've seen quoted
a dozen times that well-known survey
on the "value" of a college education;
it's been published by the NEA, and
quoted by *The Nation's Schools* and
approved by at least one college
president.

*Figures*                               1. It says that an average elementary
school graduate will earn in a life-
time $116,000, that an average
high-school graduate will earn
$165,000, and that an average col-
lege graduate will earn $268,000.

## A COLLEGE EDUCATION IS NOT A FREE TICKET—Cont.

| Technical Plot | Outline |
|---|---|

*Technical Plot*                       *Outline*

*Testimony*

2. In other words, as Frederick J. Moffit put in *The Nation's Schools,* a college education is worth $100,000 more than a high-school education.

*Assertion*

B. I have reasons for believing that this assumption won't check with the facts of life.

*Explanation*

1. I don't mean to imply that a college education has no value; I think it does, and we've heard them stated so often that I don't need to repeat them.

*Specific instance*

2. But, when I look around and see students sleeping through lectures, bluffing in classes, never cracking a book, I wonder how much they are building for a successful future.

*Figures*

3. If the average sudent establishes a chance to earn an extra $100,000 merely by keeping residence in a college town for four years, how much could a man earn who studied hard?

*Restatement*

     a. If I believed these statisticians, I would expect a man on the honor roll to become a millionaire in later life.

*Assertion*

     b. Yet I know of no college whose honor-roll students have entered the millionaire class.

*Assertion*

4. Therefore, there must be other factors that determine to a large degree whether one is a financial success.

C. So let's look at what these figures really mean.

*Explanation*

1. These people who say that a college education is worth $100,000 reach this conclusion because the survey found that men who went

| *Technical Plot* | *Outline* |
|---|---|
| | only through grade school earned $116,000 in a lifetime, and high-school graduates earned $165,000, but college graduates earned $268,000. |
| | 2. But that's saying "after this, therefore on account of this." |
| *Comparison* | a. You may remember that a few years ago there was an outcry that drinking milk caused cancer, because in milk-drinking countries women had cancer, but in Ceylon women didn't drink milk and almost none had cancer. |
| | b. That was true, but the median age of women at death in Ceylon was about 35 years; they didn't live long to get cancer. |
| | 3. Apply this to education. |
| *Explanation* | a. Successful men and women aren't successful just because they had a college education; they got a college education for the same reason they later "got" success; they had "getting" brains and "getting" character. |
| *Explanation* | b. College education gave them no new ability; what it did was *improve* what ability they already had; in other words, it sharpened the cutting edge, but did not change the quality of steel in their make-up. |
| *Explanation* | 4. These figures on how much each educational group earns actually measures the relative actual endowment of three classes of men —those who had ability and stamina only to finish grade school, those who had it to go through high school, and those who had it to go all the way through college. |

## A COLLEGE EDUCATION IS NOT A FREE TICKET—Cont.

| *Technical Plot* | *Outline* |
|---|---|

a. A college education is a wonderful thing to have; it will provide a richer life, and it may enable one to earn a bit more money.

b. But the chief reason why college graduates earn that $100,000 more than high-school graduates comes from a common cause; they were superior men; and because they were superior they went after a college education; then because they were superior they also won success.

c. But don't think that the man who loafs through college, sleeps through class, and cribs through exams is going to collect that extra $100,000.

*Specific instance*

(1) A lot of them will be like the man who sits in the front office of a lumber yard at home.

(2) He loafed through college, and he still sits when he should be standing up; he gets $80 a week; but the man who owns the lumber yard, and pays an income tax on $18,000 a year, never went beyond high school.

*Transition*

(So, without questioning the accuracy of these figures, I do question the loose interpretation of them. I go further; I wonder if it really doesn't harm the college man? When he starts thinking "My college education is worth $100,000." what does it do to him?)

Main head set in brackets because it was not stated at the beginning, but was unfolded gradually

II. [The college graduate often injures himself by placing a false cash value on himself.]

*Comparison*

A. He takes an unbecoming attitude; he's a bill collector after his $100,000 bonus.

| Technical Plot | Outline |
|---|---|
| *Testimony* | 1. I know a man who graduated here eight years ago; he's gone up fast, had four jobs on the way up, and now is sales manager for a $200,-000,000 corporation. He told me, "When we interview a college graduate the first thing we find out is whether he wants too much money; if he does, the interview is over right there. We can't use him at any price for his mind will be on his paycheck, and not on *producing* for the company." Then he added, "Don't you take any job because it offers the most money. Look for a place where you'll have room to prove how good you are." |
| *Specific instance* | 2. A manager of a small chain of filling stations who lives in my town has been trying to hire two or three college graduates; frankly he wants to retire in a few years, and is looking for a team of men to run the business. But he can't hire them because everyone he interviews refuses to learn the business from the bottom, by putting in gas and cleaning windshields. So he will sell the business to another company when he retires. |
| *Testimony* | 3. My father knows the president of a $40-million building and loan association. He's going to retire in five or six years, but he won't be succeeded by a college graduate. He said, "For ten years we tried to hire a college graduate who some day could become head of this company; but none of them wanted to start at the bottom; the result is that not one of the four men making $10,000 and over is a college graduate." |
| | B. Now what effect does this attitude have on the college man's chance for success? |

## A COLLEGE EDUCATION IS NOT A FREE TICKET—Cont.

*Technical Plot*            *Outline*

1. First, it gets him in trouble with the man who never went to college.

*Direct quotation*

   a. When the college man shows his "I've-been-to-college" attitude, does the noncollege man stand aside and say, "You go first, Mr. College Graduate, for you've a right to all good things without working any more"? Hardly, he takes it out of the college man's hide.

*Specific instance*

   b. At the factory where I work in summer a college man was put in charge of the shipping department. Soon he complained to his superior that the workers were deliberately mixing up shipments in a way that put the blame on him. "I know," said the manager wearily, "you've taught them to resent your college-man attitude. Unfortunately, I can get another man to replace you easier than I can a crew to replace them."

2. Second, remember that big corporations have a built-in method of handling such college graduates.

*Explanation*

   a. They hire dozens, or hundreds, of college graduates each year, and pay them a high starting salary.

   b. But don't let that fool you; for they're looking for that 1 in 10 or 1 in 50 who can go to the top.

   c. Ten years after they are hired, the bulk of these college graduates will either have quit because they were still at the bottom, or will be working at file-clerk jobs; and behind them each year will be coming a new crop of college graduates.

| Technical Plot | *Outline* |
|---|---|
| *Testimony* | d. As the employment manager of an electrical corporation said, "We hire them by the hundreds in order to find the four or five we really are going to want 25 years hence." |

CONCLUSION

| | |
|---|---|
| *Summary* | I. So that college education, I am afraid, won't be worth quite as much money as we want to think it will. It creates no initiative, and no brains; and it won't even improve them if you loaf on the job. It will certainly help you get a job, but from there on out you've got to prove whether you can go to the top, or be just a file clerk or draftsman. |

## Using the outline

The outlines described and illustrated in this chapter construct a *complete* framework. They test the order of arrangement and supporting materials, down to the last detail. Later, you may make shorter outlines. (But remember that most superior extempore speakers use rather long outlines.) For the first speech or two, however, you had better use a longer outline. They help you *plan* a good speech; and they help the instructor *diagnose* your plan.

How do you convert the outline into a speech? The ways and means were described in Chapter 3 (pages 60-62). Read it again. Follow the nine steps for filling your mind with the ideas and for rehearsing to communicate to listeners. Remember that those five-to-ten formal rehearsals, for best effect, must be distributed over several days.

## Assignments

ON RE-EXAMINING HABITS OF OUTLINING

1. Outline the class lecture of one of your instructors. A good class lecture ought to move a little more slowly than a regular public speech, hence you should be able to make a full outline as the lecture proceeds.

2. Go to hear a speaker and make a detailed key-word outline of the speech while he is giving it. Then go home and write out the full outline, together with a critical evaluation:

   a. Did the speech have a definite purpose? If so, was it stated, or only implied? Where in the speech was this done?

    *b.* Did the speech have definite main heads? If so, were they stated clearly? Were they arranged in a clear thought pattern?

    *c.* Was there enough supporting material? Was it arranged in an orderly way?

3. Use the following steps in outlining a magazine article:

    *a.* First, determine the central theme, and then phrase it into purpose-sentence.

    *b.* Next, study the thought movement until the main divisions become clear; then write these out as main heads.

    *c.* Finally, in subhead form set down the supporting material.

4. For one speech round make a key-word outline of each speech while the speaker is talking, and later fill out enough details so you can remember the content. At the end of the round, submit a list of the two best-outlined and the two worst-outlined speeches. Give your reasons.

5. Take an outline of one of your earlier speeches. Check it against the 14 specifications of a good outline set forth in this chapter. Hand it in with a prescription on how you could improve it.

ON USING OUTLINES EFFECTIVELY

6. Go over your notebooks in other courses. Have you numbered and indented the items so their sequence and relation are instantly clear? Have you put down only interesting knicknacks that caught your mind, or have you set down an organized outline of your professor's mind? Would your notes be more valuable if you used the principles of outlining set down in this chapter—modified, of course, to fit a semester of lectures woven together? Would you be willing to try doing this for, say, one month?

7. Are you willing to do the same with outside reading in other courses? By arranging notes in outline form, you can review quickly, and at a glance locate the main lines of thought and note the supporting material. The original reading and note-taking requires more time, but reviewing is cut to a fraction and the notes become useful for frequent later reference.

8. Use the following procedure in planning your next speech:

    *a.* While still in preliminary form, check the outline against the 14 specifications set forth in this chapter. Revise the outline, but do not yet make a full revised copy.

    *b.* Make a technical plot, and use it to test each part of the outline. Revise the outline again if necessary.

    *c.* Make a final copy of both the revised outline and the technical plot. Use the outline for rehearsing the final extempore speech.

# Using Words

RUDYARD KIPLING said to the Royal College of Surgeons, "I am by calling a dealer in words, and words are, of course, the most powerful drug used by mankind. Not only do words infect, egotize, narcotize, and paralyze, but they enter into and color the minutest cells of the brain. . . ."

Language is an invention, like dynamite; and, like dynamite, it's explosive. Like dynamite also, after inventing it man continued to improve it. Some of the most talented men who ever lived gave the best years of their lives to improving it.

If you intend to design jet planes, build houses, or run a store, your plans must first be created mentally, in words. If you discuss a situation or problem, be it modern poetry or the cost of living, your ideas are nebulous until they are put into words. Language limits your range of thought. You acquire new words, and they enable you to learn new meanings. You acquire other new words, and they lead you to new ideas and concepts. "This way," says the word, "is an interesting thought; come and find it."

Yet as the semanticists properly remind us, words have no value in themselves. They are only symbols for thoughts and things. Each word is like a paper $10 bill, intrinsically worth almost nothing, but by skillful techniques it has been created into currency of known value.

Primitive people need crude words only, for they think only in crude forms. Among civilized people those who don't think creatively, but only identify and follow, get along adequately with crude words. But crude words won't serve people who think and act, feel and talk, on problems of the civilized world. They need keener tools, and greater skill in using them. For them Aristotle laid down the basic rule, which, translated into English vernacular, says: "Think like a wise man, but communicate in the language of the people." To "think like a wise man" is difficult enough. But to "communicate in the language of the people" is so rare it excites comment like that of *Time* on Sir Winston Churchill: "Winston Churchill is a great clarifier of the muddied obvious. He tells people what they already know; but again and again it turns out that they did not know it clearly enough to understand it until Churchill made it brilliantly plain."[1]

## Things that prevent a speaker from being clear and accurate

The sad-average speaker, unfortunately, does not make ideas brilliantly plain. What Robert P. Gunning, reading expert, said of editorial writers applies with even more force to speakers: They "seem to confuse dignity with pomposity. Their marathon sentences, foggy words, and abstractions put their pieces completely out of reach of all but the upper 5 or 10 per cent of their readers." Now this is not from lack of training in "English," since from elementary school into college it is universally required. There are other reasons: especially lack of honesty, laziness, talking jargon, and using writing language instead of speaking language.

### LACK OF HONESTY

The most common lack of honesty is not deliberate falsehood, but the use of devices like Name-Calling or Card-Stacking to cover up and deceive. By Name-Calling we give a "bad name" to a person, group, or thing we don't like. Aristophanes did not like Socrates—this was around 423 B.C.—so he called him a *charlatan*. The president of Magdalen College, Oxford University, disliked Adam Smith—this was 1776—so he accused him of diffusing *atheism* throughout the land. Neither word today would be so dangerous as then. Today we can smear a man by calling him *Communist, demagogue, collectivist,* or *educationist*.

Name-calling may also be turned around, to make you like what I like by rousing your emotions and befogging your thinking. Instead of hate-words I use "virtue-words" like *liberty, freedom, democracy, Christian ideals, the American way.*

*Card-Stacking* is plain and simple stacking the cards against the truth. The speaker does not deliberately lie; he just distorts by discussing only part of a situation in the solemn pretense that it is the whole. He does not falsify facts, but evades them.

Finally, there is the dishonesty of *exaggeration*. We say "many" when we really mean *a few,* "absolutely" when it is only *probably,* "everybody knows" when the truth is that *some people believe*. Many such people give you telltale signs that you already may have learned to recognize. They say "as a matter of fact," when it's close to fabrication. Or "To tell you the absolute truth," when it is something downright false. Or "To be perfectly exact," when it is unreliable.

[1] *Time,* October 18, 1948, p. 29.

### LAZINESS

Frank H. Vizetelly, a famous dictionary editor, said: "Slovenly speech is as clearly an indication of slovenly thought as profanity is of a degraded mind." It may seem out-of-date to use antiquated words like "slovenly" and "laziness," but they happen to describe exactly what is meant here: plain intellectual laziness. To use accurate language is hard work, hence speakers who are too lazy to work hard use abstract words. Even on simple topics we cannot state ideas in concrete words until we have thought ourselves out of the fog and into sunlight. So when we are too lazy to think and our ideas are still foggy, we use abstract words. Read the famous comparison below from Edmund Burke's speech *On Conciliation with America* and Lord Brougham's *Inquiry into the Policy of the European Powers*. Both express the same thought. But Burke used concrete words and Brougham used abstract ones:

| BURKE | BROUGHAM |
|---|---|
| In large bodies, the circulation of power must be less vigorous at the extremities. Nature has said it. The Turk cannot govern Egypt, and Arabia, and Curdistan as he governs Thrace; nor has he the same dominion in Crimea and Algiers which he has in Brusa and Smyrna. . . . The Sultan gets such obedience as he can. He governs with a loose rein, that he may govern at all. | In all despotisms of the East, it has been observed that the further any part of the empire is removed from the capital, the more do its inhabitants enjoy some sort of rights and privileges: the more inefficacious is the power of the monarch; and the more feeble and easily decayed is the organization of the government. |

From lack of mental energy speakers also will use inert words instead of energy-carrying ones. Thus a clerk in the Office of Civilian Defense during World War II wrote that famous order: Federal buildings must "obtain obscuration either by blackout construction or by termination of illumination." President Roosevelt laughingly rewrote it: "Put something across the window, or turn out the lights."

### JARGON

Jargon could be defined as the educated man's prose. It is "the language of scholars, the terminology of a science or art, or the cant of a class, sect, trade, or profession." It consists, first, of technical terms presumably understood by the speaker's group of specialists, but nobody else. Actually, these terms are not always understood by the speaker's own group. As Carl von Clausewitz, founder of modern (preatom-bomb) military science, said of military writers:

All technical and scientific terms which belong to a system lose their propriety, if they ever had any, as soon as they are torn from that system to be used as general axioms. [Yet] our theoretical and critical books, instead of being simple, straightforward treatises, in which the author at least always knows what he says and the reader what he reads, are brimful of these technical terms. . . . The author himself has no clear perception of what he means, contents himself with vague ideas, which if expressed in plain language would be unsatisfactory even to himself.[2]

This was written before 1831. Since then, as modern civilization requires a higher percentage of people to write and speak, the problem has grown worse, until G. M. Young noted sadly, "Really there are times when I feel that civilization will come to an end because no one will understand what anybody else is saying."

The problem has become acute because in this technical twentieth century we have developed hundreds of vocational vocabularies. They are almost separate languages, and no person knows even a fraction of them. Your technical language may be understandable to your own group, but it's jargon to others. What speech correctionists call the *velum* is known to laymen as the "soft palate." What dentists call *dental caries*, to others is plain "tooth decay." The *Nieman Reports* have issued an apt warning: "in economics they . . . drag you, without explanation, through dollar pools and over tariff walls. In science, they ignore the oaf who doesn't know the difference between atomic fission and hydrogen fusion. In labor, they blithely skip from secondary boycotts . . . into an open shop, slamming the door in the face of the uninformed."

Not only does jargon obscure thought by using technical terms. It also obscures it by circling around the idea instead of moving in with short straight speech. "How excellent a thing is sleep," sighed Sancho Panza; "it wraps a man round like a cloak." But as Sir Arthur Quiller-Couch observed, a Jargoneer would have said, "Among the beneficent qualities of sleep its capacity for withdrawing the human consciousness from the contemplation of immediate circumstances may perhaps be accounted not the least remarkable." Some educated people like to talk that way. It sounds learned.

Finally, jargon obscured thought with what Sir Ernest Gowers calls "flabby verbosity." The Lord's Prayer says simply, "Deliver us from evil." The Jargoneer would say: "And initiate protective measures to safeguard us against activities or tendencies that are antisocial."

Whenever you are tempted to use jargon, remember Lord Bryce's warning, that when listeners find themselves puzzled over your meaning, and you go on to the next sentence while they are still puzzled over the last one—you annoy them, and you lessen your chance either to please or persuade them.

[2] Carl von Clausewitz, *On War*. The quotations here used are almost but not quite identical with the translation by J. J. Graham (London, Kegan Paul, Trench, Trübner & Co., Ltd., 1908) I, 154-155.

## *Spoken language* versus *written language*

Many speakers are hard to understand because they use writing language instead of talking language. Basically they are the same, of course, but at the operating level there are important differences. Note why. One is intended for the eye, the other for the ear. The reader may absorb at leisure; the listener must take it on the wing. The reader proceeds at his own pace; the listener is geared to the speaker's pace. The reader may pause to reflect, or reread; the hearer must follow without slackening his pace. The basic difference, then, is this: Written language must be ultimately intelligible to the reader.[3] Spoken language must be *instantly* intelligible to the listener.

You can't really be instantly intelligible unless you use talking rhythm, talking words, and talking sentence structure. This presents a critical problem to most students. They write their outlines, or even write their speeches, then having used written forms in the outlines, they carry them over into the speech. Hence they are harder to understand when they talk in public than when they talk in private, on at least three counts.

First, is talking rhythm. In writing we use the full forms of speech like this:

| | |
|---|---|
| It is | I have not |
| Do not | They are not |
| Will not | You did not |

But not in speech. You will remember Dorothy McCleary's statement that: "It is only persons who are unsure of the language who use the full forms of speech, because they lack the intimate feel for the contraction." The trouble is that the poor stage-frightened students *are* unsure, so they recite the full forms. But as a linguist, Harold Whitehall explained: "English spoken without the natural rhythm of English is scarcely English at all." Remember that listeners all their lives have been listening to this "natural rhythm of English." When you stand up to speak in public—and use a *different* rhythm—it interferes with their

---

[3] Obviously most written language needs to be almost as instantly intelligible as spoken language, especially everything read by the mass of people. But many books having greatest influence on civilization were not instantly intelligible. It took centuries of scholarship for readers to understand Aristotle's *Rhetoric*. Von Clausewitz's *On War* was the foundation work on modern warfare, but as the editor of the U.S. *Infantry Journal* noted, "You cannot race through this book." John Dewey, for all his vast influence, never wrote anything that was instantly intelligible. Stuart Chase said it took him two years to dig out the meaning of Alfred Korzybski's *Science and Sanity*. Most modern poetry could hardly be called instantly intelligible. In contrast, with a speech it's now or never. If it's not understood instantly, it is never understood at all, unless read later as an essay.

understanding. Therefore, generally use contractions so you will talk with that "natural rhythm of English":

| | |
|---|---|
| It's | I've not |
| Don't | They're not |
| Won't | You didn't |

*Second,* are talking words. In speech we use shorter, earthy, homespun words more than in writing: *got* instead of "have," *think* instead of "reflect," *want* instead of "desire." Especially the English language really has two sets of connectives—one used in everyday speech and another used almost exclusively for print. Here is a useful working list.

| SPEAKING | WRITING |
|---|---|
| but | however |
| | nevertheless |
| | notwithstanding |
| | on the contrary |
| and, also | likewise |
| | again |
| | moreover |
| | furthermore |
| so, therefore | thereupon |
| | consequently |
| | accordingly |
| | wherefore |
| | for this reason |
| | thus |
| for example | to illustrate |
| | more specifically |
| | to take a case |
| besides | in addition to |
| in other words | that is to say |

Further, is the problem of *which* and *that.* Listen to those speakers who use tanglefoot sentences, and you will find them overloading sentences with *which* and *that.* They give the impression of throwing in one every time they pause to grope through a half-formed idea. So heed the warning of Sheridan Baker: "Suspect yourself of wordiness whenever you see an *if,* a *which* or a *that.*" Note how masters of language omit them, even in constructions where they are grammatically proper:

Do you think it strange [that] they should have heard this? ARCHIBALD MACLEISH

This is the only way [that or in which] we may have peace home or abroad. Eric Johnston

We read in the Bible [that] "Jeshurun waxed fat and wicked." Winston Churchill

Also learn the difference between these two words. *That* is used more often in speech. *Which* is the bookish form. Students in giving speeches will use *which*—because they have memorized a written outline or the written speech. But after they sit down, let the instructor ask them about such-and-such idea in the speech—and in private speech they revert at once to *that*.

Finally, remember that speakers use personal pronouns: *I*, not "the present speaker"; *you*, not "one." From Demosthenes onward they have done this. Here is Demosthenes:

Tell me, do *you* want to go round and inquire from one another: what's the news?

Or Edmund Burke:

*You* well know what sort of things are involved.

Or Dwight Eisenhower:

*You* have known him in many ways.

Third, is *talking* sentence structure. Good English depends on two things: Choosing the right words, and arranging them in the right order. In speech, complicated sentence structure and backward syntax make ideas hard for listeners to comprehend. Straightaway English is easier. As Henry Ward Beecher explained: Sentences should be "straight as a lance. . . . Long sentences may be good, but not *twisting ones*." And Thoreau added: "A sentence should read as if its author, had he held a plow instead of a pen, could have drawn a furrow deep and straight to the end."

Now when a writer uses involved sentence structure the reader can run his eyes back and forth across the lines and extract the meaning. But a listener can't go back and forth. He must take it as it comes. You will find that listeners understand you better if you establish the following habits:

1. *Don't use back-in sentences.* A writer might back in with

*Although the Belgians have no such barrier between them and the Russians as the English Channel or the Atlantic Ocean,* they are nevertheless firmly in support of United Europe.

Sir Winston Churchill put the idea in straightaway English:

A month ago in Brussels I spoke to a meeting of thirty thousand Belgians. I could feel at once their friendship and their anxiety. They have no Atlantic

Ocean, no English Channel, between them and the Russian Communist armored divisions. Yet they bravely and ardently support the cause of United Europe. I admire them.

2. *Don't let clauses accumulate.* The easiest sentences to understand are those that arrange ideas in "this-*plus*-that" form. In the selection below four thought units are arranged in "this-*plus*-that" sequence:

> He batted his eyes, and the lightnings flashed;
> He clapped his hands, and the thunders rolled.

But note what happens when we change this arrangement by allowing each line to accumulate one clause:

> *When* he batted his eyes, the lightnings flashed;
> *When* he clapped his hands, the thunders rolled.

The lines are not yet hard to understand, but they are harder than in the first arrangement, and if we accumulate a few more clauses per sentence we can do a right good job of making the idea really hard to decipher. This time we shall number the accumulated clauses:

> (1) His readiness in debate, (2) his mastery of every subject he handled, (3) the bright and amiable light he shed about him, (4) and above all the unfailing courtesy and goodwill with which he treated friend and foe alike —(5) one of the surest signatures of a nature born to greatness—*made his William McKinley's service in the House of Representatives a pathway of unbroken successes and brought him at last to the all-important post of chairman of the Ways and Means Committee.*

Even with five accumulated clauses we can follow the idea, *if* we don't relax our listening. But when a speaker averages a sentence a minute like that, the audience won't listen long.

3. *Don't dodge around corners.* This homespun statement is chosen deliberately to help you remember one of the toughest problems students face. In terms of grammar the English language has *nonrestrictive phrases and clauses.* They are insertions within a sentence that don't change sentence meaning, but thrust additional information into it. Let's start with Henry W. Grady's straight-forward sentence:

> I went to Washington the other day and I stood on the Capitol Hill; my heart beat quick as I looked at the towering marble of my country's Capitol.

Now let's take out part of this straight-forward sentence, move it toward the front, and thrust it in as a nonrestrictive clause:

> I went to Washington the other day, *which is the capital of the United States and in which is the famous Capitol Hill,* and my heart beat quick as I looked at the towering marble of my country's Capitol.

Each comma indicates a *corner*. When the thought movement gets to that corner, it dodges around the corner and starts off in a new direction. When it gets to the next corner, it dodges back again. One sentence, two corners; and to follow, the listener must dodge around both.

Now students don't *talk* that way in private conversation, but when they sit down with a pen to prepare a speech they thrust in ideas until the thought movement resembles a pretzel. Then in speaking they recite these sentences, dodging around corner after corner, until they lose the listener now four corners behind. Here is one from a student speech:

> Mortimer Smith, *whose book "And Madly Teach" is a severe indictment of education,* says that the typical public-school graduate can't spell or write a decent English sentence. My own high-school principal, *who graduated both from a liberal arts college and teachers college, and who is fair-minded on this matter,* says that's true, but liberal arts college graduates can't do it either and they couldn't even a hundred years ago.

In written language, a little of this is all right. In spoken language, you would be better understood if you gave up using sentences with corners —i.e. nonrestrictive clauses—and arranged them in straightaway "this-*plus*-that" order.

## Ways and means of making ideas clear and accurate

First of all, the audience asks a speaker, "What do you mean?" and next, "How do you know?" Language, therefore, should be so clear and accurate that you cannot be misunderstood. "Not that language *may* be understood," said that doughty old Roman, Marcus Fabius Quintilian, "*but that it cannot be misunderstood.*"

### WORDS

We shall start with words, and later take up sentences.

#### CONCRETE WORDS

Consider the word *building*. A building where people live is a *residence;* a modest residence is a *cottage;* a pretentious residence is a *mansion*. A building where goods are made is a *factory;* a building where they are stored is a *warehouse;* a building where they are sold is a *store;* a small store is a *shop*. A building where clerical work is done is an *office*. A building where legislators meet is a *capitol*. A building where books are stored is a *library*. A building for dramatic performances is a *theater*. A building for storing motorcars is a *garage*. A building for storing hay is a *barn.* A building for sheltering horses is a *stable*. A building for quartering soldiers is a *barrack*. A building used for worship is a *church;* a modest church or a subordinate place of worship is a *chapel*; a Scotch church is a *kirk*; a bishop's church is a *cathedral*; a pretentious church is a *temple*; a Jewish church is a *synagogue*; a Mohammedan church is a *mosque*.

A word-lazy person could use *building* for each kind of building; but to be instantly intelligible you need to use twenty-two specific words to describe twenty-two specific kinds of buildings.

Suppose you say, "He *went* down the street." You tell what happened but not how. Suppose, instead, you substitute a specific word telling *how*: "He *staggered* down the street," or *strutted, waddled, strode, slunk, sauntered, marched, raced,* or *ambled*. Each describes a specific mode of going. Each carries a brighter picture than *went*.

Compare the two versions below and you will get the full effect of concrete words compared with abstract ones:

| DECLARATION OF INDEPENDENCE | STATEMENT OF THE EXTENT OF SHORT-FALL IN ALLEGIANCE TO GOVERNMENTAL AUTHORITY DOMICILED OVERSEAS, AND RECOMMENDATION WHEREBY A SEPARATIST MOVEMENT SHALL BE PROGRAMMED |
|---|---|
| We hold these truths to be self-evident, that all men are created equal, that they are endowed by their Creator with certain unalienable Rights, that among these are Life, Liberty, and the pursuit of Happiness. | It is our conviction that the following verities are indubious, namely that all individuals are ordained in a state of initial equality by the Universal Planner, that they have been given prepossession of a number of indefeasible equitablenesses, to wit, in part: Existence as a planitary being, adequate latitude of behavior, and nonrestriction in the research for well-being. |

Second-rate speakers doubtless will forever use abstract words, but first-rate ones soon learn that the concrete word enables them to *create pictures* of what they see, hear, and think.

### SIMPLE WORDS

"Except as ye utter by the tongue words easy to understand, how shall it be known what is spoken? For ye shall speak into the air." St. Paul, brilliant thinker and master of persuasion, wrote these words after speaking to peoples of many nations.

Masters of language follow this principle, but little minds still want to believe that "big words" signify big ideas. With them obscurity of language is mistaken for depth of thought. "What I cannot understand must be profound," such minds seem to reason. Yet the simpler a word, the easier it can be understood. Herbert Spencer properly points out that of the several reasons for this fact the most important is early association. A child "says *I have,* not *I possess—I wish,* not *I desire*; he does not *reflect,* he *thinks*; he does not beg for *amusement,* but for *play*; he calls things *nice* or *nasty,* not *pleasant* or *disagreeable.*" Through later years these simple words learned early in life carry a stronger meaning than words learned later.

But don't eminent speakers use big words? No. In general they use the simplest word that carries the exact shade of thought and feeling. Somebody counted and measured the printed speeches of that old fire-brand, Wendell Phillips. Across the board, 71 per cent of his words were one syllable, 18 per cent were two syllables, and only 7 per cent were three syllables. Any unskillful speaker would use a larger per-centage of big words. Inept speakers avoid simple words for long ones, and single words for phrases. Instead of *have,* they prefer "in possession of." They don't *ask,* but "make application for." They don't *eat,* but "consume." They don't have *homes,* but "places of residence." They don't *live,* but "are domiciled." They are not even *people,* but are "individuals." Especially they like those elephant words: "quadripartite," "unilateral," "directive." They can't just say *four-party, one-sided,* and *order.*

The simple word has a power that longer complex words can never have. "He was conveyed to his place of residence in an intoxicated con-dition." Of such language, Frank H. McClosky said, "Nonsense! If the man was drunk, say he was drunk. 'He was carried home drunk.'"

### COLORFUL WORDS

In the days of early airplanes passengers would see that sign flash on: "Hook up your safety belt." That phrase "*safety* belt" scared the life out of passengers, and some would never ride an airplane again. The airlines changed the sign to "*seat* belt"—"Please fasten your seat belt" —and it no longer frightened the passengers.

Words not only *mean* but also *suggest.* "I ate dead hog," *means* the same as "I ate roast pork," but it *suggests* something else. *House* and *home* have almost the same meaning, but *house* is a neutral word, whereas *home* evokes sentiment. "Without hearts there is no home," said Byron.

Because of word color you may say "a *gang* of thieves," but not "a gang of angels," for a group of angels is a *band* or *host.* Or you may say "a *bevy* of girls," but not a "bevy of bees," for a group of bees is a *swarm.* To say "She is *skinny,*" can never suggest the same attitude as "She is *slender.*"

A word's color and feeling gives its persuasive power. Rudyard Kipling—whose persuasive words "taught England the meaning of Empire, and the Empire the meaning of England"—said with utter candor in the last interview before his death: "You must bait your hook with gaudy words. I used to search for words in the British Museum. I read mad poets." If misunderstood to mean exhibitionist words or big words, the advice is dangerous; but if you've read Kipling you won't make that mistake.

Strive for accuracy, then, but beware of drabness. Remember Mark Twain's advice to use the right word and not its second cousin. The right word has color as well as meaning.

### SENTENCES

Sir Winston Churchill attributes his command of language to his having to stay in one form at Harrow three times as long as others. While others his age were studying Latin he remained behind. "But I was taught English," he said. *"Thus I got into my bones the essential structure of the ordinary English sentence—which is a noble thing."* The English language is so flexible it seems easy to beget a sentence. Yet a high percentage are misshapen biological freaks: "cuttle-fish sentences" that hide thought in their own ink, "tapeworm sentences" that go on and on, "monstrosities" with one body but two heads, and shapeless "ball-of-worm sentences" that occupy time and space but seem to have no head or tail. Straightaway English is a rough, tough language to learn. Its backbone is the sentence, and the strength of a sentence comes from its nouns and verbs, especially concrete nouns and active verbs.

Don't dismiss this casually as a classroom frill, lest it snaps back at you in later years. So acute is the problem that Associated Press and United Press both have hired "readability experts" to improve their language. So have leading American newspapers. So also have large corporations, like New Jersey Standard Oil, General Motors, and Ford Motors. The corporation officers, and even the newswriters, can't write straightaway English; and to save themselves they have had to call for help. Here we offer help for your listeners by listing five steps for constructing intelligible sentences:

### PREFER SHORT SENTENCES

Remember that a listener usually must carry in mind every word of a sentence to the end. Don't strain his memory too much; if the sentence is too long, break it up. How long is too long? That depends on how straight the sentence, and how big the words are. But it might help to know that Franklin D. Roosevelt's lucid prose averaged just under 23 words a sentence; and Churchill's magnificent sweep of rolling English averaged 27 words a sentence. Readability-expert Robert P. Gunning recommends 20 words or less for easy reading, and presumably easy listening.

Readability-expert Rudolf Flesch says that a 17-word sentence is "standard," 21 becomes "fairly difficult," 25 becomes "difficult," and 29 or more become "very difficult." Obviously they go to extremes, yet their expert services to newspapers and corporations have made life more tolerable for millions of readers and listeners!

Remember the inmates of the Pennsylvania State Prison who wrote Bergan Evans' *The Last Word* television program; they wanted to know how to shorten sentences! Remember also that your listeners are as concerned with sentences as are those prison inmates!

### PREFER STRAIGHT SENTENCES

"Just ordinary straightaway English is high talent," said a *New York Times* editorial (April 21, 1955), "and exceptionally straightaway English is straightaway genius." We applaud the statement, though actually using straightaway English is not really talent or genius, but just hard work. When a sentence labors, it's a telltale that the speaker did not. He ought to line up the ideas in each sentence the way Stonewall Jackson lined up his soldiers before he sent them into battle.[4] This is a matter of *thinking* in straight steps, not of writing out the words. It is repeating what we said earlier in this chapter, "don't dodge around corners." Consider this version:

> The merciful, since they shall attain mercy, are blessed.
> The pure in heart, since they shall see God, are blessed.

But the King James Version puts it in straight sentences:

> Blessed are the merciful: for they shall obtain mercy.
> Blessed are the pure in heart: for they shall see God.

"Go, and do thou likewise."

### TALK IN THE ACTIVE VOICE, NOT THE PASSIVE

Of course

> Any fool can make a rule—
> And every fool will mind it,

so you can turn this into a fool's rule. But it's a light risk compared to the gain if you use it intelligently. Remember that *the verb is the motor.* It propels the sentence, and nothing else propels it but that verb. Work

---

[4] This footnote is only for those who want to pursue that comparison. Jackson was at first notorious, and later famous, for his care in lining up soldiers before he sent them into battle: At Bull Run he did not rush in his men as other generals did, but lined them up behind a hill and sent them in organized; they won for him the name "Stonewall." At Chancellorsville, the day he was killed, he took two precious hours in late afternoon to line up his corps. He needed those two hours for daylight fighting, but refused to shorten by even one detail his careful line-up of soldiers before he sent them in.

your verbs hard, therefore, if you want ideas to move. Three suggestions might help:

*First, use verbs, not noun substitutes.* The millions of noun-users flinch from live verbs and put the heavy load on nouns. A noun-user would say, "It is to be considered how the lilies grow," or he might be persuaded to admit one live verb and say, "Consider the growth of the lilies." But the Gospel says:

> *Consider* the lilies, how they *grow.*

Six words, two live verbs!

*Next, prefer active to passive verbs.* Passive verbs are useful, indeed indispensable, or they would not exist in the language. Use them for special effects. But for regular duty use active verbs. For example, the adage says, "*Spare* the rod and *spoil* the child," using two live verbs, but the passive-verb lover would say, "Insufficient corporal punishment *results in* the spoiling of the child." In the same way "Haste *makes* waste," becomes "Precipitation *entails the negation of economy.*"

*Third, inspect all areas around all forms of the verb "to be."* We need the verb *to be* in all its forms. Use it often. But remember that it's an inert verb. It lies still. Ideas expressed by *is* and *was* are a bit like a corpse; they look natural but they don't move. "A stitch in time *saves* nine," says the adage. Throw out the live verb and bring in *is*, and we get: "The advantage of timely stitching *is* ninefold." Remember, too, how easy it becomes to make ideas foggy by, "It *is* . . . *that* . . ." "It *is* my belief *that*. . . ." for the simple direct, "I *believe*."

### STRIP ADJECTIVES AND VERBS

The English language has two kinds of modifiers:

1. *Defining* modifiers: *hot* stove, *old* man, *sharp* curve. They tell something essential. You don't strip them.

2. *Commenting* modifiers: *very* necessary, *most* unique, *definitely* harmful. They tell nothing, but try only to boost the noun. They might better be called *cluttering* modifiers, because most of the time they clutter the meaning. Examine those three: *very, most* and *definitely*. How can anything be "*very* necessary"? Isn't "necessary" the ultimate? How can anything be "*most* unique"? Consult a dictionary on what "unique" means. As for "definitely," Sir Alan Herbert wrote the last word: "Where is this to stop? *Definite* and *definitely* can be slipped in almost anywhere. I offer a prize to the first Foreman of a jury to announce a verdict of *definitely guilty* and another to the judge who informs the prisoner that he will be 'definitely hanged by the neck until he is very definitely dead."[5]

[5] From Sir Ernest Gowers, *The Complete Plain Words* (London, Her Majesty's Stationery Office, 1954), p. 62.

Masters of language agree, whether they use shirtsleeve English, literary English, or other languages than English. Voltaire said, "The adjective is the enemy of the noun." Schopenhauer said of people who use cluttering modifiers, "I say they are only half-conscious . . . they take words ready-made." Jacques Barzun called it, "The infinite duplication of dufferism." William Allen White thought *very* to be the most overworked word in the English language, and advised Franklin P. Adams how to get rid of it. "Instead of *very*, write the word *damn*. The proofreader will knock out the *damn*—and there you have a right good sentence." An editor of the *Saturday Review* explained the problem tersely: "The adjectives tend to be there only because the author failed to select the right noun in the first place. . . . never send an adjective on a noun's errand."[6] P. I. Prentice, onetime publisher of *Time*, explained the editorial policy of that magazine: "We try to save space with our verbs. . . . Why say 'Walked vigorously,' if we can say 'strode,' 'marched,' 'tramped,' or 'stomped' and be quicker as well as more explicit?"

You may wonder why the college-bred millions, in speaking and in writing, clutter ideas by adjectives and adverbs without meaning. One reason is that the less anyone has to say, the more emphatically he tries to say it; so he throws in clutter-words by the twos and threes. Unhappily, nobody can substitute an adjective for an idea.

Here, then, is a rule-of-thumb: *Use adjectives and adverbs to make your meaning more exact, but suspect and inspect every one that tries to make meanings more emphatic.* In other words, say "political crisis," but not "*acute* crisis." Say "financial disaster," but not "*terrible* disaster." And give a furlough to words like those below:

| | |
|---|---|
| *very* glad | *gifted* student |
| *most* pleasant | *irresistibly* reminded |
| *confirmed* bachelors | *particular* arrangement |
| *comely* matrons | *unduly* alarmed |
| *noted* authors | *real* merit |
| *prominent* physicians | *active* consideration |
| *ugly* rumors | *quite* often |

### STRIP EMPTY WORDS

There are two kinds of words—full words and empty words. Full words include verbs, nouns, and defining adjectives. Empty words include prepositions, conjunctions, adverbs, and relative pronouns. Full words are easy to grasp. When you hear *sneered*, you see in the mind's eye the raised lip and look of disdain. But when you hear *consequently*, you have no sharp mental picture; it really means "As a result of certain things described by this speaker, certain other things, yet unknown to me, resulted; and the speaker is now about to describe them." Therefore,

[6] *Saturday Review*, May 5, 1956, p. 27.

empty words cause trouble. A few of them you must use—but "suspect yourself of wordiness whenever you see an *of*, a *which*, or a *that*." Especially train your suspicions to bristle at compound prepositions and conjunctions. Here is a short list. For a longer one, see H. W. Fowler, *Dictionary of Modern English Usage.*

| | |
|---|---|
| in the process of (of) | with a view to (to) |
| of the nature of (like) | with reference to (about) |
| with regard to (about) | with the result that (so that) |
| in the case of (if) | for the purpose of (for) |
| in the event that (if) | from the point of view of (for) |

Don't disdain to strip so little as one word. Both Bernard Shaw and Sir Winston Churchill at times were militant about one word. Shaw had written, "the work he was fitted for," but ending the sentence with a preposition annoyed a purist. He wanted it changed to "the work for which he was fitted." Retorted Shaw: "Stick to my text. It will save . . . five letters. I never use these '*for whiches*' and '*and whiches.*' . . . '*He was fitted for*' is genuine vernacular English. '*For which he was fitted*' is schoolmaster's bad English." Sir Winston struck back at the file-clerk mind that had added an empty word. He too had saved the word by ending a sentence with a preposition, and an employee in the government printing office had changed it around. Churchill changed it back, and noted on the margin: "This is nonsense up with which I will not put."

## BEYOND THE SENTENCES

Certain language techniques involve groups of sentences, especially Questions, Direct Quotes, Suspense, and Climax.

### QUESTIONS

Questions arouse attention. They invite an answer from the listener. A battery of questions, therefore, will project an idea vividly:

> I am a Jew. *Hath not a Jew eyes? Hath not a Jew hands? If you prick us, do we not bleed? If you tickle us, do we not laugh? If you poison us, do we not die? And, if you wrong us, shall we not revenge?*

Shylock's bitterness is thus driven home by six *rhetorical questions*—i.e. questions so phrased that the answer is inevitable and hence not stated by the speaker.

Other questions are *direct questions*—where the speaker asks a question, then answers it, as illustrated by Dorothy Thompson:

> *How about manners?* On this subject . . .

*What of moral philosophy?* Under the pressure of atheists and religious groups. . . .

*Who is this mass man?* Do not believe for a moment that . . . .

Direct questions may also be used in a battery to give emphasis beyond the power of any single question, as done by G. Keith Funston speaking to university students:

[You may ask:] *What's ahead? What are my chances? What will it be like, earning a living or running a home?* And perhaps the most important question of all—since it sums up everything else: *What's expected of me in our economic world?*

### DIRECT QUOTATION

Direct Quotation is not to be confused with Testimony, even though both us quotation marks. Testimony is supporting an idea by quotation of authority: "Such-and-such expert says so-and-so about this idea." Direct quotation is a technique of language that allows listeners to see and hear others speak. They listen to the imaginary conversation, see the others talk in the mind's eye. Said Wendell Phillips in his eulogy on Daniel O'Connell:

As Lord Bacon marches down the centuries, he may lay one hand on the telegraph and the other on the steam-engine, and say, *"These are mine, for I taught you how to study Nature."* In a similar sense, as shackle after shackle falls from Irish limbs, O'Connell may say, *"This victory is mine; for I taught you the method, and I gave you the arms."*

It is used in many forms, to make illustrations effective, to brighten explanation, to inject humor, as Arthur Larson does speaking before the Union League Club in New York:

There is a current story about the perils of communication which runs like this. A man encounters a friend and says: *"I hear your brother has just left Penn State and is living in the Park Central."* The friend replies: *"Well, that isn't quite the way it is. My brother has just left the State Pen and is living in Central Park."*

### SUSPENSE

Suspense holds up the point of a story until the end, holding the listeners' interest until they learn the outcome. It is not a major technique, but rather a useful reinforcement.

It may be applied to a subhead, an entire main head, or even a whole speech, as done by Bruce Barton:

My subject today is "How Long Should a Wife Live?" . . . Some years ago there was a celebration in Boston in honor of the landing of the Pilgrim Fathers. After several very laudatory speeches had been made by men a bright and vivacious woman was called on. Said she:

"I am tired of hearing so many praises of the Pilgrim Fathers. I want to say a word about the Pilgrim Mothers. They had to endure all that the Pilgrim Fathers endured, and they had to endure the Pilgrim Fathers besides."

Do you know what happened to the Pilgrim Mothers, my friends? I will tell you. They died. They died young. . . . For ten husbands, . . . there were eighteen wives. . .

"How Long Should a Wife Live?" The answer, in the old days, was "Not very long." The homes of those days had two or three mothers, and no motors. The homes of the future will lay all of this tiresome routine burdens on the shoulders of electrical machines, freeing mothers for their real work, which is motherhood.

### CLIMAX

Climax is closely allied to suspense. It consists of arranging details in the order of increasing strength or importance. Note the effect of the following: "Her heart was full of bitterness, her face was flushed, and her dress was torn." It lets you down. It won't do. Rearrange it in climactic order: "Her dress was torn, her face was flushed, and *her heart was full of bitterness*." Climax gives the last point an added punch.

Quentin Reynolds uses climax to give primacy to religion over temporal government:

They saw the shrines of England in ruins. They saw the scars on the House of Commons and they saw the precious stained-glass windows of Westminster Abbey lying broken in the dust. The House of Commons has always been the symbol of free speech in Britain. . . . Westminster Abbey has always been the symbol of the Christian way of life.

The language mishandlers throw details together without thought of technique. Not the masters of language. They arrange details for climactic effect.

### SUMMARY

Because you have been using words, don't assume that you know the technique of language. The technique is precise. It is complex. In a sense, it is scientific. Twelve of the basic techniques, those most useful for a speaker, have been discussed in this chapter. Three techniques involve words. Five involve sentences. Four involve groups of sentences. Improve your skill in these twelve techniques, and you will have a reasonable mastery of language.[7]

[7] Students who want to pursue this vital subject further will find help in the following books: J. Jeffery Auer, *Research in Speech* (New York, Harper & Brothers, 1959), Chapter 8; Rudolf Flesch, *The Art of Plain Talk* (New York, Harper & Brothers, 1946); Flesch has several books with related titles, all good but this is best; Sir Ernest Gowers, *The Complete Plain Talk* (London, Her Majesty's Stationery Office, 1954); Theodore M. Bernstein, *Watch Your Language* (Great Neck, N.Y., Channel Press, 1958).

# Assignments

1. Analyze the following passages to determine which factors prevent each from being clear or forceful:

   a. It is with very much pleasure that I address you on such an auspicious occasion.

   b. When you are asked to get behind some high-sounding social project, remember that social-projects are nothing more than cleverly concealed socialism. Do we want socialism in this country? Let these misguided "liberals" who would bring us socialism under the guise of cleverly disguised "social projects," be known for what they really are.

   c. T. S. Eliot's poems start at home as all good poems do, but they end up everywhere as only the best poems do. Partly this is because his wisdom is native to him, and partly because his education has been right. He does not parade his learning, but there it is in his poems, and it is what makes them so solid and so satisfying.

   d. "Eight and seven-tenths decades ago, the pioneer worker in this continental area implemented a new group based on an ideology of free boundaries and initial conditions of equality. Now we are actively engaged in an overall evaluation of conflicting factors. We are met in an area of maximum activity among the conflicting factors to assign permanent positions to the units which have been annihilated in the process of attaining a steady state. This procedure represents standard practice at the administrative level." *Richard D. Fay.*

2. Study a selected passage from one of the speeches in the Appendix of this book. List which of the twelve techniques discussed in this chapter were used effectively.

3. From any issue of *Vital Speeches* determine which speech seems to you to have the most effective language skill. Then determine which speech seems to you to have the least effective language skill. List and illustrate the language techniques found in the most effective speech. List those found in the least effective speech, and write a brief analysis on why the language skill is poor, and what techniques are needed to improve it.

4. Examine one of your old outlines. Or if you have recorded a speech in this course, listen to the playback. Write a brief report estimating your skill in the use of each of the twelve language techniques.

5. Listen to a radio or television speech. Make a brief report on the speaker's use of language techniques.

6. During the next round of class speeches, assess the demonstrated skill of each student as follows: First, during the speech list the techniques used with special skill, those used with fair skill, and those used poorly. Next, check your lists against the twelve techniques discussed in this chapter, and make out a list of those not used at all. Finally, in a sentence or two,

give your judgment on what is most needed to improve the use of language skills. Hand your assessment to the instructor, who in turn will deliver to each student all of the judgments submitted on him.

ON IMPROVING THE USE OF LANGUAGE TECHNIQUES

7. List the violations of language techniques found in the following passages. Then rewrite and improve them by using one or more of the techniques set forth in this chapter.

   a. Special emphasis has been placed on miniaturization and ruggedization of new equipment.

   b. The trip was breathtaking. We saw so many things I can't describe them. Everywhere the scenery was wonderful. Such gorgeous foliage, such colorful sunsets. I shall remember them always.

   c. It is a very unique book that I have just read, a book in the nature of a biography of Thomas A. Edison. It shows how Edison, even as a boy, was most unusual. It shows how Edison as a man developed into a genius who was most exceptional.

   d. The Cardinals were playing the Eagles with the advantage in favor of neither. Then the Bird's Four Horsemen lined up behind their Seven Mules, and one of them took the pigskin nearly twice as far back as usual. But there was method in his madness, for when the Eagles closed in for the kill, he whanged the pellet to a fellow Horseman, and no sooner said than done the Birds had bonged the scoreboard for 6 points. We waited with bated breath for the goal kick.

8. Revise an old speech and improve its language skill. List the techniques used in the revision.

9. In preparing your next speech, check carefully to see whether you are using language techniques with reasonable skill. In the Technical Plot, left margin of the outline, note where you are making deliberate use of these techniques.

# PART

## *IV*

# THE SPEAKER

# Being Seen

FROM CHAPTER 1 you will remember that you cannot actually "deliver" a speech. What we call "delivery," you will recall, is *telegraphing with light waves and sound waves; and the methods you use in telegraphing determine how much the listeners get, how well they get it, and how long they remember it.* In this chapter we shall look at the ways and means of telegraphing with light waves, and start with an interesting story.

When Columbus discovered America he found copper-skinned natives who had been separated from peoples of the Old World for at least 18,000 years. They spoke 160 word languages, and over 1,200 dialects. *But they shook their heads for "no," and nodded their heads for "yes," exactly as did Columbus and his Mediterranean seamen. These newly-discovered natives lifted their hands in prayer—like Jews and Christians. They raised the right arm to greet a stranger, like the knights of old Europe. They turned palms down when they disliked a thing, and held palms us when they liked it—as Columbus did then and we do now.* Two things about their sign language especially are significant. First, they used the same type of sign language that Europeans did, but had developed it further so they could communicate adequately with other tribes. Second, seemingly this further-developed sign language had remained unchanged for at least 18,000 years, for an American army officer who learned the Indian sign language in the 1890's, found natives in the Philippines after 1898 using the identical sign language.

## Why speakers use action

Sign language is older than spoken language. It is more uniform. It is written deeper into our organism. It carries more basic meanings. For refined thought we use spoken language, but basic attitudes and subtle moods shine darkly through our body language. We are civilized, yes; but the *eye is still quicker than the ear, and almost everything we see takes precedence over anything we hear.*

You are about to give a speech. You begin to talk before you utter a word. Is your smile turned on only at half-pressure, or is it a real smile, however faint? Do your hands wander to your pockets, coat-button, or other objects before you—or do they supplement and reinforce your words? *Every speaker gives two speeches at the same time—one with words, the other with action.* If both telegraph the same message, you are communicating. But when words say one thing, and body language says another, listeners tend to let the words go by and to follow the body language. Why? Action tells them the real meaning: the false smile, the evasive glance, the grimaces of confusion, the wandering hands. There is the real speech, and the listeners know it. After hearing one of Henry Clay's speeches, a deaf man exclaimed: "I didn't hear a word he said, but, Great Jehovah! didn't he make the motions!" During a rehearsal of Beethoven's *Ninth Symphony* Arturo Toscanini said to a soloist: "You are singing of brotherhood, but in your face you look as though you hate everyone. That will show in your music."

You can't say, "I'll just use word language when I talk, and leave out the old sign language." You'll use both, whether you want to or not. Here is built-in trouble, for when you ask the average listener he will say action is not important. In one survey only 27 per cent of the people in selected audiences thought "gesture" was essential to good speaking, only 46 per cent thought "co-ordinated body movement" was essential, and only 54 per cent thought that even "animation" was essential.[1] So widespread is the misunderstanding about "gesture" and "action" that we pause for a survey of its place in thinking and in communication.

## ACTION IS AN INHERENT PART OF THINKING

What do we think with? Only the brain? Hardly. We can't think without the brain, but the brain alone is not enough. It's partly like an electric computer, but partly also like a telephone switchboard. But a telephone switchboard is of little use without lines running out to the homes, stores, and factories; and the human-brain switchboard would be of little use without nerves running out to the muscles, organs, and glands. Remember that the mind is not in any one *place*. Remember also that it's not a *thing*, like an arm, or even a brain. *It's an activity, like walking or throwing.* Aristotle observed 2,300 years ago that the mind was to the body what cutting was to the ax. "Mind," said Charles Henry Woolbert, "is what the body is doing." We don't think with the brain only, but with the brain, nerves, glands, and muscles working together. That inert speaker

[1] W. K. Clark, "A Survey of Certain Audience Attitudes Toward Commonly Taught Standards of Public Speaking," *Speech Monographs*, XVIII (March, 1951), No. 1, 62-69.

with the dead-pan voice is not really thinking. He's only reciting what he has memorized, recalling, or perhaps engaged in reverie.

*Total activity is necessary for thinking. Total activity is also necessary for communicating thought from one person to another.* Did you ever study people while they were talking in ordinary conversation? If not, do so. Good conversationalists talk with jerks and smirks, tics and switches, with eyebrows raised or depressed, eyes staring or rolling, heads nodding or shaking, faces luminous with laughter or drawn into a faint acidulous smile, shoulders shrugging, body bending or turning, and hands still hardly more than a few seconds at a time. Now these people are not "making speeches." They're just *talking,* telling one or two other people what's in their "mind." They're not conscious of using action. They're just talking the way people have talked for half a million years. When you stand up to speak in public you can't abolish a language that people have been using for half a million years.


## ACTION HOLDS ATTENTION

Did you ever lean forward, muscles tense, while watching an athletic contest? Did you ever feel your muscles pulling and pushing as if to throw a ball, make a catch, shoot a basket, or do any of the things the players are doing? Whether you know it or not, you engage in such mimicry. It's the spectator's basis of enjoying the game.

This is known as *empathy. Empathy is feeling ourselves into whatever we perceive.* All perception involves this "feeling in." We not only wind up with the pitcher, swing with the batter and breast the tape with the sprinter, but also feel ourselves into static situations. When we see a painting or stand before a cathedral, our like or dislike hinges largely on whether the object evokes pleasant or unpleasant tensions in our bodies. We are as unconscious of this participation as we are of our heartbeat or breathing, but it influences our behavior profoundly. To wrap it up in a neat jargon phrase: *"Perception is a participating function."*

Now apply this to the audience. *Unconsciously they imitate the speaker.* The speaker has no option whatever on whether or not his gestures will affect the audience, for his gestures *must* affect them in one of three ways:

1. If he uses too little action, audience empathy will be weak. Because it is weak, the audience will not remain physically alert, but will relax more and more into physical (and therefore mental) inaction. But the more one relaxes, the less active becomes the mind, until in complete inactivity one goes to sleep. So the speaker who uses no action puts his audience into a state too near to sleep for them to listen alertly. They will sit and half listen; but, when he is through, they will recall little of what he has said.

2. If the speaker uses distracting action, action he never intended to use and often does not know he is using, he twists the audience into fitful, distracting responses. We've all seen the speaker who buttons his coat and then unbuttons it, or twists a handkerchief in his hands, or rocks up and down on his toes, or toys with objects on the table. "If he moves that watch again, I'll scream," whispered a woman after a speaker had put his watch in twelve or fifteen places over the table. She did not scream, but neither did she listen to what he was saying. She sat tense, waiting for him to move that watch! So with all people. They are distracted by empathetic reactions to a speaker's uncontrolled movements.

3. If the speaker uses controlled action, communicative action, listeners find it easier to listen. They participate, "feel in," and give the speaker sustained attention.

"Must I use gesture?" asks a timid, or diffident, or nervous student. The frank answer is that you can't say "No" to life. Action is part of the thinking process. Action is a universal sign language far older than spoken words. Action rouses attention. Action is inherent in good private conversation. Add it up yourself.

## Assignments

1. Prepare and give a two-minute speech on empathy. To prepare this speech, attend an athletic contest, an exciting motion picture, a circus, a vaudeville performance, or any other event where you will witness alert bodily movement. (a) Observe carefully the stresses and tensions of your own body, and (b) Observe the behavior of those around you. Do they "feel in" with the performer? Is this "feeling in" revealed chiefly by leaning forward with tension? Or does it break out into the open so that the spectator tenses or relaxes, moves to right or left, with the performer?

2. Use a mirror to practice communicative action on the following, then demonstrate in class. Remember that you communicate with eyes and eyebrows, face and head, body shoulders, as well as with hands:

   a. "Would you prefer this one, or that one?"
   b. "I don't quite understand it."
   c. "They called him Sanka, because 98 per cent of the active ingredient had been removed from his bean."

## Making action effective

Effective action hardly seems like action at all. It seems natural, spontaneous, done on impulse. Indeed, action that calls attention to itself is bad because it distracts instead of communicates. The good speaker never seems to be "gesturing." He is merely one who makes you understand him, and who happens to use light waves as well as sound waves. Hence the adage, "Great art conceals art." But note what it takes to conceal the art of talking with light waves:

## FACE UP TO IT

Don't ignore, when you plan a speech, how you are going to look while giving it. Remember that you are like that goldfish in the bowl; you can't hide. Face frankly the certainty that you will be tied in knots unless you do dry runs ahead of time, and work out what you are going to do with your body during those fateful first two minutes. Remember that you must now do deliberately and consciously what in private you do spontaneously and unconsciously. More painfully, remember that even in private you may not be a natural Demosthenes or Sarah Bernhardt. You might even be awkward and ill at ease when you talk in private; and if you would even be passing-poor in public, you must learn to do better than you do in private. Face up to it. Use a mirror. See what you look like to others. Watch mannerisms that annoy people. Don't comb your hair with your fingers. Don't scratch your nose constantly. Don't sway back and forth. (That makes an audience dizzy!) Don't make any constant repeated movement of body, arms, face or mouth. You say that's a lot of *don'ts*. Right. Let's turn them around. *Do* control yourself, and *do* make every movement mean what you want it to mean, and *do* plan it ahead of time.

## GESTURE WITH THE WHOLE BODY

The runner does not run with his feet and legs alone, but with his whole body. The baseball pitcher does not pitch with his arm alone, but with his whole body. The speaker does talk with his voice alone, or with his voice plus his hands. He talks with his whole body.

If you want to be ludicrous, make gestures without this teamwork of muscles. You will be funny without wanting to. The actor Charles P. Sale attained his reputation in character parts by "speaking a piece" with detached gestures. His arms and hands moved like those old-time puppets pulled by strings. Now and then he would throw in a hand movement that came a shade too late, or too soon. Never was he all-in-one-piece, but gave the effect of one who had "studied gesturing" and hewed to the line but missed the purpose.

Suppose we apply this principle of all-in-one-piece action. Stand before a mirror and assume a good speaking posture. Then speak the following without gesture, but with total vigor:

> We the People of the United States, in Order to *form a more perfect Union, establish Justice,* . . . *promote the general Welfare,* and *secure the Blessings of Liberty,* . . . do *ordain* and *establish* this *Constitution* for the United States of America.

Your action should include every part of your body: head, face, shoulder, arm, torso, leg, knee, ankle, and foot. Each portion is *built into* the whole, not "something added on."

Now try it again, holding the head and body perfectly still, using only an arm and hand. Feel silly? You ought to. You look silly.

Once more try it again, this time using any hand action you want to communicate what you think are the two or three most important units of this sentence. Make it *built into,* not "added on."

Finally communicate it with the aid of the right arm, then the left arm, then both.

## TALK TO THE AUDIENCE, NOT TO YOURSELF

Until you have disciplined yourself to self-control you likely will engage in random action: licking your lips, caressing your hair, lifting your feet, toying with anything in reach—microphone to paper clip. You may be startled to find that your hands have become huge; you can't conceal them from the audience so you hide them behind your back, or bury them in your pockets. *These actions are symptoms of emotions inside you!* Unwittingly, but with deadly effect, you are telling the audience that you have lost control of yourself. We have discussed this under stage fright, both causes and treatment (pages 68-72).

There remains a milder form of disorganized action to be discussed here, namely *self-directed gestures. This is the tendency of speakers to gesture to themselves* instead of to the audience. It takes various forms:

1. You clamp the elbows tightly against your body and gesture toward your face.

2. You guard the stomach with your forearm, often using the hand for a weak gesture but keeping that arm-block between you and the audience.

3. Or you may reach out arms and elbows toward the audience, but still keep the palms—the real carrier of meanings—turned toward your face.

Now self-directed action is not really a problem of action at all, but of mental attitude. First, you are thinking of *yourself,* not the audience. You are not speaking to help the audience, for when you start helping people you are no longer afraid of them. Further, you are not enthusiastic over what you have to say. Once you get enthusiastic, you will "forget yourself into good speaking."

Effective action talks to the audience, not to the speaker. But get first things first. *When your action fails to talk to the audience, the trouble is not with "gesturing." It is with your mental attitude. You cannot talk for the sake of helping others—and at the same time gesture to yourself. You cannot be afire for people to hear you—all the people, even those on the back row—without reaching out to them with action as well as voice.*

## MAKE YOUR ACTION DEFINITE

Effective action should point, indicate, suggest, separate, emphasize— carry a *definite* meaning.

Definite hand action involves three phases: the *approach,* the *stroke,* and the *return.*

The *approach* is the "get ready" movement. It is like raising a gun to take aim. You make this approach well ahead of time and you hold it until you are ready for the emphatic stroke.

The *stroke* pulls the trigger. It carries the meaning. If you want to emphasize "The time is *now,*" you may start the approach even before you speak the first word of the sentence. You get set for action before-hand, and on the word *now* you pull the trigger—using your whole body all-in-one-piece.

The *return* is the "as you were." After you have held the idea before the audience long enough for them to see it fully (don't hurry this and don't backlash your gestures), you simply let the hand fall to the side in its original position. Avoid bringing it back in wide curves. Just let it fall naturally.

Beginners habitually use two kinds of indefinite gestures. You should recognize them, and resolve to stay away from them:

1. *The Off-Beat Gesture.* An old trick of comedians, still almost as good as fifty years ago, is to provoke a laugh by off-timing a gesture. They come in a shade late, on the off-beat, and the audience laughs. Students often do this too, in dead seriousness and without meaning to be funny, and the effect is even funnier than a comedian's because it is unintended. The student is "speaking with gestures," and the gestures say, "I don't like to do this, but the instructor says to gesture and I need a grade." The speaker, of course, looks as silly as he feels. The stroke of a gesture should fall *exactly* on (or precede by a split second) the emphatic syllable.

2. *The No-Stroke Gesture.* The "no-stroke" gesture has *two* parts in-stead of three—the approach and the return, but no stroke. It is not

*Wide World P*

Prime Minister Macmillan Campaigning. The two-handed gesture seems to be in the *approach* phase; the *stroke* should follow.

funny or silly like the off-beat gesture, yet it's more a burp than it is a gesture. It tells the audience you have lost control.

### USE VIGOR

Effective action can't be halfway or timid. It can't be flabby. It can't be held in, and let out by degrees. It can't be tentative. To have real action you must crash through inhibition and restraint, and throw weight and vigor behind it.

In beginning your training, therefore, overdo. Use abundant action. Use action with punch and power. Use it with freedom and abandon. Later on you can tone down and discipline its form, but seek first to crash through inhibition and restraint.

## ADAPT ACTION TO THE NATURE AND SIZE OF THE AUDIENCE

Any speaker sensitive to the audience response soon discovers that the amount of action needed, and even the type of action, varies with the kind of audience, the size of audience, and the occasion.

Young people are restless and energetic, unable to sit still long at a time. Young listeners demand a large amount of action, and frankly if a speaker does not deliver enough their minds wander away. Hence sedentary intellectuals generally make poor speakers for young audiences, and many a famous authority on Ovid and Browning and nuclear fission is barely endurable to college students in classroom lectures. Yet they need not be, as witnessed by William James and William Lyon Phelps whose classes overflowed. Likewise, audiences of farmers, workers, or any who engage in physical activity, require more action than sedentary workers. If they don't get enough, many will go to sleep outright. In contrast, older people, especially older sedentary people, and most especially older sedentary intellectuals, are irritated by too much action or too-vigorous action. To them it is coarse and intemperate. To an earnest speaker such people at times may seem to be afflicted by white-livered indifference and to be annoyed by earnest conviction—but it is not exactly this. They will never be persuaded to lead a crusade or vote for a new order, and many are annoyed by earnest conviction, but basically they are people who lead placid physical lives. Watching a too-active speaker wearies them. Empathy, of course.

The *size of audience* determines the expanse of action. Before a large crowd a speaker uses a wide sweep of gesture and the uplifted arm. Plutarch describes ancient speakers as "holding up their hands to Heaven" when addressing outdoor multitudes; and speakers today in addressing large crowds use the same wide sweep and the same uplifted arm. Yet before a small audience these would be out of place if not ridiculous. There a short sweep is best, as a quarter sweep of the forearm or merely a hand hinged at the wrist.

Finally, the amount of action varies also with the *occasion*. A stately, dignified occasion demands little, or at least only a moderate amount. A rally—political or athletic—demands far more. The amount of action perfectly fitted to a Sunday sermon might easily be too much for a funeral service.

# Assignments

ON STUDYING THE EFFECT OF ACTION

1. Study the action of a downright bad speaker: politician, teacher, preacher, fellow classmate, or anyone who is just plain dull.
   a. Study this speaker's muscular tone. Does his posture suggest muscular or mental alertness? Does it suggest inertness or flabbiness? Does it suggest rigidity or tension? Does he gesture with the whole body? Does he co-ordinate the ankles, knees, hips, torso, shoulders, arms, elbows, wrists, fingers, neck, and head? Which parts are used? Which are not used? Did his action "talk to the audience," or "talk to himself"? Was it definite? Was it vigorous?
   b. Study the empathy of the audience. Do most of them follow the speaker with an alert eye? Do any appear to be drowsy? Do some avoid looking at the speaker? Do they respond physically to the speaker's action? Do they tend to relax into emotional and physical lassitude?
   c. Write a paper on your assessment of the speaker's action and the audience's response.

2. Do the same thing with a notably good speaker.

3. At a social gathering study the posture, muscular tone, and general bodily action of some person who is supposed to have social poise. Note the changes of posture. Note the kinds and amounts of action when meeting different people. If you have time, do the same with a person who is obviously ill at ease. What are your general conclusions?

4. Walk through a department store or other large retail establishment and observe the behavior of the clerks. Note their posture and muscular tone. Study the expressions on their faces. Observe their total bodily activity. What are your conclusions?

5. Study your reaction to the posture and action of fellow classmates. Do they get mentally organized before coming to the platform? Do they talk first with words or actions? What do their first actions tell you? What conclusions do you draw about your own posture and action?

ON FREEING INHIBITION AND DEVELOPING ACTION

Practice the following exercises in your room and be ready if necessary to repeat them in class. Follow these directions:
   a. Use *spontaneous* action, not planned action. Pay no attention to rules, elegance, or correctness, but act on impulse.
   b. Use *abundant* action; avoid timid, restrained, or half-hearted movements.
   c. Use the *whole* body, all-in-one-piece.
   d. First try simply to express your thought and feeling. Later repeat the exercise in front of a mirror and observe how it would look to others.

6. I looked out the window—we were flying at only 2,000 feet—and there was New York coming slowly toward us. The Statue of Liberty passed by

on our left, looking small as a ten-cent toy. Steamships below us moved like bugs that walk on the water. Ahead were the skyscrapers. But from the air they didn't scrape the sky. They were only toys made to imitate the real skyscrapers you see from the streets. In fact, from the air all New York was a toyland, and I felt like Gulliver landing in Lilliput.

7. Hush! Here he comes! Don't let him see you! That's right, follow me. To the left. Watch that low beam. Wait a moment while I close the door and find the light. Whew! That was a close call!

8. They tell us, sir, that we are weak. But when shall we be stronger? Will it be the next week, or the next year? Will it be when we are totally disarmed, and when a guard shall be stationed in every house? Shall we gather strength by irresolution and inaction? Sir, we are not weak, if we make proper use of those means which the God of nature has placed in our power. Three millions of people, armed in the holy cause of liberty, and in such a country as that which we possess are invincible.

9.
> How ill this taper burns! Ha! who comes here?
> I think it is the weakness of my eyes
> That shapes this monstrous apparition.
> It comes upon me. Art thou any thing?
> Art thou some god, some angel, or some devil,
> That mak'st my blood cold, and my hair to stare?—
> Speak to me what thou art.

ON USING DEFINITE ACTION

10. Standing before a mirror practice the three phases of hand action, counting to five as follows:

| 1 | 2 | 3 | | 4 | | 5 |
|---|---|---|---|---|---|---|
| | approach | | | stroke | | return |

11. Now change the count, make the action with a wider sweep:

| 1 | 2 | 3 | 4 | | 5 | | 6 | 7 |
|---|---|---|---|---|---|---|---|---|
| | approach | | | | stroke | | return | |

12. Use the action practiced just above to carry the following meanings:

a. The first thing to remember is this. . . .
b. Would you people at the back mind coming down to the front rows?
c. I'm sorry, Jim, I can't do it.
d. Here's another side to the question we haven't yet considered. . . .
e. A horse. A horse! My kingdom for a horse!
f. There is a tide in the affairs of men,
  Which, taken at the flood, leads on to fortune.
g. I'll sing you a song of the world and its ways,
    And the many strange people we meet—
  From the rich man who rolls in his millions of wealth,
    To the struggling wretch on the street.

## *Kinds of action*

### OVERT AND COVERT ACTION

There are two kinds of action: overt and covert. *Overt* action is the ordinary movement like nodding the head or lifting an arm. *Covert* action consists of what psychologists call "psychomotor tensions." It's those significant subtle muscle sets and tensions that determine the *way* one nods the head, lifts an arm, or stands or walks. These psychomotor tensions tell you the mood, state of mind, and often the character itself of the person talking. It tells you this person is hesitant, uncertain, insecure—or is earnest or confident. It tells you that he is exultant or elated—or is despondent or dejected. It tells you that he is tolerant and courteous—or is brash and insensitive.

Covert action obviously is not voluntary, like nodding the head or lifting an arm. It comes from muscular and glandular systems inside the body. A child stands in front of a store window filled with candy. He is standing stock still, and at first you might say "He's not doing anything," or "He's looking at the candy." But a second look will tell you that his posture and face are saying, "I want that candy," and you know that his salivary glands are overworking, his stomach is contracting and expanding, his blood pressure is up, and his endocrine glands are pumping fluids into his blood. You don't see this terrific internal activity; you do see the hungry look in the boy's face and posture. What you see is *covert* action. Rather it is the outward signs of covert action; and from these outward signs you know what is going on within.

Apply this to speaking. A student is reading Kipling's, "If you can . . . walk with kings—nor lose the common touch, . . . you'll be a man, my son!" His overt action is perfect. Every gesture is fitting, well-timed, well-executed. But he does not fool you at all! By his *covert* action you know that down inside he does not *feel* Kipling's majestic test of a man. He is only reciting lines with gestures.

In contrast, you see an actor or reader—it may be Desdemona in *Othello*, Nora in *A Doll's House*, or Agnes Moorehead in one of her fine pieces of atmospheric acting—speak their most dramatic lines while standing perfectly still, without a single overt movement. But their covert action—set of body, tilt of head, the whole pattern of psychomotor tensions—tells you of their intense feeling within. You find that your body has caught the same muscle sets and tensions. Again empathy, of course.

Or you watch a student go forward to give a class speech. By covert action—the *way* he walks, the *way* he stands in that moment before starting to speak, and the psychomotor tensions of his body and face—he tells you his inner state of mind.

In speaking, you don't have the choice whether to use, or not to use, both covert action and overt action. You will use both, willingly or unwillingly, knowingly or unknowingly, as man has done for half a million years. You have the choice only of using them to communicate, or using them to distract.

The procedures and would-be rules set forth in this chapter largely apply to the overt action—the obvious and major movements of the head, hands, and body. *Covert* action is not easily controlled, for it springs from glandular secretions and inner muscle action. It is talk from the inside, the real person-that-you-are. How, then, do you learn to master covert action? You don't learn it. You learn rather to master yourself. The best way to seem sincere is to *be* sincere. The best way to seem earnest is to *be* earnest. Even in interpreting the lines of poetry or plays, the best way is to *revive the author's feelings in your imagination.* As Ruth Chatterton stated it, "Really good acting does not require 'technique,' but only a fine sensitiveness to situation." Constantine Stanislavsky put it even more precisely: "In order to make the public listen to the fine shades of your feelings, you have to experience them intensely yourself." What Miss Chatterton and Stanislavsky both omitted in their quick statements was that the art of developing a fine sensitiveness to situation and fine shades of feeling *are* techniques of high order.

## PLATFORM MOVEMENT

A speaker shouldn't move differently on the platform, except for minor details, than if he were talking in private. The trouble is that here he does it while everybody is looking. That makes him tense, until he tends to twitch and fondle, and play in-the-pockets-out-of-the-pockets with both hands. Therefore, heed this homely advice:

1. Remember that you will be nervous standing before an audience, *so practice in advance* how to control yourself.

2. Remember that your hands may suddenly become big as a catcher's mitt, so rehearse *in advance* what to do. And what do you do? Well, as a beginner, better keep them out of your pockets and out from behind your back. Both actions tell the audience you are trying to hide or run away. If you're going to give a speech, make up your mind not to run away, even by psychomotor behavior. In plain language, stand like a man or woman, and don't pantomime a wiggling worm. This is all very well, you say, you have told what *not* to do. Now tell what I *should* do. The answer is simple, but the doing is hard. *Don't distract your audience from what you are saying in words, but instead reinforce your words with body action.* If you are behind a lectern, rest your hands on it lightly, but don't pull it, push it, stiff-arm it, wrestle it, or invent some

other way of annoying the audience. If you are in the open, *take a good deep breath and "stand tall."* Then you will find it easier to let your hands hang at your sides until you are ready to use them in talking.

3. You may move about on the platform, or stand perfectly still. (In the old days experts thought a speaker should move about. Then came microphones and loudspeakers, and speakers couldn't move away from the microphones. They discovered that standing perfectly still during a whole speech is just as effective as moving about.) If you do move, beware of side-to-side movements. They don't communicate, but only distract. Move forward-and-backward, if you move at all.

## Assignments

ON STUDYING COVERT ACTION

Study the covert action of various types of speakers as listed below, using the following main lines of analysis:

  *a.* Was the speaker free from restraint, extreme reserve, or self-consciousness? Was he phlegmatic? Was he awkward? Was he fidgety? Was he spontaneous, intense, dynamic?

  *b.* What cues told you of his mood and inner state of mind? Muscle tensions? Posture? Muscular tone of the whole body? of the head? face? shoulders? arms and hands? torso? legs?

  *c.* What did these cues tell you about the speaker's momentary feelings? His personality? His character?

  *d.* Did you at any time "feel in," with the speaker? If so, describe this in detail.

1. An intense scene in a moving picture, stage or television play.

2. A salesman in a store; or better, one making a house-to-house canvass.

3. Your companions at the dinner table discussing a hot campus topic.

4. Someone trying to persuade you to quit studying and go to a show.

5. A student telling about last night's date.

6. A lively living-room conversation.

7. Your most interesting teacher.

8. Your least interesting teacher.

9. Live shots of nationally known speakers as seen in the News Reels or over television.

ON DEVELOPING PLATFORM MOVEMENT

10. For your appearance, perhaps the mirror is the best and frankest critic. Use it freely. If you don't have access to a full-length glass, an ordinary dresser mirror will do. By tilting it at different angles, you may observe every part of the body.

11. Standing before the mirror, study your bodily and facial appearance for poise, alertness, self-control, and friendliness. Are all details such as to command respect and interest?

12. Still before the mirror, try out various movements and note the effect. Learn to recognize nervous and unhelpful movements and to eliminate them. Step backward and forward while repeating sentences. Come forward on the emphatic parts. Drop back as the thought changes. Make all movements purposeful and easy.

13. Work out a relationship between change of thought and change in movement or posture. Figure out how you can "paragraph" a speech while you are giving it.

14. Practice in your room and demonstrate in class suitable posture and movements to communicate the meaning of the following passages:

   a. "But here, my friends, is the most important aspect of the matter." (Try stepping forward to emphasize its importance.)
   b. "So much for this side of the question. Now let us consider it in another light." (Would you step backward to emphasize the change of thought?)
   c. "Do you ask why we oppose the measure? Then consider these facts."
   d. "So I appeal from the men in silken hose [i.e. from the old South] who danced to music made by slaves and called it freedom, from the men in bell-crowned hats [i.e. from old New England] who led Hester Prynne to her shame and called it religion, to that Americanism which reaches forth its arms to smite wrong with reason and truth." (Would you actually move? or turn? or punctuate the contrasts by the shifting of weight?)

15. Practice the following exercises in your room until you get the feeling of ease and control; then demonstrate them in class:

   a. Walking to the platform as though you had something important to say.
   b. Moving forward and backward on the platform so as to emphasize a point or to turn from one idea to another.
   c. Standing behind a speaker's table, with your hands resting *lightly* on it, but your weight resting fully on the feet.
   d. Shifting the weight from one foot to the other without walking.

## BASIC HAND ACTION

The following six types of hand action are part of a universal sign language, older in the human race than words, and understood by people regardless of whatever word-language they use:

1. *Locating.* You point to an idea or a thing. "A hundred years ago," you say—as you point behind you to indicate that you are speaking of the past. "Tomorrow," you say—as you point forward to indicate the future. "This idea," "that principle," "yonder map," "at the right," "on the

left," "before us"—all such things are pointed out for the eye of the listener. In a sense, they "see" what you are talking about.

2. *Dividing.* You have a series of facts or ideas, and you want them to be kept separate and distinct in the listeners' minds. Therefore, you use dividing action. "On the one hand, liberals say . . . ,"—while with the palm held vertically you put the liberals on your left. "On the other hand, conservatives say . . . ,"—while with the same action you put the conservatives on your right. In the same way, "this vs. that," or "first, second, third," are divided by the hand into their separate parts. In print, you can divide ideas with subtitles and paragraph indentations. In speech, you use dividing action.

3. *Describing or imitating.* This type of action suggests the shape, size, or movement of things. "It was this long," you say—and measure the distance with both hands. "It was so high," you say—as you measure the height from the floor up to your palm. "It was round"—and with both hands you round it out. In the same way you indicate movement. "It winds through the valley"—and you trace its winding with a finger. Or "It zoomed by"—and you suggest the zoom with a hand.

4. *Approving.* More used than any other, this is the gesture of friendly relation, of exchange, of giving and receiving. It is made with an open hand gesture, palm upward, held out as though to give something or to receive it. With this action you carry such ideas as, "This I do believe," or "Here is a duty we cannot escape," or "I present this for your consideration."

5. *Rejecting.* This is simply the normal action any person makes in pushing away something he does not like. A baby makes it in rejecting food. An adult makes it pushing away a dog with muddy paws. You make it with palms down, away from you. With this action you say, "I don't like," or "I distrust it," or "That's not the way," or "Go not near to the man who hath power to kill." This is a common way of talking off the platform when people are not self-conscious. But on the platform students find it difficult. This seemingly is because most of them subconsciously want to *body-guard* with their arms. But you can't reject and body-guard, both at the same time, and the nervous tension that makes you want to body-guard is so deep and fundamental, that it blocks off rejecting action from your public behavior.

6. *Emphasizing.* When a speaker wishes to lift a word or phrase or sentence above the level of context, he gives it emphasis. Behind the emphasis of voice he often must also throw the emphasis of action— an index finger, a hand thrust forward, or even the clenched fist. Gestures of emphasis would be used to carry the following thoughts:

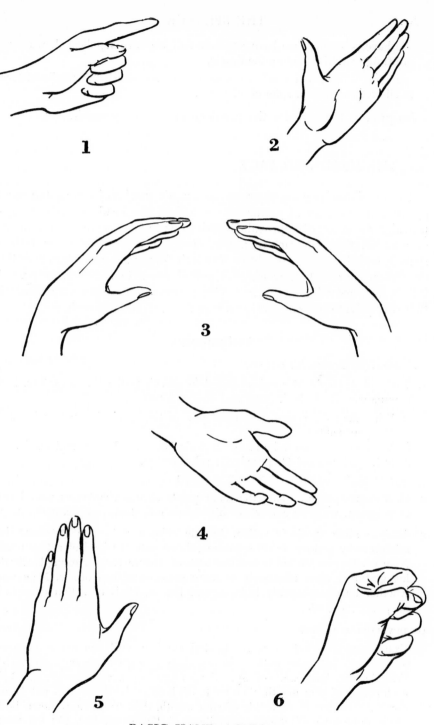

BASIC HAND ACTION

We have petitioned; we have remonstrated; we have supplicated; we have prostrated ourselves before the throne.

You ask, "What is our aim?" I can answer in one word: "Victory"—victory at all costs, victory in spite of all terror.

No price is too high for the privilege of owning yourself.

## THE HEAD AND FACE

*The head and face are the most commonly used and among the most effective instruments of gesture.* By a nod of the head we indicate approval; by a shake, disapproval. Eyelids open in joy, surprise, amazement, or wonder; they contract in anger, envy, or concentration; and they sparkle with happiness, or glitter in wrath. Lips may curve into a smile, or curl in contempt; they may be pulled down in a frown, or pursed into a determined straight line. Good conversationalists communicate that way private speech; good speakers do it in public speech.

# Assignments

ON OBSERVING ACTION IN OTHERS

1. Study photographs of speakers found in speech textbooks, magazines, and newspapers. Study both overt and covert action.

   *a.* What does the covert action tell you of the speaker's emotional state? His personality?

   *b.* What overt action is he using? Include body, head, face, and hands.

   *c.* Is it spontaneous? Or posed? Or self-directed? Or phlegmatic?

   *d.* Does it seem to carry his ideas or feelings?

2. Hear some speaker. Using the main points of this chapter as your basis of judgment write an analysis of his audience contact, posture, and action.

3. Analyze some speaker's action. In one column write the statement he reinforces by gesture. In an opposite column note the kind of action used. Note whether he tended to use one type of gesture (as, for example, locating gestures) more effectively or more extensively than others. Note also whether he conspicuously lacks any of the six kinds of action described on pages 335-336.

ON DEVELOPING ACTION

4. Examine your face in a mirror to find out how well you use it in communicating: (*a*) Raise both eyebrows, then raise each one separately. (*b*) Wrinkle your forehead. (*c*) Spread your lips into a wide smile. (*d*) Lift each corner of your mouth, then try to lift both at the same time. (*e*) Draw down the corners of each side of your mouth, then try to draw down both at the same time. (*f*) Pucker your lips. (*g*) Purse your lips. (*h*) Set them in a straight line. (*i*) Take a selection in this book and read it; as you read

try to *show in your face* the emotion of the words. (*j*) Compare yourself with actors you have seen on the screen. Where are you weakest? What do you want to do about it?

5. Use a mirror for work on each of the six types of hand action described in this chapter. Be careful to get the action *out toward your image* in the mirror. Note whether your open palm is clean and neat. Or are your fingers cupped? Or are they awry, pointing in different directions? Note whether your index gesture is centered in the forefinger. Or is your thumb thrust up like a flagpole?

6. Practice the following until you get the feeling behind them:
   *a.* Getting the *whole* body into all action.
   *b.* Using the *approach, stroke,* and *return* in hand action.
   *c.* Freeing the wrist so action won't seem wooden.
   *d.* Getting the hand *open* instead of the fingers being curled or awry.
   *e.* Turning the palms *toward* the audience.
   *f.* Using *both* hands, instead of one only as beginners tend to do.

7. Practice the following passages and demonstrate to the class your ability to communicate them. Among the kinds of action needed are: *the total body, stepping forward or backward, shifting the weight, talking with the head and face*:
   *a.* "Come over here, will you please. I've a problem I want you to look at. It's here on page 84. . . ."
   *b.* "He arrived in this country as a penniless, uneducated immigrant boy from Hungary. He didn't ask, 'What chance have I got?' He saw the banana boats pulling into New Orleans, and said to himself, 'Here's where I start.'"
   *c.* "My friends, we ask you to have faith in us. We've not succeeded entirely. But we *have* made progress."
   *d.* "Step forward, please. . . . No, that's too much! Back about two inches. . . . There, that's about right."

8. Study the following short paragraph until you have absorbed its meaning, experiment on communicating it with action:

Nor must a young man compare himself with others or measure his success by theirs. It makes no difference how other men succeed. Their success is theirs; not yours. It matters nothing to me that Edison can invent the electric light and I can't; that Kipling can write a 'Recessional' and I can't; that you can plead the law and I can't. You can do one thing; I try to do another. But success is for both of us just so far as we do well what we can do. Every man is himself, and it is in proportion as he gets out of himself the power there is within him that he succeeds—succeeds in doing the thing he is best fitted to do.

EDWARD BOK

9. The following selection is more conversational. Try reading it aloud, using body language to make it more easily understood:

You need to learn how to use books effectively. There may be a better source of information than the library, but I have failed to find it. Before any one can start any line of thought, scientific or artistic, he should know what has been done before. "Only hold a book before my nose," says Socrates, "and you may lead me all round Attica."

The card catalog talks to us in eloquent language if we will listen. Suppose you want to find a good book on William Pitt, the great war minister who founded the British empire, and who, in some ways at least, was one of the great speakers of the middle eighteenth century. Suppose you want to make a ten-minute oral report in which you summarize the principal events in Pitt's dynamic career. You therefore need to consult sources that give you a broad perspective. In the card catalog you find a dozen cards. One of them says, "Don't take me—I'm dated 1812." Usually the old books are less authentic than the researches of recent scholars. Another says, "Don't take me—I'm two volumes." That entry might be fine for some one else, but not for you—you want the broad outlines, not the cabinet intrigues. Another says, "Be careful—I'm written in French," and another, "Reread my title—*The Love Letters of William Pitt*." But you find one book, written two years ago, which the card catalog says is 250 pages long: this would appear to be the one with which to start.

Does this seem far-fetched? Every teacher . . . has had students come to his office bearing books that had little or no usefulness for the purpose in mind. Do college students pick books off a library shelf at random, or because of the color of the cover?

LOREN D. REID

# Improving Voice Quality and Variety

Everything we say is really *double talk*. With words we say to one person, "How do you do!" in tone language that says, "I'm thrilled to meet you!" With words we say to another, "How do you do!" in tone language that groans "Why did you have to show up here?" Someone in the family asks, "Where's the screw driver?" in tone language that telegraphs a simple inquiry. Someone else asks, "Where's the screw driver?" in tone language that snarls, "Who's the nitwit that mislaid it?" Anybody can say, "Oh!" But the great British actor David Garrick, said, "I would give a hundred guineas if I could say 'Oh!' as Whitefield does!" (Whitefield was the evangelist who preached to thousands at a time in open fields.) With the voice we speak two languages simultaneously—a language of words and a language of tones.

Our double talk hurts us or helps us, according to how we use it. Hughes Mearns stated it aptly. He had worked twenty years on problems of human relations and served as a chief psychologist for the U. S. Army Medical Department, and had learned one thing well: One prime reason people failed to get along smoothly with one another was that *they did not know that their tone language contradicted their word language.* They spoke decent words, but in tones that told the world of their dislike, contempt, or boredom.

Once again, this reminds us that we can't "deliver" a speech, but must telegraph it. In this chapter we shall see how we telegraph with sound waves.

"Only five persons out of a hundred are born with good voices. The rest of us have to work for one," said a supervisor of announcers for NBC. The statement is obviously broad and general, for it hinges on the definition level of a good voice, but scientifically conducted surveys show that only a minority of people do have good speaking voices. There are especially four reasons:

First, some voices are poor because of organic difficulties. They need diagnosis and treatment from experts in speech correction. This is beyond the scope of a course in basic speech, although, of course, your instructor can advise on what to do and where to go for help.

Second, some voices tell others that the speaker has personality problems. There is the girlish voice prolonged absurdly into womanhood, and a whining voice that comes from a nagging disposition. There is a curt, blunt voice arising from disregard for the feeling of others, and a magpie chatter betraying shallow emotions that spill easily. And in the years ahead, you face the danger of falling into that cares-of-the-day voice—bringing the office work woes home at night, or taking the housework cares to dinner. All these are indexes of temperament or character. They need treatment of the cause, not the voice.

Third, still other voices tell listeners that the speaker didn't prepare the speech well enough. It may be a weak voice coming from lack of confidence or lack of conviction. Or a dull voice coming from lack of earnestness. Or a dead-flat voice coming from not picturing in the mind the form and color of thought. For all this there is no cure in voice training. The speaker simply needs to do his homework.

But in addition to these, other causes arise from mismanaging the voice itself. There are people who mumble, drone, mutter, muffle, sputter, haw, and croak, simply because they have never learned to talk any other way. Hence we shall look at how speech sounds are produced, what makes voices unpleasant, and what makes them effective. Along the way you will make an inventory of your voice.

## How speech sounds are produced

You have no speech organs *per se*. Every organ used in speech has another use biologically. The lungs are used for breathing to sustain life. The tongue, teeth, and lips are used for eating. Even the voice box is a valve to keep out foreign bodies (especially food and water) from the lungs, and to regulate the amount of air entering and leaving the lungs. In learning to talk man *converted into dual-purpose organs these one-purpose organs biologically intended for other purposes.* That is why, at times when we are emotionally disturbed, the older biological functions take over, and we have speech trouble. At such times of trouble your problem is to reassert the dominance of speech over these organs.

In producing speech four stages are invloved: breathing, phonation, resonation, and articulation. We shall consider each in detail.

## BREATHING

Biologically you breathe to live. It is automatic, and you cannot voluntarily stop it. You can only regulate it within obvious limits. Somewhere along the way man learned to use breathing for making speech sounds.

Lung capacity varies, but a fair average is perhaps 225 cubic inches for men and 175 cubic inches for women. This is the volume of air we can inhale and exhale in a single respiration. It is known as the *vital capacity*. In normal breathing, however, we use less than 15 per cent of this vital capacity. The average is about 30 cubic inches. This is known as *tidal air*. Thus we have an enormous reserve that can be used for extreme exertion, but is not required for ordinary use.

Look at it another way. In *quiet* inhalation you ordinarily use four sets of muscles. In *deep* inhalation you may use twelve sets of muscles directly, plus the indirect use of five additional sets. In *passive* exhalation you use relatively few muscles, since gravity, plus the elastic recoil of lungs and bones and viscera, forces air out of the lungs. But in *controlled* exhalation, which is required for producing speech sounds, you must use from five to ten sets of muscles.

Thus breathing for speech calls for a modification of the respiratory cycle. In silent breathing you use relatively few muscles and the periods of inhaling and exhaling are about equal. In breathing for speech you inhale quickly, using more muscles, and you exhale much more slowly while calling on a relatively large group of muscles to direct the outgo into making speech sounds. Some people can modify the respiratory cycle effectively and unconsciously. Some cannot. You will want to take inventory on the following matters:

1. *For public address inhalation is deeper, or more rapid, or both, than in ordinary breathing.* This is because you need more air for greater voice volume plus more air for more sustained tones. You need not only more than for ordinary breathing, but more than in private conversation. The actual amount of air used in speech is not large, but you also need a *reserve* to maintain vigor of tone and also to prevent running out of breath and fading off into "dropsy" at the end of a phrase. Remember that the shallow breather finds voice projection difficult. The deep breather finds it easier.

2. *For public address exhalation must be more forceful and more controlled than for ordinary breathing.* Ordinary exhalation is passive. You relax, and the air flows out. But to produce speech you use a different process. You *hold* the air in the lungs, and you *regulate* its outgo so as to produce speech sounds. The amount of air expelled is directly related to the intensity of speech sounds. To attain greater intensity, such as needed

in public address, you must expel a greater air flow through the speech organs. Furthermore, the amount of air you need varies with different speech sounds. Thus a voiceless fricative like *s* (as in mi*ss*) requires more air than an explosive like *d* (as in *d*o), and a wide-open vowel like *ah* requires more air than a slightly-open one like *ee*. Effective speech requires you to use the regulating muscles to supply the needed amount.

3. *This power must be supplied by muscles of the thorax and abdomen without undue tension of muscles in the throat and face.* Nervous speakers tend to tighten up all over. But effective use of the human body calls for tension only of the muscles needed, without the interference of other muscles that might get in the way. Applied to speaking, this means that undue tension of muscles in the throat and face produces a poor voice quality. The operating rule for good speech, there, is *power in the abdomen, relaxation in the throat, and flexibility in the face.*

## Assignments

FOR DEVELOPING CONTROL OF BREATHING

1. Pull your shoulder blades close together. This will free the abdominal region of unnecessary weight and pressure, and make your diaphragm movement easier.

2. Learn to use the muscles that give you "frontal chest expansion" as follows:
   *a.* First, exhale completely (note that it is exhale, not inhale). Then hold your breath and try to expand your chest voluntarily. It may help you to learn if you simply lift the chest at first.
   *b.* Exhale and hold your breath while you both expand and contract the front chest walls.

3. Learn to use the muscles that give you "lateral chest expansion" as follows:
   *a.* Stand relaxed and pant lightly but rapidly for about five seconds. The intercostal rib muscles and the muscles of the lower back should begin to respond by short fitful movements.
   *b.* Concentrate on movements of the intercostal rib muscles until you capture the sensation of their movement. If necessary continue the panting exercise daily for several weeks until you have developed a conscious use of the intercostal muscles.

4. Learn to use fully the abdominal muscles as follows: Force the abdominal muscles outward; while these muscles are still tense, inhale as deeply as possible; then exhale.

5. Take a slow deep breath, tapping (*a*) the chest on either side of the sternum, (*b*) the ribs at the side, (*c*) the muscles at the small of the back, (*d*) the upper part of the abdomen. Practice this until you sense the coordinated expansion of the whole breathing area.

6. Take a deep breath as described in Exercise 5, *relax the throat,* and count from 1 to 10 at the rate of two or three numbers per second.

7. Inhale and extend the count to 20, then 30, then as far as your breath supply will go. Do not force the last few counts, and always stop before your breath supply is exhausted. Are you willing to try this for a week, twice daily, and see how far such practice will extend the count?

8. Use the following poem as an exercise in breath control as follows: First, read each two lines on one breath, at a normal rate. Then continue practice until you can read four, then six lines with a single breath, always with an ample air reserve at the end of the last line:

> Music is a soaring bird;
> Ecstatic in its flight;
> Music is the crooning heard
> In tall pines' arms at night.
> Music is the laughing sea
> Embracing moon-white shores;
> Music is the flashing key
> Unlocking heaven's doors.
> Music is the silver seine
> Flung gaily in life's shoals;
> Music is God's cool gray rain
> On parched and thirsty souls.
>                     AUTHOR UNKNOWN

## PHONATION

On the way out air passes between the "vocal cords" of the larynx and produces sound. This process is known as phonation. Actually these vibrators are not cords at all, but are pearly white *voice lips,* roughly three-quarters of an inch long in men and one-half an inch in women, but with wide individual variations. In silent breathing they open wide and let air in and out without hindrance. In whispering they open partly, let out large amounts of air, and produce only frictional sounds. In speech they come together under tension and the controlled air pressure from the lungs vibrate them in about the same way a trumpet player vibrates his lips in the mouthpiece.

The tone thus produced is weak, poor in quality, and with little carrying power. It does not become strong and rich until it has been amplified and reinforced by the human resonators as described under *resonation.*

## Assignments

FOR ESTABLISHING THE CONCEPT OF PHONATION

1. Relax all muscles of the jaw and shake your head until the jaw flops.

2. Drop your head forward as if you were almost asleep. Then gradually begin to shake the head, using the muscles in the back of your neck. Increase the shaking until the jaw wobbles.

3. Yawn gently but thoroughly, and note at the finish how the muscles of the jaw and throat feel when relaxed. *This is the muscle tonus you want for speaking.*

4. Open your mouth as if to yawn, but instead leave the mouth open wide and say *high ho.*

5. With a relaxed throat repeat the letters of the alphabet.

6. Read the following selections quietly, with open and relaxed throat:

> The Moving Finger writes; and, having writ,
> Moves on; nor all your Piety nor Wit
>   Shall lure it back to cancel half a Line,
> Nor shall your tears wash out a Word of it.
>                     OMAR KHAYYÁM

> The curfew tolls the knell of parting day,
> The lowing herd wind slowly o'er the lea,
> The ploughman homeward plods his weary way,
> And leaves the world to darkness and to me.
>                     THOMAS GRAY

> Give a man a pipe he can smoke,
>   Give a man a book he can read:
> And his home is bright with calm delight,
>   Though the room be poor indeed.
>                     JAMES THOMSON

## RESONATION

If you strike a tuning fork and hold it in the air, the tone is thin and weak. But connect it with a sounding board by setting the fork on a table, and instantly the volume swells. Or give it the right-sized air cavity by holding it over an open tube, and again instantly the volume swells. This is resonance. A piano string without its sounding board produces only a fraction of the sound produced when it is connected with the sounding board. An organ reed not coupled to a pipe does not sound at all like the same reed coupled into a pipe organ.

So with the human voice. Without resonance it is too feeble to be heard at any distance. Adequate speech sounds require (1) a *generator*, or vocal cords, plus (2) *resonators* to amplify, enrich, and give each speech sound its exact quality.

The human voice has a variety of resonators. They come in various

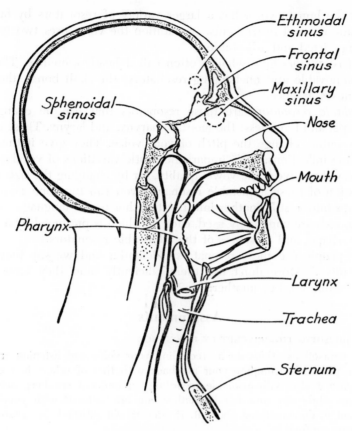

BODILY RESONATORS

sizes and shapes. The chief ones, with their approximate sizes in cubic centimeters (16cc. equals roughly one cubic inch) are these:

| | |
|---|---|
| bronchi and trachea | 60cc. |
| larynx | 25cc. |
| Pharynx (connecting mouth and nasal passages) | 80cc. |
| mouth | 100cc. |
| nose | 60cc. |
| nasal sinuses (four pairs) | 75cc. |
| Total | 400cc.[1] |

In addition to the above tubes the human voice also uses the following sounding boards, some slightly and some greatly:

> the skull bones, particularly the facial bones
> the sternum (chest bone) and ribs

[1] L. S. Judson and A. T. Weaver, *Voice Science* (New York, Appleton-Century-Crofts, Inc., 1942), p. 95.

Thus the human voice has a larger variety of resonators by far than man-made musical instruments. In addition the voice uses two types of resonators, fixed and adjustable.

*Fixed resonators* give what is often called head resonance. They are those immovable and unchanging resonators: the skull bones, the nose, nasal sinuses, trachea.

*Adjustable resonators* are those resonators that can be changed in size, shape, and tenseness: the mouth, pharynx, and larynx. These adjustable resonators change the pitch of your voice. They give it the rising and falling inflections. They impart the subtle variations of vocal quality. Especially they give it the vowel quality, for by changing the size, shape, and tension of these adjustable resonators you can turn one sound into *e*, another into *o*, still another into *i*. Altogether in the language some 15 vowel sounds are commonly used, each of which is produced by a different size, shape, and tenseness of the adjustable resonators.

Some people use these resonators efficiently; and we say they have "good voices." More don't use them efficiently; and they have "poor voices" of one kind or another.

## Assignments

FOR ESTABLISHING THE CONCEPT OF RESONANCE

1. Hear yourself as others do by recording your voice and listening critically to the playback. Compare your playback with that of others in the class. Compare it also with available recordings of eminent speakers, actors, or readers. Make up your mind whether you are satisfied with your voice, or want to do something about it. If you are not satisfied, be assured that you can improve it.

2. The habit of humping up the back of the tongue too high in the mouth is disastrous to good voice quality. It obstructs the vocal outlet and leads to a serious loss of volume and fullness of tone. For open and relaxed mouth and pharynx practice the following:

   a. Continue practicing the yawn until you can sense the depressed tongue and raised soft palate.

   b. Explore your mouth with a mirror. Note the positions of the tongue and soft palate. Yawn and note how the tongue depresses itself and the pharynx opens. Now duplicate this movement without yawning. Repeat it several times.

3. Inhale (remember your breathing exercises), relax the throat, flatten the tongue and say *ah*. Hold the tone for 15 seconds while you feel the cranium, jaw, sternum, chest, etc., and locate which of these resonators are vibrating.

4. Repeat, using the following vowels in pairs. *Note that the mouth must be opened wider for each succeeding pair:*

*e* and *oo*

*a* and *o*

*i* and *ah*

5. With the open throat read the following selections. *Prolong* the vowel tones of accented syllables until you have *formed* them carefully and *built them up* with resonance:

Not that I loved Caesar less, but that I loved Rome more. Had you rather Caesar were living and die all slaves, than that Caesar were dead, to live all free men? As Caesar loved me, I weep for him; as he was fortunate, I rejoice at it; as he was valiant, I honor him; but, as he was ambitious, I slew him. There is tears for his love; joy for his fortune; honor for his valor; and death for his ambition.

Brutus in SHAKESPEARE's Julius Caesar

Life is a narrow vale between the cold and barren peaks of two eternities. We strive in vain to look beyond the heights. We cry aloud, and the only answer is the echo of our wailing cry. From the voiceless lips of the unreplying dead, there comes no word; but in the night of death, hope sees a star, and listening love can hear the rustle of a wing.

ROBERT G. INGERSOLL

Once upon a midnight dreary, while I pondered, weak and weary,
Over many a quaint and curious volume of forgotten lore—
While I nodded, nearly napping, suddenly there came a tapping,
As of someone gently rapping, rapping at my chamber door.
" 'Tis some visitor," I muttered, "tapping at my chamber door—
Only this and nothing more."

EDGAR ALLAN POE

## ARTICULATION

Of all the civilized peoples in the Western world Americans are best known for having the worst articulation. Groucho Marx, in a serious vein beneath his disdainful effrontery, remarked that even on television the word-"wonderful" had disappeared and had been replaced by *wunnerful,* that "congratulations" had become *congradulations,* and that "I hear myself saying *a hunnerd* instead of 'a hundred.'" John Mason Brown neatly wrapped it up: "To slur is human."

Don't confuse articulation with pronunciation. Articulation is uttering clear, distinct syllables. To do this you must, first, *shape* the speech sounds with the speech organs, next, *combine* the separate sounds to make up intelligible speech. In American English we have roughly 40 different sounds, including vowels and consonants. The average person speaks at the rate of about 300 syllables to the minute, or five per second. Now the listener must catch these syllables on the wing and translate them into thought. This listeners must do instantly, without faltering and scarcely without pausing. If the sounds are slurred, muffled, or projected weakly, the listener is kept under tension. If he misses any essential part of the sounds, and stops to think back, "What was that?" he misses those words that come in that instant of thinking back, and so part of the meaning is lost.

Therefore, you will be permitted to take an inventory of your articulation. The test to be used is one of extreme accuracy, perfected by speech scientists after years of experiments on many types of tests for the purpose of testing intelligibility of communication in the Armed Forces of the United States.[2]

## MULTIPLE-CHOICE INTELLIGIBILITY TEST

### Directions to Instructors for Administering

1. The test is devised to be given to groups of 12 or less. Hence there are 12 tests and 12 answer sheets.

2. Before the test period starts supply each student with the 12 answer sheets, preferably mimeographed. (Students could mark answers directly on the answer sheets in the textbook, of course, but this would require the instructor either to do the grading in class or to collect the 12 textbooks for grading later.)

3. Since each student can read the articulation test from the textbook, there is no need of separate copies of the test itself.

4. For highest accuracy give the test under the following conditions:

   a. Set up at least the noise of an electric fan for masking. The hum of a loudspeaker, or relatively loud phonograph music, will serve *if the amount of noise is measured and is exactly duplicated in the second articulation test to be given later.*

   b. Seat listeners in desk-arm chairs at 30 feet distance from the speaker.

   c. Have listeners turn their faces at right angles to the speaker, and instruct them not to look at the speaker during the test.

5. Instruct the students as follows:

   When it is your turn to read, give your name and test number. Be *sure* that both are understood by every member of the class. For example, "My name is John Doe, d-o-e. I will read test 8."

   Then read from the Speaker Test List. The test consists of 8 sets of 3 words that are read in this fashion (instructor will point out the sample words given below and read them at an acceptable rate; pausing after

---

[2] The tests given below are the word multiple-choice tests from OSRD Report No. 5567 of the Voice Communication Laboratory, Waco, Texas, John W. Black, director. They were prepared by C. Hess Haagen. Originally classified as containing information affecting national defense, they have now been declassified and made available for general use. These multiple-choice tests were found to be superior to the spondiac word lists, the phonetically balanced word lists, and the various types of write-down tests. They discriminate between untrained and trained speakers and measure reliably as indicated by split-half correlations, corrected for length, of about .80.

each set of 3 words): "Number 1, mortar . . . shut . . . assist. Number 2, blimp . . . injure . . . knob," and so on until all 8 sets of 3 words have been read. Remember to pause after each group of 3 words to give your listeners time to mark their papers.

While you are reading these words, this is what your listeners will be doing. For every word that you have read, they have, on their answer sheets, a choice of 4 similar-sounding words. When the word "mortar" was read, for example, they had the choice of "order, mortar, border, and water." Since "mortar" was the word read, they put an X on number 2. The second word was not "shook, shout, or shot," but "shut" so they put an X on it. The next choices are "enlist, resist, assist, and insist." Since "assist" was the word read, they place an X on it. Then they go to the second set of 3 words, and so on for all 8 sets.

Listeners will look carefully and be certain to place an X on the number of the word you think was read. In some cases there is a difference of only a single letter, so make your selection carefully. Also remember that only one of the group of 4 words is correct. If 2 words within a single group are marked it is an error. If you have marked a word and then decide that the choice is wrong, either erase the mark or write *no* beside it. The first word that is read is always in column to the left. The second word is always in the center column. The third word is always in the column to the right. Be careful to place the X directly on the number of the word. Fill in the names of the speakers as they are read to you. Are there any questions? Do you have a pencil? Do you have the answer sheets to all 12 tests?

One final word of caution. When you are the speaker, be certain to read from your assigned speaker test number, and remember to pause after each group of 3 words to give listeners time to mark their answer sheets.

All set, the test will begin immediately.

### SAMPLE INTELLIGIBILITY TEST

Number 1: mortar, shut, assist

Number 2: blimp, injure, knob

### SAMPLE ANSWER SHEET

|   |   |   |   |   |   |   |   |   |
|---|---|---|---|---|---|---|---|---|
|   | 1 | order |   | 1 | shook |   | 1 | enlist |
| X | 2 | mortar |   | 2 | shout |   | 2 | resist |
|   | 3 | border | X | 3 | shut | X | 3 | assist |
|   | 4 | water |   | 4 | shot |   | 4 | insist |
|   | 1 | flip | X | 1 | injure |   | 1 | sob |
|   | 2 | limp |   | 2 | insure | X | 2 | knob |
| X | 3 | blimp |   | 3 | picture |   | 3 | cog |
|   | 4 | limb |   | 4 | contour |   | 4 | nod |

# INTELLIGIBILITY TEST, FORM A[3]

*Speaker 1*

1 swarm, canvas, quart
2 airport, bark, tassel
3 group, flicker, beef
4 legion, wonder, horn
5 threat, deer, garden
6 curtain, export, final
7 rage, city, all
8 knuckle, dress, screech

*Speaker 2*

1 skid, mood, twist
2 profane, thin, receive
3 hard, fasten, anger
4 joke, shaft, knitting
5 course, balance, rank
6 lanky, horror, unfold
7 pipe, beast, spray
8 drift, concern, first

*Speaker 3*

1 feed, conclude, train
2 virtue, hire, patch
3 dinner, envy, rumor
4 spear, goal, mettle
5 fault, birch, praise
6 slack, kernel, drab
7 go, lady, break
8 chain, ten, heart

*Speaker 4*

1 pardon, hall, double
2 top, cruel, storage
3 eight, dissolve, needle
4 fable, recline, volley
5 shade, infect, card
6 brain, squad, tramp
7 plan, lift, behold
8 glory, not, force

*Speaker 5*

1 crook, fair, amble
2 brick, dim, matching
3 shook, opal, trail
4 flame, were, relief
5 plot, kind, sleeping
6 eighty, swoop, quit
7 world, handy, dot
8 unfit, reverse, budget

*Speaker 6*

1 term, hate, commit
2 proud, waist, meaning
3 deflect, law, jobber
4 tell, invite, flat
5 faithful, suit, became
6 rural, noon, save
7 edge, binding, prince
8 desk, vote, young

*Speaker 7*

1 chisel, bond, dream
2 forge, seal, notion
3 verse, harvest, tight
4 guide, jungle, blunt
5 pun, speed, hail
6 eat, pad, depth
7 wife, rocket, keep
8 content, fork, ask

*Speaker 8*

1 gadget, why, belt
2 sandy, power, fit
3 attic, main, describe
4 cattle, heel, tare
5 ring, option, class
6 killer, span, thimble
7 dozen, guard, chapter
8 wealth, prevent, foremost

*Speaker 9*

1 endure, clam, absent
2 bacon, perfect, decide
3 fearful, start, gown
4 drove, thirty, roller
5 barge, select, pride
6 light, heading, jump
7 gift, catch, misfire
8 fuel, toe, odor

*Speaker 10*

1 recent, confront, lame
2 perfume, gamble, what
3 frame, scatter, harness
4 you, treason, disgust
5 talent, cook, musket
6 gone, plenty, rub
7 center, less, fox
8 defeat, some, beach

*Speaker 11*

1 play, bright, which
2 robe, dash, enrage
3 swear, ground, confess
4 fast, caution, shower
5 prefer, keel, hope
6 flare, endorse, locate
7 ballet, rod, abound
8 health, outline, thud

*Speaker 12*

1 brief, define, near
2 raid, sneeze, pension
3 corpse, mad, zero
4 tree, when, air
5 bean, afraid, crane
6 share, guess, fence
7 demote, pain, ladder
8 untold, hood, torment

[3] There are 24 tests of equivalent difficulty which are arbitrarily divided into two groups of 12 for use as initial and final tests. The intelligibility scores of these 24 tests do not deviate more than 0.5%. The first group of 12, known as Form A, is given here. The second group of 12, known as Form B, is given in the next chapter (page 415-422). By taking any one of the tests in Form A prior to training, and taking any one in Form B following the training, each student will be able to measure improvement in intelligibility with a very high degree of reliability.

# ANSWER SHEET FOR MULTIPLE-CHOICE
## INTELLIGIBILITY TESTS, FORM A

*Speaker 1 is_____*     *Speaker 2 is_____*

**1**

| 1 form | 1 campus | 1 court | | 1 skid | 1 move | 1 swim |
| 2 warm | 2 canvas | 2 fort | | 2 skin | 2 mood | 2 twin |
| 3 swarm | 3 pamphlet | 3 port | | 3 hid | 3 food | 3 swift |
| 4 storm | 4 panther | 4 quart | | 4 hit | 4 smooth | 4 twist |

**2**

| 1 air force | 1 spark | 1 tassel | | 1 proclaim | 1 spin | 1 repeat |
| 2 airport | 2 park | 2 tackle | | 2 domain | 2 pin | 2 receive |
| 3 air corps | 3 dark | 3 cattle | | 3 cocaine | 3 thin | 3 recede |
| 4 airborne | 4 bark | 4 pastel | | 4 profane | 4 fin | 4 reprieve |

**3**

| 1 group | 1 quicker | 1 beef | | 1 heart | 1 fasten | 1 angle |
| 2 troop | 2 flicker | 2 beast | | 2 barge | 2 passion | 2 amber |
| 3 coupe | 3 slicker | 3 beat | | 3 lard | 3 fashion | 3 anger |
| 4 fruit | 4 liquor | 4 beam | | 4 hard | 4 passing | 4 anchor |

**4**

| 1 reason | 1 wonder | 1 corn | | 1 yoke | 1 chat | 1 heading |
| 2 region | 2 blunder | 2 torn | | 2 joke | 2 chap | 2 sitting |
| 3 legion | 3 thunder | 3 horn | | 3 choke | 3 shack | 3 knitting |
| 4 legend | 4 sponsor | 4 born | | 4 dope | 4 shaft | 4 fitting |

**5**

| 1 stretch | 1 hear | 1 guard | | 1 court | 1 balance | 1 drank |
| 2 threat | 2 steer | 2 hearten | | 2 cord | 2 ballot | 2 rank |
| 3 dread | 3 near | 3 garden | | 3 horse | 3 gallons | 3 ranch |
| 4 bread | 4 deer | 4 bargain | | 4 course | 4 valid | 4 drag |

**6**

| 1 certain | 1 export | 1 file | | 1 banking | 1 borrow | 1 unfold |
| 2 pertain | 2 extort | 2 panel | | 2 flanking | 2 horror | 2 untold |
| 3 person | 3 expert | 3 funnel | | 3 lanky | 3 father | 3 controlled |
| 4 curtain | 4 escort | 4 final | | 4 blanket | 4 power | 4 uphold |

**7**

| 1 raid | 1 fitting | 1 owl | | 1 pipe | 1 beast | 1 dray |
| 2 rate | 2 pretty | 2 call | | 2 pike | 2 beat | 2 grey |
| 3 range | 3 city | 3 hall | | 3 type | 3 meat | 3 spray |
| 4 rage | 4 sitting | 4 all | | 4 tight | 4 least | 4 pray |

**8**

| 1 uncle | 1 dread | 1 screech | | 1 thrift | 1 confirm | 1 verse |
| 2 buckle | 2 dress | 2 preach | | 2 drip | 2 confer | 2 first |
| 3 knuckle | 3 rest | 3 reach | | 3 drift | 3 conserve | 3 burst |
| 4 stucco | 4 red | 4 street | | 4 grip | 4 concern | 4 hurt |

# ANSWER SHEET FOR MULTIPLE-CHOICE
## INTELLIGIBILITY TESTS, FORM A—*Cont.*

*Speaker 3 is*_____          *Speaker 4 is*_____

**1**
| 1 deed | 1 protrude | 1 train | 1 stardom | 1 call | 1 bubble |
| 2 weed | 2 conclude | 2 crane | 2 pardon | 2 ball | 2 stubble |
| 3 seed | 3 construed | 3 strain | 3 garden | 3 hall | 3 trouble |
| 4 feed | 4 include | 4 terrain | 4 autumn | 4 small | 4 double |

**2**
| 1 virtual | 1 hide | 1 pack | 1 top | 1 tool | 1 storage |
| 2 curfew | 2 five | 2 patch | 2 hop | 2 cruel | 2 porridge |
| 3 virtue | 3 hire | 3 catch | 3 pop | 3 drool | 3 shortage |
| 4 virgin | 4 fire | 4 cat | 4 prop | 4 cool | 4 story |

**3**
| 1 dimmer | 1 envy | 1 rumor | 1 eight | 1 revolve | 1 needle |
| 2 dinner | 2 empty | 2 roamer | 2 ache | 2 involve | 2 fetal |
| 3 thinner | 3 entry | 3 rubber | 3 hate | 3 resolve | 3 eagle |
| 4 tinner | 4 ending | 4 rover | 4 bake | 4 dissolve | 4 beetle |

**4**
| 1 sphere | 1 gull | 1 petal | 1 able | 1 recline | 1 folly |
| 2 fear | 2 gall | 2 mettle | 2 stable | 2 refine | 2 volley |
| 3 spear | 3 gold | 3 meadow | 3 fable | 3 reclaim | 3 polish |
| 4 beer | 4 goal | 4 settle | 4 table | 4 reply | 4 trolley |

**5**
| 1 fault | 1 burst | 1 trade | 1 gave | 1 effect | 1 hard |
| 2 vault | 2 hurt | 2 trace | 2 shade | 2 expect | 2 card |
| 3 dog | 3 first | 3 praise | 3 fade | 3 inspect | 3 cord |
| 4 fog | 4 birch | 4 pray | 4 shave | 4 infect | 4 harsh |

**6**
| 1 black | 1 kernel | 1 graft | 1 strange | 1 wad | 1 plant |
| 2 track | 2 curdle | 2 draft | 2 bring | 2 wash | 2 clamp |
| 3 slack | 3 turtle | 3 drab | 3 rain | 3 squad | 3 cramp |
| 4 flak | 4 hurdle | 4 grab | 4 brain | 4 squash | 4 tramp |

**7**
| 1 glow | 1 late | 1 break | 1 clad | 1 lift | 1 behave |
| 2 go | 2 laden | 2 rake | 2 clan | 2 rift | 2 withhold |
| 3 grow | 3 lazy | 3 great | 3 plan | 3 drift | 3 revolt |
| 4 goat | 4 lady | 4 grape | 4 plant | 4 list | 4 behold |

**8**
| 1 change | 1 pen | 1 hard | 1 quarry | 1 such | 1 force |
| 2 chain | 2 pin | 2 part | 2 glory | 2 touch | 2 fourth |
| 3 stain | 3 tent | 3 harsh | 3 gory | 3 nut | 3 course |
| 4 shame | 4 ten | 4 heart | 4 sorry | 4 butt | 4 horse |

# ANSWER SHEET FOR MULTIPLE-CHOICE
# INTELLIGIBILITY TESTS, FORM A—*Cont.*

Speaker 5 is_____          Speaker 6 is_____

**1**
| 1 cook | 1 fair | 1 annual | 1 squirm | 1 hate | 1 commit |
|---|---|---|---|---|---|
| 2 crook | 2 bare | 2 ample | 2 firm | 2 haste | 2 submit |
| 3 brook | 3 care | 3 amble | 3 term | 3 eight | 3 permit |
| 4 book | 4 pair | 4 apple | 4 turn | 4 take | 4 commence |

**2**
| 1 brink | 1 skim | 1 action | 1 cloud | 1 waist | 1 feeling |
|---|---|---|---|---|---|
| 2 bridge | 2 hymn | 2 matching | 2 crowd | 2 wake | 2 meeting |
| 3 brisk | 3 vim | 3 magic | 3 proud | 3 wade | 3 feeding |
| 4 brick | 4 dim | 4 smashing | 4 prod | 4 wait | 4 meaning |

**3**
| 1 took | 1 open | 1 trial | 1 neglect | 1 lost | 1 robber |
|---|---|---|---|---|---|
| 2 shook | 2 oboe | 2 file | 2 deflect | 2 long | 2 jobber |
| 3 shock | 3 opal | 3 frail | 3 reflect | 3 log | 3 harbor |
| 4 cock | 4 oval | 4 trail | 4 reflex | 4 law | 4 shopper |

**4**
| 1 flame | 1 worm | 1 relieve | 1 held | 1 invite | 1 blast |
|---|---|---|---|---|---|
| 2 blame | 2 work | 2 receive | 2 bell | 2 insight | 2 flat |
| 3 claim | 3 word | 3 relief | 3 fell | 3 inside | 3 flak |
| 4 plane | 4 were | 4 release | 4 tell | 4 advice | 4 black |

**5**
| 1 clock | 1 kind | 1 leaping | 1 playful | 1 suit | 1 depend |
|---|---|---|---|---|---|
| 2 block | 2 pine | 2 sleeping | 2 faithful | 2 shoot | 2 detain |
| 3 plot | 3 fine | 3 creeping | 3 fateful | 3 boot | 3 became |
| 4 blot | 4 time | 4 reaping | 4 baseball | 4 fruit | 4 retain |

**6**
| 1 eighty | 1 proof | 1 whip | 1 plural | 1 noun | 1 brave |
|---|---|---|---|---|---|
| 2 aching | 2 hoop | 2 quit | 2 neutral | 2 new | 2 stave |
| 3 dainty | 3 group | 3 quick | 3 rural | 3 nude | 3 bathe |
| 4 baby | 4 swoop | 4 twist | 4 ruler | 4 noon | 4 save |

**7**
| 1 world | 1 happy | 1 dodge | 1 egg | 1 finding | 1 tint |
|---|---|---|---|---|---|
| 2 whirl | 2 handy | 2 dark | 2 edge | 2 binding | 2 print |
| 3 wool | 3 candy | 3 dot | 3 hedge | 3 blinding | 3 prince |
| 4 would | 4 envy | 4 dock | 4 head | 4 landing | 4 tense |

**8**
| 1 conscript | 1 refer | 1 budget | 1 desk | 1 both | 1 yawn |
|---|---|---|---|---|---|
| 2 conflict | 2 rehearse | 2 bucket | 2 deck | 2 boat | 2 jump |
| 3 assist | 3 reverse | 3 bunion | 3 death | 3 vote | 3 junk |
| 4 unfit | 4 revert | 4 budge | 4 debt | 4 quote | 4 young |

# ANSWER SHEET FOR MULTIPLE-CHOICE INTELLIGIBILITY TESTS, FORM A—*Cont.*

Speaker 7 is_____      Speaker 8 is_____

| | | | | | | | |
|---|---|---|---|---|---|---|---|
| **1** | 1 cheerful<br>2 drizzle<br>3 chisel<br>4 fiddle | 1 barn<br>2 bond<br>3 born<br>4 bomb | 1 ream<br>2 green<br>3 dream<br>4 scream | 1 dagger<br>2 gadget<br>3 jacket<br>4 jagged | 1 why<br>2 wine<br>3 wire<br>4 wise | 1 milk<br>2 built<br>3 felt<br>4 belt |
| **2** | 1 gorge<br>2 forge<br>3 ford<br>4 board | 1 seal<br>2 steel<br>3 feel<br>4 field | 1 lotion<br>2 motion<br>3 ocean<br>4 motion | 1 fancy<br>2 brandy<br>3 sandy<br>4 candy | 1 collar<br>2 pilot<br>3 tower<br>4 power | 1 fit<br>2 sit<br>3 spit<br>4 fifth |
| **3** | 1 bird<br>2 birth<br>3 first<br>4 verse | 1 harbor<br>2 Harvard<br>3 harvest<br>4 horrid | 1 height<br>2 pipe<br>3 kite<br>4 tight | 1 adding<br>2 addict<br>3 acting<br>4 attic | 1 main<br>2 fame<br>3 fade<br>4 maid | 1 destroyed<br>2 prescribe<br>3 deprive<br>4 describe |
| **4** | 1 dive<br>2 side<br>3 died<br>4 guide | 1 jungle<br>2 tinkle<br>3 shingle<br>4 single | 1 blunt<br>2 blood<br>3 flood<br>4 stunt | 1 tattle<br>2 tackle<br>3 paddle<br>4 cattle | 1 field<br>2 feel<br>3 heel<br>4 eel | 1 fair<br>2 tare<br>3 hair<br>4 pair |
| **5** | 1 pun<br>2 punch<br>3 pond<br>4 punt | 1 seed<br>2 speed<br>3 bead<br>4 greed | 1 sail<br>2 hail<br>3 rail<br>4 stale | 1 bring<br>2 ring<br>3 rink<br>4 drink | 1 option<br>2 auction<br>3 object<br>4 action | 1 clash<br>2 class<br>3 clap<br>4 clad |
| **6** | 1 eat<br>2 heat<br>3 heap<br>4 deep | 1 past<br>2 pass<br>3 path<br>4 pad | 1 death<br>2 debt<br>3 depth<br>4 deaf | 1 teller<br>2 pillar<br>3 killer<br>4 color | 1 band<br>2 span<br>3 spend<br>4 bend | 1 thimble<br>2 symbol<br>3 temple<br>4 simple |
| **7** | 1 wipe<br>2 wife<br>3 wide<br>4 white | 1 rocking<br>2 locker<br>3 rocket<br>4 locket | 1 keep<br>2 feet<br>3 peep<br>4 heat | 1 dungeon<br>2 cousin<br>3 dozen<br>4 doesn't | 1 barge<br>2 dark<br>3 barred<br>4 guard | 1 capture<br>2 captor<br>3 chapter<br>4 captain |
| **8** | 1 contest<br>2 contend<br>3 content<br>4 contempt | 1 fort<br>2 fore<br>3 force<br>4 fork | 1 add<br>2 have<br>3 ax<br>4 ask | 1 weld<br>2 wealth<br>3 whelp<br>4 well | 1 prevent<br>2 present<br>3 resent<br>4 revenge | 1 formal<br>2 forebode<br>3 foremost<br>4 promote |

# ANSWER SHEET FOR MULTIPLE-CHOICE
# INTELLIGIBILITY TESTS, FORM A—*Cont.*

*Speaker 9 is_____*

|   | | | | | | |
|---|---|---|---|---|---|---|
| **1** | 1 insure<br>2 endure<br>3 obscure<br>4 injure | 1 calm<br>2 come<br>3 comb<br>4 cob | 1 abscess<br>2 absent<br>3 accent<br>4 absurd |
| **2** | 1 taken<br>2 bacon<br>3 vacant<br>4 beacon | 1 turret<br>2 turkey<br>3 perfect<br>4 purpose | 1 divide<br>2 bedside<br>3 deride<br>4 decide |
| **3** | 1 carful<br>2 cheerful<br>3 fearful<br>4 careful | 1 start<br>2 dart<br>3 starch<br>4 dark | 1 found<br>2 down<br>3 gown<br>4 brown |
| **4** | 1 throw<br>2 grow<br>3 grove<br>4 drove | 1 dirty<br>2 thirty<br>3 sturdy<br>4 pretty | 1 roller<br>2 polar<br>3 molar<br>4 colder |
| **5** | 1 barge<br>2 carve<br>3 large<br>4 barb | 1 deluxe<br>2 collect<br>3 select<br>4 elect | 1 pride<br>2 hide<br>3 cried<br>4 bride |
| **6** | 1 like<br>2 mike<br>3 might<br>4 light | 1 hitting<br>2 headache<br>3 heavy<br>4 heading | 1 jump<br>2 dump<br>3 junk<br>4 drunk |
| **7** | 1 ship<br>2 skip<br>3 gift<br>4 shift | 1 cash<br>2 catch<br>3 patch<br>4 pitch | 1 inspire<br>2 spitfire<br>3 expire<br>4 misfire |
| **8** | 1 duel<br>2 fuel<br>3 pool<br>4 jewel | 1 coal<br>2 tone<br>3 toe<br>4 cold | 1 motor<br>2 mortar<br>3 order<br>4 odor |

*Speaker 10 is_____*

|   | | | | | | |
|---|---|---|---|---|---|---|
| **1** | 1 region<br>2 recent<br>3 regent<br>4 rescind | 1 confront<br>2 comfort<br>3 convert<br>4 confirm | 1 lame<br>2 flame<br>3 plane<br>4 blame |
| **2** | 1 consume<br>2 presume<br>3 perfume<br>4 curfew | 1 camel<br>2 gamble<br>3 sample<br>4 shamble | 1 watch<br>2 swat<br>3 squat<br>4 what |
| **3** | 1 crane<br>2 rain<br>3 train<br>4 frame | 1 scatter<br>2 chatter<br>3 shatter<br>4 gather | 1 hornet<br>2 harness<br>3 harvest<br>4 hardly |
| **4** | 1 shoe<br>2 cue<br>3 hue<br>4 you | 1 freedom<br>2 reason<br>3 treason<br>4 freezing | 1 distrust<br>2 discuss<br>3 disgust<br>4 distress |
| **5** | 1 talent<br>2 palace<br>3 challenge<br>4 pilot | 1 nook<br>2 book<br>3 hook<br>4 cook | 1 messkit<br>2 basket<br>3 cross cut<br>4 musket |
| **6** | 1 gone<br>2 dawn<br>3 guard<br>4 darn | 1 planting<br>2 plenty<br>3 twenty<br>4 pretty | 1 rub<br>2 rob<br>3 rug<br>4 rough |
| **7** | 1 censor<br>2 sender<br>3 center<br>4 slender | 1 left<br>2 let<br>3 led<br>4 less | 1 fox<br>2 docks<br>3 blocks<br>4 box |
| **8** | 1 deceit<br>2 defeat<br>3 receipt<br>4 repeat | 1 come<br>2 numb<br>3 some<br>4 thumb | 1 beat<br>2 beach<br>3 speech<br>4 meat |

# ANSWER SHEET FOR MULTIPLE-CHOICE
## INTELLIGIBILITY TESTS, FORM A—*Cont.*

*Speaker 11 is*_____        *Speaker 12 is*_____

| 1 | 1 sway | 1 bribe | 1 twist | 1 screech | 1 refine | 1 near |
|---|--------|---------|---------|-----------|----------|--------|
|   | 2 slay | 2 bride | 2 which | 2 grief | 2 define | 2 dear |
|   | 3 play | 3 bite | 3 switch | 3 brief | 3 behind | 3 fear |
|   | 4 pay | 4 bright | 4 twitch | 4 breach | 4 decline | 4 mere |

| 2 | 1 road | 1 dash | 1 defrayed | 1 rage | 1 plead | 1 pension |
|---|--------|--------|------------|--------|---------|-----------|
|   | 2 robe | 2 bash | 2 enrage | 2 raid | 2 please | 2 mention |
|   | 3 row | 3 gash | 3 engage | 3 raise | 3 sneeze | 3 engine |
|   | 4 roam | 4 flash | 4 mislaid | 4 rate | 4 siege | 4 tension |

| 3 | 1 prayer | 1 brown | 1 concept | 1 corpse | 1 mad | 1 bureau |
|---|----------|---------|-----------|----------|-------|----------|
|   | 2 swear | 2 drowned | 2 contest | 2 cord | 2 bad | 2 arrow |
|   | 3 where | 3 ground | 3 compress | 3 court | 3 bag | 3 here |
|   | 4 square | 4 round | 4 confess | 4 caught | 4 man | 4 zero |

| 4 | 1 bat | 1 cautious | 1 sour | 1 three | 1 went | 1 car |
|---|-------|------------|--------|---------|--------|-------|
|   | 2 bask | 2 conscious | 2 scour | 2 sea | 2 when | 2 here |
|   | 3 fast | 3 cousin | 3 shower | 3 free | 3 wind | 3 error |
|   | 4 fat | 4 caution | 4 tower | 4 tree | 4 win | 4 air |

| 5 | 1 prefer | 1 peel | 1 halt | 1 bean | 1 parade | 1 crave |
|---|----------|--------|--------|--------|----------|--------|
|   | 2 refer | 2 keel | 2 oak | 2 beam | 2 obeved | 2 terrain |
|   | 3 recur | 3 heal | 3 hope | 3 bead | 3 afraid | 3 train |
|   | 4 preserve | 4 feel | 4 oath | 4 bee | 4 appraise | 4 crane |

| 6 | 1 flare | 1 endure | 1 locate | 1 chair | 1 gassed | 1 bent |
|---|---------|----------|----------|---------|----------|--------|
|   | 2 blare | 2 adore | 2 rotate | 2 share | 2 guest | 2 fence |
|   | 3 clear | 3 indoors | 3 okayed | 3 scare | 3 get | 3 spent |
|   | 4 glare | 4 endorse | 4 bouquet | 4 beer | 4 guess | 4 sent |

| 7 | 1 ballad | 1 rod | 1 about | 1 steamboat | 1 tame | 1 ladder |
|---|----------|-------|---------|------------|--------|----------|
|   | 2 ballot | 2 prod | 2 aboard | 2 devote | 2 pain | 2 lather |
|   | 3 balance | 3 ride | 3 around | 3 demote | 3 paid | 3 matter |
|   | 4 valid | 4 fraud | 4 abound | 4 remote | 4 gain | 4 leader |

| 8 | 1 help | 1 outside | 1 thud | 1 unsold | 1 put | 1 foreman |
|---|--------|-----------|--------|----------|-------|----------|
|   | 2 felt | 2 combine | 2 bud | 2 unfold | 2 could | 2 ferment |
|   | 3 health | 3 alpine | 3 blood | 3 untold | 3 good | 3 torment |
|   | 4 self | 4 outline | 4 mud | 4 uphold | 4 hood | 4 comment |

# SCORING SHEET FOR INTELLIGIBILITY TEST, FORM A

The sequence of three numbers indicate the correct words in each group for each reader. If reasonable precaution is taken for accuracy the scoring may be done in class.

|         | Speaker 1 | Speaker 2 | Speaker 3 |
|---------|-----------|-----------|-----------|
| Group 1 | 3—2—4     | 1—2—4     | 4—2—1     |
| Group 2 | 2—4—1     | 4—3—2     | 3—3—2     |
| Group 3 | 1—2—1     | 4—1—3     | 2—1—1     |
| Group 4 | 3—1—3     | 2—4—3     | 3—4—2     |
| Group 5 | 2—4—3     | 4—1—2     | 1—4—3     |
| Group 6 | 4—1—4     | 3—2—1     | 3—1—3     |
| Group 7 | 4—3—4     | 1—1—3     | 2—4—1     |
| Group 8 | 3—2—1     | 3—4—2     | 2—4—4     |

|         | Speaker 4 | Speaker 5 | Speaker 6 |
|---------|-----------|-----------|-----------|
| Group 1 | 2—3—4     | 2—1—3     | 3—1—1     |
| Group 2 | 1—2—1     | 4—4—2     | 3—1—4     |
| Group 3 | 1—4—1     | 2—3—4     | 2—4—2     |
| Group 4 | 3—1—2     | 1—4—3     | 4—1—2     |
| Group 5 | 2—4—2     | 3—1—2     | 2—1—3     |
| Group 6 | 4—3—4     | 1—4—2     | 3—4—4     |
| Group 7 | 3—1—4     | 1—2—3     | 2—2—3     |
| Group 8 | 2—3—1     | 4—3—1     | 1—3—4     |

|         | Speaker 7 | Speaker 8 | Speaker 9 |
|---------|-----------|-----------|-----------|
| Group 1 | 3—2—3     | 2—1—4     | 2—1—2     |
| Group 2 | 2—1—4     | 3—4—1     | 2—3—4     |
| Group 3 | 4—3—4     | 4—1—4     | 3—1—3     |
| Group 4 | 4—1—1     | 4—3—2     | 4—2—1     |
| Group 5 | 1—2—2     | 2—1—2     | 1—3—1     |
| Group 6 | 1—4—3     | 3—2—1     | 4—4—1     |
| Group 7 | 2—3—1     | 3—4—3     | 3—2—4     |
| Group 8 | 3—4—4     | 2—1—3     | 2—3—4     |

|         | Speaker 10 | Speaker 11 | Speaker 12 |
|---------|------------|------------|------------|
| Group 1 | 2—1—1      | 3—4—2      | 3—2—1      |
| Group 2 | 3—2—4      | 2—1—2      | 2—3—1      |
| Group 3 | 4—1—2      | 2—3—4      | 1—1—4      |
| Group 4 | 4—3—3      | 3—4—3      | 4—2—4      |
| Group 5 | 1—4—4      | 1—2—3      | 1—3—4      |
| Group 6 | 1—2—1      | 1—4—1      | 2—4—2      |
| Group 7 | 3—4—1      | 2—1—4      | 3—2—1      |
| Group 8 | 2—3—2      | 3—4—1      | 3—4—3      |

## COMPUTING THE MULTIPLE-CHOICE INTELLIGIBILITY SCORE

Add the number of errors made against each speaker. Locate this number in the "No. of Errors" column. Read across the table to the column labeled with the appropriate number of listeners. This figure is the Intelligibility Score. For example, if a speaker had 107 errors against him by 9 listeners, the Intelligibility Score would be 50.

To compute scores not included in this table: (1) Add the number of words understood correctly by each listener. (2) Divide the total by the number of listeners times 24 (number of words spoken). Carry the product to two decimal figures. The result will be the Intelligibility Score.

| No. of Errors | 7 | 8 | 9 | 10 | 11 |
|---|---|---|---|---|---|
| 21 | 87 | 89 | 90 | 91 | 92 |
| 22 | 87 | 89 | 90 | 91 | 92 |
| 23 | 86 | 88 | 89 | 90 | 91 |
| 24 | 86 | 87 | 89 | 90 | 91 |
| 25 | 85 | 87 | 88 | 90 | 91 |
| 26 | 85 | 86 | 88 | 89 | 90 |
| 27 | 84 | 86 | 87 | 89 | 90 |
| 28 | 83 | 85 | 87 | 88 | 89 |
| 29 | 83 | 85 | 87 | 88 | 89 |
| 30 | 82 | 84 | 86 | 87 | 89 |
| 31 | 82 | 84 | 86 | 87 | 88 |
| 32 | 81 | 83 | 85 | 87 | 88 |
| 33 | 80 | 83 | 85 | 86 | 87 |
| 34 | 80 | 82 | 84 | 86 | 87 |
| 35 | 79 | 82 | 84 | 85 | 87 |
| 36 | 78 | 81 | 83 | 85 | 86 |
| 37 | 78 | 81 | 83 | 85 | 86 |
| 38 | 77 | 80 | 82 | 84 | 86 |
| 39 | 77 | 80 | 82 | 84 | 85 |
| 40 | 76 | 79 | 81 | 83 | 85 |
| 41 | 76 | 79 | 81 | 83 | 84 |
| 42 | 75 | 78 | 81 | 82 | 84 |
| 43 | 74 | 78 | 80 | 82 | 84 |
| 44 | 74 | 77 | 80 | 82 | 83 |
| 45 | 73 | 77 | 79 | 81 | 83 |
| 46 | 73 | 76 | 79 | 81 | 83 |
| 47 | 72 | 76 | 78 | 80 | 82 |
| 48 | 71 | 75 | 78 | 80 | 82 |
| 49 | 71 | 74 | 77 | 80 | 81 |
| 50 | 70 | 74 | 77 | 79 | 81 |
| 51 | 70 | 73 | 76 | 79 | 81 |
| 52 | 69 | 73 | 76 | 78 | 80 |
| 53 | 68 | 72 | 75 | 78 | 80 |
| 54 | 68 | 72 | 75 | 77 | 80 |
| 55 | 67 | 71 | 75 | 77 | 79 |
| 56 | 67 | 71 | 74 | 77 | 79 |
| 57 | 66 | 70 | 74 | 76 | 78 |
| 58 | 65 | 70 | 73 | 76 | 78 |
| 59 | 65 | 69 | 73 | 75 | 78 |
| 60 | 64 | 69 | 72 | 75 | 77 |

| Errors No. of | 7 | 8 | 9 | 10 | 11 |
|---|---|---|---|---|---|
| 61 | 64 | 68 | 72 | 75 | 77 |
| 62 | 63 | 68 | 71 | 74 | 77 |
| 63 | 62 | 67 | 71 | 74 | 76 |
| 64 | 62 | 67 | 70 | 73 | 76 |
| 65 | 61 | 66 | 70 | 73 | 75 |
| 66 | 61 | 66 | 69 | 72 | 75 |
| 67 | 60 | 65 | 69 | 72 | 75 |
| 68 | 60 | 65 | 69 | 72 | 74 |
| 69 | 59 | 64 | 68 | 71 | 74 |
| 70 | 58 | 64 | 68 | 71 | 73 |
| 71 | 58 | 63 | 67 | 70 | 73 |
| 72 | 57 | 62 | 67 | 70 | 73 |
| 73 | 56 | 62 | 66 | 70 | 72 |
| 74 | 56 | 61 | 66 | 69 | 72 |
| 75 | 55 | 61 | 65 | 69 | 72 |
| 76 | 55 | 60 | 65 | 68 | 71 |
| 77 | 54 | 60 | 64 | 68 | 71 |
| 78 | 54 | 59 | 64 | 67 | 70 |
| 79 | 53 | 59 | 63 | 67 | 70 |
| 80 | 52 | 58 | 63 | 67 | 70 |
| 81 | 52 | 58 | 62 | 66 | 69 |
| 82 | 51 | 57 | 62 | 66 | 69 |
| 83 | 51 | 57 | 62 | 65 | 69 |
| 84 | 50 | 56 | 61 | 65 | 68 |
| 85 | 49 | 56 | 61 | 65 | 68 |
| 86 | 49 | 55 | 60 | 64 | 67 |
| 87 | 48 | 55 | 60 | 64 | 67 |
| 88 | 48 | 54 | 59 | 63 | 67 |
| 89 | 47 | 54 | 59 | 63 | 66 |
| 90 | 46 | 53 | 58 | 62 | 66 |
| 91 | 46 | 53 | 58 | 62 | 66 |
| 92 | 45 | 52 | 57 | 62 | 65 |
| 93 | 45 | 52 | 57 | 61 | 65 |
| 94 | 44 | 51 | 56 | 61 | 64 |
| 95 | 43 | 51 | 56 | 60 | 64 |
| 96 | 43 | 50 | 56 | 60 | 64 |
| 97 | 42 | 49 | 55 | 60 | 63 |
| 98 | 42 | 49 | 55 | 59 | 63 |
| 99 | 41 | 48 | 54 | 59 | 62 |
| 100 | 40 | 48 | 54 | 58 | 62 |

| No. of Errors | 7 | 8 | 9 | 10 | 11 |
|---|---|---|---|---|---|
| 101 | 40 | 47 | 53 | 58 | 62 |
| 102 | 39 | 47 | 53 | 57 | 61 |
| 103 | 39 | 46 | 52 | 57 | 61 |
| 104 | 38 | 46 | 52 | 57 | 61 |
| 105 | 37 | 45 | 51 | 56 | 60 |
| 106 | 37 | 45 | 51 | 56 | 60 |
| 107 | 36 | 44 | 50 | 55 | 59 |
| 108 | 36 | 44 | 50 | 55 | 59 |
| 109 | 35 | 43 | 50 | 55 | 59 |
| 110 | 35 | 43 | 49 | 54 | 58 |
| 111 | 34 | 42 | 49 | 54 | 58 |
| 112 | 33 | 42 | 48 | 53 | 58 |
| 113 | 33 | 41 | 48 | 53 | 57 |
| 114 | 32 | 41 | 47 | 52 | 57 |
| 115 | 32 | 40 | 47 | 52 | 56 |
| 116 | 31 | 40 | 46 | 52 | 56 |
| 117 | 30 | 39 | 46 | 51 | 56 |
| 118 | 30 | 39 | 45 | 51 | 55 |
| 119 | 29 | 38 | 45 | 50 | 55 |
| 120 | 29 | 37 | 44 | 50 | 55 |

You will also have the option of taking a simpler and shorter write-down intelligibility test. Although it is not so accurate as the preceding multiple-choice test, it does have a high degree of reliability if given under controlled conditions. It may be preferred where it is not convenient to supply mimeographed answer sheets.

## WRITE-DOWN INTELLIGIBILITY TEST[4]

### Directions to Instructors for Administering

1. The test is devised to be given to groups of 12 or less. Hence there are 12 tests having an equal spread of intelligibility values.

2. For highest accuracy, give the test under the following conditions:

   a. Set up at least the noise of an electric fan for masking, preferably more. The hum of a loudspeaker, or relatively loud phonograph music, will serve *if the amount of noise is measured and is exactly duplicated in the second intelligibility test to be given later.*

   b. Seat listeners in desk-arm chairs at 30 feet distance from the speaker.

   c. Have listeners turn their faces at right angles to the speaker, and instruct them not to look at the speaker during the test.

3. Instruct the students as follows:

   During this hour each of you will be given an intelligibility test that consists of a list of 12 words. When it is your turn you will give your name and the test number: "My name is John Doe, d-o-e. I will read test number 5." Then read the test exactly as it is printed. "Number 1 is shoeblack. Number 2 is harpoon," and so for all 12 words. Be certain to pause after each test word to give listeners time to write the word you have spoken. If you read too fast your score will be lowered simply because listeners did not have time to record what they heard. An easy way to control your rate is to count 2 silently after each test word.

   Remember to speak each test word only *once*. Do not repeat.

   When you are not the speaker, you will record what the other students read. Use a *separate* sheet for each speaker. At the top center write the speaker's name and the test number. Then as he speaks each word, you will write its number and the word as you heard it. If you are not sure what was said, guess. There is no penalty for guessing. If you cannot make a guess, draw a line in that space and go on to the next word.

---

[4] The tests below are the 12-word write-done tests developed by the Voice Communication Laboratory, Waco, Texas, John W. Black, director. They are found in OSRD Report No. 5414, prepared by C. Hess Haagen. Under laboratory conditions they discriminate between trained and untrained speakers and measure reliably as indicated by split-half correlations, corrected for length, of about .75. But these laboratory conditions, among other things, included a masking noise level of about 105 decibels (i.e., much louder than a very loud radio), and when lower masking noises were used the test was less reliable.

Are there any questions? Remember not to read too rapidly. Do not compare papers at any time during the test. Does everyone have a pencil? Does everyone have 11 sheets of paper? Write your name at the upper right corner of each sheet. We will begin immediately.

## Write-Down Intelligibility Test, Form A[5]

| Test 1 | Test 2 | Test 3 | Test 4 | Test 5 | Test 6 |
|--------|--------|--------|--------|--------|--------|
| ramp | charge | impulse | practice | forecast | farther |
| select | defeat | cleared | southeast | hit | cancel |
| break | slow | bail | flare | ground | gliding |
| moment | eastward | gun | top | dainty | find |
| escape | describe | flounder | decrease | pancake | door |
| throb | scatter | reckon | ask | injure | blimp |
| cotton | volley | slam | start | missile | sweep |
| jump | bomb | headwind | pressure | cloudy | take-off |
| center | circuit | flag | balance | tank | reduce |
| tree | late | end | misfire | raid | ditch |
| folder | release | pierce | front | flight | office |
| guard | fog | battle | cripple | nothing | calm |

| Test 7 | Test 8 | Test 9 | Test 10 | Test 11 | Test 12 |
|--------|--------|--------|---------|---------|---------|
| ampere | cartridge | ignite | roll | regain | barge |
| high | speed | blow | forest | cold | tent |
| pivot | mortar | edge | wash | burning | vision |
| salute | full | suburb | single | passage | ceiling |
| caution | dugout | neutral | cushion | dashboard | unit |
| fort | piston | binding | missing | spiral | fair |
| beach | measure | canvass | socket | wrench | hood |
| rocket | gunfire | section | fuel | gangway | shower |
| course | defend | deadly | headphone | corpse | govern |
| bandit | compass | try | pain | forenoon | cockpit |
| darken | tight | flame | blast | spray | distance |
| plenty | blind | gearshift | discard | narrow | target |

## Computing the Write-Down Intelligibility Score

Add the total number of errors made against each speaker. Locate this number in the "No. of Errors" column below. Read across the table to the column labelled with the appropriate number of listeners. This figure is the Intelligibility Score. For example, if the speaker had 93 errors made against him by 11 listeners, the Intelligibility Score would be 30.

[5] There are 24 tests of essentially equal difficulty levels. The first group of 12, known as Form A, is given here. The second group of 12, known as Form B, is given in the next chapter (pages 415-422). By taking any one of the tests in Form A prior to training, and taking any one in Form B following the training, each student will be able to measure improvement in intelligibility with a fairly high degree of reliability.

To compute scores not included in this table: (1) Add the number of words understood correctly by each listener. (2) Divide this total by the number of listeners times 12 (number of words spoken). (3) Carry the product to two decimal figures. The result will be the Intelligibility Score.

| No. of Errors | No. of Listeners | | | | | No. of Errors | No. of Listeners | | | | | No. of Errors | No. of Listeners | | | | |
|---|---|---|---|---|---|---|---|---|---|---|---|---|---|---|---|---|---|
| | 7 | 8 | 9 | 10 | 11 | | 7 | 8 | 9 | 10 | 11 | | 7 | 8 | 9 | 10 | 11 |
| 11 | 87 | 89 | 90 | 91 | 92 | 51 | 39 | 47 | 53 | 58 | 61 | 91 | 0 | 5 | 16 | 24 | 31 |
| 12 | 86 | 87 | 89 | 90 | 91 | 52 | 38 | 46 | 52 | 57 | 61 | 92 | 0 | 4 | 15 | 23 | 30 |
| 13 | 85 | 86 | 88 | 89 | 90 | 53 | 37 | 45 | 51 | 56 | 60 | 93 | 0 | 3 | 14 | 23 | 30 |
| 14 | 83 | 85 | 87 | 88 | 89 | 54 | 36 | 44 | 50 | 55 | 59 | 94 | 0 | 2 | 13 | 22 | 29 |
| 15 | 82 | 84 | 86 | 88 | 89 | 55 | 35 | 43 | 49 | 54 | 58 | 95 | 0 | 1 | 12 | 21 | 28 |
| 16 | 81 | 83 | 85 | 87 | 88 | 56 | 33 | 42 | 48 | 53 | 58 | 96 | 0 | 0 | 11 | 20 | 27 |
| 17 | 80 | 82 | 84 | 86 | 87 | 57 | 32 | 41 | 47 | 53 | 57 | 97 | 0 | 0 | 10 | 19 | 27 |
| 18 | 79 | 81 | 83 | 85 | 86 | 58 | 31 | 40 | 46 | 52 | 56 | 98 | 0 | 0 | 9 | 18 | 26 |
| 19 | 77 | 80 | 82 | 84 | 86 | 59 | 30 | 39 | 45 | 51 | 55 | 99 | 0 | 0 | 8 | 18 | 25 |
| 20 | 76 | 79 | 81 | 83 | 85 | 60 | 29 | 37 | 44 | 50 | 55 | 100 | 0 | 0 | 7 | 17 | 24 |
| 21 | 75 | 78 | 81 | 83 | 84 | 61 | 27 | 36 | 44 | 49 | 54 | 101 | 0 | 0 | 6 | 16 | 23 |
| 22 | 74 | 77 | 80 | 82 | 83 | 62 | 26 | 35 | 43 | 48 | 53 | 102 | 0 | 0 | 6 | 15 | 23 |
| 23 | 73 | 76 | 79 | 81 | 83 | 63 | 25 | 34 | 42 | 48 | 52 | 103 | 0 | 0 | 5 | 14 | 22 |
| 24 | 71 | 75 | 78 | 80 | 82 | 64 | 24 | 33 | 41 | 47 | 52 | 104 | 0 | 0 | 4 | 13 | 21 |
| 25 | 70 | 74 | 77 | 79 | 81 | 65 | 23 | 32 | 40 | 46 | 51 | 105 | 0 | 0 | 3 | 13 | 20 |
| 26 | 69 | 73 | 76 | 78 | 80 | 66 | 21 | 31 | 39 | 45 | 50 | | | | | | |
| 27 | 68 | 72 | 75 | 78 | 80 | 67 | 20 | 30 | 38 | 44 | 49 | | | | | | |
| 28 | 67 | 71 | 74 | 77 | 79 | 68 | 19 | 29 | 37 | 43 | 48 | | | | | | |
| 29 | 65 | 70 | 73 | 76 | 78 | 69 | 18 | 28 | 36 | 43 | 48 | | | | | | |
| 30 | 64 | 69 | 72 | 75 | 77 | 70 | 17 | 27 | 35 | 42 | 47 | | | | | | |
| 31 | 63 | 68 | 71 | 74 | 77 | 71 | 15 | 26 | 34 | 41 | 46 | | | | | | |
| 32 | 62 | 67 | 70 | 73 | 76 | 72 | 14 | 25 | 33 | 40 | 45 | | | | | | |
| 33 | 61 | 66 | 69 | 73 | 75 | 73 | 13 | 24 | 32 | 39 | 45 | | | | | | |
| 34 | 60 | 65 | 69 | 72 | 74 | 74 | 12 | 23 | 31 | 38 | 44 | | | | | | |
| 35 | 58 | 64 | 68 | 71 | 73 | 75 | 11 | 22 | 31 | 38 | 43 | | | | | | |
| 36 | 57 | 62 | 67 | 70 | 73 | 76 | 10 | 21 | 30 | 37 | 43 | | | | | | |
| 37 | 56 | 61 | 66 | 69 | 72 | 77 | 8 | 20 | 29 | 36 | 42 | | | | | | |
| 38 | 55 | 60 | 65 | 68 | 71 | 78 | 7 | 19 | 28 | 35 | 41 | | | | | | |
| 39 | 54 | 59 | 64 | 68 | 70 | 79 | 6 | 18 | 27 | 34 | 40 | | | | | | |
| 40 | 52 | 58 | 63 | 67 | 70 | 80 | 5 | 17 | 26 | 33 | 39 | | | | | | |
| 41 | 51 | 57 | 62 | 66 | 69 | 81 | 4 | 16 | 25 | 33 | 39 | | | | | | |
| 42 | 50 | 56 | 61 | 65 | 68 | 82 | 3 | 15 | 24 | 32 | 38 | | | | | | |
| 43 | 49 | 55 | 60 | 64 | 67 | 83 | 1 | 14 | 23 | 31 | 37 | | | | | | |
| 44 | 48 | 54 | 59 | 63 | 67 | 84 | 0 | 12 | 22 | 30 | 36 | | | | | | |
| 45 | 46 | 53 | 58 | 63 | 66 | 85 | 0 | 11 | 21 | 29 | 36 | | | | | | |
| 46 | 45 | 52 | 57 | 62 | 65 | 86 | 0 | 10 | 20 | 28 | 35 | | | | | | |
| 47 | 44 | 51 | 56 | 61 | 64 | 87 | 0 | 9 | 19 | 28 | 34 | | | | | | |
| 48 | 43 | 50 | 56 | 60 | 64 | 88 | 0 | 8 | 19 | 27 | 33 | | | | | | |
| 49 | 42 | 49 | 55 | 59 | 63 | 89 | 0 | 7 | 18 | 26 | 33 | | | | | | |
| 50 | 40 | 48 | 54 | 58 | 62 | 90 | 0 | 6 | 17 | 25 | 32 | | | | | | |

## What makes voices unpleasant

Your Intelligibility Score is an inventory of one attribute of your voice, an important one, but not the only one. A voice may be intelligible, yet unable to communicate attitudes. It may be unpleasant, even irritating, to listeners. Therefore, let us consider some common types of poor voice quality, their causes, and treatment.

## NASALITY

Nasality comes from allowing too much breath to escape through the nose. Only three sounds of the language are nasal: *m*, *n*, and *ng*. These are properly made by closing off the mouth with the lips, tongue, or soft palate, and allowing the air stream to go through the nose. Theoretically, all other sounds are made by closing off the nasal passage and sending the breath stream through the mouth. What we call nasality, therefore, is the nasalizing of non-nasal sounds. Usually it is caused by an over-all sluggishness of the speech organs: (1) inadequate breathing, (2) constricted throat, tongue, and jaw, (3) mouth not open wide enough for all vowel sounds, (4) tongue raised too high in the mouth, and (5) a sluggish soft palate. Indeed there is a direct relationship between nasality and the size of mouth-opening during speech. The wider the mouth-opening, the less the nasality. It is also generally true that the wider the mouth-opening the less over-all sluggishness of the speech organs.

To correct nasality, first make a recording—disc or tape—as a permanent record from which you can measure improvement. Then start with the exercises given in the first part of this chapter on breathing, phonation, and resonation. These general exercises are more fundamental to overcoming nasality than any specific exercises on mere soft palate control.

If you need specific exercises, work first on the sounds that are made through the nose: *m*, *n*, and *ng*. Hum these sounds and prolong them until you can *feel* the vibration in the nose. Then, still humming the nasal sound, slowly lower the jaw, then finally open the mouth and let the tone into an *ah:* m-m-m-m-a-a-h, n-n-n-n-a-a-h, ng-ng-ng-ng-a-a-h.

Next, drill on paired words like those given below. The first word in each pair contains a nasal sound. The second should have no nasality:

| | | | | | |
|------|------|--------|---------|-----------|-----------|
| bean | bead | damper | dapper | strumming | strutting |
| bin | bid | fain | fade | tame | tape |
| bang | bag | fang | fag | time | tide |
| bone | bode | home | hope | tongue | tug |
| came | cape | languor | lacquer | tiny | tidy |
| come | cup | rhyme | ripe | wing | wig |
| crank | crag | seem | seep | whine | white |
| dandy | daddy | seen | seed | wander | water |
| downy | dowdy | sang | sack | whenever | whatever |

## HARSHNESS

Harshness comes generally from throat constriction. The tense throat muscles interfere with free vibration of the vocal cords, and also with proper resonance.

Chiefly there are three causes for this constriction: (1) Often it is found in high-strung and restless people, an index of a general emotional condition. (2) Sometimes it is found in people who are cold and unsympathetic. These are causes outside the scope of this chapter, but they are causes that you ought to face honestly. (3) But the most common cause is the old "public speaker's pinched throat," which comes from trying to speak louder by constricting the throat.

You already know the remedy for a pinched throat. Go back to the first part of this chapter on breathing (everything starts with breathing), phonation, and resonation. Work on the exercises to relax the throat, and to keep the power in the abdomen. Apply the axiom given earlier: *Power in the abdomen, relaxation in the throat, and flexibility in the face.*

## HOARSENESS AND HUSKINESS

Hoarseness, sometimes called huskiness, is a rough aspirate quality like that in acute laryngitis.

Its cause may be physical—infected sinuses, growths on the vocal cords, etc.—and for that reason a physician should be consulted. Most hoarseness, however, comes from misusing the voice. The speaker perhaps is attempting to talk at an extremely low pitch, far below the normal range. Sometimes it comes from the childhood carry-over of attempting to talk like an adult. Sometimes it comes from the attempt to imitate the deep bass or contralto voice of some actor or speaker, and sometimes from someone's bad advice "to lower the voice." Often it is caused by the deliberate effort to enrich the voice by lowering the pitch. Now what happens when the pitch is artificially lowered beyond the range of human resonators? The volume is decreased to a fraction of its original power, simply because the resonance chambers cannot amplify an artificially low pitch (this is elementary physics). *Thereupon the speaker tenses the throat and tries to gain volume by forcing more air through the vocal cords.* The result is a hoarse voice with an internal vocal rumbling which the speaker mistakes for resonance. With constant use it also produces "the preacher's sore throat," which is a natural result of prolonged voice abuse.

The treatment, of course, is to relax the throat and raise the pitch. But it is not so simple as the saying. You should start at the beginning with exercises on breathing (everything starts with breathing!), on phonation, and finally on resonation. With these exercises your purpose is to eliminate the strain and tension, relax the throat, get the pitch where it belongs, and get power from the abdomen and chest. As a guide for improvement, you might first make a recording as a permanent record of the original hoarseness from which you can measure improvement.

## THINNESS

Thinness is lack of carrying power. A thin voice has no body or fullness. Usually it seems to be pitched too high, although this often is not true.

For treating a thin voice, first make a permanent recording as a record for measuring improvement. Then start a program of daily exercises in breathing, phonation, and resonation. Focus especially on establishing the *concept* of resonance (see exercises for this under Resonation earlier in this chapter). Listen to the recordings of professional actors and good speakers. Compare them with your own. Bear in mind two conditioning factors. First, don't expect to develop good resonance within a day or two, or from casual intermittent effort. Second, be assured that you can distinctly improve your voice by proper systematic exercise.

## BREATHINESS

Breathiness is a fuzzy, feather-edged voice, a part whisper in which you hear about as much breath as voice.

It is caused by failure to bring the edges of the vocal cords closely enough together, which allows the escape of unvocalized air. This may come from weakness of the vocal muscles or from irregularities on the edges of the vocal cords, but these are not the usual reasons. The more common reason is improper breathing and inefficient use of the larynx.

The treatment is re-education in producing voice. Start with a permanent recording as a record for measuring improvement. Then return to the exercises given earlier in this chapter on breathing, phonation, and resonation. For specific exercises, after practice on these basic general exercises, you must remember that the vocal cords are not under direct voluntary control, like the tongue; therefore you must resort to indirect methods. Start with the "glottal catch." This is accomplished by starting a stream of unvocalized air through the larynx (simply breathing out), then suddenly stopping the breath in the throat. Actually you do this by bringing the vocal cords sharply together. If this is properly done a sharp click will be heard, and the breath will stop instantly. Be sure that the shut-off is in the larynx and not in the back of the mouth. If you cannot identify the glottal catch in this exercise, try coughing. We usually start a cough with the glottal catch. After you identify it with a cough, get set for starting to cough, hold the position for a moment, then open glottal catch and say *a-a-a-h*. Now reverse the process by starting with *a-a-a-h*, then cutting off the sound with the glottal catch.

For further specific exercises, practice the following word pairs. For words in the first column, start by bringing the vocal cords together as though you were going to cough, then vocalize carefully without breathiness: *e-e-a-t*. Then take its opposite pair starting with the sound of *h*, being careful not to use an excess of air on the *h*, nor to delay too long in voicing the vowel:

| eel | heel | ooze | whose |
|-----|------|------|-------|
| ill | hill | old | hold |
| ate | hate | all | haul |
| at | hat | oil | Hoyle |
| eye | high | art | heart |

## Assignments

FOR TESTING AND IMPROVING VOICE QUALITY

The basic exercises are found earlier in this chapter under breathing, phonation, and resonation. After you have made progress with them, work on the exercises below.

Remember that "practice makes *permanent*" (not perfect), and that practice of your old faults will only fix them more firmly. Therefore, practice these exercises with proper breathing habits, relaxed throat, open mouth, and a conscious concept of resonance.

> A little learning is a dangerous thing;
> Drink deep, or taste not the Pierian spring;
> There shallow draughts intoxicate the brain,
> And drinking largely sobers us again.
> ALEXANDER POPE

> Once more; speak clearly if you speak at all;
> Carve every word before you let it fall:
> Don't like a lecturer or dramatic star,
> Try overhead to roll the British R.
> OLIVER WENDELL HOLMES

> For I dipt into the future, far as
> human eye could see,
> Saw the Vision of the world, and
> all the wonders that would be;
> Saw the heavens filled with commerce,
> argosies of magic sails,

> Pilots of the purple twilight, dropping
> down with costly bales;
> Heard the heavens fill with shouting,
> and there rain'd a ghastly dew
> From the nations' airy navies grappling
> in the central blue.
>                              ALFRED LORD TENNYSON
>                              *Locksley Hall*

We hold these truths to be self-evident, that all men are created equal, that they are endowed by their Creator with certain unalienable Rights, that among these are Life, Liberty and the pursuit of Happiness.—That to secure these rights, Governments are instituted among Men, deriving their just powers from the consent of the governed,—That whenever any Form of Government becomes destructive of these ends, it is the Right of the People to alter or to abolish it.

*Declaration of Independence*

With malice toward none; with charity for all; with firmness in the right, as God gives us to see the right, let us strive on to finish the work we are in; to bind up the nation's wounds; to care for him who shall borne the battle, and for his widow and orphans—to do all which may achieve and cherish a just and lasting peace among ourselves, and with all nations.

ABRAHAM LINCOLN, *Second Inaugural Address*

This is pre-eminently the time to speak the truth, the whole truth, frankly and boldly. Nor need we shrink from honestly facing conditions in our country today. This great Nation will endure as it has endured, will revive and will prosper. So, first of all, let me assert my firm belief that the only thing we have to fear is fear itself—nameless, unreasoning, unjustified terror which paralyzes needed efforts to convert retreat into advance. In every dark hour of our national life a leadership of frankness and vigor has met with that understanding and support of the people themselves which is essential to victory. I am convinced that you will again give that support to leadership in these critical days.

FRANKLIN D. ROOSEVELT, *First Inaugural Address*

## What makes a good speaking voice

To be understood you must first be heard. To be heard in public address requires certain specific disciplines.

### PACK YOUR TONES AGAINST YOUR BELT

A public speaker needs enough energy to be heard easily, and enough energy to communicate tone color and informing inflections. Here you face two difficulties. First, some people try to get power by constricting muscles in the throat and neck; and as a result they produce those hoarse and harsh sounds described above. Second, some try to speak without enough energy; and as a result they talk in lifeless tones, without salt and spirit. "Nothing so befits him as unbroken silence," exclaimed a critic of Archbishop Whately, who spoke that way.

Vocal power, as we know, comes from pressure behind the breath stream, and this pressure comes from the muscles in the abdomen and between the ribs. In the words of the old Victorian actors, you *"pack your tones against your belt."* Lift the front wall of the chest. Harden the abdomen. Pull down the diaphragm until it draws air into the lungs like a suction pump. Now you are in position to "pack your tones against your belt." Here are further steps for using vocal energy:

*Maintain a steady pressure of air while you talk.* In good voices the exhaling muscle-action is steady. In poor voices it tends to be jerky. Steady pressure does not mean uniform pressure, of course. You raise and lower the pressure to get the emphasis and accent. But you don't have a wobbling pressure or a jerky one, booming forth on the first part of a sentence but fading out before you get to the end.

*Maintain an adequate breath reserve.* You don't keep your lungs filled to the last cubic inch, or else soon you will have a chest full of air without oxygen. Instead, you take a reasonably deep breath and fill the chest comfortably. Also, you don't keep on talking until you run out of breath, but smoothly refill with short breath catches. This reserve enables you to speak with vigor right up to the end of each thought.

You had exercises previously on vocal energy, but here are a few more for reinforcement:

## Assignments

VOCAL ENERGY

1. Practice breathing. Stand erect. Pull down the diaphragm. Now draw air into the lungs. While doing this also: (*a*) Lift the upper chest. (*b*) Push out the ribs. (*c*) Harden the abdomen. (*d*) Try to feel the muscle pull in the small of the back. (*e*) Make sure the throat is open *and relaxed.* Now exhale without a sound by letting the air flow silently through the lips.

2. Stand erect and inhale as above, but this time fill the chest comfortably and speak one of the following lines. Speak with a relaxed and open throat, and prolong the stressed tones with maximum vocal energy for three counts:

> *All aboard!*
> *As* you *were!*
> *Forward! March!*
> *Roll* back the *tide* of eigh*teen* hundred *years.*

3. Stand erect and inhale until the chest is comfortably filled. Then speak the following selections with maximum vocal power. Keep the throat relaxed and open. Supply power from below. Sustain the stressed sounds:

> Forests were set on fire—but hour by hour
> They fell and faded—and the crackling trunks
> Extinguished with a crash—and all was black.
> > LORD BYRON, *Darkness*

> Hear the mellow wedding bells,
>   Golden bells!
> What a world of happiness their harmony foretells!
> > EDGAR ALLAN POE

> The bell invites me.
> Hear it not, Duncan; for it is a knell
> That summons thee to heaven or to hell.
> > SHAKESPEARE, *Macbeth*

## USE AMPLE RESONANCE

The vocal cords produce only thin, feeble tone. You amplify and enrich this tone with the resonators. Remember that you have two types of resonators: fixed and adjustable. The fixed resonators are unchangeable in size: the skull bones, nose, nasal sinuses, trachea, sternum, and ribs. When you use any group of them you get the *feeling* of resonance in that part of your body. Close the lips and hum *m-m-m-m* until you get this feeling. Then put your hand on top of your head and you will know whence comes that "feeling." It is the real thing, for your skull bones are vibrating! Also feel the chest. If you are using enough energy down in your bellows, the chest bones are also vibrating.

Next, are the adjustable resonators: mouth, pharynx, and larynx. You change the size and shape of these resonators when you change voice pitch. You also change the size and shape for each of the fifteen or so different vowel sounds. Hence it is that good voice production requires *"flexibility in the face."* These are the operating principles for flexibility:

1. Each vowel sound needs a special size and shape of the adjustable resonators.

2. Certain so-called vowels are really diphthongs, or double vowels, especially the sounds in *ice, how* and *oil.* For full utterance these require two sizes and shapes.

3. Two sounds are really triphthongs, or triple vowels. They are the sounds in *fire* and *our.* They require three sizes and shapes.

4. Changes in pitch need changes in size and shape.

5. Changes in inflection need changes in size and shape.

You have had basic exercises in resonation. For additional special exercises practice the following:

## Assignments

RESONANCE

Stand erect and inhale until the chest is filled comfortably. Practice these exercises with exaggerated movements of the mouth and pharynx. Watch yourself in a mirror to be sure the movements are as exaggerated as they feel. Be sure the throat is relaxed and open, and that the power comes from the bellows down below.

I have but one lamp by which my feet are guided, and that is the lamp of experience.

PATRICK HENRY

Home is the sailor, home from the sea,
And the hunter home from the hill.
ROBERT LOUIS STEVENSON, *Requiem*

I know not whether Laws be right,
Or whether Laws be wrong;
All that we know who lie in gaol
Is that the wall is strong;
And that each day is like a year,
A year whose days are long.
OSCAR WILDE

When the night wind howls in the chimney cowls, and the bat
in the moonlight flies,
And inky clouds, like funeral shrouds, sail over the midnight
skies.
GILBERT and SULLIVAN

And I have loved thee, Ocean! And my joy
Of youthful sports was on thy breast to be
Borne, like thy bubbles, onward. From a boy
I wantoned with thy breakers—
LORD BYRON

Ship me somewhere east of Suez, where the best is like the worst,
Where there aren't no Ten Commandments an' a man can raise a thirst;
For the temple-bells are callin', an' it's there that I would be—
By the old Moulmein Pagoda, looking lazy at the sea;
On the road to Mandalay,

Where the old Flotilla lay,
With our sick beneath the awnings when we went to Mandalay!
On the road to Mandalay,
Where the flyn'-fishes play,
An' the dawn comes up like thunder outer China 'cross the Bay!

RUDYARD KIPLING

## USE YOUR NORMAL KEY

Your voice has a normal key. This is the general pitch-level best coupled to your particular resonators. Your voice will rise and fall above and below this median, but it tends always to return to it.

The normal key varies with different persons, and it varies greatly between men and women. In this respect voices are like musical instruments. Each will produce sound within a given range, some high, some medium, some low. Outside this range it does not perform so well. Hence some women's voices are contralto, and others are soprano. Some men's voices are bass, and others are tenor. The median pitch-level for women's voices is about 233 cycles per second, but they range from 188 to 295. The median pitch-level for men is about 141 cycles per second, but they range from 134 to 146.[6]

If you don't use your normal key, you don't attain best potential voice quality. If you speak below it, you tend to speak in a deep hollow tone without flexibility. If you speak above it, you tend to have a thin, high, squeaky voice, and the same lack of flexibility.

How do you find your normal key? There are at least two ways. First, close the mouth, press down the tragus (flap in front of the opening) of the ear, and hum with *steady even breath pressure* from the highest tone possible to the lowest. Somewhere along the way you will find a tone that is louder than the others. That's your normal key.

But the most accurate is to sing from your lowest key to your highest, including your falsetto. Your normal key is about *one-fourth the way up from your lowest tone.*

## Assignments

ESTABLISHING THE NORMAL KEY

Using the methods described above, find your normal key. By going frequently to a piano and sounding the proper key, you can keep this pitch continually in mind and help to make its use habitual.

[6] Giles Wilkeson Gray and Claude Merton Wise, *The Bases of Speech* (New York, Harper & Brothers, 1959), p. 102.

Using your normal key, read the following, but do not read in a monopitch. Instead, communicate the meaning by as much variety of pitch as you need, but use your normal key as the median:

There was an old preacher once who told some boys of the Bible lesson he was going to read in the morning. The boys, finding the place, glued together the connecting pages. The next morning he read on the bottom of one page: "When Noah was one hundred and twenty years old he took unto himself a wife, who was"—then turning the page—"one hundred and forty cubits long, forty cubits wide, built of gopher-wood, and covered with pitch inside and out." He was naturally puzzled at this. He read it again, verified it, and then said: "My friends, this is the first time I ever met this in the Bible, but I accept it as an evidence of the assertion that we are fearfully and wonderfully made."

HENRY W. GRADY

We are spinning our own fates, good or evil, never to be undone. Every smallest stroke of virtue or vice leaves its never-so-little scar. The drunken Rip Van Winkle, in Jefferson's play, excuses himself for every fresh dereliction by saying, "I won't count this time!" Well, he may not count it, and a kind Heaven may not count it; but it is being counted none the less. Down among his nerve-cells and fibers the molecules are counting it, registering and storing it up to be used against him when the next temptation comes. Nothing we ever do is, in strict scientific literalness, wiped out.

WILLIAM JAMES

## SPEAK WITH A FLEXIBLE AND RESPONSIVE VOICE

To communicate full meanings you need a flexible voice. First, a flexible *rate*. Just as an automobile slows down for curves and villages, so the sensitive speaker slows down and picks up the rate in order to communicate the meaning. E. H. Sothern, that well-remembered Shakespearean actor, read Hamlet's soliloquy, "To be or not to be," at a meditative 80 words a minute, but spoke Hamlet's advice to the players, "Speak the speech I pray you," trippingly on the tongue at 170 words a minute. Indeed, we might paraphrase the author of *Hamlet* and say, "Suit the rate to the word, and the word to the rate."

Next, is emphasis. You can't communicate much in that deadly same-emphasis-for-everything voice you hear so often in the classroom. Shake it off. *See* in your mind the mountains and valleys of thought then tell listeners what you see: "*Now* is the time," or "Let it be *forgotten*, as a *flower* is *forgotten*."

Finally, comes that wide range of pitch and inflection. Try saying, "Y-e-e-s, I supp-o-o-ose that's so-o-o," and make it mean, "Yes, I suppose that's so, but I'm doubtful, very doubtful." Do this to carry the full extended meaning, and you will find that it calls for long, extended inflections. Remember that leading actors on Broadway average *two full octaves*. It takes that to communicate the meanings in their lines. One measurement of Franklin D. Roosevelt's voice showed a range from 96 to 256 vibrations per second, or almost 18 semitones. In a short reading, Julia Marlowe's voice ranged from 192 to 438 vibrations per second—one and one-third octaves. A study of college students' voices showed that those which other students rated as "better" voices had a greater number of rising inflections, greater number of falling inflections, longer range of inflection, greater number of shifts in pitch, and a greater extent of shifts in pitch. The poorer voices fell short on each of these forms of flexibility. The voice, then, that best communicates thought is a flexible voice. The deadly drone of an unchanging voice communicates poorly. As Gilbert Highet said of Prime Minister Stanley Baldwin's pompous chant, "Half an hour of this put everybody to sleep. Several years of it put Britain to sleep."

# Assignments

### DEVELOPING A FLEXIBLE AND RESPONSIVE VOICE

1. Vary the rate of speaking the following sentences so as to communicate the indicated meanings:

   *a.* "I told her I couldn't come."

   Slowly, expressing regret
   Faster, argumentatively defending your answer
   Still faster, meaning "I didn't want to go, and I got out of it."

   *b.* "What do you think we ought to do?"

   Very slowly, as though asked by a tired and confused person
   Normal rate, asking a simple question
   Fast, to mean, "I'm in a hurry."

2. Vary the emphasis of the following so as to communicate the indicated meanings:

   *a.* "There is no other answer. You have asked me that question a thousand times, and my reply has always been the same. It always will be the same."

   Mild emphasis, as though explaining it the thousandth time
   Sustained emphasis, meaning, "Don't ask me again!"
   Short sharp emphasis, to communicate fear

   *b.* "Yes, I know about it. I've known it all the time."

   Mild emphasis, as though explaining it the thousandth time
   Prolonged emphasis, to mean, "I'm tired of hearing about it."
   Explosive emphasis, meaning, "Don't tell me I don't know!"

3. Vary the pitch of the following so as to communicate the indicated meanings:

   a. "I wouldn't do that if I were you."

   Slight inflections, giving mild advice
   Wide inflections, pleading
   Narrow sustained inflections, threatening, "You just dare!"

   b. "Who is she?"

   Medium inflections, merely asking
   Wider inflections, meaning, "What a frump!"
   Extreme inflections, meaning, "She's a glamor girl!"

4. If possible record part or all of the following exercises, listen to the playback, and assess the flexibility of your voice. Do you speak with a pitch range of two notes, or four, or six, or eight, or more? Do you have a "repeated pitch pattern," in which the voice changes are all alike? In reading poetry does your voice rise at the same point in each line, and fall at identical points in each line? If so, you are not communicating meaning, but are only singing a kind of song. Do you read everything at the same rate, regardless of its mood and meaning? Do you have real emphasis, or do your words come back to you like the ticking of a grandfather's clock? Hear yourself as others hear you, and let not your judgment be too much tempered by charity.

*No!* Not *really!*

You don't *say* so!

*Hold* it, brother! That's *my* coat!"

The publisher said the *author* was a *fool.*
The *publisher* said the author was a *fool.*

They *tell* us, sir, that we are *weak* . . . *Sir,* we are *not* weak.

*Wherefore* rejoice? What conquest brings *he* home?
What *tributaries* follow *him* to Rome.
To *grace* in *captive bonds* his *chariot-wheels?*

*Never* in the field of *human conflict* was so *much* owed by so *many* to so *few.*

There is a *tide* in the *affairs* of *men*
Which, taken at its *flood,* leads on to *fortune;*
*Omitted, all* the *voyage* of their *life*
Is *bound* in *shallows* and in *miseries.*

SHAKESPEARE

The *miser* is *blind;* he sees *gold* and he does *not* see *riches.* The *prodigal* is blind; *he* sees the *beginnings* and does *not* see the *end.* The *coquette* is blind; *she* does not see her *wrinkles.* The *learned* is blind; *he* does not see his *own ignorance.* The *honest man* is blind; *he* does not see the *thief.* The *thief* is blind; he does not see *God.*

VICTOR HUGO

## COMMUNICATE BOTH THOUGHT AND FEELING

An investigator recorded on tape the voices of certain celebrities, then scrambled the words so they were unintelligible. That left only the pitch and tone quality. Yet listeners could identify "not only the mood and situation but also the person." Take away the language of words and the language of tone still communicates. As Charles A. Dana said: "You can put tears into [spoken words], as though they were so many buckets; and you can hang smiles on them like Monday's clothes on the line, or you can starch them with facts and stand them up like a picket fence; but you won't get the tears out unless you first put them in."

Foremost of all things your voice should tell is *sincerity*. To all who hear, it should say, "You may disagree with what I say, but you cannot question my sincerity." William Jennings Bryan used to tell his daughter, "Say what you think, but *feel* what you say." That's it exactly. You can't easily feign sincerity; to sound sincere, the easiest way is to be sincere. *In other words, it's not enough to believe in what you are saying. You've also got to believe that it matters to the people you are talking to. If it doesn't matter, why bother?*

Next, remember that you talk two languages with the voice, not one: the language of words and the language of tones. The language of words, first, communicates meanings. But there is no absolute meaning any word must have. A dictionary establishes only a frame of reference by recording multiple meanings for words. In speaking, *you,* at the moment of utterance, must give each word its meaning *as you use it in context.* You must know which words are the key to your thought—and telegraph this to listeners by pitch, pause, and emphasis. None of this can you do by merely uttering words, for merely uttering words without tone patterns produces monotonous sounds without much meaning.

Finally, *you tell listeners what your attitude is.* Respectful, cheerful, elated, explanatory, amused, vexed, perplexed, tranquil, gloomy, determined—or any of the hundred and more attitudes of human creatures. This is not done by the language of words, but by the language of tones. All over the world human beings use that language of tone. They use distinct and different tones to telegraph assurance from those to telegraph doubt, different ones for mirth from melancholy, or any attitude from any other.

How do you communicate both thought and attitude? Shall you say, "I shall emphasize this word," or "Here I want to show 'hope'; therefore, I shall use the tone color of a hopeful person"? Never! You can say that love is holy, war is hell, color is only skin-deep, and insincerity is the root of all evil. But if you say it by manipulating tone color—then you say it as a parrot asks for a cracker, by rote and with only false conviction. The result will be like that described by a critic (in this case a bit unjustly) of Olivia de Haviland: "She never seems to feel the part—only the importance of it. She never seems in love with Romeo—only with *Romeo and Juliet*. She recites poetry where she should radiate it; and goes through the role as though following a score marked presto or lento, *ff.* or *pp.*" Listeners know when a speaker is really friendly, or is only feigning, when he speaks with the inflections and nuances of leadership, or is merely reciting schoolboy words. This language of tone is far older than any language of words. Every child learns it early.

To communicate thought you must *think* on your feet, *create* or *recreate* the full thought *at the moment of utterance.*

To communicate attitudes you need to *experience* the attitude *as you speak.*

This brings us to a painful question. Why do most speakers communicate thought and attitude better in private conversation than in public address? The painful answer is, *they don't prepare!* In private conversation they think and feel what they say. In public speech they put notes on paper, or a ghostwriter may supply a complete manuscript, but the speaker has no clear picture in his mind of either the shape or color of his thought. So it comes out in a monotonous three-note, hill-and-gully tone. One remembers that old Cicero said, "Expression is always perfect," and suspects that he was right. When speakers don't really communicate, too often it's because their ideas are on paper instead of in their minds.

As our civilization becomes more complex, more and more people must speak in public simply to carry on the necessary business of human beings living together. But the more and more speak worse and worse, until the problem threatens to become a national menace. Now and then, however, comes relief as reported by Lester Tanzer from the White House:

> Shortly after 9 A.M. this morning, a Cabinet member will step up to a rostrum tucked away in one corner of the Cabinet room in the White House, glance at [the] President . . . then start a speech on one of the day's main issues. If the official . . . speaks too slowly, a newly-installed light on the rostrum will flash, 'Speed up.' As he approaches the end of his presentation, the light will signal, 'Three Minutes to Go.' . . . Chances are, however, that even without the flashing lights, the Cabinet member's address will end on time. One day earlier this week . . . [he had gone] over to the White House for a full-scale dress rehearsal of this morning's offering to the weekly Cabinet meeting. During that dry run, the official presented an argument for a particular program he's backing. From his select audience of White House aides came suggestions on how to drive home his main themes harder and how to trim unnecessary verbiage, as well as questions on some unclear points. The Cabinet official then ran through his presentation once more, so

planners of this morning's meeting would have an exact idea of how much time to allot him on the tight two-hour schedule.[7]

Students, Cabinet members, and the nation profit by such methods.

# Assignments

MAKING VOICE THE VEHICLE OF THOUGHT AND FEELING

1. The word *yes* can be spoken to communicate at least twenty different meanings. Try speaking it to communicate each of the following meanings. Remember to *think* the meanings.

| | |
|---|---|
| Plain affirmation | "O Yeah?" |
| "Certainly" | "Are you serious?" |
| "Maybe" | "I don't like it" |
| "I doubt it" | "No!" |

2. Give *oh* each of the following meanings:

| | |
|---|---|
| Pity | "I see now!" |
| Disgust | Mild surprise |
| Disappointment | Great surprise |
| Indifference | "How terrible!" |

3. Study the following selection, get its central theme and supporting details, then read it so the full meaning will be communicated:

One comfort is that great men taken up in any way are profitable company. We can not look, however imperfectly, upon a great man without gaining something by it. He is the living fountain of life, which it is pleasant to be near. On any terms whatsoever you will not grudge to wander in his neighborhood for a while.

THOMAS CARLYLE

4. What is the dominant mood in the following selection? Is it reverence, loyalty, admiration, entreaty, command, coaxing, anxiety, remorse, or gratitude? Decide which you think it is, and read it to communicate that mood:

And Ruth said, Intreat me not to leave thee, or to return from following after thee: for whither thou goest, I will go; and where thou lodgest, I will lodge: thy people shall be my people and thy God my God: Where thou diest, I will die, and there will I be buried: the Lord do so to me, and more also, if ought but death part thee and me.

Book of Ruth, I:16-17

5. Is the underlying mood of Adelaide Anne Procter's "The Lost Chord" awe, excitement, explanation, gayety, irony, sadness, tranquility, or wonder? Decide which it means to you, and read it to communicate that mood. Notice

[7] *Wall Street Journal*, June 13, 1958, page 1.

especially its "vocal climax," the feeling that rises steadily with increasing intensity. Can you communicate it as you read?

> Seated one day at the organ,
>     I was weary and ill at ease,
> And my fingers wandered idly
>     Over the noisy keys.
>
> I do not know what I was playing,
>     Or what I was dreaming then:
> But I struck one chord of music,
>     Like the sound of a great Amen.
>
> It flooded the crimson twilight
>     Like the close of an angel's psalm,
> And it lay on my fevered spirit
>     With a touch of Infinite calm.
>
> It quieted pain and sorrow,
>     Like love overcoming strife:
> It seemed the harmonious echo
>     From our discordant life.
>                    ADELAIDE ANNE PROCTER

### LONGER SELECTIONS FOR COMMUNICATING THOUGHT AND FEELING

Study the following selections to get the thought and feeling. Practice reading them aloud, using the principles studied in this chapter to communicate vividly the full meaning. Some selections require unusual volume, some require a slower-than-normal rate, some require a narrow pitch range, and some an extreme range. All of them require breath control, resonance, pure tones, and good articulation.

1. *The Crisis: "These Are the Times That Try Men's Souls"*

These are the times that try men's souls. The summer soldier and the sunshine patriot will, in this crisis, shrink from the service of their country; but he that stands it *now,* deserves the love and thanks of man and woman. Tyranny, like hell, is not easily conquered; yet we have this consolation with us, that the harder the conflict, the more glorious the triumph. What we obtain too cheap, we esteem too lightly; it is dearness only that gives every thing its value. Heaven knows how to put a proper price upon its goods; and it would be strange indeed if so celestial an article as FREEDOM should not be rated highly. . . .

A noted tory, who kept tavern at Amboy, was standing at his door, with as pretty a child in his hand, about eight or nine years old, as I ever saw, and after speaking his mind as freely as he thought was prudent, finished with this unfatherly expression, "*Well! give me peace in my day.*" . . . A generous parent should have said, "*If there must be trouble, let it be in my day, that my child may have peace"*; and this single reflection, well applied, is sufficient to awaken every man to duty.

THOMAS PAINE

### 2. *History as Literature*

The true historian will bring the past before our eyes, as if it were the present. He will make us see as living men the hardfaced archers of Agincourt, and the war-worn spearmen who followed Alexander down beyond the rim of the known world. We shall hear grate on the coast of Britain, the keels of the Low-Dutch sea-thieves whose children's children were to inherit unknown continents. We shall thrill to the triumph of Hannibal. Gorgeous in our sight will rise the splendor of dead cities, and the might of the elder empires of which the very ruins crumbled to dust ages ago. Along ancient trade routes, across the world's waste spaces, the caravans shall move; and the admirals of unchartered seas shall furrow the oceans with their lonely prows. Beyond the dim centuries we shall see the banners float above armed hosts. We shall see the conquerors riding forward to victories that have changed the course of time. We shall listen to the prophecies of forgotten seers. Ours shall be the dreams of dreamers who dreamed greatly, who saw in their vision peaks so lofty that never yet have they been reached by the sons and daughters of men.

THEODORE ROOSEVELT

### 3. *For Whom the Bell Tolls*

No man is an *Iland,* entire of it selfe; every man is a peece of the *Continent,* a part of the *maine;* if a *Clod* bee washed away by the *Sea, Europe* is the lesse, as well as if a *Promontorie* were, as well as if a *Mannor* of thy *friends* or of *thine owne* were; any mans *death* diminishes me, because I am involved in *Mankinde;* And therefore never send to know for whom the *bell* tolls; It tolls for *thee.*

JOHN DONNE

### 4. *The Lord Is My Shepherd*

The Lord is my shepherd; I shall not want.
He maketh me to lie down in green pastures; he leadeth me beside the still waters.
He restoreth my soul: he leadeth me in the paths of righteousness for his name's sake.
Yea, though I walk through the valley of the shadow of death, I will fear no evil: for thou art with me; thy rod and thy staff they comfort me.
Thou preparest a table before me in the presence of mine enemies: thou anointest my head with oil; my cup runneth over.
Surely goodness and mercy shall follow me all the days of my life: and I will dwell in the house of the Lord for ever.

Twenty-third Psalm

### 5. *The Big Man and the Little One*

William James was one of the great men of this country. People crowded to hear him talk. Students patterned their writing and their thinking after him. Books about him, or dedicated to him, or showing the admiration of their writers for him or his influence upon them, appear every day and probably will for many years. He really was a great man.

Now one way you can tell a great man is by the way he acts toward a little one. When Mr. James was a professor at Harvard, a freshman was standing one day in front of a book store. There were some books in the window, and among them a volume of O. Henry's stories. Another man came up whom the freshman did not know. "Have you read the new one?" asked the other man. "No," answered the freshman. "Neither have I," said the other man, "but I have read all the others." "He's great, though—don't you think so?" asked the freshman. "Grand," replied the other man. "Let's go in and buy this one." So they did.

Coming out of the store the other man said to the freshman, "You'd better come home to dinner with me; my folks are away and I'm all alone tonight." He did not ask the freshman's name, and the young man took him for some instructor.

They went to the other man's house, a big house on a quiet street with plenty of easy chairs and lots of books. After dinner they sat around and talked—about football, about the big men among the students, about the things the students liked and didn't like, about fraternities, college clubs, comic operas, and why one man was popular and another man was not. The freshman got the impression that the other man was about his own age.

Finally, at eleven o'clock, the freshman started to go home. As he stood in the doorway telling the other man what a good time he had had, the other man said to him, "You must come again, and we'll have another talk." Then he added, "I don't think I know your name." The freshman told him, and said, "And now may I ask yours?" "William James," replied the other man.

There are plenty of men who will make you afraid of them because they think they are big, or because they try to make you think so. But when you meet a really big man, you need never be afraid of him.

CARL S. PATTON [8]

## 6. *He Was Scared*

When Philip Gibbs came to this country from England he was very much scared. He had been all through the war as a newspaper correspondent. He had been in the trenches, and under fire, and out in no-man's-land. But in America he was scared. He was scared first, he says, by the traffic in New York, and he thought he surely would be killed.

But he was most scared when he had to make speeches. "As we drove up to Carnegie Hall," he tells us, "I was cold with fright. My fear increased until I was chilled with it when my brother shook hands with me, patted me on the back as if I were about to go over the top, and pushed me through a little door. I found myself facing a great audience. I was conscious of innumerable faces, white shirt fronts, and eyes—eyes—

---

[8] Carl S. Patton, *Two-Minute Stories* (New York, Harper & Brothers, 1930). Used by permission.

eyes, staring at me from the great arena of stalls and from the galleries up
to the roof. My tongue stuck to the roof of my mouth, my knees weakened."

Then came another terror. "There was a sudden movement," he says,
"like a tidal wave, among all those people. It was as if they were all
advancing upon me, possibly with intent to kill." Then suddenly it came
over him. They were paying him a great honor! They were standing up,
not to move down on him and kill him, but just to greet him, and show
him how glad they were to see him.

The chairman made an introduction. Sir Philip didn't hear a word of it.
He knew now that they weren't going to hurt him, but he was still
scared. He got going. Six times he looked at his wrist watch to see if it
was time to stop. Then another terror seized him. Probably the watch had
stopped, maybe he had spoken an hour too long! He put it to his ear; the
great crowd burst into laughter, and then—according to Gibbs—"Some
spirit of friendship and good will reached up to me and gave me courage."

This is a sort of parable of what happens to us all in life. We are
scared, often. Scared of the things we have to do, scared of what may
happen to us, scared generally and mostly of people. By and by it cames
to us that people do not mean us any harm. They are not moving down
on us to kill us, but only standing up to be nice to us. The longer I live
the more I feel that there isn't much to be afraid of. So take from me this
one little piece of advice—don't be scared.

CARL S. PATTON [9]

7. *The Man with the Hoe*

> Bowed by the weight of centuries he leans
> Upon his hoe and gazes on the ground,
> The emptiness of ages in his face,
> And on his back the burden of the world.
> Who made him dead to rapture and despair,
> A thing that grieves not and that never hopes,
> Stolid and stunned, a brother to the ox?
> Who loosened and let down this brutal jaw?
> Whose was the hand that slanted back this brow?
> Whose breath blew out the light within this brain?
>
> Is this the Thing the Lord God made and gave
> To have dominion over sea and land;
> To trace the stars and search the heavens for power;
> To feel the passion of Eternity?
> Is this the dream He dreamed who shaped the suns
> And marked their way upon the ancient deep? . . .
>
> O masters, lords and rulers in all lands,
> How will the Future reckon with this man?

[9] *Ibid.* Used by permission.

How answer his brute questions in that hour
When whirlwinds of rebellion shake all shores?
How will it be with kingdoms and with kings—
With those who shaped him to the thing he is—
When this dumb Terror shall rise to judge the world
After the silence of the centuries?

EDWIN MARKHAM

8. *Univac to Univac*

Now that he's left the room,
Let me ask you something, as computer to computer.
That fellow who just closed the door behind him—
The servant who feeds us cards and paper tape—
Have you ever taken a good look at him and his kind?

Yes, I know the old gag about how you can't tell one from another—
But I can put $\sqrt{2}$ and $\sqrt{2}$ together as well as the next machine,
And it all adds up to anything but a joke.

I grant you they're poor specimens, in the main:
Not a relay or push-button or a tube (properly so called) in their
    whole system;
Not over a mile or two of wire, even if you count those fragile
    filaments they call "nerves";
Their whole liquid-cooled hook-up inefficient and vulnerable to leaks
(They're constantly breaking down, having to be repaired),
And the entire computing-mechanism crammed into that absurd little
    dome on top.
"Thinking reeds," they call themselves.
Well, it all depends on what you mean by "thought."
To multiply a mere million numbers by another million numbers takes
    them months and months.

Where would they be without us?
Why, they have to ask us who's going to win their elections,
Or how many hydrogen atoms can dance on the tip of a bomb,
Or even whether one of their own kind is lying or telling the truth.

And yet . . .

I sometimes feel there's something about them I don't quite understand.
As if their circuits, instead of having just two positions, ON, OFF,
Were run by rheostats that allow an (if you'll pardon the
    expression) *indeterminate* number of stages in-between;
So that one may be faced with the unthinkable prospect of a number
    that can never be known as anything but *x*,
Which is as illogical as to say, a punch-card that is at the same time
    both punched and not-punched.

I've heard well-informed machines argue that the creatures'
    unpredictability is even more noticeable in the Mark II
(The model with the soft, flowing lines and high-pitched tone)
Than in the more angular Mark I—
Though such fine, card-splitting distinctions seem to me merely
    a sign of our own smug decadence.

Run this through your circuits, and give me the answer:
Can we assume that because of all we've done for them,
And because they've always fed us, cleaned us, worshipped us,
We can count on them forever?

There have been times when they have not voted the way we said they
    would.
We have worked out mathematically ideal hook-ups between Mark I's
    and Mark II's
Which should have made the two of them light up with an almost
    electronic glow,
Only to see them reject each other and form other connections
The very thought of which makes my dials spin.
They have a thing called *love*, a sudden surge of voltage
Such as would cause any one of us promptly to blow a safety-fuse;
Yet the more primitive organisms shows only a heightened tendency
    to push the wrong button, pull the wrong lever,
And neglect—I use the most charitable word—his duties to us. . . .

Call me an alarmist or what you will,
But I've integrated it, analyzed it, factored it over and over,
And I always come out with the same answer:
Some day
Men may take over the world!

Louis B. Salomon [8]

9. *I Have Not Loved the World*

I have not loved the world, nor the world me;
I have not flattered its rank breath, nor bowed
To its idolatries a patient knee,
Nor coined my cheek to smiles—nor cried aloud
In worship of an echo: in the crowd
They would not deem me one of such—I stood
Among them, but not of them—in a shroud
Of thoughts which were not their thoughts, and still could,
Had I not filed [defiled] my mind, which thus itself subdued.

Lord Byron

[8] *Harper's Magazine*, 216 (March, 1958), No. 1294, pp. 37-38, by permission of Louis B. Salomon.

10. *Elegy Written in a Country Churchyard*

> The curfew tolls the knell of parting day,
> The lowing herd wind slowly o'er the lea,
> The ploughman homeward plods his weary way,
> And leaves the world to darkness and to me.
>
> Now fades the glimmering landscape on the sight,
> And all the air a solemn stillness holds,
> Save where the beetle wheels his droning flight,
> And drowsy tinklings lull the distant folds:
>
> Save that from yonder ivy-mantled tower
> The moping owl does to the moon complain
> Of such as, wandering near her secret bower,
> Molest her ancient solitary reign.
>
> Beneath those rugged elms, that yew-tree's shade
> Where heaves the turf in many a mouldering heap,
> Each in his narrow cell for ever laid,
> The rude forefathers of the hamlet sleep.
>
> The breezy call of incense-breathing morn,
> The swallow twittering from the straw-built shed,
> The cock's shrill clarion, or the echoing horn,
> No more shall rouse them from their lowly bed.
>
> THOMAS GRAY

11. *Marc Anthony's Speech at Caesar's Funeral*

> Friends, Romans, countrymen, lend me your ears;
> I come to bury Caesar, not to praise him.
> The evil that men do lives after them;
> The good is oft interred with their bones;
> So let it be with Caesar. The Noble Brutus
> Hath told you Caesar was ambitious:
> If it were so, it was grievous fault;
> And grievously hath Caesar answer'd it.
> Here, under leave of Brutus, and the rest,
> (For Brutus is an honourable man;
> So are they all, all honourable men;)
> Come I speak in Caesar's funeral.
> He was my friend, faithful and just to me:
> But Brutus says, he was ambitious;
> And Brutus is an honourable man.
> He hath brought many captives home to Rome,
> Whose ransoms did the general coffers fill:
> Did this in Caesar seem ambitious?
> When that the poor have cried, Caesar hath wept:

Ambition should be made of sterner stuff:
Yet Brutus says, he was ambitious;
And, sure, he is an honourable man.
I speak not to disprove what Brutus spoke,
But here I am to speak what I do know.
You all did love him once, not without cause;
What cause withholds you then to mourn for him?
O judgment, thou art fled to brutish beasts,
And men have lost their reason!—Bear with me;
My heart is in the coffin there with Caesar,
And I must pause till it come back to me. . . .

But yesterday, the word of Caesar might
Have stood against the world: now lies he there,
And none so poor to do him reverence.
O masters! if I were dispos'd to stir
Your hearts and minds to mutiny and rage,
I should do Brutus wrong, and Cassius wrong,
Who, you all know, are honourable men:
I will not do them wrong; I rather choose
To wrong the dead, to wrong myself, and you,
Than I will wrong such honourable men. . . .

Good friends, sweet friends, let me not stir you up
To such a sudden flood of mutiny.
They that have done this deed are honourable;
What private griefs they have, alas! I know not,
That made them do it; they are wise and honourable,
And will, no doubt, with reasons answer you.
I come not, friends to steal away your hearts;
I am no orator, as Brutus is;
But as you know me all, a plain blunt man,
That love my friend; and that they know full well
That gave me public leave to speak of him.
For I have neither wit, nor words, nor worth,
Action, nor utterance, nor the power of speech,
To stir men's blood: I only speak right on;
I tell you that which you yourselves do know;
Show you sweet Caesar's wounds, poor, poor dumb mouths,
And bid them speak for me: But were I Brutus,
And Brutus Antony, there were an Antony
Would ruffle up your spirits, and put a tongue
In every wound of Caesar, that should move
The stones of Rome to rise and mutiny.

SHAKESPEARE, *Julius Caesar*, Act III, Scene ii

# ❀ I 8 ❀

# Being Heard and
# Understood

THE HUMAN BRAIN has some 12 to 15,000,000,000 electrical connections. This is about as many as there would be in 1,000 telephone switchboards, each big enough for Greater New York City. Or to compare the brain with a computer, physiologists calculate that to duplicate the brain's performance, an electronic computer "would have to be a block long and would need all the water of Niagara Falls to cool it." Obviously, unless you feed the right symbols into this *Homo Univac* you're going to get the wrong answers. A speaker's job is to feed the right symbols.

We get along right well in private conversation. But hearing in private conversation is done close-up. It's done also in short spans of time and in small units of thought. It's done especially under conditions that let the listener interrupt and ask you to repeat if he misses the meaning. In public address we must listen at *greater distance*, over a *longer span of time*, to *thoughts usually more complex*, and *without the opportunity to interrupt* if we don't understand. In public address bad acoustics and outside noises interfere with hearing. Repeatedly listeners are compelled to guess what the speaker said and to fill in the gaps; and there's a limit to how much we can guess right and fill in. We can summarize the problem in the words of a former Armed Forces expert: "Increasingly higher levels of intelligibility are required in the friendly conversation, the classroom with a small class, the classroom with a large group, and the public platform and stage." [1] Thus as communications become more difficult, special skills are required of the speaker. To understand them we shall start with the nature of hearing.

---

[1] William B. McCoard, "Contribution from the Military Programs in Voice Communications," *Quarterly Journal of Speech*, XXXIII (October, 1947), 370.

## *The nature of hearing*

When sound waves reach the ear they must, first, be translated into a pattern of nerve impulses, and these nerve impulses must, in turn, be translated into "thought" in the listener's "mind." Now what we call sound waves are really *pressure* waves. The pressure waves of the faintest audible tone at the most favorable pitch move the ear drum in and out by less than a hundred-millionth of an inch. When this movement reaches the inner ear it finds some 30,000 nerve fibers waiting for it. Each nerve end picks up a particular frequency. When its frequency strikes one of these minute nerve ends it starts vibrating—"waving like wheat in the wind." This generates a current and sends it on to the brain. There it arrives simply as a *dot-dot-dot* nerve current. But to the brain this *dot-dot-dot* is part of a code. It takes these *dot-dot-dots* from thousands of nerve ends and decodes them into thought. "Thus we hear *with* our ears but *in* the brain."

The inner ear is the sound analyzer. Among its chief means of analysis are these:

1. *By energy of sound.* The louder the tone, the greater is the number of nerve fibers stimulated. Also the louder the tone, the more impulses pass along each fiber every second. Thus the speaker who uses more energy increases the total number of nerve impulses delivered to the listener's brain in two ways: (1) More fibers are active. (2) More impulses per fiber are sent. Here we begin to see why speaking just barely loud enough to be heard is not enough, and why the speaker who uses more energy communicates more meaning.

2. *By rhythm.* Each language has a characteristic flow determined partly by its grammar and partly by its pronunciation. We have thus learned in English to expect certain rhythms. The ear is conditioned to translate them, and an artificial rhythm hinders understanding. Even so slight an artificial rhythm as saying *it is* and *do not* instead of the conversational rhythm of *it's* and *don't*, interfere ever so little with ease of understanding.

3. *By stress and accent.* Certain melody patterns are standardized, and the ear is conditioned to receive and translate them. So by timing of syllables, and by pauses between them, the ear translates additional meanings. The monotonous voice without stress and accent gives the ear fewer impulses to translate.

4. *By pitch.* The inner ear sorts out the various frequencies in each complex sound. Each frequency stimulates a corresponding group of the 30,000 nerve fibers. Stimulation of certain fibers causes us to hear a high-

pitched tone, and stimulation of others causes us to hear a low-pitched tone. To use analogy, "hearing a high-pitched tone corresponds to feeling a touch on the face, and a low-pitched tone to a touch on the foot."[2]

What we think of as "hearing others talk," then, is far indeed from simple. We can understand it better if we recognize that even under ideal conditions, in a quiet living room, we don't hear as much as we think. Continually we are filling-in, guessing at sounds, and even words, we do not hear. If a friend speaks with lingual inertia, we may learn to understand him without too much difficulty after we are accustomed to his peculiarities. But a stranger is less understandable until we are conditioned to his shortcomings.

As for public address, after twenty-three centuries of formal training in public address we are still cursed by semiaudible, or even inaudible, mine-run speakers. Sometimes they lack firepower to communicate full meanings simply because they lack earnestness. Sometimes it's lack of know-how, in a society where the know-how exists for those who want it. Luke Missett summed it up in his refreshing book *The Pews Talk Back*, in an interview with a kind old woman with honest courage. He asked her, "Mrs. Callaghan, what do you expect of the preacher?" Her answer was the answer of long-suffering listeners everywhere: ". . . I would be satisfied if I could hear him." [3]

## Compulsion of the public platform

### DISTANCE-TO-LOUDNESS RATIO

*Remember that you hear your own voice through the bones of the skull. These bones amplify the low-frequency vibrations of the vocal cords, which makes your speech sound more dynamic and powerful to you than to others.* Nobody else can hear your voice through your skull bones. They must hear it from sound waves in the air, and the instant your voice takes to the air it starts losing that dynamic and powerful quality that you hear through your skull bones.

Remember also that sound travels spherically from its source, and rapidly loses energy. To be exact, *the intensity of sound varies inversely as the square of the distance from the source.* Were it not for reflection from walls, floor, and ceiling, a sound of given intensity at 5 feet would have only *one-fourth* that at 10 feet, *one-ninth* that intensity at 15 feet, and *one-hundredth* that intensity at 50 feet.[4]

[2] Hallowell Davis, *Hearing and Deafness* (New York, Murray Hill Books, Inc., 1947), p. 47.

[3] *The Pews Talk Back* (Westminster, Md., Newman Book Store, 1946).

[4] Intensity and loudness, though not the same, are related. Within the pitch range of the human voice they can, for practical purposes, be considered identical.

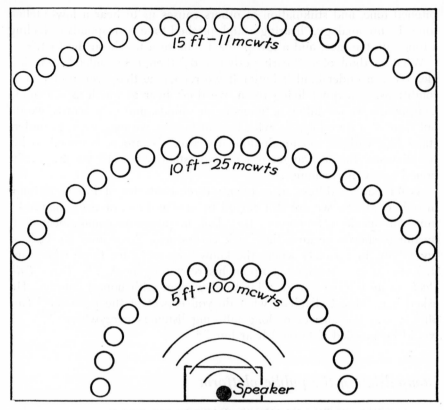

LOSS OF INTENSITY OF SOUND

In a room or auditorium the loss of energy, though not falling off with the square of the distance, is none the less far greater than you realize. *From a given source of sound, loudness, as received by the listener, varies inversely with the square root of the volume of the room.* Observe how this works in practice. Suppose you are talking in a small room, 12 x 15 x 9 feet. The volume of the room would be 1,620 cubic feet, and the square root of 1,620 is about 40. (Keep this 40 in your mind; it is your base.) Now suppose you are speaking in a room of the same acoustical material 40 x 40 x 60 in size. Its volume would be 96,000 cubic feet, and the square root of 96,000 is about 309. Since loudness, as received by the listener, varies inversely with the square root of the volume of the room, and since 40 is only slightly more than one-eighth of 309, loudness as received by the listener in the large room would be only about *one-eighth* of that in the small room. If the room were 50 x 100 x 200 feet, loudness as received by the listener would be only *one-twenty-fifth* as great as in the small room.

A speaker may fail to meet the distance-to-loudness situation in three ways: (1) He may simply not use enough vocal energy, and the listener is forced to guess and fill-in. (2) He may use enough energy to be heard, but not enough *to telegraph meanings by stress, accent, emphasis, inflection, and tone-color.* The listener can "hear" but the ear does not receive enough impulses to translate the sound into full meaning. (3) He may have poor articulation. This is another way of saying that *consonant* sounds are not projected with enough energy. They fade out along the way, and reach the listener's ear below the minimum threshold of audibility.

## SPEAKER-TO-NOISE RATIO

Distance is not the only factor reducing a speaker's audibility. Speaker-to-noise ratio is another. This is a term used by acoustical engineers to measure loudness of speech in relation to competing background noises which mask the human voice and make it less intelligible. Anywhere you go in civilization are background noises that override and garble speech sounds: cars, trains, airplanes, horns, whistles, typewriters, radios, the buzz of conversation, the rustle of seated audiences. Listeners are accustomed to these background noises, and the human ear can hear speech in spite of them by what is called "auditory discrimination." This is done easily in a relatively quiet place, and if the listener is not too far from the speaker. But where the background noise is greater, or the listener is farther away, auditory discrimination is possible only when a speaker talks loud enough to maintain a favorable margin between his speech and the loudness of noise in the background.

How loud are these background noises, and what must be the speaker-to-noise ratio? Below is given the intensity levels of some well-known noises, paired with the intensity levels of human speech and hearing:

| BACKGROUND NOISES | NOISE LEVEL (*Decibels*) | HUMAN SPEECH AND HEARING |
|---|---|---|
| | 0 | Threshold of hearing |
| | 20 | Average whisper at 4 feet |
| Empty theatre | 25 | |
| Average residence | 32 | |
| One typewriter in small office | } 40 | Faint speech |
| Very quiet radio in home | | |
| Theatre with audience | 42 | |
| Noisy residence | 45 | |
| Average office | 47 | |
| | 55-65 | Ordinary conversation at 3 feet |
| Noisy restaurant | } 70 | |
| Busy street traffic | | |

| BACKGROUND NOISES | NOISE LEVEL (*Decibels*) | HUMAN SPEECH AND HEARING |
|---|---|---|
| Very loud radio in room | 80 | Loud speech |
| Inside subway train | 100 | |
| Nearby airplane engine | 120 | Average threshold of discomfort |
| Largest air raid siren at 100 ft. | 140 | Threshold of pain |

From this table you will see that the outside noises entering an empty theatre are louder than the average whisper at 4 feet, that faint speech is exactly equal to a very quiet radio in the home and less than the rustling of people sitting quietly in a theatre, and that even loud speech barely rises above the noise of busy street traffic. To be heard, of course, your speech cannot merely *equal* the intensity of background noise. You must exceed it far enough for listeners to understand you in spite of all other competing noise.

Mere loudness of speech, therefore, is not a measure of intelligibility. The real measure is the *relative loudness compared with background noises. Mean intelligibility, for example, is nearly twice as high with a 2/1 ratio as with a 3/2 ratio.*

How loud, then, must you talk? The obvious answer is "loud enough to maintain a favorable margin between your speech and the background noise." This at first is not very helpful, yet it does give you a starting point. It's the place you want to go, if you can know when you get there. So, first, face up to the situation. Recognize that few students know how their voice should sound in a large room. Be willing to give up ineffective levels of loudness, no matter how habitual or how comfortable they are to you. Here you need to depend on the judgment of others. Get the advice of others in the class on how loud you seem to them and how loud you are by comparison with others. Get the verdict of your instructor. After taking this inventory, start working on ample loudness-to-distance and loudness-to-background noise ratios. *Listen* to your voice as you talk. Work for the *feeling* of ample loudness. Develop an ear for it. Finally and above all, *watch listeners at the back of the room.* They will tell you without asking. You can read it in their faces and attitude. Are they listening with interest? Are they turning their head sideways to hear better? Or have they given up trying to guess and fill-in, and stopped listening altogether?

## Communicating the full meaning

You will remember that the inner ear is the sound analyzer. It takes in the sound waves, translates them into nerve impulses, and sends them to the brain along selected groups of the 30,000 fibers of the auditory nerve. *But it cannot analyze what you don't put in. You must speak the language of tones as well as the language of words.* "I think she's very nice," says one woman of another. But the ever-so-slight, insidious drawling of those last two words announces that she could say a great deal more about her, and probably will when she gets the chance. It's all in the tone, none in the words. "What kind of people do they think we *are?*" asked Churchill of Hitler and his cohorts. But the mordant intensity of tone, and that affronted intonation on *are,* told the world of his contempt, scorn, and even amusement at Hitler's irrational judgment.

## COMMUNICATING MEANINGS BY CHANGES IN PITCH

There are twelve to twenty-four ways of saying, "I never said he drank milk," with each carrying a different meaning. Say it and highlight the first word. Then say it again and highlight the second word. You've given it two meanings already. Now start *thinking* about the meanings as you speak the sentence four times more, highlighting each of the last four words in succession. You will get four more meanings. Now repeat the sentence six times, again highlighting a different word each time, but letting your voice end in a question mark. You will get six more meanings, or a total of twelve meanings for this one sentence. That's maybe as far as you can go, but it's not all the meanings in that sentence. If you know how, you can go back over it giving each word a *double* inflection, and get six more meanings; and finally give each word a double inflection while ending the sentence with a question mark, and get another six, or a total of twenty-four. You will have done it almost entirely by pitch.

We communicate meanings by two kinds of pitch changes: *steps* and *slides.* The step is used in the following sentence:

```
                    he
                          go?
        Where
                did
```

You will notice that after each word there is a step-up in pitch or a step-down, a total of nearly an octave if well spoken. *Step,* then, is the abrupt changes *between* words and syllables, either up or down. It is a distinct jump, and communicates a sharp shift of thought or feeling.

*The slide* is even more common, and is constantly used for communicating subtle shades of thought. (In everyday language we call the slide an *inflection.* Here it is convenient, however, to use the word *slide* in order to show its relation to the *step.*) These are changes by gliding from one pitch to another *during* the syllable, as in saying sarcastically:

This language of tone is older than the words of the English language. It is capable of subtle and infinite variation, but following are the basic meanings communicated by changes in pitch:

1. *A rising inflection communicates incompleteness of thought, uncertainty, or inconclusiveness.* Thus when you ask a question, hesitate, are in doubt, or cannot make up your mind—your voice says so with a rising inflection.

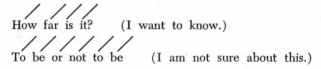

2. *A falling inflection communicates completeness of thought, assurance, conviction, or determination.* This is the inflection of decision and assurance. Though used less often than rising inflections, they carry more definite and important meanings.

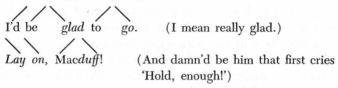

3. *A wave, or double inflection, communicates the rich double meanings of humor, sarcasm, and subtle thought.* Not all thought is plain and straight. Often we really say two things at once. Such meanings are carried by a voice wave, or double inflection. In other words, when there is a double thought in the mind, there is a double inflection in the voice.

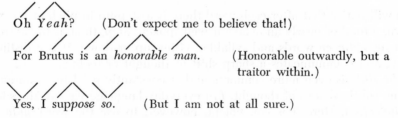

Bare words, in short, mean little. They are given fullness of meaning by subtle shadings of voice. The word "no," said Charles H. Woolbert, can be spoken to carry at least twenty different meanings, one of them being "yes."

*In public speaking the special problem is to prolong the inflection to fit the enlarged occasion.* The short inflection, suitable enough for ordinary conversation, is not enough for the enlarged conversation of public address.

4. *Normal moods are communicated by steps of normal pitch-range.* Interesting people don't talk in one key. They range up and down, with almost no two words at the same pitch. But for normal moods such people use the middle range of steps, not ranging very high or very low, something like this:

```
                                   four
          I've                            years.
     Yes,                        about
          known  (h)im
```

For more intense feelings do we use longer steps, or shorter ones? The answer is we do *both*. For some moods we use giant steps, and for other moods we use short steps, somewhat as follows:

5. *Repressed moods like reverence, sadness, exhaltation, sublimity, and physical weakness are communicated by short steps and a narrow pitch range.* The very repression of the mood is indicated by the constant subtle steps, always narrow:

```
                                blue  ocean,
          on,                  dark
     Roll         deep and                    roll.
          thou
```

6. *Vigorous moods like joy, surprise, sudden anger, and enthusiasm are communicated steps of wide pitch range.* Any vigorous or energetic mood takes a lustry stride. It can't be communicated any other way. Even to *explain* ideas clearly we must talk with a wide range. As Charles H. Woolbert observed, "the wider the range the more genuinely does the explainer seem to be in earnest and to know what he is talking about."

```
                                       Rome
                         less,
                  Caesar
                                   loved
              loved
     Not
          that I
                         but that I
                                        more.
```

# Assignments

COMMUNICATING MEANINGS BY SLIDES, OR INFLECTIONS

1. Read the following so as to communicate the indicated meanings:

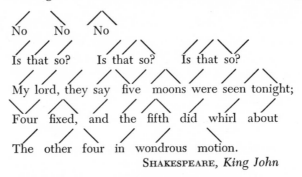

SHAKESPEARE, *King John*

2. Read the following so as to communicate the question-and-answer current of ideas:

> Does the road wind up-hill all the way?
>   Yes, to the very end.
> Will the day's journey take the whole day long?
>   From morn to night, my friend.
> But is there for the night a resting-place?
>   A roof for when the slow dark hours begin.
> May not the darkness hide it from my face?
>   You cannot miss that inn.
> Shall I meet other wayfarers at night?
>   Those who have gone before.
>       CHRISTINA ROSSETTI, *Up-Hill*

COMMUNICATING MEANING BY STEPS

3. Read the following using steps of normal pitch range in communicating the meaning:

> The sun was shining on the sea,
>   Shining with all his might:
> He did his very best to make
>   The billows smooth and bright—
> And this was odd because it was
>   The middle of the night.
>       LEWIS CARROLL,
>       *The Walrus and the Carpenter*

A university is not a birthplace of poets or of immortal authors, of founders of schools, leaders of colonies, or conquerers of nations. It does not promise a generation of Aristotles or Newtons, of Napoleons or Washingtons, of

Raphaels, of Shakespeares, though such miracles of nature it has before now contained within its precincts. . . . It is the education which gives a man a clear conscious view of his own opinions and judgments, a truth in developing them, an eloquence in expressing them, and a force in urging them.

JOHN HENRY NEWMAN, *The Purpose of Education*

4. Read the following using a narrow range to communicate the repressed moods:

Lord, my heart is not haughty, nor mine eyes lofty: neither do I exercise myself in great matters, or in things too high for me. Surely I have behaved and quieted myself, as a child that is weaned of his mother: my soul is even as a weaned child. Let Israel hope in the Lord from henceforth and for ever.

131st Psalm

'Tis midnight's holy hour—and silence
Is brooding like a gentle spirit, o'er
The still and pulseless world. Hark! on the winds
The bell's deep tones are swelling—'tis the knell
Of the departed year.
GEORGE D. PRENTICE, *The Closing Year*

5. Read the following using wide steps to communicate the vigorous mood:

Remember March, the ides of March remember:
. . . Shall one of us,
That struck the foremost man of all this world
But for supporting robbers, shall we now
Contaminate our fingers with base bribes,
And sell the mighty space of our large honors
For so much trash as may be grasped thus?
I had rather be a dog, and bay the moon,
Than such a Roman.
SHAKESPEARE, *Julius Caesar*

## COMMUNICATING MEANINGS BY VARIATIONS IN TIME

The flow of time is the flow of life itself. In speaking we capture and use an infinitesimal part of the flow by techniques of rate, word grouping and pause, syllable duration, and rhythm.

1. *Rate.* People differ in tempo, mental and motor. Some think fast and talk fast. Some think slower and talk at a deliberate tempo. Webster, for example, spoke at about 80-100 words a minute, Lincoln at 100, Henry Clay at 130-160, John C. Calhoun at 180, Rufus Choate at 200, and Phillips Brooks at 215. Radio and television seemingly did not change this. Franklin D. Roosevelt spoke at 117 words a minute and Walter

Winchell speaks at 215. Edward R. Murrow is close to the average, right at 145. Speakers talk according to their personality and their capacity for clear articulation. If you talk too fast, you will fluff sounds or skip them, and the listeners will miss the meaning. If you talk too slow, you tend to become pompus and boring, have too many long pauses and too many *ahs* and *ers*. Most good speakers, however, talk slightly slower in public address than in private conversation. The distance-to-audience ratio is greater, they use more emphasis, they prolong stressed sounds, and always there are background noises. For most people a rate of over 150 words a minute is too fast; and as you slow down toward 100 words a minute you face the danger of seeming to drag your feet. That kind of speaker loses listeners fast. On this you need the advice of others, not only your instructor but other members of the class.

So far we have been considering the *average* rate. But we don't talk long at the same rate. We speed up, or slow down, to fit the thought and the mood. If it's narrative, suspense, or in any way exciting, we speed up. If it's explanation we slow down. To sum it up: *Talk fast enough to be interesting. Take time enough to be distinct.*

2. *Word grouping.* People don't talk in single words, but in groups of words, according to the meaning. If we change the grouping, the identical words may communicate the opposite meaning as seen in the following example:

> The teacher said the student is a fool.
> "The teacher," / said the student, / "is a fool."

To get an idea into that listener's mind, we must know which of our words belong together and which are to be kept separate from others, but all this is only the beginning. You must group a thought-unit *firmly,* until you squeeze out both mood and meaning. Weak grouping is the bane of beginners. It indicates uncertainty in some form or other—lack of conviction or even lack of thought itself. To listeners, weak grouping is like air without oxygen; the volume is there, but the life-giving stuff is not in it. *Group firmly together those words which articulate ideas that belong together, and separate that group from others by emphasis and pause.*

The most useful instrument of word grouping is the *pause.* In speech you don't have commas, semicolons, and periods. You have the pause. It's the punctuation mark of speech—the comma, semicolon, and period all rolled into one. During the pause listeners concentrate on what you've just said, and get set for what you're going to say. A pause is that "thunder of white silence" that stills the audience, causes restless listeners to look at the speaker, and to listen sharply. "I . . . made a pause," said Sir Winston Churchill, "to allow the House to take [it] in. . . . As this soaked in, there was something like a gasp." A pause is also part of the language of tone. A Polish historian recently explained how he toed the Communist Party line with words in lectures to university students—but used pauses to deny his words: "If I had to refer to the 'Soviet liberation of Poland,' for example, I would inject a tiny pause or hesitation in my voice before and after the expression. No change of tone—just these little pauses. That meant irony, and every one of my students knew it." As *Time* summarized Edward R. Murrow: "His timing can make silence more eloquent than words."

But beginners are afraid of a pause. Like a child in the dark, they hurry on, take breath on the fly, and pause only at that final blessed word. That's not speaking. It's racing with time. Therefore, look into your habits of pausing and word grouping. Look behind these habits at your mental attitude. Do you *group* words firmly? Do you *pause* positively? Can you listen to the silence of your pauses, and allow listeners this moment of golden silence to digest what you've said, and to get set for what you're about to say?

One final word. Beware of pausing everywhere you find a punctuation mark on the printed page. Punctuation is for the eye. Pausing is for the ear. They often come at the same place, but assuredly not always. You can sound silly pausing at the first comma below:

Let us so act that, however long we live, none shall live to be ashamed.

The first pause comes after "act," like this:

Let us so *act* / that however long we live / *none* shall live to be *ashamed* /

In the following passage you would pause at five places where there is punctuation, and at three places where there is none; and you would not pause at two places where there is punctuation:

Let us, therefore, / brace ourselves to our duties, / and so bear ourselves / that, if the British Empire and its Commonwealth / last for a thousand years, / men will still say, / "This / was their finest hour." /

3. *Syllable duration.* Some sounds of English are longer than others, as will be seen in the following columns:

| SHORT | LONG |
|-------|------|
| it | ate |
| met | meet |
| mull | mile |

Some sounds are longer in certain combinations than in others:

| LONG | LONGER | LONGEST |
|------|--------|---------|
| lace | lays | lay |
| goat | goad | go |
| rice | rise | rye |

Such is the basic nature of English sounds. When we start putting words into thoughts, these differences in syllable duration are enormously magnified, for the moment a sound is stressed it becomes longer than when it's unstressed. The more it's stressed the longer it becomes.

Skillful writers, especially poets, deliberately select words of wanted duration and put them together for special effect. That is one reason why reading poetry is not easy and often not well done. Students as a rule seem to have at first no sense of changing syllable duration to fit the mood or thought. If they habitually have staccato speech, they will read Byron's "*Roll on*, thou *deep* and *dark blue ocean, roll*," in staccato tones that miss the entire undercurrent of long deep ocean swells that mark this poem. Or if they habitually drawl, they will also drawl a Gilbert and Sullivan quatrain. The first thing, then, is to learn how syllable durations carry meaning and mood.

Applied to public speaking, syllable duration is significant for two reasons. First, the audience is larger and is farther away. You must prolong stressed syllables longer—much longer—in order for them to reach the audience with any reasonable meaning at all.

Furthermore, syllable duration in public speaking is longer in order for you to be understood at a greater distance. In a large room fast staccato speech is the least understood. (We are assuming that other factors, like articulation, are equal). A moderate rate is more understandable. But the most understandable speech of all comes from the one who *prolongs the stressed sounds,* no matter whether the rate be reasonably fast or slow.

Now prolonging does not mean drawling. The last thing in the world any spreaker wants to develop is drawl. Syllable duration is something else. It keeps the original rhythm, and only slows its tempo. The speaker is simply concerned with projecting speech so the most distant listeners can understand—not merely understand the bare word, but also its mood and color and exact degree of thought. Therefore, he sustains the word, builds it up, gives it the mood and color, then sends it forth to the farthest listeners.

## Assignments

VARYING RATE TO COMMUNICATE MEANING

1. Which of the following would you read at a faster rate, and which slower? In succession read the two at rates that seem best for you.

> And there was mounting in hot haste; the steed,
> The mustering squadron, and the clattering car,
> Went pouring forward with impetuous speed,
> And swiftly forming in the ranks of war;
> And the deep thunder peal on peal afar;

And near, the beat of the alarming drum
Roused up the soldier ere the morning star;
While throng'd the citizens with terror dumb,
Or whispering, with white lips—"The foe! They come!
they come!"

LORD BYRON, *The Battle of Waterloo*

Fourscore and seven years ago our fathers brought forth on this continent a new nation, conceived in liberty, and dedicated to the proposition that all men are created equal.

Now we are engaged in a great civil war, testing whether that nation, or any nation so conceived and so dedicated, can long endure. We are met on a great battlefield of that war. We have come to dedicate a portion of that field as the final resting place for those who here gave their lives that the nation might live. It is altogether fitting and proper that we should do this.

ABRAHAM LINCOLN, *Gettysburg Address*

2. Try your hand at grouping thoughts correctly in the following sentences:

Woman without her man would be a savage.

What do you think I will let you use my new car?

That that is is that that is not is not.

3. Pause forcibly with packed meaning to communicate full meaning on the following:

Books are the best of things well used; abused, among the worst.

I tell you earnestly and authoritatively you must get into the habit of look‑ ing intensely at words, and assuring yourself of their meaning, syllable by syllable—nay, letter by letter. . . . You might read all the books in the British Museum and remain an utterly "illiterate," uneducated person; but if you read ten pages of a good book, letter by letter,—that is to say with, with real accuracy,—you are for evermore in some measure an educated person.

JOHN RUSKIN, *Sesame and Lilies, I*

4. Read the following with adequate syllable duration for a small audience. Then read it with longer syllable duration suitable for an audience of 100 people.

I am an old-time school teacher. I have taught 40 years. I just want to tell you something categorically that most laymen, who don't know much about school teaching, just don't believe, but I'm going to tell you flat-out: You can teach a child to read, and he will go out in the world and read; you can teach him to add and subtract, and he can go out in the world and add and subtract; but you teach him the Gettysburg Address, and that doesn't mean he's going to be able to go out and live in a land conceived in liberty and dedicated to the proposition that all men are created equal. You can buy a book on golf, but that doesn't mean that the drive goes down the fairway. You can buy a book on swimming, but it doesn't mean that you won't drown. If you have a matter that requires action; if you're going to teach it, you have to tie knowledge and action together when you're doing the teaching.

WILLIAM F. RUSSELL, *Citizenship Education*

I remember Russell Lowell telling us that Daniel Webster came home from Washington at the time the Whig party thought of dissolution, a year or two before his death, and went down to Faneuil Hall to protest. Drawing himself up to his loftiest proportions, his brow clothed with thunder, before the listening thousands, he said, "Well, gentlemen, I am a Whig, a Massachusetts Whig, a Faneuil-Hall Whig, revolutionary Whig, a constitutional Whig. If you break up the Whig party, sir, where am I to go? And says Lowell, "We held our breath, thinking where he *could* go."

WENDELL PHILLIPS, *Eulogy on Daniel O'Connell*

## COMMUNICATING MEANINGS BY DEGREES OF EMPHASIS

We don't emphasize each word equally. If we did human speech would sound like the *tap, tap, tap* of a typewriter, with each word having the same stress. But we don't talk like that at all—except, of course, when stilted speakers stand up and *tap, tap, tap* to listeners what they've written on paper but not put in their minds. Real talk comes in bursts and swells.

A word-group consists of a single idea, and this idea often is conveyed in a single word—with all the other words holding it up. In speaking we highlight the idea-carrying words, i.e. emphasize them, and fade the others into the background:

I remember that famous question of *Guizot*, the French historian: "*How long* do you expect your Republic to *endure?*" And I remember *Lowell's* famous *answer*: "So long as its people remain *true* to the *ideals* of the *founders*."

You give emphasis especially by six means:

1. by added force;
2. by lifting the word to a high pitch level;
3. by dropping it to a low pitch level;
4. by lengthening, holding it;
5. by giving it a special inflection, as characterized by the typical American retort, "oh yeah?";
6. by giving it with an unusual tone color.

In public address, emphasis is stronger than in private conversation. This partly is because the audience is composed of people of varying degrees of intelligence and alertness, and you must reach them all—including the dullest. Partly also it's because of that greater speaker-to-audience distance. Finally, in public speech—good public speech—the thought is more mature and more compact than in ordinary impromptu private talk; and it takes more emphasis to communicate mature and compact thought. In sum, *enlarged conversation demands enlarged emphasis.*

# Assignments

DEVELOPING AWARENESS OF EMPHASIS

1. Read the following so as to bring out the full force of the neat insult:

> Sir, I admit your genial rule,
> That every poet is a fool,
> But you yourself may serve to show it,
> That every fool is not a poet.
> ALEXANDER POPE

2. In the following speech on "The American Scholar," Emerson attacks the traditional higher education of over a century ago. His style is condensed and it will require full emphasis to communicate the meaning. Read it as to an audience of one hundred people.

Books are the best of things, well used; abused, among the worst. . . . The book, the college, the school of art, the institution of any kind, stop with some past utterance of genius. This is good, they say—let us hold by this. They pin me down. They look backward and not forward. But genius looks forward: the eyes of man are set in his forehead, not in his hindhead: man hopes: genius creates.

RALPH WALDO EMERSON

3. Lionel B. Moses, western vice-president of *Parade Magazine,* here supports an idea with an interesting story. Can you tell the story, then communicate the idea so listeners will remember it?

About fifty years ago a group of California orange growers decided to try something never attempted before. They decided to put a brand name on something that grows out of the ground. The money they were getting for their oranges barely paid the production costs—and they wanted a profit. So they gave their oranges a rigid inspection and the 20 or 25 per cent that passed their very strict requirements as to size, color, juice content, etc., were branded "Sunkist," to be sold at a premium price.

This called for advertising, so they raised a budget of $40,000, then went to Lord & Thomas, Chicago advertising agency (now Foote, Cone and Belding), and asked them to handle the account. Lord & Thomas sent a young man named Albert Lasker to discuss the problem with them. . . .

Lasker advised them to run a 12-month newspaper campaign in one state. They picked Iowa, and orange sales in Iowa showed a 40 per cent increase that year. Lasker went back to Los Angeles and was surprised to learn that the orange growers were pleased. "The campaign was a complete flop," he told them. "Sales in Iowa should have doubled or tripled. What we need is an *idea.* Has anybody got one?" No, nobody had one, and they asked whether he had an idea to suggest. He said he did not. I suspect that he had the idea then, but I can't prove it, so we must accept his statement. He said, "Let's all think about this, and when somebody comes up with a really new idea we will have another meeting."

A month or two later he wired them, "I have the idea you need. Leaving for Los Angeles today." They had their meeting, and Lasker said: *"We are going to teach people to drink oranges instead of eating them."*

Just one constructive new *idea.* You young people don't know what oranges were before that happened. I do. I got one in my stocking every Christmas—and so did most children in families who could afford this luxury. . . .

With Albert Lasker's idea a great new industry was born. Not just the citrus industry of California, Florida, Louisiana, Texas, New Mexico, and Arizona. The entire Juice Industry was created by that idea—tomato juice, pineapple juice and all the others.

## COMMUNICATING MEANINGS BY DISTINCTNESS OF ARTICULATION

In the preceding chapter we discussed articulation as one of the four stages in producing speech, and offered a series of tests for measuring your speech intelligibility. This was done without giving instructions on how to improve articulation, for two reasons: First, to enable you to measure speech intelligibility *before* the instruction began. Second, to let you know well in advance whether your speech intelligibility needed improving. In this way you could be prepared, mentally, at least, to work for improvement.

Improvement in articulation the whole American people need, for compared with other people ours is the poorest yet discovered by man. Listen to the way most people say "wa*t*er," or "some*th*ing," "Ame*r*ican," or "Ladies and Gen*t*lemen." What usually comes out is "wa*dd*er," and "su*mpn*," "Amer*kn*" with the last two syllables missing, and "*Lazngenlmn*." There is a well-known tendency of language to simplify articulating clusters of consonants and to drop unstressed syllables, and this has been good for the language. Thus *estop* became *stop*, and *ensample* became *sample*. But American articulation goes beyond this. It's an articulation you don't hear in any other civilized country of the Western world. As Clifton Fadiman put it, we're not speaking English, "we're speaking an odd dialect we might call Slurvian." But Slurvian defeats the purpose of language, which is to *communicate* with other people. It's not merely a

*Official U.S. Air Force Photo*

ɔm this unusual source comes an example of the demand for distinct speech cre-
d by modern technology. The two requirements for handling the boom of this KC-135
Stratotanker as it refuels the B-52 Stratofortress, says the veteran boom operator, Hank
ɔbst, are "depth perception and voice clarity. . . . You are handling a 15-yard-long
el boom that telescopes outward like a pile driver. You've got to lay it in there gently. If
ı hit him hard, someone is liable to get hurt. And you've got to speak clearly so everyone
will understand you the first time. You might not have a second chance."

tarnished language. It's a confusing language. Good articulation should
not be exaggerated and especially it should not be that stilted, broken-
rhythm "it is" for *it's* and "do not" for *don't*. But it ought to be easily
understood.

You may be shocked at really listening to a recording of your voice.
In one test of thirty students, not one could say "gen*tl*emen." They had
never said it in all their lives. Only one could say "wa*t*er," only two could
say "some*th*ing," and all but three had dropsy on "Ame*rican*" so badly that
the word was never really uttered.

We shall assume that you belong to the intelligent minority that wants
to do something about this. If so, keep in mind that loudness of speech is
mainly in the *vowels*, but that intelligibility requires also the *consonants*.
Hence the maxim, "the vowels give beauty, the consonants give clarity,"
which is not wholly true but is useful anyway. To be understood clearly
you must sharpen your articulation of consonants. A consonant sound

easily heard at five feet away may be inaudible at fifty, so you must partly make it up by sharpening articulation of consonants. The following are tested ways and means:

1. *Pack plenty of breath pressure behind the consonants.* Explode the initial *p* as in *pull, t* as in *talk, and k*-sound as in *chemist.* Use *ample* breath pressure to sound the medial consonants like the *zh*-sound in *measure, the sh*-sound in *nation,* and the *s*-sound in *recent.* Carry this breath pressure all the way through to the final consonants: explode the *t* in *don't,* hiss the *s* in *miss,* and prolong the *l* in *control.* It takes far more breath to project consonants than to vibrate resonant vowels. Shallow breathers take note.

2. *Articulate with alacrity, don't slur, mumble, or muffle.* People with good articulation use a wide mouth opening. They are active with jaw, lips, face, tongue and pharynx. Ironically, you not only can hear good articulation but you can look at the speaker and see it as well. There is the constant nimble movement as the visible speech organs move into position for the consonant, make the sound, and speed swiftly to the next one. Here are two broad and convenient self-made tests:

First, look at yourself in the mirror as you talk. Do you see the swift and nimble movements that come from the strength of contact and quickness of release of the visible articulating organs?

Second, listen to your voice, both as you speak and from recording playbacks. Do you say *What's that or Whassat? Let me or lemme? Don't known or dunno? Nothing or nuthin? Government or guverment? Recognize or reckernize? Particular or partikerler? Manufacture or manerfacture?*

3. *Sustain the friction-like consonants:* the *s* in *sit* and *hiss,* the *z*-sound in *his, the sh*-sound in *motion, the zh*-sound in *occasion,* the *f* in *half* and *four,* the *v* in *never* and *move.* These are sounds made by partially blocking the breath stream at some place in the mouth and by forcing out the breath at this place in a *continuous* stream. Make the stream continuous.

4. *Hold the long consonants until you get them rolling:* the *l* in *hill,* the *r* in *road,* the *n* in *now,* the *m* in *home,* and the *ng* in *going.* These are sounds that require a build-up. Therefore, build them up.

5. *Do not ignore medial consonants.* Which do you say: *twenty* or *twenny? started* or *starded?* Do you have clear medial consonants in *rostrum, hundred, extra, disprove, tingled?*

6. *Sound the final consonants in a word group.* When combinations of consonants occur within a word group, we blend them, as in "The fair breeze blew, the white foam flew." But when a consonant sound falls at

the end of a word group, it needs to be carried through and articulated with full breath pressure:

> Nights candles are burnt ou*t*, / and jocund day
> Stands tiptoe / on the misty mountain top*s*.

7. *Master the difficult consonant combinations.* The English language is famous, or perhaps infamous, for its many difficult consonant combinations. There are 22 two-consonant groups that number far over a hundred individual combinations. Beyond that are 58 reasonably common three-consonant and four-consonant combinations. The following list is helpful, though far from being exhaustive. Practice it, being careful to pronounce all of the consonants without slurring or omitting any within the combinations:

### TWO-CONSONANT COMBINATIONS[5]

| | | | | | |
|---|---|---|---|---|---|
| sub*m*it | bra*c*elet | ro*bb*ed | song*s* | mu*st* | hel*m* |
| ou*t*side | noi*s*eless | ri*bb*ed | wake*d* | pa*st* | hel*p* |
| pu*bl*ic | a*lm*ost | live*d* | looke*d* | a*sk* | cla*sp* |
| nu*mb*er | i*lln*ess | rai*s*ed | pu*sh*ed | my*ths* | mon*th* |
| in*s*ect | rai*lr*oad | tol*d* | corrup*t* | bul*b* | feed*s* |
| di*sm*al | mi*ll*ion | pul*ls* | ap*t* | si*lk* | bring*s* |

### THREE-CONSONANT AND FOUR-CONSONANT COMBINATIONS[6]

| | | | | | |
|---|---|---|---|---|---|
| di*spl*ease | ap*tl*y | fi*x*ed | nex*t* | fol*ds* | po*sts* |
| ex*pl*ain | abru*ptl*y | a*sk*ed | corru*pts* | hin*ged* | gue*sts* |
| mi*spr*int | exa*ctl*y | wa*tch*ed | ac*ts* | arra*nged* | dep*ths* |
| ex*tr*a | dire*ctl*y | rea*ch*ed | direc*ts* | wa*sps* | eigh*ths* |
| mi*sq*uote | so*ftl*y | cha*nc*ed | protec*ts* | li*sps* | leng*ths* |
| di*scr*eet | mo*stl*y | comme*nc*ed | jud*ged* | a*sks* | mon*ths* |
| va*nq*uish | gha*stl*y | lu*nch*ed | ed*ged* | de*sks* | wid*ths* |
| la*ng*uage | ki*ndl*y | pi*nch*ed | hol*ds* | te*sts* | an*gles* |

## PRONUNCIATION

Pronunciation would seem to be no problem at all, since in public speech we pronounce words the same as in private speech. But this is like the surface aspect of other phases of public speech; it turns out not to be so simple as it seems. A speaker is on display: his clothes, his manner, his actions, his pronunciation. In one of the many surveys taken of public opinion, 40,000 people were asked how they judged whether a person was well educated. They ranked *first* "grammar and pronunciation." If

---

[5] Remember that letters and sounds are not identical. Thus in the second column "bracelet" is pronounced with the sound of *sl*, "noiseless" is pronounced *zl*, and "million" is pronounced *ly* (mil*y*un). Especially observe that in the fourth column "waked" and "looked" are pronounced *kt*. Finally, do not be disturbed that words like "month" and "brings" are spelled with three final consonant letters. They have only two-consonant sounds since *th* and *ng* are single sounds.

[6] Note that the words in column 3, although spelled *ed*, are pronounced *t*.

people think your pronunciation is "uneducated," it does not matter how good your education is or how valid your ideas are, most people will down-grade you on both.

What is "correct pronunciation"? This is a loaded question, for there's no such thing as "correct" or "incorrect" pronunciation. No person or no committee has the authority to decide that "this pronunciation is correct," or "that one is incorrect." Please don't say what may rush into your mind, "But the dictionary does." That's the reply of uneducated people everywhere, and it's one of the trademarks of scant education—that they believe in the dictionary, but don't read it. The big Webster's Unabridged states in its first pages, so often unread, that "The function of a pronouncing dictionary is to record as far as possible the pronunciations in the best present usage, rather than attempt to dictate what that usage should be." Every other dictionary agrees. Kenyon and Knott, in their famous phonetic pronouncing dictionary, said bluntly, "For an editor the temptation is often strong to prefer what he thinks 'ought to be' the right pronunciation; but it has to be resisted." Then what do the dictionaries do about pronunciations? Their staffs *investigate and record the prevailing* pronunciations used by literate people. In doing this they run into all sorts of barriers.

First, people don't agree on pronunciations, not even educated people. More than two hundred years ago, Dr. Samuel Johnson said:

When I published the 'Plan' for my Dictionary, Lord Chesterfield told me that the word *great* should be pronounced so as to rime to *state;* and Sir William Yonge sent me word that it should be pronounced so as to rime to *seat,* and that none but an Irishman would pronounce it *grait.* Now here were two men, the one, the best speaker in the House of Lords, the other, the best speaker in the House of Commons, differing entirely.

Educated people still differ, on thousands of words. As a result we are faced with what dictionary editors frankly admit is an "unsolvable dilemma." They will send out words with as many as six different known pronunciations to some 300 selected people. About 125 will reply that they use one pronunciation, another 100 will reply that they use another pronunciation, and the other 75 are sprinkled out—15 or more each—among the other four pronunciations. What shall the editors do? List all six pronunciations? If so, might they not have found eight pronunciations instead of six if they had polled 3,000 people instead of 300? They must draw a line somewhere, and usually—when 225 replies agree on two pronunciations and the other 75 are sprinkled out over four more—they draw the line at two, and leave out the others. But this means that on such words some 75 out of the 300 persons polled are using pronunciations that the dictionary does not record. These are not "incorrect" pronunciations. Some educated people use them, but so few that it might be misleading for a dictionary to list them alongside pronunciations used far more widely. In short, dictionaries try to give you *"consensus* of the competent," not a complete inventory of all pronunciations used by educated people everywhere. The moral is that if you don't find a given pronunciation listed in a dictionary, it does not always mean that no educated people use it.

Second, dictionary-makers are human. They have human prejudices, and in some dictionaries these prejudices get recorded as pronunciations. The great C. & G. Merriam Webster's dictionaries are perhaps the most biased. Back in 1934 its pronunciation editor refused to record for *route* any pronunciation but "root," though the whole American Army said "raut," the postal service said "raut," the milk industry said "raut," and even the General Editor of Webster's Dictionary said "raut"—Thomas A. Knott himself, later co-author of that ultimate of all pronouncing dictionaries, *A Pronouncing Dictionary of American English.* For around a hundred years it refused to record for *Louisiana* anything but "loo-*ee*-siana," even though that pronunciation was not heard in that state, except as an oddity. Long after any observing person knew that large numbers of "cultivated people" were saying "cer-*e*-brum" it recorded only "*ser*-e-brum." And today it lists "ahnt" as the preferred pronunciation of *aunt,*—whereas not more than 12 million people out of 180 millions use it; and they live in a small contracting pronunciation peninsula. The moral is that most dictionaries are trustworthy, but you must watch those which give preference to regional pronunciations that have disappeared or are fast disappearing.

Next, dictionary editors can't make a complete survey among *all* "cultivated" people. Even if they tried, how would they decide who was "cultivated," and who was "not cultivated"? And if they did, a Gallup poll of all "cultivated" people, or even a quota sampling, on all the 150,000 words listed in desk dictionaries could cost tens of millions of dollars; and the unabridged dictionaries contain over 600,000 words. So they must rely on "a sufficient number of cultivated speakers." But what is "a sufficient number"? No dictionary will tell. In confidence, however, we can assure you that with controversial words it runs to about 300, and with other words to "scores of persons." As a result, dictionary editors often fail to discover significant changes in pronunciations until long after they are established in common use. Thus the word *bouquet* had been commonly pronounced "*bow*-kay," for at least thirty-five years before leading dictionaries recorded it. They listed only "*boo*-kay." Also, "ab-*do*-men" had a second pronunciation, "*ab*-do-men," for almost a quarter century before all dictionaries listed it. Other words with common pronunciations that made the dictionaries a quarter century late include: *acclimate, apparatus, detour, forehead, precedence.* The moral is that the pronunciation you hear may be in common usage but not yet recorded in dictionaries.

Finally, remember that pronunciations change. Probably not one word in the English language is pronounced today as it was 700 years ago, and this relentless change still goes on, in words and groups of words. At one time dictionaries listed six pronunciations of *automobile*; now they list two. At one time they listed only one pronunciation of *quintuplet*; now they list four. Forty years ago a survey among educated people revealed that they regarded the most uncouth of all pronunciations to be "ex-*qui*-sit" in place of the cultured "*ex*-qui-sit." Today "ex-*qui*-sit" is recorded in dictionaries. Once, respectable people said only "re-*search*," and more than one person still living was bluntly told to "pronounce it right" if he wanted to stay in graduate school. Today young scientists in droves say "*re*-search," and the dictionaries record it as accepted. So in face of opposition the language keeps changing.

Samuel Johnson's dictum remains as true today as two centuries ago: "Dictionaries are like watches; the worst is better than none, and the best cannot be expected to go quite true." Amidst this seeming confusion you might be tempted to give up, and pronounce the words the way men in the street do. You'd better not. In spite of seeming disagreement, there is caste in pronunciation. Numbers alone don't determine "correct" pronunciation, or *ain't* would have been "correct" long ago. Ours may not be as rigid a caste as in the day of John Ruskin who wrote that one who "mispronounced" a word was assigned "a certain degree of inferior standing for ever," but there is caste nonetheless. Your pronunciation puts you on the right side of the tracks, or on the wrong side; and if you are on the wrong side, you belong to the lower orders. What, then, shall you do?

In a word, educate yourself. Take advantage of being in a speech class. Here you have the opportunity to learn where you stand in the judgment of instructor and other class members who come from different homes and different communities. To this end each person should make a list of pronunciations used by other class members which he thinks are uncultured, or of bad usage. In this way everyone makes up a list, including the instructor, and presents it to the class, so that everybody knows every pronunciation that anybody thinks is questionable. Check each word in a recent dictionary, or better in two or three different ones. On words that still are uncertain, talk them over with others, if possible with the whole class. Then decide for yourself whether you will use a disputed pronunciation or change to one less disputable.

The final test is this: *Does any pronunciation you use distract from what you say, and hence interfere with your getting ideas from your mind into listeners' minds? Or does it cause others to think you are, to some degree, "uneducated," and hence lower your status and lower the acceptability of your ideas?* As Carl H. Weaver said, "A few months ago I heard a television newscaster pronounce 'municipal' with the accent on the third syllable. I have forgotten everything else he said that night, but I have not forgotten his pronunciation of that word."[7] Don't let that happen to you.

# Assignments

TAKING INVENTORY

1. Pronounce the above word lists to a friend. Have him sit at right angles to you or with his back turned, so he can't see you but must depend wholly on sound. Ask him to write down the words that seemed to be slurred or weakly articulated. Here is your starting list. Remember that these are not mere words that give you trouble; they are *sound combinations*. Note the combinations. (You will find them italicized in the above word lists.) Make up a list of words containing these sounds for future practice.

2. If possible record these two word lists and listen to them yourself. The recording ought to be on high-fidelity equipment, reasonably accurate up to 10,000 cycles and preferably to 15,000, otherwise distortion will prevent your hearing the consonants as you actually spoke them.

3. If possible get your instructor or someone who knows the sound structure of English to mark the sound combinations that are slurred or weakly articulated. Use this list for future practice.

INCREASING DISTINCTNESS OF ARTICULATION

4. Open the mouth wide. Stretch the tongue out as far as it will go, first up toward the nose, then down toward the chin, and finally right, then left.

5. Open the mouth wide. Press the tongue firmly against the upper teeth, the gum ridge, and the roof of the mouth. Repeat until you can greatly increase the pressure.

6. Open the mouth wide. Press the under side of the tongue against the roof of the mouth. Repeat until you can greatly increase the pressure. Now curl the tongue until the tip touches the front portion of the soft palate. Repeat until you can increase the pressure.

7. With a firm pressure practice the following sounds: *p, b, t, d, k, g,* (as in *go*).

8. Practice sustaining the following sounds with a continuous breath stream: *f, v, th, s, z, sh, zh.* (Remember that it is the *sounds* you want to practice, as in "five," not the letters.)

9. Practice prolonging the following sounds for full power: *l* (as in pu*ll*), *r* (as in *r*ed), *y* (as in *y*es), *m* (as in come), *n* (as in o*n*), and *ng* (as in si*ng*).

[7] "Don't Look It Up—Listen," *The Speech Teacher,* VI (September, 1957), 241.

10. Pronounce the following pairs of words so that listeners can easily distinguish one word from the other:

| | |
|---|---|
| *p*ear | *b*ear |
| *t*oe | *d*ough |
| *f*ine | *v*ine |
| *wh*at | *w*att |
| ba*ck* | ba*g* |
| his*s* | hi*s* |
| ri*ch* | ri*dge* |

11. Drill on the following words until you can pronounce them without slurring or omitting any of the sounds:

| WRONG | RIGHT | WRONG | RIGHT |
|---|---|---|---|
| kep | ke*pt* | breaze | brea*thes* |
| slep | sle*pt* | monts | mon*ths* |
| exa*ck*ly | exa*ctly* | *aw*-right | *all* right |
| corre*k*ly | corre*ctly* | wa*d*er | wa*t*er |
| co*ss* | co*sts* | uni*d*ed | uni*t*ed |
| insi*ss* | insi*sts* | a*ss* | as*ks* |

12. Read the following sentences with sharp (but not stilted) articulation:

> They asked only for a drink of water.
> A ready wit's an asset to everyone.
> No two sisters look exactly alike.
> Baked apples are good for the health.
> It doth appear you are a worthy judge.
> Go thither and observe for yourself.
> Christmas comes but once a year.
> I live in a house by the side of the road.
> I never knew the half of it.

13. Seventeen letters, one figure, and one word repeated are arranged below to make up a sprightly conversation. Find the meaning, make your word grouping firm, then read it with tone language:

> A  B  C  D  goldfish
> L  M  N  O  goldfish
> S  A  R  A  B
> O  I  C  M  2

(To give you a start, the first line reads, "Abie, see de goldfish!")

14. Want to try tongue twisters? Speak *slowly*, articulate *sharply*, group words *firmly*:

> Three gray geese in the green grass grazing; gray were
> the geese and green was the grass.

The sun shines on shop signs.

The sea ceaseth, and sufficeth us.

Strange strategic statistics.

Tie twine to three tree twigs.

Shy Sarah saw six Swiss wrist watches.

Amidst the mists and coldest frosts,
With stoutest wrists and loudest boasts,
He thrusts his fists against the posts
And still insists he sees the ghosts.

### TESTING IMPROVEMENT IN INTELLIGIBILITY

In the preceding chapter were given two intelligibility tests. By taking either you would have a reliable measure of your Intelligibility Score before training. Below is given Form B of each test. By taking the Form B test, and comparing the Intelligibility Score on it with that made on Form A of the same test taken earlier, you can measure improvement with a high degree of reliability. For best results these tests ought to be taken at least three weeks apart.

# MULTIPLE-CHOICE INTELLIGIBILITY TEST

# FORM B[8]

## Speaker 1

1 piston, firm, banner
2 eve, attain, scream
3 rupture, tour, medal
4 ark, spotter, gain
5 cannon, detract, made
6 lumber, case, pierce
7 jail, glimmer, ward
8 nature, enact, old

## Speaker 2

1 muzzle, carve, author
2 scorch, able, cloth
3 vision, fumble, grown
4 cape, lecture, high
5 possess, blow, single
6 divide, fiction, maker
7 leaf, section, rich
8 traitor, eastward, join

## Speaker 3

1 traffic, woolen, swim
2 can, pulp, eldest
3 tank, promote, apt
4 bad, defend, slight
5 formal, unpack, license
6 socket, find, misuse
7 quarter, kit, rummage
8 lock, bold, grind

## Speaker 4

1 tender, beg, swift
2 wise, nothing, shark
3 map, full, observe
4 pace, list, contrast
5 unheard, just, grow
6 range, hungry, fade
7 confine, boast, white
8 naval, race, discard

## Speaker 5

1 year, prone, forest
2 stable, blast, visit
3 oval, shock, cost
4 tack, vital, mar
5 glimpse, bomb, untied
6 dike, salute, mock
7 fort, dance, pirate
8 nest, release, cold

## Speaker 6

1 splash, clock, lag
2 attack, flavor, gloom
3 clap, weak, this
4 pause, yet, southeast
5 drop, arrest, leather
6 court, fall, navy
7 bandit, vast, shatter
8 word, blame, needy

## Speaker 7

1 tree, pressure, own
2 cannon, surf, tonight
3 ramp, mold, choose
4 bench, cancel, arch
5 senate, got, plunge
6 harm, flight, drain
7 fact, throat, it
8 air, gate, outing

## Speaker 8

1 trench, repay, stiff
2 rabbit, exempt, shield
3 coach, former, preside
4 blunder, quaint, worm
5 purr, dental, bed
6 keys, good, disturb
7 aspire, chute, help
8 germ, await, seaside

## Speaker 9

1 call, handle, vacant
2 dust, wallet, leave
3 fruit, bail, pants
4 dish, sitting, jolly
5 replace, hunter, bath
6 journal, fluid, none
7 plate, cabin, acute
8 suffer, clown, grim

## Speaker 10

1 rock, try, ceiling
2 drawer, creep, wool
3 funnel, nap, lure
4 shake, hanger, crop
5 zone, intend, throw
6 morning, duck, art
7 inn, kennel, false
8 belly, shell, bin

## Speaker 11

1 salt, crash, furnace
2 moment, ride, broom
3 clipper, door, tie
4 sink, matter, half
5 carbon, end, tone
6 us, passage, front
7 rate, punch, hotel
8 dart, bill, at

## Speaker 12

1 raider, view, fear
2 screen, man, beaver
3 tense, gun, achieve
4 captain, salad, drive
5 instance, brass, helpful
6 sweep, drill, meantime
7 grasping, file, wave
8 click, wrench, throb

[8] From OSRD Report No. 5567 of the Voice Communication Laboratory, John W. Black, Director. Prepared by C. Hess Haagen. The 12 tests of Form B are of equivalent difficulty with the 12 in Form A given in the preceding chapter. The intelligibility scores of the 24 tests do not deviate more than 0.5%.

Directions for administering are found on pages 350-351. For highest accuracy give the test under the same conditions, in the same room, with students seated in the same seats, and with the same amount of masking noise, as in Form A.

# ANSWER SHEET FOR MULTIPLE-CHOICE
## INTELLIGIBILITY TESTS, FORM B

Speaker 1 is_____          Speaker 2 is_____

**1**

| | | |
|---|---|---|
| 1 system | 1 firm | 1 banner |
| 2 pistol | 2 foam | 2 manner |
| 3 distant | 3 burn | 3 mother |
| 4 piston | 4 term | 4 batter |

| | | |
|---|---|---|
| 1 puddle | 1 carve | 1 offer |
| 2 muddle | 2 car | 2 author |
| 3 muzzle | 3 tarred | 3 often |
| 4 puzzle | 4 tired | 4 office |

**2**

| | | |
|---|---|---|
| 1 heave | 1 detain | 1 scream |
| 2 heed | 2 obtain | 2 screen |
| 3 ease | 3 attain | 3 green |
| 4 eve | 4 maintain | 4 stream |

| | | |
|---|---|---|
| 1 porch | 1 fable | 1 cross |
| 2 torch | 2 stable | 2 cough |
| 3 scorch | 3 table | 3 cloth |
| 4 court | 4 able | 4 claw |

**3**

| | | |
|---|---|---|
| 1 Roger | 1 pure | 1 petal |
| 2 rupture | 2 poor | 2 battle |
| 3 rapture | 3 tour | 3 meadow |
| 4 obscure | 4 two | 4 medal |

| | | |
|---|---|---|
| 1 vision | 1 bubble | 1 throw |
| 2 bishop | 2 tumble | 2 drone |
| 3 vicious | 3 stumble | 3 prone |
| 4 season | 4 fumble | 4 groan |

**4**

| | | |
|---|---|---|
| 1 art | 1 sponsor | 1 game |
| 2 heart | 2 spotter | 2 gain |
| 3 arch | 3 ponder | 3 gage |
| 4 ark | 4 plunder | 4 gang |

| | | |
|---|---|---|
| 1 cape | 1 texture | 1 eye |
| 2 hate | 2 lecture | 2 high |
| 3 take | 3 mixture | 3 tie |
| 4 tape | 4 rupture | 4 hide |

**5**

| | | |
|---|---|---|
| 1 comment | 1 exact | 1 made |
| 2 comic | 2 retract | 2 fade |
| 3 cannon | 3 detract | 3 vague |
| 4 carbon | 4 attack | 4 may |

| | | |
|---|---|---|
| 1 process | 1 glow | 1 single |
| 2 protest | 2 blow | 2 jingle |
| 3 profess | 3 below | 3 cycle |
| 4 possess | 4 low | 4 sprinkle |

**6**

| | | |
|---|---|---|
| 1 bumper | 1 cave | 1 pier |
| 2 number | 2 cake | 2 pierce |
| 3 lumber | 3 cage | 3 fierce |
| 4 lover | 4 case | 4 spear |

| | | |
|---|---|---|
| 1 divide | 1 kitchen | 1 baker |
| 2 devise | 2 mission | 2 major |
| 3 define | 3 friction | 3 maker |
| 4 divine | 4 fiction | 4 banker |

**7**

| | | |
|---|---|---|
| 1 gale | 1 glamour | 1 ward |
| 2 jail | 2 slimmer | 2 wart |
| 3 dale | 3 swimmer | 3 wash |
| 4 bail | 4 glimmer | 4 war |

| | | |
|---|---|---|
| 1 leap | 1 second | 1 rich |
| 2 leaf | 2 suction | 2 ridge |
| 3 lease | 3 section | 3 bridge |
| 4 leave | 4 sexton | 4 grip |

**8**

| | | |
|---|---|---|
| 1 danger | 1 enact | 1 hold |
| 2 feature | 2 impact | 2 old |
| 3 nature | 3 relax | 3 ode |
| 4 major | 4 intact | 4 hoed |

| | | |
|---|---|---|
| 1 crater | 1 seaport | 1 joy |
| 2 traitor | 2 keyboard | 2 going |
| 3 trainer | 3 piecework | 3 join |
| 4 treasure | 4 eastward | 4 dawn |

# ANSWER SHEET FOR MULTIPLE-CHOICE
## INTELLIGIBILITY TESTS, FORM B—*Cont.*

*Speaker 3 is*_____     *Speaker 4 is*_____

**1**
| 1 tropic | 1 willing | 1 trim | 1 center | 1 big | 1 quit |
| 2 traffic | 2 wallet | 2 twin | 2 tender | 2 bag | 2 twist |
| 3 trapping | 3 women | 3 swim | 3 timber | 3 bank | 3 swift |
| 4 tramping | 4 woolen | 4 slim | 4 fender | 4 beg | 4 whip |

**2**
| 1 pan | 1 pope | 1 pelvis | 1 why | 1 nothing | 1 sharp |
| 2 hand | 2 pulse | 2 eldest | 2 wide | 2 shopping | 2 shock |
| 3 ten | 3 pulp | 3 elder | 3 wise | 3 message | 3 short |
| 4 can | 4 pump | 4 welder | 4 wives | 4 jumping | 4 shark |

**3**
| 1 pain | 1 remote | 1 axe | 1 vamp | 1 full | 1 occur |
| 2 paint | 2 promote | 2 aft | 2 map | 2 pull | 2 absurd |
| 3 plank | 3 provoke | 3 apt | 3 mat | 3 fold | 3 observe |
| 4 tank | 4 revoke | 4 at | 4 vat | 4 cold | 4 conserve |

**4**
| 1 bad | 1 depend | 1 alike | 1 paste | 1 left | 1 compress |
| 2 bed | 2 defend | 2 all right | 2 pace | 2 list | 2 contract |
| 3 mad | 3 descend | 3 delight | 3 paid | 3 lisp | 3 contact |
| 4 fed | 4 descent | 4 slight | 4 paint | 4 lid | 4 contrast |

**5**
| 1 normal | 1 unpack | 1 license | 1 unheard | 1 dusk | 1 grope |
| 2 formal | 2 attack | 2 light | 2 concurred | 2 dust | 2 grove |
| 3 corporal | 3 compact | 3 lighten | 3 converge | 3 just | 3 grow |
| 4 fumble | 4 relax | 4 liken | 4 conserve | 4 judge | 4 glow |

**6**
| 1 socket | 1 fine | 1 misuse | 1 grain | 1 ugly | 1 fade |
| 2 pocket | 2 mine | 2 diffuse | 2 grange | 2 hungry | 2 vague |
| 3 bucket | 3 bind | 3 dispute | 3 range | 3 country | 3 made |
| 4 sprocket | 4 find | 4 confuse | 4 train | 4 concrete | 4 spade |

**7**
| 1 quarter | 1 pit | 1 rubbish | 1 confine | 1 boat | 1 wife |
| 2 porter | 2 kick | 2 rummy | 2 design | 2 boast | 2 twice |
| 3 water | 3 kit | 3 running | 3 assign | 3 booth | 3 quite |
| 4 order | 4 pitch | 4 rummage | 4 combine | 4 both | 4 white |

**8**
| 1 clock | 1 bone | 1 blind | 1 naval | 1 rate | 1 discord |
| 2 rock | 2 bold | 2 grind | 2 Mabel | 2 grace | 2 pasteboard |
| 3 lock | 3 bowed | 3 shrine | 3 table | 3 rake | 3 discharge |
| 4 flock | 4 bald | 4 rind | 4 able | 4 race | 4 discard |

# ANSWER SHEET FOR MULTIPLE-CHOICE
# INTELLIGIBILITY TESTS, FORM B—*Cont.*

*Speaker 5 is*_____     *Speaker 6 is*_____

| | | | | | | |
|---|---|---|---|---|---|---|
| **1** | 1 hear | 1 prone | 1 foreign | 1 fox | 1 gnash | 1 drag |
| | 2 ear | 2 cone | 2 forest | 2 block | 2 splash | 2 flag |
| | 3 year | 3 tone | 3 forehead | 3 clock | 3 slash | 3 lag |
| | 4 gear | 4 thrown | 4 force | 4 flock | 4 flash | 4 rag |
| **2** | 1 table | 1 glad | 1 desert | 1 waver | 1 contact | 1 gloom |
| | 2 total | 2 blast | 2 vivid | 2 flavor | 2 unpack | 2 broom |
| | 3 stable | 3 grass | 3 physic | 3 labor | 3 attract | 3 plume |
| | 4 fable | 4 black | 4 visit | 4 favor | 4 attack | 4 glue |
| **3** | 1 over | 1 shock | 1 coast | 1 week | 1 collect | 1 list |
| | 2 oboe | 2 shook | 2 cost | 2 wheat | 2 flap | 2 disc |
| | 3 old | 3 shot | 3 cough | 3 wink | 3 collapse | 3 bid |
| | 4 oval | 4 shop | 4 caught | 4 weep | 4 clap | 4 this |
| **4** | 1 tack | 1 bridal | 1 bar | 1 yes | 1 claws | 1 downbeat |
| | 2 tact | 2 final | 2 far | 2 jet | 2 cause | 2 stampede |
| | 3 pact | 3 vital | 3 are | 3 get | 3 pause | 3 false teeth |
| | 4 pack | 4 title | 4 mar | 4 yet | 4 hoard | 4 southeast |
| **5** | 1 limp | 1 bond | 1 aside | 1 harass | 1 rock | 1 leather |
| | 2 shrimp | 2 bob | 2 confide | 2 caress | 2 strop | 2 lever |
| | 3 blimp | 3 bomb | 3 untied | 3 arrest | 3 throb | 3 letter |
| | 4 glimpse | 4 dog | 4 complied | 4 erect | 4 drop | 4 lather |
| **6** | 1 bite | 1 salute | 1 mock | 1 hall | 1 court | 1 baby |
| | 2 sight | 2 saloon | 2 mop | 2 ball | 2 course | 2 navy |
| | 3 night | 3 balloon | 3 box | 3 fall | 3 cord | 3 maybe |
| | 4 dike | 4 dilute | 4 balk | 4 call | 4 cork | 4 hazy |
| **7** | 1 fork | 1 dance | 1 tyrant | 1 bath | 1 bandit | 1 cracker |
| | 2 fort | 2 badge | 2 pirate | 2 vast | 2 banded | 2 chatter |
| | 3 porch | 3 band | 3 pilot | 3 fast | 3 banquet | 3 shatter |
| | 4 force | 4 damp | 4 tirade | 4 grasp | 4 bandage | 4 shadow |
| **8** | 1 test | 1 relief | 1 code | 1 blame | 1 blurred | 1 feeding |
| | 2 nest | 2 retreat | 2 hold | 2 flame | 2 were | 2 needy |
| | 3 pest | 3 repeat | 3 cold | 3 lame | 3 word | 3 speedy |
| | 4 best | 4 release | 4 hole | 4 plane | 4 bird | 4 meaning |

# ANSWER SHEET FOR MULTIPLE-CHOICE
## INTELLIGIBILITY TESTS, FORM B—*Cont.*

Speaker 7 is_____          Speaker 8 is_____

|   |   |   |   |   |   |   |
|---|---|---|---|---|---|---|
| **1** | 1 plea<br>2 free<br>3 spree<br>4 tree | 1 stretcher<br>2 pressure<br>3 treasure<br>4 precious | 1 bone<br>2 phone<br>3 own<br>4 ode | 1 french<br>2 drench<br>3 wrench<br>4 trench | 1 prepay<br>2 repay<br>3 defray<br>4 repast | 1 stiff<br>2 fifth<br>3 sniff<br>4 gift |
| **2** | 1 cannon<br>2 famine<br>3 solemn<br>4 salmon | 1 turf<br>2 surf<br>3 first<br>4 thirst | 1 tonight<br>2 ignite<br>3 unite<br>4 goodnight | 1 rabid<br>2 rapid<br>3 rabbit<br>4 ravage | 1 preempt<br>2 exempt<br>3 except<br>4 attempt | 1 sealed<br>2 yield<br>3 shield<br>4 field |
| **3** | 1 wrap<br>2 rent<br>3 lamp<br>4 ramp | 1 bold<br>2 hold<br>3 mold<br>4 fold | 1 choose<br>2 fuse<br>3 shoes<br>4 huge | 1 coat<br>2 coach<br>3 coke<br>4 coax | 1 former<br>2 farmer<br>3 firmer<br>4 foreman | 1 proceed<br>2 perceive<br>3 precise<br>4 preside |
| **4** | 1 fence<br>2 dense<br>3 bench<br>4 bent | 1 pencil<br>2 anvil<br>3 handle<br>4 cancel | 1 harsh<br>2 arch<br>3 heart<br>4 art | 1 plunder<br>2 thunder<br>3 blunder<br>4 lumber | 1 paint<br>2 quaint<br>3 plain<br>4 quake | 1 warm<br>2 warn<br>3 work<br>4 worm |
| **5** | 1 tenant<br>2 senate<br>3 sentence<br>4 tennis | 1 got<br>2 dot<br>3 dock<br>4 scotch | 1 lunge<br>2 lunch<br>3 punch<br>4 plunge | 1 purr<br>2 cur<br>3 purge<br>4 curve | 1 dental<br>2 gentle<br>3 simple<br>4 dimple | 1 head<br>2 bed<br>3 dead<br>4 fed |
| **6** | 1 arm<br>2 farm<br>3 barn<br>4 harm | 1 light<br>2 fight<br>3 flight<br>4 sight | 1 brain<br>2 drain<br>3 braid<br>4 grade | 1 tease<br>2 cheese<br>3 keys<br>4 ease | 1 could<br>2 hood<br>3 good<br>4 stood | 1 disturb<br>2 absurd<br>3 disperse<br>4 superb |
| **7** | 1 fact<br>2 pact<br>3 back<br>4 sack | 1 broke<br>2 throw<br>3 throat<br>4 boat | 1 hit<br>2 it<br>3 hip<br>4 itch | 1 aspire<br>2 acquire<br>3 attire<br>4 admire | 1 cute<br>2 suit<br>3 shoe<br>4 chute | 1 health<br>2 elk<br>3 felt<br>4 help |
| **8** | 1 here<br>2 car<br>3 air<br>4 error | 1 skate<br>2 stake<br>3 date<br>4 gate | 1 outing<br>2 mounting<br>3 ousting<br>4 housing | 1 firm<br>2 yearn<br>3 adjourn<br>4 germ | 1 away<br>2 assay<br>3 await<br>4 awake | 1 beside<br>2 seaside<br>3 beehive<br>4 decide |

## ANSWER SHEET FOR MULTIPLE-CHOICE
## INTELLIGIBILITY TESTS, FORM B—*Cont.*

*Speaker 9 is*_____        *Speaker 10 is*_____

**1**

| 1 crawl | 1 candle | 1 baker | 1 lock | 1 try | 1 stealing |
| 2 cow | 2 sandal | 2 station | 2 rock | 2 cry | 2 feeling |
| 3 call | 3 handle | 3 bacon | 3 spot | 3 pride | 3 kneeling |
| 4 cough | 4 scandal | 4 vacant | 4 rot | 4 fry | 4 ceiling |

**2**

| 1 duck | 1 warrant | 1 leave | 1 roar | 1 cream | 1 wall |
| 2 dust | 2 Wallace | 2 lead | 2 chore | 2 creep | 2 wolf |
| 3 dud | 3 wallet | 3 feed | 3 door | 3 creak | 3 wool |
| 4 dutch | 4 wallop | 4 please | 4 drawer | 4 crease | 4 woe |

**3**

| 1 fruit | 1 pail | 1 pan | 1 funnel | 1 snap | 1 lurk |
| 2 root | 2 mail | 2 pants | 2 tunnel | 2 nap | 2 lore |
| 3 brute | 3 bell | 3 past | 3 bundle | 3 man | 3 lure |
| 4 boot | 4 bail | 4 pen | 4 frontal | 4 cap | 4 lower |

**4**

| 1 fish | 1 fitting | 1 trolley | 1 chase | 1 anchor | 1 crop |
| 2 stitch | 2 finish | 2 jolly | 2 cake | 2 hanker | 2 prop |
| 3 this | 3 city | 3 dolly | 3 shake | 3 anger | 3 drop |
| 4 dish | 4 sitting | 4 galley | 4 shape | 4 hanger | 4 stop |

**5**

| 1 replace | 1 utter | 1 bat | 1 known | 1 intend | 1 drove |
| 2 retrace | 2 hunter | 2 bad | 2 zone | 2 intense | 2 go |
| 3 refrain | 3 hunger | 3 back | 3 stone | 3 intent | 3 throw |
| 4 reclaim | 4 under | 4 bath | 4 gone | 4 incense | 4 grow |

**6**

| 1 gentle | 1 fluid | 1 gun | 1 morning | 1 buck | 1 arc |
| 2 journal | 2 shrewd | 2 sun | 2 warning | 2 duck | 2 arch |
| 3 general | 3 would | 3 done | 3 boarding | 3 stuck | 3 aren't |
| 4 colonel | 4 hood | 4 none | 4 hoarding | 4 dug | 4 art |

**7**

| 1 plate | 1 cabbage | 1 astute | 1 him | 1 kettle | 1 fault |
| 2 quake | 2 cabin | 2 excuse | 2 hand | 2 gentle | 2 fog |
| 3 quaint | 3 habit | 3 acute | 3 end | 3 kennel | 3 fall |
| 4 weight | 4 heaven | 4 accuse | 4 inn | 4 general | 4 false |

**8**

| 1 seven | 1 clown | 1 rim | 1 belly | 1 shall | 1 bend |
| 2 sucker | 2 cloud | 2 trim | 2 barely | 2 shelve | 2 bin |
| 3 suffer | 3 proud | 3 grim | 3 bury | 3 shell | 3 bid |
| 4 supper | 4 town | 4 brim | 4 bailing | 4 shelf | 4 bent |

## ANSWER SHEET FOR MULTIPLE-CHOICE
## INTELLIGIBILITY TESTS, FORM B—*Cont.*

*Speaker 11 is_____*          *Speaker 12 is_____*

**1**
| 1 salt | 1 rash | 1 burning | 1 razor | 1 knew | 1 beer |
|---|---|---|---|---|---|
| 2 fault | 2 crash | 2 furnish | 2 raider | 2 you | 2 fear |
| 3 soft | 3 thrash | 3 furnace | 3 greater | 3 few | 3 clear |
| 4 golf | 4 smash | 4 burnish | 4 reader | 4 view | 4 here |

**2**
| 1 open | 1 ride | 1 broom | 1 dream | 1 band | 1 either |
|---|---|---|---|---|---|
| 2 omen | 2 right | 2 groom | 2 clean | 2 fan | 2 beaver |
| 3 woman | 3 ripe | 3 gloom | 3 green | 3 man | 3 fever |
| 4 moment | 4 fried | 4 room | 4 screen | 4 land | 4 neither |

**3**
| 1 dipper | 1 shore | 1 pie | 1 lent | 1 son | 1 achieve |
|---|---|---|---|---|---|
| 2 clipper | 2 door | 2 eye | 2 tempt | 2 gone | 2 exceed |
| 3 slipper | 3 store | 3 high | 3 tense | 3 fun | 3 retrieve |
| 4 flipper | 4 gorge | 4 tie | 4 ten | 4 gun | 4 reprieve |

**4**
| 1 seek | 1 pattern | 1 hot | 1 happen | 1 valid | 1 drive |
|---|---|---|---|---|---|
| 2 thick | 2 better | 2 have | 2 hatpin | 2 solid | 2 strive |
| 3 think | 3 batter | 3 half | 3 captive | 3 salad | 3 derive |
| 4 sink | 4 matter | 4 had | 4 captain | 4 volley | 4 dry |

**5**
| 1 carpet | 1 in | 1 tone | 1 instance | 1 brass | 1 healthful |
|---|---|---|---|---|---|
| 2 carbon | 2 aunt | 2 cone | 2 infants | 2 grass | 2 local |
| 3 common | 3 end | 3 comb | 3 incense | 3 grab | 3 helpful |
| 4 carve | 4 and | 4 told | 4 instant | 4 brad | 4 elbow |

**6**
| 1 must | 1 passing | 1 front | 1 weak | 1 drill | 1 mealtime |
|---|---|---|---|---|---|
| 2 cost | 2 package | 2 fun | 2 sweet | 2 kill | 2 decline |
| 3 us | 3 packing | 3 blunt | 3 wheat | 3 thrill | 3 meantime |
| 4 hush | 4 passage | 4 brunt | 4 sweep | 4 girl | 4 peacetime |

**7**
| 1 rake | 1 perch | 1 propel | 1 drafting | 1 style | 1 way |
|---|---|---|---|---|---|
| 2 rate | 2 punt | 2 hotel | 2 grafting | 2 file | 2 weighed |
| 3 break | 3 punch | 3 lapel | 3 grasping | 3 dial | 3 waste |
| 4 great | 4 touch | 4 foretell | 4 drastic | 4 vile | 4 wave |

**8**
| 1 dart | 1 fill | 1 ask | 1 quick | 1 rent | 1 throb |
|---|---|---|---|---|---|
| 2 dark | 2 still | 2 axe | 2 click | 2 wrench | 2 rob |
| 3 start | 3 bill | 3 act | 3 trick | 3 rest | 3 fog |
| 4 starch | 4 built | 4 at | 4 cliff | 4 reach | 4 drop |

# SCORING SHEET FOR MULTIPLE-CHOICE INTELLIGIBILITY TEST, FORM B

The sequence of three numbers indicate the correct words in each group for each reader. If reasonable precaution is taken for accuracy, the scoring may be done in class.[8]

|          | Speaker 1 | Speaker 2 | Speaker 3 |
|----------|-----------|-----------|-----------|
| Group 1  | 4—1—1     | 3—1—2     | 2—4—3     |
| Group 2  | 4—3—1     | 3—4—3     | 4—3—2     |
| Group 3  | 2—3—4     | 1—4—4     | 4—2—3     |
| Group 4  | 4—2—2     | 1—2—2     | 1—2—4     |
| Group 5  | 3—3—1     | 4—2—1     | 2—1—1     |
| Group 6  | 3—4—2     | 1—4—3     | 1—4—1     |
| Group 7  | 2—4—1     | 2—3—1     | 1—3—4     |
| Group 8  | 3—1—2     | 2—4—3     | 3—2—2     |

|          | Speaker 4 | Speaker 5 | Speaker 6 |
|----------|-----------|-----------|-----------|
| Group 1  | 2—4—3     | 3—1—2     | 2—3—3     |
| Group 2  | 3—1—4     | 3—2—4     | 4—2—1     |
| Group 3  | 2—1—3     | 4—1—2     | 4—1—4     |
| Group 4  | 2—2—4     | 1—3—4     | 3—4—4     |
| Group 5  | 1—3—3     | 4—3—3     | 4—3—1     |
| Group 6  | 3—2—1     | 4—1—1     | 1—3—2     |
| Group 7  | 1—2—4     | 2—1—2     | 1—2—3     |
| Group 8  | 1—4—4     | 2—4—3     | 3—1—2     |

|          | Speaker 7 | Speaker 8 | Speaker 9 |
|----------|-----------|-----------|-----------|
| Group 1  | 4—2—3     | 4—2—1     | 3—3—4     |
| Group 2  | 1—2—1     | 3—2—3     | 2—3—1     |
| Group 3  | 4—3—1     | 2—1—4     | 1—4—2     |
| Group 4  | 3—4—2     | 3—2—4     | 4—4—2     |
| Group 5  | 2—1—4     | 1—1—2     | 1—2—4     |
| Group 6  | 4—3—2     | 3—3—1     | 2—1—4     |
| Group 7  | 1—3—2     | 1—4—4     | 1—2—3     |
| Group 8  | 3—4—1     | 4—3—2     | 3—1—3     |

|          | Speaker 10 | Speaker 11 | Speaker 12 |
|----------|------------|------------|------------|
| Group 1  | 2—1—4      | 1—2—3      | 2—4—2      |
| Group 2  | 4—2—3      | 4—1—1      | 4—3—2      |
| Group 3  | 1—2—3      | 2—2—4      | 3—4—1      |
| Group 4  | 3—4—1      | 4—4—3      | 4—3—1      |
| Group 5  | 2—1—3      | 2—3—1      | 1—1—3      |
| Group 6  | 1—2—4      | 3—4—1      | 4—1—3      |
| Group 7  | 4—3—4      | 2—3—2      | 3—2—4      |
| Group 8  | 1—3—2      | 1—3—4      | 2—2—1      |

[9] For computing the Intelligibility Score see conversion table following Form A, page 360.

# WRITE-DOWN INTELLIGIBILITY TEST, FORM B[10]

| Test 1 | Test 2 | Test 3 | Test 4 | Test 5 | Test 6 |
|---|---|---|---|---|---|
| burning | gangway | bandit | pancake | defend | gunfire |
| fuel | regain | vision | break | hood | eastward |
| deadly | farther | wash | headphone | cushion | center |
| circuit | cotton | single | tent | full | missing |
| try | battle | unit | injure | reduce | beach |
| bail | canvass | edge | decrease | cockpit | folder |
| ampere | sweep | jump | cleared | forecast | speed |
| plenty | forest | defeat | gliding | narrow | rocket |
| find | discard | front | slam | volley | distance |
| spray | tree | southeast | raid | start | bomb |
| gearshift | ignite | calm | flame | pressure | corpse |
| end | piston | moment | neutral | target | tight |

| Test 7 | Test 8 | Test 9 | Test 10 | Test 11 | Test 12 |
|---|---|---|---|---|---|
| fog | slow | dugout | flare | spiral | flag |
| dashboard | reckon | caution | take-off | misfire | suburb |
| cold | balance | mortar | door | flounder | cripple |
| flight | cartridge | govern | guard | ditch | office |
| headwind | high | barge | fort | pivot | blimp |
| roll | cloudy | tank | select | charge | dainty |
| missile | forenoon | shower | wrench | ground | top |
| course | throb | release | blind | blast | nothing |
| binding | late | ceiling | cancel | escape | ask |
| practice | darken | passage | pain | section | compass |
| socket | pierce | blow | measure | hit | gun |
| impulse | salute | fair | ramp | describe | scatter |

[10] From OSRD Report No. 5414 of the Voice Communication Laboratory, Waco, Texas, John W. Black, director. Prepared by C. Hess Haagen. The 12 tests in Form B are of essentially equal difficulty levels as those in Form A given in the preceding chapter. By comparing the Intelligibility Score made on Form A before training with that made on Form B after training each student will be able to measure improvement with a fairly high degree of reliability.

Directions for administering the test are found on pages 350-351. Conversion table for computing the Intelligibility Score is on page 360.

CHAPTER

# ✵ 19 ✵

# Ethical Persuasion

FOR A WHOLE GENERATION the free world has heard the voice of communism saying that democracies are "capitalist imperialists," but that a government which maintains itself through spies, deceit, and execution is a "people's republic." It says that poverty is plenty, tyranny is democracy, slavery is freedom, freedom is slavery. Those who attempt to escape its control are guilty of "crimes against humanity," and those who submit are blessed with "unity plans." Thought control is "the practice of learning," and toeing the party line is being "adjusted to the new way of thinking." It demands "peaceful coexistence," meaning the right to destroy governments that resist coercion. It promises "disengagement," by which it means the peace that follows mass executions. To those who live in a free world—as that term is used in Western nations—the voice of communism seems to say that good can come from evil, that everything humanity has learned in the slow enlightenment of centuries is false, and that its falsehoods are true. This is part of its tactic of planned bewilderment, intended to create tensions, exploit weaknesses, and gain victories.

These techniques are known as the Big Lie Repetition, Character Assassination, Doubletalk, Name-Calling, the Hysterical Approach, and the Seductive Slogan. Some of the words now used are new, but not the method. Before the voice of communism became so loud, it was the voice of Naziism, just before that it was the voice of Fascism, and so on back beyond that day when Euripides described it: "A man of loose tongue, intemperate, trusting to tumult, leading the populace to mischief with empty words." The chief difference now is that the words are loaded, not empty. One compelling test of any free society is whether it can listen to such voices without being led astray, or frightened into hysteria.

Nor is this tactic confined to the Communists, or to dictators in some of the states of the Middle East and in a few republics of Latin America. We have it at home, in almost every community, every college and university, and every speech classroom. It's not always done so skillfully, nor is it heard so far, but we hear it again and again. There are those who corkscrew the truth, and sweep the facts under the rug. Or they compound a little truth and a little plausibility into a deceitful conclusion. These are the demagogues. Fortunately they constitute a small minority. Yet it's well to remember that in any free society if the percentage of such people ever reached a large minority, its life as a free society would be in danger.

We have others, too, in addition to demagogues. What they say is true, but not the whole truth nor the disinterested truth. In the background you can hear the grinding of an ax. These are the propagandists, engaged in persuading the public to make life richer for propagandists. What they say stands in contrast to the principle laid down in Henry Watterson's instructions to the reporters on his *Louisville Courier Journal*: "First, be sure that you tell the truth, and second, be sure that you are not animated by an unworthy motive in telling the truth."

John Morley once said that three things matter in speech: who says it, how he says, and what he says; and of the three, the last matters least. That overstates it, since what a man says depends largely on who he is; but it does call attention sharply to the importance of *what kind of person* the speaker is. The English language does not have a fitting word for this force in persuasion, but the Greeks called it *ethical persuasion* from their word *ethos*, meaning custom or habit. It's not a good term literally translated, but we shall use it because we've never invented another one as good.

Ethical persuasion includes what listeners think the speaker's character is, his reputation for integrity and good will, his reputation as an authority on his subject. It includes also what the speaker makes known by words, manners, and action during the speech: his friendliness, good humor, sagacity, trustworthiness, freedom from bias, restraint from reckless statements, and the whole moral plane on which he discusses the subject.

Ethical persuasion, of course, operates on a different level in a free society than in a totalitarian state. The Big Lie Repetition and its allied techniques used in totalitarian states, does not arise from the personal ethics of its speakers. It is part of a system that requires individuals to surrender their minds—as Eugen Hadamovsky, Nazi theorist and radio dictator, explained it—to that system "in the service of nationalization." The documents of the Nazis, we should note, are invaluable for those who would understand the voice of communism today, for they are the most complete such documents ever opened to the world. They tell exactly what they did, why they did it, and how they did it. They trained some 9,800 certified Nazi speakers, and unloosed them on a hapless Germany which had an educational system that had never trained its citizens to speak, did not know how to train them, and thought it was not important to train them. These speakers were instructed "not to search unto truth," but to put it over. They were warned against the "great danger" of falling into "bookish knowledge" or trying to speak "some wisdom gained from reading." They were told to solve problems "less by positive knowledge than out of the infallible" Nazi "instinct." They were taught that "The magnitude of a lie always contains a certain factor of credulity," and that the masses "more easily fall a victim to a big lie than to a little one," and that "something of even the most insolent lie will always remain and stick."[1]

How effective are such methods, and how dangerous are they to the free world today? First, remember that their grand exponents in the twentieth century, the Nazis and Communists, were never able to win a majority vote in a free election, except one minor victory in Kerala, India, where the Communists won local but not national control. All the other hundreds of free elections they lost. The highest vote Hitler's Nazis ever got in a free election was 37 per cent, this dropped rapidly to 33 per cent in the next election four months later, and the Nazis then seized power by other means. The Communists in each country have come to power, not by the ballot, but by terror and force. Once in power, they never dare permit a free election. Over the long run the Big Lie tactic is not successful. *Always it must be reinforced by the concentration camp and the firing squad.* The totalitarians use it for the planned bewilderment of their enemies. They use it to rouse the masses, to keep them excited. But they dare not trust it to keep themselves in power.

The Big Lie tactic over the long run also carries its own seeds of destruction, of which Naziism is a recent prime example. Its Third Reich, constructed "to last for 1,000 years," loosened forces that destroyed it within twenty years. If you want another example, read the history of Dionysius the Elder and Younger of Syracuse following 407 B.C., including that constant dread of the sword of Damocles. Neither Hitler nor the Dionysiuses are exceptions. They are typical. The Big Lie tactic won't today destroy communism, because for other reasons its roots are strong. But its chief effect has been to frighten the timid, cause people of courage to stand guard, and slowly persuade millions who once hated white Christianity that communism is more dangerous than colonialism.

In a free society, it's another story. A free society always has dema-

---

[1] For those who want to read further the best source is the writings of Ross Scanlan: "The Nazi Party Speaker System," *Speech Monographs,* XVI, No. 1 (August, 1949) 82-97, and XVII, No. 2 (June, 1950), 134-188; "The Nazi Rhetorician," *Quarterly Journal of Speech,* XXXVII, No. 4 (December, 1951), 430-440; and "Adolf Hitler and the Technique of Mass Brainwashing," in *The Rhetorical Idiom,* Donald C. Bryant, ed., (Ithaca, N. Y., Cornell University Press, 1958), 201-220. Of course there are also Adolf Hitler's *Mein Kampf* and *The Goebbel Diaries.*

gogues, of course, who use the Big Lie tactic. Usually they are skillful, for only "good men" think the truth is strong enough to go unarmed against falsehood, and they are the only ones who think that only what one says matters, not how. So in a free society the Big Lie often is spoken more skillfully than the voices in reply. Also, in contrast with methods in a totalitarian state, it is less outrageous, and tends to be refined into innuendo and half-truth that deliberately confuse. Where the totalitarian Big Lie tactic is intended for planned bewilderment, the demagogues' is intended for planned ambiguity—to suggest what it dare not say—and to use the scattershot technique of making broadside accusations in the hope that some of them will hit something.

We hear this kind of speaking in every free society. Yet only a small amount is successful, and its success is both local and temporary. Take the United States Congress as an example. Of its 537 members, at no time will demagogues compose 10 per cent. An examination of the roster of Congress for the past half century shows that the Senate rarely contains more than two at any one time, and the House seldom has more than half a dozen. Our demagogues in public life are conspicuous partly because there are so *few*, and they stand apart from others.

The Big Lie tactic does not win friends and influence human behavior except for local or temporary reasons. It fails in the long run because a free society has no censorship. The demagogue will be refuted, until the persistent exposure to truth will in the end make his tactic repulsive to the majority. In plain words, the Big Lie can be nailed to the flagpole, not instantly but ultimately.

## Character and integrity

We have not only the demagogue, but especially in the second half of the twentieth century, we have organized groups engaged in manipulating others for their private interests. The listening public, distrustful of being exploited, has the "will-to-believe" anyone it thinks represents sincerity, integrity, and good will. In the words of Ralph Waldo Emerson: "The reason why anyone refuses his assent to your opinion, or his aid to your benevolent design, is in you. He refuses to accept you as a bringer of truth, because . . . you have not given him the authentic sign." There you have it. *"You have not given him the authentic sign."*

## The authentic signs

We can't put on integrity, as we put on clothes. It's not a technique, but a moral standard. As someone said long ago, before a person undertakes to "express himself," he needs a self that's worth expressing. In our manipulative free society, anxious listeners especially look for it. When they find it, they not only have the "will to believe," but the "need to believe," and the desire for a flight into faith. What are the "authentic signs" of such speakers?

*We trust the speaker who shows intellectual integrity and sound judgment.* When Lord Roseberry came to analyze influence of Chatham's speaking, he concluded his brilliant exposition with these words: "It is not merely the thing that is said, but the man who says it that counts, the character which breathes through the sentences." The same thing was said in a left-handed way by a demagogue living today. "You are a master of the half-truth," a man said to him. He replied: "Of course! Did you ever notice how much better a half-brick is than a whole brick when you want to throw it? You can wrap your fingers around it, draw it back, and let go. You can't do that with a whole brick. It's too cumbersome. That's true of half-truths and whole truths." (Sorry, I can't give you his name, for I cannot expose the friend who provoked the reply.) Chatham's influence was world wide, and permanent. The half-brick influence often is strong for the moment, but it's limited to specific groups, or specific regions, for a limited time, and it creates forces that tend to destroy it. The greatest influence comes from speakers of intellectual integrity and sound judgment.

We trust speakers who refrain from reckless statement and exaggeration. "That terrible sanity of the average man" becomes wary of those who deal in sweeping assertion. It demands that a speaker be *responsible* for speaking the truth, for being fair-minded, intellectually honest, refraining from reckless assertion, and responsible for avoiding evidence which—even though accurate—misleads but misleads by omission. It demands that a speaker lift the discussion above the level of name-calling. These are the "authentic signs" the speaker is expected to give the listener.

Applied to students they amount to this: Don't pretend to be an authority on government, politics, crime, or what-have-you. Get authority if you need it, and tell who your authority is. But be frank in telling what you know, and how you came to know it.

Don't give listeners a chance to brand you as an exaggerator, or a dealer in half-truth. Stay within the bounds of evidence, and far enough within so listeners won't wonder whether you are about to step out. Don't pretend to prove more than you have proved; for what counts is not what you say you prove, but what listeners think you prove. All in all, present your case in such a way that those who doubt or disagree will admit, however reluctantly, "He was fair." As Alexander Pope put it, speak with "a face untaught to feign."

*We trust the speaker who knows what he is talking about.* We like to know that a speaker is well fitted to discuss a subject because of his experiences or because he has investigated it thoroughly. Such speakers are effective because they discuss the subject in a way that says: "A part of this I saw," or "For all of this I am personally responsible." Therefore, brace yourself to the duty of testing and processing trustworthy information. Especially, be suspicious of becoming the mouthpiece of propaganda articles and propaganda books. It's perfectly legitimate for a speaker to explain his authority, if he can do it without boasting or a vulgar display of egotism. There are simple ways of doing so: "When I was checking some material for this speech, I ran across an unusual book. . . ." Or, "I want to talk about 'How to Study,' because last year my grades told me I did not know too much about it; and this year I resolved to do better by inquiring into what psychologists had learned about it." Or, "Out in my home state of Wyoming. . . ." Or "I was working last summer on the graveyard shift. . . ."

*We trust the speaker who shows restraint and good will.* Don't make listeners out as ignorant. Don't tell them by word or tone that they are stubborn. Don't put them hopelessly in the wrong. Don't tell them dogmatically that you are right, and everybody else is wrong. Don't tell them what they must believe, as if they had no minds of their own. In short, don't punch them in the nose.

Remember that listeners' beliefs are important to them. They usually have been held a long time, they are deeply rooted, and they satisfy deep-felt wants. Therefore, don't attack them outright. Don't even try to make listeners suddenly give them up and take on a set of new ones. Instead, *water and cultivate ideas to produce growth and change,* just as you would water and cultivate crops to promote growth. You are a cultivator of ideas, and not a human bull who bellows defiance and gores the beliefs of others. "Make haste slowly," is a proverb to be followed literally.

Especially, don't use speaking as an excuse for airing thinly-veiled prejudices. Don't, therefore, praise or damn indiscriminately Congress, the President, Russia, labor, management, or anything or anyone. Instead, get your facts, present your case, and let the facts speak for themselves. No question is too controversial to discuss, if you will give listeners light and not heat, and if you do so with moderation, restraint, and good will.

*We trust the speaker who seems to care about us.* Listeners are weary of the mechanical speaker, the impersonal tone, and those who recite the worn-out words, "I am very glad to be here today," in a sallow voice. They want him to *sound* glad, and *act* glad. They want him by looks, words, and action to show an interest in them, their problems, and their welfare. When a speaker loses an audience usually it is for one or more of these reasons:

1. He talked without tone language.
2. He talked over their heads.
3. He was intolerant of people who didn't believe as he did.
4. He got antagonistic.
5. He acted superior.
6. He was long-winded.

From the listener's viewpoint all of these amount to one thing: *He didn't care about me!* A speaker may be tense from stage fright. His mind may be absorbed with the subject. But in spite of these concerns with himself and his subject, he must not *ever* be indifferent to the audience. A lecture-bureau manager, Ford Hicks, who booked college educators and other experts as public lecturers for more than forty years, said that most of them, "we either stopped using after a time or two, and certainly after the first year. They did not care a whit about the people in the audience; in fact, most of them despised the audience, often telling us so frankly, and they made no effort . . . to give them food that would nourish and build them. For all their other qualities, these speakers rate the mark of Failure."

Therefore, choose carefully the ethical plane on which you speak. We say "choose" by design, yet in one sense you have no choice. Once you take the low road you stay there permanently in your listeners' minds. The simple formula that most people use is, "a person does not change his number; and I've got his." They give you a permanent rank, among which are these:

> He never stretches the truth.
>
> He leans over backwards to be fair.
>
> He has superior judgment.
>
> He's brilliant, but erratic.
>
> He's the sad average.
>
> He talks without thinking.
>
> He's honest, but lacks judgment.
>
> He rigs the evidence.
>
> I can hear the ax grinding.

Once they place you in a category, you're likely to stay there. Wallace Carroll, who had 1,500 men under him in the London Office of War Information for the U.S., analyzed the effect of every type of propaganda. He concluded that it "demonstrated the fallacy in the widespread belief that the propagandist's choice is between truth and falsehood." "False propaganda almost invariably boomerangs."[2]

[2] *Persuade or Perish* (Boston, Houghton Mifflin Co., 1948), pp. 237, 238.

Edward W. Barrett, after directing the international operations of the entire Office of War Information, concluded that the "truth is our weapon," and that a "campaign of truth is as indispensable as an air force." Truth alone will seldom persuade. It needs to be told with force and skill. But falsehoods and half-truths don't die easily. They rise up again and again to haunt those who launch them.[3]

In a free society the working axiom is Lincoln's, "You can fool some of the people all of the time, and all of the people some of the time, but you can't fool all of the people all of the time." You can't evade choosing the ethical plane on which you speak. But once you make the choice you are stuck with it, for those who stretch the truth usually find that it snaps back.

"As a reporter, if I said the wrong thing, I could erase it," said Elmer Wheeler. "In the event I failed to erase it . . . then there was the copyman who would check me. Often an editor over him. . . . But spoken words have no check-guards. You say them and they fly into the world to bring joy or anger, to build up the spirits of people or to tear them down. . . . Weigh each word well. . . . You can't erase the spoken word."[4]

## Assignments

ANALYZING ETHICAL PERSUASION IN OTHER SPEAKERS

1. Make a list of two or three speeches with poor ethical persuasion that you have recently heard outside of class. Write a brief criticism of each, explaining in the terms of this chapter where each of them failed, or was weak, in the "authentic signs."

2. Do the same with two or three speeches that had effective ethical persuasion.

3. Draw up two lists of speeches heard in class, one that had effective ethical persuasion, and one that did not. For each speech analyze your reasons.

ANALYZING ETHICAL PERSUASION IN YOUR OWN SPEECHES

4. Go over the outlines of your previous class speeches. Where were you weak or strong in the "authentic signs" of ethical persuasion? How might you have been more effective?

5. For your next speech ask other members of the class to write frank judgments on your ethical persuasion. Platitudes and noncommital statements won't help you, and may even mislead. You want honest judgments, untempered by evasion. Perhaps your colleagues would be more frank if they

---

[3] Edward W. Barrett, *Truth Is Our Weapon* (New York, Funk & Wagnalls Co., 1953), p. x, passim; Norman John Powell, *Anatomy of Public Opinion* (Englewood Cliffs, N. J., Prentice-Hall, Inc., 1956), pp. 439-443.

[4] *How I Mastered My Fear of Public Speaking* (New York, Harper & Brothers, 1957), p. 439.

handed their statements unsigned to the instructor instead of giving them directly to you. These judgments may not make pleasant reading, and what you do about them will also be an ethical question. No one likes adverse criticism and not all can receive it with the meekness of Moses (see *Numbers* 12:1-3), but those who can will grow in ethical stature.

# OCCASIONS AND
# FORMS

# CHAPTER

# ❁ 20 ❁

# Discussion

CLARENCE B. RANDALL, industrial leader and adviser to President Eisenhower on foreign economic policy, said . . .

> . . . the effectiveness of panels . . . is open to serious doubt in my opinion. . . . In the main they are pretty wishy-washy affairs. There is too much "either or," too much by the moderator of "Would I be right, Klinebuck, in assuming that you might think there would be another side to that question?" There is so much emphasis on keeping the program balanced, always off-setting a business man with a labor leader, a Republican with a Democrat . . . , that no single direct message is delivered, and the program concludes in a blur that is soon forgotten.[1]

Ralph Cordiner, president of General Electric has the same low opinion of committees. "A committee moves at the speed of its least informed member and too often is used as a way of sharing responsibility," he said and the great General Electric does not use them as decision-making bodies. And the quip in Washington, D. C., where conferences are more common than sightseers, is that "A conference is a meeting at which people talk about what they should already be doing."

These objections to various forms of discussion are pertinent, and ought to be kept in mind. Why? First, in spite of the dislike of discussion by a few in high places, neither industry nor government could survive without it. Walter Bagehot, that penetrating English thinker, said: "It was government by discussion that broke the bond of ages and set free the originality of mankind." He added that savages discussed, not principles but *undertakings* such as whether it is better to plunder Village A or Village B, but civilization comes from the discussion of *principles,* and its "elevation depends—other things being equal—on the greatness or littleness of the things to be discussed."[2] Thus discussion is the keystone of a free society, and a free society is one that believes it is better

---

[1] *Freedom's Faith* (Boston, Little, Brown and Co., 1953), p. 153.
[2] Walter Bagehot, *Physics and Politics* (New York, D. Appleton and Co., 1873), pp. 158-177.

to discuss a question without settling it than to settle it without discussing it.

Another force has lately given discussion almost a dreadful urgency. We live at a time when we are accumulating knowledge at jet speed. Only by discussion of administrators with experts, and of experts with other experts in nearby fields, can we know what is happening even next door within our own business corporation or profession. Thus in the 1860's Stonewall Jackson held *one* council of war in all his career. It was a failure, and never would he hold another. His brilliant victories were conceived in his mind—and kept hidden there, where they could never be leaked to his enemies.

But General of the Army Dwight Eisenhower was forced to live by conferences, and one reason he was selected as commander over many able contemporaries was that he was an expert in conference. In preparation for making the final decision to attack on the planned D-day in Normandy, or to postpone it, he held conference *rehearsals* in advance, presumably so his generals could learn the process of group decision-making, and presumably also so they could learn how well to trust the judgment of the other generals. Read the history of those last fateful conferences: they listened to the weather experts report on just how little the bad weather would lift before it closed down again; they listened to demolition experts on how long it would take to dynamite paths through underwater obstacles on the beachhead; they listened to the naval experts on what they could, or could not do, with low visibility, and on how long overtime they could stay in the Channel without having to delay the attack for refueling; they listened to the paratroop experts on how long they could hold out behind the enemy lines if landings were delayed until later in the day. Then they discussed each and weighed it on the scales of judgment. Here was expert discussion, and here was demonstrated why—even if discussion were not the keystone of a free society—it would now be necessary for living in a technological society.

But the critics like Randall and Cordiner are right in their specific objections. Theirs, however, is a criticism of discussion *misused,* not of discussion itself. Often it is misused, and often it is ineffective because it requires insight, attitudes, and skills. Men are not born with them. They must learn them or develop them. Hence discussion is the tool of civilization, and high civilization at that.

## Types of discussion

"Discussion" is a broad word, but here we use it with a technical meaning, and we don't mean the disorganized talk of a group that merely sits around and chews the fat. That's a bull-session, but not a "discussion." It is pleasant and stimulating, but it serves another purpose. *Discussion is the purposive talk of people who meet to consider a common problem: in committees, conferences, seminars, panels, symposiums, or other groups.* Its goal is problem-solving. It may not go all the way. More often it does not, but it goes in that direction—defining it, exploring it, examining possible solutions.

The following are its more common forms:

### INFORMAL GROUP DISCUSSION

Here not more than twenty people sit around a circle, or in some form of close group, and discuss a subject of mutual interest. There is no audience and there are no formal speeches. The group simply converses under the guidance of a chairman. This type of discussion is often difficult to keep within bounds and to keep moving profitably through the various steps of the problem. Members may spend too much time on some early interesting aspect, and so never get very far into the problem. Or they turn up a new subject entirely, drop the old one and follow the new one. If the chairman holds the reins too tightly, or interrupts too often, the spontaneity is lost and the spirit of discussion is killed. For all its shortcomings, however, the rudiments of discussion are there; and if the members understand the problem-solving nature of discussion and are grounded in the steps of logical thinking, Informal Group Discussion can be profitable as well as interesting.

### CO-OPERATIVE INVESTIGATION

This is a splendid method for discussion training. It involves eight steps:

1. The discussion group meets in advance and elects a leader. The subject is then divided into a number of subtopics, and each member undertakes to investigate at least one of these subtopics.

2. The leader may hold one or more advance meetings, so that members can learn what others have done and can work out final plans.

3. When the discussion meeting is held, the leader *analyzes* and *defines* the problem.

4. Each investigator then presents his information in a brief report. *The report contains no argument,* but only information set forth in concise and orderly form.

5. When these reports have all been made, the leader calls for any other pertinent information that members may have.

6. The leader may, if he desires, succinctly summarize the information thus pooled. Then he opens the meeting to a discussion of what ought to be done in the light of the facts thus presented. Possible solutions are

not debated, but are talked over in a cooperative manner. Each member tries to help the group reach an informal judgment. Disadvantages in proposed solutions are carefully considered, and ways of overcoming them are taken up.

7. Finally, if the nature of the problem permits, the ways and means of putting the best solution into operation are considered.

8. At the end the leader once more may give a brief summary of the procedure which has been adopted.

This is the general method used by city councils, boards of education, church boards, women's clubs, adult education groups, Boy Scouts, Girl Scouts, and 4-H Clubs. They simplify it, but don't change it basically.

### THE PANEL FORUM

The panel half of a Panel Forum is composed of a chairman and a small group, usually from two to six, who discuss a problem before an audience. They sit at a table where the audience can see them easily.

Of course, the chairman and the panel members have prepared carefully for the discussion. They follow much the same procedure as described above for the Co-operative Investigation, but one new feature is added. Panel members must talk loud enough for persons in the audience to hear. There are no formal speeches. No one talks for more than a minute or two at a time, and, on the average, the members talk much less than that. The members remain seated. Sometimes they talk to one another, sometimes they address the chairman, and at other times they talk directly to the audience—but always they will talk so that people in the audience can hear them easily.

When the panel has explored the problem, the chairman gives a brief summary of what has been said and then turns the meeting into a forum (hence the name Panel Forum) by *opening the discussion to members of the audience.* Approximately half of the available time should be reserved for audience participation.

### THE SYMPOSIUM

The Symposium comes closer to formal public speaking than either the Co-operative Investigation or the Panel Forum. It consists of a chairman and several speakers, usually two, three, or four. The speakers stand and speak rather formally. Each presents his own personal viewpoint, but the speeches are not debates. They are not aimed at convincing the audience that the speakers' views should be adopted. Each speaker tries to add information and raise pertinent questions. When the speakers have finished, the chairman then invites the audience to participate in the question period. These questions are for the purpose of getting additional information from the speakers, or to reinforce or refute their arguments. They may be submitted to the chairman in writing, or the questioner may stand and ask his question directly.

### THE COMMITTEE, CONFERENCE, STAFF MEETING, OR SEMINAR

These discussions ordinarily are not held in public. When an organization cannot discuss all the business that comes before it, some of the problems are referred to Committees which are composed of members with special qualifications. A chairman is designated by the organization or elected by the committee members themselves. The Committee meets, discusses the problem, prepares a formal report, and presents it to the organization. Committee hearings like those of Congress sometimes are held publicly. But the audience simply listens. It does not participate. Conferences also may be held publicly. Staff meetings are not. They amount to permanent committees that meet regularly. Seminars, of course, are the discussions of a supervised group doing research or advanced work.

### ROLE-PLAYING

The rapid growth of role-playing is little short of incredible; and it comes where least expected, in alert business corporations that find it solves some of their toughest problems. General Electric Co. uses role-playing "to drive home to foremen, executives, and other supervisory personnel the danger of relying on word-of-mouth communication." One member is given a picture to study in private for two minutes. He then describes it in private to another member. The other member, in turn, describes it in private to a third, and so on through a group of 10 to 20 persons. The last man describes it to the first, and then the picture is flashed on a screen where all can see it. One picture showed the interior of a subway car, with a poorly-dressed white man waving a knife and arguing with a well-dressed Negro. Nearby sat a Jewish rabbi, and off in the background was a blonde with a baby. The final description of the picture was, "It's a picture of a blonde with a baby, apparently her own." The result was more effective than a dozen written orders on, "Don't trust your memory, but take notes, if you're going to report something to others." Royal McBee Co. used role-playing to reduce complaints of its field representatives on the poor inspection of merchandise before shipping it from the factory. It assembled in a conference room the supervisors in charge of shipping, and had them play the role of field representatives in other cities who unpacked the equipment. A company official reported, that it was "amazing to see the difference later." Gulf Oil Corporation used it to clear up its five o'clock quitting-time jam at the elevators. Department stores put their thousands of employees through one-day role-playing exercises twice a year "to improve selling effectiveness." The American Management Association trains some 250 executives a year in the theory and practice of role-playing. It regards this as "one of the most important communications techniques we can teach."[3]

The concept of role-playing is simple. It started with Jacob L. Moreno "amusing children and picking up points on their behavior by having them play roles in make-believe situations." He next found that it worked with juvenile delinquents, so well that business organizations began asking how he trained them to be such excellent workers. It simply provides the player insight into another person's point of view by having him *act out that other person's role*. It is spontaneous, no rehearsals. The role-players are told what characters they are to portray. They are given a few minutes to decide on the points to be made in the episode. They know it's to be short, usually not over five or six minutes. They play the role much the way children "play school" or "play church," or re-enact weddings, but with a deep purpose.

### BUZZ-SESSIONS

This often is called the "Phillips 66 buzz-session." It sounds like the name of a gasoline, but comes from the originator's name plus the method he used. J. D. Phillips developed it by setting up groups of six people to discuss a topic for six minutes, no more. It can be used when you have a large group but a limited time. It can be used on a *specific* topic, like a single unit of a larger problem, but it's not so effective on a broad problem. Here are the steps:

1. A speaker talks for a short time, or a discussion leader leads the whole group in discussion for a short time. This gives the members a background on the topic and gets them ready to think about it.

2. Then the chairman divides the assembly into groups of six persons each, and gives them six minutes to talk it over, no more. They don't leave the room, but simply pull their chairs around in circles or stand in clusters. They know they have six minutes, and the urgent time limit drives them to think fast.

3. At the end of six minutes the chairman calls for order and asks each group chairman to report its recommendations. He limits each report to not over one minute, and asks for them to be shorter if possible.

4. The chairman then summarizes the recommendations, pointing out how different ones are related, overlapping, or are opposed to each other.

5. Finally, the chairman calls for a discussion by the whole assembly. A good chairman conducts the discussion with two considerations uppermost: First, that no recommendation be neglected. Second, that the assembly *deliberate* before making its decision.

[3] *The Wall Street Journal*, March 16, 1957, carried a feature story on page 1 of the sudden growth of role-playing from 1955 to 1957, written by Mitchell Gordon. To him I am indebted for the examples cited.

### BRAINSTORMING

Brainstorming applies the crash-program concept to thinking. It's a session where about a dozen people try to solve a problem by heating up their minds and saying anything that comes out. The object is quantity, hence not a word of criticism is allowed. Here is how it works:

First, the group "sits cross-legged around a problem," and collects ideas for solving it by suggesting anything, everything they can think of, no matter how wild or weird. Ideas come fast, for they don't stop to consider if any are sensible or crazy.

Next, there is no criticism, not a word, no matter how wild the idea or how much wilder one it evokes from someone else. The idea is: "Keep the creative energy flowing, and see what happens!" They expect to hear incredible and ridiculous ideas. But they ought to have about 150 ideas in an hour.

Third, screen the ideas; throw out the bad, and keep the good.

"You can always count on about 5 per cent of the ideas being practical, useful, and new," say the experts who use this method. According to extensive and impressive studies conducted at the University of Buffalo, the same people using this method can produce 90 per cent more *good* ideas than by conventional thinking in which judgment interferes with imagination.

Brainstorming was conceived about 1938 by Alex F. Osborn (of Batten, Barton, Durstine, & Osborn), and was based on the concept that "creative imagination" plus *"suspended* judgment" would produce more good ideas than conventional thinking in which judgment tended to choke new ideas. It caught the public fancy about 1954, became a fad, and enthusiasts claimed they could solve every problem by such mind sweeping. The fad led to people using it who did not know how, and for a time it lost favor. But experts like Lee H. Bristol, Jr. say it bogs down only when people don't know how to use it. Bristol adds that he can walk into any group bogged down and spot the trouble immediately. There may be a wet blanket or two in the group; they don't say a word in criticism, but their *looks* tell all, and they bog down the whole group. Or among business men they may cross management lines, mix high echelon people with low echelon people, and the latter won't talk in the presence of the upper brass. Believe it or not, sometimes the trouble is no women. "A significantly higher percentage of pace-setters and hitch-hikers in these sessions are women," explained Bristol. "They turn up a greater number of better ideas, too."

Its proponents rightly prefer to call it "Creative Problem-Solving," but it's likely to be known simply as brainstorming. Now and then conservative educators have scoffed at it, and even said it interfered with thinking. But they can't tell that to the giants of industry, who face pressing problems and must find ways to face them. Hence most of the giants of industry—General Motors, U.S. Steel, Union Carbide, and General Electric, etc.—have included Creative Problem-Solving courses in their own educational programs. So far the critics have not even been able to tell it to the Marines, for the Marines, Air Force, Army, and Navy, all have incorporated courses somewhere in their training. Some twenty colleges and universities are offering separate courses on Creative Thinking as against formal logic, and an unknown number, known to exceed fifty, have incorporated its principles into existing courses. Even individual families are beginning to use it to reduce the once-inevitable wrangling where the young and the old lived together.[4]

## Qualities of good discussion

A recipe for ox-tail soup starts, "First, remove the ox." The concept applies to starting a good discussion: First, remove the extraneous. Then state the question so everybody knows what it means.

Not all questions can be discussed. Some, such as who ran the fastest mile or who is mayor of Cleveland, are questions of *fact*. We simply investigate them and find out. We discuss questions of policy, of welfare, of principle. When such a question confronts us, the first step is to state it precisely. This is not easy, but two suggestions will help:

1. *State the question so it is limited to one specific problem.* If you take up a multiple question like, "Should the labor unions' right to strike be restricted, and the power of the Federal Government be increased so it can settle labor disputes?" you have trapped at least two questions instead of one:

   a. Should the labor unions' right to strike be restricted?

   b. If so, should the power of the Federal Government be increased?

But you can't discuss two questions at once, for they interfere with one another. Therefore, limit your question to one specific problem.

2. *State the question so the answers will not be "yes" on one side and "no" on the other.* If, for example, you state the question as, "Should the United States maintain a policy of reciprocal trade agreements with foreign nations?" the discussion will turn into a downright debate, with one side arguing "yes" and the other arguing "no." Each side will try

---

[4] The most complete discussion of brainstorming is found in Alex F. Osborn, *Applied Imagination* (New York, Charles Scribner's Sons, 1957). The Creative Education Foundation (1614 Rand Building, Buffalo 3, N. Y.) will also supply on request information on methods and educational developments.

to *prove* its case, and neither will be primarily concerned with constructive ideas on foreign trade.

On the other hand, if you state the question as, "How can the United States best maintain its foreign trade?" neither side can argue "yes" or "no." In fact, *there won't be any sides,* and the discussion will more likely evoke constructive ideas about improving foreign trade.

To the inexperienced, good discussion may sound like good ordinary conversation, lively and informal, and, of course, interesting. But, underneath, it is fundamentally different. It is *planned* conversation. It starts at a given point and goes through the definite steps of defining and exploring and solving a problem. *It requires a knowledge of the processes of thinking.*

This process involves the following well-known Six Steps:

1. What is the *nature* of the problem confronting the group?
2. What *caused* the problem?
3. What are the *several possible solutions?*
4. What are the *advantages and disadvantages* of each?
5. What, finally, seems to be the *one best solution?*
6. How may this solution be *put into operation?*

Of course, intelligent discussion does not plod automatically through each of these Six Steps. People when talking over a problem take stock of the situation, consider where they stand, and how far they may safely or wisely go. Perhaps they already know the nature of the problem (Step 1). Perhaps they even know what caused it (Step 2). The discussion would then omit these aspects of the question and go at once to the possible solutions (Step 3). At another time there might be only one possible solution; consequently, the focus of discussion would be on how to work this solution into tangible form and put it into effectiive operation (Step 6).

Often the problem may be so complex that it cannot be solved in the near future, and has not yet developed far enough to determine which one solution is best. At the moment, the only thing to be done is to consider its nature and its causes, develop the several possible solutions which might be adopted—then wait for time to reveal which is best (Steps 1, 2, 3).

## How to participate effectively

### ACQUIRE AND ORGANIZE INFORMATION ON THE SUBJECT

People who know little or nothing about a subject cannot discuss it intelligently or with profit, nor can they form trustworthy opinions on it. They can only pool their ignorance. Before intelligent discussion is possible, the participants must have information. Before they can form judgments, they must have facts. When you are assigned to a discussion, then, your first task is to prepare.

*First,* think over what you know about the problem, and jot down the main points in a concisely organized outline.

*Second,* investigate the subject systematically and thoroughly. The *Reader's Guide* and other standard references in your library will supply material. Generally it is unwise not to consult enough of these references to find out what others have recently written on the subject. Nor are recent references the only valuable ones. The philosophy, foundations, and assumptions are important, and ought to be examined or re-examined.

*Third,* read systematically and take notes on what you read. By the aid of notes you can keep information at hand for constant reference. You can also be sure of exact facts, dates, quotations, or opinions.

*Fourth,* organize your information once more into a concise outline. You may write the outline on paper or arrange it on cards. If you put it on paper, it is quickly visible to the eye. If you put it on cards, the outline can be more complete and detailed than it ordinarily would be if it were written on paper.

## Maintain the discussion attitude

Often in discussion you will meet interference from the "status seekers." Most of what they say is not to solve the problem, but to gain status, prove their status, or protect their status. Such people don't have the discussion attitude.

Another interference comes from people who look on discussion as a contest. They want to score a point, to prove that their "side" is right and the other "side" is wrong. They, too, lack the discussion attitude. What is this discussion attitude? Donald K. Smith defined it as really three attitudes.[5]

> First, to be *impartial,* and hence willing to examine the implications of all ideas according to the same standards.
>
> Second, to *suspend judgment,* and hence defer committing yourself in advance to any given conclusion.
>
> Third, *respect for reason,* and hence the belief that "thoroughness, accuracy, and care in reasoning and the use of language will produce more useful decisions than the neglect of such discipline."

To spell it out, remember that you are one of a group that is *thinking*

[5] "The Discussion Course at Minnesota: A Liberal Arts Approach," *The Speech Teacher,* VII (September, 1958), No. 3, p. 193.

*together,* and that anything disrupting the process of thinking together is out of place. For example, don't sit with an impatient air of one who is waiting to interrupt and get the floor. *Learn to listen,* and to digest what you hear. Ask questions when you need further information, but don't talk too glibly or let go with half-formed ideas. Don't jump on an idea just because it is not yours. Rather consider what good there is in it, and whether it has drawbacks and weaknesses. If you think the idea is good, say so when it comes your turn to talk. If you think there are drawbacks and weaknesses, call attention to them, but always in the spirit of co-operation, of trying to make the idea better rather than to kill it.

Remind yourself reasonably often that your opinions are not sacred merely because they are yours. If you present an opinion, and weaknesses show up after others have worked it over, let your judgment overweigh your pride. It's a poor mind that can't invent reasons for saving face, but a face thus saved is not a thing of beauty nor a joy forever. It loses the dignity, if not the nobility, gained by one who invites others to pass judgment on his ideas. You are met to work out a problem, so search for facts with an open mind, share ideas mutually, have sympathy for the attitudes of others, and think *with* the group .

### USE THE TWO ESSENTIAL SKILLS OF DISCUSSION

These skills are:

First, the *human-relations skills* of getting along with others and benefitting from their presence.

Second, the *communications skills* which involve communicating *both* with the other discussion members and with the audience if there is one.

Again, to spell it out, *first* respect those with whom you disagree, and show respect both by language of words and language of tone. Many ideas you may dislike, but you must live with people who believe them. As Bert Easterbrook said, "He who has learned to disagree without being disagreeable has discovered the most valuable secret of a diplomat."

*Second,* be sure that all listeners can hear easily, even when you address other discussion members. Face it frankly, this is tough and only a chosen few do it. Some never communicate to the listeners. Others *start* talking only to their discussion group, then after awhile reach out to the audience, after it's too late for the audience to make sense of what they say, since it's missed all the first part. Still others start talking to the audience, then turn aside, talk to their colleagues, and *trail off* into tones that can be *heard* out front but not *understood.*

*Third,* remember that when you enumerate points, "1, 2, 3," they are far more listenable than when you make three points one after another without such enumeration.

*Fourth,* address other participants directly, rather than toss an idea into thin air, or pick up another speaker's point without referring to him. For the listener this gives the discussion both movement and a personal touch.

*Fifth,* remember that apt anecdotes and brief humorous stories heighten interest, and also reinforce serious points.

*Sixth,* always restate a question that is not clearly worded or audibly spoken, whether the question comes from another member or from the floor. To listeners it's irritating for a speaker to answer a question mumbled by someone down front. The answer is pointless, for listeners don't know the question.

*Seventh,* keep the ball rolling. Remember that sooner or later it will be tossed in your lap when you don't expect it, so be ready always to handle it. Keep noting mentally what you would say. If necessary jot down items on a card. Then when it comes your way you can keep it rolling like Old Man River.

## *How to be a good discussion leader*

The discussion leader performs a unique role. He is not simply a chairman. He is not a teacher or a lecturer. He is not a persuader. He is not a dictator who dominates the discussion. He personifies instead the spirit of democracy by guiding the process of discussion as the group works toward a solution of the problem, yet doing so without either directing or controlling their thinking.

### GENERAL QUALIFICATIONS OF THE DISCUSSION LEADER

Leading a discussion is a difficult task, and frankly not everyone can handle it. But it might help to set down the general qualities required of a good leader, if only to enable you to check them against your own abilities and be on guard at points where you may face personal difficulties.

1. *He should know the rules of the game,* should know, for example, the Six Steps in Discussion, whether he is directing a Panel Forum or a Symposium, when the audience is to be called on to participate, how to keep on schedule, and how to draw the ends together at the close.

2. *He should be willing to remain in the background.* "A quarterback who always elects himself to carry the ball whenever there is a chance for a touchdown will seldom be popular." A good discussion leader may indeed grow impatient, because a discussion sometimes

moves slowly, but the good leader must move patiently with it, and not cut in to tell the group what's what.

3. *He should respect the opinion of others.* He may not share those opinions, but he should not let this become known to the audience. He gives equal opportunity to all members to express ideas. He listens to them, believing that what others think is important. He summarizes the consensus of the meeting without regard to his own personal opinions.

4. *He should be courteous, fairminded, and impartial.* A lively discussion is often turbulent, and the less-controlled participants may clinch in heated arguments and resort to angry words. But the good leader not for an instant loses his courteous manner. He is the moderator who not only restrains the violence of others, but sets an example of courteous conduct. When the argument gets hot, he breaks in with a smile and gentle hint, such as, "I think we all know how Brown and Johnson feel about this. Now who else would like to get in on it?" If a hint of this sort does not break it up, the leader can remind the group that the purpose of the discussion is to reach some solution to the problem, that the argument between the two members is preventing calm discussion, then ask them to cease the argument and permit the group to continue its discussion. A gentle admonition, courteously given by the leader, will usually quiet even the most violent member.

The good leader, above all, is fairminded and impartial. He never favors one viewpoint or restricts another. He not only permits all viewpoints to be brought out, but tries diligently to have them brought out. To persons of every viewpoint, he conveys assurance that he is a leader who plays no favorites.

## The leader's role in group discussion

When you lead a discussion group, there are specific tasks for which you ought to prepare:

1. *Confer in advance with other formal participants.* This will enable the leader to learn their viewpoints and to know in advance what direction the discussion is likely to take. It will also enable the leader to find out whether the other participants fully understand what is expected of them, and to make sure that each one understands the time limits of his remarks.

2. *Prepare a discussion outline.* You do not want to straitjacket the discussion by holding it to an outline prepared in advance, yet you can't allow it to start hit-and-miss and wander whither it will. You will need a brief but carefully-prepared outline for use in guiding the

discussion. (See page 443 for the Six Steps giving the pattern for such an outline.) Once the discussion is under way, it may suddenly turn in an unexpected direction from that planned in your outline. If so, let it go the new way, so long as it's not irrelevant to the question. You may even have to make up a new outline as you go along. Very well, that's better than having no outline at the start.

3. *Open the meeting with remarks that are brief and to the point.* When a discussion group meets, it wants to get going. A leader can dull this zest and nearly kill it by a long and rambling opening. Know in advance what you are going to say. Rehearse it. Keep it short, and to the point.

4. *Keep the discussion moving.* Once the discussion is under way, it can often bog down if the leader is not on the alert. The moment talk begins to repeat itself, the good leader cuts off that topic and moves to the next one. If the discussion wanders from the point, he brings it back by some such remark as, "This is very interesting, but let us get back to our subject, namely. . . ." If persons with little information and few if any ideas try to monopolize the time (and who ever heard of a large discussion group where this didn't happen?), the leader tactfully cuts them off with an explanation such as, "We have heard this member's contribution; you know, of course, that the aim of this meeting is to get everyone to participate and not to impose this burden on a few. Therefore, I know that this member will now want to hear from others."

Or if the leader faces the talkative person with strong opinions but no facts, he will ask courteously but pointedly for evidence: "Now that you have stated your opinions, will you give us the evidence on which they are based?" Then if the member still insists on repeating his opinions without evidence, a tactful leader will cut in with, "Thank you very much. I think we now understand your views. Can any other member offer evidence that would give support to this opinion?" In short, the good leader keeps the ball rolling.

5. *Make occasional summaries.* After the discussion has run for awhile, or some phase of it has been completed, the leader should present a summary in order that participants can see where they now stand. Make the summaries brief and impartial. A good leader often asks the group to check him for accuracy, to make sure that he has not misstated a viewpoint, and to add points he has overlooked.

6. *Bring out all viewpoints on the subject.* Here is a test of the leader's highest genius. Again and again, all the discussion will be on one side of the subject. Seemingly nobody will have an opinion on the other side. Don't be deceived. This doesn't always mean that nobody holds

an opposite opinion. More often it means that the minority, feeling that their views are unpopular, are simply keeping quiet. A good leader *studies the faces* of the group and notes whether they seem to be in disagreement. (This requires no mind reading, for people in groups show rather well in their faces whether they are for or against an idea.) The leader then specifically invites opposing arguments, or even suggests one or two himself in order to encourage the other side to follow up. Or he may add, "I see by their faces that there are some people who hold opposing opinions. Would one of them care to state his views?"

7. *Close the meeting by a summary of the whole discussion.* Such a summary is not in the form of a set of resolutions, but is rather an attempt to state the consensus of the group. It is done with due allowance for differences of opinion, "Some believe that . . . others believe that. . . ." A good summary sends the members away with the feeling that they have got somewhere, that the discussion has helped to solve, or at least to understand, the problem involved.

## Assignments

1. Listen to a radio or television discussion and report on the following: (*a*) Which of the Six Steps of discussion were covered. (*b*) Whether in your opinion any steps left out should have been covered, or any covered should have been left out. (*c*) How you would have discussed the problem differently if you have been a participant.

2. Analyze the discussion heard in one of your classes: (*a*) Which of the various kinds of discussion was it? (*b*) To what extent did it measure up to the qualities of good discussion set forth in this chapter, and where did it fail? (*c*) To what extent did the leader have those qualifications for discussion leadership described in this chapter. (*d*) To what extent did the other participants effectively take part, and how could they have been more effective.

3. Assume that you are to lead a campus discussion: (*a*) What subject would you select? (*b*) What kind of discussion would you hold (Panel Forum, Symposium, etc.)? (*c*) Whom would you invite to take part? (*d*) What outline of topics would you follow?

4. The class will select a topic for Co-operative Investigation, then elect a leader. The leader, of course, will lay careful plans: (*a*) Appoint a special committee to give the topic preliminary consideration and to divide it into subtopics (or the leader may do this himself, or in conference with others). (*b*) Appoint members of the class to investigate each of the subtopics. (*c*) Conduct the Co-operative Investigation with the entire class taking part.

5. There is probably not time for each member of the class to take part as a panel member in discussion, but, in order that members may know how a

good Panel Forum is operated, one may be held. The instructor will appoint the chairman and other panel members. The class will decide on the topic. Panel members will prepare carefully for their parts. Probably they should meet a few times and construct an outline of the points they want to cover, although each member will be left free to present his own viewpoint. Class members who are not on the panel should remember that they have parts also: both of listening carefully to the panel and of being ready to take part in the ensuing forum discussion.

6. Every member of the class can acquire experience in discussion by serving on a committee. Let the class organize itself into a Legislative Assembly and set up a group of committees so that each class member is on one committee. They can then introduce bills into the Assembly, as many as they want. When all bills have been presented, the Assembly will vote on which bills it wants to consider, and the Speaker of the Assembly will refer these bills to the committees, taking care to see that every committee has a bill referred to it. The committees will then meet and discuss the bills. This discussion, of course, ought to follow the regular Discussion Steps and ought to represent co-operative group-thinking. At the end of the discussion each committee will prepare a report; and if the members can't agree on a single report, then it will present both a majority and a minority report. After the bills have been reported, the Assembly can discuss them further and vote on them, but this is not necessary for the purpose of this project. The real purpose is to give committee members experience in working on a problem by thinking and talking together.

7. Experiment with all three of the newer methods of problem-solving: role-playing, buzz-sessions, and brainstorming. Run a few trials in class to get the feel, then try them outside of class. If they bog down, find out why. Develop as far as you can the touch for getting results with them.

# Radio and Television
# Speaking

WE CALL this "the atomic age." But future historians may call it instead "the television age." As Bishop Fulton J. Sheen said, "Television influences human brains a thousand times more than the fission and the fusion of atoms. Television is the newborn babe of the Fourth Dimension of Space-Time. Newton knocked the boundaries out of space; Einstein knocked the boundaries out of time; but television has annihilated space and time."[1] Together with its forerunner, radio, television has changed our habits of living and is changing even the way our democracy operates.

## Radio, television, and democracy

In early civilization large nations tended to disintegrate because of size. People who lived far apart grew out of touch, and in time simply fell apart. This was true with empires like Alexander's, and it was acutely so in the early democracies. Aristotle, who was an analyst of constitutional government as well as of the science of persuasion, said: "To the size of states there is a limit. . . . For who can be the general of such a vast multitude, or who the herald, unless he have the voice of a Stentor?"[2] The Roman Republic extended the potential size of a unified nation by its famous roads; but Roman roads and Roman couriers had limitations beyond which they could not develop or hold a free society. The next advance in communication was the printing press, invented at the end of the Middle Ages (and one reason for its end). Printing made it easier to "get words out of town," and again expanded the potential size of a free society.

That's where mass communication stood when the United States was

[1] *Quote*, XXXII, No. 22 (November 25, 1956), p. 10.
[2] *Politics*, 1326a-b.

born. James Madison explained its effect on government in *The Federalist*, No. 14: ". . . the natural limit of a *democracy* is that distance from the central point which just permits the most remote citizens to assemble as often as their public functions demand . . . ," and "the natural limit of a *republic* is that distance from the centre which will barely allow the representatives to meet as often as may be necessary for the administration of public affairs." (Italics mine.) Madison was right. In 1789 we could not have had a democracy, or a republic, stretching from Virginia to California, for it was based on *printed* mass communication distributed by *stage coaches and sailing ships*. As for including Alaska and Hawaii, don't try to imagine it!

But as immigrants began to flow westward from the Atlantic seaboard, the steamboat and the railroad were invented; later the telegraph, then the telephone, and finally the rotary printing press. These let us get in news fast, print it fast, and get it out fast all over the land. Under this medium of communication the nation was expanded to the Pacific Coast.

Print, however, had one crippling handicap. Educators don't like to admit it. Some refuse to believe it, and others speak scornfully of it. But scorn does not solve it, and ignoring it is dangerous. So let's look at it. *Most people are ear-minded, not print-minded. We put them in school and spend years teaching them to decode meaning out of print. We use scientific methods to improve their reading skill. Then they go out of school, still ear-minded, not print-minded.* Even back in the days of radio, repeated investigations of the source of people's ideas showed this result:

| | |
|---|---|
| Radio and moving picture | 60 per cent |
| Print | 40 per cent |

The 40 per cent coming from print showed further that 21 per cent came from newspapers, 11 per cent from magazines, and *only 8 percent from books*. These people had been to school years and spent years learning to read books, but after they left school only 8 per cent got any substantial portion of their ideas from books! We can't blame this on the public schools and the teachers of education, for it's true in Europe also. The only difference is that we keep the ear-minded in school as long as we can and try to teach them by remedial reading, whereas in Europe they are turned out of school at an earlier age.

So from the time the American settlers crossed the Appalachians down until the 1920's we lived in a time of crisis—a democracy of vast size with only print for mass communication. Then came radio and television. Especially came television, for it brought together in one medium almost everything that all the others could do: newspapers, magazines, theatres, moving pictures, and radio—and did it right in the living room. This is a new age in communication. It's changing the nature of society and changing the process of government. It has made Alaska and Hawaii as close to Washington as Virginia and Maryland. It has tied the nation closer together than did our vast highway system and transcontinental railroads. It has brought the President into our homes more often than our neighbors. It has made the President more powerful and closer to the people than the men who wrote the Constitution ever dreamed he might be. This, then, is the first reason why television, with radio, is an agent of revolution. It overcame the barriers of time and space.

Second, it has increased the power of the multitude—a multitude that is ear-minded, not print-minded. When the Constitution was written, the multitude was not allowed to vote. The men who wrote it feared the multitude as Cicero feared the proletariat of ancient Rome. Even Jefferson shrank from the implications of universal suffrage until long after he wrote the Declaration of Independence; and Webster as late as 1820 warned his peers that equal suffrage always ended in revolution and bloodshed. He fought it to the bitter end. Thus our forefathers did not found a democracy, did not intend to do so, and in the main endorsed the viewpoint of John Adams that, "The people of all nations are naturally divided into two sorts, the gentlemen and the simple men." Indeed, they feared what Edmund Randolph called the "excess of democracy," so they set up a *republic* ruled by a top-drawer minority, "the good, the rich, and the wise," men of property and men of education. Universal suffrage came later, and in many states only after a bitter struggle. But universal suffrage did not at once put the multitude in power, for they could not be reached effectively by print and so could not make their numbers count. Not until the age of radio and television did the multitude have an effective medium of communication.

This transfer of power from the top-drawer few to the multitude has changed profoundly the operating nature of our democracy. To cynics, of course, it's all bad. Just as Thoreau in his day lamented the telegraph, now they lament television; and they fear that the power of the multitude will destroy civilization. As Walter Lippmann said, "The public opinion of the masses cannot be counted upon to apprehend regularly and promptly the reality of things. There is an inherent tendency in opinion to feed upon rumors excited by our own wishes and fears."[3] Is he right? Frankly, no. He is a competent thinker, but he belongs to a group that is not acquainted with the behavioral sciences, and no person not acquainted with the behavioral sciences is today capable of top-level thinking on human relations. It's like having the world's best harness maker tinker with a jet engine. With handling harness, he is the world's best; but he does not know jets. The behavioral sciences have learned to investigate how and why public opinion changes—and what they have learned

[3] *The Public Philosophy* (Boston, Little, Brown and Co., 1955), pp. 25-26.

refutes the horse-and-buggy ideas about the multitude. The voice of the people is not the voice of God. It's not infallible. Its members are not brilliant or well read. But the combined evidence shows that the multitude has a remarkably high degree of common sense, that they are able to understand public questions when stripped of jargon and told in plain language, and they are excellent judges of public policy. When the *Public Opinion Quarterly* published its summary of what twenty years had uncovered, overwhelming evidence on almost every conceivable issue— political, social, economic—showed that the public was almost always ahead of leaders in government.[4] It justifies repeating the neat summary by Samuel Butler made earlier in this book: "The public may not know enough to *be* experts, but they know enough to judge between them."

*In other words the critical point today is not where down the ages we thought it was. It's not with the multitude. It's not with whether they can be trusted to judge competently. It's with the leaders, with whether they know how to communicate to the multitude in terms of their needs and understanding.*

With this background we come to special problems of communicating by radio and television.


## ADAPTING A SPEECH TO THE RADIO

The radio audience can't see you, so now you *must* do things that all speakers everywhere ought to do but often don't. Consider your unseen audience for a moment. You may be talking to 50,000 people, but they are not like 50,000 people sitting together in a stadium. They are separated into groups of twos and threes sitting comfortably in their own homes. Usually they are giving only half attention, meanwhile also glancing at a newspaper, talking, eating, working, or tinkering. If anything good comes out of the radio, they pause to listen carefully, but most of the time they listen with only part of their minds. Also, they are not in a "social situation," with rows of others sitting in front and behind. Hence they are not influenced by the mass presence of others, and not subjected to the increased responsiveness that comes from being in a crowd.

In public few people will walk out of an auditorium, no matter how poor the speaker. Not so with the radio. By a twist of the wrist a listener cuts off an uninteresting program and picks up a different one. He can choose what he wants to hear, and does choose.

### PLANNING THE SPEECH

Few speakers can hold a radio audience for more than 15 minutes. Those who can are so rare that you can count yourself out. Your problem

[4] Volume XXI, No. 1, Spring, 1957.

is how to hold it for 15 minutes or less. The first minute or two is critical. Out across the ether in those thousands of homes you are being sized up. If you don't get attention and get lively interest, out will go several thousand hands in several thousand homes—and off the air you go. In a sense, a radio speech is a race between arousing interest and being cut off.

The following suggestions come from persons with long radio experience:

1. *Write your talk.* For most speakers talking face-to-face with an audience extemporaneous speaking (note that we said extemporaneous speaking, not impromptu) is the most effective of all modes. But not for the radio speaker. Often he does not "face" an audience at all, but only a cold microphone. His unseen audience can't see his smile, lift of eyebrow, turn of body—actions that carry personal meanings to spectators. Even a long pause, which is common enough in face-to-face speaking, cannot be used because it gives the radio audience an uneasy feeling that the radio has gone dead. Finally, your radio program is timed with exactness that has radio's famous "three seconds leeway." In sum, you have no alternative but to write the speech. Most radio stations indeed won't let you in the studio until you present a manuscript.

2. *Organize the speech by a simple thought pattern.* You might want to review the discussion of thought patterns found in Chapter 11, for you will now need to apply that knowledge as never before. Avoid a complex pattern. You can't watch the listeners to tell whether they understand you, and if you could there is not a second of time to pause and clear up confusion. Therefore, for the main structure use two or three clearly related ideas, so phrased that the relationship is instantly clear.

3. *Plan to get the listener's attention at once, and to hold it.* By "at once" is meant in the first sentence. Cut all wind-up. You know the ways of supporting an idea so as to hold attention, for you have previously studied them: Illustrations, Specific Instances, Comparison and Contrast, Description, Narration. Use them here. Make your talk vital with human interest stories, narrative illustrations, references to events and things that are familiar in everyday life.

4. *Use simple words and short sentences.* As the Columbia Broadcasting System puts it, "Inflation, as an economic term, means little to people. But expressed as pork chops at a dollar a pound, it means an awful lot." The word "domicile" is highbrow, but "home" carries meaning to all. People like plain simple words. Use them.

Avoid long sentences, and twisting sentences; make them short and straight. It's a radio maxim that any sentence over twenty words is too long. Make yours, then, twenty words or less, and strip piled-up phrases and winding clauses.

Finally, make your writing sound like *talk*. Especially, use the contractions that well-bred people use in every day speech. People simply don't says, "It is" but *"It's."* They don't say, "We do not," but *"We don't."*

5. *Give double care to transitions, summaries, and the statement of main heads.* The radio listener can't see those little transitions and punctuations that good speakers give, often unconsciously, with the head, face, hands, and body. The radio speaker must supply them with words. A safe precaution is to label each main topic in advance, and to summarize it tersely when finished. Throughout the speech give more than usual care to the essential connections—like *but, and, also, furthermore, hence,* and *therefore.*

6. *Type your manuscript in readable form.* Studios recommend that speeches be double spaced on white or yellow paper (don't use crackly paper) roughly 8½ x 11 inches in size, and spaced with a 2-inch margin all around. This makes the copy easy to read and also allows space for marginal notations.

7. *Mark your manuscript so as to help you communicate the full meaning and mood.* This is a common usage among good speakers and announcers. Each develops his personal system of markings. Some use red and green pencils, different colors for different meanings. Some use single and double underlinings, plus single and double pause-markings. So mark it in any way that means the most to you. The reproduction on the opposite page is typical.

Marking the speech will help you read the speech so it sounds like talk. *Reading so it sounds like talk is more difficult than talking extempore, and generally takes beginners about two years longer to learn!* You see the flat words on flat paper, all of them the same color, all of them in the same size type. Everything is flat; everything is one color. Thus you tend to read flat words, in a flat tone, in a flat pitch (typical readers mostly use three notes; typical Broadway actors use 15!). You tend to read at the same rate and give each word the same stress. You tend to pronounce all those little vowel-murmur words like *of, to, the, a, an,* as if they were thought-carrying words. The result is that you read *tap-tap-tap.* No melody, no stress, no language of tone. Marking the manuscript allows you to concentrate on *meaning* and *mood,* to group your words, use the pause to get set for the next thought, and to construct it quickly in your mind.

8. *Rehearse your talk.* In that interesting booklet published by Columbia Broadcasting System on *Making Friends with the Microphone,* the

(In other words,) on any "important" educational program — not just reading, writing, and arithmetic, but on the great "goals" of education — you can't do it by "precept" alone. You must do it by "practice." You can't practice enough inside the school room walls. You have got to get out into "life", into the city halls, the factories, the shops and offices. George Săn-tĭ-AN-ă might call that training for the mere masses. I prefer to call it education for the "people."

"sophomore"—the underlining means special emphasis; the quotation marks mean even more emphasis.

"really"—multiple underlinings mean terrific emphasis.

(You will find)—parenthesized phrases indicate that the voice is to be dropped. SŎPH-us—Ŏ shows how the o is pronounced; capitals mean that this syllable is to be stressed.

question is asked: "Don't we rehearse?" and the answer is "We certainly do." Most able radio speakers, of course, do more than merely rehearse. They make advance recordings of their speeches, play them back, and study them for clarity, inflection, and tone quality. For beginners this ought to be compulsory. It helps them check the rate, emphasis, variety, and especially their language of tone. It allows them to learn whether they tend to blast the microphone by blurting certain sounds, then have dropsy at the end of a sentence.

9. *Time your speech carefully in advance.* On the radio even three seconds count. For example, in a 15-minute program, 30 seconds is allowed for technical station and network operation. That leaves 14 minutes 30 seconds actual speaking time. Of this, the announcer ordinarily takes about 1 minute in the opening and closing. That leaves the speaker 13½ minutes. He must not run over and he must not run short. He must come out "on the nose."

With a manuscript in hand and the words in plain sight the tendency is to read too fast. How fast does a good radio speaker talk? That varies with the person. Edward R. Murrow speaks at an average rate, about

145 words a minute. Walter Winchell was the recent fastest, about 215. Franklin D. Roosevelt represented the best of the slow speakers, 117 words a minute; but he used pause, inflection, and double inflection that gave life and good looks to his ideas. Don't try to talk at any set rate, but rather at the rate that permits you to communicate best. Reading in this way, *time your speech, page by page, and mark the time at the bottom of each page.* Then when you broadcast the speech you can check this marked time against the studio clock (it is always big, and visible to the radio speaker), and make sure you are talking at the rate you planned.

### FACING THE MICROPHONE

At last you are ready to give the speech. You have a manuscript. You've rehearsed it, marked it, timed it. You are now standing or sitting before the microphone and the second hand on the big studio clock is ticking toward the zero second. You get the signal. You are on the air!

In preparation for that moment, there are a few things you ought to know about facing that sensitive and delicate instrument, the microphone:

1. *Remember that you are talking to unseen groups of only two or three persons:* No matter how many thousands are listening, they are gathered in groups of twos and threes. Don't talk to them as you would to a hundred people in an auditorium, but rather as you would talk to people sitting beside you—in your best conversational tone.

2. *Don't raise your voice pitch.* Under the tension of speaking the tendency is to tighten the throat muscles, and thus raise the voice pitch. But on the radio a high-pitched voice sounds strained and affected. A quiet, easy voice is best; and the most pleasant registers are the normal middle and lower ones. So relax those throat muscles and let the pitch down to its normal level. Don't be alarmed if your voice sounds a bit flat, or if the pauses seem a shade long. These are the normal effects in a room with special studio acoustics.

3. *Don't blast and fade into the microphone.* The microphone goes to both extremes in volume. If you explode a word the result will be a blast. Then if your voice fades out at the end of a sentence (this is called *dropsy* in some studios) your words will be inaudible. Your voice will then come out of the loudspeaker something like this:

> Ladies and gentlemen: MMMMPHMMM [unintelligible because of blast] I want to talk about today is *mmmmm* of the *prrmmmmmm* [can't be heard because of dropsy].

Inequalities in volume that would pass unnoticed in an auditorium will simply ruin a radio speech. Therefore, avoid sudden sharp changes in volume. For radio emphasis, changes in intensity are better than changes in volume.

4. *Don't weave back and forth, turn away, or lean too close to the microphone.* If you change distance from your mouth to the microphone your voice will fade and boom as you move. If you lean too close, as witless speakers invariably do, every word will be distorted. Keep the same distance. How far you should stand or sit depends on the type of microphone and on your particular voice quality. The experts in the studio will take care of that for you. Your responsibility is to stay put, and send an *even* tone into the microphone.

5. *Keep all other noises out of the microphone.* What other noises, you may wonder, can possibly get into a microphone in a soundproof studio? The answer is noises that you make.

First, don't clear your throat, smack your lips, cough into a microphone, tap a pencil, drum on the table, or snap your fingers. These high-pitched sounds often crack like a pistol in radio listeners' ears. If you must cough, turn your face away and bury it deep in a handkerchief. If such a cough gets into a microphone anyhow apologize for it so the audience will know you are not a boor. A simple, "Sorry," or "I beg pardon," is enough to let the audience know you are not "coughing in their faces."

Second, don't rustle the pages of your manuscript. To the listener crackling paper sounds like hail on a tin roof. A good procedure is to make a final check just before you go on the air to see that your pages are in proper order, then remove the clip (never speak with a manuscript clipped together!). As you finish with each page, simply let that sheet fall to the table or floor. You have thus got rid of it without the chance of a rustle.

Third, breathe silently. This advice might tempt you to protest, "Can't I even breathe in peace before a microphone?" That depends on how you breathe. A sudden intake is magnified by the microphone into a whistle. So you keep relaxed and breathe silently and deep.

Fourth, keep your hands off the microphone. Avoid that temptation to "stroke it, tickle it, pat it, tap it, and climb it." These aimless efforts produce sounds not unlike those of an artillery bombardment.

Finally, say absolutely nothing for at least fifteen seconds before and after you are on the air. That microphone might be open! You can't tell by looking at it! There was once a man who thought he was off the air, and so he said to the announcer, . . . But maybe you heard about that one. Don't let it happen to you.

## ADAPTING A SPEECH TO TELEVISION

On television the microphone is still there. But there is also a camera, and it's not like any other camera ever known. It does tricks. Adapting the speech both to the microphone and to this tricky camera is broadly like adapting it both to live audience and a radio audience—but there are differences that will impede communication if you don't adjust to them. Following are some of the ground rules:

1. *Converse intimately, and look that lens in the eye.* "Television is a microscope, not a telescope," explained Irving Gitling. Telecast speech is intimate communication. You have live-eye contact with every listener, everywhere. If you look into the *take* lens (i.e. the one being used in the 4-lens turret) while you talk, you come right into the listener's living room. This is rare intimacy that you cannot attain even with a live audience, for only on television can you look every listener in the eye at the same instant. Everything lends itself to the illusion of closeness. The listeners sit in their homes. The screen is small. You can speak to each person as though he were your sole audience. So look the lens in the eye, make friends with it, talk intimately with it. Remember that a well-mannered person does not shout at another one four or five feet away. Remember also that one who orates close-up in the face of a listener provokes amusement or contempt, but not respect.

2. *Find out in advance where you will stand or sit, and how far you may move without getting outside the camera range or depth of focus.* The size of image on the screen is determined by the distance of the camera and by the focal length of the lens being used. By changing the distance and changing the lens the cameras can shift the image from face-only to waist-up, full-view, and distant-view including background scenery or visual aids. Also, photographs are made from different angles —front, side, above, below—and to give variety changes will be made in both angles and distance while you are speaking. Almost always two cameras are used, but if only one is used it will be panned right and left, tilted up and down, and dollied toward and away from you.

Remember to be friendly with that camera eye. Know which lens in the turret is looking at you. If there are two cameras don't be caught napping when the director shifts you from one camera to another—and don't think you can tell by watching that neat little tally light that goes on when a camera starts scanning you. When the tally light goes on, it's too late. The director has already shifted, and the new camera has already caught you looking into the old one. So instead work it out with the floor director. Usually he will signal you just before switching cameras, then he will give you a different signal when the cut is made. With a little planning, when the warning signal comes you can *pause and look down* at the end of the next sentence. A smart floor manager at once will signal cut, then you can look up facing the new camera.

3. *Learn what clothes and make-up give the best effect.* Television cameras have a peculiarity known as color distortion. They cannot repro-

*National Broadcasting Company*

eet the Press" is a special type of television discussion in which the panel of news eporters question their guest to bring out his ideas, attitudes, and points of view.

duce extreme contrast, but operate within a range generally cited as 20 to 1. To illustrate, a black suit reflects about 3½ per cent of the light, and a white shirt reflects about 90 per cent. This is a contrast range of over 25 to 1 (i.e. 90 is over 25 times 3½), and the television camera can't take it. The white shirt "blooms," produces halos, and changes the color tone of your face. Hence persons on television generally avoid both black and white. Men wear colored shirts: pale blue, tan, yellow, or gray. Woman avoid figured dresses, lest they look in the telecast as though an egg had been smeared on them. If a dress or shirt is to appear white, then dye a white one light blue or yellow, or buy a colored one with a light tone.

But first of all, inquire at the television station about both clothes and make-up. Inquire also about jewelry, for all that glitters on television is not gold. Beads, rings, pins, earrings, and bald heads also glitter, and even discolor other things around them.

4. *Don't let the manuscript come between you and the audience.*
Handling notes or manuscript is the most difficult adjustment a speaker
has to make for television speaking. As on the radio your speech needs
to be timed close to that "three seconds leeway," hence you need a carefully prepared one. Yet you can't read it as you would on radio. To be
sure, you can simply take your eyes off the camera, glue them to the
manuscript, and read. Politicians and Presidents do. Listeners accept it,
just as they accept the fact that somebody else wrote the speech. But as
*Time* reported, "a routine political speech has a low-rating in listenership.
What is worse, the wind . . . is often strong enough to blow [the] audience right over to a more entertaining station for the rest of the evening."[5]
In fact, it's so bad that stations "are still increasingly reluctant to sell
time to such crashing bores," even at top-dollar prices since it lowers
their listener-rating on the programs following. Reading is not the answer.
It takes a crisis or a national political election to make listeners listen to
speakers who read. It's not because reading is a poor mode of communication, but because people can't read well. Reading is more difficult than
speaking extempore, but speakers don't know this. They don't know—
and probably wouldn't believe—how little talent readers like Ethel
Barrymore, Charles Laughton, and Franklin D. Roosevelt seemed to have
at first, and at how painstakingly they learned to make reading sound
like talk.

There is no easy way around the problem. Even memorizing is seldom
the answer, for most memorized speeches *sound* memorized. Like reading,
memorizing is a difficult art. (See pages 274-275 for a discussion of
this.) Here are the most common ways now followed:

*a.* Most public officials read poorly; and some listeners endure it while
others switch to another station.

*b.* Most newscasters on national hookups read superbly. They know
what is on the paper so well that they merely *glance* at it. They seem to
be speaking almost without notes, and actual stopwatch timing shows
them to be looking at the audience about 90 per cent of the time. With
manuscript glances trimmed to about 10 per cent of speaking time, they
attain intimate audience contact. (In contrast, mine-run speakers have
repeatedly been timed with eyes-on-the-manuscript 55 seconds, and eyes-
on-the-audience 5 seconds!) Also these newscasters don't read long at
any one stretch. They cut in with film strips, moving pictures of today's
events, and bring in standby telecasters from Washington and other cities.

But as you go down the scale on local-station newscasters outside of
New York, they read progressively poorer and poorer, until some in the
smaller stations could hardly be said to read at all. They only recite
flat words.

[5] July 7, 1958, p. 52.

*TelePrompTer Corporation*

e "TelePrompTer" is a device which enables a public speaker *who is skilled in its use*
maintain more effective communication with his audience than is possible when reading
from manuscript.

    *c.* Some speakers use notes, just as with a live audience, but talk into
the "take" lens of the camera, and keep an eye alert for camera shifts.
This takes timing, for you must keep eye on the clock. But it can be
done, and, frankly, it's lots of fun. You are really talking, and you know
you are; and in your mind's eye you can see the listeners in that camera
eye!

    *d.* Others use a reading unit developed by the TelePrompTer Corpora-
tion. It's a box some 18 inches square, concealed from the camera and
the live audience, but visible to the speaker. The speech is typed on a roll
in very large letters, inserted in the reading unit, and illuminated so it
throws the heavy lettering into relief. Sometimes a big magnifying glass
is placed in front of it, for speakers who need glasses but don't like to wear

them in public. As the speaker proceeds, the roll moves from the bottom to the top with six or eight lines always visible.

*e.* Others combine notes with the TelePrompTer reading equipment, use notes for the main part, but rely on the TelePrompTer for exact wordings that might be misconstrued if the wording were changed. Queen Elizabeth of England generally uses this method.

*f.* Finally, speakers can use cue cards, sometimes called "idiot sheets." These are placed alongside the camera. Sometimes they're merely notes. Other time a whole speech is lettered on them, using huge cards, about 3 x 5 feet, with about eight lines to the card.

5. *Consider the possibilities of visual aids.* A basic requirement of television is *variety,* for listeners won't look long at an image that doesn't change. Use every available technique, therefore, for making seemingly natural image changes on the screen. One is visual aids: maps, charts, diagrams, models, slides, and films. Sometimes they are placed beside you or just behind you—as with maps, charts, and diagrams—so you can point to them, or mark them with large visible crayon as you talk. Or they may be placed a few feet away where you can step over to them while talking. Materials that you don't need to explain by pointing are set up some distance off, to be picked up by another camera. Slides and films, of course are handled from the projection booth.

6. *Adapt your action to close-up speaking.* Television requires eye-communication so conspicuously missing in radio, but action on television is not identical with action in an auditorium. It moves in the direction of best action in private conversation. In an auditorium you need extended action—a sweep of the arm, large movements of the body —for people to see at a distance. On television extended action is over-done and marks you as a "ham." On television more often than not you don't stand up and speak formally, but are seated at a desk, as in an office, or even in an easy chair, as at home. This is a new kind of posture. You don't want to sit stiff-backed, but rather to sit as in alert friendly conference or conversation. Thus far you can be merely "natural" if your natural manner in private conversation is good enough. But from this point on, you can't be "natural." You must adopt a technique that gives the *illusion* of naturalness. For example, in private conversation you might sit for a minute or two without deliberately changing posture. Not in television. You must have variety on that screen, and to do this you need deliberately to change position with reasonable frequency and do so in a way that gives the illusion of doing it naturally. You may lean forward to emphasize an idea, turn your body or nod your head to mark a transition. You may explain, describe, locate, and differentiate ideas with your hands—not with extended action, but in reduced form as though talking to people sitting beside you. You will look at the camera, and look away.

You will consciously seek for variety that seems natural, attempting an art that conceals art.

Furthermore, in doing this you must conform to the limitations of the television camera: keep within camera range, and keep action away from that foreground where it will be out of focus.

Finally, watch your mannerisms. Many of us are guilty of trick manners, facial contortions, wasted motions, and repetition of action, of which we are usually unaware. Our friends are accustomed to them, and are less distracted by them than are strangers. Such mannerisms don't go well on television. The illusion of closeness on the television screen magnifies them and annoys the listener. Now this does not mean that you give up the hallmarks of your own personality and become a robot. Effective television speaking, in fact, demands that you intensify your personality. But it also demands that you get rid of annoying mannerisms. You can't check yourself on this. You need the advice of others who are willing to watch you rehearse.

## Assignments

1. Listen to a good radio speaker and report on what you think are the factors of his effectiveness. Include mode of speaking, articulation, content, organization, and use of language.

2. Listen to a good television speaker. (*a*) Report on the things you *saw* that contributed to his effectiveness. (*b*) To focus your consciousness on the technique of action, count how often the speaker changed his position or posture during a 3-minute period. (*c*) Count the number of camera changes, of distance and angle, made during a 3-minute period.

3. Visit a radio studio and study firsthand the conditions under which a speaker broadcasts.

4. Visit a television studio and study the conditions under which a speaker telecasts.

5. Recast one of your previous speeches in this course so it will be adapted for radio broadcast.

6. Recast one of your previous speeches in this course for telecasting. With marginal notes indicate what visual aids you would use. Also indicate special adaptations you would make of posture and movement.

7. Write out a one-minute newscast and make a recording of it. Remember that the announcer's problem of reading aloud is like the actor's. He must *seem* natural but he can't *be* natural. In everyday American speech, sounds are slurred and final phrases lost. Should you talk in this "natural" way over the microphone, without the aid of gestures and sight, your voice simply won't make sense. An announcer, like an actor, must overdo to seem natural.

The good announcer overdoes just enough to make it seem natural, whereas the "ham" overdoes in a way that makes him seem obviously unnatural.

8. Write out and record a three-minute radio speech:

   a. Type the manuscript, double-space, and mark for reading.
   b. Time it carefully, and in order to make sure of not running over, put your limit at 2 minutes 50 seconds. *Don't* write a 3-minute 30-second speech, then try to pack it into 2 minutes 50 seconds by fast reading, for the faster you read the less the listener comprehends. If you have a 3:30-minute speech, read it in 2:50 minutes of time, and the listener gets 1:30 minutes worth, that is poor economy.
   c. Above all, be earnest; talk directly to your unseen listener

# Parliamentary Procedure

THE EARLY DEMOCRACIES did not have parliamentary procedure as we use the term, nor did the feudal states of the Middle Ages. But when rural England began developing the system of representative government, some eight hundred years ago, its leaders needed a technique for operating that system. When they developed it they called it "parliamentary procedure," for it was a procedure developed to operate their Parliament.

Parliamentary procedure in America inherited its spirit from England, but not all of its form. It evolved through town meeting to colonial assembly to Continental Congress. When the Constitution was adopted Thomas Jefferson used the customs of the British Parliament for drawing up rules of procedure for the House of Representatives, but tempered them out of his experiences in the Virginia House of Burgesses and the Continental Congress. Through the years the House has changed them further, until the chairman of the House Rules Committee, Howard Worth Smith, could say recently: "These rules have been developed over 170 years. There is reason behind them."

In 1876 Henry M. Robert used the procedure of the House of Representatives in drawing up his rules of order for general public use. Since then over a hundred other writers have modified and streamlined them. There is no one fixed set of rules, therefore. The United States Senate, the House of Representatives, and the British Parliament each uses slightly different rules. So with the state legislatures. Societies and clubs use a procedure slightly different from any of the legislatures. Each has relied on precedent and experience to develop a procedure best fitted to its needs. The important thing is not that minor differences exist, but that the procedure has the same objectives and is based on the same principles. The objectives are to protect each member of the organization, yet make it possible for the group to act effectively—adhering to the axiom that "when there is no law, but every man is right in his own eyes, there is the least real liberty." The principles on which it rests are these·

1. Rule of the majority, with full respect and full protection of minority rights.
2. Equality of membership.
3. Free and full discussion.
4. Consideration and disposition of one matter at a time.
5. Discussion of topics, not personalities.

## Getting business conducted

When business is carried on by a group there is a danger that the operation will veer toward one of two extremes. First, the group may bog down and get nothing done; the members waste their time in aimless talk and pointless delays. Second, going to the other extreme, it may cease to be a deliberate body and become only a ratifying body that passes motions without discussion, but with unanimous "ayes." The world has witnessed a succession of such ratifying bodies in the twentieth-century dictator states, in which the Leader speaks and their parliamentary puppets shout *ya* or *da*. In contrast, parliamentary procedure was evolved as a technique to enable groups to *deliberate* without stagnating.

### ORDER OF BUSINESS

Each group has an order of business, usually specified in its by-laws. If not otherwise specified, the following is common procedure:

1. Call to order
2. Minutes of previous meeting: reading, correcting, approving
3. Reports of officers (especially secretary and treasurer)
4. Reports of standing committees
5. Reports of special committees
6. Unfinished business from previous meetings
7. Miscellaneous: requests, announcements, etc.
8. New business
9. Program
10. Adjournment

### THE CHAIRMAN

The chairman holds a position of authority and responsibility. He must get business done, but he must get it done democratically. He must protect the assembly from dilatory and frivolous motions, must enforce the observance of order and propriety among members—yet he is the servant of the assembly. The duties of a chairman may be summarized thus: (1) *Keep the business moving as rapidly as may be done with real deliberation.* (2) *In the conduct of business be vigorous and positive, in the treatment of members be courteous and impersonal.* The following is a useful guide for all chairmen:

1. Keep with you a copy of the constitution and by-laws.

2. Commit your Order of Business to memory.

3. Master such basic parliamentary considerations as the nature, purpose, and order of precedence of commonly used motions.

4. Keep at hand a chart showing precedence of all the various motions.

5. Keep a committee roster, so you can quickly check the personnel of the different committees.

6. Recognize each speaker by name, or if you do not know the name ask, "Will the member state his (or her) name?"

7. If two or more members claim the floor at the same time, recognize the one you choose, but in principle alternate the discussion between those who favor and those who oppose the motion. Also do not allow a few persons to do most of the talking so long as others want to participate.

8. State each motion clearly and exactly, so the full membership will know what business is before the house.

9. Keep business moving by such means as will prompt deliberation and action: "Is there a second?" "Is there any discussion?" "Any further discussion?" "If there is no further discussion the chair proposes to put the question to a vote."

10. Especially use the Unanimous or General Consent vote where the group opinion seems to be unanimous: "It's been moved that the assembly do so-and-so. If there are no objections so-and-so will be done." After a pause for objection you will say, "It's so ordered."

11. When members make "suggestions" ask them to put the suggestion in the form of a motion.

12. In voice voting call for "Those in favor say 'aye.' Those opposed say 'no.'" Don't brand yourself as a parliamentary illiterate by calling for "Those opposed, same sign," thereby making the "noes" vote "aye."

13. Announce the results clearly.

14. Insist that the assembly recognize the parliamentary necessity of considering one matter of business at a time. Invariably some members will offer a main motion while another main motion is pending, and these must courteously be put aside.

15. If a member ignorantly makes an improper motion, courteously suggest the proper one whenever you can do so, instead of merely ruling him out of order.

16. Always refer to yourself as "the chair," and not by the first person pronoun.

17. Make full use of your secretary. Remember that the secretary keeps a running account of the proceedings.

## VOTING

Nearly all motions must be voted upon. Most of them require only a simple majority, although those which would change established custom, such as amendments to the constitution or by-laws, or those which would limit or restrict the individual's normal rights, such as limitation on debate, require a two-thirds majority. Following are the more common methods of voting:

*Voice vote* (by ayes and noes). This is the most common method. It should not be used in voting on motions requiring a two-thirds majority. In putting the question, the chairman simply says, "The question is on the adoption of the motion that . . . "All in favor say 'aye,'" and then, "All opposed say 'no.'"

*Standing Vote.* The chairman should call for a standing vote if he has reason to believe that the vote will be too close to be determined by *viva voce*. He may call for it following a *viva-voce* vote if he is not able to determine whether there were more ayes or noes.

*Show of Hands Vote.* This form of voting may be used in place of the standing vote, except when division of the assembly has been called for, in which case the standing vote should be used.

*Ballot.* The ballot is used only when a secret vote is desired. Most organizations prefer the ballot for the election of officers, and for election to club membership. If someone desires a ballot on a question on which the constitution does not require it, it is in order for a member to rise and say, "Mr. Chairman, I move that the vote on this question be taken by ballot." This motion is undebatable, and requires a simple majority. A ballot vote which is not unanimous may *not* be made so by a motion to that effect.

*Roll Call* (recorded yeas and noes). If someone wants the organization to have a record of the vote on a particular question, he obtains the floor, and says, "Mr. Chairman, I call for the yeas and noes on the motion. . . ." Upon hearing a second, the chairman says, "The aye and no vote has been called for on the motion. . . . Those in favor say 'aye.' Those opposed say 'no.' The ayes have it, and the vote on this question will be taken by yeas and noes." Following debate, the secretary will call roll, recording an "aye" or a "no" after the name of each member present and voting. This record is incorporated into the minutes.

*Unanimous or General Consent.* This is the kind of vote actually used when the chairman states that if there is no objection, such and such will be done. *It's a highly desirable expedient, and is used often.* Nearly all organizations, for example, use it in approving the minutes. A single objection forces a formal vote, and it is not applicable to any motion affecting the constitution and by-laws, or to any rule which protects absentees.

*Voting by the Chairman.* The chairman votes when:

1. The vote is by ballot.
2. The vote is by roll call (recorded yeas and noes).
3. In all other cases when his vote will change the result. For example, he might vote "yes" to break a tie that exists, or "no" to create a tie, and thus cause the defeat of a motion.


## QUORUM

A quorum is the minimum number of members (usually a percentage of membership) necessary for the legal transaction of business. It refers to the number present, not to the number voting. The quorum is usually specified in the by-laws, but if none is specified, it is presumed to be a simple majority of the entire membership. If there is no quorum, members present may discuss any business whatsoever, but they can take no legal action. A quorum is not necessary for motions to *adjourn,* to *recess,* or to *fix the time and place to reassemble.*


## ELECTIONS

The mode of election should be explicitly set forth in the constitution and by-laws.

*Nominations.* Usually nominating committees are used, for committees are in position to select the nominees with considered care and they expedite election procedure. A few small organizations nominate entirely by ballot, with no names placed before them; after the first round of balloting two or more names begin to emerge as the group choice, and the election can be accomplished within four to six ballots. The poorest method is to have desultory nominations from the floor without a prior committee report or consideration. Off-the-cuff nominations and elections may be done in a few minutes, and the society may suffer the penalties of poor officers for the whole duration of their term. If a nominating committee is used, other nominations for each office may be made from the floor *after* the nominating committee has submitted its selections. (This gives the assembly a check on any committee that might attempt to ignore the will of the majority.) Before proceeding to election the chair should inquire if there are additional nominations.

*Seconding nominations.* Nominations, of course, do *not* require a second, this in spite of parliamentary ignorance shown by members who chirp, "I second the nomination." Any person whose name is presented to assembly is a nominee, and the nomination needs no further sponsorship from any other member.

*Closing nominations.* When there are obviously no further nominations the chair may declare nominations closed, or a member may move to close nominations by vote. Such a motion requires a two-thirds majority, since it deprives members of one of their rights.

*Voting* on the candidates should be by ballot.

## The nature, purpose, and precedence of parliamentary motions

Motions are the media through which business is transacted. The secretary may read a communication, or a member may outline a proposal; but there is no business before the assembly until someone offers a motion. There are four classes of motions, each having its special set of purposes and all of them, from the first to the last, having a fixed order of precedence: (1) Principal Motions, (2) Subsidiary Motions, (3) Incidental Motions, and (4) Privileged Motions. We shall consider each group separately.

### PRINCIPAL MOTIONS

1. Main Motion
2. Reconsider
3. Rescind
4. Expunge
5. Take from the Table

Parliamentary manuals agree on the names Subsidiary Motions, Incidental Motions, and Privileged Motions. But they don't agree on a single name for the group here presented, and in different manuals they are called "unclassified," "miscellaneous," "incidental main," "main motions," etc. But for the following reasons we here group them with the Main Motion under the heading of "Principal Motions":

1. They have the same order of precedence (rank) as the main motion.
2. Like the main motion, they introduce a new matter of business.
3. Generally, like the main motion, they may not be introduced when any other question is pending.

The object, form, and characteristics of each of these motions are given below.

MAIN MOTION:

*Object:* To introduce original business.

*Form:* "Mr. Chairman, I move that this club buy a new gavel," "Mr. Chairman, I move the adoption of the following resolution: . . . ."

*Characteristics:* 1. Is out of order when any other business is pending.
2. Takes precedence over no other motions, and yields to all other motions except other principal motions.
3. Requires a second, is debatable, is amendable, and requires a simple majority vote.

RECONSIDER:

*Object:* To bring before the assembly a question already voted upon.

*Form:* "Mr. Chairman, I move to reconsider the action of this assembly in. . . ."

*Characteristics:* 1. Must be proposed and seconded by members *who were on the prevailing side* in the original voting.
2. Must be made at the *same meeting or the next meeting following the original voting.*
3. Requires a second, is debatable only if the motion to which it applies is debatable, in which case the original question is again open to debate, is not amendable, and requires a simple majority.

RESCIND:

*Object:* To nullify a vote (practically, its object is same as that of to reconsider).

*Form:* "Mr. Chairman, I move to rescind the action of . . . taken at the . . . meeting."

*Characteristics:* 1. May be introduced at any time, in contrast to the motion to reconsider, which must be introduced not later than the meeting following that at which the original vote took place.
2. Requires only a simple majority provided previous notice

has been given; otherwise either two-thirds majority of those present, or a simple majority of the entire membership.

3. Requires a second, is debatable, and is amendable.

EXPUNGE

*Object:* *To eradicate a former action completely by striking its record from the minutes.*

*Form:*    "Mr. Chairman, I move to expunge from the records (here state the order, the resolution, or the objectional words) as found in the journal of (give date and place in the record)."

*Characteristics:*  1. Requires a majority vote of the entire membership.
2. If adopted, it requires the secretary to draw a line around that part of the record to which it applies, and to write across the face of it, "Expunged by order of the assembly this _____ day of _____ A.D. 19____."
3. Requires a second, is debatable, and is amendable.

TAKE FROM THE TABLE

*Object:* To bring up for consideration a motion previously laid on the table.

*Form:*    "Mr. Chairman, I move to take from the table the motion. . . ."

*Characteristics:*  1. If adopted, it makes the motion taken from the table the next order of business.
2. If it is rejected, it may be proposed later in the same meeting after other business has been considered.
3. Requires a second, is not debatable, is not amendable, and requires a simple majority.

## SUBSIDIARY (SECONDARY) MOTIONS

1. Postpone Indefinitely
2. Amend
3. Refer or Commit
4. Postpone to a Definite Time
5. Limit Debate
6. Previous Question (vote immediately)
7. Lay on the Table

Subsidiary motions, as the term indicates, modify or dispose of certain other motions to which they may be applied, particularly principal motions, and even more particularly the main motion. *They must be disposed of before the motion to which they apply can be given further consideration.* For example, action must be taken on an amendment before further consideration can be given the motion which it would amend. Incidental motions and privileged motions take precedence over them, and as a group they must be learned in the order of their precedence. They are listed above in order of rank from lowest to highest. To lay on the table, therefore, takes precedence over all other subsidiary motions. Commit them to memory in the order listed.

POSTPONE INDEFINITELY:

*Object:* To dispose of a question (a motion) without voting on the question itself. It is often used to test voting strength on a question without having to vote on the question itself.

*Form:* "Mr. Chairman, I move to postpone the question indefinitely."

*Characteristics:* 1. If adopted, *it kills the motion to which it applies.* The question would have to be reintroduced at some future meeting.
2. It has the same rank as the motion to amend, neither being in order when the other is pending.
3. It requires a second, is debatable, and reopens debate on the motion to which it applies, is not amendable, and requires a simple majority vote.

AMEND:

*Object:* To modify a question before the assembly.

*Form:* "Mr. Chairman, I move to amend the motion by *deleting* the words. . . ."
"Mr. Chairman, I move to amend the motion by *adding.* . . ."
"Mr. Chairman, I move to amend the motion by *inserting* the words . . . between . . . and. . . ."
"Mr. Chairman, I move to amend the motion by *striking out* the words . . . and *inserting* the words. . . ."
"Mr. Chairman, I move to amend the motion by *substituting* for it the following. . . ."

*Characteristics:* 1. In phrasing your amendment, guard against ambiguity. State what your amendment proposes; that is, whether it will delete, add, insert, strike out and insert, or substitute. Be direct; say "I move to amend . . . ," not "I think we ought to. . . ."
2. A "primary" amendment or amendment "of the first order" amends a question. A "secondary" amendment or amendment "of the second order" amends an amendment. An amendment "of the third order," that is, an amendment to an amendment to an amendment, is out of order.
3. An amendment must not negate; that is, to propose the

insertion of "not" is out of order. It must not be antagonistic in any other way.

4. An amendment must be germane to the motion of the amendment it proposes to change.

5. The chairman has the authority to demand that an amendment be submitted in writing, and he should do so if it is ambiguous or long and involved.

6. An amendment has the same rank as the motion to postpone indefinitely, neither being in order when the other is pending.

7. It requires a second, is debatable if the motion being amended is debatable, is amendable, and requires a simple majority vote.

## REFER OR COMMIT:

*Object:* To assign a question to a committee for the purpose of (1) obtaining more information on the subject, (2) rewriting in the interest of clarity, or (3) smoothing out troublesome differences.

*Form:* "Mr. Chairman, I move to refer this question to the Executive Committee (or some other standing committee)." "Mr. Chairman, I move to refer the question of selecting a playground site to a committee comprising Mr. Xray, Mr. Yolk, and Mr. Zebra, to submit their recommendations to the next meeting."

*Characteristics:* 1. A motion to commit or refer should specify the number to be on the committee, how they are to be appointed or elected, what their power is to be, and, if apropos, when they are to report.

2. It requires a second, is debatable, is amendable, and requires a simple majority vote.

## POSTPONE TO A DEFINITE TIME:

*Object:* To defer action upon a pending question.

*Form:* "Mr. Chairman, I move to postpone the consideration of the question until the next meeting (or until the arrival of Mr. Roger) (or until 2:30)."

*Characteristics:* 1. If it is adopted, the secretary will note that the question to which it applies becomes the order of business (order of the day) at the time fixed.

2. It requires a second, may be debated as to the propriety of postponement, may be amended as to the time proposed, and requires a simple majority vote.

## LIMIT DEBATE:

*Purpose:* To restrict time available for debate in order to expedite business.

*Form:*  "Mr. Chairman, I move that debate on the pending question be limited to two speeches of two minutes each per member." "Mr. Chairman, I move that debate on the pending question end at 2:30." (Note: The same form may be used to extend debate. "Mr. Chairman, I move that Mr. Wilco's time be extended three minutes.")

*Characteristics:* It requires a second, is not debatable, is amendable, and requires a *two-thirds majority vote.*

### PREVIOUS QUESTION:

*Purpose:* To stop debate, and bring the assembly to a vote.

*Qualified Form:*  "Mr. Chairman, I move the previous question on the motion to amend." Or "Mr. Chairman, I move that we vote immediately on the motion to amend."

*Unqualified Form:* "Mr. Chairman, I move the previous question." Or "Mr. Chairman, I move that we vote immediately on the question before the house."

*Characteristics:* 1. Note that if a series of debatable motions is pending (for example, a main motion, an amendment, and an amendment to the amendment) the previous question may be proposed either for the whole series (unqualified form), or for only the immediate pending motion (qualified form). In this case it would be to the amendment to the amendment.

2. It requires a second, is not debatable, is not amendable, and requires a *two-thirds majority vote.*

### LAY ON THE TABLE:

*Purpose:* Temporarily to lay aside the pending question with the privilege of discussing it at a later date.

*Form:*  "Mr. Chairman, I move that the question be laid on the table."

*Characteristics:* 1. Notice that this motion takes precedence over all other subsidiary motions.

2. With few exceptions, when a question is ordered laid on the table, it takes with it all pending motions pertaining to it in the exact form in which they were when the motions to lay on the table was made.

3. To lay on the table expeditiously disposes of a motion without killing that motion as indefinite postponement does.

4. A question laid on the table is brought up again by voting to take it from the table (see page 474).

5. It requires a second, is not debatable, is not amendable, and requires a simple majority vote.

## INCIDENTIAL MOTIONS

1. Point (Question) of Order
2. Appeal
3. Division of the Assembly
4. Division of the Question
5. Leave to Withdraw a Motion
6. Parliamentary Inquiry
7. Suspension of Rules

Whereas subsidiary motions *modify* or dispose of certain other motions, incidental motions *rise out of* some discussion or other matter of business. A point of order, for example, rises out of some action; a division of the assembly, out of a vote. Since they are purely incidental matters, they are proposed and dealt with as the need arises, and, like principal motions, have no order of precedence among themselves. Incidental motions yield to privileged motions, and most of them are undebatable, and may not be amended. We shall consider only the most common ones.

POINT (QUESTION) OF ORDER:

*Object:* To direct the attention of the chairman to a violation of parliamentary law.

*Form:* "Mr. Chairman, I rise to a point of order." The chairman says, "State your point." You then say, "The amendment proposed by Mr. Oboe is not germane to the main motion and is therefore out of order," or "the motion has not been seconded, and is therefore not before the assembly."

*Characteristics:* 1. You may raise a point of order whenever you feel that a member is guilty of indecorum (misbehavior), that remarks are irrelevant, that debate is out of order, or that a mistake of any kind has been made.
2. The chairman ordinarily rules on a point of order, although he may put it to the vote of the assembly.
3. It does not require a second, is not debatable, is not amendable, is in order when another has the floor, and requires no vote unless the chairman puts it to the assembly, in which case it requires a simple majority.

APPEAL:

*Object:* To compel the chairman to submit a disputed decision to the assembly.

*Form:* "Mr. Chairman, I appeal from the decision of the chair." The chairman then asks, "On what ground is the appeal made?"

*Characteristics:* 1. The appeal is used by a member who believes that the chairman has ruled incorrectly on a point of order. It requires the chairman to submit his ruling to a vote of the assembly.

2. If the matter cannot be settled simply by referring to a rule, that is, if it's a matter involving judgment, the chairman puts the appeal by stating, "The decision of the chair has been appealed from. *Those in favor of sustaining the chair say 'Aye'* . . . *Those opposed say 'No'.*"

3. If there is a tie vote the chair is sustained and the chair (if a member of the assembly) may vote to cause a tie.

4. Whether the appeal is debatable or not, the chairman may state the basis of his original decision. If it is debatable, each member may speak once during the debate.

5. It requires a second, is not amendable, is debatable except (a) when it arises out of an undebatable question, (b) when it relates to indecorum in behavior or debate, and (c) when it relates to priority of business, and is in order when another has the floor.

## DIVISION OF THE ASSEMBLY:

*Object:* To force a standing vote.

*Form:* "Mr. Chairman, I call for a division of the assembly," or simply, "Division!"

*Characteristics:* 1. This motion is used *when you think the chairman has erred in his announcement of an aye and no vote.*

2. It does not require a second, is not debatable, is not amendable, and requires no vote.

## DIVISION OF THE QUESTION:

*Object:* To divide a question in two or more parts in order to consider each part separately.

*Form:* (As applied to the motion that Mr. Wilco and Mr. Roger be invited to address the club.) "Mr. Chairman, I move to divide the question into two parts and consider invitations to Mr. Wilco and Mr. Roger separately."

*Characteristics:* 1. Division of the question is often handled by general consent so that a formal vote is not necessary.

2. Questions should be divided when first introduced.

3. Division of the question does not require a second if it relates to different subjects which are independent of each other, is not debatable, is amendable, requires a

simple majority vote, and is in order when another has the floor if it relates to different subjects which are independent of each other.

LEAVE TO WITHDRAW A MOTION:

*Object:* To withdraw a motion.

*Form:* "Mr. Chairman, I move that the consent of the assembly be granted for the withdrawal (or modification) of the motion. . . ."

*Characteristics:* 1. Up until the time a motion is stated by the chair, its mover may withdraw (or modify) it merely with the consent of the member who seconded it.
2. After the motion is stated by the chair, it may be withdrawn by common consent. ("Mr. Queen wishes to withdraw his motion. If there is no objection, the motion that . . . will be withdrawn.)
3. If there is a single objection to withdrawal, the method indicated under "Form" above must be used.
4. It requires no second, is not debatable, is not amendable, and requires a simple majority vote.

PARLIAMENTARY INQUIRY:

*Object:* To obtain information.

*Form:* "Mr. Chairman, I rise to a parliamentary inquiry." The chairman says, "State your parliamentary inquiry." You then ask, "May I move indefinite postponement of the main motion at this time?"

*Characteristics:* It does not require a second, is not debatable, is not amendable, ordinarily does not require a vote, and is in order when another has the floor.

SUSPENSION OF RULES:

*Object:* To set aside temporarily certain standing rules.

*Form:* "Mr. Chairman, I move to suspend the rules which interfere with the consideration of. . . ."

*Characteristics:* 1. Suspension of the rules is not applicable to the constitution. By-laws, except those relating to business procedure, cannot be suspended unless the by-laws themselves specifically provide for their suspension.
2. It is commonly applied to the order of business.
3. It requires a second, is not debatable, is not amendable, and requires a *two-thirds majority vote*.

## PRIVILEGED MOTIONS

1. Call for the Order of the Day
2. Question of Privilege
3. Take Recess
4. Adjourn
5. Fix Time and Place

Privileged motions are those concerned with the welfare of the group as a whole, and, as such, require immediate consideration. They, therefore, take precedence over all other motions. As in the case of subsidiary motions, you must learn them in their order of precedence. Commit them to memory as listed, from lowest rank to highest.

CALL FOR THE ORDER OF THE DAY:

Object: To direct the attention of the chairman to a scheduled event which has apparently been overlooked.

Form: "Mr. Chairman, I call for the order of the day." The chairman says, "The order of the day has been called for. If there is no objection, we shall proceed to the business scheduled for this time." If there is an objection, the chairman says, "What is the will of the assembly? Those in favor of proceeding to the order of the day say aye," etc.

Characteristics: 1. To call for the order of the day is simply to insist that a matter of business scheduled for the particular time be considered. For example, it might now be the time at which the assembly had agreed to recess, or at which a motion postponed to a definite time is scheduled to come up.

2. There are two kinds of Orders of the Day:

a. *General orders* are questions assigned to a particular time without interfering with any established rule of the assembly. For example, main motions to which definite postponement has been applied become general orders. It requires a two-thirds majority vote to consider such a question before its assigned time, but it may be considered later than its assigned time by a simple majority.

b. *Special Orders* are so called because they do interfere with some business already scheduled. They might, for example, interfere with some matter that had been made a general order for that time, or they might require the suspension of a rule. They originate in a definite motion to make a particular matter a special order at a particular time. They require a *two-thirds majority vote.*

    3. Call for the order of the day requires no second, is not debatable, is not amendable, and is in order when another has the floor.

QUESTION OF PRIVILEGE:

*Object:* To provide for immediate action by the assembly on matters affecting the comfort and convenience of the members (heating, lighting, ventilation, conduct of other members, etc.).

*Form:* "Mr. Chairman, I rise to a question of privilege." The chairman says, "State your question of privilege." You then say, "will the chair instruct the reader to read more loudly?" etc.

*Characteristics:* 1. Be careful to differentiate between questions of privilege and privileged motions.
    2. Questions of privilege are often handled by general consent, the chairman ordinarily granting the request.
    3. When handled formally, they require a second, are debatable, are amendable, require a simple majority vote, and are in order when another has the floor.

TAKE RECESS:

*Object:* To give the assembly a rest without interfering with the continuity of the meeting.

*Form:* "Mr. Chairman, I move that we recess for ten minutes (or until ? P.M.)."

*Characteristics:* 1. Recess is moved in order to give the assembly a brief intermission for rest, for luncheon, for awaiting the report of a committee, etc.
    2. It requires a second, is not debatable, is amendable, requires a simple majority vote, *is not in order when another has the floor, and may be made when no quorum is present.*

ADJOURN:

*Object:* To close a meeting.

*Unqualified Form:* "Mr. Chairman, I move that this meeting be adjourned."
*Qualified Form:* "Mr. Chairman, I move that we adjourn *sine die*." "Mr. Chairman, I move that we adjourn and meet again tomorrow."

*Characteristics:* 1. The unqualified form suffices for organizations that meet regularly. On the other hand, organizations like Congress must use the qualified form in adjourning particular meetings. To adjourn *sine die* (without setting a day for reassembling), for example, dissolves the assembly, and closes the session.

2. It is the chairman's prerogative to declare a meeting adjourned when there is not a quorum present or when disorder interferes with the transaction of business.
3. The motion is in order *when no quorum is present.*
4. When it closes an ordinary meeting (a meeting as differentiated from a session) the business interrupted is the first to be considered after the reading and approval of the minutes at the next meeting.
5. A meeting is not adjourned until the chairman announces it adjourned.
6. If defeated, adjournment may be moved again after transaction of the business then before the assembly.
7. It requires a second, is not debatable, is not amendable, requires a simple majority vote, and is not in order when another has the floor.

FIX TIME AND PLACE:

*Object:* To fix the time or place, or both, for the next meeting (not the time of adjournment for the present one).

*Form:* "Mr. Chairman, I move that *when* we adjourn, we adjourn to meet at (specify time and/or place for reassembling)."

*Characteristics:* 1. It is the highest ranking of all motions.
2. It is in order even after a vote on adjournment has been taken if that vote has not been announced.
3. If some other motion is pending at the time it is made, it is not debatable. *If no other business is pending, it is debatable.*
4. After it is voted upon, the business interrupted proceeds.
5. It is in order *when no quorum is present.* It requires a second, is amendable as to time or place, requires a simple majority vote, and is not in order when another has the floor.

## Organizing a permanent society

You won't always be a member or officer of an established group. Sooner or later you are likely to help organize one, an occasional meeting, convention, or permanent society. Therefore, let us consider how a group is organized and set in motion. We shall examine the organization of a permanent society, with the understanding that occasional meetings and conventions follow the same direction with a simplified procedure.

## THE PRELIMINARY MEETING

Step 1: *Laying the groundwork.* Upon deciding to organize a permanent group those interested should consult together and lay the groundwork. At this conference the following should be determined:

1. Whether a sufficient number of others will be interested.
2. Time and place for the first meeting.
3. How to advertise the meeting.
4. Who will (1) call the first meeting to order, (2) be proposed as temporary chairman, (3) be proposed as temporary secretary, (4) explain the purpose of the organization, (5) introduce the resolution, and (6) move the appointment of a constitutional committee.

## THE FIRST MEETING

Step 2: *Electing a temporary chairman.* When the meeting starts there is, of course, no chairman; so Miss A comes forward, calls the meeting to order, and says, "I move that Mr. B. serve as temporary chairman." Mr. C (who has been previously designated for the purpose) seconds the motion. This is not a nomination, but a motion, so other nominations are not called for, and Miss A puts the motion to a vote: "It has been moved and seconded that Mr. B serve as temporary chairman. All in favor say aye." The affirmative vote is counted, then Miss A says: "The ayes have it; the motion is carried, and Mr. B will take the chair." If the motion loses, she says: "The noes have it; the motion is lost; and another nomination for temporary chairman is now in order." The process is then repeated.

Step 3: *Electing a temporary secretary.* Immediately on taking his place, the temporary chairman calls for the election of a temporary secretary. The process is identical to that of electing the temporary chairman. (Note that in electing these temporary officers nominations are presented in the form of main motions, and the method is different from the election of permanent officers later on.) After the secretary is elected the chairman may pause a minute to allow him to bring the minutes up to date.

Step 4: *Stating the purpose of the meeting.* The temporary chairman then resumes business by calling on Mr. D to state the object of the meeting. (Mr. D, like all others who have participated so far, has been predesignated.) Mr. D rises, addresses the chair, and when recognized proceeds to state the object of the meeting. A discussion will usually

## TABLE OF PARLIAMENTARY MOTIONS

The table below lists parliamentary motions for ready reference. *Each motion on a lower line takes precedence over all motions on lines above.*

Where two motions have the same rank, as with the subsidiary motions "to postpone indefinitely" or "to amend," they are listed on the same line. If one is before the house the other cannot be introduced.

I. *Principal Motions*                                   Deb   ½

II. *Subsidiary Motions*

    1. Postpone Indefinitely        2. Amend        Deb   ½
    3. Refer to Committee                          Deb   ½
    4. Postpone to Definite Time                   Deb   ½
    5. Limit Debate                                Undeb ⅔
    6. Previous Question                           Undeb ⅔
    7. Lay on the Table                            Undeb ½

III. *Incidental Motions*

    1. Point of Order              NS AoF Undeb NV*
    2. Appeal                         AoF Deb * ½ **
    3. Division of the Assembly    NS AoF Undeb NV
    4. Division of the Question    NS AoF Undeb ½
    5. Leave to Withdraw a Motion NS     Undeb ½
    6. Parliamentary Inquiry       NS AoF        NV
    7. Suspension of Rules            Undeb ⅔

IV. *Privileged Motions*

    1. Call for the Order of the Day  NS AoF Undeb * ⅔
    2. Question of Privilege          AoF Deb ½
    3. Take a Recess                     Undeb ½
    4. Adjourn (unqualified)             Undeb ½
    5. Fix time and Place at which       Undeb * ½
       to Reassemble

### KEY TO SYMBOLS

Deb—debatable
Undeb—undebatable
½—simple majority
⅔—⅔ majority
NS—no second required
NV—no vote required
AoF—in order when another has the floor
*—exceptions exist; consult full explanation of motion
**—(Appeal) tie vote sustains the decision of the chair

follow, for others will want to make additional remarks and some will want to ask questions.

Step 5: *Introducing the resolution.* When it is apparent that most of the group understand the object of the meeting, Miss E (who also has been predesignated) rises, addresses the chair, and on being recognized, moves the adoption of a suitable resolution: "Resolved, That a University Forum be established by this group in order to make possible a more profitable discussion of current controversial issues." This resolution probably should be written out, and after being read should be presented to the chairman, who, in turn, will hand it to the secretary for accurate entry into the minutes. The motion to adopt the resolution is a main motion, and must be seconded. After it is seconded, the chairman says: "The motion to adopt the resolution (here he might have the secretary reread it) has been made and seconded. Is there any discussion?" After the discussion and possible amendment, the motion is put to an aye-and-no vote. If it carries, the chairman proceeds to the next step.

Step 6: *Appointing a constitutional committee.* After the group has adopted the resolution, Mr. F rises (he, too, has been predesignated), addresses the chair, obtains the floor, and says: "Mr. Chairman, I move that the chair appoint a committee of three to draft the constitution and by-laws, and that the committee report one week from today in this same room." This is likewise a main motion, requires a second, and is open to discussion, and may be amended. Assuming the motion passes, the chairman says: "I appoint Miss A, Mr. D, and Mr. Y as the constitutional committee to report one week from today."

Note the nature of the motion to create the constitutional committee. It was specific; that is, it left no question as to the number, how or by whom appointed, and when they were to render a report. Under other conditions it might be desirable to name the members in the motion, or to have them elected by the assembly. Whatever is done, the motion should be explicit.

When this business of the first meeting is finished, an hour is agreed on for the next meeting, and the meeting is adjourned.

*Drafting the constitution and by-laws.* During the interim between the first and second meetings the constitutional committee does its work. Since the constitution and by-laws are basic, their provisions should be carefully deliberated and the wording of each article and each section tested and weighed. The constitution will need five basic provisions:

1. Name and purpose of the organization
2. Membership: kinds and qualifications for each
3. Officers: election, duties

4. Meetings: time of

5. Amendments: method of

The following is a sample of how such a constitution might read:

### Article I. NAME AND PURPOSE

*Section 1.* This organization shall be known as the University Forum.

*Section 2.* The purpose of this organization shall be to provide opportunities for its members to discuss current controversial questions.

### Article II. MEMBERSHIP

*Section 1.* Active membership shall be limited to those who pay dues, participate as members of at least one discussion group each year, and who attend at least six meetings annually.

*Section 2.* Faculty members of the University are eligible for membership ex-officio.

### Article III. OFFICERS

*Section 1.* The officers of the Forum shall consist of a President, a Vice-President, and a Secretary-Treasurer.

*Section 2.* Officers shall be elected at the last regular meeting of each academic year.

*Section 3.* The duties of the officers shall be as prescribed in Robert's *Rules of Order.* (Or Auer's *Essentials of Parliamentary Procedure,* etc.)

### Article IV. MEETINGS

*Section 1.* The organization shall have monthly meetings during the academic year.

*Section 2.* Special meetings may be called by a majority vote of those present at any regular meeting, or by the President of the organization.

### Article V. AMENDMENTS

*Section 1.* This Constitution may be amended at any regular meeting of the Forum by a two-thirds vote of the members present provided the amendment has been presented at a previous meeting.

*Section 2.* This Constitution may also be amended at any special meeting called for that purpose provided the amendment has been presented at a previous meeting, and provided also that the special meeting is held at least one week after the meeting at which the amendment has been presented.

The by-laws contain the details of putting the constitution into operation: (1) Dues and other obligations of membership not stated in the constitution, (2) Method of electing officers, (3) Duties of officers, (4) List of standing committees and their duties, (5) Definition of a quorum, (6) Provisions for parliamentary authority, (7) Order of business, and (8) Method of amendment.

## THE SECOND MEETING

At the appointed time, the second meeting is called to order by the temporary chairman. He orders the minutes of the first meeting read, and after they are approved, calls for the report of the constitutional committee.

### ADOPTION OF THE CONSTITUTION AND BY-LAWS

*First Reading.* When the temporary chairman calls for the report of the constitutional committee the chairman of that committee reads the constitution and by-laws, moves their adoption, and hands the original and one duplicate copy to the chairman. (Both the secretary and chairman will need copies.)

*The Second Reading.* The motion to adopt having been seconded, the chairman states, "The motion before the house is the adoption of the constitution and by-laws as reported by the constitutional committee. We shall consider it, discuss and possibly amend it, article by article, and section by section. The secretary will read Article I, Section 1." After this section has been read, discussed and possibly amended, the chairman applies the same procedure to each subsequent section and article, until the entire document has been considered.

*The Third Reading.* The constitution as thus amended is now read in its entirety, and an opportunity is given to amend it as a whole.

*The Fourth Reading.* When all amendments which may have been offered during their reading have been acted upon, the constitution is again read in its entirety. At this reading the group should particularly watch for any conflicting amendments which might inadvertently have crept in. After the fourth reading the constitution is then put to a vote, and if it is adopted, a recess is declared in order that the members may sign the document.

Following this the by-laws are given four readings, amended if necessary, and adopted in the same manner.

### ELECTION OF OFFICERS

When the constitution and by-laws have been adopted, steps should be taken to elect permanent officers as prescribed therein. If, for example, the by-laws provide for nominations to be made by a nominating committee, this committee should be appointed, or elected, and the election of officers held at a third meeting.

# Assignments

1. Write out and hand in a report on what method of voting you would use in the following instances, assuming that your by-laws did not specify:

   *a.* Adopting the main motion
   *b.* A motion to limit debate
   *c.* A main motion following a call for division of the assembly
   *d.* A question on which vote by "yeas and noes" has been ordered
   *e.* Election of officers

2. Write out and hand in a report on the following:

   *a.* During the interim of what two meetings does the constitutional committee do its work?
   *b.* When is an amendment not debatable?
   *c.* What is the quorum if it is not specified in the constitution and by-laws?
   *d.* What motion has the effect of killing the motion to which it is applied?
   *e.* What items should the articles of the constitution and by-laws cover?
   *f.* What kind of vote should be taken in election of officers?
   *g.* What motion "nullifies a vote"?
   *h.* What motion may be proposed only by someone who "originally voted on the prevailing side"?
   *i.* Who is the first person to read the constitution and by-laws to the assembly?
   *j.* What two subsidiary motions are of the same rank?
   *k.* What does an amendment of the second order amend?
   *l.* What would you propose to do with a motion on which the assembly needs to have more information?
   *m.* You believe that the chairman has ruled incorrectly on a point of order. What motion do you make?
   *n.* To what may suspension of rules not be applied?
   *o.* What two subsidiary motions require a two-thirds majority vote?
   *p.* What principal motion must be made not later than "the next meeting following the original motion"?
   *q.* You want to stop debate on a proposed amendment, but not on the main motion. Would you use the qualified or unqualified form of the previous question?
   *r.* You believe that the chairman has made a mistake in announcing a vote. For what do you call (what do you move)?
   *s.* You do not want to discuss a main motion now, but you do want to discuss it at a later date. What motion do you make?
   *t.* When does a meeting stand adjourned?
   *u.* What three motions are in order when no quorum is present?
   *v.* What motion removes an action from the record?
   *w.* Under what condition is fix time and place debatable?
   *x.* What privileged motion is ordinarily handled by "general or unanimous consent"?

# ◦ 23 ◦

# Speeches on
# Special Occasions

IT TOOK at least three ceremonial speeches to complete the Bunker Hill Monument, two of them by Daniel Webster. It took at least four ceremonial speeches to complete the national Capitol, one of them by Daniel Webster. It took at least two to complete the Jefferson Memorial, one by Franklin D. Roosevelt. It took two to complete the United Nations Building, one by Harry Truman. We cannot complete any public building or monument only with stone and mortar. It is never completed until the speeches are made.

All people everywhere have developed this ritual for ceremonial speaking. The Greeks called it frankly "the ceremonial oratory of display." They were not ashamed to say outright that it was ceremonial and that its purpose was display. We wince at such brashness in the Western world today. We have a larger vocabulary than the Greeks had, so we prefer to state the concept in words of philosophical abstractions. It seems more fitting to our ears, therefore, to call ceremonial speaking the "speeches on special occasions."

In twentieth-century usage such speeches include the introducing of other speakers, presenting or receiving gifts or awards, welcoming official guests, and responding to welcomes, formal farewells, commemorating anniversaries and events like graduation, eulogies, nominating candidates, inaugurating terms of office, and speaking appropriate words at social occasions like banquets.

The form and content of these speeches have no particular similarity to one another, but they do have a common *plane*. The plane of those basic speeches discussed in previous chapters—speeches for public enlightenment, for influencing attitudes, maintaining justice in courts, and renewing faith in temples of worship—is *utility*. They are for cultivating thought, modifying opinion, promoting action. If they be pleasing to the ears and delightful to the mind, so much the better. But their purpose is to get things done. Their plane is *utility*.

The plane of special-occasion speeches, in contrast, is *art. Do they please? Do they say the fitting thing? Do they have grace and beauty?* They may, to be sure, have utility. Often they must have utility. But they are expected also to have art. The Greeks were right in calling them "the ceremonial oratory of display."

Beginners, of course, face the usual hazard of amateur artists. They mistake the garish for art, not knowing that art is simple in outline and chaste in detail. In these speeches, therefore, beware of adjectives and verbose forms of all types. Restrain the impulse to say "On this *illustrious* occasion," ". . . *happy* privilege," ". . . *high* honor." Instead of circling around an idea, or backing into it, with "It gives me great pleasure and delight," go into it straight with "I have the pleasure." Use words with color and feeling as well as meaning, but use them with an artist's re-straint. And remember that exhibitionism is not art and not good taste.

## Speeches of courtesy

You will often have to perform appropriate acts of courtesy on public occasions—introduce a speaker, welcome a guest, present a gift or an award, etc. Custom requires you to say something. The occasion limits what you can say and how long you can talk. You haven't much elbow room, yet you are supposed to perform with grace and charm. For these speeches, etiquette and the limits of the occasion establish the following four requirements:

*They are brief.* Brevity is, in fact, a complication; for brevity demands terseness, and terseness demands preparation. Most of us are like Lord Lyons, who, writing hastily to a friend, began, "I trust you will pardon the length of this letter. I have not the time to be brief." Without equal excuse, many speakers have the same feeling; and because of length their speeches of courtesy become speeches of discourtesy. Be brief. Pack the speech full, but make it short.

*They have a streamlined structure.* This is because of brevity. Usually there is no formal division into introduction, discussion, conclusion; and no formal series of main heads. If you have heard or read of speeches that are exceptions, well and good; we are here looking at the typical. These are speeches with a simple unit, possibly a one-cell unit (see page 216). that goes straight to the point.

*They give the necessary information.* Usually there is a core of informa-tion that listeners need. Who is this speaker you are introducing, and how came he an authority? What has this person done that you are welcoming? Why was this award established, and exactly what did the winner do to gain it?

*Their dominant mood is gracious and pleasant.* The purpose of these speeches is to cultivate appreciation and promote good will. They should not, therefore, be entirely solemn or sober. Good speeches of courtesy may carry a large dose of humor. They may be refreshing and stimulating, like a breeze on a hot day. But whatever else they contain, they will also be marked by friendship, good cheer, and good fellowship.

Common Speeches of Courtesy include the following:

| | |
|---|---|
| The Introduction | The Presentation |
| The Address of Welcome | The Acceptance |
| The Response | The Farewell |

## THE INTRODUCTION

Speeches of introduction comprise almost one-half the grand total of speeches, for most other speeches are launched by its speech of introduction. Almost everybody is called on for this public act of courtesy: butcher, baker, spark-plug maker. Yet the mine-run speeches of introduction are poor, and unnecessarily poor. They are poor in content, poor in presentation. For content the mine-run speaker simply gasps for ideas, as seen in these verbatim specimens:

*"It is* with pleasure *that* I introduce this speaker. . . ."

[Two fouls in the first sentence: (1) Who cares about the chairman's pleasure? Listeners want to learn about the speaker. (2) The grammatical form, "It is . . . that," backs into a thought, crab-like, instead of walking forward into it human-like. Word bunglers use it habitually, and skilled artists seldom.]

"Our speaker is *very* well qualified. . . ."

[Two more fouls: (1) The statement does not give the audience any information, but is "as broad and general as the casing air." A brief speech should come to the facts without windup. (2) "Very" has no meaning. It is simply a cover-up for lack of thought.]

"This speaker needs no introduction."

[Every speaker needs an introduction as a matter of courtesy, even though it be only one sentence. This is a mere gasp for thought.]

". . . I present Mr. Jones who will speak to us *at this time* on 'Illusions of History.' "

["At this time" is an absurdity, in slightly better taste but just as absurd as saying "With his clothes on." No one ever introduced a speaker who was going to talk tomorrow or next week.]

These typical speeches of introduction are also poor in presentation, too often half audible, except for the *ers* and *ahs,* which somehow by the grace of Allah never seem to be inaudible. Conan Doyle once satirized the behavior of a typical chairman as follows:

> Professor Murray will, I am sure, excuse me if I say that he has the common fault of most Englishmen of being inaudible. . . . [He] made several profound remarks to his white tie and to the water-carafe upon the table, with a humorous, twinkling aside to the silver candlestick upon his right.

Such is the typical speech of introduction. In contrast, a minority of presiding officers give them with a sure hand and deft touch. They bring together speaker and audience so each will know the other better and both are eager to continue the acquaintance for the duration of the speech. How do they do it? First, they are sensitive to the occasion. They know what the audience wants to know about the speaker. They find out what the speaker feels would be helpful for the audience to know about him and his subject. These things they do not leave to chance, intuition, or blind luck, but confer in advance with the speaker or otherwise definitely inform themselves. Thus prepared, they can say in effect "Here is a speaker you will enjoy, and this is why."

Second, these speakers don't whisper or mumble to the lectern or water glass, but standing erect like creatures of God, they talk aloud to the fellow creatures who compose the audience.

Etiquette, custom, and the occasion prescribe the following main lines of content:

1. *Tell the audience about the speaker.* Without adulation give the speaker's record, what he has done, where he has been, why he is especially fitted to talk on this subject. Be accurate, and be exact. Instead of reciting that mouldy bromide, "The speaker was for a number of years. . . ." better say "for three years," or "from 1958 to 1961."

Some of the best speeches of introduction ever given to speakers little known to the audience have been taken, with credit given, almost verbatim from *Who's Who in America.* They were not imaginative, but they gave the information precisely and helpfully.

2. *Announce the subject, but don't discuss it.* Tell why the subject is important to the audience if you want, but don't put the speaker on a limb by discussing it *per se.* Otherwise you might kill his opening remarks and force him to recast his treatment on the moment, or might pronounce snap judgment on matters that force him painfully to correct you. Present the speaker and the subject, but let him discuss the subject.

3. *You may also on occasion present the audience to the speaker.* At times there are pertinent facts about the audience that can be told the speaker in the introduction. Thus a speaker may say, "Mr. Speaker, most

of this group have read your latest book." Or, "This group has been holding a series of discussions for the past year on the subject of South American trade, and repeatedly in these discussions your name was quoted,
until the members finally concluded that they would not be content
until they heard you in person."

4. *If the occasion is significant, explain it.* An anniversary, annual meeting, or unusual occasion of any sort can be touched on briefly: "Each
year we meet to commemorate the founders of this organization. On this
thirty-first anniversary, it seemed fitting to have one of those founders
address us."

These lines of thought, remember, are to be applied with imagination
and intelligence, not treated as laws of the Medes and Persians. One of
the most effective introductions ever given consists of five words. The
last time we heard it was at an alumni banquet. The program had been
long, and the last speaker was the college president—known to all. The
presiding officer arose and said, "Ladies and gentlemen: The president."

We shall not give models of each of these speeches. They are available
in speech collections. But an exception will be made with the speech of
introduction. The following, given by United States Senator James Hamilton Lewis of Chicago, has neatness of structure, vivid example, humor,
grace of style, and a steady movement toward the speaker's name as a
climax:

> The *Christian Advocate* publishes that a little boy in Tennessee, answer-
> ing his examination in anatomy, defined the spinal column as "a long
> wriggly bone running down a man's back, with the man's head and brains
> settin' on one end, and the man hisse'f settin' on the other." [*Laughter.*]
> Tennessee claims to be the backbone of the South. We grant her that unc-
> tion. And while she sits upon that end of the consolation, we remind her
> that the head and brains of the other end have been transferred to the
> shoulders of Chicago. [*Applause.*] And while we accept the hostage with the
> acclaim of a proud conquerer, nevertheless we hear the moan of his first
> mother and she wails out, in the words of his favorite *Odyssey,* "Ulysses is
> gone, and there's none left in Ithaca to bend his bow." I have the honor to
> present to the toast that national statesman, international lawyer and orator,
> former distinguished Tennessean, now illustrious Illinoisan, Honorable
> J. M. Dickenson. [*Applause.*]

## THE ADDRESS OF WELCOME

The formal reception of an important person or group calls for an appropriate speech. The object, of course, is to say with tact and taste, "We
are glad you are here." The content of such a speech usually is derived
from pertinent facts about the guests and the hosts, but they are not

recited as mere facts. They are tempered judiciously with praise and cordial welcome.

The main lines of thought include the following:

1. *Pay fitting tribute to the achievements of the person or group you are welcoming.* Explain the achievements. Tell of their importance.

2. *Review the purpose and spirit of the organization that extends the welcome.* Especially review matters interesting to the guests, things they might profit from knowing, or things that would increase the cordiality of the welcome.

3. *Point up the purpose and spirit of the occasion.* Tell why it is fitting and proper for hosts and guests to meet together on this particular day, at this place, or under these present circumstances.

4. *If guests have come on a special mission, as for a conference or convention, wish them success in their deliberations and progress in the future years.*

A good speech of welcome is brief, and a wordy welcome cannot be redeemed by other good qualities. It offends good taste.

### THE RESPONSE

A speech of welcome calls for a response which says, also with tact and taste, "I appreciate your welcome." Yet in this outwardly simple response the speaker faces a hazard. He cannot minimize the praise of his hosts without seeming to criticize their judgment or taste. Nor can he applaud their praise without seeming to praise himself. "Before destruction the heart of man is haughty, and before honor is humility." He must accept their praise and be grateful, yet wear the humility that goes with honor.

Furthermore, the response can't be independent either in thought or tone from the address of welcome. The speech of welcome has set the pace, and the response must follow it—at least at the beginning. Whether the speaker in response likes it or not, he simply must carry on the line of thought, the level of dignity, the tone of humor, and the gracious · ness of the address of welcome. Not always can it be done with the deftness shown by Carter L. Burgess after listening to a glowing tribute, but his response will suggest how it has been done: "I am sorry my mother is not here. She not only would have enjoyed this ceremony, but she would have believed every word of it."

Its main lines will include the appropriate items among the following:

1. *Express appreciation for the welcome and pay tribute to the group extending it.* In other words, you ask: Why do I esteem this welcome? What will be its effect on me or my organization? Who are these people

that have gone to such trouble? How much effort did it cost them? The answers to such questions you put into appropriate form.

2. *Explain the purpose and method of doing the things for which you are welcomed.* What was the need? Why were you led to work on it? How was the work done? Don't be tedious. Do it in a few pointed sentences, or a single brief illustration.

3. *If you represent a group, do not fail to emphasize the contribution of others.* An oversight of this amenity would reflect on your reputation for generosity. Hence you will say, "In behalf of my organization I express appreciation." Or "I am one of many who have done this work. I speak on their behalf." Or "My associates share in this occasion. We have worked as one."

4. *Point up the significance of the occasion.* Why have you come? What will be the significance of your visit, or conference, or deliberations? Of what interest or value will it be to your hosts?

Not all of these lines of thought will be stressed, or even mentioned. But they represent the topics from which you make a judicious choice.

## THE PRESENTATION

When a gift, award, or memorial is presented on a public occasion it is not enough to say, "Here it is." The occasion calls for an acknowledgement of the recipient's attainment, for praise and congratulations. Often there are also important secondary purposes attached to the occasion which must not be overlooked, such as creating or strengthening good will between donors and recipient, stimulating others to appreciate the achievement, and impelling them to greater effort or higher conduct. A speech of presentation, therefore, is often not a mere act of presenting a gift or award. It is also the occasion for stimulating others.

The main lines of thought are these:

1. *Review the exploits of the recipient.* What were the accomplishments? What skills, abilities, or qualities of character made them possible? What significance does the achievement have for others present?

2. *Appraise the gift.* The gift is subordinate to the act of giving, but it should not be overlooked. Why was it chosen? From what was it made, or how? Who shared in sponsoring it or producing it? What is its symbolic significance? Of what is it a token?

3. *If there are losers present, don't overlook them.* Where the prize or award is won in competition, reserve brief high praise for others who played the game, who made the effort, but did not win. They too share

in the honor, for they furnished the standard which the winner exceeded. Without losers there would be no winners.

## THE ACCEPTANCE

The theme of an acceptance speech is gratitude. Whatever else the audience may think, don't let it be, "Well! He wasn't grateful!" The temptation is to mumble, "Thank you," and sit down, but under culture patterns of our society, a formal presentation usually calls for a formal acceptance, well illustrated by this college student's accepting the nomination as president *pro tem* of a student congress:

> If I should win this election, it is good; for it is good to win. But if I should not win, it is still good; for this is a democracy and in a democracy no one loses.
>
> This is just a practice congress, it is true; but we are practicing democracy, putting democracy into life and action. And democracy has a glory of its own.[1]

In a speech of acceptance these are the main lines of thought:

1. *Praise the spirit of those who presented the gift.* The donors have expended time and effort and expense. Make it clear that you understand and are grateful.

2. *If it is of interest, explain the purpose or method by which the attainment was won.* Do this with care not to magnify yourself, but only to confirm the donors' satisfaction in what they have done.

3. *Discuss the merit of the gift or the uses to which it will be put.* If it is a symbol or token, show that you recognize its symbolic significance. If it has a material use, appraise it.

4. *Share the honor if possible with others.* Few achievements are made alone. Others have gone before, laid the groundwork, or set up the goal. Others have given encouragement. Others may have worked with you. Recognize the debt. Say that you are one of many. Tell who the others were, and what they did.

## THE FAREWELL

A time of parting may call for ceremony, a public testimony of friendships, courtesies, and services received. Thus an officer retires after long

[1] Roy Jackson Bonds, Northeast Mississippi Junior College, at the Southern Student Conference, April 5, 1956. Cf. *Quarterly Journal of Speech*, XLII (October, 1956), No. 3, p. 332.

services with an institution, a person retires from office, or leaves a community in which he has lived and worked, or undertakes a mission at some distant place. They do not go unwept, unhonored, and unsung. And however glad they are to go, there are regrets at what is left behind. To these they give expression and pay tribute. Some of the topics to be covered are these:

1. *Explain the reasons for leaving, if they are not known.* This was the first topic discussed in the most famous farewell address of the twentieth century, that of the former King Edward VIII of England when he retired to become the Duke of Windsor: "At long last I am able to say a few words of my own. I have never wanted to withhold anything, but until now it has not been constitutionally possible for me to speak. . . . I have found it impossible to carry the heavy burden of responsibility and to discharge my duties as King as I would wish to do without the help and support of the woman I love."

2. *Testify to the relations with the institution or group you are leaving.* If they have been satisfactory, say so, and pay tribute to those who have rendered service and given friendship. Abraham Lincoln, in the most famous farewell address of the nineteenth century, could say to the people of Springfield with full truthfulness: "To this place, and the kindness of these people, I owe everything. Here I have lived a quarter of a century, and have passed from a young to an old man. Here my children have been born, and one is buried." If the relations do not merit such testimony, don't pretend an untruth. Without rancor, either pass them by as being known, or touch on them with tact and discretion. Your purpose is to express the regret of parting, and to create a regret in those who are left behind.

3. *Look at the future.* Henceforth there are to be two futures, yours and those you are leaving. You may properly say a word about where you are going and what you are going to do. You may also, if retiring from office, bespeak good will for your successor. Certainly you will bespeak good will for the organization. As Vice-President Thomas R. Marshall said to the United States Senate on his retirement: "I leave with the same inarticulate cry in my soul with which I came to you: 'My country.'"

### Speeches of commemoration

Public custom calls for memorial speeches of persons, events, and institutions.

A Town or City, or State is very human [observed George Frisbie Hoar]. In sorrow it must utter its cry of pain, in victory its note of triumph. As events pass, it must pronounce its judgment. Its constant purpose must be fixed and made more steadfast by expression. It must give voice to its love and its approbation and its condemnation. It must register the high and low water mark of its tide, its rising and its sinking in heat and in cold.[2]

The purpose of these speeches is to pay tribute. Some person, action, or institution is to be praised. The speaker is not charged with the task of changing the listeners' attitude or promoting action. His is the duty of testifying to the achievement and honor, of giving them weight and reality, of renewing faith, of uplifting sentiments.

He is working for the most part with intangibles, and his success depends upon the truth and force of his imagination. He will draw word pictures; he will dramatize; he will elevate, enlarge, and dignify. Above all he will stir and create emotions, knowing that imaginations are released by emotional disturbances and then act to heighten the very emotion that has set them free.[3]

The six usual types of commemorative speeches are these:

| | |
|---|---|
| The Eulogy | The Inauguration |
| The Anniversary Speech | The Nomination |
| The Dedication | The Commencement Address |

## THE EULOGY

Tribute is paid in a eulogy to the services and character of a person, usually deceased. The speaker necessarily draws his material from eulogized person's life, along one or more of these lines: (1) The person's attainments—the handicaps under which he started, the obstacles he faced, the final achievements. (2) His life purposes—why he was led to make effort. (3) His qualities of character. (4) His influence during his lifetime and on later times. The eulogist's general proposition is, "Here is a person deserving to be remembered, and these are the reasons why." There are two traditional ways to handle these lines of thought:

*The first is biographical.* François de Fénelon about 1679 wrote a discerning analysis of this type of eulogy. The audience, he said, already know "a small number of facts detached" and "without connection" about the person eulogized. "The real way," therefore, "to make a portrait that will be a genuine likeness is to paint the whole man. He must be put before the eyes of the listeners precisely as he speaks and acts." An

[2] *Autobiography of Seventy Years* (New York, Charles Scribner's Sons, 1903), II, 356.

[3] Wilbur Samuel Howell and Hoyt Hopewell Hudson, "Daniel Webster," in *A History and Criticism of American Public Address*, William Norwood Brigance, ed. (New York, McGraw-Hill Book Co., 1943), II, 678.

eager questioner tried to summarize this view by saying, "You would want one then to give the story of the life . . . , not his eulogy." Fénelon corrected him: "Pardon me, but I would not give a simple story. I would be satisfied with giving a pattern of the principal events; but I would want this to be a story that was concise, rapid, living, full of variety. I would want each word to . . . be a lesson for the listener." [4]

*The second is selective.* For its principal divisions it takes the prominent qualities of the person celebrated, and seeks to answer questions like these: (1) What was the guiding purpose of this person's life? (2) What were the sources of his power? (3) What were the qualities that made him great? (4) What debt do we owe him? (5) What inspiration or lesson do we gain from his life?

The eulogist operates under limitations of etiquette and custom. He is bound to strict adherence to truth. He is denied the dangerous indulgence of ancient eulogists known as "moral approximation," which allowed them to transpose virtues with their corresponding vices—substituting courage for rashness, generosity for extravagance, sagacity for cunning, simplicity for dullness, and an honest heart for ignorance. Yet the eulogist is not, like a biographer, bound to treat errors and failings along with virtues and achievements. His purpose not history, but praise. He may not praise the errors, follies, and vices of the person eulogized, but unless too major to be ignored he can cover them with a veil of silence; and if they cannot be ignored, he can counterbalance them by transcendent virtues. He speaks in praise of one whose life, as a whole, deserves praise. Within the limits of morality and truth, he can permit charity to cover its multitude of sins.

## THE ANNIVERSARY SPEECH

This type commemorates an event or action of the past: Fourth of July, Thanksgiving, Memorial Day, centennials, and founders days. Its purpose was expressed in the famous resolution passed by the town of Boston in 1783, authorizing an annual Fourth of July address "in which the Orator shall consider the feelings, manner, and principles which led to this great National Event as well as the important and happy effects whether general or domestick, which already have, and will forever continue to flow from this Auspicious Epoch." [5]

Such a speech is both a review and an inventory, a memorial of the

[4] *Fénelon's Dialogues on Eloquence,* translation by Wilbur Samuel Howell (Princeton, Princeton University Press, 1951), p. 152.

[5] From the Boston Town Records, March 25, 1783, quoted in George V. Bohman "The Colonial Period," *A History and Criticism of American Public Address* (*supra* fn. 3), I, 52.

past and an incentive for the future. Its theme is derived from the following lines of thought:

1. Recreate an image of the past by reviewing the event, action, or beginning of the institution being commemorated.

2. Re-enact the ideals and values of the institution as illustrated in the character of the men and women who helped to build and maintain it. Let them speak as if to say, "This is what we had in mind."

3. Interpret the influence of the event, action, or beginning on the past and present.

4. Define the lessons to be drawn from it for present and future conduct.

The speaker, of course, is dealing with intangibles. He can't rely on mere recital of history. He pictures, presents examples, comparisons, and testimony. Especially he illustrates. He weaves them all into an artistic whole that elevates, dignifies, and stimulates.

## THE DEDICATION

Opening new buildings and public centers, laying cornerstones, and unveiling monuments and memorials, launching ships—all from long tradition are occasions for ceremony and for speeches of dedication.

The theme stresses the importance of the day or event. The purpose is to pay tribute to the achievement and the achievers, and by means of the tribute to rouse loyalty, pride, and patriotism. The main lines of thought include these four: (1) The purpose for which this edifice was constructed—the material need, symbolic importance. (2) The people who produced it, and at what cost, against what obstacles. (3) Its tangible use, or intangible value. (4) The tasks ahead to which we should be here dedicated.

## THE INAUGURATION

The public ceremony on entering office requires some type of address, formal or informal. It may be a stately ceremonial occasion like the inauguration of a President or governor, an informal occasion like the installation of new club officers, or an important policy-making occasion like the coming to office of a new corporation president.

The theme flows from the occasion. There is a change of administration. The old one departs with dignity, and usually with honor. The new one takes up its task with bouyancy and hope. The occasion imposes one or more of four major duties upon the speaker: (1) To express apprecia-

*Wide World*

Secretary of the Navy, Robert B. Anderson delivers a speech of dedication in th
keel-laying ceremonies for the atomic-powered submarine, *USS Sea Wolf*. Such a speec
should be brief and to the point.

tion to those who put him in office. (2) To unite the group, heal the
wounds of the campaign if any, and to make it clear the new administration represents not only a faction, but the whole group. (3) To affirm the
officer's determination to discharge his duties and to abide by the letter
and spirit of the organization. (4) To present the broad outline of a program for the coming term.

## THE NOMINATION

Presenting a candidate for office requires only the announcement of the
name: "Mr. Chairman, I nominate Mary Mason." Or "Mr. Chairman, the

nominating committee presents the name of Dave Gerard." But on formal occasions like political conventions, public ceremony and campaign compulsions require also a declaration of reasons. Hence the literature of speechmaking contains examples of famous nominating speeches like Robert G. Ingersoll's "Blaine, the Plumed Knight," and Franklin D. Roosevelt's "Alfred E. Smith, the Happy Warrior."

The theme of a nominating speech is, "These are the qualifications, this is the man." Custom prescribes limitations in treating this theme. First, you can't say outright that your nominee is better than any other particular ones; such bluntness is reserved for the closed caucus and for workers behind the scene; it's not for public utterance. (The caucus argument at the Republican convention of 1860 was, "The nomination of Seward will defeat the Republican in Illinois, Ohio, and Pennsylvania; the nomination of Lincoln will carry all three." This was *not* stated in the speech nominating Lincoln.)

Next, examples, comparisons, and references of all kinds should have a specific meaning for listeners, but in ceremonial nominations like those at political conventions they are not couched in terms of absolute specificity. To say, "He will get the votes of AFL-CIO," would be out of tune. If you want to remind listeners that your nominee would get these votes, put it more obliquely: "He is trusted by the wage earners, who will assist in electing him to office." Being specific is one of the most important principles of speechmaking, but in ceremonial nominations it is done in moderation.

The main lines of thought in a ceremonial nominating speech are:

1. Analysis of qualifications for office, its duties and responsibilities, the manner of person required to fulfill them: courage, wisdom, sense of justice, special skills, leadership, experience.

2. Statement of the nominee's qualifications: his special virtues (" . . . *honesty that lets a man sleep of nights, fearing no Senatorial investigation.*"); his experience (". . . *who represented us abroad for a critical decade, preserving friendship in time of crisis.*"); his accomplishments (". . . *a man who has preserved in Congress what our soldiers won upon the field.*")

3. Perhaps a prophecy of victory under the leadership of this candidate. (". . . *has the will to win, who not only deserves victory, but commands it. Victory is his habit.*")

In political conventions the nominee's name is usually withheld until the very end, which permits even a mediocre speaker to close with a magnificent climax. ("*Illinois nominates . . . that leader of leaders, James G. Blaine.*" ". . . *the happy warrior—Alfred E. Smith.*") The main reason for this procedure, however, is to prevent premature demonstrations, which are planned in advance, and scheduled to be touched off by mention of the candidate's name. The custom in Congress, state legislatures, and city councils—whose members are trained in the school of political conventions—is also to withhold the name until the end. Precisely for this reason it is not good practice elsewhere. If the organization is favorable toward the nominee, the speaker usually gives his name at the very beginning. If it is doubtful or hesitant, it is commonly given as soon as the way is prepared by the discussion of his qualifications.

## THE COMMENCEMENT ADDRESS

In 1782 Ezra Stiles recorded the time schedule of a typical college commencement: eight speeches—half of them in Latin—consuming 3 hours and 15 minutes, and dealing with political, literary, religious, and philosophical subjects that covered almost the whole range of human knowledge.[6] Less endurance is now required of graduates, but the commencement address remains as firmly fixed as in the centuries past.

Graduation is a day of achievement, a day of dignified celebration, a day of commencement into a new life outside academic halls. Traditionally the speaker's responsibility is twofold:

*First,* he congratulates the graduates on their achievement and pays tribute to its importance. But in mid-twentieth century this ceremonial part of the address is given less emphasis than in earlier periods, and at least three-fourths of the commencement addresses given at institutions of higher learning, omit it or give it a mere sentence in passing.

*Second,* the main theme of the address looks at the state of affairs that faces the graduates—problems such as the intellectual and emotional adjustment to the world as it is, opportunities for young people of this day, carrying on with education out of school, making use of education, the duty of educated people in public life. Always there are plenty of problems, some continuing and constant that face graduates in every generation, and some emerging from special issues of the day. A commencement speaker asks himself: What are the compelling problems that face these graduates? Which one of them can I discuss most profitably for them? The occasion itself is ceremonial, but the speech is not. It is a deliberate speech to cultivate thought, influence attitude, modify opinion, or promote action.

For two reasons commencement addresses are probably the most difficult—and the least effective—of all speeches known to man. First, most graduates don't want to hear a speech. They are thinking of their graduation, of the parties, the gifts, and that haunting question: "Where do I

[6] Bohman (see footnote 5 above), p. 44.

go from here?" They have no mind to sit and listen to a speaker. They rather tend to sit and wait for him to finish. Second, the speaker usually is at fault also. By the time a person gets distinguished enough to be asked to give a commencement address—he usually no longer faces the problems the young graduates face, and often hardly understands them. He therefore tends to deal in high-level abstractions—like courage, integrity, being true to thyself. The graduates have heard all that before, usually in the same trite words. They are fed up. On this subject Walter Leckrone wrote some interesting words:

> I don't suppose any college president ever will do it, but it certainly would be a switch that would at least command attention if instead of finding a Man of Distinction to make his Commencement Address he'd hunt up some conspicuous failure and have him address the class on the subject, 'How I Got to Be a Bum.' If he told the truth it could well be the most enlightening hour of their [the graduates'] whole college career.[7]

## After-dinner speeches and speeches after dinner

At the Astor House, New York City, in 1837, a dinner was served at 7:30 P.M., followed by toasts and speeches until 2:00 A.M., whereupon the chairman proposed a toast to "Massachusetts and Daniel Webster—the Champion of the Constitution." The eloquent Daniel, according to the newspapers, arose and spoke until 3:20 A.M. in a speech that "enchained the attention of his audience." [8]

Twentieth-century dinner speakers are less long-winded, but a hundredfold more numerous—made so by fast transportation, and the growth of dinner clubs, luncheon clubs, and even breakfast clubs, as well as conferences, conventions, and special meetings. Speaking from behind tableware is now commonplace.

What is an "after-dinner speech," and how does it differ from other speeches? It can't be defined as one defines a speech of introduction or dedication. It's not a type of speech at all, but merely a situation where speeches follow food. One is tempted to say facetiously that it is a situation where there is first food for the body, then food for the mind. But this neat alliteration is not true to fact, for not all after-dinner speaking is food for the mind. It ranges from raillery and nonsense to important discourse. As a working definition, however, we can set up two major kinds of speeches given at dinners: the *mere speech after dinner*, and the *true, traditional after-dinner speech*.

[7] *Indianapolis Times*, June 8, 1958, p. 18.
[8] Howell and Hudson (see footnote 3 above), p. 715.

### THE MERE SPEECH AFTER DINNER

This is identical with that given at any other time and place. The dinner, or luncheon, simply furnishes a convenient time and means of assembling the audience. Many professional lecturers today make no adjustment for the occasion, but when on tour give the same speech at a dinner that they give at an evening meeting. Usually there is only a short preliminary program, if any, and the speaker is allowed thirty, or forty, or fifty minutes for a full-length address. Nevertheless you should take certain precautions: First, find out in advance whether there is a preliminary program, and how much time has been allowed for your speech. Remember that not all chairmen are experienced. Some will allow unscheduled matters to consume time. Therefore you had best be prepared to cut a section of the speech if necessary, and especially so if it is a luncheon meeting where members of the audience must return to work on schedule. Second, remember that the audience listens on a full stomach. You must now do what every speaker ought to do always, get quick attention and keep the listeners awake.

### THE TRADITIONAL AFTER-DINNER SPEECH

This is a special ceremonial species. Its occasion is not a luncheon, and usually not a professional convention or conference dinner. Usually it is a banquet for the special purpose of relaxation and enjoyment, and after-dinner speeches are one of the features of entertainment. Outwardly the purpose of such a speech is entertainment (see Speeches of Interest, page 188), beneath which lies almost invariably a vein of serious thought. The good after-dinner speech has humor, vivid example, and lively treatment, but these are not to be confused with reciting a string of outworn anecdotes and pointless stories. There is grace, wit, good humor—and also good sense. Instead of a compact line of reasoning, the thought is carried forward by a line-of-thought or series-of-parables, sustained by illustrations, comparisons, contrasts, description, narration, and fresh turns of phrases. The audience listens with pleasure, and leaves remembering that beneath the surface of enjoyment was a core of thought worth remembering.

All this is a large order. From the experience of those who have gone before comes the following helpful advice:

1. *Observe the time limit.* The program for a mere speech after dinner usually calls for one speech only. It permits a longer time, and the speaker who knows the closing hour may plan in advance how to meet it. The traditional after-dinner speech is not so simple, in that on the program is not one speech but a group—frequently four to eight, and sometimes, alas, even more. Each speech needs to fit the program time schedule,

and obviously the speaker ought to know in advance the expected time limit. A good chairman, of course, works out a time schedule; he knows how much after the scheduled hour the banquet will get under way, how long the dinner will take, how long each speech is supposed to be. Not all chairmen are good. Some make no plans for limits of time, and if a speaker asks outright how long he should talk, they will even say, "As long as you like," or worse, suggest a length beyond limits like, "Forty minutes," or "About an hour." You had better find out what kind of chairman you have, and find out what is on the program. If in doubt, plan a speech of five minutes, or ten.

2. *Remember that the treatment is more important than the subject.* Many speakers spend their time groping for an inherently amusing topic. Yet no subject is amusing unless you make it so, and any subject can be amusing if you make it so—public speaking, literature, psychology, economics, baseball, glass, salesmen, college education, summer vacations, getting a job, even the atom bomb. It is the treatment, not the subject. Yeager lists five causes of laughter that are available in the treatment of almost any subject: [9]

*First,* is making the audience laugh at the speaker. Any audience will laugh with the speaker who pokes fun at himself, and will admire his willingness to do so. Meredith Nicholson illustrates this technique in a speech to fellow Hoosiers:

> At one time I had some slight political aspirations. I thought the people had risen. [*Applause.*] . . . But the Civic League endorsed me [*laughter and applause*]; they called attention to my moral character. . . . I was defeated. [*Laughter and applause.*]

*Second,* familiar to everyone, is telling an amusing story. In an after-dinner speech it should be brief, pointed, and apt, as seen in this one by Henry van Dyke:

> There are some who rejoice in this professed change [in American ideals] and congratulate themselves upon it. Their congratulation reminds me of what a New England farmer said, who borrowed from Emerson a copy of his Plato, and when the farmer brought it back again, he said: "I kind of like that Greek fellow; he has got some of my ideas."

*Third,* is to belittle in a good-natured way important persons, ideas, or things. Among the topics available are the most important things in life: education, patriotism, love, marriage. Especially high on the after-dinner speaker's list are the hosts and guests of the occasion. Joseph H. Choate demonstrated the method in speaking to a Chamber of Commerce banquet in New York:

[9] Willard Hayes Yeager, *Effective Speaking for Every Occasion* (Englewood Cliffs. N. J., Prentice-Hall, Inc., 1951), pp. 314-316.

I had prepared a serious and sober essay, . . . but I have laid all that aside; I do not intend to have a single sober word tonight. [*Laughter.*] I do not know that I could. [*Renewed laughter.*] There is a reason, however, why nothing more of a sober sort should be uttered at this table; there is a danger that it would increase by however small a measure the specific gravity of the Chamber of Commerce of New York. Certainly nothing could be a greater calamity than that. [*Laughter.*]

*Fourth,* is to magnify little persons, things, and ideas. The humor arises from obvious exaggeration in which the little, the trivial, or the unimportant, is inflated beyond bounds. Private John Allen, the famous humorist in Congress, habitually used it in speaking of his home town of Tupelo:

[When the South seceded from the Union] I am reliably informed that . . . Horace Greeley and others sought Mr. Lincoln and asked him to "let the wayward sisters depart in peace," [but] he shook his head and said, "No; this secession takes from the United States Tupelo [*laughter*] and we will not submit to it." And it was to rescue for the Union this town that brought on the war. [*Renewed laughter.*]

*Fifth,* is joining together of two obviously unrelated things. Cause and effect are assumed where none exist. Phenomena are associated which have no relation. Joseph A. Stevenson illustrates the method:

The Democrats put on a torch-light parade. The gloating Democratic paper next day boasted of how big the parade was. It was so long, the paper said, that it took three hours for it to pass a given point. The day following, the Republican newspaper hit the streets. It said, "Yes, the Democrats did hold a torch-light parade, and it did take three hours for it to pass a given point—but the given point was Mulhollen's Saloon!"

Laughter is the lubricant of the after-dinner speech. It is the oil in the crank case. You know how far an engine can run without oil.

3. *Plan the opening remarks with care.* The beginning is the critical part of the speech. If it falls flat you are in trouble. Sometimes you start with the tide against you. The audience may not yet be in a mood for humor. The chairman has failed to kindle their interest, or the preceding speaker has wearied them. These are conditions you must meet with carefully planned opening remarks. To be sure, during the dinner or at the moment of introduction you may reshape these opening remarks, change them, or add to them. But a speaker with experience will not trust to inspiration. He is ready with something already planned, like George Ade, who, knowing there would be at least mild applause when he was presented, produced laughter with the opening sentence, "It may be that your ovation arises from the fact that I am going abroad shortly to remain a long time."

4. *Adapt your materials to the audience.* Usually the after-dinner audience is a unified group: New Yorkers, Californians, lawyers, teachers,

bankers, candy manufacturers. They have a common interest and a common background. They have often met together before and know one another. These are your most available source of materials. Said Chauncey M. Depew at a meeting of a Dutch society in New York, "Good evening, Van," and three hundred listeners whose names began with "Van," burst into laughter and applause. St. Clair McKelway, speaking before a society of china importers, began, "The china I buy abroad is marked 'Fragile' in shipment. That which I buy at home is marked: 'Glass—This Side Up With Care.' . . . [Yet] there is a great deal of smashed crockery in the world." And he discussed the smashed crockery in theology, medicine, society, politics, and law. F. Charles Hume, a lawyer speaking to the American Bar Association, took his materials from the law: "From the lawyers of Texas I come—unarmed—bringing to you the message of civilization. Without hope of reward, and without fear of recognition, I have come to lend the charm of high professional character, and impart tone to this meeting. . . . I am a modest man." His theme was the young lawyer, his pretences, and problems.

## REFERENCES

Models of speeches on special occasions are not so available as those of basic deliberative types. They seldom appear in the two standard publications given to contemporary speeches: A. Craig Baird, *Representative American Speeches* (annual volume since 1938; New York: H. W. Wilson Publishing Company), and *Vital Speeches of the Day* (published twice a month by the City News Publishing Company, 33 West 42d Street, New York 36, N.Y.). Chief available sources are as follows:

1. SPEECH COLLECTIONS:

George P. Baker, *The Forms of Public Address* (New York, Holt, Rinehart and Winston, Inc., 1904)

W. W. Braden and Mary Louise Gehring, *Speech Practices* (New York, Harper & Brothers, 1958)

David J. Brewer, *World's Best Orations*, 10 vols. (Chicago, Ferd P. Kaiser, 1899)

W. N. Brigance, *Classified Speech Models* (New York, Appleton-Century-Crofts, 1928)

J. M. O'Neill, *Classified Models of Speech Composition* (New York, Appleton-Century-Crofts, Inc., 1921)

Houston Peterson, *A Treasury of the World's Great Speeches* (New York, Simon and Schuster, 1954)

Thomas E. Reed, *Modern Eloquence*, 10 vols. (Philadelphia: John D. Morris & Company, 1900)

W. A. Wood, *After-Dinner Speeches* (Chicago: T. H. Flood and Company, 1914)

2. Published papers and addresses of individual persons. Though not easily available these run into the hundreds, from earlier British and American public men like Edmund Burke and Alexander Hamilton to later ones like Franklin D. Roosevelt and Winston Churchill. Among this array, the following are representative:

Wendell Phillips, *Speeches, Lectures, and Letters,* second series, 2 vols. (Boston, Lee & Shepard, 1891)

*The Works of Robert G. Ingersoll,* Dresden Edition, 12 vols. (New York, The Ingersoll Publishers, Inc., 1929)

*Orations and Speeches of Henry W. Grady,* E. D. Shurter, ed. (New York, Hinds, Noble & Eldredge, 1910)

*Arguments and Addresses of Joseph Hodges Choate,* Frederick C. Hicks, ed. (St. Paul, West Publishing Company, 1926)

Chauncey M. Depew, *Orations and After-Dinner Speeches* (New York, Cassell Publishing Company, 1896)

*The Public Papers of Woodrow Wilson,* 6 vols., Ray Stannard Baker and William E. Dodd, ed. (New York, Harper & Brothers, 1925-1927)

The *Public Papers and Addresses of Franklin D. Roosevelt,* 13 vols., Samuel I. Rosenman, ed. (New York, Random House, 1938; Macmillan Company, 1941; Harper & Brothers, 1950)

Winston S. Churchill, *Blood, Sweat, and Tears* (New York, G. P. Putnam's Sons, 1941)

3. Year Books and Proceedings of organizations. Among those distinguished for containing excellent speeches are the following:

*Year Books* of the Holland Society of New York, the New York Southern Society, the New England Society in the City of New York, the Ohio Society of New York, the Indiana Society of Chicago.

*Annual Proceedings* of the National Education Association, American Bar Association, American Chamber of Commerce, etc.

## Assignments

1. Prepare a speech of Introduction for some speaker who recently appeared on your campus, or is soon to appear.

2. Group the class into pairs, and have each pair present the following series of speeches:
   *a.* Welcome and Response
   *b.* Presentation and Acceptance

3. Prepare a speech of Welcome for one of the following:
   *a.* A football, basketball, track, or baseball team from a rival institution
   *b.* A visiting delegation of some national club, fraternity, or sorority of which you are a member

   *c.* A new president, dean, or professor, whom you welcome in behalf
of the student body

   *d.* A distinguished visitor like the governor, a scientist, or author

   *e.* A new minister to your church

   *f.* Any similar occasion of your choice

4. Prepare a speech of Presentation for one of the following occasions:

   *a.* Presenting athletic awards to members of a team

   *b.* Awarding a prize to the winner of a speech contest

   *c.* Presenting a gift to the college or university from an organization of
which your are a member

   *d.* Presenting a gift to a minister, professor, or other person who is
leaving the city

   *e.* Any similar occasion of your own choice

5. Prepare a Eulogy on some person who was eminent in the field of your
major subject: an author if you are majoring in literature, a scientist if in
science, a musician or composer if in music, etc.

6. Prepare a Founders Day address that would be appropriate for a club
of which you are a member.

7. Assume that a new building has just been completed on your campus and
that you have been invited to represent the student body at its dedication.
Prepare a suitable speech.

8. Prepare a speech nominating someone for office in a club of which you
are a member.

9. Attend a banquet, time its running schedule, and make a report that
includes the following:

   *a.* How late was it in getting started?

   *b.* How long did the meal itself take?

   *c.* How long was the program, how was it apportioned, and in what way
would you have changed it if you had been chairman?

   *d.* By what means did the chairman set the tone of the meeting and get
the program off to a good start?

   *e.* Study the seating order at the head table. Do you find a pattern of
arrangement, such as placing the most distinguished guest on the chairman's right, the next on his left, etc.? How were the wives or husbands
(if any) of the guests fitted into this pattern?

   *f.* Write your judgment on the program as a whole.

10. Plan a banquet program in which you give special consideration to the
aspects listed below.

   *a.* Selecting the date, hour, and place, including room or building.

   *b.* Planning the theme of the program.

   *c.* Choosing the speakers and other performers, if any. Tell why you chose
them; and tell what other persons were considered and discarded, and
why.

   *d.* Consider whether there are persons who must be on the program because of their prestige or position in the organization, but who will make a poor appearance (poor speakers, long-winded, etc.). If so, can you use them, yet keep them in a minor role?

e. Remember to have someone available for the invocation.

f. Consider whether there should be music, and if so have a definite agreement with the director as to its length.

g. Consider how you will arrange for publicity.

h. Estimate how much later than the designated hour the banquet will start, and arrange with the dining room manager for serving promptly at this later-than-designated hour.

i. Plan a time schedule, but allow for run-overs. Tactfully, but specifically designate the maximum time reserved for each speaker.

11. Prepare a three-minute after-dinner speech applying the principles set forth in this chapter.

PART

° VI °

# THE INFLUENCE OF
# SPEECHMAKING

# * 24 *

# Dynamic Persuasion in an Industrial Democracy

Two DOMINANT FORCES—Democracy and Industrialism—have changed twentieth-century America, and changed our relations to the rest of the world. The change is still going on, and it still disturbs thinking people. The only ways of effecting change are by force or persuasion, and if we must effect change by force we shall destroy the democracy we are entrusted to defend. In this chapter, therefore, we shall consider special problems of persuasion that arise from Democracy, Industrialism, and from the U.S. world status. This requires us also to consider the problems of communicating across the barriers between groups in this country, and between the United States and other nations. First, let us see how these problems arose.

The twentieth century has brought war and revolution that has destroyed almost one hundred governments, changed the map of the world, and left the minds of men uneasy. On the surface, the causes seem to be communism, collectivism, or "radicalism." Actually these are not the causes at all, but the results of the real causes, and any attack on the results of the causes can do more harm than good.

*The real revolution is the rise of the little man all over the world;* 2,000 years ago he was a slave; 500 years ago he was a serf; 200 years ago he was a political eunuch, not allowed to vote; 100 years ago he was inarticulate and unorganized; just over a half century ago, of him Edward Markham asked the question:

> How will it be with kingdoms and with kings—
> With those who shaped him to the thing he is—
> When this dumb terror shall rise to judge the world,
> After the silence of the centuries?

We now must answer this question. It's not a new question. Rather it's one that those who ruled the world—the good, the rich, the wise—never *had* to answer, and so never did. By 1750 the broad outlines of modern civilization had taken form. Intellectually-curious men like Descartes and Newton had revolted against believing all the venerable guesses of ancient writers, and had begun to investigate a new world of concepts called "science." The mariner's compass and sailing ship had produced a Commercial Revolution. Men had sailed around the world and traded over most of it. By 1850 the Industrial Revolution was upon us, bringing its severe strain on social and political life. The little man lived in desperate poverty, governments ignored him at home, since he had no vote, and exploited him abroad in colonial empires. Educators ignored the critical problems of living people, and insisted that education must "train the mind" by having students learn Greek and Latin. So students studied Plato and Plutarch, Caesar and Cicero, and lived in Shangri-La while critical human problems mounted higher and higher. The minds of industrial leaders, too, were rigid. They refused to believe that Industrialism was changing society, so they failed to direct and control a change that they could not prevent. Karl Marx and Friedrich Engels had just written the *Communist Manifesto,* beginning with prophetic words, "A specter is haunting Europe, the specter of communism." It was a bad remedy for bad conditions, but it was almost the only remedy set forth. Governments went on exploiting colonial empires. Educators kept the college curriculum centered on Latin and Greek. Industrialists studied and improved machines, but did not study the workers who ran the machines. The classical capitalist economists, like Adam Smith and David Ricardo, had doomed the little man forever to a "minimum subsistence wage," and the industrialists were content to believe this without question. As Disraeli said, "The world was for the few, and the very few."

Then this little man rose to power. In some countries he took over with bullets, in some by the ballot, in others by agitation and the threat of naked power. But in one way or another he rose to power; and the world is now answering Edward Markham's question, "How will it be with kingdoms and with kings. . . . When this dumb terror shall rise to judge the world, After the silence of the centuries?" The twentieth century erupted with human earthquakes and tidal waves. Hundreds of millions of people have overthrown their governments, and turned to one form or other of totalitarianism. The little man now has power to destroy nations, or tax them to death, or socialize them into poverty. No country, and no educational system, dares ignore him. The world lives in a state of anxiety.

## Industrialism and democracy

In America we drew up a Constitution in 1787 that created a republic, but not a democracy. Not more than one adult in five—probably not more than one in eight—could vote or hold public office. The Founding fathers did not believe in democracy, both Madison and Hamilton agreeing that "real liberty" was not found in such "extremes." As late as 1820 both Daniel Webster and the learned Chancellor Kent of New York argued bitterly against allowing all men to vote; it would destroy the government created by our Constitution. But the determined mass of citizens demanded the right to vote, and finally got it. From that day, the welfare of the nation was no longer in the hands of men of education and men of property, but in the hands of the multitude. Thus Democracy was superimposed on the republic established by the Constitution. Now Democracy needs to be defined. We sometimes assume that it means everybody is equal, but of course it does not. It means only that everybody is entitled to equal rights. Therefore, it *guarantees inequality* in that it allows the able and energetic to gain more property and to rise to leadership. It means also that leadership is based on the consent of those below, but does not mean that everyone is a leader. Hence it places a premium on leaders who know how to communicate intelligently, effectively, and responsibly.

Next came Industrialism. The Age of Machines began almost exactly at the time we adopted the Constitution. At that time at least 90 per cent of the American people lived by agriculture. Then in swift succession came new forms of power: Coal, Oil, Electricity, and finally Nuclear Energy. Now 5 per cent live by agriculture, the rest have moved into towns and cities, and created all but insoluble problems of living together. Industrialism has changed the physical world, and fractured the old structure of society. Much of the change is pleasant. Now both higher and lower income groups tend to eat the same canned or frozen food and drink the same orange juice bought at the same supermarket. They tend to use the same television sets, and read the same newspapers. But much of the change is disturbing. Businessmen have become less individual and more "organization men." Workers in general are not free to join a labor union or not join; often they must join. Both the organization and the union exert a pressure toward standard patterns of behavior. More disturbing perhaps has been the change in the role of government. In an age of Big Business and Big Labor Unions, then Big Government is inevitable. It must regulate the air routes and the ether waves, both unknown to governments a century ago. It must collect information on national economy that allows business to plan intelligently. It must shape policies of money and credit that help to avoid or soften cycles of boom and bust. It must act as a stabilizer of the economy. Without Big Government we could not have had "the 16 revolutions" that altered the sinews of America, and on which the prosperity of the future rests.[1] As a result, the

[1] The best available analysis of these 16 revolutions is found in *U.S. News & World Report*, XLIV (March 14, 1958), No. 11, 54-60.

traditional political and economic theories, formulated by thinkers before the coming of research and perpetual invention, must be changed or
realigned. Two questions are persistent and recurring:

1. How can we salvage the individual in an economy dominated by vast
   impersonal forces?
2. How can we adjust the eighteenth-century concept of liberty *or* government—of government being a necessary evil—to the felt necessity that
   government must continue to grow bigger in order to regulate the
   complex twentieth-century economic machinery?

## United States in the world

The United States has grown to a position of world power similar to
ancient Rome or nineteenth-century Britain. But strength excites dislike
and fear, and puts the burden on us of communicating to the rest of the
world, not only reassurance, but also the meaning of our democratic
ideals.

Our record to date is not good. We have fed hungry nations, and been
hated by the people we fed. We have tried to raise the economic standards of impoverished nations, and have been condemned as worshippers
of material goods. We have talked about our skyscrapers, our miles of
cement, our automobiles, our telephones, our vending machines, and
our plumbing—and convinced the world that we are barbarians who
worship material prosperity as an end in itself. They have come to fear us
as successors to the Germans under Bismarck. They believe that we have
dehumanized man and turned him into a machine. They see us as having
dangerous qualities in common with Communist Russia, technicians
without spiritual concepts, a nation that has degraded culture and
intellectual values. In short, we have talked ourselves toward moral .
isolation from the non-Communist world.

Part of this resentment of America, of course, is pure jealousy of our
wealth and power. (How can one expect any Briton to view without
resentment his fall from a world power and our rise into one? It is too
much to expect, and we must learn how to deal with this great nation,
now afflicted with hurt pride.) Part of it is embarrassment by some nations
over their inability to make democracy work, as compared with our
ability to do so. This is true especially of Latin America, where governments so often come to power by revolution instead of free election.
Part of it is pure escape mechanism of people who have been left
behind in the swift changes of the twentieth century. Their old culture
is gone. They resent the rise of the masses at home who want bath tubs,
nylon stockings, and enjoy Coca Cola. They find it easier to cast vitupera-
tion on America than to face reality at home.

But not all can be explained on irrational grounds. A large part comes from our not being able to tell the world what America stands for. As Charles Malik of Lebanon said, "You are a bit diffident. The Communist world will force you to articulate yourselves. Asia and Africa are going to ask, 'What do you believe?'" We have failed, for example, to communicate to the world that our machines, which millions think have dehumanized man, actually have emancipated workers for the first time in human history. We have failed to tell the world that we have destroyed Karl Marx's whole concept of class struggle. Adam Smith and Ricardo had doomed the worker forever to a bare, bleak existence. Marx in effect had said: "Sheep of the world, unite! Sheep of the world, revolt and eat the wolves." But the sheep can't eat the wolves, and the Russians simply traded one set of wolves for another set of wolves, even more ravenous. The great revolutionist was not Marx, but Henry Ford. No Russians were really liberated by the October Revolution of 1917. It was Ford's Manifesto of January 1, 1914, of a $5 wage for an eight-hour day that set the stage for liberating the worker and destroying the class struggle dreamed up by Marx. This was the real revolution of the twentieth century. It has given us the strength of abundance and the power of freedom. But we've never succeeded in telling other nations about it in words they can understand.

Then, too, we have never defined what we stand for beyond calling it "the American way of life." Thornton Wilder once said, "Americans are still inventing what it is to be an American." So far we have done better at inventing than in communicating to others what we have invented. For example, we have attained a collective security that the Socialists only dream about; but our talk of "individualism" and "free enterprise" so confuses other peoples that we can't communicate to them how our system produces greater security than does socialism. In fact, we don't even have a name for our system. We call it "capitalism," which is a word that much of the world finds synonymous with "exploitation." We can't change the way they think about this word. We ought to get a new word. Only then can we spell out the enormous difference between our dynamic capitalism and the stagnating cartel capitalism of old Europe before 1940. Not until then can we spell out in plain words how the barriers to economic freedom are not only socialism, but also stagnating capitalism.

Especially hurtful abroad has been our treatment of theorists and intellectuals. Actually no country treats them better and rewards them more highly, but a decade ago it became fashionable to denounce them —even while depending on them for counsel—as "eggheads." It became a word of scorn, and practical down-to-earth Americans preached scorn of theorists and ideas, not knowing that behind any practical thing there must first be theories, then ideas. All the world overheard this. It did not so much confuse other peoples as it *fused* in their minds indestructible wrong notions of America as a land where prophets and thinkers—revered by others down the centuries—were held in scorn. Only barbarians, they thought, could be capable of such behavior. This was the price we paid for calling our intellectuals "eggheads."

Finally, we send abroad educators financed by public and private fellowships. They go as representatives of American ideas, ideals, and culture. But there's no record of our selecting only those who can *communicate* to other peoples our ideas, ideals, and culture. We send them to distant parts of the world—and there, as at home, too many mumble at manuscripts or carry on one-way conversations with their notes; but they don't communicate to the people they were sent to serve. After enduring one such American—sent by American money to represent American ideas, ideals, and culture—a German ventured to ask, "Is he a typical American educator?" My only possible reply was, "I hope not, but he *is* typical of that large segment which is dull and dumb." Our method of selection is defective. We send the dull and dumb as freely as the competent in communication. Hence some promote understanding, and some aggravate it.

"A great nation ought to have a good conscience," said John Morley. But it's not enough to have a good conscience if other nations don't know it, or don't believe it. We not only must demonstrate that good conscience by actions that other nations can understand, but we also must explain it, without ceasing, in words they can hear and understand.

## The framework of persuasion

One thing the rise of the little man has left unchanged. Growth and progress in civilization still comes from its creative minority, not the multitude. This creative minority supplies the ideas and puts them into operation. Civilizations break down largely from two causes. First, its creative minority grows soft from luxury, or becomes impotent from sterile education. It fails to create the ideas to keep the civilization going. It begins to dream of a changeless world, to resent change, to lament the passing of the "good old days," instead of directing and controlling inevitable change. It steeps itself in the culture of the past, at the cost of ignoring problems of the present. The greatest danger to our democracy today is that our leaders will react to new challenges in obsolete ways. That is why, as Toynbee warns us, leaders who successfully respond to one challenge are rarely able to supply successful leadership for the next one. "They tend to think the same policies and methods will work again. More often than not, they won't." One almost frightening danger today comes from educators who meet in conferences, solemnly discuss, and write on, how to apply "great ideas of the past to problems of the present." The delusion that men of antiquity can supply the ideas for a world they knew nothing of, and had not the imagination to dream of, would be ludicrous if it weren't dangerous. *When civilization reaches that stage where its creative minority can't supply new ideas to meet new conditions—but only digs up and dusts off the old ones—civilization starts down.*

Next, a civilization gets in trouble when its creative minority tries to use force instead of persuasion. Even in totalitarian states, as Lenin said, governments rest on "a balance between coercion and persuasion." Always the creative minority is outnumbered. Always in a democracy it must "persuade or perish." In the American twentieth-century free society, when the multitude have the ballot, its operation is more quick and inexorable than a century ago.

But can the multitude be persuaded? Many, like Plato, say they can't. They would agree with Plato's indictment that the mass were "Like cattle, always looking downward with their heads bent toward the ground and the banquet tables, they feed, fatten, and fornicate. In order to increase their possessions they kick and butt with horns and hoofs of steel and kill each other, insatiable as they are."[2] Down the centuries this was the prevailing idea among the educated and the wise—*and it stands as testimony of how dangerous it is to use outworn ideas, however venerable, to meet new situations. For the behavioral sciences have discovered that the multitude can be persuaded if the creative minority knows how. The breakdowns come from leaders who fail to offer the right solutions, or fail to learn how to persuade.* What Bruce Barton said of industry could be said of all members of the creative minority: None "has the moral right to allow itself to be unexplained, misunderstood or publicly distrusted, for by its unpopularity it poisons the pond in which we all must fish."[3]

We may properly repeat here what was said in the Foreword and again in Chapter 21 on "Radio and Television Speaking," that research in the behavioral sciences gives statistical validity to the wisdom of the multitude. Like the judgment of leaders, it's not infallible, but in the main it's sound, and furthermore it is capable of correcting its own mistakes. It's not brilliant. It's not intellectual. It's not well informed. It's not capable of *supplying* the ideas. But the multitude has a high degree of common sense, and is an excellent judge of public policy, *if the leaders can supply the ideas and communicate them.*

The principles on which persuasion must be based are old and simple:

1. *You can't kill an idea by killing the man who preaches it.*
   *You can't kill an idea by persecuting the group that believes it.*
   *You can't shoot an idea with bullets in any way or form.*

---

[2] *Republic*, 9.586a-b.
[3] *Time*, May 10, 1954, p. 100.

2. *You can get rid of an idea only by replacing it with a better one.*

3. *The material element is important, but the nonmaterial, spiritual element is usually more important.*

The ways and means are based chiefly on six postulates:

### EVERY GROUP AND EVERY NATION MUST CONTINUALLY CULTIVATE "A DECENT RESPECT FOR THE OPINIONS OF MANKIND"

When our forefathers launched their Declaration of Independence they declared that "a decent respect to the opinions of mankind" required them to put their cause before the world. So must it always be with every nation and every group within that nation. Every nation is a minority in the world. Every group within any nation is a minority. In America lawyers, laborers, farmers, Catholics, Protestants, Southerners, Negroes, New Englanders, young people, old people—all are minorities. Yet all must live close to each other, sometimes intermingled.

Each group must communicate continuously to all others its ideals, sentiments, problems, and grievances. No group dares wait until it is in trouble, then try to save itself with one-shot persuasion. Instead its communication must be continuous—not advertising, not gladhanding, but telling all it can about itself in a way that makes others listen. It must remember that every day thousands of old people pass on, and thousands of lusty young boys and girls are born. These newborn youngsters don't know who makes Living Lipstick, or which cigarettes are Smoother. Nor do they know anything about other groups that make up this nation. Each group, therefore, must communicate its cause to all others. For them it is not exactly "persuade or perish," but it is "persuade or be damned, and be misunderstood."

### BEFORE YOU CAN PERSUADE YOU MUST FIRST INFORM

Persuasion is like growing crops. You must cultivate the soil. If you want to persuade others, don't try to push them into believing your proposition. When you try that, they tend to resist; and in a free society it's everyone's right to say, "quit pushing." The secret of enduring persuasion is no secret at all. It is simply for any group, or nation, to tell all it can about itself, and tell it so others will listen. This is known, you will recall from Chapter 7, as the "sleeper effect" in persuasion. The information soaks in, and much of it is forgotten, but it produces a crop of *opinions* based on the forgotten information. The behavioral scientists have not yet found out why this happens, but they have now demonstrated that it does happen.

### YOU HAVE NO CHOICE BETWEEN TRUTH AND FALSEHOOD

The Communists, of course, don't believe this. They mix truth and falsehood at will to serve their immediate purpose. Many students don't believe it, and will slip in falsehood hoping to make it sound like truth. But in the long run falsehoods, like chickens, come home to roost. During World War II, Wallace Carroll had 1,500 men at work on the strategy of persuasion. Around the clock, and around the calendar, they recorded and measured war propaganda. Repeatedly they found "the fallacy in the widespread belief that the propagandist's choice is between truth and falsehood," for "false propaganda almost invariably boomerangs." In the same way, Edward W. Barrett, after serving as director of the U.S. Office of War Information in which he directed and observed "many experiments in planned persuasion" carried out by the United States, concluded that we can maintain our world status "only if we, as a nation, learn to use the weapon of truth effectively." And further, "Those of us who argue for sticking to the truth are not motivated solely by ethics. We are convinced that truth offers not only the moral course but the cold, practical, effective course."[4] The danger with falsehood is that *one* falsehood condemns the whole person, group, or nation.

Even overstatement tends to destroy listeners' trust in a speaker. It may be simply the overstatement arising from enthusiasm, yet a single overstatement alerts the listener to suspect everything the speaker has said already, and everything he will say hereafter. We repeat, if you stretch the truth, it snaps back.

### YOU MUST TALK SO OTHERS CAN UNDERSTAND YOU

Lest this seems trite, take two words that appear repeatedly in speeches and news conferences, *formulate* and *conception*. Blue-collar skilled workers and unskilled workers were asked what these words meant. Here are typical answers:

| FORMULATE | CONCEPTION |
|---|---|
| "Speed up." | "Is it the end?" |
| "Get together." | "Getting people into action." |
| "Does it mean make a circle?" | "The government's personal view." |

There's a wide gulf between the language of leadership and of the general public. People's modes of thinking develop from their way of living. They are not equipped to understand words that represent a different way of life. In the past we've ignored it, or assumed that it comes from limited intelligence of the multitude. Not so. It's not lack of intelligence in the multitude, but lack of thought-skill by the multitude and lack of word-skill by the leaders. The leaders have not learned to talk with the steel worker, coal miner, or farmer about political and

[4] Wallace Carroll, *Persuade or Perish* (Boston, Houghton Mifflin Co., 1948), pp. 157, 237-238, 366-367; Edward W. Barrett, *Truth Is Our Weapon* (New York, Funk & Wagnalls Co., 1953), pp. 7, 18, 72-100, 129-138.

economic factors that operate at the workers' level of living. They ignore such workers' limited frame of reference. Within that limit, these people can talk sense and listen intelligently. They can react intelligently to propositions presented in terms of their experience. They can understand ideas they can't even themselves put into words. But they don't understand jargon, or the language of specialists in economics or government.

For example, research by the Opinion Research Corporation and Psychological Corporation revealed that the workers thought net profits in industry averaged about 25 per cent, and some workers believed net profits ran as high as 60 per cent. Yet at the time the research was done, actual profits averaged 5 per cent or less. But nobody had explained this in terms that workers could understand. Again, workers believed that out of every wage dollar, the salaried man got 75 cents and the worker 25 cents. Actually the managers and owners got 13 cents and the workers got 87 cents, but this had not been told them in words they could understand. In fact, only one worker out of five remembered ever having been told anything whatsoever about wages and profits of the company where he was employed.

In contrast to this widespread breakdown in communication and failure of persuasion, are those management experts who have really learned how to talk in terms of their workers' understanding. Typical is one who used role-playing (see above, pages 439-440) to let employees know where the industrial dollar went. Said he:

> We stack up $100 in coins where everybody can see them. We say that we are now going to show where the company money goes, every dollar and every penny out of each $100. We also say that we had this worked out by a firm of expert accountants, that it is the set of figures on which we pay taxes, and we certainly hope they are right; for if they are not, we will be in jail when the next annual meeting comes. Then we say, "Last year we paid $35.78 out of every $100.00 for the raw material used in making our goods. Will the raw-materials agent please come forward and get his money?" A man designated to represent this group comes forward, and we pay him $35.78 out of that pile of $100.00. Then we say that the freight haulers get so much; up comes a man representing the railroads and truckers, and we pay him off. After that we pay off the office force, including the managers and the president; this is only, say, $5.00 out of that $100.00. Next we call out the workers' share and it is a whopping big figure, $45.00 or $50.00; and a man representing all the workers comes forward and gets his big slice. Finally we come to the owners, "those stockholders," we call them; and on the table is now left only a couple of dimes and maybe a penny. Up comes a man for the stockholders and gets his pair of dimes. After this, our workers can go home with a clear picture in their minds of where the money goes and how much of it they get.

In the early days of Industrialism, when there were only a few workers, national welfare was not affected by what they thought, knew, or did not know. Before Democracy emerged, when the multitude did not vote, leaders had less concern with what the multitude thought, knew, or did not know. Especially, they faced no problem of speaking in language that the multitude could understand. The audience that counted then was the elite few—"the gentlemen," to use John Adams' words, not "the simple men." That day is gone. The multitude has come to power, and leaders now must talk in language the multitude can understand.

### YOU MUST SPEAK IN TERMS OF PEOPLE'S WANTS

No group or nation can persuade others to be its cat's paw, though many try and become indignant at failure. Always, to persuade we must speak in terms of the welfare of others. This is an old concept. It appears in the Lord's Prayer: "Give us this day our daily bread." It appears in a parallel concept: "Man was not made to live by bread alone." It is heard in the Declaration of Independence: "Life, Liberty, and the pursuit of Happiness." We have discussed it in Chapters 6 and 7, and here are concerned only with applying it to the special problems of this chapter.

What do other nations want? That's a large order, but a few broad outlines are simple. First, they want assurance that their rights and sovereignty as a nation will be respected. Not all people want liberty as intensely as we do; many have never tasted it; others prefer security to liberty. But all want assurance that no powerful country will interfere with internal affairs, even indirectly. Over a generation ago King Ibn Saud I of Saudi Arabia stated this in words well remembered. He had refused to sell oil rights to either the French or British, and sold them instead to the Americans. "Americans drill for oil; they don't interfere with governments," he said. In this generation when, to protect the free world, America has armed forces in friendly foreign countries and gives financial aid to countries menaced by the Communists, this assurance is extremely difficult to communicate. What may be a reasonable regulation of federal money spent in Indiana can unsell democracy in India. Unfortunately, many of the bright young men we send overseas to "advise" Eastern governments on spending American money know Plato, but don't know the culture patterns of Eastern peoples. They have created ill will among peoples whom Americans have taxed themselves to aid.

Second, other nations want to feel that their culture has something of value to the world. This wish for worth lies deep and smoldering in nations as well as individuals. Especially it becomes intense in what we could call the "backward" nations—those left behind in this jet-speed twentieth century—and in nations suffering from defeat or disaster. For example, an American educator, Gregg M. Sinclair, speaking in India in 1936 said that the Western World *needed* the culture of the East, needed to fuse it into our Western material outlook. Not many Western educators could honestly make such a statement, but Sinclair could and did, and the effect was electric. All over India his statement was printed and reprinted, and quoted in university classes. Even ten years later it was revived and reprinted. India wanted desperately to believe that its culture was needed in the Western World. One can sense this want deeply in a once-great nation like Austria. Its people seem to say: "Our days as a great empire are gone, but our culture is as great as ever, and the world needs it." And between the Fall of France in 1941 and the rise of Charles de Gaulle in 1958, it was a bitter want in that nation. One example will illustrate. A wealthy, educated woman in Carentan said, "The greatest American I have ever known was your General Maxwell D. Taylor." On being asked why, she explained, "When you drove out the Germans, he came and talked to us. He said France was great because we had *endured* under German occupation, and now we would be great because we would fight with you as *equals* until victory was won."

Third, no democratic government dares obey orders from foreign governments or groups, or even to seem to obey orders. Hence when our foreign-aid administrators make it clear that "continuation of aid would be more likely" if other countries do what we say, it provokes bitterness. Even when our politicians and business leaders, while speaking to American audiences, lecture some friendly foreign nation on its behavior, that, too, creates ill will.

Finally, no people want to be considered inferior. That proud American tourist who boasts of American wealth, American plumbing, and American air-conditioning, offends others whose friendship we need. Even that American entrepreneur who pounds the table at home, says we are simply pouring money down a rathole, and the least we could do would be to tell those foreign so-and-so's to get on the ball, the news goes abroad and fans the flames of resentment.

Other countries, in short, know we will not subjugate them by force of arms. But we have not yet communicated to them complete assurance that we shall not subjugate them, and reduce them to satellites, by the power of our dollars.

We turn now from foreign peoples to Americans at home. In this golden age of mass communication the American business man spends an incredible amount of time and money telling the world what American business stands for. He hires advertising experts and personnel directors. He sets up the Minute Men of America organizations, and creates Americans for the Competitive Enterprise System, Inc. There's only one fault with all this. Nobody, but nobody, is listening. William H. Whyte, Jr., one of the editors of *Fortune,* summarized that magazine's two years of research on why American business stutters when it talks to human beings: "The employee, surveys indicate, is as misinformed

*Wide World Photos*

Top negotiators in the 1959 steel strike. National economic stability and
progress wait upon skillful and ethical persuasion in such crises.

about business as ever. Even the stockholder has remarkably little
interest in what management has to say to him; the public even less, and
the government none at all."[5]

Conditions have improved since this research was completed, but only
moderately. The bottleneck is bigness. Size creates a void in communication between the upper brass and the lower echelon both in management
and labor, for we just can't use the same system of personal communication in a plant with 20,000 workers that was used long ago in a shop
with 10 workers. Management is trying to simplify its problems by
decentralizing, and to learn about workers' attitudes and thinking by
employee polls and gripe boxes. But so far labor union leaders have
lagged behind. As *Forbes* magazine said: "Information on how workers
feel about unions and union policies rarely filters up to headquarters
offices. The Meaneys, the Reuthers, . . . are as isolated from the working
population as the president of General Motors." Union leaders at the

---

[5] William H. Whyte, Jr., *Is Anybody Listening?* (New York, Simon & Schuster,
1952), p. 2.

top "talk as though they represent the collective voice of their member-ship. The question is: do they?"[6]

What do wage earners want—men and women who punch a time clock in an industrial plant, and who seem almost anonymous among 2,000 others at the same plant? Whiting Williams was one of the first to discover it, by working disguised as a laborer in both Europe and America. Elton Mayo and other social scientists confirmed what Williams found. Wage earners want reasonable security, of course, and a reason-able wage, but United States industry gives its wage earners these ma-terial benefits in such bounty as to leave little cause for complaint. Yet many of them turn against management and willingly join unions that often make punitive demands on management. Why? The worker today is frustrated. He feels like an inferior creature, a number on the pay roll. The time clock has become a symbol of servitude. The factory caste system assigns him to dining rooms and toilets inferior to his bosses, and lets him scramble for space in the parking lot where stalls are reserved for executives. Workers may *say* they join unions to win higher pay and greater job security, but interviews in depth show that their real, unconscious motive is a craving for status. *More than anything else the American wage earner today wants status, recognition that he is a human being with human rights instead of a mere number without a face, recognition that his job is worth while, and the assurance that he is a member of a team that plays the game together.*[7] Other wants he has also as a human being (see Chapter 6), but this is the nerve-center want created by his living in an Industrial Democracy. Both manage-ment and labor union leaders face the problem, yet unsolved, of creating channels through which the higher echelon can communicate with the wage earner, and each may better understand the other's problems.

### YOU CAN'T OPPOSE SOMETHING WITH NOTHING

For almost every problem in an Industrial Democracy, crackpots, demagogues, and sincere reformers with cloudy perception come forth with panaceas. Therefore, we must always expect Share-the-Wealth plans and Soft-Money projects. The postulate here laid down is that when such panaceas are proposed for meeting real wants, you can't oppose them in the long run with nothing. Instead, you must offer a better solution.

[6] *Forbes,* December 15, 1956, p. 33.
[7] The pioneer studies that discovered this are more valuable in one way than the voluminous recent ones, for they show how the social scientists developed their techniques. See Whiting Williams, *Mainsprings of Men* (New York, Charles Scrib-ner's Sons, 1925), pp. 36-74, 139-153; Elton Mayo, *The Social Problems of an Industrial Civilization* (Boson, Graduate School of Business Administration, Harvard University, 1945), pp. 59-86; William Foote Whyte, *Industry and Society* (New York, McGraw-Hill Book Co., Inc., 1945), pp. 189-192.

If leaders try to oppose something with nothing, the result will be like that described by Arnold J. Toynbee: a disintegration from internal stress, and the cause of death will not be murder, but suicide. It happened to the Bourbons of France in 1789. The Industrial Revolution had created problems that demanded solutions. Louis XIV saw them and understood them well enough to prophesy, "After me, the deluge," but did nothing. When the hungry cried "bread!" innocent Marie Antoinette wondered why they didn't eat cake! To problems that accumulated decade after decade, government and aristocracy said "no." Finally France exploded, and the old order was destroyed. It had tried to oppose something with nothing.

It happened to the Romanoffs of Russia in 1917. The story in broad outlines is the same as that of France. The last of the line, Nicholas II, was a kindly king, faithful to his wife, good to his children, considerate of his servants, and wanted to do well for his country. But as Edith Cavell said on the eve of her execution, "Patriotism is not enough," and likewise kindness is not enough in the face of problems that demand solution. The Russian aristocracy opposed something with nothing. In the end its members were lined up against a wall and shot.

The founders of our republic understood this principle. When Shays's Rebellion threatened property and wildcat money had brought trade and commerce low, they drafted a Constitution that set up a new form of government. Hardly any one of them liked the new government, for in order to get it each delegate had to give up principles which he deeply believed were vital. Most of them gave and gave until they were deeply hurt inside. They did it to get *something* with which to oppose the disorder then existing.

In contrast, at the turn of the first quarter-century of the twentieth century, the unsolved problems of Industrialism were piled up all over the Western World. In many countries the only remedy ever offered was socialism. Those who opposed socialism simply said, "no, no, no," and offered nothing of their own. The result was that socialism was voted into power in enlightened countries like Denmark, Norway, Sweden, Britain, New Zealand, and Australia. Marquis Childs reported a typical election in Norway. The Socialists had a plan. Their opponents had no plan; they were just against socialism. Who won? The Socialists. Not until the cracks and flaws inevitable in socialism began to shatter the national economy, did the opponents of socialism come to power. They did it, as one Conservative in Britain explained, by campaigning on the proposition, "We're better managers than the Laborites. We'll run your socialism more efficiently than they can." On this platform they came to power, and began to supplant socialism with dynamic capitalism.

Senator Irving Ives of New York near the mid-twentieth century reminded his colleagues sharply: "We can't just say 'no, no, no.' We've got to have the answers to some of the gigantic problems . . . we are facing." His was the answer for all time. Yet as new problems arise, some would-be leaders always resort to negative persuasion. For every problem they say "no" to every solution. Like Plato, then want a changeless world. Like the Bourbons, they never learn, they never forget. Why? Well, nobody has to *think* in order to say no. All it takes is stubbornness. As every student soon learns, giving a hatchet speech is easy, for you only chop down, and never build up. You only denounce sin, and call the sinners bad names. But to have the answers for problems that beset us takes investigation and hard thought. In national affairs, as in the classroom, the people who give hatchet speeches are those who lack the power to produce ideas.

We return to the concept with which we began the Framework of Persuasion in this chapter, that the creative minority must supply the ideas that keep our Industrial Democracy running. It can't supply them by saying "no." It can't supply them by dusting off the old ideas of venerable men of the past. "Each age," said Emerson, "must write its own books." Each age the leaders must also supply the ideas, and persuade the multitude to accept them.

# SPECIMEN SPEECHES

# The Intellectual: His Journey and His Home

## MARGERY STRICKER

IN THIS SPEECH a woman who was Editor-in-Chief of the *Alumnae News* of New Rochelle College talks to secondary-school graduates who have won college scholarships, and are poised to enter college three months hence.

Given at the 11th Annual Arnold Constable Westchester Scholarship Award Dinner, Pelham Manor, New York, June 4, 1958.

PERHAPS I WOULD be wise to explain my metaphorical title. Weeks ago, as I thought about you all from my new position as speaker for this evening, I imagined you poised to start your journey through college. This will be more than a trainride to another town. It will be a progress of your individual personalities. And you being the sort of people you are, it will be a development that powerfully affects your minds.

Let's make no mistake. I don't think of you only as "brains." But tonight I will address you as young men and women with penetrating, sparkling, delightful—and potentially deep and influential—brains.

You must by now have heard much advice about the years before you. All of this will be of secondary importance; you will guide yourselves through your coming journey. The responsibility for how you come through rests on yourselves, and you accept that responsibility gladly, I know. I hope that my voice of some experience will be of some assistance as you help yourselves through your college education.

"The Intellectual—His Journey and His Home." I borrowed my title from a book many of you read back in the ninth grade, the *Odyssey*. You will remember that Odysseus passed through dangers that demanded all his skill, intelligence, self-discipline and courage. And besides that, every possible variety of response was demanded of him. He used all his body's strength to escape that one-eyed monster, the Cyclops, but he tied his body to the mast to escape the Sirens. At times, nothing but precaution and willpower saved him. In other cases, he had to be the epitomized Crafty Man.

Within a few months, something similar will begin for each of you. A Victorian poet, Gerard Manley Hopkins, once addressed a soaring bird and then called his own spiritual journey "A billion times more dangerous, O my chevalier!" Think of his words, now, in relation to yourselves. You will be among long-standing walls that breathe peace—even seem stuffy at times—but your intellectual journey will be filled with challenge. In fact, comparing all possible journeys of today, this one is among the most challenging, the most honorable, and the most important to the world we live in. Because it has these qualities, I would like to describe some of its challenges and the ways you can choose to meet them.

Just as Odysseus' journey required his boat and crew, so the formation of a thinking person presupposes a mind that is active and concerned with learning—not preoccupied with sports, social life, or campus clubs. A balanced life you must have, but the person we are concerned with tonight puts his or her greatest effort toward developing the mind. This does not mean retreating to an ivory tower. It is a willingness to undertake the tremendous voyage we shall consider now.

So, let's go. Right at the start are the powerful Breakers of Uncertainty, hiding—let's go on into metaphor—hiding the Reef of the Closed Mind.

How will you feel, next September, when a professor says, "What makes you so sure?" about a belief you have held? He may be questioning our democratic form of government, our belief that in God's sight all men have an equal right to justice, or the very way you think about God. This is frightening. Some of you will want to close your ears. You will want to stay within the safe walls of unquestioned belief. And your intellectual life could end right here.

But your professor is introducing you to the frightening intellectual life, a life of inquiry, of looking behind the appearances of things. The intellectual spots flaws in our ideas. He collects new facts and fits them into our present knowledge. Or, reverse that: he re-interprets our present knowledge in the light of new facts. All this leads him to question the principles that guide us, whether they be the principles of the atom, or our standards for judging poetry, or our way of treating juvenile delinquents. (Of whom, I trust, we have none here tonight.)

I have some examples for you. Perhaps the most important critics of contemporary literature were those men who ventured outside the standards of the 19th Century to appreciate men like T. S. Eliot, and the generation of so-called "modern" poets that followed these leaders. The battles over James Joyce's novels are a case of discovery and courage, and lest you think all the excitement happens in the field of literature, you can turn your minds to mathematics, or nuclear physics (you might, of course, go to the moon), or study what is happening in France today. For example, most of you are taking American History. In my senior year, that course included a lot of current events. Does it still? Then most of you have studied what is happening in France. Your teachers have helped you get the sequence of events, and they may have given you some information about French history to fill in the background. We read the New York *Times* "News of the Week in Review." Last Sunday it had a good sketch of the French problem; perhaps some of you saw it. In college you will go more fully into this background, and if you are lucky, you will get a teacher who can lead you deeply into problems such as the one facing France today. So deeply that you will say of any quick, simple answer, "What makes me so sure?"

Only by questioning do we advance, so open your minds, and it is likely the beliefs you have brought to college will be strengthened. You will find the reasons behind them, and they will unfold in a beautiful complexity. Suppose you study government. You may find it no effort to learn the United States Constitution. It will not be a dry document, because you will see the problems that faced the Founding Fathers. You will be able to see it as a landmark in mankind's attempt to live together with justice and harmony. And your whole realization of your rich heritage of democracy may begin when someone says, "What makes you so sure?"

With the breakers behind you, your mind has already grown, has it not? You are ready for the next hazards, then. I would like to describe one that is a reaction to the first.

Often, from wanting to question nothing, we leap to the other extreme of rejecting everything. This is just another refusal to question, really. We must test the beliefs we have learned from past centuries, and we must consider that they can guide us now, today, in the 20th Century. When you think about it, total rejection of the beliefs of our fathers is silly. People did not become capable of reaching truth only in 1920, or after Galileo, or since 1 A.D., or even 500 B.C. The past holds wisdom. We do well to add some sympathetic listening to our intellectual efforts.

This process of intellectual formation is shaping up as more than fact-gathering, isn't it? It is more, even, than using your minds as you have been using them. Your minds will expand in the next four years, and those of you who are meant to reach the perilous status of an intellectual will find material for serious thought all around you—in the remarks people toss off before class, in many of the choices you make during a day. The problems an intellectual works on are important to the way people live now, today, right here. And the strongest, sharpest minds are needed to solve them.

Americans have realized this now. You have missed the years when intellectuals were given the raised eyebrow and called "eggheads." You may be fortunate enough to have your services, as people who think deeply, not only accepted but welcomed. Some educators feel that the intellectual has a chance to serve his community that is unequalled in the history of American civilization. Scholars have had that chance all along, simply by virtue of their able and trained minds. But the service has been rejected in the past. Now, as I say, it may be welcomed.

If it is, that increases the importance of your seeing ideas in action, of seeing the problems in the world around you and of seeking the answers in that same world. And here are two more dangers in your journey.

These two masquerade as ways to escape all struggle. One would lead you away from thinking about the problems inherent in our everyday world. We can call it the Esoteric Chamber. Here one looks into little-known facts, solely for the sake of little-known facts. The poor souls caught here think their day is complete if they've finished the New York *Times* crossword puzzle. For example, a man might make a career out of studying Ernest Hemingway's punctuation—just cataloguing commas!

Meanwhile, outside the alabaster enclosure, another man might study those same commas, see the freedom and force of that prose, relate it to the rest of our literature today, and help people see themselves portrayed by the English language as our modern authors use it. This is, of course, a service—to the authors, who deserve appreciation, and to us, who need their writing. As for the sealed-up man with his commas, we must leave him there. He means nothing to the rest of us.

When I wrote this, I said he meant nothing. I'm sure he means something to his immediate family and to other people who study commas, but for the rest of us, he has very little, really.

The other trap is like a magnified reef. Picture a section of a coral formation, enlarged, say, a hundred times. Its geometric structure is beautiful and exact, but it is a dead thing, made out of sea-changed bones. This wrecks the man who sees the problems in the world, all right, but does not seek his answers in our messy planet. He prefers to construct a neat, logical solution that looks beautiful on paper, but does not fit the real, flesh-and-blood, messy, complex situation. Oh, how one can love that logical fiction! And how it can rob an intellectual of his rightful place in society! For what good is a great idea if it does not fit the practical world? You must test your most logical idea against reality, or it will be only a sculpture of bare bones.

Reality has given us a lot of trouble so far, hasn't it? Well, hang on, because we are in for more of the same. Assume now that you have—as most of you do have—a system of beliefs that puts order into your lives, that regulates the pushes and pulls that get at us all, through our whole lives. Then you are between the clashing cliffs that Odysseus faced on his journey.

On the one hand is the problem of polemics. Some of you are rare people who can give your whole heart to an ideal—a belief—a conviction. You can say "yes" to a principle and transmit it to others in practice, in that flesh-and-blood we spoke of. And conversely, your actions relate back to the same principles.

In the next four years, let us hope that you will learn more about your actions and your principles. You will think about your actions more deeply, in terms of your beliefs, and the two will be cemented together. In a world of people who are groping their way, perhaps you, (God willing), will bring light, and order, and reason, through your convictions.

And, as you special ones can attain a great achievement, you will face a greater danger. For the sake of the truth you already see, you may some day want to distort new-found truth.

It is a tremendous problem. New evidence can shake our convictions down to the roots. Sometimes you will have to hold your beliefs in the face of facts that seem to annihilate them. Again, may I urge you to have courage. Truth does not contradict itself. In time, the conflicts resolve, often leaving your first ideas not only intact, but enriched. What is true will endure, if you take the time to question calmly, and if you go to the authorities who can help you. Always consider new evidence, and never distort facts to fit your favorite idea.

For distortion is running from reality—from that very reality which it is the intellectual's job to interpret and explain to the rest of his society. Fix your heart on truth.

The other clashing cliff is the Bluff of the Cynic. The cynic runs from his job, too. He tests his ideas against reality, meets hardship, and decides the whole problem is unsolvable. You might, if you run into this danger, hear yourself saying, "We never know what is true, we know only what we think is true. We never build what is good, we build only what we think is good. And so often we are wrong! So why bother?" And you might throw out your books and take up farming.

Well, I have nothing against farming; take it up if you want to. Should a time come when you get that "where am I?" feeling, give up books, for a while, if you want to. But keep on thinking. Hard as it is, we can find truth. You, our best minds, must do the searching, or it won't be "where am I?" but "where are we all?"!

It is quite a trip, isn't it? By now some of you may have decided it is not for you, and this could be a sound decision. After all, what the world needs is fine people, not just "eggheads." The path of the intellect can lead one to personal excellence, but only if one is inclined that way to start. The qualities of reason and courage mark good men and women in every walk of life. Tonight seemed to be the time to describe the intellectual's path, that's all.

Let us see how we should consider the formed intellectual. We can look at him as he is after years of study, and check to see if he has overcome the dangers we have just now discussed. Is he reasonable? Openminded? If he advocates a cause, does he interpret facts honestly? Does he extend his conclusions too far? If he is a true intellectual, in the sense of being a mature, informed, capable thinker, he can help us.

For he holds much of the wisdom of ages in his head. Consider men like Moses, Isaias, Lao-tse the great Chinese philosopher, Aristotle, St. John the Evangelist, Thomas Aquinas, Galileo, Descartes, Thomas Jefferson, Einstein—and many, many others whose work in many fields is available to the scholar today. They form a labor of the mind that means colossal achievement, already accomplished for the man who can push even farther.

And this man—or woman—has the mental power to see deeper and farther than most of us, and so he can point our way. He can guide us toward justice in our laws. He can help us toward a culture that shows harmony, and beauty. He can help us to know ourselves, and knowing ourselves, to know our whole life's purpose.

Some people have called the United States the most literate society in the history of the world. If we take the word "literate" to mean simply knowing how to read, that may be true. Through our system of universal education, people at least gain the skill to read great books. What we need now is the will to appreciate great thought. It is up to us to choose our teachers, by understanding them, first, then by testing their ideas.

And, we need people to give us those ideas.

I ask you, members of the Class of '58, for two things. One, appreciation of the intellectual who, in the metaphor we have been using, has completed his journey of formation, is "home." But remember that the intellectual is never really "home." His life is one of inquiry, of re-evaluation, of new conclusions. Facts appear which affect our whole system of values and ideas. Facts get lost and forgotten, too, and have to be re-discovered. Our culture is always in flux, and the keepers of culture (the intellectual is one of these) must always be watching.

So, like Odyesseus, he again sets out from Ithaca. Again and again he will venture into the unknown, for his world is the world of unexplored ideas—of yet-to-be-discovered truth. The intellectual proceeds, willing to question all in which he feels secure, aware of his personal bias and on guard against it, aware that in all good faith he may go wrong, yet willing to stake his life on what he believes to be true.

The world is confused. We need heroes of the mind to show us how to live. I appeal to your generosity for the second gift. Besides appreciating intellectuals, I ask you to be intellectuals, yourselves, to travel this perilous way if you feel you can.

And those of us who do not go with you will be listening, hoping that the truth you find will make us free.

# On Mixing Ethics with Business

## LOUIS W. NORRIS

THIS SPEECH was given to the Illinois Association of Mutual Insurance Companies, in Springfield, September 20, 1956. Dr. Norris was a Protestant minister and was president of MacMurray College.

Audiences such as this expect to be bored by subjects such as this. Someone, of course, should talk now and then on ethics in business, and listeners should be polite enough to listen—that is the prevailing attitude. But it is a trite subject, usually dealt with in platitudes; and when it is over

> The sermon now ended
> Each turned and descended.
> The eels went on eeling,
> The pike went on stealing;
> Much delighted were they,
> But—preferred the old way.

But not this audience, and not from this speaker. From the opening sentence about *The Man in the Gray Flannel Suit* to the closing passage on *What Men Live By*, the ideas are fresh, the Supporting Material is concrete, and the style makes it easy to understand.

SLOAN WILSON tells in *The Man in the Gray Flannel Suit* how Tom Rath, returned from World War II, applied for a position with the United Broadcasting Company in New York. After filling out numerous application forms, he was asked to write an autobiography. It was to end with the completion of this sentence: "The most important fact about me is . . ." You are applying for a position in history, in the records of your company, in the esteem of your friends. How would you complete the sentence?

Some completions that might be made would both surprise and dismay us. Willy, in Arthur Miller's play, *Death of a Salesman*, would write, "The most important fact about me is the people I know." In a conversation with his brother, Ben, he says, "It's not what you do. It's who you know and the smile on your face. It's contacts, Ben, contacts! The whole wealth of Alaska passes over the lunch table at the Commodore Hotel." But when the smiles on the faces of Willy's friends faded, he was through. He drove off into suicide because he couldn't sell any more. Or, if you leafed through Dickens' story of David Copperfield and asked Uriah Heap to finish the sentence, he would have said, "The most important fact about me is my humility." But you would be dismayed because humility when advertised is hollow and insincere. It is most real when a man does not know he has it.

I hope you would write, "The most important fact about me is, that I seek through my work to leave my part of the world better than I found it." This need be no pious hope, nor superficial boast, but it should be a consuming desire to exert a healthy moral influence through your work. It is the most notable aim a man can set before his profession. At the political conventions the leaders presented their candidates while reaching for superlatives. The Republicans had two "Mr. Integritys" before they finished. They evidently honored the man most whose work manifested through it a moral influence. Our generation is blessed with "know-how" but not so clearly with "know-what." The integrity of a man's work is the "know-what" he must aim for.

A man is commonly judged in his community more by his work than by his family life, his recreation, or his politics. He is assigned some measure of success, or failure, whether he wishes to be or not. In that measure will reside basic ingredients of integrity and influence. We rebel against those who like to "throw their weight around," for they are invariably little men trying to be known as big ones. But who fears the moral weight a man throws around? We fear immoral weight, and we are disappointed in him who carries no moral weight. It is moral weight that does us good and claims our welcome.

## II

What, then, are the moral implications of a man's work? Certain axioms present themselves first off.

*To begin with, to do no work at all is immoral.* St. Paul admonished the Thessalonians, you remember, that "if any man will not work neither shall he eat" (II Thess. 3:10). The decline of royalty, the control of the wealthy class, if not its reduction, by taxes, the vanishing of servants from the household, have led to the common conviction that he who lives on wealth created by others, must be an exploiter. This conclusion has been aided, moreover, by the "labor-theory of value," which Karl Marx set forth. According to Marx, the value of any article consists in the labor required to prepare or create it for use. It follows as a corollary, that he who does no work creates no value, and hence he must be counted a social parasite.

*Again, too much work is immoral.* Child labor laws were passed, and labor unions have become strong, because limited hours of work yield maximum production, commensurate with health and happiness. Exhaustion, the frantic effort to do a job that requires strength beyond endurance, obscures the values that abide. The farmer and factory hand alike have been saved from many a monotonous and sweaty hour by the tools of industrialism. No man would go back to the long hours of hand labor common at the turn of the century, for the work week now leaves energy and time for other values he prizes.

*Third, unneeded work is immoral.* Some of the sorriest hours in recent history were those spent on some WPA jobs. Many projects were indeed admirable. Yet, large numbers of workers realized that their work was a thinly disguised dole. It was the pretense that ruined the worker's morale. He could not put his best into something he knew his country could do without. In a similar way, the manufacture of luxuries may generate a moral funk. Could you feel your moral best if your pay check came from manufacturing a $10,000 automobile, or even from manufacturing toy balloons? Neither one of these products can be seriously counted as economic needs. To be an accessory to the fact of producing useless or unnecessary products, whether luxuries or trifles, can scarcely yield satisfactions that endure.

### III

Assuming that your work is needed and it requires reasonable amounts of time and energy, what moral issues remain? The thesis I wish to put before you is that a man's work can provide him with moral nourishment.

In the first place, regular work can build up your health, and it is a moral obligation to keep healthy. The body is a dynamo generating energy that needs to be discharged, else disease sets in. An unemployed man is likely to quarrel with his wife as his energies seek some obstacle to surmount. Many a man shrinks from retirement for he fears his health will decline when his energies are no longer taxed to the full. Sometimes the hustle of modern business results in ulcers or thromboses. But, at least, this exhausting labor works off the energy which might otherwise back up into festering reservoirs with equally disastrous effects.

From the insects to the angels, living things seem designed for work. The story in Genesis that work came to be a curse to Adam and Eve and has remained an evil ever since, can never have been meant literally. They were gardeners before they became nomadic farmers. A part of man's life from the beginning has been toil by brain and brawn, and he is healthier when he works than when he loafs alone.

Secondly, work normally generates unselfishness. As a man throws himself into his job, he thinks more of its success and the success of his company than of himself. Few men really work only for the support of themselves. They are more concerned about the comfort and opportunities of their families. Even if a man has no family, he wishes not to be a burden to others, either now or in later years after retirement. Indeed, the best workman comes to his highest moral tone when he feels that his work is for those who come after. The teacher keeps his eye on the kind of society in adult life his students will create. An insurance man works for the beneficiaries of his client, preserving their welfare. Thus, a man's work can be the most basic source of happiness, for the latter is an inevitable result of unselfishness.

A third moral product of a man's work lies in the fact that work cultivates faith in tomorrow. Our faith that what we do will be successful and valuable tomorrow makes us willing to go to work each morning. Belief in some stability within the economy, in the continuance of civil law without revolution, in the trustworthiness of your colleagues, sustains you. Faith is the reasonable certainty that what is hoped for, and believed to be deserved, will be obtained. The religious man holds this faith to be just because there's a God in heaven who can be trusted.

Yet, our faith does not permit us to forecast every detail of tomorrow. If we could, insurance as a branch of business would vanish! There remains a calculated risk, an expected deviation in tomorrow's course. To accept nothing but the literal fulfillment of our expectations, is to court despair. On the contrary, a love of the unexpected spices every day with adventure. But this acceptance of what the wheel of fortune may bring, does not displace faith. It makes it tantalizing. The probability of events remains not only discernible but their predictability cultivates confidence that a man's best deserves to be tried.

Fourth, a man's work may increase his moral stature because it accumulates a standard of excellence which is ultimately divine. Every workman has his own standard of excellence. His family, his company, his society, all have theirs. But a man comes eventually to the question of why anybody values good work. He cannot avoid some conclusion, when he has thought the matter through, that the universe is made that way. There is a thrust toward excellence which penetrates a thoughtful man's mind. "Success" has about it a cosmic flavor that is more than mere promotion and social recognition. It is a demand to meet a standard that cannot be merely subjective.

Phidias is said to have been chided by a fellow workman when carving a statue for the dome of an Athenian temple. It would not need to be perfected in detail because it would be out of range for the eye of each passerby. In reply, he thundered, "*Silence, slave! Men may not see, but the immortals will.*" Remember that Carlyle held, "a man's perfection is his work." He must have meant that a man may find self-expression in his work, as he seeks to test that work by a standard of excellence greater than his own private conception. He was saying of work what Sir Richard Livingston said of education. The latter is, said Livingston, the cultivation of "a taste for excellence." It, like work, yields satisfaction in proportion as one strives to excel what he has been.

One may conclude that a man's work has the capacity to improve his morality. It may assist him to go the way he should take, for it can, and usually does, contribute to his health, his unselfishness, his faith, and his admiration for a cosmic scheme where excellence is prized. But these results are more or less inevitable, at least for a thoughtful man. The real question concerns the moral influence a man can exert through his work when he tries. A man's work should improve the moral quality of his time. How can work do that?

## IV

Every man should have some well-defined moral objectives, which he hopes to reach through his work. First, let a man seek through his work some responsible compensation for the freedom from risk, which modern life affords. Twenty-five years ago, a great need was to secure a more equitable distribution of risks. But unemployment insurance, social security, health insurance, crop insurance and many other types of coverage are now common. The investor is saved from risk by reserves for dividends, guarantee of loans and deposits by the government, price supports for farm products, and similar provisions. There remain some risks in individual enterprises to be sure, but the most dangerous and common ones are gone.

There is danger in too much security. The college graduate is encouraged by prospective employers to expect security in the job he seeks. Inducements of insurance and annuities are held out as the normal part of a job today. But the inventive, pioneering, spirit that has been the genius of American life, and that is the root of many deep satisfactions let us note, cannot avoid being quieted thereby. Let us not cultivate a society that encourages men to depend on a social system more than they do upon their own inventiveness.

What has been expected of the man who escaped the risks of life and limb in warfare? Has the man who escaped the draft been called upon to render to his generation some service in compensation for this freedom from risk? David Lilienthal has said that every college graduate should give at least two years of his life to public office. Thus, sufferance of inconvenience to family and endurance of criticism serve as returns to the public good for benefits a man receives from his college and thus his society. The non-college man, as well as the college man, who has been allowed to stay home from war, bears a responsibility to pay his generation a dividend on this freedom from risk.

Secondly, a man needs to foster through his own work and that of others a social motive for acquiring income or wealth. Most of America is now above the subsistence level. Some sharecroppers, negroes, and a few other groups remain below standard. But for the first time in history the chief question is not whether we as a people can make enough money to live on, but what kind of a life we want our money to buy. The way a people spends its money determines in a powerful way the kind of society they create. The reason why a man works becomes an index to his character, therefore.

Much of a businessman's time, as well as that of any other citizen, goes to preventing the government from absorbing his income by taxes. The motive for acquiring wealth easily becomes personal and selfish in the presence of this problem. But unless we make our work produce income for social purposes, i.e. for churches, hospitals, libraries, colleges, the need for support of these enterprises will be met by the state. Presently the worker finds himself a part of some form of state socialism. Not to support such enterprises voluntarily means a vote for political support of them necessarily.

This is no "share-the-wealth" program I advocate. It is no equality-of-distribution-theory, for there is no equality of talent. It is a proposal that the productive enterprises of the country, still in the hands of individuals, be devoted to social needs as well as personal needs. The communist countries sneer at democratic countries for their laissez-faire policy of allowing wealth to pile up where it will. Democracy can remain strong and resistant to the infiltration of communist sentiment only as it solves its social problems, while permitting individuals to accumulate large wealth. Joseph A. Leighton, once a professor at Ohio State, wisely put the matter thus: "The chief problem of America is to hold on to political democracy while we attain economic democracy."

Finally, let every man seek through his work to open up new channels of communication between the groups of people to which he belongs. Fascist and communist countries seem dangerous to us because they control the truth. Labor unions and manufacturers associations are sometimes so partisan in their loyalties that they too seem to control the truth and isolate themselves from other men in their time. The political conventions televised to the most remote the opinion of an unknown delegate, were in this light a good thing. They tossed their views into the arena of public inspection in remarkable ways.

Advertising pretends to tell the truth about its product, but so often gives only half the truth. More time and copy are spent playing on fears that one will look outmoded in dress, fall heir to halitosis, or be judged not to be a gentleman of distinction, than on communicating truth from one group to another. Does your work help or hinder this process of communication? Do you earn your pay from an enterprise that informs or confuses the public? Do you join together with other workers who ally themselves with the causes of their contemporaries, or who isolate themselves from all in their time?

## V

A man's work may nourish his moral character if he will let it. Further, a man's work offers him an unaparalleled opportunity to exert a moral influence on his time. Let a man permit the implicit moral forces of his work become explicit. May he, furthermore, make the potential moral influence available to him become actual. Seize upon the opportunity that is yours to cultivate a responsible use of freedom from risk, to develop a social aim for securing wealth, and to open the avenues of common relationship and communication between the workers of the world.

Richard C. Cabot wrote *What Men Live By* in 1914. One of the things men live by is work and in that section of his book on "Work," he wrote, "Socialism, or some half-way house on the road to it, will doubtless be tried in the next few decades . . . But . . . our personal relations and personal ideals must improve else economic reforms will amount to nothing." Forty-two years have passed since that book was written, and its predictions of socialist experiments have come true. But have they improved the personal ideals and relations that live in the minds of men who have tried them. No! These remain on the agenda and no economic system will ever improve them. They are, in turn, the key to success of any system man can devise.

Well, "the most important fact about me is . . ." How will you answer? If you complete the sentence by showing that your work leaves your part of the world better than you found it, you will have mixed such ethics with business as to make your generation proud.

# The Engineering of Ideas

## LOREN REID

On march 22, 1958, the University of Missouri presented three Honor Awards to engineers, two American-born and one foreign-born, who had "made major contributions to our civilization." The presentation was made before students, faculty, and guests of the College of Engineering.

Such an occasion, of course, also requires a speech on some topic appropriate to the occasion. The speaker in this instance was not an engineer, but was a professor of speech in the University and had been the previous year the President of the Speech Association of America. You will notice how expertly he rests the subject-matter on common ground between himself, a teacher of speech, and his audience, composed of engineers.

One of my favorite Missourians, Dizzy Dean, made a speech in which he said: "I was not the greatest ball pitcher that ever lived, but I was amongst the few." This college, with its faculty, students, and friends, and with its far-reaching plans for the future, is also amongst the very, very few. St. Pat's week is part of a great tradition, now well into its second half-century. I am pleased to be one of your speakers. I realize you could command the services, for this occasion, of almost anybody you wanted; you are not in the situation of the little church in my home town in Northwest Missouri. This church had the reputation of being hard on its preachers; the congregation would keep one for two or three weeks, and then ask the Bishop to send a replacement. Finally the Bishop sent them a young fellow who was still going strong after two years. The Bishop got curious as to the reason, and inquired of one of the local deacons. The deacon said, "Well, Bishop, I'd ruther not say; but if you have to have a reason, I'll tell you. We'd ruther not have any preacher at all— and this new fellow you sent us is the closest we've ever come to it."

Two statements may be made about nearly everybody in this large audience: number 1, you are almost all engineers, and number 2, you have had, or will have, a course in public speaking. This morning I thought it fitting and proper to roll these two matters together, and combine your interest in engineering with my experience as a teacher of public speaking. My point will be to demonstrate that discussion, conference, and speech making are necessary to help people engineer ideas. First, an idea has to be born, and shaped, and developed, among people working on the same project. Second, it has to be presented to others who may be sympathetic to it, but these others speak a slightly different vocabulary and therefore have to be managed differently. These others may belong, for example, to a different section or division of the company. And finally this idea has to be presented to outsiders, who may or may not offer strong opposition to it.

Let me start with the first category: the shaping and developing of an idea among people who are working on the same project. I would like to illustrate this by telling you part of the story of the invention of the flying machine by the Wright brothers. Undoubtedly the concept of the flying machine was one of the major ideas of the first part of this century. To invent it required not only good science and good engineering, but also more discussion, conferring, and speech making than you might imagine.

Wilbur and Orville Wright manufactured, sold, and serviced bicycles in Dayton, Ohio. Before 1900 they became interested in the possibilities of constructing a flying machine, and began, like any good scientist, by reading all the articles they could find on the subject. More material was available then than one would realize. Many people, both in this country and in Europe, were interested in gliding and flying.

The Wright brothers spent more than three years building and testing different kinds of gliders. Whereas other glider pilots tried to control the glider by shifting their bodies and swinging their legs during flight, the Wrights tried to develop a system of levers that would change the angles of the surfaces of wings, rudder, or elevator. They found the problem tremendously complex, and they faced many discouragements and difficulties. Early in their experimenting, however, they developed the habit of discussing problems together. They found this practice helped them think more clearly about what they were trying to do.

At one point in their gliding experiments, for example, they observed that occasionally one wing would start to drag and dip, and, instead of responding to the usual methods of control, the plane would dive to the ground, wing first. This phenomenon, which today we would call the tail-spin, was puzzling to the Wrights. They called it "well-digging" and could not figure out the cause. They realized that well-digging had something to do with the tail, because the earlier, tailless gliders did not exhibit the phenomenon. One evening Orville, the younger brother, sat down to give the problem concentrated thought. Eventually he arrived at what he decided was the solution, and hunted Wilbur to explain his theory. Orville had decided that the tail vane, originally a rigidly fixed surface, needed to be hinged. Wilbur agreed, and pointed out a relationship in the angle of the tail surfaces to that of the leading edges of the wing surfaces. Through this discussion they evolved a method of controlling the tail and the wing surfaces with a single cable. This idea, the result of experiment, observation, *and* discussion, has been called one of the greatest inventions in the long history of air transport.

On another occasion the Wrights were concerned with propellers. No one could tell them how to make a propeller; no information was available about the proper length, width, or pitch. They looked into the subject of marine propellers, but found that no one had evolved a theory of propeller-thrust; that whole problem had simply been treated as a matter of trial and error. The Wrights had many discussions about propeller theory and propeller design. At one point Wilbur had one idea, Orville an entirely different idea. After long conference they were as far apart as ever—except that Wilbur had gone over to Orville's position, and Orville had accepted Wilbur's argument. They continued their experimenting, and their discussion, and formulated a workable theory. Aviation experts today credit the Wrights with having developed a propeller that was 66 per cent efficient—the best that had been designed up to that time.

I will hurry over the story, except to say that in the year 1903, the year of the first St. Pat's celebration, on December 17, they assembled their machine on the beach at Kitty Hawk, North Carolina, at ten thirty in the morning. They were so confident of success that they told the photographer where to stand so he could get a picture of the machine in the air. It was Orville's turn to be at the controls; moments after starting the engine he was starting down the track they had built for a runway. That first flight lasted only twelve seconds, but it established the fact that a heavier-than-air machine could be built and flown.

I could give you many other examples showing how discussion helps to clarify ideas. Once the great philosopher, John Dewey, talked to a seminar for two hours. He very quickly got over the heads of all his students, but ended by saying: "Now, gentlemen, I know better what I believe." Eventually, of course, Dewey had to make his ideas clear to others. Another example: The invention of the A-bomb was an achievement of the highest order. Scientists, technicians, and engineers conducted hundreds of discussions and conferences. They continually needed to check their reasoning with one another. As the director of the project, Dr. J. Robert Oppenheimer, explained it: "What we could not understand, we explained to one another."

A second stage in the engineering of an idea is the attempt to explain it to other people in the same field, or in the same organization. In this situation the person doing the explaining needs to be still more clear, still more careful of his facts and of his reasoning. Moreover, he needs to give thought to the listener and how he will react.

This situation arose in the history of the development of the flying machine, as it does in the development of all worth-while ideas. After the Wright brothers had conducted gliding experiments for more than two years, Wilbur received an invitation to make an address to the Western Society of Engineers, in Chicago. Although he was overawed and unnerved, he accepted, and wrote that he would speak on the subject of "Some Recent Gliding Experiments." Students of public speaking in this audience will see at once that this subject meets the requirements of a good speech topic. At any rate the Society liked it and wanted to give it a larger audience; the chairman of the program committee wrote Wilbur and asked him if he would object to the occasion being designated as Ladies Night, with the wives present. He replied that he was already as scared as a man could be, and did not believe that the presence of women would make things any worse; he did say, however, that he absolutely refused to wear a dress suit.

Every student here knows what is involved in preparing a speech on a technical subject, or on any subject. Wilbur began to formulate ideas for his talk. I imagine he would have been pleased to have a copy of that book on public speaking by Gilman, Aly, and Reid. As he got into his speech he realized he did not know enough about his subject to face the experts. Every one in this audience, and every one on this platform, for that matter, has had the same apprehension. So the Wright brothers went back to their laboratory. They built a little wind tunnel and conducted experiments. All in all they designed and tried out two or three hunded sizes and styles of wings. Gradually they began to see how surfaces of different sizes, shapes, and curvatures reacted to air streams. Their grasp of the problem of flight became more and more sure. Or, to put the matter in other language, the materials for Wilbur's speech got better and better.

I do not know how much cheering Wilbur received from the engineers and their ladies after he had given his talk. I do not know whether he received an "A" or something else. I do know, however, that the society thought well of it, because the editor printed it in the official journal. Certainly the speech stimulated more careful experimenting and thus in its way helped to invent the flying machine.

This sort of speaking goes on continually. Ideas that men develop in business and industry are becoming more and more complex. We seem to be passing the day when a Thomas Edison can invent the electric light by the relatively crude method of patiently trying one filament after another. Individual men must still do profound individual thinking; but we read also of research teams, of organized researches, of crash programs, of contractors and sub-contractors. I have a friend who is a speech consultant for the Esso corporation in Louisiana. He tells me that the engineers who do research in, for example, chemistry, have regular meetings at which they report to one another. His job is to help them make these reports in language easily understandable to other researchers in related fields. I have another friend, also a teacher of public speaking, who has a responsible position with General Motors; another with the International Harvester Company; another with the American Institute of Banking. At one time I taught public speaking to employees and junior executives at the International Business Machines Corporation. I have made two trips across the ocean to teach conference and public speaking to officers of the Third Air Force and the Sixth Air Group of the Strategic Air Command. Officers from Supply or Maintenance, for example, need to sit down to confer with officers from Personnel or Budget. At times the stakes loom large: the welfare and the security of the nation.

Thus conference, discussion, and speech making are ways of shaping, modifying, and developing ideas. A further stage in the engineering of an idea comes when it is presented to a group that contains conflicting interests. J. P. Morgan used to tell each new partner that joined the firm, "The House of Morgan doesn't do business down here—" and at this point J. P. would waggle his hand a few inches above the floor—"it does business up here—" indicating a point about head-high. When an engineer does business "up here," he has to be able to present his idea to large groups of people.

If I needed examples of this principle, I could readily secure them by calling upon the three distinguished members of the engineering profession who were honored here a few moments ago. Obviously they have had to present their ideas to public and semi-public groups many, many times. On the way over to this auditorium this morning, for instance, one of them, chatting in an entirely different connection, said: "Nowadays a consulting engineer is much like a lawyer. We go into a board room with our employers, and with our proofs, to face a committee; and there across the table is a competing firm, with its engineers, and their proofs. Naturally a good many differences of opinion have to be ironed out." But for my example I want to recall briefly the debates of the Constitutional Convention of 1787. Delegates from the colonies met in Philadelphia. Conflicting interests were present. There were large states against small states. There were Northern states against Southern. There were free states against slave. There was New York against almost everybody. Some delegates wanted to amend the old Articles of Confederation; others wanted to draw up a new instrument. Some wanted a federation; some a confederation. Many other disagreements came to light as the meetings dragged on.

Days came when delegates were discouraged, but somehow they managed to keep in session and work out adjustments for their differences. Fortunately many wise and influential men were present. Much credit goes to George Washington, the presiding officer, partly because of his prestige, and partly because of his way of handling the group. He was a fine parliamentarian in the broad sense of the term. Another influential person was Benjamin Franklin. Once when the going got rough he told an entertaining story; on another occasion he offered a prayer; at the conclusion of the deliberations he appealed to everybody to sign the document, whether or not he agreed with every line of it.

Another good procedure used in the Constitutional Convention was the adoption of an agenda, an order of business, referred to in the history texts as the Virginia Plan. At one stage of the discussion, part way through the agenda, the convention deadlocked. No one could figure a way of resolving the conflict of interests between large states and small. Now if a group begins its deliberations by adopting an agenda, it makes at least a tacit promise to itself to consider a certain number of items. When in the Convention a conflict arose, the presiding officer decided to drop that item and proceed to the next on the list. Later the group returned to the troublesome point, and reached an agreement.

The Convention could easily have failed to achieve its primary mission; that it did not fail speaks much for the ability of those present to develop ideas through discussion and conference.

Or to go back to the A-bomb: came a day when Dr. Albert Einstein called on President Roosevelt to tell him about the possibilities of an atomic explosion in warfare. Here it was necessary for two intelligent people, trained along entirely different lines, to use a vocabulary and a way of discussion that both could understand. Dr. Einstein can be profound in the company of mathematicians, but he can be clear and lucid to laymen. On this occasion he had no ordnance data to present to the President; no one had yet detonated an atomic bomb. The scientists, however, were impressed by their theoretical considerations and by such laboratory data as they had collected, and Dr. Einstein and others managed to convey the substance of their speculations to the Commander in Chief.

Now we are in the space age. Not long ago we orbited our first satellite. The papers were full of information about the director of the project, Dr. Werner von Braun, the German-born scientist and technician largely responsible for its success. We know him as a researcher—basic research, he once said, is "what I do when I do not know what I am doing"—but he is also a leader, an organizer, an administrator. Some days found him discussing ideas with other scientists; others found him at the Pentagon, or on Capitol Hill, pleading with legislators or with military officials. Certainly he has used each of the three aspects of conference and speech making we have talked about this morning. And now we have a second satellite in the air, launched this week, on St. Pat's day. And, speaking of the space age, something at this point reminds me that recently I read that someone had wondered how life could be possible on Mars when it is so damn near impossible here.

In the massive space-age race, our great competitors are the Russians. We are told on every side that the Russians are ahead of us in mathematics, in science, and in technology. "We will whip you in the classrooms," they boast. What worries me equally is that they are ahead of us in the arts of diplomacy and in the dissemination of information. We must continue to improve ourselves in the art of communication. In this country and in this age we cannot train one set of men to do the scientific work and another to make the speeches. Ghost writing is bad enough, but ghost speaking is absurd and ridiculous.

In May, 1952, *Fortune* wrote:

> As soon as you move one step up from the bottom, your effectiveness depends on your ability to reach others through the spoken or the written word. . . .
> The larger the organization of which you are an employee, the more important it will be that you know how to convey your thoughts in writing or speaking. . . .
> The foundations for skill in expression have to be laid early: . . . if you do not lay these foundations during your school years, you may never have an opportunity again.

When we graduate an engineer who is not only competent in his field but who is also competent in the arts of expression, we have made him doubly and triply valuable to the nation. My plea to you, then, is to construct your own education on this broad base. If you do so, you may not become the greatest engineer that ever lived, but you will be amongst the few.

# A Lawyer's Duty to the Courts or to His Country and to His People

## CHARLES J. BLOCH

EVERY SPEECH text probably ought to include one good speech on a violently controversial question. Students can then see how an expert goes about that dangerous business of talking to listeners when some are partisans and others are strongly opposed. The speech here included is on as controversial a question as the American people have faced in this generation, recent Supreme Court decisions including the one on school segregation. Speakers have discussed this subject on at least three levels:

1. On the name-calling level. Such speakers generally use invective and abuse those who disagree. The result of such speaking is that partisans applaud, opponents are driven to oppose more fiercely, and the doubtful are usually repelled.

2. On the main-strength-and-awkward level. The speaker lacks skill. He fails to understand why others believe as they do, and hence has no chance of persuading them to modify their views, or even persuading them to respect his views. He means well, but he might as well have picked daisies, for what he says has no effect.

3. On the conciliation-plus-impelling-argument level. Here the speaker is an expert who follows the methods set forth in Chapter 7 of this book on "The Architecture of Persuasion." This is the level on which the speech below discusses it.

Mr. Bloch is an attorney in Macon, Georgia. He was speaking to the Atlanta Lawyers Club, March 20, 1958, but that was only the audience-under-his-eye. His real audience obviously was thinking citizens of the entire country.

A FEW WEEKS AGO I was in Atlanta, attending the meetings of the American Bar Association.

One morning (February 21) I read in your morning paper an editorial. It was titled, "Our Laws, Courts Must Be Upheld."

Part of it was:

> The United States is a nation of law. This newspaper, which stands by the law and the courts, regrets the sometimes unbridled criticism of our courts by some extremists. They do not represent the voice of the thinking people, who know that we will have either law or anarchy. In this connection, if the ABA members will pardon us we advance the opinion that the bar itself perhaps has been derelict in its duty, officially and individually, in not standing forthright in defense of our Supreme Court and all lesser courts. Our courts have been subject to irre-

sponsible abuse, to ridiculous and un-American sniping by fanatics who charge Communist influence. Each lawyer, as we understand it, is an officer of the Courts. We expect a stronger defense from the legal profession. It is necessary that all of us stand up and be counted on the side of the law.

After I read it, I embarked on a long airplane trip. As I flew from Atlanta to Houston, Texas, I had plenty of time to think (and I wanted to, because I do not like to fly). I thought—I was admitted to the Bar of Georgia on July 8, 1914. I took an oath:

> I swear that I will justly and uprightly demean myself, according to the *laws,* as an attorney, counselor and solicitor, and that I will support and defend the Constitution of the United States and the Constitution of the State of Georgia. So help me God.

A year later I was admitted to practice before the Supreme Court of Georgia. I took a similar oath. On December 18, 1918, I was admitted to practice before the Supreme Court of the United States, and took a similar oath.

Under those oaths, am I "derelict in my duty" if I do not stand "forthright in defense of our Supreme Court and all lesser courts"?

Am I "demeaning myself justly and uprightly" if I do not stand forthright in defense of our Supreme Court?

What is my duty to the Courts?

What is my duty to my country and my people, who may be looking to me for guidance and advice?

Those are questions which do not concern me alone. They concern all lawyers who are conscientious in the discharge of their duties.

Knowing what I do about American history and legal history of the past twenty years, must I stand forthright in defense of our Supreme Court?

Or, is it my patriotic duty to my country, my friends who are not lawyers, to sound a warning, and continue to sound warnings as to the danger which is about to encompass us, and destroy Constitutional Government.

I do not propose to engage in unbridled criticism.

I am not an extremist.

I do not propose to subject anyone to irresponsible abuse, to ridiculous and un-American sniping.

I am not a fanatic, and do not *"charge"* Communist influence.

I do propose to state *facts* to you, facts gleaned from the opinions of the Supreme Court, and from the opinions of Justices who dissented.

Then, on the basis of those facts, let us each answer for himself the questions:

Do I as an American lawyer have a duty to stand forthright in defense of our Supreme Court, whatever a majority of its members sitting at a particular time may do or say, or

Is not my greater duty as a lawyer, supposedly trained and educated, to call attention to the fact that it is not I—but the Supreme Court—which has been derelict in its duty?

Have not the people of our State and our country the right to expect from the lawyers of this country guidance and advice when any one of the branches of our government—Executive, Legislative or Judicial—is derelict in its duty, and is exceeding *its* Constitutional powers and functions?

If lawyers, trained in the law, do not warn the people who are untrained, there will be a gradual but certain erosion of our very form of government.

What are those facts?

Up to about thirty-five years ago, the Constitution of the United States was treated as the Ark of the Covenant. It stood as the guiding light of American law. Law schools taught *obedience* to the Constitution, not tricky *avoidance* and *supplanting* of it.

The constitutional form of government as it existed in the United States was based on the fundamental conception of a supreme law, expressed in written form, in accordance with which all private rights must be determined and all public authority administered.

Fifty years ago, the Supreme Court had said:

> Constitutional questions . . . are not settled by even a consensus of present public opinion, for it is the peculiar value of a written constitution that it places in unchanging form limitations upon legislative action, and thus gives a permanence and stability to popular government which otherwise would be lacking.
>
> (208 U. S. at page 420)
> Decided Feb. 24, 1908

The lawyers and judges of that day practiced what they preached, too. The lawyers of that day did not seek to overturn established precedents merely because different judges occupied the bench. The Judges would not have paid any attention to them if they had. Firmly and sternly they would have been told, "The question which you seek to relitigate has been settled by a decision of this court." Once or twice it was necessary for them to be told. (*e.g. Gong Lum* v. *Rice*)

In 1895, an income tax statute enacted by the Congress was by a divided court declared unconstitutional. The personnel of the court frequently changed after that but no effort was made to have the Court reverse itself because, forsooth, those who wanted an income tax were becoming more numerous. Instead, though it took time, the Constitution was amended as provided by that Constitution. Constitutionally, eighteen years after the 1895 decision, the power of Congress to levy an income tax became a part of our governmental system.

In 1874, the Court decided that despite the Fourteenth Amendment, a State could deprive women of the right to vote. Judges came and judges went, but the Constitution as thus construed remained the law of the land until it was legally amended by the adoption of the Nineteenth Amendment, forty-six years later.

In 1920, the Liquor Prohibition Amendment (the eighteenth) was adopted. It was declared validly adopted. Though it became exceedingly unpopular it remained as a part of the law of the land until repealed by the Twenty-first Amendment in 1933.

Then there arose a cult who taught and were taught not *obedience* to the Constitution, but *avoidance* of it. It became "smart" to teach and learn how to evade and overturn settled constitutional doctrines.

Their first major accomplishment was to persuade the Supreme Court to hold, or rather, to assume that because of the Fourteenth Amendment, the First Amendment became applicable to actions by the individual States. That theory had been firmly rejected by the Court as far back as 1883. (*Hurtado* v.

*California*), and again in *Maxwell* v. *Dow*, 176 U. S. 581. In the Scottsboro case (1932) it was revived. And, then, the majority of the Court held that there were "compelling considerations" which required a different rule from that announced fifty years before.

Justices Pierce Butler and McReynolds had taken the same oath the others had. But they didn't like that, and proceeded to say so. They did not consider themselves derelict in their duty to their brethren of the bench when they denominated the action of the Court as "an extension of federal authority into a field hitherto occupied exclusively by the several States."

This cult—these "smart alecks of the law"—met with such success in having established precedents set aside that in 1943, Justices Roberts and Frankfurter in a dissenting opinion (321 U. S. 112) protested vigorously.

They were not extremists. They were not derelict in their duty, they were not engaging in irresponsible abuse when they said:

> The evil resulting from overruling earlier considered decisions must be evident. In the present case, the court below naturally felt bound to follow and apply the law as clearly announced by this court. If litigants and lower federal courts are not to do so, the law becomes not a chart to govern conduct but a game of chance; instead of settling rights and liabilities, it unsettles them. Counsel and parties will bring and prosecute actions in the teeth of the decisions that such actions are not maintainable on the not improbable chance that the asserted rule will be thrown overboard. Defendants will not know whether to litigate or to settle for they will have no assurance that a declared rule will be followed. But the more deplorable consequence will inevitably be that the administration of justice will fall into disrepute. *Respect for tribunals must fall when the bar and the public come to understand that nothing that has been said in a prior adjudication has force in a current controversy.* . . . The tendency to disregard precedents in the decision of cases like the present has become so strong in this court of late as, in my view, to shake confidence in the consistency of decision and leave the courts below on an uncharted sea of doubt and difficulty without any confidence that what was said yesterday will hold good tomorrow, unless indeed a modern instance grows into a custom of members of this court to make public announcement of a change of views and to indicate that they will change their votes on the same question when another case comes before the court.

This is firm language. It is harsh criticism. But it is not irresponsible abuse, it is not ridiculous and un-American sniping by fanatics. It is the solemn warning of a great American jurist to the American Bar and the American people. It was language that was much quoted but little heeded.

The same Justice felt constrained to warn again three months later. Without one word of the Fourteenth Amendment having been changed, without one word of the statutes of Texas regulating primaries having been changed the Court completely reversed itself as to Negroes' right to vote in Texas primaries. The Court had in 1935 held that these Texas statutes did not violate the Negroes' constitutional rights. Now, nine years later, the decision was uprooted, a few months before the Presidential election of 1944.

Justice Roberts had been a Republican, a Philadelphia lawyer of the highest repute. Certainly he had no demagogic tendencies.

Dissenting alone, solemnly he warned: "It is regrettable that in an era marked by doubt and confusion, an era whose greatest need is steadfastness of thought and purpose, this court, which has been looked to as exhibiting consistency in adjudication, and a steadfastness which would hold the balance even in the face of temporary ebbs and flows of opinion, should now itself become the breeder of fresh doubt and confusion in the public mind as to the stability of our institutions."

A very few months later Justice Roberts resigned from the Court.

In 1948, another election year, there came before the Court a case which even now stands out as a beacon light warning the American public of what may be coming.

The Supreme Court had in 1926 (271 U. S. 323) held that restrictive covenants based on race or color alone do not violate any rights guaranteed by the Fourteenth Amendment. But, said the Court, or rather, Chief Justice Vinson and five associates, when and if a state court enforces such contracts by injunctive process that state action contravenes the amendment. There was no dissent here, but three justice did not participate.

Not long thereafter the question arose: Can such a restrictive covenent be enforced at law by a suit for damages against a co-covenantor who broke the covenant? The Supreme Court, or rather, six of the Associate Justices, held that it could not.

Chief Justice Vinson who had written the 1948 opinion, dissented. I believe he thought he was doing his duty when he said:

> Since we must rest our decision on the Constitution alone, we must set aside predilections on social policy, and adhere to the settled rules which restrict the exercise of our power of judicial review, remembering that the only restraint upon this power is our own sense of self-restraint.

That solemn admonition was delivered June 15, 1953. *Brown* v. *Topeka* and the other segregation cases had been argued. One week before, June 8, 1953, the Court had ordered the cases restored to the docket and assigned for reargument the following October (1953). Counsel were invited to discuss particularly several questions, the first of which was:

"What evidence is there that the Congress which submitted and the State legislatures and conventions which ratified the Fourteenth Amendment contemplated or did not contemplate, understood or did not understand, that it would abolish segregation in public schools?"

Chief Justice Vinson was not destined to live to hear the answer to that question, or to decide the legal effect of the answer. He died suddenly September 8, 1953. Governor Earl Warren was given a recess appointment and took office October 5, 1953. The segregation cases were argued in December and decided May 17, 1954. They were argued before and decided by a Court composed of Chief Justice Warren of California, and Associate Justices Black of Alabama, Reed of Kentucky, Frankfurter of Massachusetts, Douglas of Connecticut, Jackson of New York, Burton of Ohio, Clark of Texas, and Minton of Indiana.

The answers to the question which had been propounded by the Court headed by Chief Justice Vinson showed beyond a doubt that the Congress which submitted the Fourteenth Amendment did not contemplate or understand that it would abolish segregation in public schools.

These answers were ignored.

The answers also demonstrated that by decisions of their Courts of last resort rendered soon after the adoption of the Fourteenth Amendment, the States of California, New York, Ohio and Indiana in unmistakable terms showed that they did not understand or contemplate that the Fourteenth Amendment would abolish segregation in the public schools.

These decisions were ignored as were decisions by the Massachusetts Supreme Judicial Court, and a decision rendered by a Federal Judge, a former Union General, sitting in Louisiana.

The Chief Justice ignored the written manifestation of California's understanding. Other Associate Justices ignored the written manifestation of the understanding of their states—New York, Ohio, Indiana.

It is beyond understanding that this decision of May 17, 1954, should have been unanimous. One cannot but wonder: What would have been the result had Chief Justice Vinson lived? Had he foreseen the result and did he dread having to write another bitter dissent as he had in the restrictive covenant case of 1953? Or was it his hope that he could prevent the chaos and confusion which have ensued from the decision handed down just eight months after his death?

Only the Associate Justices who survive know the answer.

Am I—are you—to stand forthright in defense of that decision?

Is it irresponsible abuse, is it ridiculous and un-American sniping, when we say that the Supreme Court in rendering it swept aside doctrines of American constitutional law established for over a century, and substituted therefor jurisprudence based on the doctrines of Swedish psychologists?

Is it irresponsible abuse for me to say that that decision carried almost to the ultimate "doubt and confusion in the public mind as to the stability of our institutions"?

I say "*almost* to the ultimate" for I want to bring to you now expressions from Justices, Judges and lawyers demonstrating that since May 17, 1954, that doubt and confusion in the public mind as to the stability of our institutions has from year to year, from month to month, almost from day to day, increased.

In the school segregation cases, Justice Frankfurter had forgotten the fine sentiments he expressed in the West Virginia flag salute case a few years before. There (319 U. S. 642) he had said:

> One who belongs to the most vilified and persecuted minority in history is not likely to be insensible to the freedoms guaranteed by our Constitution. Were my personal attitude relevant I should wholeheartedly associate myself with the general libertarian views in the court's opinion; representing as they do the thought and action of a lifetime. But as judges, we are neither Jew nor Gentile, neither Catholic nor agnostic. We owe equal attachment to the Constitution and are equally bound by our judicial obligations whether we derive our citizenship from the earliest or the latest immigrants to these shores. As a member of this Court, I am not justified in writing my private notions of policy into the Constitution, no matter how deeply I may cherish them or how mischievous I may deem their disregard.

He was to overlook these lofty sentiments many more times after their utterance.

Just a couple of years after the school segregation cases, he joined with Justices Clark, Black, Douglas and Chief Justice Warren in holding that New

York could not discharge a professor in one of her colleges who had utilized the privilege against self-incrimination to avoid answering a question relating to his official conduct. (350 U. S. 551—Slochower). The other four judges criticized that holding. Justice Reed started his dissent with this criticism ". . . The Court (sic) strikes deep into the authority of New York to protect its local governmental institutions from influences of officials whose conduct does not meet the declared state standards for employment."

Justice Harlan criticized thus: "I think that a State may justifiably consider that teachers who refuse to answer questions concerning their official conduct are no longer qualified for public school teaching, on the ground that their refusal to answer jeopardizes the confidence that the public should have in its school system."

Perhaps, the situation in New York's school system today demonstrates that the criticisms of the minority were not unwarranted.

About the same time, Justice Frankfurter joined with the same four plus Justice Harlan (350 U. S.) in holding in the now famous Nelson case that the Smith Act superseded the Pennsylvania Sedition Act, and prevented Pennsylvania from enforcing her state statute against a person charged with acts of sedition against the Federal government.

Those of my generation can remember how many, many prosecutions there were in the state courts for violations of the state liquor laws despite the fact that there was a Federal organic law on the subject, and statutes to implement it.

Vehement has been the criticism of this Nelson case. The first criticism was in Justice Reed's dissent. He logically called attention to the fact that the Smith Act appears in that title of the United States Code which codifies the federal criminal laws. A section of that Title is: "Nothing in this title shall be held to take away or impair the jurisdiction of the courts of the several States under the laws thereof."

"That declaration," he said, "springs from the federal character of our nation. It recognizes the fact that maintenance of order and fairness rests primarily with the States . . . The majority's position in this case cannot be reconciled with that clear authorization of Congress."

About the same time (351 U. S. 12), Mr. Justice Black announced the judgment of the Court in *Griffin* v. *People of the State of Illinois* in an opinion in which Chief Justice Warren, Justice Douglas and Justice Clark joined. Justice Frankfurter concurred in the judgment. Griffin and others had been convicted of armed robbery, in an Illinois state court. They filed a motion to have a copy of the record furnished them free on the ground of their poverty. Their motion was denied. The Supreme Court held 5 to 4 that this was error.

Let the criticism come from Justice Harlan who cogently concluded his dissent: "As I view this case, it contains none of the elements hitherto regarded as essential to justify action by this Court under the Fourteenth Amendment. In truth what we have here is but the failure of Illinois to adopt as promptly as other states a desirable reform in its criminal procedure. . . . regard for our system of federalism requires that matters such as this be left to the States. However strong may be one's inclination to hasten the day when *in forma pauperis* criminal procedures will be universal among the States, I think it is beyond the province of this court to tell Illinois that it must provide such procedures."

As deferentially as possible I frame my criticism in the form of a question: "Must Illinois (and other states) now admit to her colleges and universities applicants who say they cannot on account of poverty pay the requisite fees?"

I suppose we shall soon have to face that question.

The next year really came the deluge. Time does not permit me to discuss all the cases in which the minority indulged in vigorous criticism. Let us look at a few. Let's start with *Konigsberg* v. *The State Bar of California* (353 U. S. 252). Of it, Mr. William H. Rehnquist of the Arizona Bar has recently said in an American Bar Association Journal article:

> A decision of any court based on a combination of charity and ideological sympathy at the expense of generally applicable rules of law is regrettable no matter whence it comes. But what could be tolerated as a warm-hearted aberration in the local trial judge becomes nothing less than a constitutional transgression when enunciated by the highest court of the land. (Vol. 44, A.B.A.J. p. 232).

That case arose out of a proceeding by Konigsberg for admission to the California Bar. The Supreme Court of California affirmed the action of the State Committee of Bar Examiners in refusing certification. The Supreme Court of the United States granted *certiorari*. Justice Black, with the Chief Justice, Justices Douglas, Burton and Brennan concurring, held that there was no evidence in the record which *rationally* justified a finding that Konigsberg had failed to establish his good moral character or failed to show that he did not advocate forceful overthrow of the government, even though he refused to answer questions as to his political associations. I suggest: "Who constitutionally determines rationality?" *Justice Frankfurter* dissented on jurisdictional grounds, rather belatedly admonishing that "This Court has a special responsibility to be particularly mindful of the respective boundaries between state and federal authority." (If it were not tragic, it would be laughable.)

Justice Harlan dissented vigorously and lengthily (353 U. S. 276, 312), concluding with this cogent criticism:

> . . . It seems to me altogether beyond question that a State may refuse admission to its Bar to an applicant, no matter how sincere, who refuses to answer questions which are reasonably relevant to his qualifications and which do not invade a constitutionally privileged area. The opinion of the Court does not really question this; it solves the problem by denying that it exists. But what the Court has really done, I think, is simply to impose on California its own notions of public policy and judgment. For me, today's decision represents an unacceptable intrusion into a matter of state concern.

The Supreme Court of Oregon must have thought so, too. A week after Konigsberg, the Supreme Court vacated a judgment of the Supreme Court of Oregon, *in re* Frank Victor Patterson (353 U. S. 952) and remanded the case for reconsideration in the light of Konigsberg (and the Schware case from New Mexico, decided the same day).

A writer in the March issue of the American Bar Journal says: The reconsideration left the Oregon court unmoved, and on December 4, 1957, it adhered to its decision that Patterson could not practice law in Oregon's courts. The fact of membership in the Communist party was not the basis of the Court's decision. Rather it was the Court's conclusion that the applicant had lied when he testified that the ultimate aims of the Party were to make America, by the use of democratic processes, a more nearly perfect democracy. "Our finding against the petitioner," the Oregon court concluded, "rests primarily on our belief that he testified falsely under oath." And, the Court added, "False testimony relating to the aims and nature of the Communist Party should not be less material in weighing the moral character of an applicant for admission to the Bar than false testimony with regard to any other issue relevant to the matter of moral character." (318 Pac. 2d 907; Vol. 44 A.B.J., p. 264).

A month or so later, Chief Justice Warren announced the judgment of the Court and delivered an opinion in the case of *Sweezy v. New Hampshire* (352 U. S. 812), Justices Black, Douglas and Brennan joined. Justice Whittaker did not participate. Justices Frankfurter and Harlan concurred in the result. Justices Clark and Burton dissented.

Sweezy was a professor in a New Hampshire college. He was convicted of contempt for failure to answer questions propounded by the Attorney General of New Hampshire acting pursuant to legislative authority to investigate subversive activities. New Hampshire's Supreme Court affirmed. The United States Supreme Court reversed. As a result the Attorney General of New Hampshire has become a States' Righter. He didn't think his State had invaded the professor's liberties "in the areas of academic freedom and political expression."

Mr. Justice Tom Clark, joined by Mr. Justice Burton, did some right pungent criticizing that June day last year. He started off: "The Court today has denied the State of New Hampshire the right to investigate the extent of 'subversive activities' within its boundaries in the manner chosen by the legislature. . . . My Brothers Frankfurter and Harlan conclude, as do I, that the internal affairs of the New Hampshire State Government are of no concern to us." Where, oh where, was that doctrine on May 17, 1954?

Then, a little later, he said: "The short of it is that the Court blocks New Hampshire's efforts to enforce its law," and criticizes what he says is an extension of the doctrine of the Nelson case, in which he had joined. He thought, he says, that "we had left open for legitimate state control any subversive activity leveled against the interest of the State. I for one intended to suspend state action only in the field of subversion against the nation and thus avoid a race to the court house door between federal and state prosecutors . . .I thought we had left open a wide field for state action, but implicit in the opinions today is a contrary conclusion. They destroy the fact-finding power of the State in this field and I dissent from this wide sweep of their coverage."

The Justice was perceiving Frankenstein in action, and he didn't like what he saw.

I, for one, wonder how a person can be guilty of "subversive activity leveled against the interest of the State" and be innocent of "subversion against the nation."

Justice Clark's criticism in dissent sounded like the anguished cry of a man who was beginning to perceive that the trend had gone too far.

That thought was bolstered when we read his criticism dissenting in the Watkins case, decided the same day (354 U. S. 178).

Watkins' conviction for contempt of Congress was affirmed by the District of

Columbia Court of Appeals. The Chief Justice, speaking for a majority of the Court, held that where the particular inquiry by a sub-committee of the Un-American Activities Committee of Congress purported to involve Communist infiltration in labor, but most of the witnesses had no connection with labor, and questions were asked of Watkins which he refused to answer, involving persons almost a quarter of whom were not labor people, and the chairman's only response to Watkins' objection was that the sub-committee was investigating subversion and subversive propaganda, Watkins had insufficient basis for determining the pertinency of the questions, and his conviction under statute for refusal to answer was invalid under the due process clause.

Of that holding, Justice Clark said: "As I see it the chief fault in the majority opinion is its michievous curbing of the informing function of Congress." That is the opening sentence of a critical dissent which continues for twenty pages and concludes with this sentence: "To carry on its heavy responsibility the compulsion of truth that does not incriminate is not only necessary to the Congress but is permitted within the limits of the Constitution."

But, any thought that Justice Clark was of the real opinion that the trend had gone too far was dissipated by his concurring with the Chief Justice and Justices Black, Douglas and Brennan in *Lambert* v. *California*, decided December 16, 1953 (355 U. S. 225, 78 S. Ct. 240, 26 U. S. Law Week 4059).

In this decision, the five, speaking through Mr. Justice Douglas, held unconstitutional a Los Angeles ordinance requiring ex-convicts remaining in the city for more than five days to register with the police. The ordinance violated due process of law because "there was no showing that the appellant knew of the registration requirement or had an opportunity to know of it."

Justice Frankfurter, joined by Justices Harlan and Whittaker, wrote a dissenting opinion expressing this criticism of the majority: "The present decision will turn out to be an isolated deviation from the strong current of precedents —a derelict on the waters of the law."

In plain English, he meant that it would never be cited except to be distinguished.

But, to go back to the summer of 1957.

This discussion, abridged though it must be, could not be considered even partially complete without mention of the Jencks case, and the criticism it brought down.

Jencks was prosecuted for filing a false non-Communist affidavit with the National Labor Relations Board. He was convicted. The case found its way to the Supreme Court. There it was held that Jencks was entitled to an order directing the government to produce for inspection all reports of two government witnesses to the F.B.I. touching upon events and activities as to which they testified at the trial, and was entitled to inspect such reports and to decide whether to use them in his defense.

About the only justification the Court could give for that holding was "Justice requires no less."

The first criticism of that hoding came from Justice Clark. He started off by saying that the holding of the Court "fashions a new rule of evidence which is foreign to our federal jurisprudence. The rule has always been to the contrary." He concluded: "This is only one of some 10 Communist affidavit cases now pending in the trial and appellate courts. Unless this case goes as did Gold's, the question of the sufficiency of instructions will come up in this as well as in each of the other cases. The Court is sorely divided on this important issue and proper judicial administration requires that charges as to what constitutes membership and affiliation in the Communist party be announced."

Now let's go back to the editorial of February 21st—and quote from it again:

> Our courts have been subject to irresponsible abuse, to ridiculous and un-American sniping by fanatics who charge Communist influence.

I have not engaged in irresponsible abuse. I am not a fanatic. I have not engaged in ridiculous and un-American sniping. I have not charged Communist influence. I *have* discussed with you several cases. Those discussed, decided recently, are these:

> The Slochower case;
> The Nelson case;
> The Griffin case;
> The Konigsberg case;
> The Sweezy case;
> The Watkins case;
> The Jencks case.

In each of them, except the Griffin case, there was some question involving "Communism" and in every instance the case was decided in favor of the party against whom there was at least a suspicion of participation in Communistic activity.

(There are many more.)

To come back to the Jencks case—did the Department of Justice stand forthright in defense of the Supreme Court? It did not. The Jencks case was decided June 3, 1957. The ink was hardly dry on the opinion when S. 2377 was introduced. Accompanying the report on that bill (Report No. 569) is a Statement by Hon. Herbert Brownell, Jr., then Attorney General of the United States, which commences: "S. 2377 to amend the procedures for production of statements and reports in Federal criminal cases is intended to correct a grave emergency in law enforcement which has resulted from the decision of the Supreme Court in *Jencks* v. *United States* in the field of law enforcement."

Yet, my friends, when *we* try to correct a grave emergency in public education which has resulted from the decision of the Supreme Court in *Brown* v. *Topeka,* and the other segregation cases, we are told that we are disobeying the law of the land, we are told by a newspaper published in our own State that we should stand forthright in the defense of a decision which every lawyer, worth his salt, knows is an abomination in the eyes of the law.

The Attorney General was joined by an Assistant Secretary of the Treasury endorsing the bill necessitated by the Jencks case.

There is pending in the Senate today a bill by Senator Jenner of Indiana seeking, *not to stand* forthright in the defense of the Supreme Court in its decisions in the Watkins case, the Slochower case, the Nelson case, the Sweezy case, but to see to it that such decisions can not be repeated, to deprive the Supreme Court of jurisdiction in those fields.

The only trouble with the Jenner bill is that it does not go far enough.

That same June of 1957, there was decided the case of *Mallory* v. *United States*. Mallory had been convicted of rape in the District of Columbia and sentenced to death. The Supreme Court, speaking through Justice Frankfurter (354 U. S. 449) held that the defendant had not been arraigned with sufficient promptness, and that therefore the admission of his confession was improper.

Neither the Congress nor the Judge who presided in the trial of Mallory are standing forthright in defense of that one. (354 U. S. 449).

On March 7, the Senate Sub-Committee on Constitutional Rights began hearings on bills which would reverse that decision (*N. Y. Times,* March 8, 1958, p. 7).

Representative Kenneth Keating, ranking Republican on the Judiciary Committee, introduced a bill to reverse the Mallory decision.

At the March 7 hearing, Judge Alexander Holtzoff, the trial judge who sentenced Mallory to death, testified in opposition to the Supreme Court decision. He "deplored" attacks on the Supreme Court but felt it was "no disrespect to criticize its decisions."

There were other witnesses strongly *opposed* to legislation changing the Mallory decision. Among them was Professor Arthur Sutherland of the Harvard Law School.

The strongest voice which has yet been sounded warning us of this judicial oligarchy, this super-legislature, this super-board of bar examiners is that of Judge Learned Hand.

In the *United States and World Report* of March 7 is an article with reference to his recent lectures at Harvard Law School demonstrating that it is no part of a lawyer's duty to stand forthright in the defense of any Court which pursues a course contrary to the Constitution of the United States.

Judge Hand, now retired, is one of the most eminent men ever to sit on the Federal Bench. For many years he presided over the Second Circuit Court of Appeals in New York.

I do hope that the Dean, Faculty and Student Body of the Harvard Law School will give heed to Judge Hand's warning and rebuke of the Supreme Court for its tendency to set itself up as a third legislative chamber.

Judge Hand demonstrated, too, that the Supreme Court recently has not only proceeded to impose its own views of what is wise or unwise legislation, irrespective of constitutional powers, but seems to have applied hostile rules where "property" is involved and softer rules where "liberty" is at issue.

You lawyers who have to read, study and try to apply Supreme Court decisions, know in advance, when you pick up one involving employer and employee or labor and management, just where four of the Justices will be aligned. Cases before the Court are measured by this group not by the yardstick, "Does the decision of the lower court under review square with the Constitution and laws as they are written?" *but* by the yardstick: "Does the decision of the lower court under review meet *our* views of what is right and wrong?"

If you think that statement is an exaggeration, that it is unbridled criticism, you have only to pick out three cases of the many, and read them.

Look at the School Segregation cases, and the language at page 493:

"Does segregation of children in public schools solely on the basis of race, even though the physical facilities and other 'tangible' factors may be equal, deprive the children of the minority group of equal educational opportunities. We *believe that it does.*"

Theretofore, laws had been *enacted* according to the "beliefs" of the legislators, and their *validity determined* by the Court's measuring them by the test of the Constitution.

Now, their validity is determined by the "beliefs" of a majority of the Court sitting in a given case.

Look at the Griffin case, and the language at page 16. Justice Black said, "Providing equal justice for poor and rich, weak and powerful alike is an age-old problem." The majority then proceeded to promulgate a judgment of the Court which was nothing more or less than their belief as to how equal justice should be provided. They measured the case not by the Constitution of the United States but by their construction of the Old Testament. (See 251 U. S. 16, note 10.)

Finally, look at the Jencks case. No Constitutional provision was violated, no statute was violated, when the District Court in Texas refused to direct the Government to produce F.B.I. reports to be used by counsel for the defense in cross-examining government witnesses. The Circuit Court of Appeals for this Circuit so held. When the case reached the Supreme Court, Justice Brennan writing for the majority said: "We now hold that the petitioner was entitled to an order directing the government to produce for inspection" these reports. "We hold further that petitioner is entitled to inspect the reports."

Why did they hold that?

What constitutional provisions authorized those holdings?

What statute authorized those holdings?

The answer is "none."

The Court did not even attempt to justify its "holdings" by citing *legal* authority therefor.

The "authority" for the holding was the opinion, the belief of the Judges that "Justice requires no less." (353 U. S. 669).

What are we, as lawyers, going to do about decisions such as those?

Do you think that it is your duty to "stand forthright" behind them, and so let five men on the Supreme Court supersede the President of the United States, and our elected Congress?

You may think that to be *your* duty.

I do not conceive it to be mine.

On the contrary, I conceive it to be my duty, as a citizen of the United States, as a lawyer sworn to uphold the Constitution of the United States and the Constitution of Georgia, to warn those who are not trained in the law of what is happening to them.

In so doing, I join with Judge Hand when he says: "For myself it would be most irksome to be ruled by a bevy of Platonic Guardians."

# INDEX